MANAGING
A Contemporary Introduction

Fifth Edition

Joseph L. Massie

Alumni Professor and Professor of Business Administration
University of Kentucky

John Douglas

Raymond E. Glos Professor of Business
Miami University, Oxford, Ohio

PRENTICE HALL, Englewood Cliffs, New Jersey 07632

Library of Congress Cataloging-in-Publication Data

MASSIE, JOSEPH L.
    Managing, a contemporary introduction / Joseph L. Massie, John Douglas. -- 5th ed.
        p.   cm.
    Includes bibliographical references and index.
    ISBN 0-13-544859-X
    1. Industrial management.   I. Douglas, John, (date).
    II. Title.
    HD31.M337 1992
    658.4--dc20

                                            91-40437
                                            CIP

Cover Photo: Oskar Schlemmer. *Bauhaus Stairway* (1932). Oil on canvas; 63 7/8″ × 45″ (162.3 × 114.3 cm). Collection, The Museum of Modern Art, New York. Gift of Philip Johnson.

Executive Editor: Alison Reeves
Editor-in-Chief: Garret White
Coordinating Production Editor: Anne Graydon
Production Editor: Judy Winthrop
Advertising Manager: Lori Cowen
Senior Marketing Manager: Sandra Steiner
Scheduler: Liz Robertson
Copy Editor: Carole Crouse
Designer: Thomas Nery
Cover Designer: Thomas Nery
Prepress Buyer: Trudy Pisciotti
Manufacturing Buyer: Bob Anderson
Supplements Editor: David Scholder
Interior line art: Network Graphics
Photo Researcher: Teri Stratford
Photo Editor: Lori Morris-Nantz

© 1992, 1985, 1981, 1977, 1973 by Prentice-Hall, Inc.
a Simon & Schuster Company
Englewood Cliffs, New Jersey 07632

Printed in the United States of America

10 9 8 7 6 5 4 3 2 1

ISBN   0-13-544859-X

Acknowledgments appear on page 540, which constitutes a continuation of ther copyright page.

Prentice Hall International (UK) Limited, *London*
Prentice-Hall of Australia Pty. Limited, *Sydney*
Prentice-Hall Canada Inc., *Toronto*
Prentice-Hall Hispanoamericana, S.A., *Mexico*
Prentice-Hall of India Private Limited, *New Delhi*
Prentice-Hall of Japan, Inc., *Tokyo*
Simon & Schuster Asia Pte. Ltd., *Singapore*
Editora Prentice-Hall do Brasil, Ltda., *Rio de Janeiro*

Brief Contents

Contents

v

Preface

Never has the field of management been so exciting and challenging. There is worldwide evidence that a nation's management talent is one of the most important factors in the growth and survival of its economy and society. There is also evidence that, as we enter the twenty-first century, the problems will be complex.

Daily events remind us that the contemporary world is complicated and changing. We face such persistent topics as: How do we improve the vitality of American industry? Can we effectively compete with Japan, Europe, and other nations? What responsibility do American corporations have in protecting the environment and providing jobs for a diverse world population? Is total quality management possible in all of our organizations? Are labor unions outdated in the American scene? Must the introduction of new technology adversely affect the quality of work life?

Our text is an introduction to the field of management. We begin with a managerial perspective of the field that includes information about the contemporary manager's world, the roots of management, the present international challenge, and why ethics and social responsibility are important. In Part Two, we explain the fundamentals of management. We address the important area of the behavioral sciences in Part Three before turning to the contemporary challenges in management information systems and operations management. Because we believe that the truth about effective managing comes from many sources, we end our book with insights and lessons learned from the experience of practicing managers and companies.

SPECIAL FEATURES

To effectively communicate the scope of management, we have created a number of special features, which should add to the readability of the text.

Learning Objectives
The objectives listed at the beginning of each chapter state what is to be learned and how the material is organized. At the end of a reading assignment, the student can check to see if the objectives were reached.

Opening Cases
These real situations set the stage for chapter materials and give students a reference and a starting point for what follows. If the instructor so desires, students may do library research to update these cases.

Key Terms
We haven't introduced professional and technological language to impress our readers. In fact, we have avoided unnecessary academic jargon. However, in

learning a new language, a new athletic game, or any other subject, one must understand certain words. In management there are key words that have a common meaning among managers. These words have been placed in the margin and defined.

Glossary/Index
As a means of educational reinforcement and student convenience in searching for terms, all key words are defined in the margin, at the end of each chapter, and in the glossary/index.

Margin Questions
The margin questions indicate the relevance of the adjacent text discussion. Many paragraphs contain the answers to questions that we have just asked in the margin. In some cases, however, the marginal question is meant to stimulate the students' search for answers and the answer will not be found in the text.

Application and Issue Boxes
In the first eighteen chapters, we highlight **management applications, global applications,** and **ethics issues** so that students may see the relevance these topics have to particular chapters. In most instances, these boxes contain examples from very recent sources to give each chapter a contemporary flavor.

Select Photos
Relevant photos are included for each opening case to add to the sense of reality. In addition, photos with related captions appear at appropriate spots throughout all chapters to add a visual example of text material.

Study Assignments
The study assignments for each chapter serve as minitests for student review of selected and important ideas from chapter materials.

Cases for Discussion
At least one and often two cases are placed at the end of each chapter to provide students the opportunity to demonstrate their ability to apply concepts and skills. These actual situations reinforce many of the ideas developed in each chapter.

SUPPLEMENTARY MATERIALS

- *ABC News/Prentice Hall Video Library for Managing, 5th ed.* Prentice Hall and ABC News have joined forces to create the best and most comprehensive video materials available for the management course. From ABC News' wide range of award-winning programs such as *Nightline, Business World, This Week with David Brinkley, World News Tonight, 20/20* and *Prime Time Live,* we have selected one feature-length, documentary-style video per chapter to help emphasize the relation of management concepts to the world of work. Complete teaching notes are in the *Instructor's Resource Manual with Video Guide.*
- *Management Live! The Video Book.* This video-based experiential workbook supplement is available at a discounted price when shrinkwrapped to this text. The

companion *Video Collection* is free upon adoption of the shrinkwrapped package, **one per department.** An *Instructor's Manual* to *Management Live* is also available.

- ■ *Acumen Edition.* Acumen is a professional managerial assessment and development program (for IBM PCs) used in many world-wide organizations. The *Educational Version* is available, in both 3.5″ and 5.25″ disks, at a discounted price when shrinkwrapped to the text.
- ■ *Instructor's Resource Manual with Video Guide.* This manual provides annotated lecture outlines with a cross-reference to the color transparencies, answers to the text's study assignments and case questions, and a video guide for using the ABC News/Prentice Hall Video Library with the text.
- ■ *Transparency Masters.* Full-page black and white transparency masters are available for all text figures.
- ■ *PH Color Transparencies for Management—Series C.* Over 150 full color, full-page color transparencies from sources outside the text. Each transparency is accompanied by an interleaf with an extended explanatory caption.
- ■ *Test Item File.* A comprehensive test bank with over 2,000 objective questions, keyed as to level of difficulty, whether factual or applied and text page reference. It is also available in computerized format (*PH DataManager*) for the IBM-PC.
- ■ *Management and Organizational Behavior: A Contemporary View.* Prentice Hall and the New York Times brings today's business into your classroom through these specially-designed dodgers containing articles related to topics discussed in the text. This supplement is available free to students upon adoption of the text.
- ■ *Student Guide.* Pre-tests, review questions, post-tests and application exercises to reinforce student learning.
- ■ *Management Applications: Exercises, Cases & Readings* by John Samaras. This for-sale student supplement provides additional exercises, cases and readings to extend key concepts in *Managing,* 5th ed. A separate *Instructor's Manual* is available.
- ■ *Readings in Management* by Philip DuBose. Background readings organized by management functions.
- ■ *Managing an Organization: A Workbook Simulation* by Garry Oddou. A non-computerized, team-oriented simulation with *Instructor's Manual.*
- ■ *Modern Business Decisions* by Richard Cotter and David Fritzsche. A computerized, team-oriented decision-making simulation for the IBM-PC which consists of a *Player's Manual, Student Decision Disk, Professor Program Disk* and *Instructor's Manual.*
- ■ *Micromanaging Site License.* These Lotus-based software exercises help students better understand how microcomputers apply to the process of management.
- ■ *Hypercard Simulation Site License.* For MacIntosh users, a simulation called "Desktop Order" shows students how such software can help managers manage their desks.

ACKNOWLEDGMENTS

This fifth edition represents our continued efforts to bring the many new developments in the field of management to the beginning student in a concise and readable manner. Many people have helped in these efforts; many students have used past editions and have provided useful feedback to the authors; professors throughout the country have supplied helpful suggestions. We particularly want to remember faculty reviewers of previous editions who contributed lasting ideas.

We also want to thank the reviewers of the manuscript for the fifth edition:

Godwin C. Ariguzo
Marshall University

Aline Arnold
Eastern Illinois University

Carnella Barber
Glendale Community College

Don Baynham
Eastfield College

James W. Bleck
Mansfield University

Stephen C. Branz
Triton College

Richard H. Brever
Jersey City State College

George R. Buls
Johnston Technical College

Edward Butler
Gloucester County College

William Carlson
University of LaVerne

Jack Chandler
Herkimer County Community College

Douglas E. Ciolfi
Jacksonville University

Charles R. Clarke
San Jacinto College

Quentin P. Eagan
Brevard Community College

Roosevelt D. Fabris
Trenton State College

M. Jean Flint
Owensboro Community College

James Genseal
Joliet Junior College

Rita B. Hamburg
Jacksonville State University

Donna Harmon
Middlesex Community College

Nathan Himelstein
Essex County College

Roger C. Hiten
Murray State University

Paul Horsford
University of Utah

Robert N. Jones
Lenoir-Rhyne College

Charles E. Kime
Bristol Community College

John L. Kmetz
University of Delaware

John W. Lloyd
Monroe Community College

Barbara A. Maroun
Salve Regina College

Leroy J. Moore
Hawaii Pacific College

Nikki Paahana
DeVry Institute of Technology

Patsy K. Rich
Louisiana State University–Alexandria

Walter Schoenfeldt
University of Southern Indiana

Richard Shapiro
Cuyahoga Community College

Carla Lemley Simmons Jr.
Pensacola Junior College

Jim Sylvia
Northeastern Junior College

John G. Thomas
Erie Community College

Roger Volkema
The American University

Curtis R. Wehner
Eastfield College

Charles A. White
Edison Community College

Bob S. White
Reynolds College

A number of faculty colleagues and former colleagues at Miami University, Oxford, Ohio, helped in the development of the manuscript. Thanks go to Judy

A. Barille, Robert M. Harp, William J. Madison, II, and Lewis E. Welshofer, who provided insights from their careers in business, the military, and education. David Luechauer made significant inputs in the chapters on Decision Making, Communicating, and Directing; Gary Shulman also contributed to the chapter on Communicating; Richard Luebbe added his insights to the chapter on Managing Information and Production and Operations; and Ellen J. Dumond of California State University at Fullerton rewrote most of the material on Production and Operations, provided comments on the chapter on Managing Information, and contributed materials to a number of the applications and issues boxes.

Two colleagues gave a great deal of themselves in this work. W. Graham Irwin wrote some of the opening and ending cases, researched and wrote chapters on The International Challenge, Ethics and Social Responsibility, Planning and Strategic Management, Managing Information, and Lessons from Managerial and Organizational Performance. His willingness to stay with this project over the years will always be remembered and appreciated.

Amy Milholland deserves thanks beyond words. She served in every possible role. Every chapter contains some of her research and thoughts, especially the chapter on Controlling. She wrote many of the applications and issues boxes and helped develop most of the special features mentioned earlier.

The staff from Miami University also receive recognition for those moments when deadlines cried for extra efforts. These people were Kathy Bradbury, Margaret DePalma, Hazel Spencer, Mark Jensen, Carol Ault, and Nicole Quotson.

Key people at Prentice Hall deserve special mention. Executive Editor Alison Reeves was able to bring another edition to fruition, and we believe this edition is her best effort; Judy Winthrop served well in her role as Production Editor, as did Teri Stratford as researcher for the photographs, Anne Graydon as Coordinating Production Editor, and Tom Nery as designer.

To all who helped, we say thanks and realize that the best reward is knowing that students will gain from our combined efforts.

John L. Massie

John Douglas

Chapter 1

The Manager's World

Learning Objectives

1. **State** the distinction between managers and nonmanagers.
2. **Describe** the three worlds of a manager.
3. **Identify** four important future trends in the manager's job.
4. **Define** the terms organizational tradition, life style, and life cycle.
5. **Identify** at least three challenges in each world of a manager.

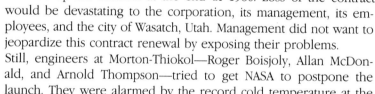

January 28, 1986. As families, schoolchildren, NASA staff, reporters, the nation, and the world watched, stunned, the Space Shuttle Challenger lifted off from the Kennedy Space Center and exploded.

The "first teacher in space," Christa McAuliffe, and the astronauts—Judy Resnik, Greg Jarvis, Mike Smith, Ron McNair, Ellison Onizuka, Dick Scobee—were killed.

The subsequent investigation by the Rogers Commission, NASA, and others determined that the cause of the explosion and loss of the crew and spaceship was the failure of the O-rings. (The O-rings were the flexible synthetic rubber, doughnut-shaped seals that were supposed to prevent the passage of gases that occurred during ignition. Without the O-rings, the containers holding the rocket fuel could not withstand the tremendous forces involved in the ignition and liftoff. The O-rings failed, the gases leaked out, and the Shuttle exploded.)

Morton-Thiokol, the primary contractor for the Space Shuttle and the company responsible for the O-rings from start to finish, had known for over a year that there was a problem with the O-rings. Morton-Thiokol knew that such a failure would result in the loss of the crew and the Space Shuttle. They knew that it would cost $350 million to "fix the problem." That money was not in the budget. They also knew that for over thirteen years, they had held a monopoly on the contract from NASA and that the monopoly could be jeopardized if anyone—particularly anyone from Congress—found out about the design flaw. Their contract was up for renewal at the end of 1986. Loss of the contract

would be devastating to the corporation, its management, its employees, and the city of Wasatch, Utah. Management did not want to jeopardize this contract renewal by exposing their problems.

Still, engineers at Morton-Thiokol—Roger Boisjoly, Allan McDonald, and Arnold Thompson—tried to get NASA to postpone the launch. They were alarmed by the record cold temperature at the launch site—only 18 degrees Fahrenheit—which they felt sure would have an adverse impact on the O-rings. They strongly recommended that NASA wait until temperatures reached at least 53 degrees before launching. For the first time in the history of the Space Shuttle launches, the engineers refused to give their approval to the launch. They were, of course, overruled by Morton-Thiokol management, who gave their approval.

NASA was having its own problems. NASA had been one of the first victims of Congress's attempts to reduce the federal deficit. Its budget cuts had eliminated staff and some safety practices and had led to the cannibalization of the Space Shuttles. (One reason that Challenger's launch had been delayed was to give the NASA staff time to pull used parts off the Space Shuttle Columbia, which had just completed a mission and landed in California, and put them into Challenger.) What staff remained generally worked twelve-hour days and had not taken a day off in months. Everyone was exhausted. NASA was on an ambitious schedule, and they were failing to stay on schedule. The Challenger flight was only the twelfth at a time when NASA should have been launching number 23.

The pressure to launch was strong. NASA needed to prove to Congress that it was productive, that it could carry cargo into space for business concerns and perhaps someday be self-supporting. In the meantime, NASA needed money from Congress to survive. Any more flight delays would be worse than just embarrassing—they would prove to Congress that NASA was not worth the investment.

The potential O-ring problem was considered an "acceptable risk" and the launch was approved.[1] ∎

The Challenger tragedy provides an opening for this first chapter on managing. All parties to that episode intended for things to go right. There is no evidence of sabotage, no evidence that people deliberately worked against the project. The NASA objectives had the support of the American people—space exploration at that point captured the imagination of most. But the disaster highlights the world that today's managers face. Good intentions, committed people, and an excited population are not sufficient ingredients for the successful completion of projects. Not all the managerial problems you will face will be life-threatening, nor will they have the same impact and consequences if failure occurs. But the managerial problems of today are truly complex and difficult, and you'll see the evidence when you read Chapters 3 (The International Challenge) and 4 (Ethics and Social Responsibility). While it is easy to assign blame and to criticize the highly publicized failures of management, it is not as easy to suggest remedies. Never before has management faced such serious challenges and dilemmas. It is crucial that the managers of the future learn as much as possible about the field of management—theory and practice—so that they can handle these challenges and dilemmas as well as possible.

This book is a contemporary introduction to the fundamentals of managing. We offer you the opportunity to learn some of the language of management—a language that will enable you to converse with practicing managers of organizations. You'll also have the opportunity to add to what you already know about managers. For example, you may know something about managers of manufacturing firms like John Deere or General Electric but not about managers of service institutions like a Children's Hospital or the University of Virginia. You may have knowledge of management in large firms—for example, General Motors—but not small firms like Becker's Neighborhood Lawn Care Service. You may be familiar with the management of profit-making organizations like Chrysler and McDonald's but not with the management of nonprofit entities like the Red Cross and the Girl Scouts. By depicting management in a very broad context, we intend the coverage to be as complete and real as possible. This first chapter describes the setting in which managers perform their activities. It provides an overview of the business environment of the 1990s, in which managers have increased in importance.

What do managers do?

MANAGERS: A GENERAL DESCRIPTION

Managers The people in an organization who are primarily responsibile for seeing that work gets done through the efforts of others.

Managers see to it that work gets done. This very simple and broad statement includes all kinds of managers—the president of a large steel corporation, a football coach, the director of a day-care center, and the administrator of an educational institution.

In most instances, the work of managers differs markedly from the work of nonmanagers. The president of a steel firm does managerial work; such a per-

Ethics Issue

Shades of Gray

Ethics and social responsibility are an important part of a manager's world. No book can tell you how to be ethical in every situation. Ethics is based upon an individual's—your own—values and perceptions. In this text, we will attempt to raise ethical issues, to ask ethical questions, to present situations and ideas. Black-and-white, right or wrong answers to ethical questions are not always possible. Perhaps the answers are only in shades of gray.

For example, you read at the beginning of this chapter about acceptable risks at NASA. Everyone had very good intentions. No one wanted the astronauts to die. The managers at Morton-Thiokol knew that the O-rings could fail at low temperatures; yet, they approved the launch because they wanted to protect their own jobs, the jobs of their employees, and the economic health of their community. The managers were doing what they thought was right. There will be different opinions, different ideas, different values on each issue.

Some people, for example, are very upset that tobacco companies continue to operate even though it has been proven that both smoking and second-hand tobacco smoke cause cancer and death. The tobacco industry contends that if they went out of business, thousands of people would lose their jobs and their homes. Besides, no one forces anyone to buy tobacco products.

Alcohol—beer, wine, bourbon, whiskey—is a leading cause of death on our highways. Twenty-five percent of the people in prison to-day have alcohol-related problems. Yet, the alcohol industry is thriving, as are bars and nightclubs, providing thousands of jobs to thousands of people and economic stability to their communities.

Some people are horrified that abortion clinics exist, but the managers of the clinics feel that they are providing a service to society by eliminating unwanted babies and freeing the women from the responsibilities of motherhood.

Animal-rights activists do not want animals used in the testing of new products, but scientific researchers know that they cannot develop new products, like the artificial heart, without testing the products on animals.

There are numerous ethical questions and situations. How thoroughly should a company test a new drug before it is used on an AIDS patient? Should obsolescence be built into products so that the consumer must buy a new product every three years? Should white men be discriminated against so that black men will have a better chance to succeed in the business world? Should the government continue to legislate how businesses should act? What responsibility does a company have toward the homeless? the unemployed? the environment? society?

Ethics is one of the themes of this text. It is the subject of Chapter 3. In addition, we will have boxes, like this one, in each chapter. We may not have the answers, but we will raise some of the questions.

son does not operate a machine. Football coaches manage the staff and the players; they do not play the game themselves. The director of a day-care center sees that revenues equal or exceed costs, that health care standards are maintained, that parents are satisfied with the care, and that a qualified staff follows a planned program; he or she does not necessarily deal directly with the children. An academic administrator anticipates the student enrollments for the next few years, develops committee assignments for the faculty, represents the higher administration to the faculty and the faculty to the higher administration, prepares budgets and reports, and manages one or more secretaries and perhaps student help; he or she may not teach in the classroom. There is a distinctive set of activities performed by managers and administrators. See Figure 1-1 for some classified advertisements describing the positions of managers and nonmanagers.

FIGURE 1-1 Classified Ads: Managers and Nonmanagers

We are a leading national distrubutor of pharmaceuticals and allied health products with the following challenging management position available:

MANAGER, PURCHASING AND MERCHANDISING

We seek a talented professional to manage the merchandising and purchasing of three major product lines while supporting the sales objectives of two divisions.

Primary responsibilities will include: purchasing Rx, OTC and HHC merchandise, overseeing the creation of advertising/promotional pieces; directing pricing of products in accordance with market forces/corporate goals; developing product lines; and supervising, training and developing staff.

To be considered, you should have: a Bachelor's degree in an appropriate discipline; five years related industry experience; and strong interpersonal and communication skills.

We offer a competitive salary, an excellent benefit package and a dynamic work environment. Submit your resume including salary history and requirements. Principals only. No phone inquiries, please.

moore medical corp.

JOHN P. DRAKE,
HUMAN RESOURCES MANAGER
MOORE MEDICAL CORP.
389 JOHN DOWNEY DRIVE
NEW BRITAIN, CT 06050 EOE/M/F/H/V

CREDIT MANAGER

National commercial finance company seeking individual to fill the position of Credit Manager. Qualified candidate will perform duties of underwriting new commercial transactions of potential loans from $250M to $20MM. Qualifications include but are not limited to: Degree in finance or accounting, strong credit skills, excellent communication skills, and experience in asset based lending desirable.

ACCOUNT EXECUTIVE

We also need qualified candidate for Account Executive. As an Account Executive you will be assigned a specific client base and will be responsible for monitoring and maintaining those client accounts. Responsibilities include: Analyzing all client financial reports, preparing client files for credit line renewals, and evaluation of client performance. We seek a career oriented professional with 1-3 years credit analyst banking experience, and/or asset based lending experience, and/or consumer credit lending and collection experience. The successful applicant must have demonstrated superior analytical and communication skills.

For consideration please forward your resume with salary history and requirements in confidence to:

Transamerica Commercial Finance
P.O. Box 800806
Dallas, Texas 75380
Equal Opportunity Employer

TRANSAMERICA
COMMERCIAL FINANCE

Employee/Labor Relations Manager

Major downtown Cleveland firm is seeking a dynamic individual to be challenged by the daily Personnel/Labor Relations activities in this fast paced union/non-union environment.

Qualified candidate has 5 years experience in contract negotiation/administration, arbitrations, management training/program development and workers' compensation. Experience with computerized personnel system desirable.

We offer an excellent starting salary and an exceptional benefits package. Qualified applicants should send their resume, including salary history to:

Box BB258
Plain Dealer.
An Equal Opportunity Employer

Opportunities at Ericsson

Ericsson Network Systems Inc., a subsidiary of one of the world's largest telecommunications companies, has the following openings available:

Product Manager – Power Systems

Responsibilities include marketing and product management throughout the U.S. of Ericsson's power products; providing support for power and grounding related matters within all of Ericsson's U.S. operations; and gathering/analyzing information about customers, competition, and general trends in the American market.

A minimum of 7 years' experience in power and grounding related matters, coupled with 3 years' managerial responsibilities required. Marketing experience is essential, as well as exceptional communication/interpersonal skills. Bachelor's degree in Electrical Engineering or equivalent experience required; MBA preferred.

Technical Writer

Responsibilities include planning, coordinating and developing technical documentation; interfacing with system designers, engineers and supervisors; writing and producing assigned documents/special projects; and evaluating and organizing information for end user.

BS degree or equivalent is required, along with 2+ years' experience with technical writing in a telecommunications or electronics field (operations and maintenance preferred), and experience working with documents conforming to Bell Standards. Excellent written, oral, and interpersonal skills are essential, as well as working knowledge of electronic word processing systems. Formal training in electronics, computer and/or telephony preferred, as well as central office switching and project planning experience.

For immediate consideration, please forward your resume to: Ericsson Network Systems Inc., Dept. CPD/217, P.O. Box 833875, Richardson, Texas 75083-3875.

An Equal Opportunity Employer m/f/v/h

ERICSSON
Network Systems Inc.

ELECTRONIC TECHNICIAN

ELI LILLY AND COMPANY IS CURRENTLY SEEKING QUALIFIED INSTRUMENT MAINTENANCE TECHNICIANS IN THE FOLLOWING AREAS

- PROCESS CONTROL INSTRUMENTATION-A MINIMUM OF 4 YEARS EXPERIENCE IN PROCESS INSTRUMENTATION OR RELATED WORK. PNEUMATIC AND ELECTRONIC PROCESS CONTROL INSTRUMENTATION BACKGROUND DESIRABLE.
- ANALYTICAL INSTRUMENTATION-A MINIMUM OF 4 YEARS EXPERIENCE IN ANALYTICAL EQUIPMENT REPAIR OR RELATED WORK. EXPERIENCE IN HPLC, GC AND RELATED SYSTEMS DESIRABLE.
- COMPUTERS AND PERIPHERALS-A MINIMUM OF 4 YEARS EXPERIENCE IN PERSONAL COMPUTER OR PROCESS COMPUTER SET-UP AND REPAIR.

THESE POSITIONS REQUIRE A TWO YEAR ASSOCIATE DEGREE IN ELECTRONIC TECHNOLOGY OR EQUIVALENT.

INDUSTRIAL ELECTRICIAN

ELECTRICIAN OPENINGS REQUIRING 6-8 YEARS EXPERIENCE IN INDUSTRIAL TROUBLESHOOTING AND REPAIR OF CONTROLS, MOTORS, PRODUCTION EQUIPMENT AND RELATED EQUIPMENT. ELECTRONIC EXPERIENCE WOULD BE ADVANTAGEOUS.

APPLY IN PERSON AT: EMPLOYMENT LOBBY, 1200 SOUTH KENTUCKY AVENUE OR SEND RESUME WITH EMPLOYMENT HISTORY AND EDUCATIONAL BACKGROUND TO: CRAFT RECRUITMENT, ELI LILLY AND COMPANY, LILLY CORPORATE CENTER-MAIL DROP 3111, INDIANAPOLIS, INDIANA 46285

ELI LILLY AND COMPANY
AN EQUAL OPPORTUNITY EMPLOYER

Data Processing

HENRY Vogt MACHINE CO.

NC PROGRAMMER

VOGT, a leading manufacturer of forged steel valves and fittings, heat transfer products and commercial ice making equipment, is seeking an NC Programmer. This 2nd shift position shall be responsible for developing NC programs either manually or through the use of CADAM or CATIA for machines with three axis or more of control.

The ideal candidate will possess journeyman level experience as a Machinist or Toolmaker with NC machining experience. A background in CATIA or CADAM would be beneficial. For the successful applicant, VOGT offers a progressive, team-oriented work environment with an attractive wage and benefits package. Qualified applicants should send a resume to:

Personnel Manager
Henry Vogt Machine Co.
P.O. Box 1918
Louisville, KY 40201-1918
Equal Opportunity Employer

	By title	By position	By level		By level	
	Executives	Top	4th	level	1st	level
	Managers	Middle	3rd	level	2nd	level
			2nd	level	3rd	level
	Supervisors	Bottom	1st	level	4th	level

FIGURE 1-2 Three Sets of Terms Used to Classify Managers

How are managers classified?

Supervisors First-level or bottom segment of management within an organization; has hourly employees as subordinates.

Managers may be classified by title, position, or level. Figure 1-2 shows three different sets of terms used to identify the management work force.

Generally speaking, **supervisors**, first-level personnel, and the bottom segment of management are all part of the same class—a group that usually has subordinates in the hourly work force. People in the supervisory class usually have moved into this managerial rank from the hourly work force. Often, they have some college education or vocational training, and they have a good knowledge of the technical aspects of the jobs held by those who work under them.

Middle managers Managers at the mid-level of the organization who supervise first-level managers; judged on managerial skills, they are usually working toward being in top management.

Middle management, managers, and second- and third-level personnel, on the other hand, frequently supervise people who are part of the first level of the firm. **Middle managers** manage other managers, usually have advanced education or have graduated from college, aspire to move up the executive ladder, have less technical training than the first-level personnel, and are evaluated for their managerial skills.

CEO (Chief Executive Officer) The top management position in an organization.

Another level of management manages managers; this is the top level, the one containing the executives. The people at this level have titles such as Vice President of Operations, Vice President of International Marketing, Vice President of Human Resources, Divisional Vice President, and President or Chief Executive Officer (usually addressed as the **CEO**). The skills demanded at this level cover a broad spectrum of activities, from negotiating with the head of national labor unions during contract discussion, to representing the corporation at congressional hearings in Washington, D.C., to addressing a group of stockholders at the annual meeting, to deciding the long-range strategy for developing and selling new products in overseas markets. Michael Eisner and Frances Hesselbein are examples of very good managers.

As CEO of the Walt Disney Company, Michael Eisner is credited with saving the company from financial ruin. Walt Disney, the founder of the Disney Company and the creator of Mickey Mouse and Disneyland, died in 1966. Between 1966 and 1984 (when Michael Eisner took over), profits dwindled, the stock price declined, the Disney television show was canceled (for the first time in three decades), and even attendance at the two Disney theme parks—Disneyland and Disney World—fell. The movies being produced by the Disney Studios—including *The Black Hole*—were innocuous and definitely disappointing at the box office. Eisner revitalized the company.

His first goal was to get Disney back on the air. According to Eisner, the television shows sell merchandise based on Disney characters and promote Disneyland and Walt Disney World; the amusement parks then stimulate enthusiasm for the movies; and the movies can be used to help keep the parks fresh. Eisner has been very successful in meeting his first goal: The Disney Sunday movie returned to the air, and the Disney Studios produced top-rated Saturday

Michael Eisner, shown here with the symbol of the Disney Corporation, Mickey Mouse, is an excellent manager. His efforts led to the revitalization and growth of the Disney Company. He is the CEO (Chief Executive Officer) of the organization, managing the Disney theme parks in Anaheim, Orlando, Paris, and Tokyo; managing the movie and television studios (Disney-MGM, including Touchstone), and managing the Disney retail stores.

morning cartoon shows and prime-time television such as the critically acclaimed and commercially successful *Golden Girls*. The studios returned to producing successful movies in 1986 with *Ruthless People* and *Down and Out in Beverly Hills* and continued through the late 1980s and early 1990s with such movies as *The Little Mermaid, Who Framed Roger Rabbit?, Dick Tracy, Pretty Woman,* and *Scenes from a Mall.* (As president of Paramount, his previous position, Eisner was responsible for turning out such hits as *Raiders of the Lost Ark* and *Terms of Endearment.*)

Both Disneyland and Disney World have been updated, and additional amusement parks have been developed and opened in Japan and Europe. Disney World and Epcot Center have been expanded, and in 1989, Disney added MGM/Disney Movie Studio Theme Park as a third component in the Disney World/Epcot Center complex in Orlando, Florida. Disney World now has the distinction of being the number one vacation and honeymoon spot in the world. In addition, Eisner has added retail stores called "The Disney Store" to the Disney Empire; fifty-five stores have already been opened across the United States. Eisner plans to quadruple that number within the next few years.[2]

Business Week calls Frances Hesselbein, executive director of the Girl Scouts from 1976 through 1990, the "Grande Dame of American Management."[3] In her book *The Female Advantage*, author Sally Helgesen describes Hesselbein as "the epitome of a distinctively feminine management style that executives would do well to emulate."[4] Managers at leading businesses like IBM and Motorola watch videotapes describing Hesselbein and her ideas. Even MBA students at Harvard study her management techniques.

When Hesselbein took over as executive director of the Girl Scouts in 1976, membership had been in a solid decline for at least eight years. Many considered the Girl Scouts to be irrelevant—a white, middle-class organization in a society that was rapidly becoming more aware of its cultural diversity. The "badges" that the girls could earn in scouting were in cooking and sewing, whereas the interests of the girls were in potential careers, technology, and contemporary issues. In addition, the Girl Scouts had competition from the Boy Scouts; the Boy Scouts were making overtures to girls to join their ranks. Hesselbein took a failing organization and turned it into an efficient, innovative, and responsive organization. She "managed with a mission." She says, "We kept asking ourselves very basic questions: What is our business? Who is the customer? And what does the customer consider value?" Hesselbein recognized cultural diversity by advocating "equal access" to the Girl Scouts; she started troops in neighborhoods that had never been a part of the organization and created programs for low-income girls. Today, 15 percent of the Girl Scouts are minorities; that is triple the percentage of a decade ago. Hesselbein recognized that girls wanted more than cooking and sewing; the two most popular badges today are "Computer Fun" and "Math Whiz." Publications for the Girl Scouts today cover topics like teenage pregnancy, drugs, sex education, and child abuse instead of good grooming and how to host a party. Hesselbein also excels in crisis management. In 1984, rumors were circulating that pins had been found in the famous Girl Scout cookies. Hesselbein managed to contain the damage to the organization and appeared on television news shows with a representative of the Food and Drug Administration to face the problem. New tamper-resistant packages were designed for the cookies. The FBI later determined that the rumors were a hoax. Under Hesselbein's administration, membership in the Girl Scouts has grown to 2.3 million, and the annual budget is $343 million.[5]

Frances Hesselbein is the former director of one of the largest nonprofit organizations in the world, the Girl Scouts. Business Week has called her the "Grande Dame of American management." She was the manager of the Girl Scouts from 1976 through 1990, developing the Girl Scouts into a contemporary organization responsive to the needs of its 2.3 million culturally diverse members.

THE WORLDS OF THE MANAGER

The manager works in three worlds simultaneously: personal, organizational, and socioeconomic. Every decision the manager makes is influenced by those three worlds. Figure 1-3 shows some of the factors and influences of each world.

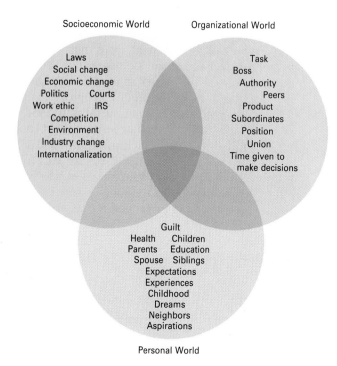

FIGURE 1-3 The Worlds of the Manager

The Personal World

What factors make up your personal world?

Each manager relates or responds to a job in a unique and very personal way. Who that person is, what that person wants to become, what forces exist in that person's home life—all these influence how a manager behaves and responds to work. Since no two managers share identical backgrounds and personalities, no two managerial jobs are performed in the same way.

Although we could have provided you with many examples of factors from a manager's personal world, the one selected is a truly contemporary issue: guilt. Many managers today are part of a dual-career household. *Fortune*, in conjunction with New York's Bank Street College of Education and the Gallup Organization, recently completed the first nationwide study of certain parental anxieties and how they carry over into the workplace. The study shows that fathers in dual-career couples share both the responsibility and the guilt, stress, and worry connected with obtaining care for their children.[6] (Another study, conducted by Stanford University, showed that husbands in dual-MBA career couples actually have more anxiety about the children than their wives do.) In *Fortune*'s study, nearly 30 percent of the men had refused a new job or a promotion or transfer because it would have meant having to spend time away from their families. Almost 25 percent of both men and women sought less-demanding jobs so that they could spend more time with their families. This study and others have also shown that children affect productivity, since working parents miss work because of a child's illness or a school function. Some of the results of the survey are in Table 1-1.[7]

Table 1-1 A Source of Managerial Guilt		
WHAT WORKING PARENTS SAY ABOUT CHILD CARE		
	MEN	WOMEN
Report that both spouses share equally in child care responsibility	55.1%	51.9%
Say the job interferes with family life	37.2%	40.9%
Sought less-demanding job to get more family time	20.5%	26.5%
Refused a job, promotion, or transfer because it would mean less family time	29.6%	25.7%
Felt nervous or under stress in past three months	49.2%	70.2%
Missed at least one workday in the past three months due to family obligations	37.8%	58.6%
Think children of working parents benefit by having interesting role models for parents	77.5%	86.3%
Think children of working parents suffer by not being given enough time and attention	55.4%	58.2%
Would like their companies to provide a subsidized child care center	38.5%	54.1%
Would like their companies to offer flexible working hours	34.8%	54.1%
Think companies can do more to help manage work/family responsibilities	34.5%	30.9%

Though working fathers and mothers pretty much agree that they share equally in child care responsibilities and that their jobs interfere with family life, more fathers say that they have refused a new job, promotion, or transfer that would take away from family time. Mothers are more likely to report that they feel stress. Only 30.9% of the women polled in *Fortune's* nationwide survey of 400 working parents wanted more child care help from their companies. But over half said they would like their employers to offer flexible working hours and provide subsidized day-care centers.

The Organizational World

In the organizational world of a manager, many elements exert a direct and usually immediate response or influence. These elements may include the nature of the task or product, the number and type of subordinates, and the relationships managers have with their bosses, peers, and subordinates.[8] The manager is also affected by company politics, communication systems, corporate culture, subordinates, and, quite possibly, a union. All of these influence what a manager does and does not do. This world differs from organization to organization. The work world of a bank, for example, differs from that of a hospital, and both differ from the work world of a governmental agency, a business unit, or a military group. In some organizations, social relationships are formal, dress is standardized, and colleagues are addressed by surname; in others, the atmosphere is informal, dress is casual, and first names are freely used. Recognition of these organizational differences is particularly important for managers in getting things done.

Tradition and Life Style

Each person is unique, with a personality and behavior that belong to that individual. So, too, with organizations. The U.S. Marine Corps, for example, has developed a *tradition* from the experiences and behavior of its personnel through the years. The psychological expectation that others have of Marines gives the Corps its tradition and its *life style*. The same process applies to other organizations.

Many corporations attempt to develop a life style among their managers by insisting that they wear similar clothing on the job, that they drive similar automobiles, and even that they reside in certain areas within a city. Perhaps an example will highlight what we mean by this tradition or life style. Many people consider banking a rather conservative industry. That is, you do not walk into a bank and find the employees wearing loud, wild, or bizarre clothing. Bank managers usually greet you in business suits. There are some banks that even insist upon white shirts or blouses as part of the uniform that generates a particular *image*. What they are trying to convey to the customer is the impression of stability, credibility, and security. These managers feel that casual clothes and eccentric behavior suggest flightiness, uncertainty, and rapid change—features that might be perceived negatively by potential customers. Thus, the tradition and the life style are perpetuated through the behavior, practices, policies, and procedures of management.

In every industry, then, you find different but definite traditions. There are some industries that tend to lead in innovation and risk taking. Some companies within an industry lead in establishing prices, in introducing new products, and in moving against the trend. In many such industries, there are also followers—those firms that have decided that the leadership costs are too high and whose heritage confines them to a follower role. That is not to say that only in the leader role can an organization be profitable. What we are saying here is that there is a niche or place that an organization fits best into, and it is an intelligent organization that is able to identify the features that give it its definite tradition and life style.

The awareness of life style and tradition is valuable to managers, who are in the position of developing objectives and establishing the long-range plans of organizations. Managers who do not know their company's tradition or life style may be making decisions that run counter to the productivity of the company, for, as mentioned earlier, industries, companies, departments, and functions all have an interdependence. A follower of the sports world is aware of what we mean by tradition and life style, for certain teams are known primarily as offensive teams in football, or run-and-shoot teams in basketball, or pitching teams and low-hit teams in baseball. The Cincinnati Reds have a different tradition, life style, and image from those of the New York Mets. Notre Dame's Fighting Irish differ in image from the Chicago Bears. What holds true in the world of athletics also exists in the organizational world.

The life style of an organization can be changed. A basketball manager who has had to play defensive basketball because of the inability of higher management to recruit tall players may change the life style of the team with some successful recruits—a number of seven-footers. *Fortune, Business Week,* and the *Wall Street Journal* are filled with stories of organizations that have, with managerial innovations, changed trends inherent in their tradition and life style.

Organizational Life Cycle

In a very simple way, you might say that organizations have three principal stages in their **life cycle**—a start-up stage, a keep-going stage, and a slowdown or start-again stage. Obviously, organizations get started. Once created, they tend to expand and get larger. The second stage in the evolution, then, is the period that could be labeled the *stabilizing stage,* when an organization, finding itself in the industry or economy, is adjusting to changes and is attempting to survive in perhaps a very competitive situation. The third stage of organization has two possibilities. An organization that has been unable to adjust will move to a slow-death or bankruptcy stage and terminate its existence. Or it may apply new ideas and new approaches to its problems or merge with other firms to start another growth cycle in its history. Organizations, therefore, have a starting point, a stabilizing point, and a kind of termination/start-again point.

Books about the history of business management are filled with case histories of defunct companies. Although small businesses are most susceptible to failure, giant firms are not immune. For example, W. T. Grant was a giant firm in the retail merchandising industry. With over 1,300 retail stores nationwide, it was a much larger organization than Sears, but it closed all its doors in the mid-1970s. The Chrysler Corporation had to look outside for new top management and to the U.S. government for financial aid to survive in the automobile industry in the early 1980s and again in the early 1990s. No industry is protected against "organizational cancer." Hundreds of banks and savings and loans closed their doors during the 1980s. The demise of Laker, Braniff, People Express, and Eastern in the airline industry; Daniel Boone, Arthur Treacher, and Minnie Pearl in the fast-food industry; Osbourne and others in the computer industry, and other companies in both growing and mature stages illustrates that all organizations, no matter how large or previously successful, must continually revitalize themselves.[9] In fact, all of American industry has been passing through a period of reflection and self-evaluation as international competition has uncovered elements of decay. Thus, the idea of a life cycle extends far beyond human life to all types of organizations.

A knowledge of the position of a company in its life cycle may help a manager with a number of career-cycle decisions. Only three examples of such decisions are offered here; they are related to the idealized life cycle of an organization in Figure 1-4.

Knowing where a company is in its life cycle may help managers match their own needs with those of the company. For example, if a manager's pri-

Life cycle The stages in the life of an organization that include a start-up and growing stage, a stabilizing stage, and a declining or revitalizing stage to avoid extermination or death.

What is the value in knowing an organization's life cycle?

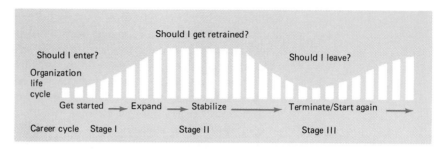

FIGURE 1-4 Relation of Career Cycle to an Organization's Life Cycle

mary assets are innovating, contributing new ideas, and accepting change, a company in the early stages of growth would value that manager. A company that has stabilized its growth (and is thus in its second stage) would find such managerial characteristics disruptive. On the other hand, a manager who does not particularly like constant change might enjoy working with an organization that is in the stabilizing stage; in such a stage, his or her particular assets would match those of the company. At any point of a growth cycle, managers would do well to make an assessment of their own abilities and characteristics to see if they match those demanded by the situation.

The knowledge of a company's life cycle can help managers direct their own efforts. Managers should reassess what they have been doing relative to the company's stage of growth and ask whether what they have been doing is consistent with what the company seems to need at that point in its life cycle. If there is no match from the reassessment, managers may be able to train or develop themselves to be more in line with the company's stage of growth.

Knowledge of the stage of a company in its life cycle can be very helpful to managers in determining when to change jobs. The worst time for managers to go into the job market searching for other managerial opportunities is when they have been released from a company in its last stage. The best time to move is when they are still mobile and the organization is still respected as a source of employment. It is possible for managers to sense the characteristics of "organizational cancer" and to make plans to move to other organizations before the final stage is reached.

The life-cycle concept is not restricted to industries or corporations. The idea can be applied to departments or functions. For example, during a time of high employment, the personnel manager is very important because of the search for capable managerial talent. Similarly, when an organization is in the early stages of growth with a new union, a great deal of uncertainty exists and the personnel function is again vital. At a later stage in the growth of the company and the union, the personnel function may not be as critical. Knowledge of life cycle as an organizational characteristic is important in matching a manager to the organization and in directing personal efforts.

The Socioeconomic World

Are there recent changes in a manager's world?

The socioeconomic world contains all those elements of the political, legal, economic, social, and physical world outside the organization. This world includes customers, suppliers, competitors, social institutions, technology, and

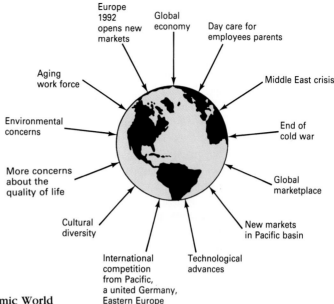

FIGURE 1-5 The Dynamic Socioeconomic World

all other factors directly or indirectly affecting the manager's organization in either the domestic or the international context. All of these can have a lasting impact on what managers do or should do on their jobs. The socioeconomic world is dynamic. Figure 1-5 illustrates some of the recent changes in a manager's socioeconomic world. Economic factors, including interest rates and levels of employment, clearly affect managerial strategies. Energy issues, including unstable crude oil prices, deregulation of natural gas, and nuclear energy, have served as environmental shocks felt by all managers. New growth opportunities have developed in rapid-growth high technology such as communication and information processing, personal computers, artificial intelligence, expert systems. More job opportunities exist in the small- to medium-size firms than in the large companies.

Some industries have tended to merge and others to split apart. Hostile and friendly "takeovers" of one company by another were common in the 1980s but have declined in numbers in the 1990s because of economic and political pressures. Thousands of managers have been "let go" in recent years as corporations undergo **downsizing** to become more competitive. Deregulation of the banking, airline, and trucking industries has caused fundamental structural changes and problems for those industries. The "aging of America" is having a definite effect on managers. Older Americans—particularly the baby boomers[10]—are creating new markets for health care, recreation and travel, and more expensive homes and cars. At the same time, there is a shortage of young people for entry-level jobs in service industries such as fast food and amusement parks.

One of the most far-reaching developments in recent history has been the internationalization and globalization of many business organizations. Technology has forced all nations to face increasing competition. Few contemporary decisions can be made in isolation; borders are now defined by satellite communication stations; the ongoing changes in the USSR, Central Europe, South

Downsizing The process of reducing the size of an organization to cut costs and more aggressively meet competition; many employees, including middle and upper level managers are laid off.

What is the impact of globalization?

America, Africa, the Middle East, China, and the Pacific Rim are causing daily reassessment of organizational plans and strategies.

American companies are closing down factories in the United States and moving their operations to other countries, such as Mexico, to take advantage of the cheaper labor costs. The closing of the production plants has an immediate impact for laid-off workers and managers and a longer-term impact for neighborhood schools and governments as a tax base is eliminated.

At the same time, foreign companies are moving into the United States. Sanyo has opened production facilities in Richmond, Indiana, and San Diego, California; Honda is producing automobiles at plants in Ohio; and Toyota has put a major plant in Kentucky. Competition between the states to obtain new foreign plants is fierce as each outbids the other with tax reductions, incentives, and promises to give the foreign countries everything they need to be successful—including a highly motivated work force. And foreign corporations own many of the firms in the United States.

Global Application

American Firms Owned by Foreign Corporations

Most Americans know that Shell Oil sells gasoline in many sections of the United States. Some Americans realize that this well-established oil company is a Dutch-owned firm. The movement by foreign corporations to own traditional American firms is on the increase, and a few of the recent acquisitions are listed here. To some Americans, this shift in ownership is alarming, and they fear that the United States is losing control of its industrial base; to other Americans, it is an example of the globalization of corporations.

American Firm	Foreign Owner
■ Pillsbury	■ Grand Metropolitan (England)
■ Uniroyal/Goodrich Tire	■ Michelin (France)
■ CBS Records	■ Sony (Japan)
■ Rockefeller Center	■ Mitsubishi (Japan)
■ Genentech, Inc.	■ Hoffman-Roche (Switzerland)
■ MGM-UA	■ Pathe Communications (France)
■ Firestone	■ Bridgestone (Japan)
■ Poulan/Weedeater	■ Electrolux (Sweden)
■ Glidden	■ ICI (England)
■ Andrew Jergens Company	■ Kao Corporation (Japan)
■ Sohio	■ British Petroleum (England)
■ Shaklee Corp.	■ Yumanouchi Pharmaceutical Corporation (Japan)

FUTURE TRENDS IN THE MANAGER'S WORLD

Futurists, those people who focus on predicting changes in the 1990s and the twenty-first century, see that significant redirections are currently taking place, based on the happenings of the last decade or so. Some of these people concentrate on technological innovations; others see a rapid shift in the total external environment. All these trends will have an impact on managers.

One of the most famous futurists is John Naisbitt. His well-researched, best-selling book *Megatrends: Ten New Directions Transforming Our Lives*[11] was originally published in 1982. What he predicted then came true during the rest of the 1980s. At that time, his list of trends included

1. A move to synthesize the dual direction of high tech and "high touch" (humanizing high tech)
2. A move from short-term to long-term orientation
3. The decentralization of all aspects of society, not just of managerial organization
4. A shift from dependence on institutional help to dependence on individual and self-help
5. A shift from representative government to participatory democracy, where each citizen is directly involved in important issues
6. A change from vertical, hierarchical structures to horizontal "networking"
7. The geographical move in the United States from the North to the South
8. A change from "either/or" to multiple options
9. A movement toward a world economy
10. Rapid movement into an information society

Naisbitt, together with Patricia Aburdene, has since published a second book, *Ten New Directions for the 1990s: Megatrends 2000.*[12] Their new predictions are listed below.

Naisbitt calls his new predictions the "Millennial Megatrends: Gateways to the 21st Century." They are

1. The Booming Global Economy of the 1990s
2. A Renaissance in the Arts
3. The Emergence of Free-Market Socialism
4. Global Lifestyles and Cultural Nationalism
5. The Privatization of the Welfare State
6. The Rise of the Pacific Rim
7. The Decade of Women in Leadership
8. The Age of Biology
9. The Religious Revival of the New Millennium
10. The Triumph of the Individual

These predictions are already well on the way to being a reality, particularly in the areas of global economy and the age of biology.

Perhaps never before in the short, 100-year history of management has change played a more critical role.[13] There is no question that the nature of a manager's job will change.

What are the weaknesses of the twentieth-century manager?

Reports, studies, and articles done by *U.S. News and World Report, Business Week,* and *Fortune* in recent years have pointed out the weaknesses of twentieth-century managers: They focus on short-term profits while sacrificing long-term goals; they are unable to implement technological innovations, unable to turn new technology into salable products; they are too narrow-minded about geographical boundaries—they want to work only within narrow geographical lines, within only the United States, for example; they do not cooperate enough with other managers, either within their own firms or in other firms; they do not adequately train and motivate their employees.

What should be the characteristics of the twenty-first-century manager?

After interviewing many executives, management consultants, and business-school professors, *U.S. News and World Report* came up with the following list of must-have traits for successful managers in the twenty-first century.[14] The manager must be

1. A Global Strategist. Managers must be able to manage in an international environment, not just a national one. Managers must identify and use markets worldwide.

2. A Master of Technology. Managers must be able to take innovations in technology and make better products and better decisions.

3. A Politician par Excellence. Managers must be politicians and be able to deal with international and national politicians, laws, treaties, and regulations. Knowing the right people can cut out a tremendous amount of red tape.

4. A Leader-Motivator. Managers must be able to lead their organizations and to coach their employees to reach the organization's goals and objectives. Twenty-first-century managers must be able to lead their organizations to their goals and objectives in a global economy with rapid changes.[15]

THE MANAGEMENT CHALLENGE

We began this chapter with a brief reminder of the Space Shuttle Challenger tragedy, an event that will be remembered for many years and that highlights the world that today's managers face. Good intentions, committed people, and a supportive population are not sufficient ingredients for the successful completion of projects.

In the rest of this chapter, you read about the worlds managers face: personal, organizational, and socioeconomic. In Figures 1-3 and 1-5, you saw the scope of the manager's world through the use of such terms as "Personal Guilt, Stress, Expectations"; "Organizational Authority, The Task, Bosses"; and "International Competition, Society's Work Ethic, Changes in the Environment." You probably could add many more to this sample, because each person has a unique set of forces from these three worlds that affect that person. Our point is very straightforward. Your behavior and performance as a manager are products of the special way you respond and relate to those forces in your unique worlds. A reading of this introductory chapter provides you with the base from which to expand your knowledge of and insight into the practice of managing the resources of an organization to successfully meet goals and objectives.

It is important that you approach the remaining sections of this book with a realistic frame of mind. Your managerial world is neither doom-and-gloom nor Pollyannish. The manager's world is a very complex one, and many of the forces in the three worlds are serious and even threatening. We believe that people aspiring to positions of leadership in organizations must view the forces as realistic challenges. Therefore, we end this first chapter with a series of challenges that you and others will face as members of the Manager's World.

Challenges in the personal world

- Must responsibilities to self, spouse, children, parents, friends, and community be sacrificed for corporate demands and expectations?
- Can personality growth and development exist outside the organizational work world?
- Will the win-lose model of personal development among family members be replaced with a more healthy model?

Management Application

Managing Cultural Diversity: Rainbows and Colorblindness

Statistics and analyses provided by the U.S. Census Bureau and other organizations that study population growth indicate that the population mix is changing in the United States and in the world. The traditional majority in the United States—white with European ancestry—is decreasing in size. Birth rates for this group have leveled off or somewhat declined. At the same time, birth rates for blacks, Hispanics, and other groups have escalated. Some have predicted that by 2010, whites will be the minority in the United States and blacks and Hispanics will be the majority. Already in some cities, notably Chicago and Detroit, blacks are the majority. Hispanics and other groups are the majority in Los Angeles. In today's overall world population, whites are already the minority, making up only 30 percent of the population. Of the 1.3 billion people who will be added to the world's population by the year 2000, 92 percent will live in Africa, Asia, and Latin America. This rainbow of colors and cultures will continue. The shift in population mix will have long-lasting effects on society, politics, and business.

Du Pont and other companies are holding workshops for their employees to help them work through their prejudices and develop a should be treated as equals, with equal respect, colorblindness. The idea is that all people regardless of color, culture, or origin. Other companies are sending employees to Columbia University in New York and other universities throughout the country to attend workshops in managing cultural diversity. Some companies are working closely with elementary and secondary schools to identify students with promise early in their academic careers, particularly blacks and Hispanics, to give them support, encouragement, and career counseling. The companies are hoping these students will go into fields such as engineering and science, where shortages have been predicted. The companies are also working with secondary schools to develop technical programs for the high school students who may be their potential employees.

Source: Current Population Reports, Population Estimates and Projections, Series P-25, no. 1018, U.S. Department of Commerce, Bureau of the Census, *Projections of the Population of the United States, by Age, Sex, and Race: 1988 to 2080* by Gregory Spencer; "The Biggest Secret of Race Relations: The New White Minority," *Ebony* (April 1989), pp. 84–88; Nancy J. Perry, "The Workers of the Future," *Fortune*, Special Issue: The New American Century (Spring-Summer 1991), pp. 68–72.

Challenges in the organizational world

- Can our economic-industrial system accommodate all those who want to make a meaningful contribution, regardless of age, sex, or racial origin?

- Is management able to create an environment that is cooperative rather than adversarial, innovative rather than routine, sharing of surplus rather than protective of it?

- Must American industry be locked into destructive economic cycles?

- Will American managers open their doors to the growing number of minority people in the work force? Will opportunities be created for meaningful contributions rather than token compliance with governmental regulations?

- What are the social and ethical responsibilities of American corporations in a world frequently using different norms of behavior?

- Is it possible to simultaneously seek short- and long-term goals? Must American firms be addicted to the short run?

- Will there be a new form of corporate structure that is responsive to destructive attacks from global competition, unfair government involvement, stock manipulators, and acquisition raiders?

Challenges in the socioeconomic world

- Will the United States have the will to assume an important leadership role in global problems and issues while at the same time addressing the domestic needs of Americans?

- Is it possible to simultaneously meet the competing objectives of a healthy economy, a healthy environment, and a healthy population?

- Are we doomed to continual confrontations between the haves and the have-nots on this planet?

- Can world competition become a positive force in bringing out the best performance from all people? Can the concept of quality be infused into all aspects of organizational life?

- Is it possible for a balance to exist between opportunities and threats in the three worlds?

KEY TERMS

Managers The people in an organization who are primarily responsibile for seeing that work gets done through the efforts of others.

Supervisor First level or bottom segment of management within an organization; has hourly employees as subordinates.

Middle managers Managers at the mid-level of the organization who supervise first level managers; judged on managerial skills, they are usually working towards being in top management.

CEO (Chief Executive Officer) The top management position in an organization.

Life cycle The stages in the life of an organization that include a start-up and growing stage, a stabilizing stage, and a declining or revitalizing stage to avoid extermination or death.

Downsizing The process of reducing the size of an organization to cut costs and more aggressively meet competition; many employees, including middle and upper level managers are laid off.

STUDY ASSIGNMENTS

1. What does the Challenger accident suggest about the managerial process?
2. Identify some managers that you know, and describe what they do that makes them managers.
3. What are the differences in roles and responsibilities of a manager, like Michael Eisner, of a "for-profit" organization, from the roles and responsibilities of a manager, like Frances Hesselbein, of a "not-for-profit" organization?
4. Why does "having subordinates" help classify an individual as a manager?
5. How do the roles and responsibilities of a manager differ according to the various levels of management?
6. How might the individual life style of a manager's personal world be different from or similar to the life style of the manager's organizational world? Could there be a conflict if they are different?
7. Why would an understanding of organizational life cycle be helpful to you in looking for a job or in considering career options?
8. Why are some businesses and organizations able to survive for a long time when others fail? Should businesses be allowed to die?
9. How will growing numbers of women and minorities in the work force influence the way managers manage in the future?
10. Why is it important for you to know and understand how various environmental factors influence a manager's job? What is the value of this information to you?
11. How do all the different demands of the personal, organizational, and socioeconomic worlds affect a manager's ability to perform his or her job?
12. After considering some of Naisbitt's observations, what future trends can you think of that will shape and influence the manager's world of tomorrow?
13. How would you respond to the various managerial challenges noted at the end of the chapter?

Case for Discussion

ANDERSON BAKERY, INC.

In 1932, Aaron Anderson began a small bakery in San Jose, California, a small farming community. Anderson's, as it soon became known, won wide acceptance in the community for its oven-fresh breads and tasty line of pastries. As San Jose grew, so did Anderson's. The twenty-fifth anniversary was a grand occasion, for it was not only a silver anniversary for the company but also the date Aaron Anderson, Sr., formally relinquished control of the company to his son, Aaron, Jr.

In his farewell talk at a banquet given for the company's twenty employees and their families, the senior Mr. Anderson said, "This is a very happy time for me. We all have worked hard to make this company what it is today. What started out in a converted warehouse with only two ovens, a second-hand truck, and two men plus myself has grown into something we can all be proud of."

Aaron, Jr., was only twenty-three years old when he took over his father's bakery, but he was well liked by the employees and extremely effective in dealing with both employees and customers. And why not? He had grown up with the bakery and had worked in every aspect of the business.

Largely because of his talents and hard work, the years from 1957 to 1980 brought tremendous growth and change for the bakery. Not only did the younger Anderson have a knack with people; he also had a good sense for business. His greatest strength lay in his ability to anticipate change and to translate his forecasts into future-oriented strategy.

For one thing, he was quick to see how supermarkets would, as they did, capture the bulk of food sales and ease the neighborhood "mom-and-pop" stores out of business. He recognized that this would mean that the nationally known brands of bakery products would be a major competitor, since the larger markets preferred products whose advertising was done nationally, by the producers themselves. Through skillful selling, he countered this threat by persuading nearly all the major local supermarkets to set up in a corner of their stores a display of freshly baked Anderson's bakery goods. Anderson's and the supermarket would share the profits. The bulk of the baking was performed at Anderson's central bakery, and the products were rushed fresh, only minutes out of the oven, to the stores.

Between 1970 and 1980, Anderson Bakery grew still further. By changing its form of business from a proprietorship to a corporation in 1951, Anderson was able to get the financing necessary to double the baking capacity. He built a new, modern, more efficient bakery in 1973 on the outskirts of the most rapidly developing residential section of town. This brought about further expansion in the firm's delivery fleet. By the close of 1980, Anderson's had nearly 1,500 employees and a fleet of more than 600 trucks that carried the firm's bakery goods to neighborhoods as far away as Santa Cruz, Redwood City, and even South San Francisco.

By 1987, Anderson, Jr., was thirty years older than the day he took over the business, but considerably better off financially and a good bit busier. It was worth it, he thought. "I guess if it weren't for the challenges and problems I faced and solved, life would be pretty dull. I can't complain. I just wish my son, Aaron, were more interested in the business. I guess that's what I get for spending so much money for his piano lessons—well, his mother wanted the boy to study music. Now he is twenty-two and a college graduate. But I don't think he's got a sense for business. As a matter of fact, all he talks about is going on to graduate school in New York City to study music. I'd like someone in the family to take over the business. The only other one is his sister and she lives in Modesto, married to a rancher. There is no way I can get her and her husband to leave what they've got there. I don't know what I'll do. I'd like to slow down and start taking life easier."

By 1990, Anderson Bakery, Inc., started to experience difficulties, even though it still produced the highest-quality fresh bakery goods in the area. It was difficult to find dependable employees. Costs seemed to be growing faster than revenues. As a matter of fact, in 1990, the board of directors decided not to declare a dividend, for the first time in the history of the corporation.

Other problems surfaced. For one thing, the federal government had sent a team of safety inspectors to the plants to check their compliance with the Occupational Safety and Health Act. Close to $500,000 in changes were ordered as a result of the inspection. For another thing, the firm was charged by the state's human rights commission with racial discrimination and ordered to meet certain quotas or be fined severely.

By the middle of 1991, Aaron Anderson, Jr., decided he had had enough of the business. It was clear that his son had no interest in the bakery, and there seemed little sense in continuing to try to move at the pace he did when he was much younger. After all, he still had his health and had always wanted to retire early and do some traveling. So, when a handsome offer was made to buy the business, he sold out.

Chapter 2

The Roots of Management

Learning Objectives

1. *Define* management and explain its meaning.
2. *State* the basic functions performed in the managerial process.
3. *State* the basic ideas of scientific management and the contribution of Frederick W. Taylor and his colleagues.
4. *Outline* the framework of the classical writers Henri Fayol and Mary Parker Follett.
5. *Discuss* the significance of the Hawthorne Studies.
6. *State* the implications of Douglas McGregor's Theory X and Theory Y.
7. *Describe* the manager's job as analyzed by Henry Mintzberg.
8. *Show* how the contingency approach provides a basis for integrating classical and behavioral theories.

OVER the years, the standard brown trucks of United Parcel Service (UPS) have become a familiar sight throughout the country, and the firm has gained a reputation for productivity and dependability. Although the firm's managerial practices and policies have earned the admiration of its competitors and the respect of its customers, many observers have noted that these same practices and policies have created considerable bitterness and resentment among the firm's approximately 80,000 nonmanagement employees.

At times, the firm's supervisory practices have been characterized as paramilitary and its labor relations as medieval. Every dimension of the job has been designed to maximize productivity and promote efficiency. Drivers are given precise procedures for entering and exiting the vehicle to minimize the time involved in making deliveries and pickups.

Although nonmanagement employees generally acknowledge that the firm's wages and benefits are good, they often complain that the extreme push for productivity results in considerable job stress and continuing conflict with management. Everything is timed. Drivers receive a daily performance evaluation that compares the miles they drive and the number of deliveries and pickups they make with a computerized projection of what their performance should have been for that day. These evaluations are used to compare drivers with one another to identify poor performers. Any individual classified as the "least-best driver" receives additional supervisory attention until that individual "gets it right." Failure to improve performance and meet the computerized performance projections results in warnings, suspension, and firing.

The UPS managers can be characterized as highly dedicated and committed. These managers, most of whom started at UPS in nonmanagement positions, are expected to take the initiative, assume responsibility, work long hours, and accept the notion that hard work today will yield substantial rewards in the future. In addition, regardless of their positions in the firm, managers are expected to work with one another as "partners" in achieving the firm's goals of high productivity, reliability, and customer service. In return for this commitment and working together as partners, managers share in the success of the firm through substantial bonuses and the opportunity to purchase UPS stock (98 percent of UPS stock is held by active and retired UPS managers).

The style and practices of management at UPS have not only enabled the firm to be highly successful, but also contributed to the creation of a "unique corporate mystique" that has gained widespread recognition and admiration throughout the business world. However, from the perspective of the nonmanagement employees, is the admiration of the firm's success and image justified? ■

Are management practices the same in all companies?

You have just read a brief description of the management style and practices at UPS. The styles and practices of IBM, GM, McDonald's, Hewlett-Packard, or Ford would differ from those of UPS. Why the differences? What theories, concepts, or goals serve as the benchmark for management styles and practices? There are many possible answers.

One of those answers might come from the historical experience of the top management. The field of management itself also has a historical base. Management styles and practices have been studied for almost 100 years. The theories, models, and concepts of management practices have roots in industrial settings from the late 1800s to last week. The theme of this second chapter is history. It is our belief that history has a message for all of us.

In this chapter, we first define management and summarize its essential functions. Second, we summarize some of the basic ideas of early writers that underlie contemporary management thought. Third, we examine the transition from the classical approach to management to the behavioral approach. Finally, we show how today's managerial environment requires more of a contingency approach to management, an approach that responds to both competitive forces and social changes in the workplace.

THE MEANING OF MANAGEMENT

What is the meaning of management?

The terms *management* and *manager* are so widely used that it would seem that everyone would know exactly what they mean; yet, as with many commonly used words, there is considerable confusion as to their exact meaning. For one thing, the word *management* often identifies a special group of people at the top of an organization. For another, the words *managers, administrators, entrepreneurs, leaders, commanders,* and *bosses* are often used interchangeably. Obviously, we should first clearly identify our subject.

The role of a manager focuses on the coordination of activities performed by others and the unifying of their efforts. It involves problem solving and the optimum use of a variety of specialists using analytical techniques adapted from many other fields of study, such as psychology, engineering, economics, statistics, and accounting.

Management The process by which a cooperative group directs the use of resources (money, people, things) toward common goals.

What, then, is a definition of management that will be the foundation for our discussion in this book? **Management** is the process by which a cooperative group directs the use of resources (money, people, and materials) toward common goals. The key ideas in this definition further clarify its meaning. First, management is a *process*—it is not merely a body of knowledge, theories, and ideas; it is active and involves clearly defined functions, such as planning, organizing, staffing, leading, communicating, and controlling. These functions form the basis for study in this book. Second, management involves *cooperation* of individuals and thus deals with the behavioral components of how people in groups can best work together. Finally, the aim of management is the achievement of common *goals*. Management thus involves how the group is directed toward the achievement of objectives. In short, it is purposive and provides a common pattern that reduces random, undirected efforts.

This process is handled by a distinguishable group (managers) who coordinate the activities of others. Managers work through others and facilitate joint efforts by the individuals in the organization. Since managers are action-oriented, the first step in our study is to summarize the functions that managers typically perform.

FUNCTIONS OF MANAGEMENT

What are the functions of management?

Management is frequently defined in terms of the types of activities managers should do. This book is devoted to a somewhat detailed description of not only what managers do but also how they do it. To keep our attention on all functions as a group, let us summarize the functions of management that are later discussed in detail in Part II (see Figure 2-1).

1. Managers *make decisions*. Alone or in groups, they select from alternatives or options the direction to be taken by their unit. Chapter 5 describes decision making.
2. Managers *plan* for the future before taking action. They attempt to anticipate developments in the environment and to adapt their organization to expected social needs. Chapter 6 discusses strategic or long-run planning as the process for selecting the direction suitable to the organization's resources and available opportunities.
3. Managers *organize* activities by designing formal structures and responsibility. Chapter 7 explains the theories and techniques of organizing.
4. Managers *staff* the organization by selecting, training, and evaluating people for the needed positions; that is, the staffing function matches the people to the requirements of the structure. Chapter 8 explains the nature of the varied activities involved in the management of personnel.
5. Managers *direct* or *supervise* the work of others; in other words, they lead others toward the organization's goals. In Chapter 9, we explain the different theories of leadership and the styles that have emerged.
6. Managers *communicate* with subordinates, colleagues, and superiors. We see in Chapter 10 how this linking function involves the transmission of ideas so that actions are coordinated.
7. Managers *control* activities; that is, they utilize processes that measure actual performance and guide it toward some predetermined goal. Chapter 11 explains the essentials of all control systems and outlines the specific characteristics of particular types of control systems.

FIGURE 2-1 Functions of Management

These seven functions are closely interrelated and often occur simultaneously or in different sequences. Today, these functions seem a simple and straightforward way of defining management. Only within the last 100 years, however, have they been recognized as a unified and separate group of activities, even though people have been doing them for centuries. Before they were so recognized, you could not have studied management as a subject or been trained in school to be a manager. Of course, some people have performed some of these functions for a long time, but they could learn only by example, from family members or as apprentices. Since a knowledge of the development of these ideas can help explain the meaning of managerial functions, we now turn to this historical perspective.

HISTORICAL FOUNDATIONS OF THE PRACTICE OF MANAGEMENT

The practice of management has a long history. First, we shall summarize the evolution of the most important ideas that preceded the formation of the unified field. We take the position that the history of management is analogous to a river, which consists of different sources and tributaries, all flowing together and providing tremendous power when combined into a consistent and directed flow. By recalling the broad scope of early ideas, we indicate that management thought is not restricted to narrow channels or pools of knowledge but involves the flowing together of many ideas from varied sources. Then you can better understand the interrelationships of the many ideas in this rich heritage, and you will be better able to appreciate both contemporary contributions and their classical foundations.

Early History

What are the roots of management?

In early civilizations, management activities were handled by priests, chiefs, armies, and governments. Basic management concepts, therefore, flow from the earliest times. Having evolved over a long time, they offer you a perspective for studying management.[1] In management practice, we may search for broad generalizations, but we must adapt them to conditions that we face at the time action is needed. In other words, our generalizations depend upon particular situations as they change from time to time. To save space and cover a long historical period, we have consolidated in Table 2-1 the pre-twentieth-century sources of management ideas, the situational demands that fostered those ideas, and their implications for managing today. This table will enable you to understand the heritage preceding the emergence of management as a separate field of study. It further indicates that changes in situations require new ideas and adaptations of old ideas.

Table 2-1 not only demonstrates how environmental conditions help determine new concepts and techniques but also lays the foundation for your understanding of the nineteenth-century setting in which the separate field of management emerged. The Industrial Revolution beginning in the late eighteenth century called for larger organizational size and focused on refinements in methods for management.

Table 2-1   Early Streams of Managerial Ideas

DATES	SOURCES	IDEAS	SITUATIONAL DEMANDS	RELEVANCE TO TODAY'S MANAGEMENT
5000 B.C.	Sumerian civilization	Written records	Formation of governments and commerce.	Recorded data are essential to life of organizations.
4000–2000 B.C.	Egyptian	Planning, organizing, controlling	Organized efforts of up to 100,000 people for constructing pyramids.	Plans and authority structure are needed to achieve goals.
2000–1700 B.C.	Babylonians	Standards and responsibility	Code of Hammurabi set standards for wages, obligations of parties, and penalties.	Targets of expected behavior are necessary for control.
600 B.C.	Hebrews	Organization	Leaders organized groups to meet threats from outside.	Hierarchy of authority is a basic idea.
500 B.C.	Chinese	Systems, models	Commerce and military demand fixed procedures and systems.	Patterns and procedures are desirable in group effort.
500–350 B.C.	Greeks	Specialization, scientific method	Specialization laid foundation for scientific method.	Organizations need specialization; scientific attitude promotes progress.
300 B.C.– A.D. 300	Romans	Centralized organization	Far-flung empire required communication and control by Rome.	Effective communication and centralized control are necessary.
A.D. 1300	Venetians	Legal forms of organization	Venetian commerce required legal innovations.	Legal framework for commerce serves as foundation for ventures.
1400	Pacioli	Double-entry bookkeeping	Effective classification of cost and revenue demanded by increased trade.	Accounting systematizes record keeping.
1500	Machiavelli	Pragmatic use of power	Governments rely on support of masses. Expectations of leader and people must be clear. Opportunistic use of personal power makes leaders effective.	Realistic guidelines for use of power are a key.
1776	Adam Smith	Division of labor	The competitive system resulted from specialization.	Specialization and profits are key to private enterprise.
1800	Eli Whitney	Interchangeability of parts	Mass production is made possible by availability of standard parts.	Modules, segments, and parts are building blocks for organizations.
19th Century	Western nations	Corporation	Large amounts of capital required by entity with long life and limited liability.	Separation of owners from managers increases demand for professional managers.

Roots of Scientific Management

One of the first to respond to the challenge of this revolution was Charles Babbage, a mathematician and inventor. He wrote an essay that proposed "principles of manufacturing," and he pioneered the scientific investigation of specialization.[2] He also developed an early prototype of a mechanical computer, 100 years before modern electronic computers. Other writers also began to focus on the requirements for the new field of management. After 7,000 years, the many streams of ideas flowed together in response to the new demands by the economy and the society. With this heritage and in this setting, a group of pioneers gave birth to a new field of study—management—that unified many of the streams of ideas.

Another pioneer whose interest stemmed from operation problems was Frederick W. Taylor. In response to a technical paper presented to an engineering meeting in 1886 by Henry R. Towne, Taylor observed that he, as operating manager of a steel plant, needed to develop the concept of objective standards for methods and times of production. He observed that workers limited production (he called it soldiering) because their only standards were rules of thumb that they developed by trial and error. Taylor argued that too much of management's job was being left to the worker. He felt that it was management's job to set up methods and standards of work and to provide an incentive to workers to increase production.

Taylor's ideas of management were explained in two influential books, *Shop Management*[3] and *Principles of Scientific Management*.[4] He received further national attention in 1912 during congressional committee hearings when public opposition developed to his "efficiency" approach. His 1911 book and the congressional hearings led to his being called the "father of scientific management."

Taylor contributed a number of techniques for improving production management—time study for setting standards, functional specialization of managers' duties, and incentive systems—but his greatest importance to our overview of management thought lies in his identification of management as a separate field of study, with explicit guidelines for scientific study of the management functions. His guidelines for **scientific management** can be summarized in four general areas:

1. Discovering, through the use of the scientific method, basic elements of work to replace rules of thumb
2. Identifying management's functions of planning work, instead of allowing workers to choose their own methods
3. Selecting and training workers and developing cooperation, instead of encouraging individual efforts by employees
4. Dividing work between management and the worker so that each would perform the duties for which each was best suited (specialization), with a resultant increase in efficiency

Although these guidelines for scientific management appear today to be both helpful and appropriate,[5] their proponents came under continual attack from other groups, both practitioners and academics. We'll see later in the chapter that a number of contributors developed responses to these criticisms, recognizing that Taylor and the scientific managers laid the foundation for the study of management as a distinct and separate group of activities. Further-

Is scientific management alive today?

Scientific management
An approach to studying management that uses scientific guidelines to explain the functions of management and the role and responsibility that managers have in seeing that work gets done.

more, they met the challenge of their times in increasing productivity and efficiency during the rapid industrialization in the early twentieth century in the United States.

In addition to Taylor, there were a number of other contributors to scientific management. Henry L. Gantt, a Taylor associate, emphasized morale and psychological factors and offered a new incentive wage system and a bar control chart for production. (The Gantt chart will be discussed in detail in Chapter 18.)

Frank Gilbreth concentrated on time and motion studies and the improvement of methods of work. Building upon his experience in bricklaying, he offered approaches for studying individual motions (called therbligs, which is merely Gilbreth spelled backwards with the *t* and the *h* transposed), used motion pictures and specialized machines for studying motions, and developed a group of principles of motion economy. His approach was to seek the best way and then to have managers teach all workers in that best way. Lillian Gilbreth joined her husband in this one-best-way quest by contributing her expertise in psychology to guide management in dealing with the human element.

Scientific management first recognized management as a separate discipline, promoted scientific methods, advanced a new attitude toward studying management, and developed new specific techniques of analysis, including time and motion study. Generally, its proponents viewed management as a new, specialized area of engineering, in which the physical aspects of the workshop were paramount. Comprehensive approaches for all levels of management came from a closely related, but different, group of pioneering writers and practitioners, now called the classical-management pioneers. Their contributions provide the basis for present-day study in management.

Classical Contributions to Management Thought

Contributors to classical thought included a large number of writers, most of whom were practicing executives during the first half of the twentieth century. For our purposes, we shall concentrate on two writers who developed concepts of what managers *ought* to do: Henri Fayol and Mary Parker Follett. Figure 2-2 outlines the flow of concepts and techniques from scientific management to classical management.

FIGURE 2-2 Basic Concepts and Techniques in Early Literature

Scientific managers (Taylor et al.)

- Use of scientific method
- Set objective standards

- Search for the best way (method)
- Planning, scheduling—a job for managers
- Training workers
- Use of incentive systems

Classical pioneers (Fayol et al.)

- Identify management functions
- Management—a separate group of activities
- Principles to guide management
- Management—a dynamic and changing field

Ideas of Henri Fayol and Mary Parker Follett

Henri Fayol (1841–1925), a French contemporary of Taylor's, was the earliest classical pioneering writer. His chief contributions can be grouped in two parts: (1) his view of management as a process consisting of five elements (functions) and (2) his proposal of fourteen principles to serve as prescriptions for managers' actions. All these were developed from Fayol's experiences as a successful managing director of a French coal-mining firm; they were not the result of empirical testing, since the infant area of management had not attracted the interest of researchers.

Before Fayol's work, management had been viewed as a skill depending upon personal capacities of the individual that could not be learned in school. Fayol argued that his own success as an executive was due not to his personal capacities but to his system of management, consisting of five functions: (1) planning, (2) organizing, (3) command, (4) coordination, and (5) control. (Fayol's functions were quite similar to those around which this book is organized, especially if you substitute leading—directing and supervising—for command, and add staffing and communicating as a means of achieving coordination.) Today, with minor variations in terminology, Fayol's fundamental idea of analyzing management by functions remains basic to most discussions of management.

Fayol's fourteen principles were advanced as prescriptions for managers, although he emphasized that they were not the only ones and warned that they should be considered dependent on individual situations. (In his words, application was a matter of "proportions.") Figure 2-3 outlines Fayol's principles.

FIGURE 2-3 Fayol's Fourteen Principles of Management

1. *Division of work.* Specialization makes greater expertise possible and facilitates training.
2. *Authority.* The right to give orders and the power to exact obedience, with responsibility flowing "wheresoever authority is exercised."
3. *Discipline.* The "outward marks of respect observed in accordance with the standing agreement between the firm and its employees."
4. *Unity of command.* An employee should receive orders from one superior only.
5. *Unity of direction.* Each group with the same objective should be in the same department.
6. *Subordination of individual interest to the common good.* Interests of employees should not take precedence over the interests of the undertaking as a whole.
7. *Remuneration of personnel.* The rate of remuneration depends on (1) the circumstances of the situation—for example, cost of living, business conditions—and (2) the value of the employee.
8. *Centralization.* Decentralization is the degree of importance of the subordinate role; centralization reduces this role: The choice depends upon the situation.
9. *Scalar chain.* The chain of superiors ranging from the top authority to the lowest ranks may be supplemented by a "gangplank" by which subordinates deal with each other horizontally.
10. *Order.* Both materials and people should be located in their proper places.
11. *Equity.* "Desire for equity and equality of treatment are aspirations to be taken into account in dealing with employees."
12. *Initiative.* An employee should be encouraged to think and act within the constraints of authority and discipline.

13. *Stability of tenure of personnel.* Since successful firms need a stable group of personnel, practices should reinforce long-term commitment to the firm.
14. *Esprit de corps.* Harmony and union among personnel are great strengths of an organization, achieved by avoiding the abuse of written communications.

Henri Fayol's contributions succeeded in raising the status of management practice by supplying a framework of analysis and study. His functional approach clarified the job of managers, and his principles, although quite general and vague, have served as guidelines for more detailed development by later writers and researchers.

Mary Parker Follett (1868–1933) held views consistent with those of other classical contributors, but she filled in the gaps in the areas of psychology and sociology. Her published speeches[6] provided keen insight into management problems and served as a transition between classical and modern approaches.

Like other classical writers, she proposed principles. Her four principles were (1) coordination by direct contact of the responsible people concerned, (2) coordination in the early stages, (3) coordination as the reciprocal relating to all factors of the situation, and (4) coordination as a continuing process. The underlying idea of her approach was that management is dynamic and continually in need of change to fit the "total situation."

Follett viewed management as a behavioral process. Her thought is best identified by four terms that she used continually:

1. Evoking—drawing out from each individual the fullest potentials by emphasizing training and development to meet new challenges
2. Interacting—adjusting between individuals and the situation, with resulting changes in both
3. Integrating—searching for new positions by responding to the relationships between people and the total situation
4. Emerging—bringing new ideas into use to meet changing and new situations

Mary Parker Follett delivered many lectures to executives in both Great Britain and the United States when management was young and developing. Her realistic and practical interpretation of classical principles, with emphasis on human relationships and the total situation, is still timely. For example, John Naisbitt built upon Follett's idea of the "total situation" in the best-selling *Megatrends* (1984) to support his thesis of long-term orientation as one of the ten trends transforming our lives.

Resolving conflicts among people in organizations received Follett's special attention. Arguing that conflicts could be expected in changing situations, she explained that the usual managerial reaction of dominating or compromising led to only temporary adjustments. She advocated a process in which parties in conflict would interact in the light of the existing facts and allow a new solution to emerge that none of the conflicting parties had previously considered. She called this approach to resolving conflict an integrating process. For example, if you find that two people have opposite views for action, you should encourage each party to work out a new view not previously held by either and to integrate this new position into the situation. The emergence of this new position through interaction would result in a lasting solution, since neither person would win or lose but each could feel he or she had been a part of discovering the new solution. As a manager, you would achieve coordination through direct contact with the people concerned, and your authority would flow from the situation, not be handed down from superiors.

The early writers responded to the increasing needs of large organizations for management guidelines in the first half of the twentieth century. They were primarily practicing executives who attempted to build a theoretical base for the new discipline. Although the scientific method was applied to physical conditions at the shop and work level, the propositions were based on experiences and reflective logic.

THE TRANSITION YEARS: SCIENTIFIC MANAGEMENT CHALLENGED

Why change from scientific management?

The ideas of many of the classical writers were born in the stresses and strains of the American factory. Machines frequently broke down; replacement parts had to be created on the spot; on assembly lines, the rates of the machines and the workers did not always mesh; dirt, heat, and noise made working conditions difficult for employees and supervisors; labor was plentiful, although not all workers spoke the same language. To many workers, however, employment in the American factory was a superior alternative to working underground in dangerous mines, to working as migrant labor on farms, or to working in slavelike situations where the pay and human dignity were low.

That the writings and teachings of Taylor, Gantt, Frank Gilbreth, and others found receptive disciples among American factory managers should come as no surprise. The problems uppermost in their minds involved engineering, mechanics, and manufacturing. These American managers attempted to harness an industrial giant through work design and simplification, human engineering, and simplistic assumptions about manufacturing, workers, and management. A few examples will demonstrate their positions.

- Most problems can be reduced to a simple cause-and-effect relationship. If a machine stops, find the cause and fix it. If a worker is slow, bring in a replacement.
- Workers are individuals who work to better themselves financially. They respond best to financial rewards.
- The military system of organization is best. Certain workers are put in charge of others. These "captains" are given authority and the power to command.
- The workplace lends itself to a form of scientific decision making. Managers gather the data, analyze it, and make the decisions.
- All jobs can be broken down into functions, and those functions can be taught. Managers, like workers, will improve their efficiency by learning a set of managerial functions.

The rapid and successful growth of American industry during the early 1900s proved to many that the American way of managing was the answer to the questions of manufacturing efficiency. Did the scientific management people have all the right answers, and were their answers applicable to other forms of business enterprise? Were the management principles universal and timeless, as claimed by proponents?

During the 1930s and 1940s, many changes in society occurred that produced changes in management thinking. First, workers became more educated, which increased the complexity of their needs and expectations. Workers' rights became institutionalized in new laws and labor unions. Manufacturing and marketing processes became more sophisticated. Publicly owned corporations increasingly replaced owner-operated companies; thus, the demand for professional managers increased. Business schools began to turn out more graduates.

The industrial society, with its strong emphasis on manufacturing, was gradually transformed into the postindustrial society, in which marketing and service activities became predominant. Government's influence on business increased through regulation or deregulation. In short, these and other changes in the environment called for changes in the orientation of management thinking. In some instances, changes occurred in a natural manner so that the concepts of scientific management produced a gradual evolution. In other instances, research findings and the ideas of insightful persons challenged many of the earlier assumptions about work, the worker, and the workplace.

The Hawthorne Studies

One landmark in management thinking was the study conducted during the 1920s and 1930s in the Hawthorne plant of the Western Electric Company near Chicago. Researchers in this major manufacturing facility of AT&T initiated an ambitious study of the effects of physical factors (lighting, humidity, temperature, working conditions, fatigue, working hours, and rest periods) on productivity. Workers were divided into experimental groups, in which changes were made in these physical factors, and into control groups, in which no changes were made.

At the early stage, the Hawthorne Studies were aimed at determining the effects of lighting on productivity. Over a twelve-week period, lighting was increased and then decreased. The researchers expected to find a direct relationship between lighting and productivity of the workers, but these early studies showed a most surprising result. Productivity tended to increase when light was increased, but also when light was decreased. In fact, productivity remained higher than normal even when the light was reduced to an amount near that of moonlight. From these results, it was apparent that some other forces, entirely unrelated to lighting, were affecting the workers' output.

The workers at the Hawthorne plant of General Electric, near Chicago, were studied during the 1920s and 1930s to determine the effects of physical factors like lighting on productivity. Researchers were surprised to discover that productivity increased both when lighting was increased and when lighting was decreased. The results of the Hawthorne Studies showed that the increased attention given to the workers was one factor increasing productivity.

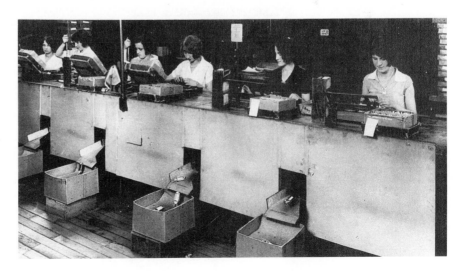

Elton Mayo, a Harvard social scientist, and other researchers became associated with the experiment; they expanded its scope to include the human factors of cooperative efforts by groups of workers. By the time the Hawthorne Studies were completed, over 20,000 employees had participated in one way or another. The researchers' findings have been reported in a number of books, providing factual evidence of both the research methodology and the results.[7] Since the Hawthorne experiment became recognized as a monumental advancement in research in management, we shall summarize its key findings, which set the stage for modern approaches.

The findings of the Hawthorne Studies may be described in both broad and specific terms. Many of the findings challenged the assumptions of scientific management, stated earlier in this chapter. The most significant broad finding was that, regardless of variation in physical factors (such as changes in lighting), productivity was significantly affected by the human reactions of those being observed; that is, the increased attention and recognition given those in the experiment increased individual pride and motivated them to produce more. This insight has been called the **Hawthorne Effect**. The human element was thus found to be a most important subject for study.

A second broad finding was that informal groups of workers that emerged in the workplace were an important force in managing that had not been recognized by classical writers.

Third, the experiment illustrated a critical characteristic of true research: the readiness of researchers to redesign a project to include new variables when results indicate that preconceived hypotheses are insufficient to explain results. They had started the experiment to explain the effect of physical factors but concluded it by studying the importance of human factors in management.

Although the Hawthorne Studies were conducted in the late 1920s and early 1930s, knowledge of their conditions, methods, and findings is of fundamental value to contemporary management. The Hawthorne experiment introduced interdisciplinary cooperation into the study of management, so that today new ideas are flowing into the field from a variety of scholarly disciplines—psychology, sociology, engineering, and economics. See Table 2-2.

What were some results of the Hawthorne Studies?

Hawthorne Effect People behave differently when they receive special attention and recognition from others in the organization.

Table 2-2 Workplace Ideas

Pre-Hawthorne	Post-Hawthorne
1930s	
1. Workers respond primarily to money.	1. Social and psychological needs are as important as monetary needs.
2. People hire in as individuals and continue to work as individuals.	2. People become members of a work group and take on the values of the group.
3. First-level supervisors know exactly what goes on during work hours.	3. An informal organization exists. This informal group influences the output of individual workers, sets standards, and controls the information management receives. A social system exists.
4. Employees respond to the chain of command—they do as they are commanded by the supervisor.	4. Informal groups have informal leaders—these leaders have an impact on the productivity of the worker and the work group.

Global Application

Social Dislocation and Malaysian Working Women

The industrialization of a society usually brings with it important changes in the lives of its people. One change is the social dislocation that occurs when men and women move from one environment (usually the rural, farm situation) to another environment (usually the city, factory situation).

Malaysian women are involved in a tremendous social and economic change that will affect them forever. They are part of a rural–urban migration that is spreading rapidly to many Pacific Rim countries.

Taiwan, Singapore, South Korea, and now Malaysia have discovered one road to economic improvement. These countries find that they have large numbers of women in their population, women who match the needs of the electronics and textile industries. In 1991, there were approximately 120,000 women workers in the textile and electronics industries of Malaysia. Women held 80 percent of the 85,000 jobs in electronics, and 70 percent of the women are Malaysian.

The development of the electronics and textile industries, in which the technology encourages the use of women, is strongly supported by the Malaysian government. Histori-

cally, the Chinese live in the cities and run the businesses and the Malays live in the countryside. The Malaysian government would like to correct that imbalance. Their policy, however, brings with it many social problems.

Many of the Malaysian women are Muslim, and their religious principles conflict with the government's New Economic Policy. Their faith means searching for something more than materialism even though, in some families, the woman's paycheck makes her the primary wage earner. Many of the women are in the *dakwah* movement (using the veil), and clothing thus becomes a symbol. The factory women have been addressed as *Minah Karan*, which means "hot stuff" and is best represented by tight jeans. Thus, the Malaysian Muslim woman finds herself in a very confusing and ambiguous role.

At this point in history, Malaysian workers, especially women, have no advocate for their concerns and rights in either the government or the labor unions.

References: John Douglas, Stuart M. Klein, and David Hunt, *The Strategic Managing of Human Resources* (New York: John Wiley, 1985), p. 116; Margaret Scott, "Brave New World," *Far Eastern Economic Review*, December 21, 1989, pp. 32–34.

Chester I. Barnard

What is the acceptance theory of authority?

A practicing chief executive of the New Jersey Bell Telephone Company, Chester I. Barnard, supplied new concepts of management and modified some of the classical prescriptions.[8] His concepts and observations laid the foundation for many of the contemporary approaches discussed later in this book. Some of Barnard's most important observations were these:

1. Managers must encourage cooperative efforts by members of the organization. Barnard viewed interpersonal relations of members as central to his thesis and was interested in explaining why members cooperate and what managers can do to induce cooperation.

2. Informal organizations, as observed in the Hawthorne Studies, are important in all cooperative efforts. They can be used to provide useful support for formal organization if they are recognized and understood.

3. Inducements to cooperate include not only monetary incentives but also nonmaterial rewards and persuasion.

4. Communications among members of an organization implement cooperation and encourage members to accept instructions.

5. The art of decision making is an important area of analysis. Later, this received close attention by theorists and the quantitative school of thought.

6. The traditional concept of authority must be revised. Acceptance of an order is critical for managerial effectiveness. Managers, therefore, must realize their dependence on subordinates.

The last observation by Chester Barnard is a very important contribution to an understanding of how to manage others. Barnard adds another element by suggesting that the right to issue commands and the power to enforce do not necessarily ensure that subordinates will behave or perform in the expected way. Acceptance by subordinates is essential for authority to be effective. If people blindly do as they are told, managers need not be too concerned about subordinates as thinking human beings.

Acceptance theory For managers to be effective, their authority must be accepted by others. A manager whose authority is not accepted will not be effective.

The **acceptance theory** of authority highlights the behavioral dimensions of the work relationship.

Herbert A. Simon

Probably the strongest attack on classical-management thought, using the most interdisciplinary approach, was made by Herbert A. Simon in 1947 in his book *Administrative Behavior*.[9] Simon built on Barnard's pioneering work in management. Simon's early prominence was as a political scientist in the area of public administration, which led him to fundamental work in management. With his focus on decision making, he found the disciplines of economics and psychology most useful. During the infancy of computer science, Simon used the computer to simulate decision-making processes, and he continues to make contributions in even wider fields as a professor of computer sciences. He was awarded the Nobel Prize in Economics in 1978.

Simon's attack on classical principles was based on the fact that they had not been tested and, furthermore, could not be tested without substantial revisions. He then proceeded to reconstruct administrative theory, using Barnard's decision-making approach.[10] Since communication of information is essential to good decisions, he sought a means of analyzing human mental processes by employing electronic computers to simulate rational processes. He observed that the economist's assumption of an economic human being rationally attempting to optimize decisions was impractical in real administrative situations; therefore, his administrative human being has "intended rationality"—that is, seeks to be rational within the limits of human capabilities—and thus usually seeks a satisfactory but not necessarily optimal solution.

Douglas McGregor

Probably the most concise summary of the theory that emerged from behavioral research was made by Douglas McGregor in 1960.[11] McGregor identified the basis for differences in managerial theories by stating their different assumptions about human nature. He referred to the theory based upon the assumptions tacitly made by classical writers as Theory X, and the theory based upon assumptions consistent with the behavioral studies as Theory Y. He stated the assumptions of Theory X as follows:

1. The average human being has an inherent dislike of work and will avoid it if possible.
2. Because of this dislike of work, most people must be coerced, controlled, directed, or threatened with punishment to get them to put forth adequate effort toward achieving organizational objectives.
3. The average human being prefers to be directed, wishes to avoid responsibility, has relatively little ambition, and wants security above all.

McGregor recommended his opposing Theory Y, based on different assumptions, as being more suitable to modern management:

1. The expenditure of physical and mental effort in work is as natural as play and rest.
2. People will exercise self-direction and self-control toward objectives to which they are committed.
3. Commitment to objectives is a function of the rewards for achievement.
4. The average individual learns, under proper conditions, not only to accept but also to seek responsibility.
5. The human capacity for imagination, ingenuity, and creativity is widely distributed among individuals.
6. In modern industrial life, the intellectual potentialities of the average human being are only partially utilized.

These explicit statements of the different assumptions of two theories tended to clarify the dichotomy in management concepts and techniques. The assumptions about human nature of Theory Y are basic to the behavioral emphasis in management since the 1960s.

CONTEMPORARY APPROACHES TO THE MANAGER'S JOB

We now turn to some contemporary approaches that have their roots in concepts and techniques of the classical writers and the transitional challengers: (1) a refocus on the nature of managerial work, (2) a contingency approach for selecting concepts, techniques, and styles tailored to specific situations, and (3) approaches for special needs.

The Nature of Managerial Work

The classical writers identified managerial functions as descriptions of what a manager should do. However, only a few studies focused on what managers actually do. In the early 1970s, Henry Mintzberg showed interest in the nature of managerial work.[12] A summary of Mintzberg's findings gives us a more complete picture of what a manager actually does. Based on his study of the activities of five practicing chief executives and the studies of other investigators,

Mintzberg generalized his description of the nature of managerial work in current practice. Mintzberg found that about one-third of a manager's time is spent dealing with subordinates, about one-third dealing with external (outside the organization) matters, and the other one-third in a variety of activities, including contacts with superiors, tours of the workplace, and thinking.

1. Managers feel compelled to work hard at "an unrelenting pace." They often take their work home, since they cannot fit it into a standard workday.
2. Managers' jobs are characterized by brevity, variety, and fragmentation. Efforts have a short duration; at one minute, the manager must handle one matter; and at the next, a completely different one. Seldom do managers complete one activity without interruption.
3. Managers prefer live action and deal with specific rather than general issues.
4. Managers prefer verbal contacts by telephone or in face-to-face meetings, for example, they devote little time to handling mail and written memos.
5. Managers seek brevity and adjust to continual interruptions. They live with pressures to allocate their time to the most pressing matters.
6. When they know the parties well, managers use informal contacts, but when they deal with outsiders and ceremonies, they schedule formal meetings.
7. Managers appear to have little control over the use of their time, but they attempt to initiate their commitments and requests for necessary information.

What are Mintzberg's managerial roles?

Mintzberg grouped ten basic roles performed by managers into interpersonal, informational, and decisional roles, as illustrated in Figure 2-4. These roles—organized sets of behaviors belonging to a position—describe what managers actually do, whereas functions of managers had historically described what managers should do.

FIGURE 2-4 The Roles of a Manager

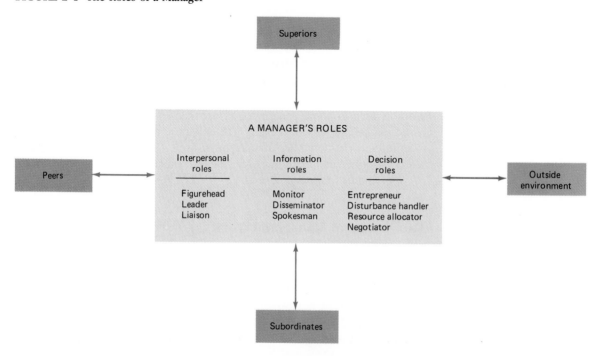

Ethics Issue

Labor Exploitation Revisited

In the early days of the Industrial Revolution (in both Europe and America), it was common for employers to pursue a policy of worker exploitation. Creative minds had produced machines that could perform the skills of a worker. To some, these inventions were a blessing; to others, they were a curse.

To workers who endured horrible conditions in the mines or who faced starvation from unemployment, factory jobs became a blessing. To others, the oversupply of unskilled labor was a curse, because it permitted owners and managers to maintain the lowest-cost work force so as to be competitive in the marketplace. Long hours were common, and men, women, and children worked on machines in factories where there was more concern for speed and output per hour than for the safety of the machine operators. People who complained about low wages were easily replaced by the eager unemployed.

The unsatisfactory employer-employee relations led to a war in many industries in the 1920s and 1930s and precipitated action by the U.S. Congress. Committee hearings on such practices resulted in the enactment of labor laws and, eventually, the right of workers to organize themselves into labor unions.

In the early 1990s, there was a development at the international level that is reminiscent of the exploitation of the early 1900s. A six-month investigation by *Business Week* revealed that China is using labor from work camps and prisons to manufacture exports targeted for markets in the United States, Germany, and Japan. This labor force is a vast one, numbering close to 10 million, and what disturbs many is that these people are often imprisoned without trial and for political reasons. They work long hours, up to fifteen hours per day, and receive low pay, if any at all.

Because many global corporations use subcontractors or buying agents or engage in joint ventures with companies in another country, such practices have escaped the notice of these firms, especially American ones. It is a violation of U.S. law to import goods produced by prison labor, and many believe it is a violation of human rights to use political prisoners to create an inexpensive work force and thus a competitive advantage in world markets.

Other countries, especially Taiwan and Japan, view China as a source of cheap labor and they have invested capital and machinery in Chinese labor camps.

Does America's experience provide a perspective needed in the global marketplace? Should the United Nations, the International Court of Justice at The Hague in the Netherlands, or the International Labor Organization in Switzerland demand hearings on and studies into the exploitation of prison labor as a cheap way to gain a competitive edge? Is the practice a violation of human rights? Is there a need for an international labor-relations policy?

References: John Douglas, Stuart M. Klein, and David Hunt, *The Strategic Managing of Human Resources* (New York: John Wiley, 1985); "China's Ugly Export Secret: Prison Labor," *Business Week*, April 22, 1991, pp. 42–46.

The Contingency Approach

A review of the evolution of management thought shows that managerial concepts developed to fit the needs of the conditions of the time. Yet, as management emerged as a separate field of study, writers continually searched for a single approach that would provide the framework for all managers in all situations. Each group of writers, using the ideas from their own particular discipline, overgeneralized and advocated new approaches as substitutes for those previously developed. Many of these different proposals tended to be in conflict, and separate schools of thought developed. Scientific managers viewed management as primarily a matter of using physical resources efficiently. Classical writers viewed management as primarily a matter of structuring formal authority. Human-relations consultants maintained that management was simply a matter of dealing with people. Others insisted that management was chiefly a psychological and sociological discipline involving individuals and groups. Some built their framework around the economists' focus of allocation of resources; some viewed it as dependent upon quantitative methods and the computer. Most of these new ideas, in fact, contributed to the growth of management thought and supplied concepts and techniques for the manager's use. None succeeded in offering a single general theory.

As management matured after 1960, research studies continually pointed toward the observation that many of the apparently conflicting ideas were useful in some situations and not in others. Some theories fit for certain managers, and some theories were applicable to others. This body of literature gave rise to a school of thought called **contingency theory**: There is no one best way to manage, organize resources and work, plan projects, direct and supervise people, communicate to others, and control the operations of a firm. What is "best" depends (or is contingent) upon the environment of the organization, its technology, the variety of industries, and the varying natures of competitors, products, and markets.

You would be in error to conclude that any approach works or that the toss of a coin will give you the direction of your firm. The remaining chapters of this book will provide you with some of the personal, organizational, and environmental forces that help define the contingencies of each situation. Figure 2-5 illustrates the contingency approach to contemporary management.

If you are searching for a single cookbook set of propositions appropriate to all situations, you will be disappointed. The contingency approach provides a basis for selecting appropriate managerial actions. It stresses the conditions

How does the contingency theory work?

Contingency theory (approach) The concept that ideas and techniques of management depend upon the situation, including technology, the external environment, and the people of an organization.

FIGURE 2-5 The Contingency Approach

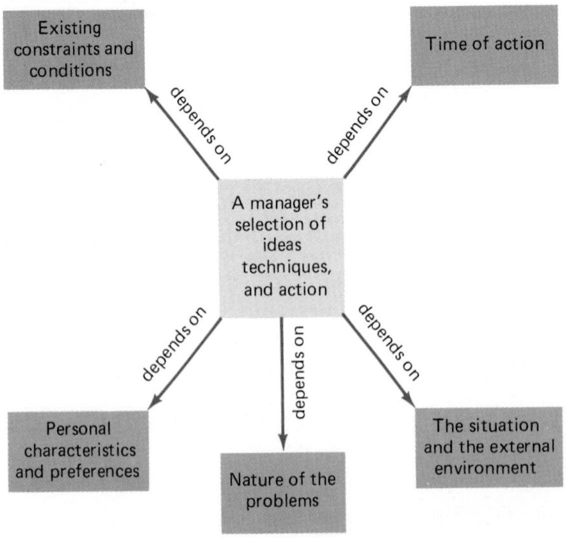

under which the propositions would be valid. It aids in proceeding through the jungle of conflicting schools of thought by distinguishing the strengths of each school to fit them into an overall approach for selection in different situations. We offer, as an end to this section, a few examples of contributions to management thought that were responses to specific needs. The needs came from the success of Japanese management, and the reality of radical uncertainty.

Approaches for Special Needs

Theory Z The managerial theory that is built on family ties, social institutions, moral duties, and cohesion of individuals, e.g., Japanese related.

Theory Z[13] is a title selected by William Ouchi in 1981 to explain the basis of an industrial society that emphasizes values not considered in McGregor's Theories X and Y. The popularity of Theory Z has been due to the success of Japanese management in producing high-quality products and increased worker productivity. Underlying the elements of Theory Z is a cultural environment, such as that of the Japanese, that places high importance on group identification with a corporate unit or an industrial clan, on consensus in decision making, on a cooperative rather than a competitive attitude, and on stability of human relationships. Theory Z prescribes that if such a cultural environment does not already exist in a nation, it should be created. In this chapter, we summarize the assumptions about human nature upon which Theory Z is founded.

Theory Z assumes that industrial workers

1. Seek intimate and cooperative work relationships with peers, subordinates, and superiors, supported by a strong and well-defined corporate philosophy.
2. Are alienated by a work environment in which family ties, traditions, and social institutions are minimized.
3. Have a strong sense of moral obligation, cohesion of individuals, discipline, and order.
4. Can be trusted to do the right thing if managers can be trusted to look out for the workers' welfare.

The essence of these assumptions is the importance of the group, not the individual. All members can trust one another to seek the group good with minimum individual cost. Characteristics of these ideal groups are lifetime employment, infrequent individual evaluation, nonspecialized careers, implicit controls, collective decision making, and collective responsibility where risks are spread among the group.

One challenge from the Theory Z example is important in a chapter describing contemporary approaches to managing. How many present American management practices are constrained and limited by assumptions about the nature of men and women and their workplace? How many other theories are out there yet to be identified, described, and analyzed? As more and more Japanese, German, British, Canadian, Chinese, and Soviet firms (to name a few) establish plants, distribution centers, and offices in the United States, staffed by people of varied backgrounds and cultures, is there not a need for new theories? Cultural diversity is moving into American corporations at a fantastic pace, and all in the field of management must be prepared to meet the new challenges of the twenty-first century.

Many other examples could be given, but the point is probably clear to you. The field of management is under tremendous pressures from rapid changes in all parts of the world. Few things are sacred anymore. More and

Management Application

How to Manage Uncertainty

Uncertainty seems to be the word of the day throughout the world. There is hardly an area on any continent where someone can look to the past, experience the present, and predict the future with confidence. Few foresaw that the unification of East and West Germany would occur before the twenty-first century, and there seems to be no end to the changes in the Soviet Union.

Many academic and professional voices are calling for a revision in all aspects of running an organization. They are asking what theories of economics best explain the behavior of markets; what assumptions are appropriate for the marketing of goods and services to consumers; what methods are best for the production of quality products; and what strategy and structure are appropriate for dealing with constant conditions of uncertainty.

Popular lecturer and author Tom Peters believes there is a need for new models of organization to meet "radical uncertainty." In an in-

sightful article, Peters describes the traditional approaches that many firms take to the management of their resources. In one of his models, he calls the traditional approach "The Inflexible, Rule-determined, Mass Producer of the Past."

Peters and others believe that the traditional approaches to management have been a burden and a handicap to those firms that must relate to the dynamic changes in their environment, their competitors, their customers, and their technology. He goes on to call for a new model of organization: The Flexible, Porous, Adaptive, Fleet-of-Foot Organization of the Future.

Although some believe Peters has overstated his case with such a request for a new model, Peters is serious in his concern for the future of American organizations.

Source: Thomas J. Peters, "Restoring American Competitiveness: Looking for New Models of Organizations," *The Academy of Management Executive* (1988), pp. 103–9.

more organizations are moving toward greater employee participation in decision making, greater use of team and project management, and temporary or ad hoc structural arrangements. There are pluses and minuses in this situation.

You may be tempted to believe that anything that is historical has no place in a dynamic, changing world. You may think that effective managing is just responding to the immediate. The challenge is to find those concepts and practices from the past that have value and utility in present situations.

A definite advantage of this situation is the realization that there will be opportunities for people to create new ideas and approaches to the problems organizations face. Those of you who like flexibility, change, and challenge will be in high demand.

SUMMARY

The manager's job can be described in terms of functions that should be performed, the roles to be assumed, certain characteristics that have been observed, and a number of approaches that have been advanced. A knowledge of the evolution of thought lays the foundation for appreciating the context of contemporary discussion. A general understanding of the types of knowledge a manager needs and the types of problems to be faced is the framework for more detailed study.

Chapter 2 ends your introduction to the manager's world. The chapter continued giving you an insight into the development of the field of management.

You read of the changes brought to the scientific management approach by the questions raised from the Hawthorne Studies, the thoughts of Chester Barnard, the criticisms of Herbert Simon, and the reflections of Douglas McGregor.

The contemporary picture of the management field became complex as you read of the more recent contingency approach and the examples of recent issues that demand new theories and approaches.

Chapter 2 ends with a sense that the evolutionary process in management is continuing, that there is value in the lessons from the past, and that there is a challenge to all who enter this field. In some cases, theory will help you in selecting the best practice; in other cases, your practices may be new or may even violate traditional ones.

KEY TERMS

Scientific management An approach to studying management that uses scientific guidelines to explain the functions of management and the role and responsibility that managers have in seeing that work gets done.

Hawthorne Effect People behave differently when they receive special attention and recognition from others in the organization.

Acceptance theory For managers to be effective, their authority must be accepted by others. A manager whose authority is not accepted will not be effective.

Contingency theory (approach) The concept that ideas and techniques of management depend upon the situation, including technology, the external environment, and the people of an organization.

Theory Z The managerial theory that is built on family ties, social institutions, moral duties, and cohesion of individuals, e.g., Japanese related.

STUDY ASSIGNMENTS

1. What is your opinion of the management approach of UPS?
2. Management is sometimes defined simply as "getting things done through others." What are the strengths and weaknesses of this definition?
3. What are the differences between managers and nonmanagers? Give some examples from your own experience.
4. Why is Frederick W. Taylor generally recognized as the father of scientific management?
5. Comment on how each of Fayol's Fourteen Principles of Management would or would not apply to managing in today's environment.

6. Why is knowledge about the Hawthorne experiment important to an understanding of the shift in emphasis from classical and scientific management orientation to the contemporary approaches?

7. Compare Barnard's contribution with those of the classical pioneers. What ideas did Barnard stress that had not been recognized by Fayol and Taylor?

8. Summarize the assumptions of McGregor's Theory X and Theory Y. From your own experience, which assumptions about human nature are more realistic in modern society?

9. How does Ouchi's Theory Z differ from McGregor's Theory Y? Since Theory Z is patterned on Japanese practices, can it be applied in the United States or other countries?

10. How do the roles and characteristics of managers described by Mintzberg explain the manager's job better than do the classical managerial functions? Should a course in management concentrate on what managers do or what managers should do?

11. What problems and challenges do you see facing the manager of the twenty-first century? Which ones are the most important? Why?

Case for Discussion

MANAGEMENT STYLE AT FEDERAL EXPRESS

Since its founding in 1972, Federal Express not only has proven to be an extremely successful enterprise, but also has received considerable attention and praise for some of its unique and innovative managerial practices. Many observers attribute Federal Express's success in establishing the overnight air express package business to a management style that focuses on people, encourages change, and accepts a wide range of managerial approaches.

Preserving Federal Express's dynamic management style has not been easy. The firm's founder, Frederick W. Smith, has frequently expressed the concern that as the firm grows, there will be a continuing problem of how to keep the organization's structure from getting out of control. If not controlled, the structure might evolve into a bureaucratic form that would inhibit the firm's dynamic management style, particularly with respect to the way people are managed. As a result, the top management of Federal Express has initiated management practices designed to keep the firm's organizational structure lean while at the same time ensuring adequate control.

One way to preserve a lean and responsive structure is to limit to five the number of organizational levels between any nonmanagement employee and the CEO. Having too many levels creates distance between people and breeds a bureaucratic staff that can retard responses to changing situations.

Federal Express uses a variety of approaches to help reinforce and preserve its focus on people. For instance, managers have incentives based on how they reward their nonmanagement subordinates who have demonstrated exceptional performance. In addition, top management attempts to communicate with every employee in the firm. They use closed circuit television to inform and to maintain contact with their geographically dispersed employees.

At Federal Express, there is a willingness on the part of management to use, innovate, or adapt whatever approach is necessary to achieve a high degree of performance. Managers are encouraged to implement successful techniques that have been used by other firms. Although this approach has proven to be quite beneficial to Federal Express and has contributed to its highly motivated workplace and market success, some observers believe this management style results in organizational inefficiencies and major mistakes. For example, in the late 1980's, its Zapmail venture failed.

Chapter 3

The International Challenge

Learning Objectives

1. **Define** the terms multinational corporation (MNC), supranational corporation, transnational corporation, and direct foreign investment.
2. **Identify** the reason that nations trade with one another, and state the economic principle explaining international trade.
3. **State** the reasons companies develop multinational companies in choosing the modes of foreign involvement.
4. **Outline** six modes by which multinational companies develop foreign involvement.
5. **Describe** the variables to be considered by multinational companies in choosing the modes of foreign involvement.
6. **Define** the terms ethnocentric, polycentric, and geocentric.
7. **Define** the terms culture and culture shock.
8. **Identify** the differences in management functions when operating in an international environment.

I N 1983, in the quiet community of Marysville, Ohio, the Honda Corporation of Japan began assembling automobiles for sale in the United States. To many people, Honda's decision to initiate manufacturing operations in the United States was simply crazy. It was hard to believe that a Japanese company known for quality products and manufacturing know-how would attempt to make cars in a country where the auto industry was in such bad shape and where the work force was made up of highly paid individuals who had a reputation for low productivity and poor workmanship.

Some industry analysts suggested that Honda's action was a public relations effort intended to relieve the pressure on the U.S. Congress to impose import quotas on Japanese auto manufacturers. Others argued that this action was a part of Honda's bold global strategy to continue its expansion beyond its basic motorcycle business, into a relatively new venture for Honda, automobiles.

At the time, many people were skeptical about Honda's plans for Marysville. Some analysts doubted that American workers could ever achieve the performance and quality standards of Japanese workers. They believed that the typical American auto worker was unmotivated and hardly dedicated to his or her job. Therefore, these observers questioned whether any of the well-known Japanese managerial practices would ever work in an American manufacturing setting.

By the end of the 1980s, it was clear that Honda's commitment to its U.S. manufacturing operations was more than a political gesture. Marysville was so successful that Honda not only expanded its capacity but enlarged the scope of its operations as well. Initially, the operation was designed simply to assemble kits shipped from Japanese plants, but by 1989, the Marysville operation included engine, drive-train, and parts manufacturing. All of this was done at a time when GM, Ford, and Chrysler were continuing to reduce their wholesale purchases of cars from Japanese manufacturers.

Honda's Marysville operation also demonstrated that Japanese managerial practices could be successfully adapted to the American context. At Marysville, Honda was able to assemble a car in 18.2 hours, which was significantly better than the best of any American producer, 25.8 hours. In addition, Honda was able to produce the same number of cars as GM, but with half the work force and a third of the production space.

Honda has integrated the usual Japanese managerial approaches of teamwork, job security, participative decision making, and incentives into the plant's operation. Application of these approaches has resulted in the development of a highly motivated, quality-conscious work force. The firm's absenteeism rate is an amazing 2 percent. Among the "associates" in the plant, there is a feeling of "us" against the competition and not "us" versus "them," the management. Not surprisingly, the United Auto Workers Union was unsuccessful in its attempt to organize Honda's work force.

But perhaps the ultimate demonstration of how well the Japanese management approach has worked at Marysville was the 1988 decision by Honda's management to begin exporting cars from Marysville to Europe and to Japan.

Honda's Marysville plant demonstrates how effectively firms can manage foreign operations when the managerial approach has a global orientation. ■

Honda's experience with its Marysville operation reflects the changes occurring in international management. Business is no longer a domestic matter, and international business is no longer a concern of or an opportunity for just larger multinational corporations. Business has been globalized beyond fundamental import-export activities.

One driving force behind this globalization is the new era of economic partnership for the twelve countries of the European Common Market (known as the European Community or EC). The year 1992 is the target date for the creation of the Single European Act, when many of the barriers (physical, technical, and fiscal) to integration will be removed. The lure of the large common market (estimated at 350 million people) and the prospect of regaining competitiveness are encouraging many Europeans to put their differences aside for the sake of oneness.[1] The dream, however, is not without some difficulties, the most recent being the problems with the unification of East and West Germany and the political and economic unrest within the former communist bloc.[2]

A complementary development to the oneness concept of a geographic market is the activity between the United States, Canada, and Mexico. A Free Trade Pact exists between the United States and Canada, and President Carlos Salinas of Mexico advocates a similar pact for his country. In the United States, there are those who favor and those who oppose the idea of a "Canamerico." [3,4]

This globalization of business presents a considerable challenge to today's managers.[5] Whether you work for a large multinational firm operating on a worldwide basis or for a small retail outlet whose market is simply Main Street, you will need to understand the concepts and dynamics of international management. In this chapter, we introduce you to this critical topic and to the issues associated with managing in the international environment, which includes Tokyo and London, as well as Main Street, U.S.A.

Historians in the year 2000 will have identified many reasons for the dramatic changes in Central Europe, the U.S.S.R., and the communist form of government. The tearing down of "the wall," so long a symbol of the East German control over its people, will live in the memories of Germans and the rest of the world for a long, long time. At the Brandenburg Gate in East Berlin, thousands of Germans of all ages braved the guns of the border guards to bring the wall down in 1990.

We will begin by examining the internationalization of America's domestic market, and then consider the nature and managerial dimensions of foreign operations. We will spend some time looking specifically at multinational companies. Finally, we will consider some variations in managerial approaches that one will encounter in the international business environment.

TOWARD A GLOBAL MANAGERIAL ORIENTATION

Will U.S. companies move toward a global orientation?

Although international management has grown considerably in the past decade, many managers still do not appreciate its significance. Until the late 1970s, most American managers believed that international management pertained only to someone who worked at an overseas subsidiary. Even management textbooks ignored the subject. This attitude existed primarily because U.S. demand had been satisfied by domestic producers. European and Japanese firms were hardly considered a competitive threat to most U.S. manufacturers.[6]

In the early 1980s, the impact of foreign competition was quite clear for many Americans. As countless factories closed throughout the country, foreign competition meant growing unemployment and a decline in the standard of living for millions of families. This impact was more evident to many individuals who watched the industrial heartland of the Midwest rapidly turned into the "rust belt."[7] Even the giants of the steel, auto, electronics, and machine tool industries acknowledged that important segments of their markets were being lost to the imported products and services of foreign producers.

At the time, many Americans, together with business, labor, and political leaders, argued that the federal government needed to enact trade policies to protect American manufacturers from what they perceived as the "unfair trading practices of foreign firms." They believed that American manufacturers were unable to compete against foreign producers. They maintained that foreign producers typically had the unique advantages of cheap labor, government subsidies, and trade barriers in their own domestic markets, which eliminated the need for them to commit resources to defend their principal market. These individuals further argued that if American producers could compete on a "level playing field," they would beat the foreign producers hands down.

Another group of Americans took a different view. They suggested that situations such as Honda's Marysville operation demonstrated that the real problem was not one of "level playing fields." The decline in America's industrial sector was not caused by foreign producers but was the result of U.S. industry's failure to adopt a global perspective. They argued that over the past decade, American businesses had failed not only to recognize that the domestic markets of the world, including the United States, had become international markets, but also to adopt managerial practices that would enable them to compete internationally.

Which position was correct? As the U.S. economy moves into the twenty-first century, there is growing evidence to support the argument that the real problem was the lack of a truly global managerial orientation.

For instance, in the mid-1980s, G.E., Maytag, and Whirlpool accepted the idea that their appliance market was international and not simply domestic. As a result, they were able to develop strategies and products that effectively neu-

There Is No Monopoly on Scandals

The recent round of scandals suggests that "there is no one country or people who engage in unethical or illegal behavior." Three recent scandals have been particularly noteworthy in their attack upon symbols of traditional values.

There is probably nothing more American than the concept of the savings and loan association. The S & Ls were the foundation for small homeowners and farmers. The idea of community investment in the mortgages of neighbors was particularly appealing to those in the vast Midwestern section of America who valued the practice of people helping each other.

In 1990, a 42-count California indictment against Charles H. Keating, Jr., president of the Lincoln Savings and Loan Association, alleged that Lincoln sold high-risk "junk" bonds by using false statements or omitting key information. None of those activities had been approved by regulators. The fires of the scandal were fanned by the investigation of the relationship between Mr. Keating and five U.S. senators. The cost to the American taxpayer has been estimated at $2.6 billion.

A second scandal dispels the notion that Japanese economic success has come from a stronger sense of national pride, a more homogeneous culture, a more productive work ethic, and higher business ethics.

In 1988, the Japanese finance minister, Kiichi Miyazawa, resigned because of the scandal in Recruit Cosmos Company. In 1989, Recruit's president, Hiromasa Ezoe, was arrested for bribery, and Prime Minister Noboru Takeshita resigned. In 1990, stock speculator Mitsuhiro Kotani was arrested for rigging stocks, and the chairman of Sumitomo Bank, Ichiro Isoda, resigned because of illegal loans made to Kotani. In 1991, Japan's top brokerages (Nomura, Daiwa, Nikko, and Yamaichi) revealed the names of 200 top clients who were paid $900 million to offset losses in the stock market. In addition, there were revelations that the *yakuza* (Japanese mobsters) invested with both Nomura and Mikko Securities, leading to the resignation of the president of each brokerage house.

To many foreign competitors of the Japanese, the scandal is sweet news, it should dispel the idea of the supremacy of Japanese values and encourage global equity in the regulation of securities transactions.

The last value under attack is the practice of secrecy by various world banks. Banks in the United Kingdom, Luxembourg, and Switzerland created reputations and profits by providing secret deposit accounts for customers throughout the world. The accounts were kept secret from regulators, government investigators, and national and international police agencies. The accounts have held the monies of Nazi war criminals, U.S. gangsters, and international terrorists. The recent scandal centered on the Bank of Credit and Commerce International (BCCI).

The BCCI, founded in 1972, was the brainchild of Agha Hasan Abedi, a Pakistani Muslim. By 1991, it was the world's largest corporate criminal enterprise as well as the world's largest money-laundering operation. Its clients included Saddam Hussein, Manuel Noriega, Ferdinand Marcos of the Philippines, and even Colombian drug barons. It created dozens of shell companies, branches, and subsidiaries in seventy countries. Incorporated in Luxembourg and headquartered in London, BCCI owned the First American Bankshares of Washington, D.C., the Independence Bank of Encino, California, and the National Bank of Georgia.

Regulators in sixty-two countries shut the banking empire down in July 1991. The corruption and bribery of public officials span the globe, and the finger of blame points to such traditional bastions of trust as the Bank of England, the U.S. Justice Department, the U.S. Attorney General, and the FBI. Some Pakistanis and Third World peoples are suggesting that the shutdown is for political reasons that it is a plot by the West to drive the Arabs out of international banking.

References: Thomas D. Elias, "Keating Trial Beginning Today," *Cincinnati Post,* August 2, 1991, p. 1; "Japan Cleans House—Again," *Business Week,* July 8, 1991, pp. 26–30; "Japan Scandal Grows," *Cincinnati Post,* July 29, 1991, p. 8a; Jonathan Beaty and S. C.. Gwynne, "The Dirtiest Bank of All," *Time,* July 29, 1991, pp. 42–47.

tralized a powerful attempt by Japanese and European appliance producers to move into the U.S. market. Campbell Soup's Pepperidge Farm division discovered that there was a cookie market beyond the United States. They successfully entered the Japanese market by working together with the Southland Corporation, whose 7-11 stores were well established in Japan. Such efforts required new managerial approaches and a willingness to adapt products and operations to a market's unique character.

There are even some U.S. firms, such as Westinghouse and Caterpillar, who are reestablishing U.S. manufacturing operations that had been either moved or outsourced to Japan, Asia, or Third World countries in the early 1980s. They had accepted the argument that one could not competitively manufacture products in the United States. In time, they also realized that by adapting some of their managerial practices, and operating their U.S. facilities as global concerns, these facilities could be operated competitively.

The ultimate irony of the renewal of American manufacturing in the 1990s is that much of the momentum for this resurgence has come from the Japanese and European firms who have either acquired or established manufacturing operations in the United States.[8] These foreign firms have come to view the United States as a worldwide manufacturing base with a stable environment, consisting of a highly skilled, "low-cost" labor force, which is increasingly productive and quality-oriented.

As Table 3-1 shows, more than two million automobiles can be manufactured annually in the United States by foreign companies such as Toyota, Nissan, Honda, and Mazda. In addition, other foreign firms, such as Michelin, Bridgestone, Phillips, British Petroleum, Electrolux, Sony, and Siemens, have acquired or established U.S. manufacturing facilities that produce products for

TABLE 3-1 1990 Foreign Assembly Capacity in North America	
COMPANY	1990 CAPACITY
Honda	440,000
GM/Toyota	250,000
Toyota	250,000
Mazda	240,000
Mitsubishi/Chrysler	240,000
Nissan	240,000
GM/Suzuki	200,000
Volkswagen	200,000
Fuji/Isuzu	120,000
Hyundai	100,000
Daihatsu	40,000
TOTAL	2,320,000

TABLE 3-2 Ten Key Industries in U.S. Foreign Trade, Their Estimated Trade Balance, and Some of the Companies in Each Category

AEROSPACE	COMPUTER EQUIPMENT	OILFIELD MACHINERY	MEDICAL EQUIPMENT	CHEMICALS
1988 surplus: $13.2 billion	1988 surplus: $2.8 billion	1988 surplus: $2.2 billion	1988 surplus: $1 billion	1988 surplus: $10 billion
► Boeing's exports total $6.3 billion	► Hewlett-Packard's exports are up 14%	► Dresser Industries expects surge of compressor exports	► Bard's exports of cardiovascular products to Japan up sharply	► Allied-Signal's exports of industrial fibers up 30%
► Pratt & Whitney's exports are now $1.67 billion	► Sun Microsystems' exports have quadrupled to $177 million	► National-Oilwell sells drilling rigs to India and Yugoslavia	► PyMaH's exports to Asia, Europe, elsewhere reach 45% of total sales	► Union Carbide had record exports of U.S.-made products to Asia in 1987
► McDonnell Douglas's 1987 exports, including military sales, are up 15.6%	► Mentor Graphics' exports are up 37% to $110 million	► Baker Hughes's exports total 9% sales	► Stryker sees 30% hike in exports of power surgical instruments	► Loctite forecasts 25% increase in exports to $25 million

CARS & TRUCKS	TEXTILES & APPAREL	ELECTRONICS	STEEL	MACHINE TOOLS
1987 deficit: 1988 deficit: $42 billion $45 billion	1987 deficit: 1988 deficit: $23.4 billion $25 billion	1987 deficit: 1988 deficit: $1.9 billion $2.0 billion	1987 deficit: 1988 deficit: $18.6 billion $18.7 billion	1987 deficit: 1988 deficit: $1.4 billion 1.1 billion
► GM imports $910 million worth of autos from Japan	► The Gap boosts imports from Hong Kong by 6%	► GE imports $100 million worth of microwaves from Korea	► USX's U.S. Steel subsidiary exports less than 1% of its total sales	► South Bend Lathe imports a range of machines from Spain and Asia
► Ford doubles imports of Korean-made cars to $225 million	► May Department Stores increases imports from Hong Kong by 10%	► Motorola buys silicon for DRAM semiconductor chips from Japan for eventual U.S. sale	► Allegheny Ludlum exported 3% of its 1987 sales, vs. 9% in 1979	► Hitachi Seiki imports half of $50 million to $60 million in equipment it sells here
► Chrysler is a net importer of $750 million	► Reebok's imports of shoes jumped 52% in 1987	► Zenith imports VCRs and camcorders from Asia	► Armco's Advanced Materials unit sells just 5% of its specialty steel abroad	► Cross & Trecker exported 8.8% of its 1987 sales, down from 19.1% in 1981

both U.S. markets and export. Like Honda, they have discovered that they can gain a competitive advantage in the international markets by integrating U.S. manufacturing operations with their other international activities.

Today, American managers realize that the changes brought about by the invasion of foreign goods and services have gone beyond simple competition. We are now operating in an environment where calculators are assembled in Mexico from parts made in Taiwan, Brazil, and the United States. People in New Hampshire are drinking Coca-Cola produced by a local bottler owned by Japan's largest brewer, Kerwin Brewery. Sweden's Electrolux has captured close to 10 percent of the European microwave oven market by having the U.S. plants of its White Consolidated division produce and export 500,000 microwave ovens annually to Europe. Even the small Black Box Corporation of Pittsburgh can achieve $70 million in worldwide sales of data communications and computer devices, using nothing more than the telephone and catalogs published in eight languages.

The challenge, then, for American managers and for you is to broaden your perspective on the international business environment.[9] Your next customer may be in Italy, and you may discover that your competitor is from Ireland. You may have to borrow money from a banker in Tokyo, and your new boss may come from India. For many firms and managers, the globalization of their business has resulted in surpluses and deficits as noted in Table 3-2.

As for those firms and managers who continue to believe that they are immune from international competition or that it has no relevance for or impact on them, it is only a matter of time until they are proven wrong.

INTERNATIONAL TRADE

What is America's comparative advantage?

Comparative advantage theory All nations can gain if each country specializes in producing goods in which it has comparative advantage and trades with others that have advantages in other goods.

For several centuries, economists have developed theories to explain why nations trade. The basic concept of international trade of goods has been that of **comparative advantage.** The basis of the theory of comparative advantage is that each nation possesses different combinations of productive resources such as land, labor, and capital.[10] The supply of these resources is not spread evenly throughout the world. Some nations are rich in natural resources. Others have a large supply of labor. Some have acquired large quantities of capital goods and finances. The theory states that under a certain set of assumptions, all nations can gain if each country specializes in the production of those goods in which it has a comparative advantage and trades with other nations who have comparative advantages in the production of other goods. The theory argues that all nations can find goods in which they have comparative advantages even though they may not have absolute advantages.

Trade, then, exists among nations as a result of the differences in the endowment of productive resources. Examples of some specific groups of differences are climate, natural resources, population density, and the supply of available capital. Orchids can be grown more efficiently in the warmer climate of Malaysia, whereas roses flourish in the cooler climates. Some nations have been endowed by nature with an abundance of extractive resources: oil in the OPEC nations, iron ore in Canada, uranium in Zaire, bauxite in Jamaica, tin in Bolivia, copper in Zambia, and so forth. Other nations, like Japan, have none

Saudi Arabia is a country that had a comparative advantage with its vast inventories of oil. Iraq attempted to create its own comparative advantage with the takeover of Kuwait in August 1990 and resulting threat to Saudi Arabia. Soon allied forces from Great Britain, France, the United States, and other countries responded to a United Nations' mandate and the Gulf War became headlines. The war was a short one and Kuwait was freed of Iraqi occupation.

or little of such resources needed for industrial development. Population density differs, with the result that some nations, like Korea and Taiwan, have advantages in labor-intensive industries because of lower wages, whereas other nations have a greater abundance of capital and thus specialize in capital-intensive industries.

Thus, American companies that have comparative advantages in agriculture and aircraft manufacturing, for instance, seek to exploit their *competitive advantage* through exporting American products.[11] Foreign companies with cost advantages in other industries have increased exports to the United States. Nations seek to encourage companies to expand exports and to set tariffs and other obstacles to limit the importation of foreign products. From the viewpoint of managing these international companies, the issue is mainly a marketing one—that is, the purchasing of raw materials and parts internationally and the sales of finished products internationally. Courses in marketing management, therefore, concentrate on these aspects of international selling and purchasing. Although international trade has increased in the last decade, the greatest increase in international activities has been in the development of global companies with sales, operations, and finances on an international scale. Managing these companies is the subject of primary interest in this chapter.

Multinational corporation (MNC) A firm that operates in more than one country and allocates resources across national boundaries with the intention of maintaining managerial control of operations.

THE MULTINATIONAL CORPORATION (MNC)

A **multinational corporation (MNC)** operates in more than one country (often, in many countries) and allocates company resources of capital, technology, employees, and managers across national boundaries with the intention of maintaining managerial control of operations. It is this managerial control that distinguishes a multinational company from other types of international com-

International trading company An international company that sells goods and products across national boundaries.

panies. It differs from the international trading company because it not only trades goods through imports and exports but also manages operations within other countries. An **international trading company** buys and sells goods and products across national boundaries, whereas a multinational company manages not only purchases and sales but also warehousing, maintenance and repair services, research, and manufacturing in foreign countries from its headquarters in another country. The foreign countries in which operations are conducted are referred to as host countries. The nation in which the corporation has been chartered and in which its headquarters is located is referred to as the home country.

Multinational companies can be relatively small and operate in only a few countries;[12] however, they are typically quite large and operate in many countries. Some operate in more than 100 countries. Table 3-3 lists some of the larger American multinational corporations.

In addition to American multinationals, we all have become aware of foreign multinational companies operating in the United States, such as the Japanese companies Bridgestone, Toyota, and Sony, the German companies Volkswagen and Bausch and Lomb, the French companies Michelin and Renault, the British companies British Petroleum and Baskin-Robbins, the Dutch companies Phillips and Heineken, and the Swiss companies Ciba-Geigy and Nestlé.[13] In view of this trend toward an increase in the number and the size of multinational companies, some observers have estimated that within the next decade, over 50 percent of the combined gross national product (GNP) of all countries will be generated by multinational companies.

Transnational company An international company that controls operations, has stockholders in many countries, and employs citizens from all parts of the world.

Some writers and international institutions use the term **transnational company** interchangeably with multinational company. For example, the United Nations has an agency that deals with transnational companies. Other writers make an important distinction between the two terms. These writers define a transnational company as an international company that not only controls operations but also has stockholders spread through the host country as well as many other countries and that employs citizens of many countries as managers.

A final distinction of international management is at present of only theoretical importance, but it raises interesting possibilities for future international management. The multinational or transnational company is chartered in one country and thus has a single home country. A company that might be chartered in the future by an international agency with managers and ownership

TABLE 3-3   Some of the Major American Multinational Corporations
Apple
Exxon
Ford
General Electric
General Motors
Hewlett-Packard
IBM
John Deere
Motorola
Procter & Gamble
Squibb
Texas Instruments

Supranational company
A company that has no national boundaries, operates in many countries, and has managers, employees, and owners from many parts of the world.

spread in a number of countries would be referred to as a **supranational company**. Such a company would not be viewed as an American, a German, a French, or a British company but as a world company, without national ties. Although there are no examples today of a purely supranational company, because no international agency has been granted the powers to grant charters of incorporation, some examples of pseudosupranational companies do exist, and others have been attempted through mergers across national boundaries. Royal Dutch Shell, the large international oil company, and Unilever, the international consumer goods company, have for years had dual home countries: Great Britain and the Netherlands. The stock of these companies is owned by citizens of many nations, and their managers come from Great Britain, the Netherlands, and other countries.

An example of an attempt to create a company with multiple nationalities is the merger in the 1970s of two large rubber companies (Dunlop Tyre, Ltd., of Britain and Industrie Pirelli, SpA., of Italy) by means of a holding company in Switzerland. Fiat and Citroën also attempted a cross-national merger in the early 1970s. Both of these attempts ran into trouble, partly because they had difficulty developing integrated strategies for the unified company.

Most international operations today fit our definition of a multinational corporation, and the term *multinational corporation* is generally used. In this text, we refer to all companies with operations across national boundaries as multinational corporations (MNCs) or multinational enterprises (MNEs).[14]

REASONS FOR MULTINATIONAL OPERATIONS

Why become multinational?

Why, then, have an increasing number of companies become multinational and made direct investments in foreign countries? Many companies retain a domestic orientation because they fail to consider the great opportunities outside their own country. Some purely domestic companies have been very profitable because their domestic industry is expanding, and, therefore, they see no reason to scan international opportunities. Some fear the unknown pitfalls of moving outside their familiar environment. They feel that they lack the expertise to operate in exotic, frustrating environments that are undergoing rapid changes and unstable developments. In short, some domestic companies do not see the need to expand outside their traditional sphere because their management training has not been oriented toward managing in an international environment.

The reasons for a company to become multinational are numerous and varied. However, for our purposes in this chapter, we can summarize four reasons.

1. One basic reason for expanding internationally is to seek and gain control of raw materials at a satisfactory cost. Earlier in this chapter, we noted that natural resources are not spread evenly over the globe but are often clustered in a few countries. A company that requires a stable supply of basic raw materials for its operations must seek these raw materials wherever they may be found. Even in a large and well-endowed country like the United States, companies find that certain essential raw materials are not found within their country's borders or that a sufficient supply is not available at reasonable cost (for example, oil). When a large per-

Integrate backward
Extending operations into stages toward raw materials to gain managerial control of supplies.

centage of the raw materials is required from foreign sources, U.S. companies find it desirable to **integrate backward;** that is, they expand backward toward the source of supply to gain managerial control of their raw materials to support their manufacturing and marketing operations. Their reasoning is that since their entire manufacturing and marketing operations need critical raw materials from other countries, they should ensure a dependable supply by expanding their managerial control over foreign operations. Furthermore, the additional profits from the extractive or agricultural stage of operations are very attractive. In many cases, the foreign nations and foreign private companies lack sufficient capital to exploit their own natural resources.

2. A second basic reason for becoming multinational is to develop new markets and to satisfy the demand of foreign consumers for products produced by the company.[15] Companies with successful domestic markets recognize that many of these products could reach vast new markets in other countries. These companies discover that continued growth depends on moving into other countries, especially if their domestic market has become relatively saturated or mature. Of course, these companies might initially export products from their domestic operations without expanding their managerial control outside their own nation. Yet, they tend to recognize that they need greater control of their marketing efforts and **integrate forward;** that is, they expand their operations and managerial control from manufacturing toward sales to the ultimate consumer.

Integrate forward
Extending operations into stages toward the ultimate consumer to gain control of distribution of finished goods.

Many present-day companies have developed multinationally to secure greater managerial control over the marketing of their products. Automobile companies such as Ford and General Motors integrated forward through sales divisions in many foreign countries. Pharmaceutical companies such as Eli Lilly and Hoffman-Roche today are often multinational. General Electric, Phillips, and other electrical manufacturers have become global companies. Unilever, Nestlé, and other food and soap companies have also integrated forward. International airlines, shipping companies, and hotel chains such as Hilton and Holiday Inn have become multinational to serve the international traveler. In many other industries, the search for new markets has caused companies to grow internationally.

3. A third reason for becoming international is to reduce the production and transportation costs of parts and assemblies. In labor-intensive industries, the cost of labor may vary widely among nations as a result of the varying supplies of different types of labor and the local demands for that labor. A number of places, such as Hong Kong, Korea, Taiwan, India, and many Latin American (Mexico, especially) and African countries, have a significant labor-cost advantage, especially in assembly-type industries. Companies with plants in advanced industrial countries have experienced rapid wage increases and have the opportunity to reduce manufacturing costs greatly by building plants in foreign countries. With a good supply of capital, these companies can invest their funds in capital equipment in a foreign country and secure higher payouts and returns on investment than manufacturing in the home country. Most nations with an eye on increasing employment of their citizens are quite receptive to companies that will supply the necessary investment and will help meet long-run development plans of their governments. Companies that have developed local markets and have obtained raw materials in these countries can also reduce the costs of transporting raw materials and finished goods by building plants in these nations.

There are many examples of companies that have developed multinationally to reduce their production and transportation costs. Ford is a good example of a company that has developed worldwide manufacturing operations to supply foreign markets. Recently, Ford has developed a strategy of producing a "world car" in which auto components such as transmissions, engines, and bodies are manufactured in different countries (for example, Great Britain, Brazil, Germany, and Singapore) in addition to managing a widespread system of assembly plants. In the radio, television, and calculator and computer industries, large multinational companies have expanded to save manufacturing costs.

Horizontal integration
The establishment of plants at the same stage of production in different countries.

An increasing number of manufacturing companies have used a strategy called **horizontal integration** of international operations—that is, the establishment of plants at the same stage of production in different countries. These strategies reduce risks through geographical diversification and enable the company to shift production from a plant in one country to a plant in another country when cost changes or labor problems develop.

4. A fourth reason for a company to become multinational is simply to keep up with or to get ahead of its competitors.[16] In oligopolistic industries with a few large competitors, each company's management keeps an eye on its competitors' strategies. If one company in an industry attempts to seize foreign opportunities, competitors will also move to prevent the first one from becoming entrenched in the new markets. For example, for years General Electric aggressively sought international business. In the 1970s, Westinghouse moved to become multinational for fear that G.E. would gain a commanding lead in the growing market. Recently, to acquire new technologies developed in other countries, European, American, and Japanese MNCs moved into global operations to remain competitive. In such high-technology industries as computer chips, the rate of change is so rapid that every company must search for international opportunities to avoid losing competitive advantages through a new discovery by a foreign competitor.

In view of this summary of the basic reasons for "going international," it is not surprising to find more companies managing internationally. In the next section, we shall see that these companies can use a number of different modes of involvement for their international development.

MODES OF FOREIGN INVOLVEMENT

How can a domestic company go international?

The modes of foreign operations differ in both the amount a firm commits to foreign operations and the percentage of resources located at home or in host countries. Among the many modes available to the company, the following six are the principal ones:

1. **Export** of products from home country. If a company wishes to minimize risks and costs of exporting, marketing, and manufacturing abroad, it might secure an export broker or another specialist to handle all foreign negotiations and procedures. The company can, thereby, avoid the complexity of managing multinational operations and can thus simply trade internationally. Usually, this mode of operation is preferable for a company that has little experience in international operations. Exporting can be followed by one of the other modes.

2. **Licensing.** Under an international licensing agreement, a firm (the licensor) grants rights to a foreign firm (the licensee). The rights may be exclusive or nonexclusive and may refer to patents, trademarks, copyrights, or special know-how. Under licensing, the licensee agrees to exercise its rights aggressively and to compensate the licensor for services rendered. For example, a publishing company may grant rights to its copyrighted books to foreign publishers; a drug company may license foreign companies to sell its patented products in other countries.

3. **Franchising.** Franchising is essentially a way of doing business in which the franchisor gives an independent franchisee use of trademarks, patents, or other valuable intangible assets; the franchisee conducts the business within an agreed area under the limitations of the agreement. Sometimes, the franchisor provides sup-

The "Golden Arches" of McDonald's were reduced in size but the symbol of American enterprise was never more visible than at the opening of a "Big Mac" store in Moscow at Pushkin Square. A two hour long wait did not discourage Soviets (and tourists) from standing in line. At one point, 3,500 customers were served daily.

plies, managerial assistance, and other resources not generally available to the franchisee. Foreign hotel chains such as Holiday Inn and Hilton, rental-car agencies including Hertz and Avis, and fast-food outlets like McDonald's and Kentucky Fried Chicken widely use franchises as a means of securing local acceptance in foreign markets and as a mode for rapid expansion.

4. **Joint ventures.** The joint venture involves sharing ownership with others and is usually formed for the achievement of a limited purpose. Joint ventures have increased in use because many countries give preference to local businesses. A multinational company with foreign ownership and control can often interest a locally owned and operated business to join with it and thereby provide local identification. Many joint ventures are on a fifty-fifty basis; some involve 51 percent ownership by the local company in countries requiring local control. The greatest advantage of joint ventures is their flexibility and adaptability. The Japanese early recognized the advantages of joint ventures as a means of implementing their expansion into foreign markets.

5. **Management contracts.** In the last decade, the management contract has become a popular form of MNC involvement, since it is merely a service contract requiring no capital investment. In communist countries, which, by definition, restrict private company operations, and in some developing countries such as Saudi Arabia, where management skills and other operating services are limited, the management contract may be the only means by which the MNC can participate. The MNC can receive compensation for its management skills without any direct foreign investment. Occidental Petroleum, Pullman Company, and others experienced in dealing with controlled economies have used management contracts extensively.

6. **Foreign subsidiary.** The foreign subsidiary, often 100 percent owned by the MNC, makes initial direct investments in other countries and operates foreign plants as part of its global network of manufacturing and marketing. This mode is preferred by those MNCs desiring maximum managerial control and willing to assume greater risks of foreign operations. The selection of the subsidiary as a mode of foreign involvement requires rigorous analysis of many variables, since it commits the company to the greatest exposure to risks of foreign operations and management. The amount of direct foreign investment in subsidiaries over the past thirty years is shown in Table 3-4.

TABLE 3.4   Where Have All the Lire, Marks, Dollars, Yen, etc., Gone?

Increasingly overseas, as multinational businesses set up shop abroad. Most direct investment from advanced industrial economies ends up in other developed countries.

Direct investment in other countries
(including reinvested earnings) in millions of U.S. dollars

	1960	1970	1980	1986
U.S.	$2,940	$7,589	$19,220	$28,050
Japan	79	355	2,385	14,480
W. Germany	139	876	4,180	8,999
Britain	700	1,308	11,360	16,691
Canada	52	302	2,694	3,254
France	347*	374	3,138	5,230
Italy	−17*	111	754	2,661

*1961 figures.   SOURCE: OECD
Cover Stories: Looking Ahead: Entering a New Age of Boundless Competition, Richard I. Kirkland, Jr., *Fortune,* March 14, 1988, p. 46.

What should you consider before going international?

With these six modes available, it is crucial that a company choose the best one for a particular situation. Among the many variables that need to be considered, the following ones are the most important in selecting the best mode.

- *Risks.* The degree of risk associated with each mode is of utmost importance. In a joint venture, the risks of investments can be shared; in licensing and franchising, the risks of investment are assumed by the licensee or franchisee, thus relieving the foreign company of owning property in the country; in management contracts and exporting, capital is not required outside the home country, and thus the risks are considerably less than when a foreign subsidiary is used. For companies without foreign experience, the less-risky modes are initially more attractive. After gaining valuable experience, other modes with greater risks can be used.

- *Legal restrictions.* The MNC must operate within the legal restrictions of both the home and the host countries. The home country may restrict actions through extensions of its antitrust laws, foreign exchange controls, and tax structure. The host country may restrict the amounts of profits that can be repatriated and may prohibit private ownership in sensitive industries such as extractive ore, banking, and those critical to economic development. The host country can restrict foreign exchange and use its tax structure to regulate operations of foreign companies. Finally, host countries may have different legal systems from those of the home country. An MNC with a home office in a country having a common-law system may have complex legal problems in operating in countries using a civil-law system or a Moslem legal system.

- *Competition and markets.* The selection of the mode of foreign operations depends upon the modes used by competitors and by the intensity of competition in the prospective market. The size of the market and the sales potential, together with the intensity of competition from local companies and other multinationals, are important, for example, in choosing whether to build a plant in the host country or merely to export from the home country.

- *Foreign expertise and experience.* Companies with extensive experience in foreign operations can better afford to make the commitment of investing in a foreign subsidiary, whereas a company with limited expertise in foreign operations would choose to export, license its product, or use a franchise agreement.
- *Degree of managerial control.* Probably of greatest importance in selecting a mode of involvement is the degree of managerial control desired. A 100 percent ownership in a foreign subsidiary offers maximum control. Exporting and licensing offer limited managerial control.

Global Application

VW Gives Up

During the summer of 1988, while major Japanese auto producers were working at a hectic pace to build or expand production facilities in the United States, Volkswagen closed its Westmoreland, Pa. production facility after little more than ten years of operation. Volkswagen had been the first foreign automobile manufacturer to establish production facilities in the United States. At the time, VW's management was concerned about the possibility that the U.S. Congress would impose trade barriers on cars imported into the United States. They felt that a U.S. production facility would help VW avoid any import restrictions and would minimize the effects of fluctuating exchange rates, which had been a problem for some time.

In setting up operations at the Westmoreland plant, VW decided to operate the facility like any other U.S. auto plant. Not only did VW hire experienced American managers to fill the principal managerial positions; it also immediately recognized the United Auto Workers as the bargaining agent for VW's hourly workers. So when production began, the only noticeable difference between the Westmoreland facility and any other U.S. auto plant was that the VW plant was producing what was considered a foreign car.

Unfortunately for VW, the similarities between its plant and other U.S. auto plants were all too real. There were chronic quality problems, labor conflict, supplier problems, and much more. Like its American counterparts, VW was taking a beating in the marketplace as the Japanese moved in to take as big a market share as possible. Then there were the internal problems. Initially, the Westmoreland operation had been set up to be independent of the U.S. sales operation. As such, there was no obligation for the sales operation to acquire the Rabbits (a particular style of Volkswagen) from the Westmoreland plant. Dealers even made a point of promoting Rabbits produced in Germany over the ones manufactured in the United States. Customers complained about the lack of German quality and engineering in an automobile that was supposed to be exactly the same as those being imported from Germany.

There were periodic attempts to restructure the Westmoreland operation, but nothing seemed to work. Instead, VW's management concentrated on other, more successful overseas operations in Mexico and Brazil. When the losses of the U.S. operation began to wipe out the profits from its other, more viable ventures, VW's management decided to call it quits and to allocate Westmoreland's resources to other segments of their business. In the end, VW found itself in the same position as the other U.S. auto producers, managing a retreat.

The nature of the environments of host countries is basic to the selection of the mode of foreign involvement and to many other decisions, and so we turn to a description and an analysis of the environments of international operations.

ENVIRONMENTS OF INTERNATIONAL OPERATIONS

From the discussion of the increasingly rapid development of multinational companies, we turn to the factors that affect the managing of multinational companies. Of course, if there were few or no differences between managing domestic and international operations, this chapter would have less importance; however, the differences are great. They are chiefly the result of the differences in the environments faced by MNCs.

The differences may be grouped in two classifications: (1) global environmental factors relating to interactions among the various nations and (2) comparative environmental factors involving the variety of separate environments within the different nations. The global factors relating to the international institutions are summarized in the following section; the comparative basis for identifying elements of the separate national environments are discussed in the following section.

Global Interaction among Environments

The managers at headquarters of an MNC face risks and problems in maintaining a unified strategy for the company to guide all country units in a common direction. Many international institutions have emerged in the last four decades that facilitate international operations. Table 3-5 summarizes the most important of these institutions with which top management may be involved.

The contingency approach to management, introduced in Chapter 2, is especially important in global operations. The management of an MNC must adapt to different host environments with the help of international institutions; yet, it should develop a compatible, unified global approach that handles the interactions among the varied environments.

Howard V. Perlmutter has observed three types of managerial attitudes that may be adopted by managers in adjusting to the global environments: ethnocentric, polycentric, and geocentric.[17]

Ethnocentric attitude
The tendency of human beings to orient to their home environments and to hold that their beliefs and customs are best for others.

An **ethnocentric attitude** is oriented toward the home environment. Managers who are inexperienced in international operations often have an ethnocentric viewpoint; that is, they are imbued with the beliefs and customs that have worked well at home and assume that they are suitable to all countries. This attitude ignores the impact of the diverse environments on managerial practices. Comments illustrating this attitude are "Americans have the best managerial approach," "My job is to teach the American way to others and to bring foreigners around to our way of thinking," "Japanese and Latin Americans are sure peculiar—why don't they do things the way we do?" and "I'm right and foreigners are wrong." A person may unconsciously take an ethnocentric view unless he or she is alerted to cultural factors of the nations in which he or she participates.

TABLE 3-5   International Institutions

INSTITUTION	ROLE AND OBJECTIVES
International Monetary Fund (IMF)	Created by the Bretton Woods Agreement in 1944. Objectives: (1) to promote exchange stability; (2) to promote international cooperation in monetary problems; (3) to eliminate foreign exchange restrictions; (4) to provide a source of reserves to correct short-run maladjustments in foreign exchange rates; and (5) to provide an orderly exchange mechanism. The role has changed to meet new monetary problems: it supplies Special Drawing Rights (SDRs) to expand amount of reserves, provides funds to nations with credit difficulties; and exerts power to impose strict constraints on economies of debtor nations.
International Bank for Reconstruction and Development (World Bank)	Created by the Bretton Woods Agreement in 1944. Objectives: (1) to facilitate capital flows between nations; (2) to provide reconstruction capital to ravaged nations after World War II; (3) to provide development capital to developing countries. The role of the World Bank has been to provide capital for infrastructure projects in developing countries, financed through quotas from member countries and by bonds sold to private investors. It conducts feasibility studies for projects and offers expert consulting to developing nations. Its services have expanded through the creation of sister institutions—the International Finance Corporation and the International Development Association.
General Agreement on Tariffs and Trade (GATT)	Originating in 1948 as a series of rounds of conferences of member nations, its principal objective is the lowering of tariffs and other discriminatory barriers. The Kennedy round of the 1960s (the sixth round) was successful in reducing tariffs significantly, the Tokyo round of the 1970s attempted to extend its efforts to reduction of other restrictions, for example, industrial standards, subsidies, and other nontariff barriers.
European Economic Community (EEC)	Created in 1957 by the Treaty of Rome signed by France, West Germany, Italy, Belgium, Luxembourg, and the Netherlands. It has been the most successful example of regional integration of nations. As a common market, it has expedited the flow of goods, capital, labor, technology, and management across national boundaries. Great Britain, Ireland, Denmark, and Greece as new members have expanded the scope of the area. Its growth and success have been major factors supporting the growth of multinational companies.
United Nations Conference on Trade and Development (UNCTAD)	A permanent agency of the United Nations created in 1964 to represent the interests of developing nations. Its objective is the redistribution of income through trade. In a series of conferences, it has challenged industrial countries to improve trade with developing countries. Its success has been limited, but it has provided pressure for easing credit to developing countries.

Polycentric attitude
An understanding that each country has unique cultural characteristics and that visitors should adapt to each, e.g. Do as the Romans do.

A **polycentric attitude** understands that each country has unique cultural characteristics that require an international manager to attempt to do things the way they are done in the host country. In short, "When in Rome, do as the Romans do." With extended first-hand experience outside the home country, a manager may develop a polycentric viewpoint. The problem is that every move to a different country requires that the manager "learn the ropes" in a new environment. The manager might "go native" and lose contact with the home culture and its management fundamentals. A polycentric manager may react against earlier cultural experiences and cause increased difficulties with superiors at headquarters. Many problems between foreign subsidiaries and home-country headquarters are conflicts between ethnocentric superiors and polycentric host-country managers. In such conflicts, headquarters may treat foreign-resident managers as though they were in "Siberia." In such cases, managers located outside the home country may not be considered for promotion. Polycentric managers have trouble fitting into the global orientation desirable in multinational companies.

The experienced top manager, in trying to resolve the conflicts between the two attitudes, attempts to develop a third viewpoint—a **geocentric attitude.** This global view recognizes the strengths in one's home environment (ethnocentrism) and the strengths of other nations' cultures (polycentrism). The managers at headquarters need to integrate these strengths to develop a unified, world perception. The geocentric, or global, view accepts the differences in cultures as conditions of reality. Cultures may not be superior to one another—they are just different. A geocentric view maximizes the advantages of these differences. The result may be that adaptions will strengthen a company's managerial approach, facilitating the transfer of ideas and practices tested in one environment and potentially useful in others. (See Table 3-6)

The modern world has become increasingly interdependent. International institutions have emerged to facilitate the interchange. We now turn to the problems faced by international managers as they adjust to this interchange across environments.

Geocentric attitude
Imbued with the beliefs from a global view, recognizing pros and cons of home and foreign environments, and attempting to integrate these differences.

TABLE 3-6 International Environmental Factors Affecting Managerial Functions

MANAGERIAL FUNCTIONS	EDUCATIONAL	SOCIOCULTURAL	LEGAL-POLITICAL	ECONOMIC
Planning	Technical capability For budgets and scheduling For long-range planning	View of change Quantitative orientation	National planning Legal framework	Inflation Industries Business Fluctuations
Organizing	Types of education group versus individual decision making	View of authority Decentralization Formal versus informal	Predictability of legal actions Political influence	Division of labor
Staffing	Supply of functional specialists Literacy level Languages	Class structure Individual mobility	Labor laws Status of management	Unions Unemployment
Leading	Management development	View of achievement Need for supervision	Tolerance to bribes Relation of government to business	Incentives Fringe benefits
Communicating	Language barriers	Customs Nonverbal methods	Validation in writing Faith in superiors	Cost of technology
Controlling	Focus on feedback	Attitude toward scientific method	Reports by government Availability of data	Private property

Problems Faced by International Managers

Diverse environments create many problems for the international manager that are not faced by the domestic manager. A geocentric attitude helps keep the problems in perspective. In this book, we can list only some of these problems.

Foreign exchange rates
The value of the currency of one country stated in the currency units of another country.

- Different languages create problems of translation and communications. Interpreters may be needed for oral communications; translators may be required for written communications. The best method for handling this problem is undoubtedly for managers to be multilingual or, at least, to learn the languages that enable them to communicate in the language of the home country and the languages of the host countries.

- Different currencies are used by the many sovereign nations. The values of these different currencies introduce risks of changes in **foreign exchange rates**—that is, the value of one currency stated in the units of another currency. Companies with profitable operations may have financial difficulties solely from losses resulting from currency fluctuations. Companies with otherwise efficient operations have faced bankruptcy simply as a result of losses in the foreign exchange market.

- Laws and regulations differ among governments and political systems. Common law, which is used in the United States, differs from civil law (the Napoleonic code, which is predominant in Europe) and religious law (such as Moslem law, which is used in the Middle East).

- Differences in accounting systems introduce problems in reporting and comparing operations in different countries.

- Systems of measuring weight and distance pose adjustment problems. For example, items sold in countries using the metric system (liters and meters) require conversion from quarts and yards.

- Customs duties (tariffs) and health, safety, and business practices imposed by different sovereign governments make international operations more difficult in spite of advances made by GATT (General Agreement on Tariffs and Trade) and other international institutions.

- Diplomatic and political pressures call for policy decisions concerning the degree of company involvement. The fact that an MNC is viewed as an outsider may make life more complicated.

These problems faced by international managers result from the differences among the national environments. A multinational company, in its attempt to maintain a unified strategy, must bridge these differences and transfer resources and managerial techniques to gain optimum performance. We now turn to these issues.

Convergence, Diversity, and Transferability

The handling of the differences and problems just noted can be improved by using the geocentric view. In spite of vast differences, increased international interchanges have resulted in some convergence of business environments. Scholarly exchanges and professional meetings have resulted in some similar terminology and managerial approaches. This increase in similarity has emerged from the following forces:

- Technological developments in communications via satellites and electronic information transfer have promoted a common basis for operations. For example, quantitative analysis and communication in numerical form are more similar than are words and sentences. New technology tends to flow across national boundaries with less cultural interface. Engineers and technicians can use similar mechanical and electronic apparatus as a common denominator for interchange. For example, TV and video tape recordings demonstrate ideas better through pictures than do merely oral and written communications.

- Increased knowledge of languages has emerged in many countries. The United States is the chief exception to this multilingual tendency. Although English is now widely used in international interchange, the American with less study of foreign languages has greater difficulty managing operations within countries using different national languages. The fact that many emerging nations have been emphasizing their own national languages requires the multinational manager to know these local languages.

- Travel by executives, students, and tourists has encouraged the standardization of jet travel and hotel accommodations. Travelers experience similar airport and convention facilities, so that while inside these buildings, they cannot tell from the setting whether they are in London, São Paulo, Hong Kong, Tokyo, or New York.

- Industrializing new countries creates similar problems of modernization. Social problems of urbanization, pollution, economic inequalities, family identification, and upward mobility of races and women are common to an increasing number of countries.

In spite of the trend toward convergence, multinational managers still find that the diversity of cultures and other aspects of environments make it harder for them to do their jobs internationally. In developing countries, the local governments have stressed the retention of their unique identity, emphasizing national languages and rediscovering their cultural roots of unique handicrafts, heritage, family tradition, and religious beliefs. They try to eliminate any evidence of past colonial ties and other outside influences with new country names, new national flags, and new national anthems.

International observers differ in their estimate of the overall effect of these tendencies toward convergence and diversity. The subject is particularly important to multinational managers, because both sets of forces directly affect their planning and directing operations. The geocentric attitude is easier to maintain if convergence in the long run is predominant. The issue is also basic to the ease of transferring ideas, skills, and managerial approaches to different countries in which the company operates. A great advantage a multinational company has over a purely domestic one is its flexibility in moving goods, technology, people, equipment, and ideas across national boundaries. For a student of management, the potential for discovering new techniques and concepts through international exchange offers enriching and rewarding opportunities. Thus, the transferability of managerial concepts, techniques, and skills across national boundaries is promising; yet, the success of each transfer depends upon the adaptability of the idea to the different environments.

Can and should American management concepts be transferred *in toto* to other countries? Is it possible for American management to import new ideas from Japan (see Management Application: Ford Europe), Germany, Yugoslavia, or other countries?

These questions can be better answered if managers (1) understand their own culture and the assumptions underlying their principles and practices and (2) understand the cultural characteristics of the countries in which they operate. With this understanding, managers can successfully transfer some management concepts and techniques across national boundaries. Without this understanding, managers may transfer techniques and concepts that are incompatible with the local environment. Furthermore, with this understanding,

Holiday Inn and other lodging chains expect international travel to expand dramatically. Kuwait, a country occupied by Iraq and then freed by allied forces, has a Crown Plaza Holiday Inn in Kuwait City.

management concepts can be enriched by transferring valuable ideas that are compatible.

The introductory chapters of this book have given greater emphasis to managing in the American domestic environment. As we widen our scope from traditional domestic to more contemporary international, we must be explicit about the cultural assumptions of American approaches, so that we have a solid basis for comparison with other cultural assumptions. This comparison can help us better determine the degree of transferability of ideas across cultures. In attempting to adopt a geocentric attitude, the multinational manager will be better able to relate the managing approaches of the home-country managers to those of the number of host-country managers.

Cultural Assumptions Underlying American Management Concepts

Global managers must not only understand the interactions among environments but also learn to operate within each environment. For this reason, we first look at the idea of culture and then identify the cultural assumptions of the American managerial principles to be developed in this book.

Culture Those acquired and learned behaviors which have persisted in human groups through traditions.

Culture is defined as those acquired and learned behaviors that have been found to persist in human groups through traditions, mores, and customs and that have passed down from generation to generation. In other words, culture is not inherited through one's genes but is developed through social experiences involving how one expresses oneself, how one thinks, and how one moves. George Murdock, an early anthropologist, identified seventy cultural universals, or common denominators of cultures, including such things as education, religion, language, values, division of labor, and social structure. In a developed culture, all elements are interrelated. A change in one element affects all others; the successful introduction of a new managerial approach de-

Management Application

Ford Europe

During the 1980s, Japanese firms gained a reputation not only for their product innovations and aggressive marketing but also for their unique managerial approaches. While many non-Japanese firms were not pleased about having to compete against the Japanese, they were nevertheless willing to incorporate some of the Japanese managerial techniques into their own operations. In both the United States and Europe, Japanese approaches such as J-I-T, lifetime security, and participatory management were implemented, with the hope that these techniques would improve productivity and quality.

Although management may have embraced some of these Japanese approaches, hourly employees often vigorously resisted any attempt to institute Japanese work rules. One of the most notable incidents occurred in 1988. Ford had been very successful in instituting Japanese work practices in its U.S. facilities and, as a result, wanted to implement the practices in all its manufacturing facilities. However, when it attempted to do so at the twenty-two plants of its British subsidiary, 32,500 auto workers responded by striking. The strike came as a surprise to Ford's management, who had even offered a substantial wage increase as an incentive to accept the new program. Although the auto workers were pleased about the raise, they objected to having the structure of their workplace changed from traditional craft-oriented specialties to Japanese-style production teams and quality circles. One Ford worker noted that the issue was more than money. It was a matter of what was important in life, for "the Japanese live to work; we work to live." To settle the strike, Ford's management agreed to a wage increase and to make any changes to Japanese-style assembly techniques a negotiable item.

---

pends on its compatibility with its new cultural setting. The difficulty of transferring ideas is in being aware of the cultural implications, since one's culture is often acquired unconsciously and one may not realize the foundations for one's actions.

As long as a manager is managing domestically, the cultural assumptions may be subtle and not recognized. Actions within the same culture appear simpler if all managers have the same orientation. But when managers cross national boundaries into different cultures, the cultural differences may cause problems. The manager may develop **culture shock,** a reduction in efficiency and a disorientation caused by subtle conflicts with a new environment. The problem may be greater for managers, since executives often change from one culture to another quickly via jet transportation. It may be reinforced by "jet lag," since managers often immediately plunge into business conferences before their bodies have become adjusted to the new time zone. An American executive expects to leave a jet and to begin important negotiations, often with serious cultural consequences.

Margaret Mead, a well-known anthropologist, once observed that people do not know their own culture until they experience at least one other culture. Likewise, managers who have operated within only one culture (the home, do-

Culture shock   The reduction in efficiency and disorientation caused by subtle conflicts within a new culture.

mestic culture) may never be conscious of the cultural assumptions underlying their managerial practices. When they move across national boundaries, they discover that a first step in adjusting to a new culture is to understand their own culture.

As a basis for a manager's departure into another culture (or nation), William H. Newman compiled six sets of attitudes and values assumed by U.S. management concepts. These assumptions are tacitly assumed; thus, an explicit discussion of them provides a base from which to move into other cultures. In addition, they provide those from other cultures and nations with an understanding of American behavior.[18]

1. The "master of destiny" viewpoint. The typical American considers that he or she has the power to make choices that affect future actions. Self-determination is in sharp contrast to a fatalistic viewpoint—for example, the Moslem view of "Allah's will." Chance, luck, and random results are, of course, possible, but the American manager has developed techniques based on probability theory to make "calculated risks." Furthermore, American managers assume a "Protestant ethic"—persistent, hard work will pay off. Planning as a key function of management depends upon the assumption that a manager has the power to make changes. Thus, in India and other traditional societies, where little has changed and where there is little hope of future changes, managers tolerate the status quo and can see no point in planning to take charge of the future.

2. Independent enterprise—an instrument for social action. American managers assume that business is a separate social institution; it is separate from the family, the church, and the government. The vitality of the enterprise is built on the employees' obligation to the enterprise and loyalty to its objectives.

   The assumption of independent enterprise is particularly important to the organizing function. The legal theory of the corporation creates a legal "person" who is separate from the life of executives and other social institutions. In some places, such as India and the African countries, the business enterprise is built upon family relationships and tribal kinships. In others, such as Latin American countries, the church and business enterprises are often merged. In communist countries, the government and the Communist party tend to be merged with the enterprise's management. In many countries, the American emphasis on avoiding conflicts of interest is not understood. Recent American scandals involving bribery by Lockheed and other American companies in Arab countries illustrate how this American assumption differs from assumptions in other countries. In the United States, securities laws and the SEC monitor the separation of the company's interest from an "insider's" personal gain.

3. Personnel selection based on merit. American management seeks the best man or woman for a position and offers rewards based upon the quality and quantity of performance. Nepotism (family connection) is minimized. Political pressures are frowned upon. Promotions based upon seniority or length of service are subordinate to productivity measures. In India and in Chinese companies outside the People's Republic of China, family connections are key factors in recruitment and promotion.

   In the United States, if performance is unsatisfactory, a person can expect to be replaced. If performance is superior, one can expect rapid advancement. Children are taught that "everyone has a chance to be president," indicating the unlimited opportunities available to those who develop superior characteristics for growth and success of the organization. The focus on merit provides a foundation for the implementation of the staffing function of management.

4. Decisions based on objective analysis. American management attempts to be scientific, that is, it searches for factual, objective, and rational support for decisions. A

significant portion of a professional manager's education involves mastering analytical techniques that provide a factual foundation for decisions. Judgments, intuitions, superstitions, or other nonrational aspects of managerial decisions are avoided if possible. The explosion of data collection and research is evidence of the validity of this assumption. Furthermore, managers have the freedom to express their interpretations of and opinions on issues that affect them. This orientation toward participation of all members of an organization in managerial decisions is the result of this assumption and is important to the planning and leading functions.

5. Shared decision making. Decision making in American management tends toward participation of all parties in the process. The individual is assumed to have unlimited potential, which can be exploited with further education. Management development programs are built upon the expectation that all employees can improve themselves and thus qualify for advancement. Initiative with proper motivation is basic to the growth of the enterprise. Investment in human capital is considered to have high payoffs. The leadership and other behavioral sections of this book are based on this assumption.

6. The never-ending quest for improvement. Since the United States is a relatively young country and has always assimilated immigrants looking for new opportunities, the culture underlying management has always viewed change as normal, expected, and preferable. In many other countries, however, the need for change is viewed as reflecting a failure on somebody's part. In the United States, change is usually attributed to an aggressive and alert management. American management is accustomed to ferment, challenges, and experimentation. The appearance of change is sought. For example, management texts, such as this one, must be continually revised to add new concepts or at least to reflect new terminology. Traditions, so valued in other countries, are viewed as evidences of "getting in a rut."

In American management literature, the manager is considered an "agent of change." In short, the function of a manager is to create change, not only to adjust to change. Thus, the assumption is that changing environment and technology force managers to seek change, not only to adjust to change; in addition, a strong management will view research and development, new ideas from outside consultants, and innovations of management techniques as means by which they will, in turn, create changes in technology and the environment.

An understanding of these six assumptions of American management provides a firm foundation on which American multinational managers can build management approaches to adapt to varied environments in other countries. A global manager must appreciate the strengths of American management principles and practices that have evolved from these assumptions. Yet the global manager must seek to understand the assumptions inherent in other cultures that may differ from American assumptions. Many of the conflicts between American expatriates and nationals of countries in which they operate are the result of failures to recognize these differences. An ethnocentric view should give way to a polycentric view and finally to a geocentric view, in which a synthesis of management approaches is predominant.

SUMMARY

This chapter has discussed the development of a global managerial orientation, the internationalization of America's domestic markets and the increasing importance and dynamics of multinational companies. It has focused on the managerial aspects of world business and has left to other books the related discussion of the political, economic, sociological, and historical details.

A large portion of this chapter has been devoted to the environmental factors that affect international management. The view has been geocentric or global. Within this view, an international manager will wish to develop a detailed comparison of the culture and environment of the home office with the cultures and environments of specific countries or regions and to consider how home-office managerial practices apply or how they should be adapted to meet the firm's long-term goals.

Much of this chapter has emphasized the differences and complexities of international management; however, it has concluded with a discussion of assumptions of American managers that may block U.S. entry into a global world.

KEY TERMS

Comparative advantage theory All nations can gain if each country specializes in producing goods in which it has comparative advantage and trades with others that have advantages in other goods.

Multinational corporation (MNC) A firm that operates in more than one country and allocates resources across national boundaries with the intention of maintaining managerial control of operations.

Multinational enterprise (MNE) Also called multinational company (MNC). It operates in more than one country and allocates company resources across national boundaries.

International trading company An international company that sells goods and products across national boundaries.

Transnational company An international company that controls operations, has stockholders in many countries, and employs citizens from all parts of the world.

Supranational company A company that has no national boundaries, operates in many countries, and has managers, employees, and owners from many parts of the world.

Integrate backward Extending operations into stages toward raw materials to gain managerial control of supplies.

Integrate forward Extending operations into stages toward the ultimate consumer to gain control of distribution of finished goods.

Horizontal integration The establishment of plants at the same stage of production in different countries.

Export One way of having involvement in international trade; in some instances an easier method of entry into another country.

Licensing The granting by a firm to a foreign firm (licensee) the right to use patents, trademarks, copyrights, or special know-how.

Franchising The granting by a firm to an independent company (franchisee) the right to use trademarks, patents, or other valuable assets while the firm (franchisor) agrees to provide assistance in operations.

Joint ventures The sharing of ownership and operations by two or more companies, often with different national homes, to achieve joint managerial control.

Management contracts A contract that usually describes providing specific services for a firm or party in another country; they usually do not require any capital investment.

Foreign subsidiary A firm owned and controlled by an MNC that operates in another country.

Ethnocentric attitude The tendency of human beings to orient to their home environments and to hold that their beliefs and customs are best for others.

Polycentric attitude   An understanding that each country has unique cultural characteristics and that visitors should adapt to each, e.g., Do as the Romans do.
Geocentric attitude   Imbued with the beliefs from a global view, recognizing pros and cons of home and foreign environments, and attempting to integrate these differences.

Foreign exchange rates   The value of the currency of one country stated in the currency units of another country.
Culture   Those acquired and learned behaviors which have persisted in human groups through traditions.
Culture shock   The reduction in efficiency and disorientation caused by subtle conflicts within a new culture.

STUDY ASSIGNMENTS

1. How does Honda's United States operation reflect the changing pattern of international business?

2. Why have businesses been assuming a more global orientation in their operations and activities? What does globalization of business mean for U.S. managers?

3. Why have a large number of Japanese and European firms chosen to acquire U.S. firms to have manufacturing operations in the United States? What does the acquisition of American firms by foreign businesses mean for American managers?

4. What are the characteristics of a multinational corporation (MNC)? Identify a firm that you think is a multinational and explain how it reflects the characteristics of an MNC.

5. What are some of the reasons why businesses expand the nature and scope of their operations to function on a more global scale?

6. Compare and contrast some of the different modes of foreign operations.

7. What must be considered when establishing foreign operations? How do these considerations vary if the firm going global is a large or a small venture?

8. Discuss some of the problems that managers can encounter when they work in foreign environments or when they manage international operations.

9. How does the managerial process change when operating in the international context?

Case for Discussion

COMET PETROLEUM

Winston Goode had earned himself a well-deserved reputation as a top-notch petroleum engineer and troubleshooter at his company's largest refinery, just outside of Wilmington, Delaware. He had been with the Comet Petroleum Company in various capacities throughout the United States for seventeen years, having served his last three years as assistant superintendent at Comet's Wilmington refinery.

When a replacement was needed for the chief engineer's position at Comet's refinery in Bangladesh, which was just coming on-line, Winston was sent there on a special short-term assignment. Upon his arrival, Winston discovered considerable confusion and a general state of disorganization amid all the problems associated with starting up a new refinery. To him, this was to be expected, and not being one to shrink from formidable challenges, Winston went about his duties with vigor and a strong sense of determination. Aside from his personal reputation and career being at stake, Winston felt a need to get the refinery into full production as quickly as possible because of the millions of dollars already invested in it.

Winston's assistant was Adel Abebbe, a Bengali who was trained as a petroleum engineer at the University of Oklahoma. Winston had not become fully acquainted with Adel when one day three weeks after his arrival, a serious problem arose. Winston moved with full force to solve this problem quickly, but he soon realized that it would require several days and the attention of a majority of his staff. He told his assistant and several others to be on the job first thing the next morning. He was shocked by their response. Adel told him, "I'm sorry, Mr. Goode, but tomorrow is Eid" (the Muslim holiday right after Ramadan).

Winston did not feel the excuse was legitimate.

"We've got a job to do here, and I want you and the others to be on the job tomorrow," said Winston.

"We're sorry, but we just can't come to work tomorrow," said Adel. "We thought you knew about our holiday and how important it is."

"I don't care if it's Christmas. You'd just better be here tomorrow morning, and early!"

With that, Winston left the outer office, where he and Adel had been standing, and returned to his private office. Several employees heard the exchange.

An hour later, Winston received a frantic telephone call from Ed Higby, the general superintendent. "Goode, what the heck is going on? The refinery is shut down. All the men have walked off their jobs. I asked a few of them and they told me something about you insulting their religion."

Chapter 4

Ethics and Social Responsibility

Learning Objectives

1. *Identify* some of the current ethics issues facing today's managers.
2. *Discuss* the difficulty in applying a single view of morality and ethics in the workplace.
3. *Explain* the concept of social responsibility from two different points of view.
4. *Compare* IBM's approach to social responsibility with Beech-Nut's approach to social responsibility.
5. *Discuss* how Johnson & Johnson used its ethics creed in deciding how to handle the Tylenol incident.
6. *Explain* the role of corporate culture in promoting and sustaining an organization's commitment to ethical practices.

FOR a number of years, the Hewlett-Packard Corporation has been recognized as one of the best corporations in the United States. Many observers believe that Hewlett-Packard has achieved such outstanding technological, financial, and market performances because its founders, William Hewlett and David Packard, developed an organizational culture that emphasizes social responsibility and ethical managerial practices. This culture is reflective of a core of values known as the "HP Way." The HP Way serves as a philosophical foundation and guide for employee behavior and managerial action. Values such as maintaining confidence in and respect for people are essential elements of Hewlett-Packard's organizational culture.

Hewlett-Packard's managers are expected to assume the belief that men and women will want to do a good job if they work in a proper environment, one in which they are treated with respect. To reinforce that expectation, Hewlett-Packard's top management has developed policies and procedures that are an extension of the firm's core values. One of the principal policies used to that end is Hewlett-Packard's "Standards of Business Conduct."

The "Standards of Business Conduct" document addresses the obligations that Hewlett-Packard's employees have to Hewlett-Packard, the firm's customers, its competitors, and its suppliers. These obligations include

- Avoiding conflicts of interest
- Refusing gifts from customers, competitors, or suppliers
- Not making payoffs to foreign governments or agents
- Not making derogatory comments about competitors
- No trading of inside information

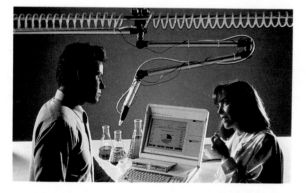

- No involvement in industrial espionage
- Promoting Hewlett-Packard as a good corporate citizen

Hewlett-Packard's management does not intend for this standard of conduct to be an explicit ethics statement. Rather, top management believes that these standards, together with other policy statements, should convey to all Hewlett-Packard's employees, customers, and suppliers that there is a moral and ethical way to conduct business activities.

The policies and statements developed by Hewlett-Packard's management regarding moral and ethical behavior are not static documents that are written, read, and then filed. Rather, they are dynamic documents that are continually reviewed and revised in response to changing social and operational conditions. At Hewlett-Packard, ethics and values are tailored to the culture of the firm.

Hewlett-Packard's managers understand that they have an obligation to instill in their subordinates a commitment to the values and ethical behavior that constitute the "HP Way." To ensure that this obligation is being fulfilled, internal auditors routinely monitor and evaluate Hewlett-Packard's managers. Managers are required to demonstrate that they have a copy of Hewlett-Packard's

Standards of Business Conduct and that they are knowledgeable about its contents. Managers must also demonstrate to the internal auditors that they periodically discuss the meaning and intent of the standards with their subordinates and that they promote the use of Hewlett-Packard's Open Door Policy to report and resolve any violations of the Standards of Business Conduct. Upon completion of the review, the internal auditors are required to certify that the managers being evaluated are in compliance with the firm's Standards of Business Conduct.

Some Hewlett-Packard employees and outside observers question the merit of these policies and procedures. They argue that Hewlett-Packard's management has simply created an institutionalized form of ethical and moral behavior. They doubt that such behavior is sincere and wonder how the firm will be able to sustain it once the firm is no longer subject to the considerable influence of William Hewlett and David Packard. For others, the issue is not the motivation, nature, or sincerity of the commitment to ethical behavior at Hewlett-Packard. What matters is that Hewlett-Packard and its employees are doing business in a socially and ethically responsible manner. ■

When news reports revealed that General Dynamics had charged the Air Force $600 for a common hammer, there was a public outcry about the lack of business ethics at General Dynamics. When Wall Street financiers Ivan Boesky and Michael Milken were accused of making enormous personal profits through insider trading, there was an outcry about the lack of ethics in business. When gasoline prices jumped dramatically in the wake of the Alaskan oil spill caused by the *Exxon Valdez,* oil companies were accused of profiting from a major environmental disaster. When Gordon Geco in the movie *Wall Street* made a speech arguing that "greed is good," business, educational, political, and social leaders began to ask why the public believed that the business community was interested in only one thing, making money.

Why the concern about business ethics?

In recent years, these and other well-publicized questionable business practices have brought business ethics to the forefront of concerns in the business community.[1] Until the late 1980s, business ethics was little more than an esoteric debate among some scholarly business professors. But in the wake of these events, businesses, business leaders, and academic institutions tried to put greater emphasis on developing ethical standards and fostering an appreciation for adherence to ethical business practices.

Many of those efforts, however, have proven to be more image than substance. Part of the problem is that the sudden push for ethical standards focused on addressing the clear-cut good-versus-bad, right-versus-wrong type of ethical issues. No one would question that pollution is bad, embezzlement is wrong, supporting the United Way is good, and honoring product warrantees is right. What the advocates of business ethics have discovered is that the real ethical issues are not black and white; rather, they are gray and complex, with no obvious solutions that enable everyone to win.[2]

A good illustration of this difficulty is the major oil spill in Alaska caused by the grounding of the *Exxon Valdez* in 1989. In the aftermath of this incident, the Exxon Corporation was criticized for staffing the ship with a captain who was known to have an alcohol problem. For many individuals, Exxon's behavior was inexcusable and represented a clear case of a company's failing to act in a socially responsible manner.

But there were other, not so clear-cut ethical issues involved in this situation. Exxon, like many organizations, had established an employee assistance

Clean-up crews arrived later than they should have after the *Exxon Valdez* dumped millions of gallons of oil into the Prince William Sound in Alaska causing irreparable damage to the environment. Many felt that the clean-up crews also left too soon, before their work was completed. Exxon was severely criticized for its seeming lack of social responsibility and ethics. It appeared that Exxon cared more about profiits than about people and the environment.

program designed to provide employees the opportunity to receive treatment for substance-abuse problems. To induce employees to participate in these programs, Exxon, like most firms that offer such assistance programs, promised to reinstate their problem employees to full duty upon their successful completion of a rehabilitation program. This practice is generally considered a vital part of an employee's long-term rehabilitation. The captain of the *Exxon Valdez* had completed just such a program. In this situation, Exxon's effort to act in a socially responsible manner resulted in adverse consequences to the society and the environment.

In this last chapter of Part I, we will see that the difficulty in dealing with issues of business ethics goes beyond how ethics can be related or applied to specific business situations. Business behavior and practices are influenced by factors such as the environment, circumstances, individual values, and organizational philosophy and culture.[3]

In our opening case, Hewlett-Packard illustrated how a variety of factors shaped the firm's standards of conduct and how those factors provided direction in defining the firm's orientation toward ethical behavior. The important aspect of Hewlett-Packard's approach was not the specifics of the "Standards of Business Conduct"; rather, it was how the firm fostered the idea that Hewlett-Packard employees have an obligation to conduct their business activities in a socially and ethically responsible manner.

But promoting ethical behavior and developing a commitment to social responsibility within a business and in its employees is not an easy proposition. For instance, in light of the recent concern over business ethics, the Harvard Business School began to incorporate the study and consideration of business ethics and social issues into its M.B.A. programs. Faculty and administrators alike were surprised that students had a less than favorable response to the introduction of ethics into the curriculum. Few students saw any merit in learning how to develop an ethics policy statement or how to motivate employees to act in an ethical manner. As one student put it, "A manager is paid to make the most profit possible. When you start getting into sociology, you lose sight of what job you're supposed to do."

In this chapter, we will examine the issue of business ethics, both in orientation and in practice. As the Harvard student noted, the factor of profit shapes, motivates, and directs individual and organizational behavior. It is not a factor that can be casually dismissed when considering ethical issues, nor is it incompatible with ethical business practices. But likewise, the factor of social responsibility raises the question of individual and organizational obligations. In this chapter, we will consider both situations. In doing so, we will demonstrate that the question of business ethics and social responsibility must be approached from a wide variety of views and perspectives. Ethical behavior and a commitment to social responsibility are vital to the success and viability of both a business venture and a society.

MORALITY AND ETHICS

It is difficult to find a universally accepted definition of the terms *ethics* and *morality*. The meaning and application of these two words are shaped and influenced by a variety of social, cultural, and situational factors. For instance, there is a variety of ethical and moral views concerning bribery. In the United States, bribery has traditionally been viewed as improper behavior and is considered an illegal activity when used to influence business decisions. However, in much of the Third World, bribery is a routine and expected part of doing business, an absolute necessity in securing contracts.[4] Such conflicting attitudes toward ethical and moral behavior can raise very complex questions: Which view of bribery is right—the American view or that of the Third World? Similarly, could we make an argument that American managers are more ethical in their business practices than Third World managers merely because the American managers do not engage in bribery? Unfortunately, as you will discover, there are no simple answers to these questions, because it is impossible to consider the issue of business ethics and morality in terms of black and white, right and wrong.

To have a meaningful discussion of ethics and morality in business, we need to establish what we mean by the terms *ethics* and *morality*. Therefore, we will use the following definitions as the basis for our discussion. **Morality** concerns how behavior conforms to established, socially accepted codes. Morality attempts to address cultural notions of right and wrong. These codes or notions are more conceptual in nature, and represent very broad-based, generally unwritten tenets that hold a society together. **Ethics** are more precise, socially derived standards and are generally written guidelines that govern the behavior of individuals, organizations, and segments of the society. Ethical standards typically address the more difficult questions of equity, righteousness, and compromise, and they provide guidelines for identifying what constitutes appropriate behavior and practices.

With those working definitions in mind, we will examine a variety of viewpoints concerning the nature and character of business ethics and morality in the workplace. In the process, we suggest that you reflect on what you believe constitutes moral behavior and ethical business practices. As you do this, you should recognize that ethical and moral behavior in business, while reflective of social and cultural factors, is highly individualistic, shaped by one's own values and experiences. However, an organization's culture and the practices of its senior managers can influence the moral actions and ethical behavior not only of its employees but also of other individuals and other entities associated with the organization.

To illustrate some of the varied dimensions of morality and ethics in business, consider the following true story. A newspaper reporter was working on a story about odometer tampering by used-car dealers. To get some background on the problem, the reporter contacted an old friend who happened to own a used-car lot. The friend acknowledged that odometer tampering was a common practice and that it was done to increase the selling price of a car. When the reporter asked his friend if he had tampered with any car sold on his lot, the car dealer replied without hesitation that he had. The reporter was surprised at his friend's revelation, particularly since he believed that his friend was a reputable businessman. When the reporter asked his friend why he had engaged in an illegal business practice, the friend replied that he had to stay in business. The car dealer argued that he had an obligation to make money to provide for his family and to provide employment for his employees. He maintained that since everyone was engaged in odometer tampering, he had no choice but to adopt the same practice.

The reporter was troubled by the interview. He felt that his friend's behav-

Morality Conceptual codes concerning how behavior conforms to established, socially accepted norms; addresses cultural notions of right and wrong.

Ethics The decision area dealing with moral behavior of individuals.

Is the car dealer dishonest?

ior was morally wrong, that it was unjustifiable for one individual to cheat another. The reporter considered the tampering an act of dishonesty. At the same time, the reporter was having a difficult time answering the argument that if his friend did not tamper, the business would go bust and people would lose their incomes. The reporter understood that his friend was not a bad individual but merely someone who was acting in the best interests of his employees and their families.

This situation shows us a variety of moral dilemmas and ethical problems and also demonstrates some of the complexities involved in addressing moral and ethical questions. It is important to note that the right or wrong of an action may change merely by taking a different perspective. The moral tenet that people should be honest in their dealings with one another is overshadowed by the moral responsibility to ensure the well-being of one's family and friends. If the practice of odometer tampering is so widespread, what benefit would there be if one used-car dealer, or a few, adhered to an ethical code of conduct? The reporter's moral responsibility to publish the truth conflicts with an ethical responsibility based on a journalism code of conduct, to protect his sources from any consequences resulting from their providing information to the press. Does the reporter tell the public that his friend tampers with odometers? For the reporter, the question is, What matters more, the need to preserve his friendship or the need to preserve his professional integrity? As with all questions of morality and ethics, the answers and required actions are not easily defined.

Although many individuals might wrestle at length with the moral and ethical dimensions of this situation, there are some individuals who would view the whole problem from a completely different perspective. They would argue that there are no moral or ethical issues involved in tampering or in the reporting of tampering practices. They base their argument on the premise that businesses are morally neutral entities; therefore, the behavior and performance of any business will be directed and shaped solely by market forces. In this case, the practice of tampering might be a natural part of the market process, or if it is not, market forces will cause the practice to stop (a promotional campaign in which used-car dealers guarantee that there is no tampering with the odometers).

But there is considerable debate over the premise that businesses and business activities are morally neutral. Many business, academic, political, and social leaders question whether the idea of business ethics can be totally eliminated. This group argues that businesses are first and foremost social institutions created by the society. Furthermore, since society gives businesses the right to exist, society has the right to determine what is expected of them and how they should act. These expectations are derived from the society's moral values, which in turn are used to define what constitutes ethical business practices. From this perspective emerges the notion that a business has a social responsibility and that its managers must conduct business in a socially responsible manner. That notion is not without confusion, or even cost, however.

For many years, the business community has received considerable criticism for its lack of social responsibility in environmental issues.[5] In particular, environmentalists have focused attention on the way businesses package their products. In response to this criticism, many businesses are beginning to make a concerted effort to be more environmentally responsible.[6]

The effort to use recyclable or recycled materials, however, has resulted in some unusual complications and "Catch 22" situations for many businesses. For instance, McDonald's responded to environmentalists' concern about their packaging by trying to eliminate the use of Styrofoam containers. McDonald's began using containers made with recyclable paper materials. Since the recyclable materials were to be used with food, McDonald's had to treat them with a special coating that subsequently reduced the biodegradability of the containers. Environmentalists then began to complain that the new recyclable containers had a more adverse impact on the environment than the old Styrofoam containers.[7]

Businesses have also discovered that there are financial costs and legal complications associated with their efforts to act in a socially responsible man-

Management Application

Ethics Consultants

In the wake of the insider-trading scandals of the late 1980s, many firms felt the need to develop and institutionalize ethics programs within their organizations. In reponse to this need, a large number of firms providing "ethics consultants" suddenly emerged on the scene. These consultants specialize in providing ethics training, guidance in developing and implementing ethics programs, and assistance in formulating written ethics policy statements for their client companies. Although many business and managerial consultants were amused by the services offered by the ethics consultant and were concerned about their validity, demand for such services was quite high.

Consumers and consumer groups were very skeptical about the motivation of firms that utilized the services of ethics consultants. Most viewed this action as nothing more than a way to improve a firm's image and limit damage caused by questionable activities and business practices. For instance, with the stockmarket crash of October 1987 and the bad publicity surrounding insider trading, many brokerage houses and financial services employed ethics consultants, hoping that the high visibility of this action would help restore investor confidence in the integrity of their operations.

Employees were even more critical of the ethics consultants. Subordinate managers viewed such programs as little more than top management's lip service to the concept of ethical business behavior. Many employees scoffed at the creation of lengthy statements of corporate ethics and employee codes of conduct, particularly when a firm suddenly announced a plant closing or forced the early retirement of senior employees.

Outside observers also questioned the merit of corporate ethics programs and the work of the ethics consultants. One study found that firms that created highly formalized ethics programs were more likely to be facing criminal and civil charges of questionable products or services and business practices than those firms that did not institute an ethics program. Other studies have concluded that ethics programs were merely for show, without a real and sincere commitment by top management. Overall, few observers felt that the ethics consultants had any impact on the actual ethical nature of a firm's culture and managerial practices.

Source: "Ethics Consultants," *Newsweek,* May 9, 1988, p. 56.

ner. There is a maze of conflicting federal and local laws governing recycling practices and environmental labeling. The H. J. Heinz Company had planned to promote environmental awareness by placing the word *recyclable* on the front of 104 million plastic bottles of ketchup. They had to cancel those plans at the last minute, however, when they discovered that they might not be able to distribute the ketchup because of conflicting state regulations that restricted the use of the word recyclable on a product's label. A Heinz spokesperson noted, "We cannot risk having our product being banned from one state to the next because of wording on the product's label."

Procter & Gamble, who has been a leader in the recycling effort, has encountered numerous problems in trying to address environmental concerns. P & G planned to include on its product labels information about emerging recycling technology. But P & G stopped that initiative when it discovered that California and Maryland had laws restricting the type of recycling information that can be included on any label. Some states have even restricted manufacturers' use of the "chasing arrow" recycling symbol because many communities are unable to handle recyclable materials.

Complicating the efforts of businesses to take an active role in the recycling movement are the jurisdictional conflicts among state governments and among federal agencies. Sometimes, the conflict is over something as simple as terminology. State regulatory authorities have been arguing about the meaning of *recyclability, recyclable content,* and *reusability,* and what is acceptable terminology in one state may not be acceptable in another. Similarly, the Environmental Protection Agency is in conflict with the Federal Trade Commission over who has the authority to issue and enforce marketing guidelines.

The business community now finds itself in a difficult position with respect to environmental issues. On one hand, many businesses have responded to public concerns about recycling. On the other hand, their efforts to act in a socially responsible manner have been frustrated by the costs and operational complications of complying with a maze of governmental regulations.

SOCIAL RESPONSIBILITY IN BUSINESS

Most of the arguments about the nature and meaning of ethics in business are based on the opinion that businesses, like individuals, have certain social responsibilities. Organizations are social institutions, whose right to exist originates with society itself.[8]

Central to this concept of social responsibility is the idea that organizations and businesses have an obligation to act in the best interest of the society. Although there is little disagreement over the point that businesses exist by the authority of the society, there are two significantly different arguments about the nature of their obligation and what constitutes socially responsible behavior.

To Professor Milton Friedman, the only social responsibility that any business or any individual has is to make as much money as possible for the shareholder. Accordingly, decisions and actions are to be based solely on whether they will yield more profit than any other alternative. The logic of this argument is that such behavior will result in the most efficient and effective use of individual, organizational, social, and environmental resources.

For those individuals and organizations who accept this view of social responsibility, there is no need to address questions of ethical behavior and business practices. For instance, the decision to close a plant would be purely an economic decision, regardless of its impact on employees and the community where the plant was located. The argument in this case would be that although closing a plant may be painful for some individuals and groups, the society as a whole benefits more in the long run because the firm is acting to eliminate inefficient and inappropriate uses of valuable resources.

Another example of how this view of social responsibility is applied is the tobacco companies' attitude that they must do whatever is necessary to maximize the profits from their products. They take the position that there are no ethical issues involved in their lobbying efforts to promote tobacco subsidies, nor is there anything ethically wrong in creating promotional campaigns that encourage young adults to start smoking. In this case, if they fail to effectively and efficiently use their resources (tobacco, employees, production facilities), then they will, in the end, not be acting in a socially responsible manner.

There are individuals and businesses, however, who believe that their first priority is to conduct all business activities in a socially responsible manner. These individuals and businesses would argue that by emphasizing ethical behavior and social responsibility, they maximize their shareholders' wealth in the long run. Accordingly, corporate donations to charitable activities and community projects would be considered morally appropriate behavior and not a misuse of corporate funds that rightfully belong to the stockholders. That is not to say that they will not take the same actions as firms that believe that the first priority should be to maximize profit. Rather, firms that emphasize social responsibility endeavor to consider and address the consequences and impact of any decision or action that they make.

IBM showed social responsibility by relocating employees from its closed Greenville, Indiana, plant to other IBM plant locations like this one in San Diego. IBM also helped the community of Greenville by giving the closed plant site to the city, helping to develop the plant site for use by the city, and by providing financial assistance to the city for retraining of the employees who chose not to transfer to another location.

When IBM makes the economic decision to close one of its plants, it also considers the impact such a closing will have on its employees and the community where the plant is located. A few years ago when IBM closed its Greenville, Indiana, distribution center, all employees were guaranteed new positions at other IBM facilities, and IBM aided the employees in their relocation. In addition, IBM gave the plant site to the community of Greenville and provided financial assistance to the community to support retraining programs and the redevelopment of the site. IBM's follow-up activity lasted more than two years after the plant was closed. IBM was under no obligation to relocate its employees, nor was it obliged to help Greenville overcome the economic loss that resulted from the plant closing. Nevertheless, IBM's management took those actions because they believed that it was the organization's social responsibility to do so.

But was IBM acting in the best interests of its shareholders? Those who believe that a business's only social responsibility is to maximize profits would categorically say no. The closing of the plant yielded IBM no profits, nor did the firm gain sales as a result, and there was little publicity given to its action. On the surface it would appear that the shareholders were the ones who bore the costs of closing the plant. IBM's management would argue that there is a long-term benefit to the firm's competitive position in acting in such a socially responsible manner. In turn, IBM's enhanced competitiveness means that its shareholders' wealth will be maximized in the long term.

Both of the views of social responsibility that we have considered focus ultimately on what managerial and organizational behavior benefits the shareholder. However, in recent years there has been some discussion that these points of view have been rather limited and that the notion of social responsibility should extend beyond the bottom line. Some business leaders are now arguing that managers and businesses should act in a socially responsible manner to maximize the benefit to the organization's stakeholders, not just to its stockholders. An organization's stakeholders consist of shareholders, employees, customers, communities, institutions, suppliers, competitors, governments, and environments affected either directly or indirectly by the activities of the organization and its members. Each of these stakeholders has different priorities and different relationships with the organization. Only a few are concerned about the impact that the firm's actions and ethical practices have on profitability. Most are concerned about other factors that are influenced by the organization's activities. The NCR Corporation was one of the biggest proponents of this stakeholders concept. It developed a major advertising campaign around this stakeholders concept, and Figure 4-1 shows some of this promotional material.

Consider the issue surrounding "right to know" laws. An organization that accepts the broad notion of stakeholders, with respect to social responsibility, would not need legislation to motivate its management to provide full and public disclosure of the chemical composition of its products and chemical reactions involved in its production process. The firm would feel obligated to let its employees know of the hazards involved in the production process. It would inform the community of the potential environmental impact that its production process has on the community's health and resources. In this instance, such disclosure would make it easier for fire fighters to manage any fires or accidental toxic spills that occur at the firm's facilities. Communities could measure the risks and benefits involved before permitting hazardous activities within the community. But few firms, even those that are recognized as outstanding examples of socially responsible businesses, would provide such disclosure. Unfortunately, there are consequences to fully satisfying all the stakeholders' expectations of social responsibility. Full disclosure would reveal valuable trade secrets, which could result in lost business. Such disclosure might also prompt public protest, which could result in serious legal restrictions on production processes. There are some very difficult trade-offs in doing business, trade-offs that generally create both winners and losers. Two examples will make this point clear.

SOCIAL RESPONSIBILITY AND CRISIS MANAGEMENT

Why do crises raise questions about social responsibility?

An organization's true commitment to social responsibility and ethical business practices often surfaces during crises. Society assumes that organizations or managers will not consciously or deliberately develop products or provide services that will cause injury or adversely affect the society. However, there are events that have an adverse and unintended impact on the organization, its employees, its customers, the community, the environment, and society as a whole: an accidental chemical leak, an oil spill, a bank failure, a train derailment, a fire, or a natural disaster. In these situations, how the organization responds demonstrates the influence that corporate culture, ethics, and personal values have on decision making and organizational actions. Sometimes, these stressful circumstances reveal a limited commitment to social responsibility.

FIGURE 4-1 NCR's Stakeholder Promotional Material

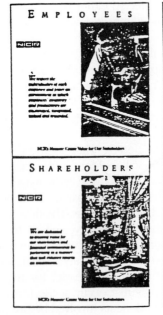

(Source: Public Relations Office, NCR Corporation, Dayton, Ohio, 1989)

Global Application

Oil Spills, Nuclear Meltdowns, and Other Global Disasters

The *Exxon Valdez* oil spill in Alaska, the nuclear meltdown in Chernobyl, the chemical explosions in Bhopal: All of these were disasters with global implications. A disaster in one country results in damage to the environment and to people's health, not only in that country, but in all the countries of the world. A nuclear cloud from Chernobyl, for example, can travel thousands of miles.

Experts feel that as the world becomes more and more industrialized, with more oil, nuclear power, and chemicals being produced and used, disasters will increase rapidly.

There is good news. Experts also feel that nearly all disasters can be prevented. Researchers have traced each disaster to its source: the people involved in the situation. For the most part, the disasters were not the result of faulty equipment or technology. The researchers feel that responsibility for disasters rests with the executive managers of the organizations who set the rules and the productivity goals. They recommend the following disaster-prevention guidelines:

1. Don't overwork employees. A tired employee is much more likely to make a fatal mistake than a well-rested one.
2. Communicate. Make sure that everyone in the organization always knows what is going on.
3. Train and train again. Training can make employees aware of potential dangers and how to handle them.
4. Let those closest to operations make decisions, particularly during times of crisis.
5. Don't let technology interfere with the employees' ability to control a situation.

Source: John Carey, "Getting Business to Think about the Unthinkable: Can New Management Strategies Prevent Another Exxon Valdez or Bhopal?" *Business Week*, June 24, 1991, pp. 104–7.

The nuclear disaster at Chernobyl provides a good example of crisis management and of global implications of disasters. Management moved quickly to contain the damage, but after the nuclear meltdown in its power plant, the town of Chernobyl had to be abandoned. The fallout from Chernobyl's nuclear radiation cloud increased cancer cases, increased birth defects, increased deaths and caused permanent damage to the environment.

Background on the Beech-Nut Story

In November 1987, the Beech-Nut Corporation pleaded guilty in federal court to fraud and to the willful violation of food and drug laws.[9] Beech-Nut's management admitted that the firm had produced and sold fake "100% All-Natural Apple Juice." The "apple juice," made for infants and toddlers, was some unknown chemical concoction that contained no apple ingredients. Beech-Nut's admission was a surprise to the firm's employees and to many executives in the food industry, especially since Beech-Nut had a long-standing reputation for quality, purity, integrity, and the use of natural ingredients in its children's foods.

News accounts of what exactly had happened at Beech-Nut led many observers to wonder why the management of such a reputable firm had allowed the fraud to occur. Some reports indicated that Beech-Nut's top executives not only had known for years that there was something wrong with the concentrate but also had rejected numerous recommendations by subordinates to stop using the suspicious apple concentrate. Instead, some of Beech-Nut's top management reasoned that all they were doing was a little harmless cheating to improve the firm's financial position. This kind of executive thinking caused many observers and Beech-Nut employees to wonder why there had been such a breakdown of both individual and corporate ethical behavior.[10]

Beech-Nut's problem began in 1977, when it started to purchase apple concentrate from the Universal Juice Company. Beech-Nut was in financial trouble when it decided to purchase Universal's concentrate, which was 20 percent cheaper than any other concentrate. Some employees at Beech-Nut were suspicious of the offer. A few employees initiated inquiries about the real composition of the concentrate. However, their efforts were ignored, particularly when Beech-Nut's apple juice products became its biggest source of revenues (30 percent of sales).

Despite improved revenues, led by growth in the sales of apple juice, the financial condition of Beech-Nut continued to decline. In 1979, Nestlé, the Swiss food conglomerate, purchased the company. At the time of the acquisition, Nestlé was the subject of a worldwide consumer boycott because of its marketing of its infant formula in the Third World. Nestlé made a number of changes in Beech-Nut's top management and made it clear that these managers were to return Beech-Nut to profitability.

Even with new ownership and new management, Beech-Nut continued to use Universal's apple concentrate. Then in 1981, Jerome LiCari, Beech-Nut's director of research and development, wrote a memorandum to Beech-Nut's president and operations chief expressing his concern that Universal's concentrate was nothing more than some chemical concoction. No one responded to the memorandum. LiCari persisted in his effort. Eventually, he was warned that his job was at risk and that he would have to prove beyond a doubt that the concentrate was a fake, before the firm would switch to a more expensive producer. LiCari never succeeded in getting Beech-Nut's management to terminate Universal's contract. However, in the 1987 court case, LiCari was the principal witness for the prosecution.

Although LiCari's effort failed, outside events ended the use of Universal's concentrate. In June 1982, investigators from the Processed Apple Institute informed Beech-Nut's executives that there was proof that Universal's concentrate was a fake and that they had initiated a lawsuit to close Universal. Beech-

Nut's management ignored the allegations and refused to support PAI's effort to shut down Universal's operations. Even when PAI and federal authorities closed Universal in July 1982, Beech-Nut chose not to cooperate in any investigation. Despite requests from the authorities to initiate a product recall and internal recommendations urging the destruction of all remaining inventories (valued at $3.5 million), Beech-Nut's top management decided to continue to sell the fake apple juice and to use its remaining supply of Universal's concentrate. Finally, when Beech-Nut refused to cooperate in the investigation of Universal, federal authorities began the legal actions against Beech-Nut that led to its 1987 conviction for fraud.

The impact of Beech-Nut's use of fake apple concentrate went far beyond the legal consequences. Beech-Nut's reputation and image suffered. Employee morale and performance also were undermined. And finally, Beech-Nut sustained major financial losses, caused by a 20 percent drop in market share. In the end, many observers wondered if there had been any real benefit from using the low-cost concentrate.

Discussion

The Beech-Nut incident illustrates the problems and consequences that organizations, managers, employees, consumers, and society can face when moral and ethical concerns are not included in the decision-making process. In addition, this situation demonstrates that one cannot judge what happened at Beech-Nut simply in terms of right and wrong, good and evil. There are other perspectives, issues, and concerns.[11]

Beech-Nut's directors could argue that in purchasing the concentrate from Universal, Beech-Nut's management was acting in the best interest of the company and society. They provide jobs and income. They support and stimulate the economic and social vitality of the communities where they operate. They benefit consumers by both providing needed products and services and stimulating competition. In this context, the argument is that if the decision had been made to terminate Universal's contract, necessitating the purchase of another apple concentrate at a higher price, Beech-Nut's competitiveness and financial situation would have deteriorated rapidly. From the organization's perspective, management was justified in taking all actions necessary to prevent the financial failure of Beech-Nut.

The Beech-Nut managers who made the initial decision to purchase the low-cost concentrate and those who chose to continue to use it in Beech-Nut's apple juice were viewed by their peers and the community as honest, well-respected citizens. The managers never considered their actions criminal in any way. They were acting in the best interest of the company. The managers also stated two other justifications for their actions. The first was that they assumed that all their competitors were doing the same thing. The second was that no one was getting hurt by the product. After all, there were no customer complaints and Beech-Nut's apple juice had the largest percentage of market share. For these managers, the actions were necessary to restore Beech-Nut's profitability; they had done what was expected of them.

Beech-Nut's competition took a rather different view of Beech-Nut's use of a fake concentrate. Some Gerber managers suggested that Beech-Nut should have known right away that something was wrong with the concentrate. The price was too good to be true. Universal's concentrate was priced 20 percent lower than any other apple concentrate. Gerber's managers also commented that they would have immediately cut off any supplier that could not demonstrate that its product was genuine. At Gerber's, what was most important was preserving the firm's integrity and maintaining consumers' trust.

Consumers were particularly sensitive about Beech-Nut's actions. In their minds, Beech-Nut had a higher responsibility than most manufacturers, since Beech-Nut's products were used primarily by infants and toddlers. Parents purchased food for their children, trusting that the producer would go to all lengths to preserve the quality and purity of the product. Beech-Nut's use of the fake concentrate was viewed as a breach of that trust, and parents responded by purchasing other brands of infants' and toddlers' food.

As you can see, the responses to Beech-Nut's behavior are varied. Some observers might suggest that Beech-Nut's managers were merely rationalizing actions that they themselves viewed as being wrong. Others might argue that Beech-Nut was being treated unfairly, that its actions were honestly motivated by its social commitment to preserving jobs and the economic well-being of its community. But in each of these instances, there existed a conflict of values. Li-Cari, in attempting to get top management to stop the use of Universal's concentrate, had to consider not only his own values, but also the welfare of his fellow employees and the interests of the community as a whole. In the end, the courts judged that Beech-Nut had violated its public trust and committed fraud.

A Different Approach at Johnson & Johnson

In sharp contrast to Beech-Nut's handling of the fake apple concentrate is Johnson & Johnson's response to the tampering incidents involving its Tylenol products.

When the first reports appeared about people becoming ill from poisoned Tylenol, Johnson & Johnson employees took the initiative and began removing Tylenol from store shelves without waiting for instructions to do so from their corporate headquarters. They knew that what they were doing was right, and they believed that top management expected such behavior. While the employees were taking action to remove, examine, and destroy the Tylenol on the shelves and in inventory, top management moved to assure the public that the company was taking every action possible to correct the problem and to prevent it from happening in the future. (Johnson & Johnson eventually developed tamperproof capsules and packaging at a tremendous cost.) Clearly, the first priority for Johnson & Johnson was not preserving short-run profits but protecting its consumers from any harm.

Why did Johnson & Johnson employees act to correct the problem, when the Beech-Nut employees would have stonewalled the situation? The reason is that the top management of Johnson & Johnson fosters and reinforces an organizational culture that stresses that all employees have a moral obligation first to the customers, then to the communities where Johnson & Johnson operates, and lastly to the firm's shareholders. These values are formally expressed in the Johnson & Johnson Credo, shown in Figure 4-2, which provides basic guidelines for ethics and socially responsible behavior.

This kind of ethical emphasis resulted in organizational, managerial, and employee behavior that earned Johnson & Johnson praise from government agencies, the media, consumer groups, and the business community for its

Does Beech-Nut have a higher responsibility because of their products?

OUR CREDO

- We believe our first responsibility is to the doctors, nurses and patients, to mothers and all others who use our products and services.
- In meeting their needs everything we do must be of high quality.
- We must constantly strive to reduce our costs in order to maintain reasonable prices.
- Customers' orders must be serviced promptly and accurately.
- Our suppliers and distributors must have an opportunity to make a fair profit.
- We are responsible to our employees, the men and women who work with us throughout the world.
- Everyone must be considered as an individual.
- We must respect their dignity and recognize their merit.
- They must have a sense of security in their jobs.
- Compensation must be fair and adequate, and working conditions clean, orderly and safe.
- Employees must feel free to make suggestions and complaints.
- There must be equal opportunity for employment, development and advancement for those qualified.
- We must provide competent management, and their actions must be just and ethical.
- We are responsible to the communities in which we live and work and to the world community as well.
- We must be good citizens—support good works and charities and bear our fair share of taxes.
- We must encourage civic improvements and better health and education.
- We must maintain in good order the property we are privileged to use, protecting the environment and natural resources.
- Our final responsibility is to our stockholders.
- Business must make a sound profit.
- We must experiment with new ideas.
- Research must be carried on, innovative programs developed and mistakes paid for.
- New equipment must be purchased, new facilities provided and new products launched.
- Reserves must be created to provide for adverse times.
- When we operate according to these principles the stockholders should realize a fair return.

(Source: Public Affairs Office, Johnson and Johnson Corporation, 1990)

FIGURE 4-2 Johnson & Johnson's Credo

handling of the Tylenol incident. The cost of removing all Tylenol from the shelves ran into the millions of dollars, but the payoff for Johnson & Johnson was that its customers remained loyal and continued to buy Tylenol. As a result, Johnson & Johnson experienced virtually no loss of market share in the aftermath of both the first and even a second Tylenol poisoning incident. In the end, Johnson & Johnson strengthened its image, market position, and long-term profitability.

The difference between the way Beech-Nut acted and the way Johnson &

Is there a lesson in the comparisons of Beech-Nut and Johnson & Johnson?

Johnson acted was based on the attitude that each firm had toward social responsibility and on the commitment each firm made to ethics and moral behavior. Each firm's response was also a reflection of its organizational culture and of how ethics and social responsibility are incorporated into that culture. As we noted earlier, you acquire most of your attitudes, values, and ethical orientation from your family and through the experiences of your formative years. The same is true of organizations. An organization's ethics and commitment to social responsibility evolve over time, and they become part of the organization's culture. In business, employees acquire and adopt the prevailing values, ethics, and orientation toward social responsibility from the organization's culture.

In the last segment of this chapter, we will examine how organizations and senior management can develop a culture that promotes and reinforces ethical and socially responsible behavior.

ETHICS AND SOCIAL RESPONSIBILITY WITHIN A CORPORATE CULTURE

Throughout this chapter, we have talked about the ethical practices and social responsibility of organizations and businesses. We have referred to IBM, Johnson & Johnson, Hewlett-Packard, and others as socially responsible firms that have displayed strong ethical practices. However, you may recall that organizations and businesses are artificial entities created by society. As such, it is awkward to suggest that an organization or a business should be able to address human moral issues of right and wrong. But because organizations are shaped and managed by people, how do organizations create an environment and a culture that develop, promote, and reinforce ethical behavior for the people involved with the organization?

The ethical standards and social responsibility of most organizations and businesses reflect the personal values and commitment to the ideals of the organizations' founders or the dominant managers. Over the years, those values and ideals become institutionalized and become integral to the corporate culture.

At IBM, it was Charles Watson's personal values and ethics that formed the basis of its corporate culture. At Johnson & Johnson, it was the ideals of General Robert Wood Johnson. At Hewlett-Packard, the culture reflects the personalities and beliefs of Bill Hewlett and David Packard. At General Motors, Alfred Sloan was credited with being the moral voice of GM's corporate culture. Those individuals were the sources of their organizations' experiences, values, and principles. They were the behavioral role models for the firm's ethical behavior and commitment to social responsibility. Therefore, the challenge facing an organization is how to successfully develop, sustain, renew, and adapt its ethical standards and its commitment to socially responsible behavior. There are a variety of approaches to achieving this end, which we will now consider.

To preserve the ethical and social responsibility agenda set forth by an organization's founders, many organizations have developed and instituted formal standards of conduct or statements of ethics. Typically, these statements cover a wide range of issues and potential problem areas. They serve as moral and ethical guidelines for managers and, in some instances, become the basis for establishing continuity and uniformity in organizational and managerial action. In some organizations, these statements have been characterized as the "unifying force," the "glue" that holds the organization together so that its employees can act in a cohesive socially responsible manner. Two examples of these kinds of statements, Champion-International and GTE, are shown in Figure 4-3.

Sometimes, these statements are a part of a whole series of policy guidelines that the organization has issued. Each statement addresses a unique dimension of the organization's operation, with some statements providing very specific and detailed policies on how to address a given situation, and other statements attempting to define and explain the organization's cultural values and ethical standards from a philosophical perspective.

For instance, Xerox has a number of documents that address a wide array of issues. These include "An Understanding," which is a running commentary on the rights and obligations of Xerox's employees. Then there is "Managing at Xerox," which addresses the firm's emphasis on employee integrity, its concern for people, and the importance of being sensitive to the customer. In addition, there is the "Xerox Policy on Business Ethics," Xerox's guide to "Business Conduct," a publication on "Policy Understandings," and finally Xerox's "Business Policy Manual."

Unfortunately, some organizations get carried away with creating very detailed statements of conduct or with publishing a multitude of policy statements that address every conceivable ethical question or situation. When that happens, either employees attempt to rigidly adhere to the statements' directive nature, or they merely pay lip service to the intent of the document. In either case, the effectiveness of such policies is limited. Under those circumstances, employees tend to go through the motions and never recognize the need to adapt and balance their handling of ethically questionable situations. More often than not, their response does more harm than good.

Given the dynamic nature of the marketplace, other organizations have recognized that statements of ethical standards and socially responsible behavior have to be dynamic and provide a degree of flexibility. These firms have found that a simple creed or policy statement is a more practical guideline for determining ethical practices and socially responsible behavior. McDonnell-Douglas Corporation uses the simple creed that its employees are "honest and trustworthy in all relationships" to govern its ethical practices. J. C. Penney's simply adopted the Golden Rule: "Do unto others as you would have them do unto you." These types of statements serve more as a general reference point, an anchor that provides an ethical and social responsibility perspective while allowing flexibility of action in dealing with a wide variety of situations. These types of statements place more responsibility on the individual manager or employee for defining the ethical standards that he or she can exercise within the prevailing corporate culture.

Ethics statements and social responsibility policies are not sufficient in themselves to cause people to behave in a socially responsible manner. A twenty-page policy statement by General Dynamics failed to prevent wide-

FIGURE 4-3 Formal Statements of GTE and Champion International

GTE's Governing Values

- *Quality* in products and services, "a goal which we will not compromise."
- *Benchmarking* is the collection of data comparing GTE performance to its best competitors. The value thus designated is the preference for excelling competitors in critical factors identified in the strategy of each business unit.
- *Employee Involvement and Teamwork.* A commitment to sharing information, participation in problem-solving, and opportunity for contribution of ideas is announced. Employee involvement is to become an integral part of the management process.
- *People.* In striving to "maintain a motivating and rewarding work environment" GTE will try to "attract, retain, develop, and reward capable individuals who help us meet our business goals and attain our vision".
- *Innovation.* Innovation will be nurtured by encouraging rather than discouraging new ideas, by supporting risk-taking experimentation.
- *Technology.* Supported by research and innovative application, a competitive technological position across diverse businesses will be sought.
- *Market Sensitivity.* Constant focus on the needs of customers and competitive activity requires intense customer contact at all levels.

(Office of Human Resources and Administration, GTE Corporation, 1988)

The Champion Way

- *Champion's* objective is leadership in American industry. Profitable growth is fundamental to the achievement of that goal and will benefit all to whom we are responsible: shareholders, customers, employees, communities and society at large.
- *Champion's* way of achieving profitable growth requires active participation of all employees in increasing productivity, reducing costs, improving quality and strengthening customer service.
- *Champion* wants to be known for the excellence of its products and service and the integrity of its dealings.
- *Champion* wants to be known as an excellent place to work. This means jobs in facilities that are clean and safe, where the spirit of cooperation and mutual respect prevails, where all feel free to make suggestions, and where all can take pride in working for Champion.
- *Champion* wants to be known for its fair and thoughtful treatment of employees. We are committed to providing equality of opportunity for all people, regardless of race, national origin, sex, age, or religion. We actively seek a talented, diverse, enthusiastic workforce. We believe in the individual worth of each employee and seek to foster opportunities for personal development.
- *Champion* wants to be known for its interest in and support of the communities in which employees live and work. We encourage all employees to take an active part in the affairs of their communities, and we will support their volunteer efforts.
- *Champion* wants to be known as a public-spirited corporation, mindful of its need to assist—through volunteer efforts and donated funds—non-profit educational, civic, cultural, and social welfare organizations which contribute uniquely to our national life.
- *Champion* wants to be known as an open, truthful company. We are committed to the highest standards of business conduct in our relationships with customers, suppliers, employees, and shareholders. In all our pursuits we are unequivocal in our support of the laws of the land, and acts of questionable legality will not be tolerated.
- *Champion* wants to be known as a company which strives to conserve resources, to reduce waste, and to use and dispose of materials with scrupulous regard for safety and health. We take particular pride in this company's record of compliance with the spirit as well as the letter of all environmental regulations.
- *Champion* believes that only through the individual actions of all employees—guided by a company-wide commitment to excellence—will our long-term economic success and leadership position be ensured.

(Executive Office Champion International Corporation 1988)

Ethics Issue

Social Responsibility Exemplified: Du Pont Corporation

Faith Wohl is the social conscience of the Du Pont Corporation; it's her job to make sure that Du Pont is "employee-friendly" and "family-friendly." Du Pont, with Wohl's leadership, is considered to be a corporate groundbreaker in helping employees to balance career and family. She and her nineteen-person staff work on employees' personal and social concerns, with a strong emphasis on family.

In the last three years, Du Pont has spent over $1.5 million to build and renovate child-care centers near its principal work sites throughout the country. In Du Pont's home state of Delaware, Wohl used $250,000 to establish the Child Care Connection, a day-care referral system that is used by over seventy-five companies throughout the state. Wohl has also started a program called Flying Colors to give grants to day-care centers to improve facilities and services.

Du Pont has one of the most generous leave policies in the United States for employees who need time off for the birth of a new baby, adoption, and illness (including illness of a relative). For the first six weeks of the leave, the employee receives full pay and benefits. If necessary, the employee may take off the next six months without pay but with full benefits. A job is waiting for the employee after the leave.

Du Pont offers job sharing and flexible schedules to allow employees to pursue other interests in life, and is trying to provide more part-time jobs and flex-time for employees. (Wohl had conducted a survey of Du Pont employees and discovered that 40 percent of the men had considered working for another employer to obtain more flexibility in job scheduling. That encouraged her to start the flexible scheduling program. Fifty-six percent of the men and 76 percent of the women favor the option. Many of Wohl's programs are started after she has done a survey to determine what employees need.)

Wohl's staff runs programs for employees on prevention of rape and sexual harassment. They run three-day workshops to help employees recognize, confront, and work through their prejudices, particularly against minorities and women. The goal is to have the multicultural work force work together with respect for all. Other programs help employees develop both as employees and as individuals.

Wohl has several other programs in mind, including scheduling month-long vacations for employees and providing bus transportation to summer camps for the children of employees. Wohl's goal, she says, is "to someday make my job obsolete."

Source: Joseph Weber, "Social Issues: Meet Du Pont's In-House Conscience'," *Business Week,* June 24, 1991, pp. 62–65.

spread lapses in ethical conduct involving government contracts, most of which were significantly more questionable than the famous $600 hammer. The real challenge for top management, then, is how to create an environment that sustains, promotes, and develops ethical behavior and a commitment to social responsibility.

The foremost means to create such an environment involves top management.[12] Without the leadership, commitment, and role modeling of top management, beginning with the CEO, no organization can hope to attain high ethical standards or consistently behave in a socially responsible manner. Top management must also ensure that the organization's expectations of ethical behavior are clearly conveyed to its employees and to all parties, the stakeholders, involved with the organization. This requires extensive communication among all parties. In the end, an organizationwide commitment to socially responsible behavior comes from communication that fosters understanding and that promotes involvement by facilitating an exchange of ideas. Employee and managerial "ownership" of the organization's values and ethical standards is essential for creating a strong corporate culture that embodies a meaningful commitment to social responsibility.

But these efforts alone cannot sustain organizational and managerial commitment to ethical practices and socially responsible behavior. What is needed to make this a comprehensive and viable component of the organization's culture and operational character is a means of monitoring and reinforcing ethical and socially responsible performance. There are many ways to accomplish this, from making an assessment of individual ethical commitment and behavior a part of the performance appraisal, to using a process known as a social audit. A social audit measures specific compliance with ethical standards and measures

FIGURE 4-4 Baxter Travenol Principles of Ethical Management

FOUR PRINCIPLES FOR ETHICAL MANAGEMENT

- *First, hire the right people.*
  Employees who are inclined to be ethical are the best insurance you can have. They may be the only insurance. Look for people with principles. Let them know that those principles are an important part of their qualifications for the job.

- *Second, set standards more than rules.*
  You can't write a code of conduct airtight enough to cover every eventuality. A person inclined to fraud or misconduct isn't going to blink at signing your code anyway. So don't waste your time on heavy regulations. Instead, be clear about standards. Let people know the level of performance you expect—and that ethics are not negotiable.

- *Third, don't let yourself get isolated.*
  You know that managers can lose track of markets and competitors by moving into the ivory tower. But they also can lose sight of what's going on in their own operations. The only problem is that *you* are responsible for whatever happens in your office or department or corporation, whether you know about it or not.

- *Fourth and most important, let your ethical example at all times be absolutely impeccable.*
  This isn't just a matter of how you act in matters of accounting, competition, or interpersonal relationships. Be aware also of the signals you send to those around you. Steady harping on the importance of quarterly gains in earnings, for example, rather easily leads people to believe that you don't much care about how the results are achieved.
  ("A CEO Looks at Ethics," Business Horizons, March–April 1987, Vol 30 #2, pg. 2)

how well the organization and its employees have done in achieving established goals of social responsibility.

What is whistle-blowing?

There is another means of monitoring the ethical conviction of the organization and its top management, but it is one that raises some difficult procedural, group dynamics, and managerial problems. This other means involves professional dissent—or, as it is more commonly known, whistle-blowing—and how the organization handles it. Although whistle-blowing typically exposes unethical practices, how it is done and how it is handled may also be ethically questionable. It can also create considerable internal conflict.[13] Some firms have established ways for professional dissent to occur, such as a variation of the old "open-door" policy, so that it is not disruptive to the organization while at the same time allowing individuals to expose unethical practices or lapses in socially responsible behavior.

A good example of how one organization approached the problem of establishing an ethically oriented culture is that of Baxter Travenol Laboratories. The firm's CEO established four principles of ethical management to guide his managers in making ethical decisions. Those principles are detailed in Figure 4-4.

In the end, there is no magic formula for creating an environment that promotes ethical behavior, but in many cases unethical behavior contributes to stress.[14] Ethics should be viewed as a system issue, looking at the total organization, and not as a problem concerned with a few "bad" individuals. However, creating an ethically oriented environment remains an elusive and somewhat intangible objective.

ETHICAL PITFALLS AND DEFINING DIRECTION

At some point, all managers will find themselves caught in a compromising position that will result in ethical conflict. There will be those times when it is necessary to tell "little white lies," to rationalize that the "end justifies the means," and to be faced with the directive "just do it, but don't tell me how." Sometimes, your actions will be based on friendships; sometimes they will be done because you owe someone; and sometimes they will be a matter of organizational politics, political survival. In these circumstances, there is no cookbook solution, no set of guidelines that give you the right answer.

There is a very disturbing point that we have not considered, yet. The reality is that there are times when unethical behavior will not have a consequence. Think about the cost of unethical behavior involving the Ford Pinto. Was Ford any less profitable, did it sell fewer cars, did its reputation suffer in the long run? Have any firms (like General Dynamics, Nestlé, General Electric, and Union Carbide) associated with serious incidents involving unethical behavior really suffered as a consequence? Consider that two-thirds of the Fortune 500 companies have been involved in some sort of illegal activities in the past ten years, and yet most remain highly profitable and viable enterprises. There are firms that openly acknowledge that their commitment to social responsibility is limited to their own enlightened self-interest and that there is no such thing as charity for charity's sake.

These should be disturbing observations. For better or worse, though, they are realities of the business world, and because of the nature of the marketplace and the business environment, these types of situations will continue to exist. It is very difficult to address all the varied and sometimes conflicting interests of the stakeholders involved with any organization. There will be compromise, there will be inequities, and there will be lapses in ethics.

Will U.S. companies become more ethical and socially responsible?

The challenge that you face, as does any organization, is how to define your own ethical and moral boundaries. You, like an organization, have to determine the extent and level of commitment to act and manage in a socially responsible manner. You, like an organization, will draw upon your experiences, values, and culture to shape and define those boundaries. It is a difficult and uncertain process, but it is a vital one for society and for your performance as a manager. Organizations are realizing that a strong corporate culture and a commitment to ethical standards and socially responsible behavior are essential to organizational survival and profitability in a competitive environment.[15] To succeed and to be an effective manager, you will likewise need a strong cultural base and commitment to ethical and socially responsible behavior.

SUMMARY

In Chapter 4, we have examined the rather complex and controversial area of business ethics and social responsibility. There are a variety of issues and perspectives to consider when addressing ethics and social responsibility. In addition, it can be a very personal area, in which individual values may influence decision making and conflict with organizational values and objectives. What is critical at this point is that you learn to understand the relationship between the cultural character of the organization you will work for and your own values, ethics, and commitment to social responsibility. By developing such an understanding, you will become a more responsible manager.

KEY TERMS

Morality Conceptual codes concerning how behavior conforms to established, socially accepted norms; addresses cultural notions of right and wrong.

Ethics The decision area dealing with moral behavior of individuals.

STUDY ASSIGNMENTS

1. What is your evaluation of Hewlett-Packard's Standards of Business Conduct? Why is it that so few businesses adopt this kind of ethical standard for their employees?

2. How does the *Exxon Valdez* accident illustrate the issues and debate associated with the concept of corporate social responsibility?

3. From a managerial perspective, what is the difference between morality and ethics? If you were the owner of a used-car lot, how would you handle the issue of odometer tampering?

4. Compare and contrast Milton Friedman's position on the social responsibility of business with the view taken by advocates of the stakeholders concept.

5. Compare and contrast Beech-Nut's approach to handling the fake apple juice incident with Johnson & Johnson's handling of the Tylenol incident.

6. Where do the ethical practices of an organization originate? What role should individual managers play in the development of an organization's ethical practices?

7. What is the managerial and organizational benefit of establishing policies and guidelines like "The Champion Way" and the "GTE Governing Values"?

8. How can an organization and its managers create an environment and a culture that promote ethical behavior?

9. What are some of the ethical pitfalls that managers must face in getting the job done?

10. Discuss whether ethics should be a concern of managers and whether business ethics should be discussed in the classroom context.

Case for Discussion

PETRO-CHEMICAL CORPORATION

For Jim Easton, vice president of human resources at the Petro-Chemical Corporation, it had been a long and difficult morning meeting with the firm's chairman, Joseph L. Mickens. As he sat in his office, he reviewed the events of the past few hours. He hoped to gain some insights from those events so that he could develop a proposal that would address the chairman's concern about how to limit the consequences of employee exposure to toxic chemicals.

Mickens had called the meeting to discuss the results of a class action lawsuit that had been filed on behalf of all past and present employees of the Petro-Chemical Corporation. Yesterday, a jury had awarded this group $58 million, after finding Petro-Chemical negligent in not ensuring the safety and well-being of its employees, who were either exposed to or worked with the toxic chemical dioxin. The jury had agreed with the plaintiffs' position that Petro-Chemical had failed to inform its workers of the dangers of dioxin and that it did not adequately protect the workers from exposure to the substance while they performed their jobs. Because of that negligence, the employees of Petro-Chemical were unnecessarily exposed to the cancer-causing substance. The jury found Petro-Chemical liable for the damage and injuries incurred by employees who had developed cancer as a result of their exposure to dioxin while working for the Petro-Chemical Corporation.

During the meeting, Mickens repeatedly expressed his anger and outrage about the outcome of the lawsuit. In response, the president and the vice president of operations emphasized to Mickens that the corporation's attorneys had repeatedly stressed to the jury the firm's outstanding safety record and employment policies. However, they commented that apparently the attorneys' arguments were not enough to persuade the jury to find in favor of the corporation. The president maintained that the firm did all that it could do in its defense, and he urged that Petro-Chemical not alter any of its policies with regard to the use and handling of toxic chemicals. The vice president of operations suggested that there were higher priorities to consider in the matter, such as the need to preserve trade secrets. A number of other executives attending the meeting endorsed his position, arguing that full disclosure of the extent to which toxic chemicals were used in the production process would enable Petro-Chemical's competition to discover the firm's product formulas.

The discussion continued for over an hour. Then Mickens abruptly cut off any further debate after the vice president of marketing remarked that the whole issue was being blown out of proportion, particularly since the firm could still appeal the court decision. Mickens responded by saying that the lawsuit and the continuing exposure of employees to toxic chemicals without their knowledge was a serious matter. He indicated that the financial well-being of the corporation could no longer be jeopardized because of issues related to employee exposure to toxic chemicals. In addition, he noted that it was highly unlikely that the firm could win the case on appeal: The firm had already lost a similar case on appeal and dioxin had received a great deal of public attention. He felt that the corporation was in a no-win situation and urged everyone to work toward overcoming this problem so that the firm could get back to the business of producing chemical products. This was to be done even if it meant that the firm would have to significantly alter its policies and practices concerning the use and handling of toxic chemicals by its employees. Mickens closed the meeting by stating that the problem now rested with Petro-Chemical's top management, and he directed everyone attending the meeting to develop a proposal that would resolve the situation.

In considering his own proposal, Jim Easton reviewed the corporation's involvement with toxic chemicals and some of the policies concerning the use and handling of those chemicals. The firm's involvement with dioxin began in the early 1960s. Initially, Petro-Chemical used dioxin as a component in some of the firm's chemical products. Later on, the corporation began producing dioxin under a licensing agreement and sold the product to the Defense Department. From the beginning, the firm made no effort to warn its employees about the potential health hazards associated with exposure to dioxin, primarily because the firm was unaware that there were any dangers involved in the use and handling of dioxin.

In 1971, the corporation ceased production of dioxin. However, it continued to obtain the chemical from other sources, since it had become a critical component in a number of Petro-Chemical's major products. About that time, some of the firm's chemists noticed articles suggesting that exposure to dioxin could cause cancer. An in-house study was done in 1974; it showed no evidence that any employee had developed cancer as a result of working with dioxin. The study did show that the employees had a higher-than-average rate of cancer but did not give any explanation for that. Management decided that nothing needed to be done; they felt that they did not need to inform employees of any potential risks associated with dioxin.

Public awareness of dioxin grew in the late 1970s and early 1980s as newspapers printed more and more stories about the adverse effects of Agent Orange (dioxin) used in Viet Nam. Both Viet Nam civilians and American soldiers were suffering and dying from cancer as a delayed reaction to Agent Orange.

Management dismissed employees' concerns, saying that the employees had nothing to worry about. About that time, Petro-Chemical was identified in the newspapers as the primary manufacturer of the Agent Orange used in Viet Nam during the 1960s. Employees demanded answers and explanations from management.

Management responded with new safety procedures, including a statement that the women working with the dioxin chemical would be reassigned if they became pregnant. This only increased the concerns of the employees, as they discussed the hazards of working with other chemicals in the plant.

Soon, the employees learned that a former employee who had had to quit working in 1975 after developing cancer had won a lawsuit against Petro-Chemical. Further investigation showed that two similar suits had been settled out of court, with Petro-Chemical making payments to the plaintiffs.

Jim spent the entire day reviewing the material from all the court cases, and he focused his attention on the evidence obtained from his division. It had grown late in the day, so Jim decided to put off any further action until tomorrow.

Chapter 5

Decision Making

Learning Objectives

1. **Describe,** in a general sense, decision making.
2. **Identify** three basic observations about managerial decision making.
3. **Define** the term decision.
4. **Explain** two conceptual models of decision making.
5. **State** the meaning of behavioral and political decisions.
6. **Explain** the differences between the rational and adaptive models.

U NTIL the early 1980s, Consolidated Printing was a highly profitable enterprise and a leader in the printing of custom business forms. Over the years, it had developed a reputation as a premium-priced printer, noted for its high quality and good service. However, by the mid-1980s, the firm found itself facing serious financial and operational problems. Fortunately, Consolidated's management realized that if the firm was to survive, they needed to make some significant changes in the nature and scope of their business.

Consolidated is a medium-size firm with over 200 employees. Its annual sales average $12 million. In the past, it was able to charge premium prices for small printing jobs because of its reputation and its versatility (there were thirty different types of printing presses). However, in the 1980s, Consolidated's situation changed as a result of major technological advances in the printing industry. This new technology fostered the growth of instant printers, who, because of their lower operating costs, were able to compete against Consolidated in terms of price, quality, and service.

Consolidated's management realized that the firm could not survive if it continued to print business forms and if it continued to operate the way it always had. Based on an evaluation of the firm and of the printing industry,

they decided to remain in the printing business but to abandon the custom printing of small orders. Instead, the firm would print large orders of mailer forms (computer-processed printed forms, such as bills), a high-volume segment of the printing business.

In addition to changing the direction of the company, Consolidated's top managers altered the firm's management and decision-making practices. The mailer group (made up of nonmanagement employees) would manage their own activities (without supervisors) and thus make decisions on hiring and firing, work schedules, equipment purchases, services, supplies, and materials.

This new managerial approach caused some decision-making conflicts. For instance, because of the concern about bankruptcy, management wanted the mailers to emphasize output (printing at a minimum revenue rate of $1,000 an hour). On the other hand, the mailers were concerned about the 12 percent rate of customer returns, a condition they thought would eventually result in a bad reputation and lost business. They wanted to focus on better quality. However, they felt they could not make the decision to reject shipping defective products, because management decided to measure the group's performance against the $1,000-per-hour output rate.

Two years after Consolidated's management began implementing the changes in the firm's direction and managerial practices, the firm is still struggling to survive and it is clear that not everyone supports those changes. ■

DECISIONS, DECISIONS . . .

An Introduction

Since early childhood, we have all made thousands of decisions. Making decisions is a very natural activity. We have felt that some were good and some were bad. Many of us like to make decisions; many of us try to avoid them. For many, the right to make one's own decisions is a matter of principle; yet, even though we sometimes like to feel that we have the power to make decisions, we may be happier when someone else "sticks his or her neck out" and makes the troublesome ones.[1]

What were some tough decisions?

History is filled with tough decisions, and many political ones stand out over the past half century:

- President Harry Truman decided to drop the atomic bomb on Japan to bring a quick end to World War II. The war ended quickly.
- President John Kennedy decided to invade Cuba by landing a group of Cuban exiles at the Bay of Pigs. The effort failed.
- President Lyndon Johnson decided to fight a war in Vietnam and to increase social spending for the Great Society. Our national debt exploded.
- President Richard Nixon decided to allow the Watergate cover-up. He was forced to resign.
- President Jimmie Carter found the Iranian hostage situation too difficult for bold decision making. He lost the next election decisively.
- President Ronald Reagan decided to allow subordinates to deal with the Iranians and attempt a swap of arms for hostages. The Irangate affair raised serious Constitutional questions about covert activity by the CIA and the national security advisers.

It's unlikely that you will ever have to make such momentous decisions, but you may face decisions similar to the following:

- Jessica Drenk read of takeover rumors of U.S. Shoe and decided to buy stock.
- Alan Staus, president of Fosdick Interiors, Inc., decided to purchase an IBM-XT computer system for his small furniture store so that sales, accounts receivable, and inventories could be better managed.
- Robert Campeau, CEO of the Toronto-based Campeau Corporation, bought Federated Department Stores for more than $8 billion.
- Sharon Peterson, director of a nursing home in Phoenix, Arizona, decided to approve an expansion of a new wing for Alzheimer's patients.
- Richard Heckert, CEO of DuPont, decided to phase out CFCs, even though DuPont produced 25 percent of the world's supply, after an international team of scientists confirmed that CFCs damage the earth's ozone layer.
- President George Bush sent U.S. forces into Saudi Arabia in August 1990, began an air offensive against Iraq on behalf of Allied forces on January 16, 1991, initiated a ground offensive on February 24, 1991, and called for a cease-fire 100 hours later.

Decision making
A course of action consciously chosen from alternatives to achieve desired result.

In this chapter, we discuss managerial **decision making.** All management functions involve decisions; you can imagine the decisions involved in planning the direction of a firm or in organizing resources of a project or in staffing personnel. A manager is oriented toward making decisions; it is part of

Ethics Issue

Decision Making in Medicine: To Give Life and to Take It Away

In California, a family watched their 18-year-old daughter become weaker and weaker. They knew that without a bone-marrow transplant she would die. Their other child, a son, was not a suitable donor, and they had been unsuccessful in locating any person whose bone marrow matched their daughter's. Their only hope seemed to be to have another baby who could be a donor. The doctors told them there was a one-in-four chance that a new sibling would be a match for their daughter. The husband had his vasectomy reversed; the doctors told him that there was only a 40 percent chance that the reversal would be successful. Then they had to beat the statistics on older mothers, including increased risk of having a baby with Down's syndrome; the mother was 43. Their baby was born healthy, and she was a good match for their daughter. At 14 months, the baby donated bone marrow to her sister. The parents had announced that their sole purpose in having this baby was to provide bone marrow for their dying daughter.

In Florida, a 78-year-old man faced murder charges for killing his wife. He claimed that he could not stand to see her suffer any longer. Alzheimer's disease had destroyed the quality of her life; she no longer knew where she was or who her husband was. Her mind no longer functioned. Her healthy body, however, still worked fine. He gave her an overdose of sleeping pills.

In Arizona, a family said goodbye one last time to their daughter, who had been in a coma after a car accident. The doctor said that there was no hope that she would ever recover and that if by some miracle she did recover, she would be a vegetable for the rest of her life. The family pulled the plug on the daughter's life-support system.

In Michigan, a doctor invented a suicide machine to make it easier for people to end their own lives when they feel that the quality of life is no longer good enough to continue.

In Indiana, a doctor ordered that no food or water be given to a severely deformed baby who was born in the hospital. The baby lived for a week before dying of starvation and dehydration.

Is it right to have a baby solely to use as a source of a transplant? Should the transplant donor have the right to say whether he or she wants to donate bone marrow? Is this a start of a trend to produce babies to be "harvested" for heart, kidney, liver, and other transplants? Is there anything wrong with mercy killing? What if a person had a living will that described when he or she wanted to die if debilitated by Alzheimer's or some other devastating condition? Who should decide when the patient should die? Who should decide when it is time to pull the plug on the life-support system? Who should decide who is good enough to live or bad enough to die?

the nature of organizational life, and each day a manager is provided opportunities to make decisions.[2]

There is no question, therefore, that managers will make decisions, whether or not they have read books on decision making. The real question is whether their decision making can be improved.

Recall for a moment the opening case in this chapter, Consolidated Printing, to get a sense of the nature of managerial decision making. A few of your reflections might be:

■ Many decisions were required to respond to serious financial and operational problems.
■ After an evaluation, Consolidated decided to remain in the printing business but to abandon the custom printing of small orders and enter the high-volume business known as mailer forms.
■ Consolidated changed its managerial approach to corporate decision making.
■ The changes created conflicts and other problems, thus requiring more decisions.

The review of Consolidated Printing shows that managerial decision making is a very complex process. It is our objective in the remaining pages to provide you with insights to prepare you for managing this complex process.

Basic Observations

Are there any basic observations?

Create in your mind a personal data base of decision-making examples. Some will involve only yourself—a decision to purchase a product, to apply for a loan, to quit a job and hunt for a new one, to select a major or a career path for your life. Some will be simple, some complex. If you've had work experience, you'll think of decisions involving other people. Daily news events will provide most readers with many examples of situations in which one decision led to another problem, which led to another decision, which led to another, and so on.

For our purposes, we want to focus on decision making within organizations even though much of the material in this chapter is relevant to your per-

A disaster, like the earthquake in San Francisco in 1989, causes managers to make nonroutine decisions. Managers of fire departments, police departments, hospitals, and government officials must first assess the damage, and then determine how to contain or reverse the damage. Victims had to be pulled from crushed cars where bridges had collapsed on the interstate system; people who were homeless after their apartments were destroyed had to be cared for and housed; families had to be reunited; fires had to be extinguished; communication lines and utilities needed to be reestablished.

sonal decision making. What are some basic observations that can be made about managerial decision making?

First, decisions stem from problems, and both problems and decisions seem to range from (1) those that are **routine** and recurring and for which information is certain and (2) those that are **nonroutine,** nonrecurring, and filled with uncertainty.[3]

Second, organizational decision making can never be perfectly rational; organizational members "contaminate" perfect rationality through personal interpretations and individual differences.

Third, no single decision-making approach applies in all situations.

These three observations on managerial decision making form the base for the remaining materials in this chapter. Remember, one of our objectives is to provide you with information, insights, understanding, and some skills in this important managerial function, one that touches on all other functions. In the next section, we will expand on each of the three observations by looking at a conceptual model and two approaches of decision making, by discussing the behavioral and political aspects of decision making, and finally by viewing some helpful quantitative concepts and techniques.

Routine Situations or decisions that contain recurring items with high certainty.

Nonroutine decisions Decision situations filled with uncertainty that lack routine and occur infrequently.

THE NATURE OF MANAGERIAL DECISION MAKING

We are now prepared to begin the more formal presentation of the managerial decision-making process. You have read the examples of decisions and probably have an idea of what a decision is. To us, a **decision** is a course of action consciously chosen from alternatives for the purpose of achieving a desired result. Thus, a decision is (1) a choice, (2) the result of conscious mental activity, and (3) directed toward a purpose. For example, if we have no choice among alternatives, we cannot make a decision; if we act without conscious effort, we merely act without a decision; if we have no purpose, we have no target for desired results.

This definition could apply to recent personal decisions: You may have a career goal in mind and may have selected your present class to move you toward that goal. You may have had a choice of sections or instructors, and you always have a choice about the amount of effort you will put into this experience. This definition also applies to the decisions managers must make in organizations.

There is a relationship between organizational decisions and organizational problems. That most decisions relate to problems should be fairly obvious to you. But what is the relationship between the two, and what are sources of organizational problems? What are some helpful ways for aspiring managers to address the decision making that stems from problems?

What is a decision?

Decision A course of action consciously chosen from alternatives to achieve desired result.

The Objectives-Plan-Action Model (OPA).   In this model (see Figure 5-1), you have the simplest description of how managers operate in an organization. Much effort at managerial, staff, and operational levels is directed toward organizational **objectives,** the plans selected to reach those objectives, and the actions necessary to implement the plans.

OPA Model An operational model that describes the topics of many managerial decisions.

Objectives Specific statements of what an organization hopes to achieve.

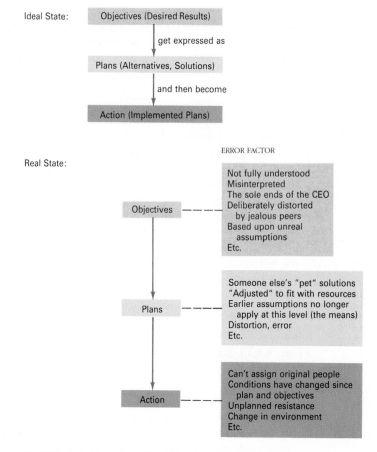

FIGURE 5-1 The Objectives-Plan-Action Model

- OBJECTIVES—Describe *where* you want to be
- PLANS—Describe *what* alternatives get you there
- ACTION—Describes *how* you will implement the plans

Decisions are obviously needed in all three areas as men and women create and then select from alternative objectives, plans, and actions that set which will be a guide for their behavior and performance. How do the decisions become problems that then demand decisions and solutions?

Objectives (also called budgets, targets, goals) may have error in them. Perhaps they are not fully understood, or perhaps certain assumptions behind the objectives prove to be wrong, or perhaps the objectives are not very realistic. Any of those situations would create problems for organizational personnel. This error factor also exists for corporate plans and the action phase of implementation.

Another source of problems is the disparities that may exist between objectives and specific plans and specific implementation. A third source of problems is changes made in the OPA between its original construction and the present time. Error, disparity, and change ensure that managers will constantly be working on decisions that are problem-related. The following examples will add to your understanding of the relationship between objectives, plans, and implementation.

Why are objectives important?

President Saddam Hussein's ambition led him to order his troops to invade and occupy Kuwait in August 1990. The United Nations asked him to withdraw from Kuwait. He ignored the request. The Allied forces used force to free Kuwait in early 1991. If Hussein had plans for a defense, they were poorly implemented, perhaps because of poor communication between Hussein and his troops.

If Chrysler Corporation sets a sales target of 25 percent of the market for domestic autos (they usually have a market share in the low teens), problems will plague the company for the complete year. So, one of the first questions a manager asks when searching for problems or causes of problems is: Is the objective feasible? Decision making without an acceptable answer to that question will cause unnecessary frustration and failure.

Suppose that the goal for a basketball team is a winning season and that such a goal is realistic based upon past performance. The plan for achieving this goal might be to rearrange the schedule so that more teams of equal or lower caliber make up the competition. It could take years, however, to change a schedule, and the coach might not have the luxury of time, especially if the alumni are calling for a victorious season soon. The coach might then decide that the solution is to find better ball players. This plan has the advantage of immediate returns to the team because it provides talented personnel who will enter as first-year students or who may be recruited from junior colleges. In this example, we have a realistic and feasible goal and a plan that relates to the objective and the capabilities of the organization. The decision making in our second example may achieve the results wanted if the implementation dimension is also successful. (Think of the states and even the high schools to which recruiters would go for basketball players. If such an analysis were not done, a sound objective and a good plan would fail because of poor implementation.)

A third example comes from the military. President Saddam Hussein of Iraq had objectives and plans for the invasion of Kuwait and the subsequent battle with Allied forces during the 1991 Gulf War. There is some question about the value of many of his plans and especially about how certain plans were implemented. The inability of Iraq headquarters to effectively communicate with its frontline forces highlights the importance of the implementation part of the plan. To a manager, the lesson here is the importance of having the appropriate resources to implement the best plan to achieve realistic objectives.

Decision making occurs to find realistic objectives, to select the best plan, and to organize the resources of the firm to reach its goals. Reference to this process suggests there are decision-making approaches that managers use.

Decision-Making Approaches

The Six-Step Approach

The basic decision-making approach is depicted in Figure 5-2. The approach shows six steps in managerial decision making: understand the situation; diagnose and define the problem; find and evaluate alternatives; select the "best" alternative; identify and inform the chain; secure acceptance.[4]

Understand the situation. Managers get paid to make decisions but our interest is in showing you that effective managerial decision making is not as easy as it may appear. Decision making usually occurs in response to some situation or problem. For example, you hear a rumor that your competitor is developing a new product that may put you out of business; you receive a printout that shows sales in your unit are continuing to decline; one of your subordinates mentions that morale among the staff is at its lowest point in months; you receive phone calls from two suppliers—one in Morristown, New Jersey, and one in Denver—and both are fuming over a change in corporate

1. Understand the situation.
2. Diagnose and define the problem.
3. Find and evaluate alternatives.
4. Select the best alternative.
5. Identify and inform the chain.
6. Secure acceptance.

FIGURE 5-2 The Managerial Decision-Making Process

policies that you had objected to at the last staff meeting. Are all these examples problems? Do all the problems require decisions?

Before jumping to conclusions, a manager must get a sense of the situation. Understanding the situation requires that there be consciousness of the problem.

From our earlier definition, we know that a good decision depends upon a conscious awareness of the factors that set the stage for the decision. The following questions will give you an idea of the factors that might relate to your situation:

- Did past actions or history contribute to the situation?
- How long has the present situation existed?
- Are the forces influencing the situation from an internal or external source?
- Can facts be found that shed any light on the situation, or is the situation dominated by opinions and interpretations?
- What are the clues to the causes of the problems?
- Is a decision called for?
- If yes, when is it needed?
- What is the cost of not making a decision?

At this stage, confusion is common and healthy, since the decision maker cannot possibly consider all the facts and must develop a selective approach for identifying the most important and relevant ones. Your creativity is put to the test. If time is available, you may find that allowing the facts to simmer in your mind will provide you with insights.[5] Some people find that discussing the situation with others tends to lubricate their own thought processes. You may "brainstorm" with a group of your associates. The key is to refrain from jumping to a single conclusion no matter how good it sounds, or from laughing at a contribution no matter how silly it appears. This first step, understanding the situation, is too often neglected, and such neglect may be costly.

Diagnose and define the problem. After becoming aware that something needs your attention, you must diagnose the situation so that you may define the problem to be solved. Since it is impossible to obtain all the facts, the manager must develop a means of finding the relevant ones. This set of questions will aid in that process:

- What is the source of the "problem"?
- Who says it's a problem?
- Who gains or loses if a certain situation becomes a problem?
- Are you dealing with symptoms and not the real problem?

- Which symptoms are the cause and which are the effect?
- What limiting organizational factors exist in defining the problem?
- Does the problem remain if we assume some symptoms away?

A good diagnosis includes both why a decision is needed and the obstacles to achieving the objectives. The diagnosis consists of a search for symptoms. The search must be based on a clear recognition of the desired results, the obstacles faced, and the limits within which a solution must fall.

The Gulf War in 1991 provides examples of the difficulty of making an accurate diagnosis. Heavy aerial bombing, the heaviest in history, was to have weakened Iraqi forces—forces who were thought to be superior to Allied forces in numbers of soldiers and tanks and in battle experience in desert conditions. Intelligence reports could not validate the damage from the bombing, and a ground war was delayed until additional bombing "assured" the commander of an advantage. The results of the ground war surprised many: 100 hours long and minimal casualties.

A clear definition of the problem is needed. Consider a doctor who is informed by a patient that her stomach aches; the doctor does not merely record "stomach aches," but also uses tests to determine exactly what is causing the ache and the limitations of the solution. An aspirin may relieve the ache, but it may not treat the cause of it. Or perhaps you have seen someone trying to get a car started. The driver says, "The car won't start"; this may indicate a problem, but it is not a good diagnosis or a definition of the problem. An experienced mechanic will check to see if the battery is turning the engine over. You would not look for problems in compression, the generator, or the distributor until you had determined the exact problem—it might merely be a dead battery!

Find and evaluate alternatives. Often, finding alternatives is the easiest step in decision making. If you have taken the time to understand the situation and define the problem, the solution or alternatives may simply jump off the page at you. A recommendation to inexperienced managers is to "suspend" their solutions to problems until they have put time into the first two steps of decision making.

Many consultants to organizations will tell you that there is no shortage of recommendations, alternatives, and suggested solutions to perceived problems. The challenge is to connect the "pet" solutions of the work force with the critical problems facing the company.

With your set of alternatives before you, evaluate each alternative to find the best one. As you analyze each one, you may find these questions useful:

- What are the advantages and disadvantages of each, or what are the costs and benefits of each?
- What are the pros and cons of each?
- Which alternatives are feasible?
- Which alternatives really solve the problem or achieve the desired state?
- Who in the organization will support or resist the solution?
- When can each alternative be implemented, and how important is the time factor—must the decision be acted upon immediately?
- Are any of the alternatives illegal or unethical?
- What unintended consequences might come from each alternative; can the organization afford the consequences?

Global Application

The OPEC Decision

In October 1973, oil negotiations that would shake the economic foundations of the Western world took place. At the time, neither side realized the magnitude of the discussions or the decision.

Sheik Yamani, oil minister of Saudi Arabia, represented the oil-producing countries of the Middle East, who had formed a cartel (the Organization of Petroleum Exporting Countries—OPEC) to negotiate with the oil-processing and oil-distributing companies. George Piercy of Exxon represented the oil companies, most of whom were American companies. The price of oil before the negotiations was $3.00 per barrel. OPEC demanded an increase to $6.00 per barrel. Mr. Piercy countered with $3.75 per barrel. Mr. Yamani countered with $5.00, but the American headquarters personnel told Piercy not to budge. The Arabs were incensed, broke off the talks, and flew home.

The price of oil during the next ten years peaked at $34.00 per barrel (March 1983). The impact on costs and revenues was severe. For example, the annual oil output of Saudi Arabia in 1985 was 3.5 million barrels per day!

Some economic observers believe the subsequent shock to the oil-consuming nations (the United States, Europe, and Japan) contributed to the decline of the U.S. automobile and steel industries, created severe unemployment in the Midwest, and stimulated increases in the prices of most products.

Some political observers believe this event in 1973 gave the predominantly Muslim countries their first real taste of economic power. They quickly translated that economic power into political power.

Source: David Halberstam, *The Reckoning* (New York: Morrow, 1986).

OPEC (The Organization of Petroleum Exporting Countries) has been a powerful force in the global economy and in local economies. Some experts believe that decisions made by this group have helped to cause the decline in the automobile and steel industries in the United States with resultant massive unemployment, particularly in the Midwest, and inflation throughout the world. Shown in the accompanying photograph is OPEC Secretary General Subroto (left) of Indonesia and OPEC President Rilwanu Lukman as they read the OPEC agreement negotiated in November 1989.

Select the best alternative. The answers to the preceding questions will eliminate certain alternatives and will show others to be good options for you. Which one is "best" rests upon many factors. For example, you might decide to expand your production to a third shift rather than building a new facility or subcontracting the work to others. Each of these three options has many pros and cons, but you may feel that going to a third shift achieves immediate results, whereas a new building will require added debt and subcontracting will result in your losing control over the quality of the production. What is "best" for one manager is not "best" for another; what is "best" at one time is not "best" at another time.

Far too many managers stop the decision-making process too soon. They naively believe that their responsibility ends when they select the best alternative. "Reassign Tom, Curt, and Sonya to our Paris office . . . reduce the work force in Bozeman, Montana . . . hire some high-powered college kids for the finance division . . . shut down our offices in Tampa, High Point, Augusta, and Morgantown." These managers assume that others will deal with the nitty-gritty aspects of implementation; the chain of command will ensure that subordinates understand and comply with directives from on high. Such assumptions are often nothing but false hopes. It is the manager's responsibility to complete the decision-making cycle, to follow through to the last phase—managing the decision. In this last phase, there are at least two procedures that might make your decision more effective: Identify the people along the decision chain, and secure the acceptance of those who will implement the decision.

Identify and inform the chain. In this step, you identify the people in the decision chain who have a need to know or who have insights or knowledge basic to the decision. Marilyn Thomas, for example, was a project report specialist who had to do the analysis and synthesis of data for a report to a major accrediting organization of a university.

She received many suggestions from faculty and administrators on the report format, style of presentation, even the date due at the national headquarters. Much of that advice conflicted with procedures she had used to file similar reports. She drew up a simple chart and identified people inside and outside of her unit who had to be informed or who probably had knowledge about the report. She called national headquarters and located a person who gave her the expected arrival date of the report, number of copies, and unique format features. She also identified important people within her unit and contacted them. From Alice in the word-processing pool, she learned the best layout of the questionnaire from the perspective of the one who would have to process the data. Marilyn also asked Alice about the demands on the word-processing center and when the best time was to send her data. The report, correctly done, reached headquarters on time. In the process of identifying and informing the people in the decision chain, a manager gains insight before a decision is made or before it is improperly implemented, and may also ensure the acceptance of the decision.

Secure acceptance. Few in the organization will be as knowledgeable about and committed to a decision as you will be. To see that it is effectively implemented, you must manage the decision into the organization. Identifying the people along the chain of the decision helps, for communication with them will provide two benefits: First, they will be given information about a project that will have an impact upon them and they can prepare to respond to that impact; second, some on the chain will provide you with information about the implementation of the project that you or your people may have missed during the analysis of alternatives. Response from those in the chain may well save you costly mistakes later; it is better to delay the implementation of a plan than to face the results of a subsequent failure.

Thus, insight has been offered on the first set of basic observations about decision making. Many decisions stem from problems, and many problems and decisions develop from two types of situations: those in which the conditions are routine and information is relatively certain and those in which the conditions are nonroutine and information is often uncertain.

The Adaptive Approach

Throughout this chapter, we have talked of two types of problems and decisions: programmatic or routine and nonprogrammatic or nonroutine. In earlier sections, you also saw that managers at the lower levels of the organization who work in jobs with high certainty and predictability will face more programmatic decision making.

Managers at middle and top levels or in uncertain, hard-to-define, changing jobs face more nonprogrammatic decisions. Although some of the approaches discussed here work well for programmatic problems, a different approach may be called for if your problems are more unstructured. An approach finding favor among decision makers who face complex, unknown, and changing environments is called the **adaptive approach.**

Adaptive approach
A decision making approach that places value on understanding that many environments are filled with complexity and change; what is important is to adapt your approach to the reality of the situation. Also called the "Muddling Through" approach by some.

Muddling Through
A decision making approach that faces the reality of the situation; it sees curved and crooked lines rather than straight lines. Also called the "adaptive approach".

Credit for this approach goes to many people, but Charles E. Lindblom was an early contributor, and he labeled it "The Science of **Muddling Through**."[6] Table 5-1 shows one way to understand this approach.

Lindblom believes that the approach in the first column was the recommended one in most organizations for the first sixty years of the twentieth century. In some firms, it still is the first approach tried. He argues for a more adaptive approach (as seen in the second column).

The authors of many management texts use different and perhaps more sophisticated symbols to describe the statements just presented, but their intention is the same. They assume that decision making is a rational, comprehensive, step-by-step process that is amenable to learning, quantification, computerization, and perhaps simulation. The disciples of this approach believe that most organizational problems can be analyzed and that what stops people from conquering their problems is their inability to use the rational approach.

Lindblom's approach pictures a different kind of world—a world filled with curved and crooked lines rather than straight lines. Notice the language that Lindblom uses when he says that clear objectives may not always be possible; that a means–end analysis does not always apply; that agreement among analysts defines the real test of a "good policy." The language in the right-hand column for item 4 (Table 5-1) could almost be a reaction to the scientific management of the early 1900s. You may recall that the early engineer-type contributors to management were searching for the "one best way." They believed that the problems of management could be solved much as the problems of machines could. Lindblom suggests to us in his method that the manager's world, unlike a machine-type world, is an interacting world. The manager must make marginal and incremental comparisons between policies and find the

TABLE 5-1 The "Muddling" Adaptive Approach	
PROGRAMMATIC SITUATIONS	NONPROGRAMMATIC SITUATIONS
1. The administrator identifies values, objectives, or ends, and then seeks the means (policies) to reach the ends,	*but* this is almost impossible to do, since determination of values and objectives is usually intertwined with the empirical analysis of the alternatives. Often a means–end analysis does not apply or is limited.
2. Thus a "good" policy is one most appropriate for meeting the desired ends,	*but* the real test of a "good" policy should be whether there is agreement among analysts that the policy is good in itself (workable), not that it is the optimum means to an agreed objective.
3. And all important factors are considered, analyzed, and evaluated. The process is a comprehensive one,	*but* in dealing with real, complex problems, all important factors cannot be known, analysis must be limited, some alternative policies will be neglected and important values overlooked.
4. And theory is often used; goals and values are maximized by selecting the best solution,	*but* in reality, and dealing with so many limitations, theory would be restrictive and inappropriate in most cases. The administrator gives up the search for the "best" solution and makes marginal and incremental comparisons between policies and/or solutions and finds the better one.

better one—a satisfactory one, not necessarily the best one. Adaptive approaches to decision making may fit better into more situations facing today's managers.[7]

Behavioral and Political Decision Making

Earlier, we mentioned that decision making touches upon all the managerial functions and you will read examples of that in the remaining chapters of Part II.

Why isn't managerial decision making rational?

In this section, we discuss the meaning of a previous statement—that managerial decision making is not necessarily a rational process. This means that managers will frequently face situations that do not lend themselves to neat, deductive, orderly processes for identifying and defining the problem or for finding, evaluating, and selecting the best alternative or for implementing the solution. It also means that the decisions of managers are influenced by their own values and preferences,[8] the expectations of their bosses, peers, and subordinates, and the numerous people in the organization who will be involved in implementing the plan of action. These people factors in management command a full section in this book, Part III—a four-chapter part that views the behavioral and political dimensions of contemporary managing. Information

Routine decisions are more likely to occur where the same process is used day after day and where automation plays a large role in production. In this automobile plant paint mixing room, for example, many of the decisions are routine—what colors to mix together and when to obtain desired results. Routine decisions are more likely to be made by first-level managers or supervisors.

about the behavioral and political dimensions of decision making comes from people who have researched what managers actually do on the job or from people who themselves have managerial experience. From them, we can see that decision making is affected by the work context and the people involved in the decision-making process.

In Chapter 2, we presented various descriptions of what a manager does. You read Professor Henry Mintzberg's description of the three categories of manager's roles: interpersonal, informational, and decisional. There is research to suggest that sales managers spend more time in interpersonal roles than other managers do, that staff managers spend more time in informational roles, and that production managers spend more time in decisional roles. Thus, the very nature of the job will determine which managers will spend more time in decision making.

You also read that managers exist at different levels in the organization and that the work demands at each level will vary in much the same way as work demands in different functional areas (for example, sales, production, human resources, finance). Figure 5-3 shows that the top and middle levels of management tend to deal more frequently with problems (thus decisions) that are nonroutine, nonrecurring, and filled with uncertainty. Their problems may come from suppliers, competitors, state or federal legislators, or stockholders—an environment external to the firm. In most instances, there are no company procedures to follow, nor are there useful models that provide assistance in the decision process. Managers at the bottom levels, on the other hand, operate in an environment that is more limited to the organization (a plant in Dallas, a warehouse in Orlando, a distribution center in Florence, Kentucky).

FIGURE 5-3 Decision Types by Management Level

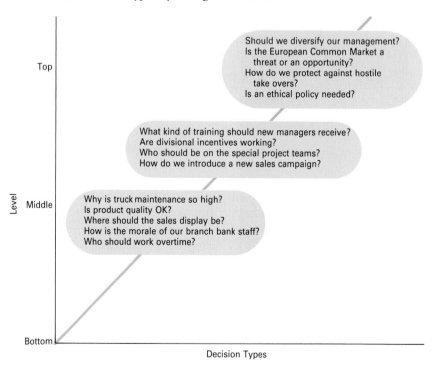

In many cases, the problems have occurred before and company solutions and procedures may be incorporated almost instantly to keep the production areas operating. Thus, the nature of the work and the level of management have an influence on the type of problem and the subsequent decisions made by managers.

One last dimension should be mentioned, that being the personal dimension of decision making. Is it not clear to you that no two people facing a similar situation will make the same analysis and decision? It's even unlikely that the same person would perform an identical analysis and come to the same decision one year later. The limitation of a rational approach to decision making was brought to the attention of management people by Herbert A. Simon, mentioned in Chapter 2.

To Simon, a decision maker cannot possibly have all the information necessary to make the perfect rational decision.[9] The decision maker also may not have the luxury of unlimited time to perform a thorough analysis and evaluation of all alternatives; in other words, it's not always possible to perform all the steps of the decision-making process as one would like. Instead of striving for the best or optimal decision, managers must move toward decisions that **satisfice**—that is, decisions that meet minimal objectives. Making satisficing decisions is more the norm or is more realistic than using elaborate steps and processes in decision making.[10]

Satisfice The search for a satisfactory solution by managers instead of the economists' focus on optimizing.

Decision makers also cannot remove from the process those personal elements of values, perceptions, motives, interpretations, and aspirations that make up the emotional character of a person. Thus, the rationality of a decision becomes "bounded" by all those factors and Simon refers to this as **bounded rationality**.

Bounded rationality People are rational within the limits of human capabilities.

Throughout this chapter, we have given examples of decision making in various organizations. You looked at two general approaches in decision making: those related to the programmed types of problems and those related to the nonprogrammed, nonroutine, and nonrecurring types. Managers may want to use quantitative concepts and techniques when facing some decision situations.

Quantitative Concepts and Techniques

Conditions under which managers make decisions vary along a continuum from those of perfect certainty to those of complete uncertainty. You can assume certainty and use a deterministic model, in which all the factors are assumed exact, with chance playing no role; or you can treat chance quantitatively in a probabilistic model, in which a quantitative representation of probability is included.

Conditions of certainty, uncertainty, and risk

Since the idea of chance implies that there is a large number of unknown forces about which we have little information, a decision involving chance will never turn out to be correct 100 percent of the time. The best we can do is to "play the averages" and make decisions that will be satisfactory more times than they will be unsatisfactory. The manager's attitude is that when faced with chance, one must still make a decision, for indecision is viewed as a cardinal weakness. Thus, managers must take chances, but they must develop ap-

Management Application

The Honda Opportunity

During the early 1970s, Ford Motor Company was engaged in debate over the downsizing of its auto line in response to government pressure to reduce fuel emissions and increase fuel efficiency. Lee Iacocca and his product man, Hal Sperlich, were strong supporters of a small front-wheel-drive vehicle. Henry Ford II and his finance people opposed the idea on the grounds that "small cars mean small profits" and that it would be too expensive to convert the production lines for a new assembly process.

After many years of frustration, Iacocca decided to explore an idea that might meet all the cost criticisms of his project. He flew to Japan to see Soichiro Honda and asked Honda if his company would supply Ford with an engine

and a front-wheel-drive transmission for the proposed Fiesta. Honda was delighted and said he could deliver 300,000 such units quickly at a price of $711 per unit.

Iacocca believed his inspiration would convince the doubters in Detroit. No Ford factory would have to be retooled, and Iacocca felt that the new Fiesta could be in the dealers' showrooms in only eighteen months.

When Iacocca told Henry Ford of his discussion with Honda and the successful results, Ford was angry. "No Jap engine is going under the hood of a car with my name on it." That killed the Honda idea.

Source: David Halberstam, *The Reckoning* (New York: Morrow, 1986).

---

proaches by which they can better understand the possible outcomes and be-able to estimate the probable outcomes. A first step in facing the uncertainty-certainty issue is to be aware of the existence of chance in the decision situation.[11]

When a manager has sufficient information about all the elements affecting the outcomes of the decision, permitting perfect prediction, we can say that operations are under conditions of **certainty.** For example, if the decision involves actions that are repeated a number of times with the same results, the manager knows and can determine the expected outcome. Under such rare conditions, you do not need to analyze the chance elements. We may view this degree of certainty as one extreme along the certainty-uncertainty continuum illustrated in Figure 5-4.

Certainty Situation in which you have sufficient information to make decision; perfect chance of predicting the outcome of the decisions.

FIGURE 5-4 Degrees of Knowledge Available in Decision Situations

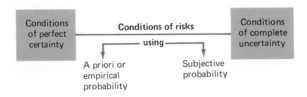

Uncertainty Situation in which you have no information on which to base decision; no chance of predicting the outcome of the decision.

Maximax Selecting a strategy for the possibility of receiving the greatest return.

Maximin Selecting a strategy for the possibility of maximizing the least favorable result; minimize possibility of worse case scenario.

Risk A condition in decision making where a manager has sufficient information for estimating the probability of outcomes.

If a decision involves conditions about which the manager has no information, about either the outcome or the relative chances for any single outcome, we say that operations are under conditions of **uncertainty,** as illustrated in Figure 5-4, at the opposite extreme of certainty. Under these conditions, you have no information upon which to develop any analysis, and thus, the best you can do is to be aware that there is no chance of predicting the events.

Even in cases of total ignorance, however, under conditions in which the decision maker has no historical data or any idea of the effects of states of nature or what action others will take, several approaches have been suggested for making decisions.

First, if you think optimistically, you may select a strategy for the possibility of receiving the greatest return, referred to as the **maximax** criterion. Using this criterion, you ignore possible losses or failures. Probably, prospectors for gold, buyers of lottery tickets, or the most venturesome entrepreneurs who "go for broke" use the maximax criterion. Second, if you decide to believe that only the worst possible outcome will occur, a strategy that maximizes the least favorable result, the **maximin** criterion, is needed. Viewing uncertainty in this pessimistic manner, the manager seeks to make the best of adverse effects of states of nature, assuring the best outcome under the worst conditions.

Finally, if you have no information about the probability of states of nature, you will select an approach that assumes that each state of nature has the same chance of occurring. In the absence of any knowledge, you merely assume that the chances for each possible state of nature are equal.

Thus, even in the case of complete uncertainty, the decision maker has options for making decisions. The foregoing criteria provide some framework for choice even in the most uncertain situations.

We are fortunate that in modern society, we have developed a great many facts and much technical scientific data that provide enough information so that the managers do not normally operate under conditions of pure uncertainty. A third condition, a condition of **risk,** illustrated in Figure 5-4, makes other analytical devices possible. Under conditions of risk, the manager has sufficient information for estimating the probability of outcomes. Probability (usually represented by the symbol P) can be defined as the percentage of times a specific outcome would occur if an action were repeated a very large number of times.

All the analytical aids for dealing with probability depend upon the various methods by which the manager can estimate P. Probability is usually stated as a fraction or a percentage; for example, $P = 0.5$ means that the chance of the occurrence is one out of two, or that it would occur 50 percent of the time.

When you do not have sufficient knowledge of conditions to quantitatively determine P, you may still estimate P by using judgment. This less exact type of probability, called subjective probability, is available in most situations. For example, you might state the subjective probability of your passing this course as 0.90; since you have no "track record" in this course and no logical basis for predicting the actions of your present instructor, your statement is purely a matter of opinion. This approach has been criticized because it encourages the manager to pull a probability estimate out of the air; however, subjective probabilities make it possible for the manager to state assumptions to someone else explicitly and quantitatively. (Your estimated grade in this course can be compared with your estimate for passing other courses you are now taking and can help you in your study plans. Your estimate of 0.90 is also a more precise way of telling your parents that you really think you will pass.)

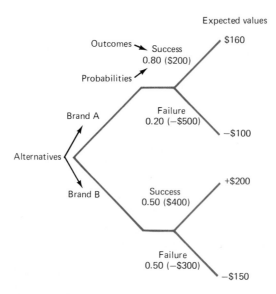

FIGURE 5-5 Decision Tree

Decision tree
A graphical method of visualizing the alternatives and outcomes of a decision assuming certain probabilities.

A graphical method for identifying alternative strategies, estimating probabilities, and indicating the resulting expected payoff is a **decision tree.** This graphical form visually helps the decision maker view alternatives and outcomes. A decision tree for the choice between Brands A and B is illustrated in Figure 5-5.

Note that in the decision tree, the decision maker states in some form the estimate of the expected outcome for each of the expressed alternatives. One approach would be to state these expectations in verbal form, such as "almost certain, very likely, likely, unlikely, very unlikely, and almost never." However, it is very useful to make these statements of expectations in quantitative values of P, perhaps making a subjective estimate. The key to this step is to state explicitly the various probabilities that might be attached to each act—outcome situation (as is shown in Figure 5-5), the alternatives, each of the outcomes for each alternative, and the probabilities for each outcome. All we need do is develop some measure that will distinguish among each of the outcomes, for there will probably be greater value for certain outcomes than for others. A useful yardstick is a monetary unit—for example, dollars. In this last step, we merely designate the value of each outcome as a certain number of dollars (as was done in parentheses on the middle limb of the tree in Figure 5-5).

Cost

Cost Sacrifices that must be made in the future to achieve an objective.

The basic idea of **cost** is that it is a sacrifice. Measurement of cost involves an attempt to determine the amount of sacrifice that will be made in a particular decision. Because a decision is made in the present with consequences that will occur in the future, the manager's judgment may be important in estimating the total costs or sacrifices involved in the decision. Several cost principles are basic to this analysis.

Future costs Costs not yet incurred; the only costs relevant to a manager's decision.

Future costs are the important costs.[12] Only those costs not yet incurred are relevant to a manager's decision. The manager makes decisions for future action. This viewpoint requires concern with future as well as with past costs. The basic criteria for current decisions are the expected benefits to be realized as a result of the decision as compared with the expected sacrifices that will need to be made. The regular books of an accountant show past costs only, and thus the manager cannot depend solely on the financial accountant's cost information, but must look to the future, using the economist's viewpoint, and to budgeting expected costs.

Opportunity costs
The costs of an action or decision consists of the opportunities sacrificed by taking that action.

Since managers are interested in selecting the best alternative, they must concentrate on the various opportunities open to them. What the manager has to give up to pursue a course of action is called the **opportunity cost** of that decision. In deciding to use an hour of your time to file correspondence, you are sacrificing the chance of doing anything else with that hour. What is the cost of your filing correspondence for one hour? It depends. If you would otherwise have been waiting for someone and thus would have been idle, the cost is zero. If the services you could perform in this hour were very valuable—say, worth $100—the cost of filing the correspondence would be $100. Of course, it is difficult to comprehend all the alternatives available, and thus it is difficult to know all opportunity costs; yet, the basic idea of opportunity cost is invaluable in helping to allocate resources properly. (Thus, your cost of reading this chapter is your sacrifice in not doing something else with your time.)

A most valuable concept in decision making is incremental cost, defined as the additional (change in) cost that results from a particular decision. Incremental analysis involves a comparison of changes in revenue and changes in cost associated with a decision. The idea is simple: You will want to do something if, and only if, you can expect to be better off than you were before. In a business firm, the manager would want to make sure that the additional total revenue would be greater than the additional total cost. The logic of incremental reasoning is clearly sound. The greatest problems in the use of this reasoning are the search for all variables that should be considered and the measurement of all costs.

Fixed costs Those costs that remain fixed regardless of the rate of production.

Variable costs Those costs that vary with the rate of operations and that can be changed in the short run.

Managers often distinguish between **fixed costs** and **variable costs** when making a decision. Some costs will vary with the rate of production or level of services, but other costs will be fixed—that is, they will remain constant regardless of the quantity of output.

Sometimes it is easy to identify a cost as variable. For example, when a worker's pay is based on the number of pieces produced and that worker produces no output, the cost of wages is zero. If the worker produces a number of pieces, the cost can be computed by multiplying the number of pieces by the rate per piece. (See Figure 5-6) On the other hand, certain costs are clearly fixed—that is, they continue regardless of the rate of production. For example, the cost of the fire insurance premium on an office building continues unchanged regardless of the output of people within the building.

Most costs are partly variable and partly fixed; in this case, the manager must analyze in more detail just what part of the cost varies with the rate of production and what part remains constant. For example, an electric bill may be composed of electricity for lighting, which will be constant regardless of the number of people in the building, and electricity for operating machines, which will vary with the rate at which the machines are used. We turn now to a second technique useful for management decision making, break-even analysis.

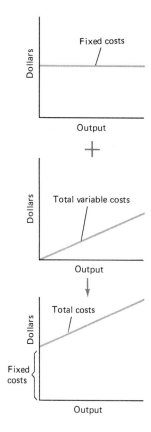

FIGURE 5-6 Derivation of the Total Costs Curve

Break-Even Analysis

Break-even analysis implies that at some point in the operations, total revenue equals total cost—this is the break-even point. The break-even point can be calculated with this equation:

$$\text{Break-even point (in units)} = \frac{\text{Fixed Costs}}{\text{Revenue per unit—Variable cost per unit}}$$

We can also handle this analysis by setting up a break-even chart. However, before we can use the equation or construct a break-even chart, it is necessary to classify total costs into fixed and variable.

The break-even chart is a graphic representation of the relation between cost and revenue at a given time and shows the point (volume) at which they are equal (break-even). Figure 5-7 is a typical break-even chart. Many times, fixed costs are shown as a base, with variable costs shown above this base. For purposes of understanding the idea of incremental cost, it is preferable to use the form in Figure 5-7. The simplest break-even chart makes use of straight lines that represent revenue, variable cost, and total cost. The construction of this chart requires only that the cost and the revenue be known at two points (volumes of output), because only two points are required to draw a straight line. The point at the y-intercept (left-hand side of the chart) is given by definition: The revenue line will start at zero (zero volume); variable costs will also start at zero (zero volume); fixed costs will be a given level on the y-axis, because by definition they will exist even if there is no production. Cost and

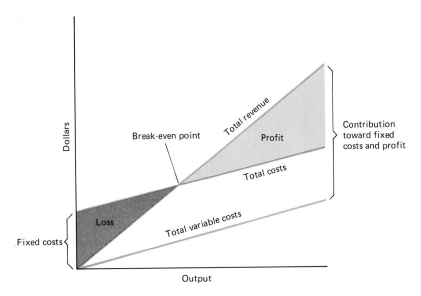

FIGURE 5-7 A Simple Break-Even Chart

revenue data at an actual volume level provide the basis for the necessary second point. All other points on the lines are the result of the assumption of linear relationships for both revenue and cost.

The simple analytical device is very useful if interpreted properly but can cause trouble if the following assumptions upon which it is based are forgotten:

1. The linear revenue line indicates an assumption that the price at which any quantity of the output can be sold is fixed and does not change with output. In other words, at any given point on the line, the value is determined by multiplying the price by the number of units sold.

2. Variable costs are assumed to be proportional to output. In other words, the variable cost per unit does not increase or decrease with the rate of production.

3. The product mix (the percentage of each of the several types of products produced) remains constant.

4. Fixed costs and variable costs are clearly distinguishable.

5. All products produced are sold by the company.

The value of the break-even chart lies in the simple and straightforward manner in which it illustrates some important economic concepts. One obvious observation is that profits do not appear if any costs are fixed until a given volume of output is reached. Once this break-even point is reached, profits appear and increase at a faster rate than do total costs.

The idea of contribution toward fixed cost and profit is clearly indicated in Figure 5-7. This idea is one of the most basic for a manager to understand; yet, many errors creep into managers' decisions on this point. We can simply state that a decision to produce extra volume depends upon whether the extra revenue will more than cover variable costs; in other words, will new revenue provide extra funds to contribute toward fixed costs and profits?

Many forms of break-even charts have been developed. Figure 5-7 shows costs and revenues plotted against output or volume in number of units. At times, you may want to use gross sales or percentage of capacity of operations instead of output in units. You can easily adapt this simple technique to your own particular situation, be it a newspaper route, a benefit dance, or a commercial airline, and thus better understand whether activity relating to revenue and expenses is sound.

In our discussion of break-even analysis, we find that with an increase in volume, the extra revenue is greater than the extra cost. We said that the difference was a contribution to fixed cost and profit—in other words, the increment gained by deciding to increase volume. If the revenue realized from each unit of production is less than the variable raw-materials cost, obviously you would lose on each additional unit produced. Break-even analysis is a very simple analytical tool, but it has power in improving decisions, since it applies basic economic theory using data usually available from accountants. After costs are segregated into fixed and variable, the number of units that must be sold to break even is simply the amount of fixed costs divided by the contribution of each unit (which, as we have seen, is the price of each unit less the variable cost per unit). Charting of different values for price, fixed cost, and variable cost per unit enables a manager to visualize the effects of alternatives within his or her control.

There is an expanding number of rigorous techniques for helping the decision maker; these techniques are important but beyond the scope of this introductory text in managing.

SUMMARY

In this chapter you were introduced to a basic function of management, decision making. You read about the relationship of organizational problems to the practice of managerial decision making. After some basic observations about decisions and an understanding of different types of problem/decisions (programmed-nonprogrammed), you read of the Objectives-Plan-Action model, which provides you with possible insights into locating sources of problems and their ensuing decisions. From there, you were introduced to a five-step process of decision making and an adaptive approach that recognizes the importance of flexibility. We also added that there are behavioral and political aspects of decision making; the process is not a sterile one.

Finally, quantitative concepts and techniques were offered for your understanding of available aids in decision making. Most managers will combine approaches to fit the needs of the situation.

KEY TERMS

Decision making A course of action consciously chosen from alternatives to achieve desired result.

Decision A course of action consciously chosen from alternatives to achieve desired result.

Routine Situations or decisions that contain recurring items with high certainty.

Nonroutine decisions Decision situations filled with uncertainty that lack routine and occur infrequently.

Objectives Specific statements of what an organization hopes to achieve.

OPA Model An operational model that describes the topics of many managerial decisions.

Adaptive approach A decision making approach that places value on understanding that many environments are filled with complexity and change; what is important is to adapt your approach to the reality of the situation. Also called the "Muddling Through" approach.

Muddling Through A decision making approach that faces the reality of the situation; it sees curved and crooked lines rather than straight lines. Also called the "adaptive approach".

Satisfice The search for a satisfactory solution by managers instead of the economists' focus on optimizing.

Bounded rationality People are rational within the limits of human capabilities.

Certainty Situation in which you have sufficient information to make decision; perfect chance of predicting the outcome of the decisions.

Uncertainty Situation in which you have no information on which to base decision; no chance of predicting the outcome of the decision.

Maximax Selecting a strategy for the possibility of receiving the greatest return.

Maximin Selecting a strategy for the possibility of maximizing the least favorable result; minimize possiblity of worse case scenario.

Risk A condition in decision making where a manager has sufficient information for estimating the probability of outcomes.

Decision tree A graphical method of visualizing the alternatives and outcomes of a decision assuming certain probabilities.

Cost Sacrifices that must be made in the future to achieve an objective.

Future costs Costs not yet incurred ; the only costs relevant to a manager's decision.

Opportunity costs The costs of an action or decision consist of the opportunities sacrificed by taking that action.

Fixed costs Those costs that remain fixed regardless of the rate of production.

Variable costs Those costs that vary with the rate of operations and that can be changed in the short run.

Break-even analysis Determining at what point total revenues are equal to total expenses.

STUDY ASSIGNMENTS

1. Discuss why managers, such as the managers of Consolidated Printing, would be resistant to letting nonmanagers make decisions or participate in the decision-making process?

2. It was suggested that a decision takes place only if (1) there are alternatives to choose from, (2) the process is a conscious effort, and (3) there is a purpose for the action. Why do you need alternatives to make a decision? How many alternatives are enough or too few?

3. What constitutes a "good" decision? If things go wrong as a result of acting on a particular decision, does it mean that the decision was a "bad" one?

4. Compare and contrast the Objectives-Plan-Action Model with the five-step decision-making approach. Which one is the more appropriate for a manager to follow?

5. Many writers do not consider "securing acceptance of decisions" as part of the six-step approach. Give some reasons why "securing acceptance of decisions" should be a part of this approach.

6. How do problems and decisions that are routine in nature differ from problems and decisions that are nonroutine and for which the information is uncertain?

7. Think about an important decision that you have made recently or one that you are currently considering. How would you approach making this decision if you used the Objectives-Plan-Action Model? How would you approach making this decision if you used the five-step approach? Would there be any difference in the final decision if you used one approach or the other?

8. How are the kinds of decisions and problems considered by executives different from the kinds of decisions and problems faced by supervisors? Which group of managers has decisions that are more difficult, that are more important to resolve?

9. Why is it so difficult for individuals, groups, and organizations to make decisions and resolve problems in a "rational" manner?

10. For decision making and problem solving, how does the adaptive approach compare with the Objectives-Plan-Action Model?

Case for Discussion

WESTOVER RETIREMENT COMMUNITY

Westover Retirement Community is a nonprofit organization located in Hamilton, Ohio. Its roots are in Hamilton, with many important Hamilton families being the primary sponsors and financial supporters. The fifteen-member executive board includes influential people from Hamilton and surrounding areas. There are M.D.'s, Ph.D.'s, attorneys, professionals, small-business men and women, corporate executives, and lay people whose parents are residents in the Community.

Westover has a number of features: one-floor living, private residential rooms as well as one-, two-, and three-room apartments, 24-hour intermediate nursing care, a chapel and weekly church services, housekeeping services, professional dietetic services, two complete whirlpool/bathing systems, and a ratio of more than two staff members to every three residents.

You are the director of the facility and it is Wednesday morning. You take the mail from your in-basket and start through the items. Some are listed below. What decisions would you make on each?

1. A memo with a phone call with an offer to give you two free tickets to a Cincinnati Reds baseball game.

2. A letter from A. Fitton, a local prominent attorney, requesting that accommodations be found for his elderly sister in New York City.

3. A report from a Miami University intern student on the security systems throughout the Community. It shows that security can be breached; residents are able to leave the rooms and the facility without detection.

4. A request from the local AARP chapter for you to address them on the topic of care of the elderly in the twenty-first century.

5. A complaint from Mrs. Lotty, a long-term resident. She lists problems with the food, linens, security, relationships with the staff (they don't treat her with respect), and the smoking habits of the male residents.

6. A budget you had requested showing deviations from budgeted to actual expenses.

7. A memo re a phone call from a local attorney who will be representing one of your employees filing a sex discrimination suit against the institution. She claims wage discrimination as well.

8. A request from your head nurse for an appointment to discuss her recent performance evaluation.

9. A return-call memo from Robert Cottrell, Chairman of the Board.

Chapter 6

Planning and Strategic Management

Learning Objectives

1. **Explain** how strategic management and planning contribute to an organization's ability to adapt to changing conditions.
2. **State** why planning has increased in importance in modern society.
3. **Describe** three forecasting techniques available to estimate future conditions.
4. **Explain** the process of developing a strategic plan.
5. **Define** the terms mission, goals, strategies, and policies.
6. **Explain** the notion of creating value for the stakeholder.
7. **Identify** the factors and determinants in the formulation of an organization's strategies.
8. **State** the advantages of clear policies and the characteristics of good policy statements.
9. **Explain** how plans and strategies can be successfully implemented.

THE changes in the tire industry over the past two decades illustrate how environmental and technological changes can dramatically affect an organization's strategies. At the beginning of the 1970s, the U.S. tire industry was dominated by Firestone, General Tire, Uniroyal, Goodrich, and the number one tire manufacturer in the world, Goodyear. As competitors, these firms shared the same markets, the same labor problems, and the same production technology for their bias-ply tires, and were dependent on the U.S. auto industry. Overall, the U.S. tire industry was considered to be very profitable, stable, and predictable—that is, until the radial tire appeared on the scene.

In the early 1970s, the French tire manufacturer Michelin developed and introduced the radial tire. This was a tremendous technological advance, for the radial tire not only performed better than a bias-ply tire but also lasted more than twice as long. Unfortunately, most of the U.S. tire producers initially failed to recognize the implications of this technological change: In time, the demand for tires would be cut in half as more and more cars were equipped with radial tires.

For the U.S. tire manufacturers, the problems from new technology were compounded by the decline of the American auto industry. As more and more foreign cars entered the United States equipped with radials manufactured by Michelin, Dunlop, and the Japanese producer Bridgestone, the output of the U.S. manufacturers fell dramatically. Akron, the tire capital of the world, experienced one plant closing after another.

In response, Firestone, General Tire, Uniroyal, and Goodrich decided to diversify their businesses so that they would not be dependent on tires for their survival. They pursued a wide range of ventures—aerospace, films, radio and television, airlines, wallpaper, and many more. However, most analysts thought that these actions showed little direction and that the firms were diversifying for the sake of diversification. Typically, the ventures had little in common with the tire industry, and very few of them succeeded. Even the Uniroyal and Goodrich merger did not succeed.

By the end of the 1980s, these firms existed in name only. The tire operations of Firestone, General Tire, and Uniroyal-Goodrich were acquired by foreign tire producers. No one produced tires in Akron anymore.

Goodyear, on the other hand, was able to preserve its leadership position in the tire industry by revitalizing its production facilities and by introducing new products, including the all-season radial. It also adapted its operations to the world market, aggressively selling tires in Japan, the Far East, and Europe. But like its U.S. counterparts, Goodyear also attempted to diversify in the early 1980s, and like its counterparts, it failed. As a result, Goodyear was the subject of a damaging, but unsuccessful, corporate takeover attempt, which allowed Michelin to take a giant step toward becoming the number one tire producer. This time, Goodyear's management responded quickly and refocused its business, getting back to the basics that would move Goodyear into the twenty-first century as the number one tire producer in the world. ∎

The substantial changes in the tire industry since Michelin introduced the radial tire in the 1970s have been rather mild in comparison with some of the changes in other industrial sectors of the economy. During that period of time, the United States shifted from an industrial economy to a service economy. There were also oil embargoes, the creation of the "rust belt," a major recession/depression, and a revolution in computers. Thousands of firms went out of business, while thousands of other firms, with names like Apple, Wendy's, Compaq, Blockbuster Videos, Rolm, Domino's, Toys 'R' Us, and Federal Express became household names and billion-dollar operations.

The question of why some firms succeed while others fail can be answered by examining how those enterprises responded to changing conditions. Those that have succeeded have done so because they recognized that they operate in a dynamic and sometimes hostile environment. They developed and instituted managerial practices that are sensitive to the present and oriented toward the future.

Strategic management and planning are critical managerial concepts and processes. They are the means whereby managers and their organizations can become sensitive to changing conditions and responsive in developing future-oriented courses of action. Adaptive managers and organizations understand that success in the past does not guarantee success, or even survival, in the future. Organizations need to know where they are going. They need plans that provide direction and serve as guidelines in making decisions.

As our opening case demonstrates, an organization's survival depends on its ability to maintain momentum and direction and on its ability to adapt operations to changes in technology and the competition. Goodyear was sensitive to its environment and, as a result, was able to develop strategies appropriate to the situation and reflective of its own capabilities. Goodyear's managers effectively used strategic management concepts and planning techniques to ensure Goodyear's long-run survival and to preserve Goodyear's leadership position in the tire industry.

The success of companies such as Toys 'R' Us demonstrates that opportunities for new approaches still exist. "Traditional" beliefs that the toy market was just seasonal or belonged in department stores did not stop Toys 'R' Us from becoming a new concept, a successful operation, a highly recommended stock on Wall Street, and an international firm with operations around the world.

THE NATURE AND IMPORTANCE OF PLANNING

Planning is a basic function of management. The functions of organizing, leading, controlling, staffing, directing, and communicating facilitate the implementation of the manager's plan and the decisions made during the planning process.

Studies done by a variety of people and organizations—including Peters and Waterman,[1] Porter,[2,3] Ansoff and Associates, Thune and House, Wood and LaForge[4]—have shown that the most successful organizations are the ones that first plan and then implement and control their plan. Planning is the most important controllable factor in determining success for organizations.

With all the research that has been done, you would think that planning would be the top priority for all managers who want to be successful, but unfortunately it is not.

Some managers tend to say, "What's the use? We can't keep up as it is, let alone take time to figure out what to do next week, next month, or next year. We'll just try to survive. Maybe things will get better." These managers "fight fires" or practice management-by-crisis. They solve each problem as it comes up, as soon as it becomes a crisis. They don't even attempt to reach a goal; they drift. They do not manage the organization's progress—how can there be progress when there is no goal? They are overwhelmed by changes in the external and internal environments, changes that are occurring at an ever-increasing rate, complicating the situation even more.

Perhaps the only constant in a manager's life is change. We will summarize here some of the changes that are occurring in the external and internal environments.

What changes affect planning?

First, technology changes so fast that an organization's plant and equipment may become obsolete almost overnight. Robots, artificial intelligence, and expert systems are becoming commonplace. Products must reflect the cutting edge of technology, since an organization's customers and clients demand advanced products to replace older models. (For example, the electric typewriter was hailed as a vast improvement over the manual typewriter, but the electric typewriter has been replaced by electronic typewriters with memory and built-in spelling checkers and automatic correction features. And the electronic typewriter has been replaced, for all practical purposes, by word processing and desktop publishing through microcomputers.) An organization could conceivably lose its customers overnight to a competitor with a more technologically advanced product. Managers need to avoid such surprises by planning for technological changes.

Second, changes in government control, regulations, and public policy require many changes in the conditions (external environment) in which managers must work. Just keeping up with the tax laws is a staggering task. Even more important, the federal government has deregulated and continues to deregulate numerous industries, from trucking to communications. Deregulation has a tremendous impact on organizations; some companies have been forced out of business as a result of innovative competition. Even innovative competition, however, does not guarantee success.

The government also has the power to break up businesses that are perceived to be monopolies. For example, in 1983, the Justice Department and the federal courts forced AT&T to spin off its local Bell Telephone System from its

Management Application

The People Express Story

In January 1980, Donald Burr resigned as president of Texas International Airlines because he wanted to start his own business. Within a few months of his resignation, Burr took advantage of the recent deregulation of the airline industry and founded People Express. When it began operations, People Express's mission was to provide the leisure traveler with a low-cost, no-frills form of air transportation.

People Express was a phenomenal success. By 1985, it was the fifth largest airline in the United States, with revenues in excess of $1 billion. Many observers attributed People's early success to Burr's exploitation of deregulation, to his development of the leisure travel market, and to strategies that considered profit secondary to providing service, achieving growth, and developing his people to their fullest potential. Because of its lower operating costs and lower fares, People Express gained a competitive advantage over the older airlines. But Burr

and his management team failed to appropriately adapt their strategies after they achieved their initial success.

People Express continued to expand its capacity beyond the demand levels of the leisure market, and when the more established airlines (who traditionally provided a higher and more reliable level of service) began matching People's prices, People's load levels (passenger volume) fell. In response, People attempted to attract business flyers, but its reputation for delays, late arrivals, and lost luggage made People Express very unappealing to the business flyer. Conditions at People soon deteriorated as the airline failed to improve its reputation and attract new passengers. In September 1986, when it was clear that People Express could not adapt to changing conditions, Donald Burr sold the airline to his former employer, the Texas International Air Corporation.

manufacturing, research, and long-distance operations. The government hoped that the creation of seven independent "baby bells" would improve competition in the telecommunications industry. Managers need plans by which they can adjust to these changing constraints.

Third, changing economic conditions—shortages of raw materials, shortages of available labor, the aging of both the work force and the consumer as the baby boomers get older, recessions and depressions, inflation, high interest rates, the declining value of the dollar against the Japanese yen and vice versa, foreign competition, hostile takeovers, mergers, global forces in economics—challenge managers to be ready for shifts and the effects of such shifts in economic forces.

Fourth, changes in social norms, attitudes, life styles, and people's expectations create new situations that require new approaches. Health concerns increasingly affect the workplace. People worry about being infected with AIDS by a co-worker who has the disease. People are concerned about remaining physically fit, and employers have responded by building exercise centers and health spas at the work site. (A healthy employee is, after all, a more produc-

Not all American firms believe that older workers are no longer productive. McDonald's began a program to hire retired men and women. Early results show these people to be good role models to the younger staff, responsible and productive in their positions, and an attraction to the older generation who come to McDonald's in increasing numbers.

tive employee. In addition, such programs help reduce the costs of medical and life insurance benefits.) Managers and employees are concerned about child care—who is watching the children and are the children safe? Racial attitudes have changed—but not enough—during the past hundred years. Women are now attempting to move into upper-level management positions. (They are making little progress. In the "Big 6" accounting firms, for example, 1 percent of all partners are women.) People want to protect the environment. And people want to have more time for themselves. The work force is getting older, and there is a shortage of teenagers and young adults to fill entry-level service positions. (Retired people are taking up the slack at Carl's Jr. and McDonald's.) America's melting pot is still melting as more and more legal and illegal aliens enter the country from Mexico, Viet Nam, and other places. It is important that the manager take all of these—and more—social changes into account when he or she looks into the future to make plans.

Planning is the managerial function that determines the pattern of actions needed for meeting future situations to attain organizational goals. Plans are predetermined courses of action made in the present to guide future implementation toward the goals of the organization. Plans and planning are means by which managers can influence the future of the organization. See Figure 6-1.

Different types of plans are made by managers at different levels in the organization. These types form a hierarchy, with general overall plans serving as patterns for detailed short-range plans. Top management prepares broad, general plans for the entire organization. Strategic plans generally seek to look further into the future, for periods of two to ten years or longer. Lower-level managers prepare plans that include greater detail but have shorter time horizons of days and months.

Plans can be classified by their subject matter, such as production, marketing, and finance. For example, the production manager uses plans for supply-

Planning The function performed by managers that determines the pattern of actions needed for meeting situations in the future in order to attain organizational goals.

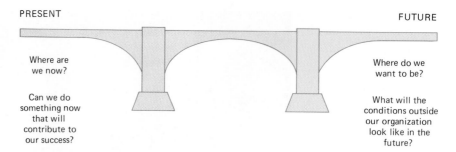

PRESENT

FUTURE

Where are
we now?

Where do we
want to be?

Can we do
something now
that will
contribute to
our success?

What will the
conditions outside
our organization
look like in the
future?

FIGURE 6-1 The Nature of Planning

ing raw materials and parts, use of equipment, assignments of personnel, amount of funds required, and quantity of output to be delivered. The marketing manager plans the sale of products and their prices, the markets to be entered, the types of promotion to use, and the channels of distribution through which to sell. The financial manager makes plans for sources of capital, the flow of funds in operations, capital expenditures, and the expected general financial condition. Other managerial specialists, such as personnel managers, engineers, and lawyers, develop plans that provide details of their activities expected when the strategic, top-level plans are implemented.

LOOKING INTO THE FUTURE: SOME FORECASTING TECHNIQUES

Each manager must identify explicitly how future conditions will affect operations.[5] The conditions in the external environment are outside one's control, but they must be estimated so that the organization can quickly adapt to changes that are occurring rapidly. Although it is impossible to predict exactly what will happen in the future, the manager should attempt to forecast the following critical groups of developments:[6] (1) economic conditions in the region and the nation, to include leading economic indicators of inflation, consumer confidence levels, unemployment rates, and consumer debt and willingness to spend even more money; (2) new laws and regulations, including those pertaining to taxation, credit, commerce, and affirmative action; (3) community pressures and social changes; (4) availability of resources and financial backing; (5) technological changes; (6) consumer demand for the firm's products and services (that is, give the customers what they want); (7) reactions of suppliers and customers; (8) availability of personnel for operations; (9) demographics; and perhaps most important, (10) actions and reactions of the competition.

The large number of factors to be forecast, the imprecision of forecasting techniques, and the limited time available for studying the future make prediction a difficult area in planning.[7] Often, the best one can do is to gather information from published sources and to prepare a qualitative estimate. With this information, the manager determines the premises or assumptions that best fit

Forecasting customer demand is a challenging task. In some countries, companies estimate production from the needs of the market. In other countries, the planning is highly centralized and the market responds to what the central planners have decided to produce. One major reason for the failures in the economies of the U.S.S.R. and some central European countries was the inability to have production and distribution relate to consumer needs. Long lines and shortages were the trademarks of the failure as depicted by the people standing in line for groceries in Leningrad, U.S.S.R.

the situations. For example, if a manager wanted to forecast general economic conditions, the following components of the gross national product (GNP) provide a framework for the approach: consumer purchases (including durable consumer goods, nondurable consumer goods, and services); private investment expenditures (construction, durable equipment, and inventory build-up); government expenditures (federal, state, and local spending); and net exports or imports (the difference between imports and exports). Using the GNP model, the manager can make general estimates of specific values for each of these components, and, with the help of published forecasts, can arrive at an estimate of general economic conditions—for example, they will improve by 5 percent in the next year, will stay about the same, or will contract by 5 percent. One can extrapolate (extend a time series into the future based upon past tendencies), or one can use percentages of GNP as guides.

After making forecasts of the general economy, the manager could focus on analyzing industry trends. Such an analysis would examine demand patterns: sales of products to new customers, sales of additional products to old customers, replacement sales for products that have worn out, and sales affected by recent technological developments.

There are a wide range of forecasting techniques that managers use in making predictions:[8]

1. Quantitative time series analysis. This is a study of past data, such as monthly sales figures or shipping volume. These data are plotted on a chart and are examined mathematically to find trends and periodic fluctuations. This method assumes that the future will closely resemble the past, and, thus, can be estimated by projecting the past data into the future. (This is not always a safe assumption.)
2. Derived forecasts. If a manager can discover another phenomenon that has been forecast by a government agency or expert, and if that phenomenon is closely associated with the variable that we need to predict, a forecast can be derived from

these other estimates. For example, if a company sells household furnishings, it can use facts about housing construction (new housing starts, for example) to help predict demand for furnishings.

3. Causal models. If an underlying cause for the variable can be determined, the forecast can be handled mathematically and produce quite accurate results. For example, one might find that sales are the direct result of the number of contacts by salespeople and predict that from every five contacts, one sale will result.

4. Survey of plans and attitudes. For a number of years, the University of Michigan has been successful in using statistical samples of consumers for determining their plans and attitudes about purchasing in the future. The forecast is then inferred from the answers to questionnaires completed by the sample respondents.

5. Brainstorming. On the assumption that two heads—or more—are better than one, one method for predicting the future is to assemble a group of people with knowledge of and interest in a specific problem and encourage free flow of creative comments. The conditions required for these brainstorming sessions are important: (a) No participant may criticize any idea, regardless of how farfetched it may be; (b) each participant is encouraged to supplement the comments of others and to provide suggestions for future estimates; (c) after recording the comments during the meeting, a manager may construct a forecast built on the variety of ideas from the group.

6. Delphi Method. The judgment of experts is sometimes the best and most feasible method of forecasting. The Rand Corporation developed the Delphi Method as a means of forecasting by seeking expert opinions. The method differs from brainstorming in that experts complete a detailed questionnaire independently and without knowledge of the responses of other experts. After all responses are in, each participant considers the (anonymous) comments of the others in the succeeding rounds. The experts tend to revise their views in the light of the others' responses, and three or four cycles of the process usually result in a consensus by all experts without direct debate or discussions.

7. Contingent forecasting scenarios. Even when several of these forecasting methods are used, the results may fail to predict future events accurately. One approach for handling the lack of precision in forecasting is contingent forecasting and planning. At the heart of this approach is the development of several scenarios, each scenario providing a different set of assumptions about future events. The scenario describes a logical sequence of events that might occur in the future. In the construction of each scenario, the manager explores the details of what might happen in the future and what the results might be if it does. With the cluster of scenarios, the manager is not dependent upon the accuracy of a single prediction but has already estimated implications of a number of possibilities and can prepare different plans to fit the different scenarios.

8. Instant analysis. The need by executives for indicators to help formulate production and marketing strategies has resulted in forecasters producing more timely estimates through instant analysis. This effort is based on data that are available several times a month, including initial unemployment claims, ten-day auto sales, the *Business Week* Index, commodities prices, money supply, steel, paperboard carloadings, and business loan demand. Such short-run forecasts can help managers respond quickly to changes, although at times, they may result in overreaction and irregular behavior.[9]

Planning and forecasting will help the manager move toward developing and accomplishing the corporate mission and goals.[10] The process reduces the temptation to manage only in response to crises, to listen only to the squeaking wheel, and to be at the mercy of everyone else's priorities. There is value, therefore, in exploring this process in greater detail.

COMPONENTS OF STRATEGIC MANAGEMENT

Strategic management
The setting of long-range
plans, selection of strategies
and policies, and allocation
of resources for reaching .
a goal.

Strategic management is the formulation and implementation of a strategic plan, with feedback/monitoring/evaluation and control of that plan.[11] Although strategic management emphasizes that planning is just one part of its process, our focus here will be on the formulation of the plan, or strategic planning, and the implementation of the plan through policies, and procedures. The specific components of strategic management, and their relationship to one another, are depicted in Figure 6-2.

To meet the challenges of modern society, more and more organizations are concentrating on formal approaches and concepts for planning their long-range progress. Specifically, these challenges result from (1) the increasing rate of changes, (2) the growing complexity of managers' jobs, (3) the increasing importance of fitting the organization into its external environment, and (4) the increasing lag between the preparation of plans and their implementation.

Plans may be based on dreams, aspirations, intuition, hopes, and expectations, but they are developed through a process that translates them into specific and concrete guides for future implementation. Planning answers these questions:

FIGURE 6-2 Components of Strategic Management

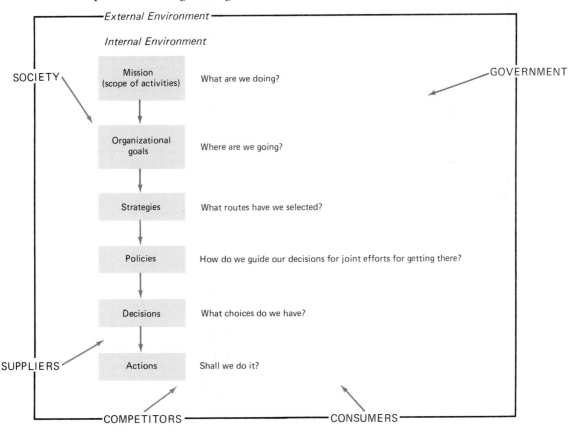

- Who, what, and where are we now?
- Where are we going? or, Where do we want to be 5 years from now? 10 years? 20 years? 100 years?
- How do we get there?

Global Application

Predicting International Strategies

As the twenty-first century quickly becomes a reality, events throughout the world remind us of the challenge of being strategic managers. What adds to that challenge is the rapid pace of change; this change makes uncertainty the most natural state of the economic, political, and social condition. Another factor is the change in the nature of constraints on strategy making.

From the 1900s until the mid-1980s, the political strategy of nations was limited or influenced by wars. Deciding the mission of your country or the objectives of your industrial power is not too difficult when your survival is threatened. During the Cold War period, the "Communist Threat" gave direction to much of the foreign policy of the noncommunist countries; the "Capitalistic Threat" gave direction to the foreign policy of the communist nations. Today, the threats, limits, and constraints upon policy making have changed. For example, the remaking of the Soviet Union will be one of the most remarkable changes of all time and one of the most difficult to predict.

The changes in the Soviet Union present the United States, the European Community, the Japanese, and other trading partners with opportunities and challenges. Few have had the experience to be able to predict what will happen or to know what posture or strategy is the most appropriate.

The plan to create a single European market has been in the making for years (at least from 1950, when the French foreign minister, Robert Schuman, put forth a plan for France and Germany to pool their coal and steel production, and many of the original assumptions are no longer valid. On January 1, 1993, the Community becomes a reality, and many businessmen and government officials are having second thoughts. Once again, no one can really predict the response of other countries to the creation of a 320-million-person market.

The Sony Corporation faces the same future, although its focus is more narrow. Sony wants to become the world's one-stop shop for entertainment and, with that mission in mind, is moving ahead with strategies to reach its goal. In 1988, Sony purchased CBS Records, Inc., for $2 billion and then spent $3.4 billion for Columbia Pictures Entertainment, Inc. On February 27, 1991, Michael P. Schulhof—the highest-ranking American at Sony, the vice chairman of Sony USA, and president of Sony Software Corporation—announced the creation of an electronic-publishing company to sell electronic games and all other multimedia computer software. The move into software for a company known for its excellence in hardware is a result of Schulhof's belief that there is a strong linkage between software development and hardware revenues. He seeks synergies between all the units of the corporation. The future will tell if this strategy works.

References: 1992 (Brussels: Arthur Andersen and Co., March 1989); "Remaking the Soviet Union," *The Economist,* July 13, 1991, pp. 21–23; "Media Colossus," *Business Week,* March 25, 1991, pp. 64–74.

Who, What, and Where Are We Now?
The Organization's Mission

The first step in the development of a plan is to specify the organization's mission, its goals, and its strategies. This requires that managers perform a little organizational self-analysis and that they answer a wide range of questions, such as: What is the organization doing now? What business are we in? Who are our customers? What do we want to accomplish? And given environmental conditions related to the economy, the competition, resources, governmental actions, and managerial abilities, managers also need to analyze and address the questions of how well the organization is doing and where it should be going in the future. It is from this evaluation that managers can begin formulating a mission statement for the organization.

The mission statement expresses and explains the purpose or reasons for the organization's existence, its *raison d'être*. It defines the nature and scope of the organization and establishes organizational direction. Mission statements are distinctive, enabling firms, managers, and others to distinguish one organization from another. Mission statements serve as the basis for allocating resources and for making strategic and operational decisions. These statements help employees understand what makes their organization distinct from their competitors. The mission statements of the Zale Corporation and the Niagara Power Company are good examples of mission statements.

Mission statement: Zale Corporation

Our business is specialty retailing. Retailing is a people-oriented business. We recognize that our business existence and continued success is dependent upon how well we meet our responsibilities to several critically important groups of people.

Our first responsibility is to our customers. Without them we would have no reason for being. We strive to appeal to a broad spectrum of consumers, catering in a professional manner to their needs. Our concept of value to the customer includes a wide selection of quality merchandise, competitively priced and delivered with courtesy and professionalism.

Our ultimate responsibility is to our shareholders. Our goal is to earn an optimum return on invested capital through steady profit growth and prudent, aggressive asset management. The attainment of this financial goal, coupled with a record of sound management, represents our approach toward influencing the value placed upon our common stock in the market.

We feel a deep, personal responsibility to our employees. As an equal opportunity employer we seek to create and maintain an environment where every employee is provided the opportunity to develop to his or her maximum potential. We expect to reward employees commensurate with their contribution to the success of the company.

We are committed to honesty and integrity in all relationships with suppliers of goods and services. We are demanding but fair. We evaluate our suppliers on the basis of quality, price and service.

We recognize community involvement as an important obligation and as a viable business objective. Support of worthwhile community projects in areas where we operate generally accrues to the health and well-being of the community. This makes the community a better place for our employees to live and a better place for us to operate.

We believe in the free enterprise system and in the American democratic form of government under which this superior economic system has been permitted to flourish. We feel an incumbent responsibility to insure that our business operates at a reasonable profit. Profit provides opportunity for growth and job security. We believe growth is necessary to provide opportunities on an ever-increasing scale for our people. Therefore, we are dedicated to profitable growth—growth as a company—and growth as individuals.

Mission statement: Niagara Mohawk Power Company

Niagara Mohawk is an energy company with diversified interest and resources committed to providing for the current and future needs of its customers through economical products and services of superior quality.

The Company is dedicated to maintaining an efficient, progressive, cost-conscious organization that provides a fair and equitable return to its owners.

Management is committed to retaining and motivating talented, productive, effective employees by providing reasonable compensation, incentives, and a good working environment.

The Company pursues opportunities to improve the economic climate and well-being of citizens, industry and business within the markets it serves. Appropriate actions are taken to meet socioeconomic responsibilities. Such actions include seeking those necessary improvements in the regulatory and legislative environment that best serve the interests of the Company's customers, employees and owners.

Management maintains high ethical standards and strives for open communications with all its constituencies.

The Company takes an active role in the development of technologies and opportunities advantageous to its customers and owners. It is dedicated to maintaining and developing dependable energy resources and delivery systems that are safe and environmentally sound.

Management will actively pursue strategies in support of objectives to accomplish this mission.

The choice of a mission can have significant and long-lasting effects. For example, Theodore Levitt observed that the railroad industry during the last century continued to consider railroading as its mission when significant changes in society were pointing toward a redefinition. If a railroad company had defined its mission more broadly as a transportation service, it would have been able to adjust to changes in the environment and technology by integrating railroads with air, auto, water, and pipeline transportation. Levitt argued that management's myopia doomed the industry to its critical present-day problems.

On the other hand, during the 1960s, a number of conglomerates attempted to expand their missions in broad, vague terms and failed to focus clearly on any limit to the scope of activities that they would perform. They failed to recognize that the opportunities offered by new activities carried with them serious problems that exceeded their expertise and resources. As a result of their ill-defined missions, a number of the conglomerates ran into trouble; some even went bankrupt.

After the OPEC actions in the early 1970s caused skyrocketing prices, gasoline shortages, research in alternative energy sources, and demands for a national energy policy, many oil companies changed their mission, which had limited them to the oil production, refining, and marketing business. By redefining their mission, firms like Exxon, Shell, and Mobil became energy resource firms engaged in the business of supplying coal, solar, nuclear, and other forms of energy, as well as oil products. In recent years, it has become clear that this change of mission not only has influenced the management and operations of these firms but also has had an impact on the social, political, and economic fabric of society as a whole. This raises the point that an organization's mission and purpose extends beyond the organization itself, and that there are a number of constituencies affected by the scope, nature, and intent of an organization's mission.

Historically, the view has been that the underlying mission of an organization is to maximize shareholders' wealth. For instance, the Nobel laureate Milton Friedman has consistently argued that the mission of an organization should be to use its resources to continually increase and maximize profits. This means that a notion such as social responsibility should not be factored into the organization's mission, nor should it influence strategic and operational decision-making processes. As a result, the principle of maximizing the shareholders' wealth has served as the justification for corporate actions such as dramatic raising of oil prices during various Middle East crises and the closing of domestic plants to relocate production operations in the low-cost labor environments of Third World countries.

Some factions are now arguing that this emphasis on maximizing shareholders' wealth is reducing the competitiveness of many corporations, and therefore the missions of many organizations are viewed as being inappropriate for today's highly competitive global environment. Out of this debate has emerged a new movement, one that believes that there are many constituencies that influence and have a stake in the fortunes of any organization. For many individuals and organizations, the concerns and interests of these **stakeholders** should be incorporated into an organization's mission. Furthermore, the underlying mission of any organization should not be to maximize shareholders' wealth but to create value for the stakeholders. These stakeholders include the shareholders as well as customers, employees, communities where the organization operates, social and governmental institutions, the organization's suppliers, and even the organization's competitors.

It is interesting to note that firms that have accepted the stakeholder concept often have mission statements that place meeting the needs and concerns of customers, employees, and society ahead of maximizing the wealth of the shareholders. For instance, the concluding paragraph of the Johnson & Johnson mission statement stipulates that a number of other concerns must be addressed before the firm considers the shareholders' return.

> Our final responsibility is to our stockholders.
> Business must make a sound profit.
> We must experiment with new ideas.
> Research must be carried on, innovative programs developed, and mistakes paid for.
> New equipment must be purchased, new facilities provided, and new products launched.
> Reserves must be created to provide for adverse times.
> When we operate according to these principles, the stockholders should realize a fair return.

Another example of how the stakeholder concept is incorporated into an organization's mission is the mission statement of the NCR Corporation (1990 Annual Report):

Mission statement: NCR Corporation
NCR's mission: create value for our stakeholders

> NCR is a successful, growing company dedicated to achieving superior results by assuring that its actions are aligned with stakeholder expectations. Stakeholders are all constituencies with a stake in the fortunes of the company. NCR's primary mission is to create value for our stakeholders.

Stakeholders All those groups that have an interest in the actions of a firm; includes the shareholders, customers, employees, suppliers, and communities.

> We believe in conducting our business activities with integrity and respect while building mutually beneficial and enduring relationships with all of our stakeholders.
>
> We take customer satisfaction personally; we are committed to providing superior quality in our products and services on a continuing basis. We respect the individuality of each employee and foster an environment in which employees' creativity and productivity are encouraged, recognized, valued and rewarded.
>
> We think of our suppliers as partners who share our goal of achieving the highest quality standards and the most consistent level of service.
>
> We are committed to being caring and supportive corporate citizens within the world-wide communities in which we operate.
>
> We are dedicated to creating value for our shareholders and financial communities by performing in a manner that will enhance returns on investments.

Once again, the shareholders are the last constituency to be addressed in the mission statement. In addition, the emphasis is not on maximizing shareholders' wealth but on creating value for the shareholders by "performing in a manner that will enhance returns on investments." Firms such as Johnson & Johnson and NCR Corporation believe that by placing emphasis on customers, employees, and the community, the shareholders will benefit more in the long run and thus will realize a higher rate of return.

The debate over whether the organization's mission should be to create value for the stakeholder or to maximize the shareholders' wealth will continue for years to come.[12] If anything, the debate will intensify. For instance, NCR assumed a leadership role in the stakeholder movement and has been viewed as one of the best examples of how a firm can "successfully" incorporate the stakeholder concept into its mission and actual practice. Ironically, NCR's success resulted in a takeover by AT&T in 1991. In its takeover effort, AT&T argued that NCR had failed to adequately address the needs of the shareholders, sacrificing the shareholders' returns to meet the needs of the other stakeholders. The two firms had extensive ad campaigns in which each questioned what NCR's mission should be. AT&T argued that NCR belonged to the shareholders (they offered to pay $100 a share for NCR stock), and NCR's management argued that it was acting in the shareholders' long-term interest (before the AT&T takeover, NCR was trading in the mid-50s range).

The mission statement, therefore, is the cornerstone of any organization. It establishes the direction of and creates the framework for the organization.[13] Regardless of whether the mission is based on the shareholder's perspective or on the stakeholder's perspective, it provides management with the basis for setting the organization's agenda and committing its resources. Knowing who we are, what we are, and where we are going, as defined by the mission, is essential in reaching managerial decisions and actions.

Where Are We Going?
The Goals or Strategic Objectives
of the Organization

The goals or strategic objectives of an organization are the statements of what the organization wants to achieve. In a sense, they are the organization's success criteria. The organization measures its performance against these goals and then, based on that measurement, determines how well it is doing. The following are typical goal statements of many organizations:

- To be the industry leader in product quality and service
- To have a 25 percent return on investment
- To be a low-cost producer
- To be recognized as a socially responsible organization
- To have an annual growth rate of 10 percent
- To have a reputation for innovative designs
- To become the number one firm, in total sales, for the industry

As you can see, different organizations have different goals, including long- and short-term goals. Notice the role of profits in the list above. Some people believe that the desire for profits drives the organization. There are some who believe that an organization derives its goals from the needs of society and will exist only as long as its goals relate to the needs of the environment in which it operates. The assumption of the private-enterprise system is that profits will exist only as long as the products satisfy the needs of the customers and clients. And the businesses will exist only as long as the profits exist.

How Do We Get There?
Strategies

Strategy The choice of routes and directions a firm takes to achieve its goals.

Management has many alternative routes and directions available for reaching its goals. The choice of routes and directions becomes management's **strategy.** Strategies may be defined as plans that direct and outline a way to achieve some end, like a game plan. They are conceived in advance of the circumstance to which they will be applied, and they are the product of a conscious and purposeful effort. But the idea of strategy is broader than this definition.[14]

The term *strategy* has its origins in military history. The word comes from the Greek *strategia,* meaning generalship. Webster defines strategy as

> (1): the science and art of employing the political, economic, psychological, and military forces of a nation or group of nations to afford the maximum support to adopted policies in peace or war, (2) the science and art of military command exercised to meet the enemy in combat under advantageous conditions.

Military history is full of examples of generals using key strategies to turn the tide of battles. In World War II, MacArthur's strategy of bypassing islands in the South Pacific and concentrating on key bases proved successful in saving many lives; Rommel's use of rapid movements of armed forces in the North African desert demonstrated superior use of strategy.

Strategy is also used in athletics. A coach in basketball or football or a manager in baseball develops a team strategy for adjusting to changes in the strategies of opponents. Substitutions of tall or short players, fast or heavy players, left-handed pitchers or batters—all affect the outcome of the game.

Likewise, businesses use strategies for entering markets, developing new products, and most of all, dealing with competitors.[15] An example of a business using strategies to direct and allocate the resources of the firm is Chrysler.

When Lee Iacocca became president of Chrysler in 1979, Chrysler parking lots and the Michigan State Fairgrounds were filled with thousands of unsold, unwanted, rusting new Chryslers, Dodges, Plymouths. (The employees of

Ethics Issue

Corporations Plan for the Environment

Each year, *Fortune* publishes a list of America's Most Admired Corporations. In 1988, Exxon was number seven on that list, surpassed only by such perennial favorites as Wal-Mart and Merck. Then came the *Exxon Valdez* oil spill in Prince William Sound. Millions of gallons of crude oil filled the Sound, killing wildlife, covering beaches, and causing what many believed was irreparable damage to the environment. For the most part, Americans were willing to accept that accidents happen. What flabbergasted many Americans, however, was that Exxon did not move immediately to clean up the oil spill. This became a symbol of big business's not caring about anything except making money. Consumers were noticeably upset. Many cut up their Exxon credit cards and sent them back to the company. Many avoided buying Exxon products. Sales dropped. Admiration of the company plummeted. By the 1990 listing of America's Most Admired Corporations, Exxon had dropped to number 110. Experts feel that Exxon will recover from the lost economic income; they are not sure that Exxon can recover from their lost reputation. Prevention of disasters and pollution is now imperative; cleanup is no longer an acceptable option.

A 1991 *Wall Street Journal/NBC* poll found that eight of ten Americans are environmentalists, trying to make changes in their life styles that will help the environment. They are trying to recycle or to buy products that are environmentally friendly. They want corporations to do more for the environment—for example, use less packaging and use recyclable materials.

At the same time, state governments are creating legislation for the environment. California has been the leader in this area, considering banning gasoline-powered lawn mowers and open grill fires for cookouts, and establishing very strict pollution-control standards for automobile emissions. (The car companies are responding to this legislation because over 11 percent of all new cars sold are sold in California.) Many local governments are closing landfills effective in 1992; this alone will cause substantial changes in the life style of Americans. At the federal level, consumers are be-

coming dismayed by the lack of action on the part of the environmental president, George Bush.

The *Exxon Valdez,* growing consumer awareness of environmental problems, and governmental legislation have caused many companies to rethink their positions on pollution, dumping of toxic waste, and landfills.

The environment is becoming part of the mission statements and strategic plans of corporations. Some companies are actively seeking environmentalists to serve on their boards of directors to help plan the future of the business. Research is being done to create more environmentally friendly products. Companies are also trying to educate consumers about what is good for the environment.

Du Pont, McDonald's, and 3M are environmentally friendly companies. Du Pont is pulling out of a $750-million-a-year business—producing chlorofluorocarbons (CFCs)—because CFCs are considered to be harmful to the ozone layer. At the same time, Du Pont has spent over $170 million to find a safe alternative to CFCs to be used in refrigeration units, air conditioners, and spray cans. Du Pont uses environmentalism as one of the factors in determining managers' compensation. Du Pont's goal is zero pollution.

McDonald's produces hundreds of millions of pounds of paper and plastic annually. The corporation has become a leader in recycling, both in using recycled paper and in recycling the paper it uses. McDonald's is also active in environmental education.

3M is planning to meet governmental regulations years before they are required to comply. In addition, the company is going above and beyond what the government requires; its guidelines for air and water quality are stricter than the government's. Its goal is to eliminate pollution.

References: Rose Gutfeld, "Shades of Green: Eight of 10 Americans Are Environmentalists, *Wall Street Journal,* August 2, 1991, p. 1; David Kirkpatrick, "Managing/Cover Story: Environmentalism: The New Crusade," *Fortune,* February 12, 1990, pp. 44–45; David Woodruff, Than Peterson, and Karen Lowrt Miller, "Cover Story: The Greening of Detroit," *Business Week,* April 8, 1991, pp. 54–60; Jaclyn Fierman, "The Environment: The Big Muddle in Green Marketing," *Fortune,* June 3, 1991, pp. 91–101.

Chrysler used to say that they could tell whether the company was having a good or a bad year by the number of cars that were left over in the parking lots.) Maybe worst of all, cars were coming off the assembly line with loose doors, chipped paint, crooked moldings, and unidentified rattles. In addition, the foreign automobile manufacturers were gaining a reputation for producing quality cars, which meant that more and more consumers were choosing Toyotas, Hondas, and BMWs over Chrysler products. In looking at this situation, Iacocca identified a number of problems that he considered unique to Chrysler. For instance, Chrysler had a marketing system that was pushed instead of pulled (cars were produced and then salespeople were told to hard-sell the cars that had been made instead of using the pull strategy of listening and responding to consumer demand); and there was no centralized communication system—no way to get at the data needed for decisions. Iacocca also identified problems shared by Chrysler and the United States economy as a whole:

1. The quality of United States products had declined.
2. Work practices had shortchanged productivity.
3. The government had become an enemy instead of an ally.
4. Foreign countries that the United States had defeated in war and rebuilt in peace were beating this country in its own markets.

Iacocca had a decision to make: let the company go under (many people had suggested this, and Chrysler was very close to going under anyway) or try to save it. Iacocca obviously chose the latter. Iacocca claimed that saving Chrysler was also saving "the American way of doing business—with honesty, pride, ingenuity, and good old-fashioned hard work."

Iacocca and Chrysler identified and implemented numerous strategies, including the following:

1. Reduce wage and salary expenses by half the 1980 level. (Chrysler ultimately reduced its work force from 160,000 to 80,000 and received over $1.2 billion in wage and benefit sacrifices.)
2. Reduce fixed costs by over $4 billion. (Chrysler closed twenty plants and modernized the remaining forty with state-of-the-art robot and computer technology.)
3. Reduce the number of different parts by one-third. (Chrysler reduced the number of parts from 75,000 to 40,000, shaking $1 billion out of inventory in the process.)
4. Improve its weak balance sheet. (Chrysler retired its U.S. bank debt by converting $1.3 billion into preferred stock, and some preferred into common stock.)
5. Improve the quality of components and finished products. (Chrysler reduced warranty costs by 25 percent in 1982; it reduced scheduled maintenance costs to a level up to $200 below that of the competition.)
6. Implement a $6-billion product-improvement program. (Chrysler has a lead in front-wheel-drive technology; it has the best fuel economy in the industry; it offers the industry's most extensive 70,000-mile warranty.)[16]

As you can see from the Chrysler example, strategies can be very diverse in nature and scope, and they can address a wide range of organizational, managerial, and competitive concerns. Some strategies are concerned with labor costs, some with finance, some with capacity, and so forth. What is important is that strategies must be tailored to the specific situation in which an organization finds itself. A strategy that has been successful for one company may not be good for another. For instance, focusing on the development of front-wheel-drive technology would not have been appropriate for Ford. Instead, Ford focused on improving quality and gambled with a strategy to use a radically different automobile design, like its Taurus/Sable model, as a means to regain market share. This demonstrates that if a competitor successfully uses one strategy, it may mean that another organization should adopt a different one so as to take advantage of unfilled market niches. Thus, the purpose of strategy is to give an organization a competitive advantage so that when it "meets the enemy," its competition, it will win.

Although management strategies are usually set by top executives, all levels of management need to be involved in the planning of objectives and the strategies to meet the objectives, and in the implementation and control of the plan. Strategies tend to provide a base on which managers coordinate and adapt their decisions and actions to changing conditions in the external environment.

Levels of Strategy

As previously noted, strategies can address a wide range of concerns and actions. Strategies, however, seldom stand alone. They are interrelated with plans and actions, and they typically fall into an integrated hierarchy. Strategies can be classified according to three levels of organization. See Figure 6-3.

Corporate strategies
Usually determined by top management, these strategies serve as an umbrella for the organization and are based on a two- to five-year time horizon.

Corporate strategies are determined by top management and are intended to identify sets of businesses in which the corporation operates or plans to operate and provide guidelines for diversification, acquisitions, and divestitures. They serve as a guide to managers in each distinct business activity, and they are based on a two- to five-year time horizon.

Business strategies
Strategies that determine how a firm will conduct its activities in a single industry or market.

Business strategies determine how the firm will conduct its activities in a single industry or market. At this level, managers identify the niche of the industry to be served, the firm's competitive posture, and the types of customers to be targeted. Of course, for single-business enterprises, corporate and business strategies are the same.

Operating-level strategies
Strategies and tactics for the lower-level operators that provide specific guidelines for day-to-day activities.

Operating-level strategies or tactics offer lower-level operators specific guidelines as to how they will carry out day-to-day activities.

Operating-level strategies enable the firm to be flexible and adaptable in response to sudden and unexpected changes in the external environment. Business strategies serve as the underlying pattern and route used to guide managers so that their efforts will be in harmony with the decisions and actions of other managers within the same business. Corporate strategies may offer the opportunity for the corporation to shift from one business to another, to adjust to basic industrial and economic changes, or to specialize in well-defined activities.

To understand how all these levels of strategies work together, consider the analogy of sailing a boat in a race: Corporate strategies determine which race or races to enter; business strategies set the general course and position of the boat in relation to its competitors in the races entered; operating-level strategies or tactics require the pilot (manager) to "tack" or maneuver in response to changes in the wind to gain an advantage over the competition. Winning the race, as in succeeding in business, requires that all levels of strategies are integrated in a way that exploits the resources of the team or organization to their fullest potential.

What are some modes of planning?

Strategic Planning and Strategic Modes

Strategic planning can take any of three modes: (1) an **entrepreneurial mode,** in which decisions are made by intuition with bold, risky leaps; (2) an

Entrepreneurial mode
Strategic planning that is characterized by intuition and bold risky leaps.

Adaptive mode
Strategic planning that is characterized by managers who study the environment as a set of given constraints and adapt to the situation.

Planning mode
Strategic planning that is characterized by managers who use all techniques to test the probable results of available plans before taking action.

adaptive mode, in which the manager studies the environment as a set of given constraints and adapts to the situation, and (3) a **planning mode,** in which one uses all techniques available to systematically test the probable results of available plans before taking action. Each of these modes can be viewed as a possible alternative in the selection of overall strategies.

The entrepreneurial mode has obvious advantages, particularly in businesses just getting started—witness Steven Jobs and Apple Computer—but there are problems with it too. Since the direction of the firm is determined by the mental attitude of the manager, the organization may shift direction in jerks and fail to gain the advantage of momentum from experience in proceeding in a clear, consistent direction. Furthermore, this mode may boil down to indiscriminate acquisitions and purchases of anything that is a bargain or that has short-run attraction. The grass tends to look greener across the fence; when

FIGURE 6-3 Levels of Strategy for a Petroleum Company

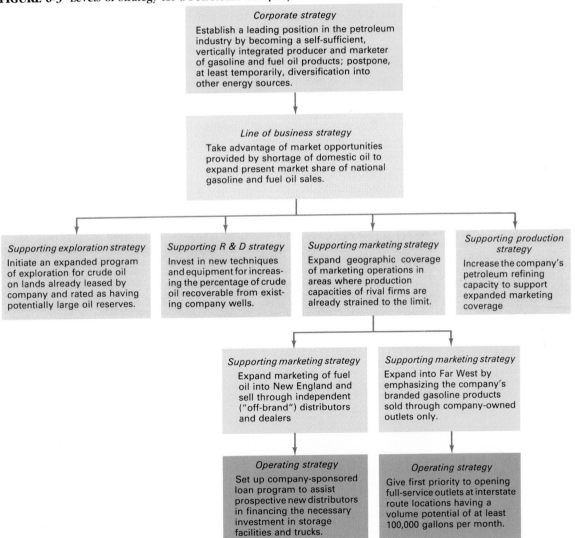

Source: Arthur Thompson, Jr., and A.J. Strickland, III, *Strategic Management: Concepts and Cases,* 3rd ed. (Plano, Tex.: Business Publications, Inc., 1984), p. 61.

entrepreneurs see another firm making good profits, they may assume that they can also make profits (even if the other firm has developed resources and competences not available to them).

For smaller firms and for firms operating in industries experiencing rapid changes, the adaptive mode for strategies can be effective. But it is important to note that there is no single mode that is best for all firms, even when they are competing in the same market. For instance, IBM and Hewlett-Packard have been competing in the computer business for years. IBM was considered to be a centrally managed firm, and Hewlett-Packard was considered to be a decentrally managed firm. IBM maintained that its approach enabled it to operate as a low-cost producer, and Hewlett-Packard argued that its approach enabled it to provide highly customized products and services to its customers. However, in 1988, both firms concluded that their respective managerial approaches were inappropriate for competing in the computer industry in the 1990s. IBM initiated a restructuring effort that attempted to decentralize its operation so that it could be more responsive to customers' needs and changing conditions. On the other hand, Hewlett-Packard felt that its decentralized approach was very inefficient, and its management decided to restructure the firm on a more centralized basis. The two firms were using different modes in an effort to adapt to what they saw as unique situations requiring their own unique solutions.

Thus, strategy is fundamentally a search for a basic direction for the organization. This search is continual, and it involves a continuing effort to identify emerging opportunities that can be exploited by the organization's changing competitive strengths and resources. For the organization, the benefit of such an approach goes beyond ensuring the organization's survival. It results in recognition, profit, success, competitive advantage, and the creation of even more opportunities.

Selection of Strategies

The selection of suitable strategies for an organization depends upon the circumstances and the environment in which the firm operates. There are a number of factors that managers need to consider when selecting strategies for their organization, business activity, or operation, as noted in Figure 6-4.

FIGURE 6-4 Important Factors in the Selection of Strategies

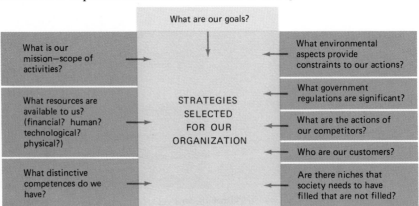

What is the most basic question?

An organization's management must address a number of questions, concerns, and issues in determining which strategies should be used. Essentially, management must first decide what the mission is, or what it should be. You would be surprised at how many businesses and managers have difficulty answering that fundamental question. Under such circumstances, it is not surprising that many organizations end up selecting strategies that are totally inappropriate. There are many other questions managers need to ask when deciding upon the organization's mission and the strategies within that mission:

- Who are our customers, or who should they be?
- What are the prospects for the industry in which we have chosen our mission?
- What unique advantages do we have?
- What advantages do our competitors have that will operate to our disadvantage?
- What resources do we have that make our mission feasible?
- Do we have distinctive competences?
- Should we develop our resources internally, or should we acquire those already in existence from outside the organization?
- What is the right time to take action?
- Should we try to change some of the environmental factors, or should we attempt to remain flexible and adapt to the environment?
- Are there niches in markets, services, and products not occupied by other organizations?
- Should we integrate vertically?
- Should we diversify or specialize?

The number of pertinent questions goes on and on! In fact, good strategic planning depends as much on identifying such critical questions as on attempting to answer them.

It is important to note that these questions should be asked on a continuing basis. Managers need to consider whether changes in the environment, technology, competition, and consumer preference make an organization's mission obsolete. An organization may need to redefine its mission, and subsequently its strategies, to continue as an enterprise. For instance, Toyota moved out of textiles into automobiles when the Japanese textile industry went into decline. The Greyhound Corporation moved out of the interstate-bus transportation business into consumer products (becoming the Greyhound-Dial Corporation) when deregulation of the airline industry made airline transportation affordable for people who traditionally had ridden the bus. In each case, the firm recognized that if it retained its mission, its future would be in doubt.

In summary, the strategy concept is important for all managers, because it tackles the important questions affecting the direction an organization takes. Its complexity is due to the following characteristics of strategies:

1. Strategies are tailored to each organization, to fit the complexity of its external environment.
2. Strategies are means for handling the uncertainty of the future.
3. Strategies change as a result of changes in the situation.
4. No strategy or group of strategies will fit all situations.

Many examples from existing businesses illustrate cases in which the strategic choice has been the basis for success and a poor choice has been the cause of failure. Furthermore, one strategy may be correct for one period of time, but a different one may be needed for another.

The use of the strategy concept is relatively new to management literature. Successful operating executives have in the past adopted appropriate strategies without publicizing their intentions in advance to competitors, for secrecy in regard to strategy is often important for its success. You seldom find a manual that explicitly states all the organization's strategies. However, you will find valuable interpretations by outside researchers and observers of past organizational strategies in books and in periodicals such as *Business Week, Fortune,* and the *Wall Street Journal.* Autobiographies of chief executive officers such as Iacocca and Pickens also provide insights into corporate strategy. If you are looking for the "secrets of success" of existing organizations, you will probably find them in their strategies.

While the idea of strategy involves charting a course within the market and external environment that uniquely fits the resources of the firm, managers also need clear guidelines for decisions and actions that enable members of the organization to coordinate their activities efficiently in planning to meet the firm's goals. We now turn to a companion concept that relates to the internal planning necessary for individuals to work as a team to implement the strategic plan.

POLICY

Policies Predetermined basic decisions that guide day-to-day decisions toward organizational goals.

Policy is the last concept associated with strategic planning that we will discuss. **Policies** are used to implement strategies. Policies are predetermined basic decisions that guide the managers of an organization in making decisions and in taking actions that lead toward the organizational goals. Whereas strategies primarily help relate the activities of the organization to its environment, policies help managers coordinate the activities and functions of people within the organization. Policies are not only decisions; they are standing long-term decisions concerning how the organization plans to accomplish its mission.

How do policies help a manager?

Policies help managers in making day-to-day decisions by providing channels and boundaries. The boundaries reduce the necessity for each manager to rethink all the factors anew; they simplify decision making by reducing the alternatives that must be considered in each situation. At times, the manager need only interpret and select the policy that applies to the individual case. Policies yield the following advantages:

1. Policies serve as precedents and reduce the need to repeatedly review all the factors in individual decisions; they save time.
2. Policies aid in coordination; if a number of managers are guided by the same policies, they can predict more accurately the actions and decisions of others in the organization.
3. Policies provide stability in the organization and reduce frustrations of members.
4. Clear policies encourage definite and forceful decisions by individual managers. Knowing the range and boundaries within which one can make a decision reduces the uncertainty about whether a decision fits in with the ideas of superiors.
5. Policies serve as a framework for guiding decisions by subordinates and enable managers to delegate authority for individual decisions.

6. Greater equity is achieved through clear policies by increasing the consistency of decisions.

Managers at all levels can make policy. Of course, the broad basic policies are made by top-level managers and are usually stated in writing. Many of these policies are long-lasting and can be collected in manuals that are available to subordinates for quick reference. Many policies, however, are unwritten and emerge through time as precedents set by individual decisions that have been made consistently in the past. In fact, if a clear policy has not been set by superiors on a particular matter, a subordinate should consider the policy implications of a single decision. What effect will the decision have on future decisions in similar situations? For example, if a manager decides to allow one subordinate to complete a report at home instead of requiring all the work to be done in the office, another subordinate, knowing of this decision, may consider it a precedent and expect that it will apply in other, similar cases in the future. If many decisions are made continually to do something in a certain way, a policy tends to emerge.

Every manager is involved in making decisions that have policy implications. In fact, if a written policy is continually ignored by a number of managers and if the superior knows of this practice and does nothing about it, it means that a new policy has emerged—to ignore the previously written statement of policy.

What does a good policy look like?

A good manager attempts to seek the advantages of using clear policies. Such use makes the job easier and more effective by allowing subordinates to make their own decisions within clearly stated limits. A good policy has the following characteristics:

1. It should guide action toward the goals of the organization and be explained to all those to whom it applies.
2. It should be stated in understandable words and usually should be in writing.
3. It should prescribe limits and channels for future action.
4. It should be subject to change but generally remain stable.
5. It must be reasonable and capable of being implemented.
6. It should allow for discretion and interpretation by those responsible for carrying it out.
7. It should be subject to periodic review.

Although policies are basic to strategic management and are generally made by top management, it should be clear from our discussion that the knowledge of how policies guide managers at all levels, and the knowledge of specific policies of one's own organization, make the idea of policy important to even the first-level manager. If you should find yourself in an organization without clear policies, you can make your job as a manager easier and more effective by asking your superior to state a policy for a particular situation that will guide you in your decisions in similar situations in the future; this action will help both you and your superior. Misinterpretations of the meaning of policies in strategic management often reduce their value. Policies are clearly distinguished from rules and procedures.

Policies are channels for making decisions, but they allow discretion by managers within certain boundaries. Rules state in precise terms what is to be done (or not done) in the same way every time, with no permitted deviations; rules permit no discretion or choice by subordinates. For example, a safety rule would state, "No explosive matter will be left in stairwells." The subordinate manager is expected to enforce this rule without deviation. No room is left for discretion; the rule serves the function of a law for fire prevention. Procedures are detailed steps to be taken to accomplish a job. For example, a clerical procedure may identify the route for the flow of a purchase order and the manner in which it will be completed. Procedures usually apply to details in planning actions; policies usually apply to boundaries in which decisions are made.

EFFECTIVE PLANNING AND STRATEGIC MANAGEMENT

Many organizations and managers use the concepts we have examined in this chapter in formulating strategic plans for their organizations. They go to great lengths to develop one-year, five-year, and ten-year plans that are beautifully printed and distributed in colorful binders. Unfortunately, the plans are filed away or stuck on shelves to collect dust. Then, one day someone decides to evaluate how well the plan worked. Typically, the evaluators discover that there was no follow-through on executing the plan. In addition, they usually determine that the plan would not have worked anyway, noting that consumers and competitors did not behave as expected and that environmental events and conditions did not occur as predicted. As a result, they conclude that the whole exercise was pointless. Nevertheless they begin the whole planning process all over again, because every organization has to have a plan.

Why do plans and strategies fail?

The reason so many plans and strategies fail is not the manner in which they were developed or the assumptions that were made. Rather they fail because the "finalized" form of the plan was not designed to be a flexible guideline for managerial actions. Most plans are written as fixed courses of action, which become invalid as soon as there is any deviation in the plan or a change in any of the operating assumptions. Effective strategic plans are those that are designed to be responsive to the dynamic and hostile environment in which an organization must operate. Although it is essential that they do establish a clear target, the "what we want to accomplish," managers should design their plans to be adaptable to the "how to get there" dimension of the plan.

Consider what happened to the Gulf Oil Company. Until the 1960s, Gulf Oil viewed itself as a fully integrated oil company. However, Gulf's management recognized that its future in the oil business was ultimately limited by the fundamental nature of its principal product, oil. Gulf knew that it would eventually run out of oil to sell. After evaluating their situation, Gulf's management decided to redefine its mission from being an oil company to being an energy resource company. Management established the goal of becoming an industry leader in the area of energy resource development. Their strategy was to focus on development and marketing of uranium resources. By the early 1970s, it was clear that their plan was a resounding success, for Gulf controlled over 50 percent of the world's known uranium deposits and supplied more uranium to nuclear power plants than all its competitors combined. Then came the nuclear disaster at Three Mile Island. Overnight, Gulf's uranium business collapsed. The firm's top management was replaced, nonoil-related ventures were terminated, and the new management adopted a wait-and-see attitude toward environmental changes. In a matter of years, Gulf's operational and financial position deteriorated so badly that it became a prime target for corporate raiders and takeover attempts. Eventually, management realized that there was nothing they could do to save the company and, in 1984, agreed to be acquired by the Chevron Corporation. In this situation, the problem was not with the plan or the strategy, the problem was management's failure to adapt the plan and the strategy to changing circumstances.

In contrast, there is AT&T. When AT&T agreed to accept the court decision in 1983 requiring that it divest itself of its local telephone operations, it developed a strategic plan for making the transition from utility company to market-driven telecommunications organization. The initial plan called for the creation of a new division, known as American Bell, which would be responsible for marketing AT&T products. After a year of operation, AT&T's management realized that the American Bell approach was not going to work. They revised their plan and restructured their operation accordingly. Over the next few years, AT&T's management continued to revise their plans and restructure their operations in response to changing competitive forces and environmental factors. But revisions and restructures were always made with an eye to moving AT&T toward being the number one telecommunications organization in the world. For AT&T, there has been much trial and error, but, unlike Gulf, it has applied the concepts of effective strategic management and planning to continue to move the organization forward.

The challenge facing today's managers is how to effectively employ strategic management and planning concepts. The world is such that organizations can no longer just tread water; they must be responsive and adaptive if they are to remain competitive. Strategic management and planning are means to achieve success and enable an organization to survive in the long run.

SUMMARY

Many concepts and principles from the chapter on decision making formed the base for this chapter on planning and strategic management. After an early section on definitions, examples, and the importance of planning, you read of some forecasting techniques. The bulk of this chapter dealt with components of strategic management. Here you read of companies that succeeded and failed; frequently, the difference could be found in each company's attention to strategic management.

To see how a firm's mission and strategies become a part of the manager's behavior, we introduced you to the important management concept of policies.

KEY TERMS

Planning   The function performed by managers that determines the pattern of actions needed for meeting situations in the future in order to attain organizational goals.

Strategic management   The setting of long-range plans, selection of strategies and policies, and allocation of resources for reaching a goal.

Stakeholders All those groups that have an interest in the actions of a firm; includes the shareholders, customers, employees, suppliers, and communities.

Strategy The choice of routes and directions a firm takes to achieve its goals.

Corporate strategies Usually determined by top management, these strategies serve as an umbrella for the organization and are based on a two- to five-year time horizon.

Business strategies Strategies that determine how a firm will conduct its activities in a single industry or market.

Entrepreneurial mode Strategic planning that is characterized by intuition and bold risky leaps.

Operating-level strategies Strategies and tactics for the lower-level operators that provide specific guidelines for day-to-day activities.

Adaptive mode Strategic planning that is characterized by managers who study the environment as a set of given constraints and adapt to the situation.

Planning mode Strategic planning that is characterized by managers who use all techniques to test the probable results of available plans before taking action.

Policies Predetermined basic decisions that guide day-to-day decisions toward organizational goals.

STUDY ASSIGNMENTS

1. Why has planning become so important in today's competitive environment?

2. Knowing that the worldwide demand for tires was just about cut in half with the introduction of the radial tire, what strategic actions could the management of Firestone, General Tire, Uniroyal, and Goodrich have taken in order to redirect the resources of their firms in a way to ensure organizational survival?

3. Why is it essential for today's manager to understand and be sensitive to the changing conditions, and how can managers use that awareness in developing a response to that change?

4. Why do businesses like People Express so often fail after achieving some degree of success? (A suggestion: First, identify some businesses, small or large, that have failed; then, examine the reasons why they failed.)

5. How can the various types of forecasting techniques aid managers in making decisions and in planning future operations?

6. Compare and contrast the mission statements of the Zale Corporation (a retail business) and the Niagara Mohawk Power Company (a utility).

7. Prepare statements to support the argument that the mission of a corporation should be:
   a. To maximize the shareholders' wealth
   b. To create value for the stakeholders

8. Throughout the 1980s, GM, Ford, and Chrysler struggled to compete against the Japanese automobile manufacturers. It appears that this struggle is continuing in the 1990s. With that in mind, develop some strategies for the American automobile manufacturers that are designed to improve their ability to compete against the Japanese automobile manufacturers.

9. Compare and contrast the missions, goals, and strategies of a small mom-and-pop restaurant in your community and a large national fast-food chain (like Wendy's or Pizza Hut). What factors influence the types of strategies that a small restaurant uses, as opposed to the types of strategies that a fast-food chain uses?

10. Explain the distinction between strategies and policies.

11. Many observers have argued that Gulf Oil made the right decision in redefining its mission as an energy company and in implementing a strategy that focused on developing the uranium resources. What do you think about Gulf's decision to redefine its mission and subsequently enter the uranium market? What action should Gulf's management have taken to prevent the demise of the firm?

12. As we move toward the twenty-first century, what changes in the economic, social, and political environment do you envision that will influence a manager's ability to develop and execute effective planning and strategic management?

Case for Discussion

THE KYLE CORPORATION

The success of the Kyle Corporation was considered quite remarkable by many observers of the automobile accessories industry. Since its founding five years ago, the firm has developed and marketed one of the best radar detectors, the Ranger, sold in the United States. Both the success of the product and the financial performance of the corporation exceeded the expectations of the firm's founders, John Teteris and Blake Covington. What was even more remarkable was that the demand for the Ranger had remained strong and was continuing to grow. However, this unexpected level of success was creating problems for the Kyle Corporation, problems that would lead unexpectedly to business failure.

The firm began operating during the last year of the CB equipment rage, which was a time when many CB manufacturers were beginning to experience a rapid decline in sales. Although most analysts predicted that the Kyle Corporation would do well during its first two years of operations, many believed that its performance would follow the same pattern as a number of CB manufacturers. The analysts believed that in the beginning there would be a substantial demand for radar detectors but that the market would quickly become saturated, demand would sag, and most of the firms making detectors would be bankrupt within five years.

But the analysts were wrong. As it turned out, demand for radar detectors did not follow the quick rise and fall experienced by CB equipment. Instead, demand remained strong, and many firms that had a reputation for manufacturing high-quality detectors, such as the Ranger, found that demand for the product exceeded their production capabilities.

Because the Ranger had been rated as the best radar detector by a number of car magazines, demand for it was exceptionally high. John and Blake viewed this situation as a mixed blessing. They were concerned that their limited production capacity was leaving a considerable amount of the demand for the Ranger unfilled and that over time, this condition would result in lost customers and market share. The corporation's financial advisers were also concerned about this problem, and they were pressuring John and Blake to expand the firm's capacity by building new production facilities. Currently, the

Kyle Corporation is located in a renovated warehouse. There is no room at that location either to build an addition onto the warehouse or to construct new facilities. As a result, the Kyle Corporation could only expand its capacity by building new production facilities at another location.

Despite additional encouragement to expand from the firm's investors, John and Blake were unsure that the cost of an expansion would be in the best interest of the corporation. They were concerned that the firm was too vulnerable to expand solely because of demand considerations. They realized that the firm was a one-product operation. In addition, they recognized that the detector's technology could be easily duplicated. On the other hand, they were aware of market research that indicated that demand for state-of-the-art detectors would remain strong in the United States for the next ten years. The researchers also pointed out that the European market had yet to be exploited by any radar detector manufacturer. But the researchers also noted that in the future, manufacturers would have to market their detectors through major retailers if they wanted to continue profitable operations. Everyone realized that the Kyle Corporation did not have either the management or the production capacity to distribute the Ranger through the major retailers. As a result, John and Blake believed that the corporation was in a no-win situation.

The management team of the Kyle Corporation consists of twelve individuals. All the managers are less than thirty-five years' old and, with the exception of John, Blake, and the vice president of sales, they all began working at the Kyle Corporation immediately after graduating from college. As for John and Blake, they were both electrical engineers, who previously worked as electronics designers for a leading high-tech manufacturer. Neither John nor Blake had any operational management experience before starting the Kyle Corporation. Blake assumed most of the operational responsibilities because he had earned an M.B.A., and John assumed most of the technical and design responsibilities. From the beginning, the two realized that their lack of managerial expertise might prove to be a handicap. However, they were able to achieve success by virtue of having a quality product and a bit of luck, by avoiding any serious managerial screw-ups, and, according to John and Blake, by the hard work, dedication, and motivation of their employees.

There are about sixty full-time and twenty-five part-time production workers employed by the Kyle Corporation. Most of the employees enjoy working for the firm, mainly because of the cooperative spirit that exists between management and the employees. The firm offers a compensation and benefit package that is above average for the type of work the employees do. In addition, there are various incentive and profit-sharing plans and considerable overtime, which provides the employees with added income. The employees are not unionized, and there has not been any effort to organize them.

The production of the Ranger is rather simple. Only a few parts, such as the detector casing, are manufactured at the firm. All the other electronic parts are easily assembled. Production consists of simple assembly-line tasks, such as soldering. These tasks require only minimum training, and the employees need to have only basic skills to perform them. Because of the simple technology involved in putting together the Ranger, the employees can perform a variety of tasks. As a result, they are allowed to change jobs with one another at their own discretion. The only area of production in which there is considerable managerial involvement is that of quality assurance. But even in that area, the management of employees has been relatively easy, because employees are highly motivated and they have become committed to making a quality product. In addition, employees are urged to suggest ways to improve quality or production, and they receive financial rewards if their ideas are implemented.

John and Blake know that their firm is at a critical point in its existence. Although they like the way the firm operates and the family environment they have created, they realize that continued success can be achieved only by reducing the corporation's vulnerability and expanding its production capabilities as well as its capacity. They have scheduled a meeting next week with their financial advisers, principal investors, and key management personnel. At that time, John and Blake plan to make some strategic decisions that will define the future direction of the Kyle Corporation.

Chapter 7

Organizing: Designing The Formal Structure

Learning Objectives

1. **State** why specialization calls for organizing.
2. **Identify** the basic means available for coordinating activities.
3. **Construct** an organization chart illustrating line, staff, and functional authority.
4. **State** six classical principles of organizing.
5. **State** the basic guidelines for organizing using the bureaucratic mechanistic form.
6. **State** the basic guidelines for organizing using the organic form.
7. **Discuss** five groups of contingency factors affecting the appropriate form for a specific organization.
8. **Illustrate** two new types of structure found to be useful in modern organizations.

"D R. Sharp, I've asked you to meet with me," said Sam Price, President and chief executive officer of Price Construction Company, "to advise us on the proper organization for our company. Frankly, I don't see any problems with our present structure, but we haven't taken a look at the question for ten years, during which time we have increased total revenue from $5 million to $17 million and have changed some activities. When I started this business twenty-five years ago, I ran the company myself. Now we operate in three regions for our paving jobs, with supporting rock quarries and asphalt plants; participate in three joint ventures internationally; operate a coal tipple with sales to large users; and, from time to time, we've developed several residential subdivisions and other activities that appeared to promise profit. Although I don't plan to retire completely even though I am sixty-five, I have three sons who have graduated from college; one with an arts degree is learning the company operations in hopes of taking over from me. You have been here several days surveying our personnel and operations. What have you found?"

"Well, Mr. Price, I have studied your records, interviewed your key executives, and learned a good deal about your growth from the beginning. I would say that your organization has evolved over the years from a small, aggressive proprietorship to a somewhat diversified operation. As I see it, you have always been interested in venturing into new areas; in short, your interests are those of an entrepreneur. Now, you would like to be free to search out new opportunities and withdraw from day-to-day management. With a couple of experienced general managers and several sons who might become more active, you

want to plan your organization structure for the future to accommodate your sons and also retain the necessary skilled engineers and nonfamily management personnel. A good organizational structure could help your key personnel understand their authority and expectations for advancement in the company."

"Also," said Price, "I'm very concerned about the fact that even though we have made good profits on individual contracts over the last five growth years, our overhead has increased so rapidly that our net income is not much greater than it was when we were much smaller. We've added to our staff departments of personnel and accounting and now have a nice computer operation; yet, even with these added organizational support groups, our efficiency seems to be less. When we were small, we made good money, but as we have increased our gross revenue, we seem to stand still in profitability."

"Mr. Price, your recent experience is not unusual. When you were small, you didn't worry much about organization, since you could supervise most of the operations yourself, but as you have obtained new business, you have had to depend on others to help manage operations. You cannot do everything yourself, and therefore we must develop a structure so that your managers can work more efficiently as a team."

"I guess you're right. I said at the beginning that I didn't see any problems with our present structure. After this brief talk with you, I can see that we should have given more attention to organizational matters long ago. I've added expensive technical people, such as engineers, accountants, and lawyers, who seem to be motivated but lack coordination of their efforts, resulting in slippages and inefficiency. I've observed, however, that my friends in other construction companies have structures that wouldn't fit our situation. Is there some ideal design that we all should have?"

"No, it is generally agreed now that there is no universal pattern that fits all. Your structure will need to be tailored to your specific situation. Your best structure depends upon a number of factors. First, your increase in size has created new demands by adding personnel that have increased your overhead costs. Second, many changes have occurred in your environment—such as changing demands by customers, increased government regulations, inflation, the labor market, and many others. Third, your engineers have been keeping up with new technological improvements, but your structure has not changed to adjust to this technology. Fourth, your strategy of entering new activities has created new demands on your structure. Your variety of activities has resulted in more complexity than you had as a small, single-product company. Finally, your style of leadership and the attitudes of your management personnel have a strong effect on your structure. For example, although you have hired a number of well-educated managers who can make good decisions, you tend to want them to refer to you many matters in which you feel your experience is required—in short, more delegation seems to be in order. To arrive at a better design of organization, we'll have to consider all these factors." ■

The opening case identifies some of the problems of organization that develop as a company grows. Mr. Price did not need to worry about structure as long as he could perform all functions himself by means of direct supervision. With increasing size and complexity of activities, the company needs to take a close look at other methods of coordinating its activities. As the Price Construction Company grew, it sought help from management seminars and books on organizing but found that many fashionable ideas used by larger companies in other industries tended to increase costs. Although gross revenue increased greatly, net profits did not increase accordingly. In short, while division of labor was necessary, the pattern for coordinating these additional parts was sketchy; Price needed to focus on organizing, a second management function. In Chapter 2, you saw that the organizing function received considerable attention from early classical writers. In fact, some believed that they had discovered certain basic principles of organizing that all types of companies could use in all situations. Although those principles proved to be useful in a number of firms of that day, later contributions have raised serious questions about how well they fit changing conditions and types of operations.

In this chapter, we examine the organizing function in five sections. First, we discuss its essence, definition, and key conceptual components. Second, we summarize the classical principles. Third, we explain the bases of two different theories of organizing. In the fourth section, we recommend a contingency theory for selecting an appropriate structure. Finally, we introduce two types of structure that have proved valuable in practice.

THE ESSENCE OF ORGANIZING

Why organize?

First, why do managers need to organize? The answer is that when people attempt to engage cooperatively in any activity, two forces must be considered:

the specialization of tasks and the coordination of efforts. This cooperative effort may be to win a baseball game, to offer health services in a hospital, to provide community services by a government agency or a voluntary service group, or to produce a product or service for a profit. In all these activities, people need to know what tasks they will perform and how they can coordinate those tasks; they need to organize.

Organizing The function of determining the structure for allocating individual (specialized) tasks and coordinating activities toward the organizational structure.

What is involved?

Organizing is the process of determining the structure for allocating individual (specialized) tasks and coordinating activities toward the organization's goals. Thus, organized effort involves (1) selecting the activities that must be accomplished to achieve the organization's objectives, (2) allocating those activities in some pattern so that each part can perform its required duties, and (3) developing a means by which each part can achieve coordination.

Methods for Gaining Coordination

Coordination A condition where departments, people, and tasks are designed or managed so that their activities merge into achieving a unified goal.

Coordination is a condition where departments, people, work groups, tasks, etc., are designed or managed so that their activities merge into achieving a unified goal. When Mr. Price first went into business, he was able to organize by determining what needed to be done, hiring several people, allocating specific tasks to each, and coordinating the operations by direct supervision.

Managers must constantly ask themselves if they need to restructure their organization. More people are being assigned to projects, teams, or short-lived task groups. Managers will need to be aware of the changes in peopie, assignments, equipment, and relationships. New organizational designs may be called for.

Whenever employees wanted to know what to do, they merely asked him for instructions. Thus, Price used one simple method of coordination—direct supervision of each member of the organization. The firm was small enough so that Price could mentally picture the structure, since he tended to do the coordination himself. Mentally, he visualized the necessary relationships of the tasks; he did not place his thoughts on paper in a chart or another observable form.

As this small organization grew, the number of employees increased, and no longer could each person repeatedly seek instructions for every needed activity; the employees tended to become acquainted with the tasks expected and to understand how their work related to that of others. When Price was absent, and without a written description of the tasks, each spontaneously and naturally learned to work with fellow employees without depending upon an explicit design. At that stage, Mr. Price still may not have needed to consciously design a structure.

Coordination was achieved not only by direct supervision but also by mutual adjustment of the members among themselves. In the language of management, the employees tended to form informal organizations—that is, interpersonal groups in reaction to situations—naturally, without conscious design. Individuals who work together learn what needs to be done; what others can do best; what others' interests, attitudes, and skills are; what actions others tend to take in different situations; and how to work together to achieve their individual and group objectives. Even if Price did not, at that stage, consciously design a formal pattern of tasks for each group of employees, the organization may have become coordinated through the skills of individual members. This second method of coordination (mutual adjustment) may be both effective and efficient as long as employee turnover remains low; however, groups may form informal organizations that conflict, and as new people are added, each will require time "to learn the ropes" from other members. In the meantime, Price would become too busy performing other managerial functions, and perhaps marketing and production functions as well, to gain coordination through direct supervision.

When the organization arrives at the stage where coordination can no longer be gained through direct supervision or through mutual adjustment, Price will be forced to organize members into logical components (departments) and to focus on providing an explicit plan for the structure. At this stage, he needs to design a formal structure to maintain coordination. Coordination, then, must be planned before the work is accomplished. He may decide (1) to standardize the content of the work by describing exactly what is expected of each individual and group, (2) to standardize the results of the work by setting specifications and performance standards, or (3) to standardize the types of skills required and group together people having similar skills.[1]

Many operations of the Price Construction Company require that certain tasks be performed, such as rock crushing, grading, paving, maintaining safety, and keeping records. In such cases, the content or description of the tasks could be the basis for coordination. Other operations, such as the construction of a road or a bridge, or producing a given quantity of rock from a quarry, could be grouped by projects organized to achieve a desired result. In addition, certain activities may require similar skills, such as surveying, making engineering designs, maintaining an accounting system, or interviewing applicants for jobs. Coordination could be attained by placing together all personnel with specified education, training, or skills. For example, accountants, engineers, lawyers, and other professionals could be grouped into different departments.

What Organizing Involves

Increasing specialization of activities, projects, and skills requires that managers look to elements within their control to gain coordination by designing, mapping out, and deliberately planning the duties and relationships of people in the organization. In summary, the organizing function seeks

1. To establish efficient and logical patterns of interrelationships among members of the organization
2. To secure advantages of specialization whereby the optimum utilization of talents can be realized
3. To coordinate activities of the various parts to facilitate the realization of the goals of the organization

The design of a formal structure to achieve these three objectives requires that management construct a clear flow of **authority** throughout the organization. Earlier, we defined authority as the right to decide or act, and so we need to provide a clear picture for each member of the organization of the duties and authority necessary to accomplish the organizational objectives.

We turn now to a basic technique for explicitly showing the authority relationships. As you observe how authority is organized through structure, remember that effective authority still requires acceptance by subordinates (Chester I. Barnard's Acceptance Theory of Authority).

Organization Charts

Authority The right to decide or act.

How do organization charts help?

Organization charts are nothing more than maps of positions and their authority relationships. In the field of management, there are three types of authority used in designing organizations: line, staff, and functional.

Line authority The direct and general authority over subordinates in an organization's most important activities.

Line authority is the broadest and simplest. Each position has direct authority for taking actions, with complete authority over lower positions in the hierarchy. A manager with line authority is the unquestioned superior for all activities of subordinates. The flow of authority is simple, direct, and uncomplicated, so that conflicts of authority are reduced and quick action is possible.

Staff authority Advisory authority that provides expert specialists for line authority.

Staff authority is purely advisory to the position of line authority. A person with staff authority studies a problem, seeks alternatives, and decides on recommendations, but has no authority to put the recommendations into action. A position with staff authority may be generalist in nature (as an "assistant to") and may serve as an extension of the line position to relieve it of any details it has limited time to handle. Staff authority also provides specialists who have expert abilities for such functions as planning, fact finding, and analysis.

Functional authority Permits specialists in a given set of activities to enforce directives within a clearly defined scope of authority.

Functional authority focuses on achieving advantages of specialization and permits the specialist in a given set of activities (such as accounting, engineering, or law) to enforce directives within a limited and clearly defined scope of authority. In one sense, the staff person with functional authority has really been given line authority over certain areas. Staff becomes desirable when the line needs advisory help; however, the coordination of a staff complicates the problems of the superior. Functional authority reduces such problems by permitting orders to flow directly from specialists at higher levels to specialists at lower levels without involving line managers with routine technical instructions.

Figure 7-1 illustrates the simplest organization chart; it shows only line authority. Each position is represented by a box, and the flow of authority is represented by straight lines. Mr. Price might have used this simple chart soon after he organized the construction company.

Figure 7-1 shows the flow of authority by lines from the top manager down through the middle managers to the workers. It shows the positions of managers and the location of responsibility. It further shows the lines through which reports are made by subordinates in accounting for their actions, and the route of delegation of authority. It does not attempt to show communication channels, nor does it picture informal relationships and mutual adjustments among subordinates.

Figure 7-2 illustrates a structure expanded to include all three types of authority. The staff position is connected by a line of authority from the top, with the returning line for flow of advisory reports. The functional position differs from the staff position, since the line of flow of its limited authority goes to its counterpart at a lower level of the organization. For example, the upper functional position may be the central accounting department, with directives flowing to a subordinate accountant reporting to the middle line manager. Such a functional flow of accounting enables the subordinate accountant to receive specific accounting directives without their flowing through the middle line manager.

Line authority is the backbone of hierarchy; staff and functional authority merely supplement the line. In designing an actual organization, the practicing manager must choose how to use each of these types. Table 7-1 summarizes the advantages and disadvantages of each to provide a basis for this choice.

Figure 7-1 Chart Showing Flow of Line Authority Only

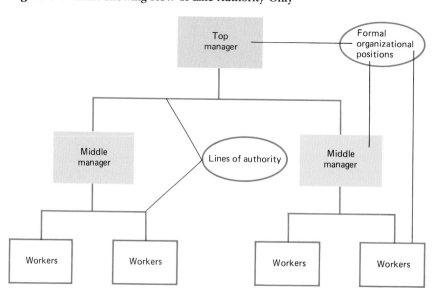

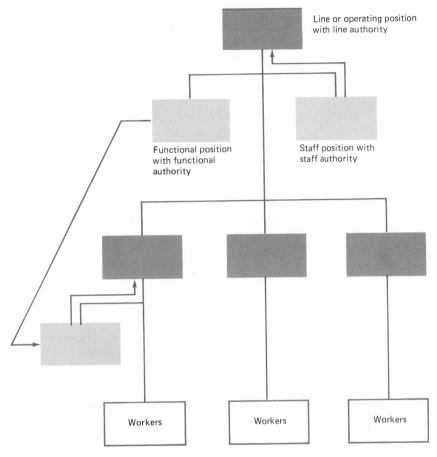

Line or operating position with line authority

Functional position with functional authority

Staff position with staff authority

Workers

Workers

Workers

Figure 7-2 Chart Showing the Three Types of Authority in Organizations

TABLE 7-1 Comparison of Line, Staff, and Functional Authority	
ADVANTAGES	**DISADVANTAGES**
Line Authority	
Maintains simplicity	Neglects specialists in planning
Makes clear division of authority	Overworks key personnel
Encourages speedy action	Depends on retention of a few key people
Staff Authority	
Enables specialists to give expert advice	Confuses organization if functions are not clear
Frees the line executive of detailed analysis	Reduces power of experts to place recommendations into action
Affords young specialists a means of training	Tends toward centralization of organization
Functional Authority	
Relieves line executives of routine specialized decisions	Makes relationships more complex
Provides framework for applying expert knowledge	Makes limits of authority of each specialist a difficult coordination problem
Relieves pressure of need for large numbers of well-rounded executives	Tends toward centralization of organization

These charts represent plans for authority flow. If changes evolve in actual exercise of authority, the charts will need continual changes or they may not represent changing authority flows.

Charts have important uses in the design of a logical structure:

1. They identify the positions in the structure.
2. They aid the manager's mental process in designing authority relationships.
3. They are especially useful for orienting a new person or an outsider to the structure.
4. They provide the point of departure for making changes in authority relationships.

CLASSICAL PRINCIPLES OF ORGANIZATION DESIGN

You may now be asking, "Okay, with these basic concepts and a charting technique, what guidelines are there for securing coordination by planning and standardizing specialized units?" We now turn to six principles proposed by classical writers. Although these principles are no longer considered applicable to all organizations, they continue to offer a foundation upon which managers can build a workable structure.

Unity of Command

Unity of command
No member of an organization should report to more than one superior on any single function.

One of the traditional principles, generally referred to as **unity of command,** states that no member of an organization should report to more than one superior on any single function. The application of this principle is easy in a pure line organization, in which each superior has general authority; however, it becomes a complex problem in actual cases in which some form of staff or functional organization is used. In practice, instructions may be received from several sources without loss of productivity. The central problem is to avoid conflict in orders from different people relating to the same subject. You should recognize immediately that the actions of a subordinate may be influenced by many people who are not recognized in the formal hierarchy of authority. The unity-of-command principle simply means that subordinates need to know from whom they receive the authority to make decisions and take actions.

Exception Principle

Exception principle
The concept that recurring decisions should be delegated, allowing superiors time to make the most important, nonrepetitive decisions.

The **exception principle** states that recurring decisions should be handled in a routine manner by lower-level managers, whereas problems involving unusual matters should be referred to higher levels. This principle emphasizes that executives at top levels of an organization have limited time and capacity and should not become bogged down in routine details that can be handled as well by subordinates. Thus, it is an important concept in the delegation of authority in an organization.

The exception principle can be very useful to a manager by focusing attention on those matters that should receive attention first. It is applicable at all levels and, if kept in mind, can help the inexperienced manager compensate for the human tendency to concentrate on the immediate, concrete, and detailed problems at the expense of the more fundamental, difficult, and abstract issues.

The principle has remained important in modern applications because of the distinction it makes between programmed and nonprogrammed decisions. Programmed decisions are those that are repetitive and routine and can be handled by a definite procedure. Nonprogrammed decisions involve new, one-shot, and unstructured elements that require tailored handling by superiors. Programmed decisions may be easily delegated; nonprogrammed decisions often need the attention of the superior.

Span of Control

Span of control The limit of the number of subordinates that one superior should supervise.

A third principle involves the manager's **span of control**: There is a limit to the number of subordinates that one superior should supervise. This principle becomes highly controversial when it states the exact number of subordinates that should report to a superior. The determination of the optimum number depends on many factors in a given organization and should always be tied directly to the number of levels in the hierarchy. If it appears that a small span of control for each manager is desirable, then the number of necessary levels will be larger than would be the case with a larger span of control. With the downsizing of most corporations during the 1980s and the resultant elimination of many levels of middle management, a larger span of control, with a flatter structure, is much more common. The organization with more levels is considered "tall," whereas the organization with a larger span of control is "flat." Figures 7-3 and 7-4 illustrate tall and flat organizations. A tall structure with small spans of control assumes that coordination can be attained only by direct supervision. A flat structure with large spans of control assumes that mutual adjustment among subordinates can handle much of the coordination of members.

The appropriate span depends upon four principal factors:

Figure 7-3 A Tall Organization Structure with Geographical Departmentation

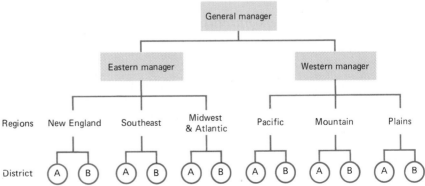

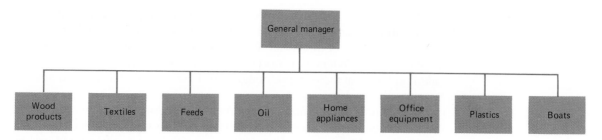

Figure 7-4 A Flat Organization Structure with Product Departmentation

1. The competence of managers in delegating authority and responsibility varies, and thus the optimum span in an organizational structure depends on the skills of the managers. The span for those who can delegate more authority can be much larger than for those who can delegate little authority.

2. The level of motivation of subordinate personnel is both a determinant and a result of the span of control. Increased motivation permits a larger span; interestingly, it has also been found that a larger span increases motivation.

3. The existence of a good information system and free communication flow is the basis for increased span. If subordinates have access to necessary information, they can take action without close supervision from above.

4. The nature of the job affects span, since a routine, stable operation can be handled by subordinates without close supervision, whereas a diverse and changing job requires a smaller span of control.

One useful approach in applying these factors is to analyze the need of subordinates for services of their superior and the rate at which the superior can supply those services. The optimum span can be determined by balancing the cost of the subordinates' waiting time against the cost of the superior's time.

Span of control refers to the number of people that one person can supervise directly. A related and probably more useful idea is the span of management, which refers to the number of people whom one superior can assist, teach, and help reach their objectives—that is, the number who have access to the superior. The span of management can probably be larger than the span of control.

Scalar Principle

Scalar principle The concept that holds that authority and responsibility should flow in a clear, unbroken line or chain of command from the highest to the lowest manager.

A fourth principle, the **scalar principle**, states that authority and responsibility should flow in a clear, unbroken line, or chain of command, from the highest to the lowest manager. One writer describes this vertical relationship as a job-task pyramid. The principle simply states that an organization is a hierarchy.[2] The importance and usefulness of the principle is evident whenever the line is severed. The splintering of one organization into two or more results from a permanent breach of this principle. Temporary breaches, however, are not uncommon, although they are frequently subtle and unrecognized. The tendency of an aggressive executive to fight the control of superiors can create an environment for forming an "empire" that is uncoordinated with the larger organization.

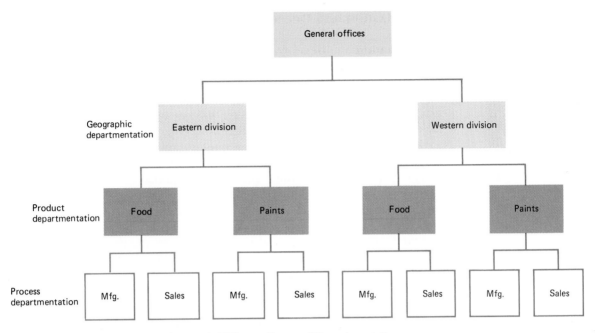

Figure 7-5 An Organization Chart with Different Types of Departmentation

Departmentation

Departmentation The manner in which activities should be divided and formed into specialized groups.

How can activities be grouped?

The manner in which activities should be divided and formed into specialized groups is usually referred to as **departmentation**. The purpose of departmentation is to specialize activities, simplify the tasks of managers, and maintain control. Several types of departmentation are possible: geographical, by customer, by process or equipment, by product, or by professional skills. Often, different types are used at different levels of the organization structure. For example, Figure 7-5 illustrates geographical departmentation at the top level, product at the second level, and process at the third.

No single formula for departmentation applies to all situations. The following criteria may help the organization planner:

1. Similar activities may be grouped together, based upon similarity of qualifications or common purpose—for example, medical and dental personnel.
2. An activity may be grouped with other activities with which it is used—for example, safety with production.
3. Functions may be assigned to that executive who is most interested in performing them well.
4. Activities may be grouped to encourage competition or to avoid friction among departments.
5. If it is difficult to make definite distinctions between two activities, they may be grouped together.
6. Certain functions that require close coordination would increase problems of higher-level managers if they were separated; such functions should be grouped together.
7. All activities related to the completion of a project can be grouped together.

Centralization and Decentralization

Centralization
A condition in an organization where authority and decision making is primarily positioned at the top of the structure.

Decentralization The process of delegating authority to lower-level managers.

Centralization and **decentralization** refer to the location of authority and decision making in the organization. If authority and decision making are positioned primarily at the top of the structure, centralization exists. If authority and decision making are distributed to lower levels, decentralization exists. Centralization and decentralization are matters of degree, and a practicing manager continually faces the question of whether to centralize or decentralize. Centralization is warranted when the decision must be made at a higher level, when status in dealing with outside people is important, when consistency of policies and procedures is of special importance, in some cases of extreme emergency, such as fire or civil disturbance, or when the organization is relatively small, the people are untrained or uncommitted, and there is a high need for coordination. Two important considerations determine the degree of decentralization desirable in a given situation. First, the amount of skills and competence possessed by subordinate managers influences the success of any program of decentralization; managers must be developed who can adequately handle the authority delegated to them. Second, the distribution of the necessary information to points of decision is critical to any delegation process; an executive with insufficient information available for making a decision will have little chance to make a good one.

Decentralization has certain advantages: (1) Authority can be spread and actions can be implemented quickly, without awaiting approval from higher levels; (2) managers at lower levels have more flexibility to adjust to changing conditions; (3) managers tend to develop more quickly in, and initiative is encouraged by, a more challenging situation.

On the other hand, the disadvantages are significant: (1) control and coordination at the top level are more difficult, since the top manager may not be aware of critical problems as they emerge; (2) duplication of effort by the more autonomous divisions tends to reduce the advantage of specialization in activities provided for the organization as a whole. Also, a unique professional specialist or an expensive special-purpose machine or computer system may be hoarded by one decentralized unit and not shared with other units.

The reason that the principle of decentralization has become increasingly important is that in modern society, more people are becoming highly educated and thus more competent to make decisions, and these people continually press for greater "democratic" participation in organizations. It would be wrong, however, to conclude that all companies are moving to a decentralized form. Honda Motor Company is centralizing certain functions because it feels it has grown too big for democracy.[3]

These six design principles give managers means by which they can build coordinative mechanisms into their structure. We now turn to the different organization design models that have been used by practicing managers. The first, the mechanistic model (also called the bureaucratic model) applies classical principles; the second, the organic model, emphasizes the opposite features.

Global Application

Joint Ventures

Joint ventures, the sharing of ownership and operations by two or more companies, often with different national homes, is a structural arrangement that is being used more frequently as global opportunities expand.

Many American corporations have worried that the European Common Market planned for 1992 will set up barriers, making Europe a "fortress" and blocking U.S. involvement. As a measure to protect themselves, American firms have increased their direct investment in Europe, as the following examples show.

- PepsiCo paid $1.4 billion for two leading makers of snacks—Smiths Crisps and Walkers Crisps (United Kingdom).
- Pfizer bought Medinvent, a manufacturer of medical equipment, for an undisclosed sum (Switzerland).
- Ford bought carmaker Jaguar for $2.5 million (United Kingdom).
- AT&T bought 20 percent of Italtel for $135 million (Italy).
- International Paper paid $300 million for papermaker Aussedat Rey (France).
- GM acquired half of Saab-Scandia's passenger-car operations for $600 million (Sweden).
- Businessland bought Bowee Systemvertrieb, a personal-computer dealer, for an undisclosed price (Germany).

The Americans are finding the process filled with frustration. The uncertainty in the Soviet Union spreads to all the agencies involved in the joint-venture process. Some firms are willing to be patient in expectation of the potential payoffs; others are turning to the countries of Eastern Europe.

American students visiting communist countries in the early 1990s found that their blue jeans made for great trading on the black market. The desire for American products led Levi Strauss to produce blue jeans at its factory in Kiskunhalas, Hungary, and the venture with Texcoop has proved to be successful, as have the joint venture between General Electric and Tungsram Company and the joint venture between Schwinn Bicycle Company and Csepel in Budapest. Such experiences excite Europeans who seek to become more market oriented in both business planning and production.

When joint ventures involve the giants of an industry, however, there is no excitement; there is fear. Such was the case when Daimler Benz and Mitsubishi announced their plans for intensive cooperation among their auto, aerospace, and electronics divisions. The shock waves rolled across North America, Europe, and Asia.

References: "America's New Rush to Europe," *Business Week,* March 26, 1990, pp. 48–49; "Big Deals Run into Big Trouble in the Soviet Union," *Business Week,* March 19, 1990, pp. 58–59; "Ventures in Hungary Test Theory That West Can Uplift East Block," *Wall Street Journal,* April 5, 1990, p. 1; "A Waltz of Giants Sends Shock Waves Worldwide," *Business Week,* March 19, 1990, pp. 59–60.

MECHANISTIC AND ORGANIC MODELS

Using the elements just discussed, theorists have advocated two opposing models for designing work and relationships: mechanistic (also known as bureaucratic) and organic. Although these two models are at opposite ends of a continuum (see Figure 7-6), they reflect developments at different stages of economic history. When the machine age of the Industrial Revolution (1750s) moved into the factory system (1830s), managers understandably viewed organizational problems as if they were machine problems. Max Weber,[4] a German sociologist of the early twentieth century, saw the parallels between the mechanization of industry and the design of other forms of organization, primarily bureaucracies.

Until the middle of the twentieth century, the mechanistic model was the only comprehensive model available for designing structure; therefore, it was assumed to be applicable to all organizations. Then, some 75 to 100 years after the beginning of the factory system in the United States, behavioral scientists using the results of research on individual and group behavior advocated a second general-purpose model, which we shall call the organic model. Chris Argyris, Warren Bennis, Rensis Likert,[5] and Douglas McGregor were the leading contributors to this model, which they proposed as a general-purpose theory for all organizations, conflicting directly with the highly formalized mechanistic model. Until the last two decades, organization design involved a choice between these two opposed models, both claiming universal applications. Since both serve as the foundation of a unifying approach to be discussed in the next section, we will first clarify the components of each.

Mechanistic model
A model that suggests that the best way to organize a company is by planning rationally, objectively, and in advance; subjective and interpersonal adjustments are to be minimized.

The Mechanistic (Bureaucratic) Model

The objective of the **mechanistic model** is to formalize organizational behavior of individuals by planning rationally and objectively an efficient structure for coordinating authority without subjective, interpersonal adjustments among the human components. Standardization of jobs, work flows, or skills would lead to predictability and stability. Confusion would be eliminated; all person-

Figure 7-6 Mechanistic and Organic Models: A Continuum

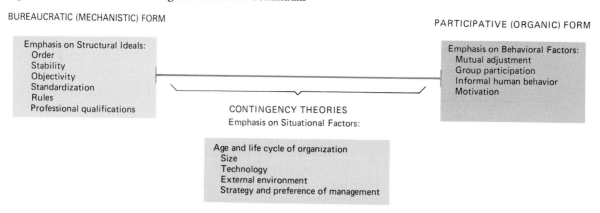

BUREAUCRATIC (MECHANISTIC) FORM

PARTICIPATIVE (ORGANIC) FORM

Emphasis on Structural Ideals:
  Order
  Stability
  Objectivity
  Standardization
  Rules
  Professional qualifications

Emphasis on Behavioral Factors:
  Mutual adjustment
  Group participation
  Informal human behavior
  Motivation

CONTINGENCY THEORIES
Emphasis on Situational Factors:

Age and life cycle of organization
  Size
  Technology
  External environment
  Strategy and preference of management

nel would know exactly where they stood and what to do. Uncertainty would be reduced and order increased by specific rules. Fairness would be built into the plan. Routines would decrease variability. The organization would run like an efficient machine, well oiled by predetermined rules, descriptions, channels, specifications, and programmed instructions. The result would be ideal coordination, since all factors would be considered in advance of implementation, objectively, equitably, and efficiently. This ideal could be achieved if certain guidelines offered by Weber were used:

1. Regular activities aimed at organization goals are described as official duties.
2. The organization follows the principles of hierarchy, in which each lower official is under the supervision of a higher one.
3. Operations are governed by a consistent system of abstract rules covering all individual actions.
4. The ideal official operates as a formalistic impersonality, based on competence, not on favoritism, personal judgment or bias, subjective preferences, or family or political connections.
5. Employment is based on technical qualifications and is not subject to arbitrary termination.
6. Administrative acts, decisions, and rules are recorded in writing to provide stability, objectivity, and predictability to operations.

The mechanistic model used the principles advanced by the classical writers discussed in Chapter 2. It offered a neat, cookbook list of ideal criteria for designing structure of authority. It had appealing features during a period in which industry and governments grew in size and a large proportion of the people had limited education. Why, then, did such an ideal model run into trouble?

The term *bureaucracy* itself tended to become a bad word, connoting red tape, insensitiveness to human feelings, and inefficiency. Those connotations resulted from built-in shortcomings:

1. A bureaucratic organization was viewed as inhuman and not attuned to the needs of human beings placed in the mechanical structure. With increasing education, worker expectations, affluence, and informal-group interactions, the rigid structure created dissatisfactions.
2. Rapid changes in society, technology, and situations demanded a more flexible and adaptable approach. It was not possible for a designer to plan for these rapid changes.
3. As organizations grew in size, the top managers became further and further removed from the grass roots of new employees who entered with creative ideas and higher levels of education.
4. The attempt to coordinate specialists by standardization itself became specialized, resulting in the design of the structure becoming an end in itself, not a means to an end.

The Organic Model

After the Hawthorne experiment and later research on individual and group relationships, behavioral scientists focused on the important element omitted in the bureaucratic form—human behavior. With this shift in attention, a different model for organizing developed that was diametrically opposed to the bureaucratic one. Assumptions about human nature shifted from Theory X to Theory Y (discussed in Chapter 2). With this new orientation, leading theorists such as McGregor, Likert, Argyris, and Bennis contributed elements for a new, nonmechanistic, organic model, of which participation by all members in an organization was the foundation.

Organic model A structure that is flexible and adjusts through the interaction of its members; one that evolves from the needs and goals of members, where coordination is by mutual adjustment and where informal groups provide the cohesion; the community of interests should determine a network structure.

What are the features of the organic model?

The **organic model** of design evolved first as a reaction to the formalization and prescription of the mechanistic model. Since it was built as the antithesis of the opposing extreme, clear guidelines for designing structure were stated as the negative of mechanistic propositions. However, as more research was done on the human element, certain positive guidelines for design emerged. Individual writers tended to identify these as basic to alternative approaches to design, such as Likert's System 4 (which was the opposite of his classical System 1), McGregor's Theory Y (which was the opposite of his classical Theory X), and Argyris's project type of structure. The models were similar, and for the sake of conciseness and explicitness, we shall group the guidelines into a composite organic model:

1. A structure should be flexible and continually adjustable through interaction of members.
2. Structure should evolve from the needs and goals of the members through their participation.
3. Coordination of specialists should be by mutual adjustment, not by rules, official directives, and rigid position descriptions.
4. Informal groups, connected not only by vertical, hierarchical channels but also by horizontal communication, influence, and cooperative efforts, should provide the cohesion needed.
5. The design of structure for humans should be similar to organic processes in biology rather than rigid, mechanistic routines of machines.
6. A community of interest of individuals and groups should determine a network structure, rather than contractual and official flow, of authority.

One explicit formulation was made by Rensis Likert in which he developed several concepts for using these guidelines for the organic model.[6] His System 4 was built on three prescriptions:

1. The principle of supportive relationships
2. The use of group decision making where appropriate
3. The establishing of high performance goals instead of job descriptions and formal authority

The principle of supportive relationships emphasizes that all relationships of members in an organization should be consistent with individual backgrounds, values, and expectations, so that the members will view the experience as supportive and one that builds and maintains a sense of personal worth and importance. This principle, therefore, results in a design tailored to the needs of the members and adaptable to the members, who not only are part of the organization but are the organization.

Linking pins Structures should be organized so that groups will overlap both horizontally and vertically; there would be no tight chain of command.

The components of a well-designed structure are viewed as groups of members rather than as positions held by individuals. Thus, Likert viewed organization structure as consisting of **linking pins** of groups, not of individuals. (See Figure 7-7.) Each group should overlap horizontally and vertically so that there is no tight chain of command. Groups serve as "linking pins" with superiors and subordinates. Each manager is in at least two groups, one with

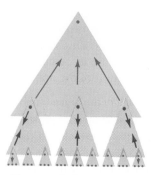

(The arrows indicate the linking-pin function)

Figure 7-7 The Linking Pin

superiors and one with subordinates, and all management functions as organic tissue for coordination rather than as discrete, mechanical meshing of parts.

Likert's third focus was on achieving high goals by emphasizing results rather than prescribed means for achieving the results. The structure best suited to achieving high goals avoids the tendency for structure to become an end in itself.

The organic model for design of structure can be summarized as focusing on behavior of members in an organization instead of on a mechanical flow of authority. The structural aspects emerge from increased participation in committees, conferences, and consultation. In such a design, shared leadership is made possible by the absence of sharp distinctions between levels of authority. All participate in reaching goals through group interaction.

The design of structure using the organic model differs completely from the design using the mechanistic model. The resulting question is, Which model is better? The answer is, It depends. Studies indicate that some organizations are successful using the mechanistic structure, some are successful using the organic structure, and some are hybrid forms. For this reason, attention has increasingly turned to studies that search for the factors to be considered when selecting an appropriate structural form. These studies have contributed to the knowledge necessary for building structures contingent upon a number of factors characterizing the situation faced by the specific organization. We turn now to these contingency theories.

CONTINGENCY THEORIES OF ORGANIZATION

Is there one best style?

During the conflict between proponents of the two forms of structure, studies began to indicate that neither model was better for all organizations. For example, Burns and Stalker found that mechanistic structures worked well under stable conditions, but that during changing conditions, a more participative type was needed.[7] Crozier, in a study of two government bureaucracies, found that certain people who prefer security and clearly defined routines were happier and more effective in bureaucratic organizations.[8] Others found that members at higher levels of the organization needed organic approaches, whereas those at lower levels needed mechanistic approaches to be effective. In some industries, certain departments could best be organized using one form and certain departments could best be organized using another.

The evolving contingency theories state that either the mechanistic or the organic form may be appropriate in certain situations. Five factors have been found to be keys in the selection of the appropriate form:

1. The age and life cycle stage of the organization
2. The size of the organization in number of people to be coordinated
3. The type, complexity, and sophistication of the technology used by the organization
4. The nature of the external environment
5. The strategy and personal preference of the top management

Age and Stage of Life Cycle

New organizations face unknown challenges and thus tend to refrain from formal planning of structure. The situation calls for members to adjust quickly, and mutual adjustment for gaining coordination is appropriate. As the organization gets older, it gains experience and confidence. Members develop routines for authority flows. With better knowledge of problems and past successful answers, the organization becomes better able to standardize authority flows to perpetuate the successful experiences. The advantages of a mechanistic form become more attractive; for example, in the opening case, Mr. Price began to see that formal structure had become more important as the company became older.

Old organizations, such as railroads, steel companies, government agencies, and established university departments, tend to seek order and stability in authority relationships by adopting mechanistic forms of structure. In such cases, changes require formal reorganizations as problems emerge.

In Chapter 1, we observed that organizations tend to experience a life cycle—birth, rapid growth, stabilized maturity, and threatened decline. This life cycle implies changes in situations faced by the organization. During rapid growth, it adapts its authority flows to the changes by means of mutual adjustments, since formal structures tend to become obsolete before they can be implemented. During the stabilizing period, formal structures become feasible and a more mechanistic structure tends to be constructed. Faced with decline in a later stage, the elaborate administrative superstructure may be too costly to maintain and the structure may need pruning and consolidation. Many organizations faced this decline in the later stage in the 1980s, including Apple Computer and General Motors. The life cycle is an important factor in reorganizing.[9]

Size of Organizations

Structure depends on the number of workers and managers who must be coordinated. Typically, organizations are grouped into small—those with 1–250 employees; medium—those with 250–1,000 employees; and large—those with 1,000 or more employees. As the number of employees increases, attention to

These two pictures show two points in the life of an automobile company. Demands of the market stimulate change and innovation. This innovation is vividly portrayed in terms of people, equipment, machines, and work processes.

coordination becomes more critical. Managers in small organizations may be successful in operations without worrying much about formal structure. In large organizations, managers need to focus on planned authority flows.

Downsizing of organizations was not the only phenomenon to affect organization structure in the 1980s—hostile takeover was another devastating trauma. One corporation, called the "raider," attempted, through the stock

A major challenge for managers is to address the problems caused by increased job specialization. During the early years of the American factory system, job specialization led to highly routine and boring jobs; the outcome in many cases was employee dissatisfaction and low productivity. In the 90s the picture at the right is fairly common and thus the need for a manager's imagination and innovation when designing the formal structure of organizations.

market, to take over, split up, or merge with another corporation, called the "victim" or "target." The raider generally borrowed large sums of money to purchase the majority of the stock of the victim, gained control, transferred the debt to the newly acquired corporation (the victim), generally kicked out the victim's management team, and restructured the organization. The victim's management team strongly opposed the takeover in one of three ways: (1) "bitter pill," or making themselves look unattractive to the raiders; (2) "greenmail," or paying a ransom to the raider by buying back the shares at an inflated price; or (3) "white knight," finding someone less objectionable to take over the corporation. (Another possibility, one that has proven to be less effective, is that management could somehow develop a constituency of support from the stockholders themselves. Stockholders generally responded more to the possibility of profit than to loyalty to corporate management.)

Hostile takeovers were first used by large companies wanting rapid growth and diversification, but they became a specialty for people who are in the "hostile takeover business," people like Carl Icahn, T. Boone Pickens, and Ted Turner.

Most observers would agree that these two forces—downsizing and hostile takeovers— had tremendous impact on American business organization and perhaps on the organization of the economy itself. Staffs are now "leaner," "streamlined," and "more efficient." Short-term results were higher profits and better earnings per share for the downsized companies. Wall Street was applauding, but the long-run impact is still unknown.

Size increases result not only in increasing the number of employees but also in (1) greater specialization of jobs, (2) greater differentiation of departmental units, and (3) more levels in hierarchy. Specialization creates needs for planned structures. Increased use of different types and skills of workers introduces the possibility of tailoring organizational approaches. For example, a

Ethics Issue

Downsizing in the Fortune 500

General Motors used a euphemism, "right-sizing," and other organizations used the term "efficient-sizing" to describe a painful process that most refer to as downsizing, or cutting people to cut costs. In the 1980s, numerous organizations used this process. When Iacocca took over near-bankrupt Chrysler, one of his first actions was to cut from the payroll over 30 percent of Chrysler's employees. When Sculley took over ailing Apple Computer, he laid off over 20 percent of Apple's staff. Cummins Engine Company reduced its staff by 33 percent.

GM closed entire plants across the nation. In just the four states of Ohio, Illinois, Michigan, and Missouri, GM eliminated over 29,000 people. Across the country, Exxon laid off 48,000 and AT&T "let go" over 35,000 people. Some of the other corporations involved in downsizing include General Electric, over 35,000; Eastman Kodak, over 13,700; and Du Pont, over 12,000. Of the total estimated 2 million people who lost their jobs, at least 500,000 of them were middle managers.

These layoffs had a devastating impact on the personal lives of the laid-off employees and a tremendous impact on the organizations themselves. Entire plants and departments disappeared, and numerous positions in other locations were eliminated. Organizations were shattered and rebuilt. The "survivors"—those people still left in the organizations after the layoffs—were shaken and distrustful and wondered if they would be the next to go. At the managerial level, managers either concentrated on short-term profits to justify their jobs or were frozen in place, unwilling to make decisions, afraid that their jobs would be in jeopardy if they made errors. Survivors attempted to find new positions, to leave the company, before a new round of layoffs hit. Corporate loyalty became an issue as employees realized that the corporations were showing no loyalty to the employees. Why should the employees be loyal to the corporations? Loyalty and commitment were highly prized values in a firm. Is that value a thing of the past?

unit that performs research may need a participative form of structure, whereas an assembly operation may call for a formal structure. Sales and marketing may need a hybrid form. With increased levels in the structure, the upper managers may use more participation, since their numbers are small and their experience and skills are greater; lower levels tend to need explicit identification of their authority.

These simple tendencies do not necessarily mean that large organizations require the bureaucratic form. Increased differentiation and levels increase the opportunities for using both bureaucratic and participative structures in different parts of the organization. Other determinants offer additional guides for organizing activities.

Technology The instruments, machines, control devices, and techniques needed in an organization to attain its objectives.

Technology

A third factor affecting structure is the type of technology used in the organization. **Technology** has been defined in different ways, but we use this simple definition: the instruments, machines, control devices, and techniques needed in operations to accomplish the organization's objectives. For example, the introduction of computer systems demands a restructuring of authority flows. Machine-paced in place of worker-paced production requires new structures. Complexity and sophistication of technology tend to require supporting administrative staffs of technical experts for control and maintenance.

How does technology affect the organization?

The pioneering studies by Joan Woodward and her associates in Great Britain focused on the importance of technology as a contingent factor affecting structure. Woodward classified production technology into three types: (1) small-batch production, (2) large-batch and mass production (assembly lines), and (3) long-run, continuous-process production (such as oil and chemical production).[10] She found that the more successful firms using each of these three technological processes had different organization structures. As complexity increased from small-batch to continuous-process, the number of levels and the span of control increased. Likewise, line organization was more suitable to the simpler processes, and line-staff-functional patterns were best in the more complex. In general, organization of firms with small-batch and continuous-process production tended to be consistent with the participative form. The large-batch and assembly operations were organized along classical and bureaucratic lines.

More recent studies[11] have modified Woodward's interpretations of the effect of technology on structure and enable us to identify some underlying technological characteristics that have an influence on structure:

1. The degree of skill required by the instrument or machine
2. The degree of sophistication of operations
3. The diversity of technology used in the organization
4. The rate of change in technology employed
5. The degree to which operations are subject to automatic (computer) controls

As one might expect, recent studies indicate that technology has a greater effect on structures at the operations level and less at the top. Changing technology requires the greater flexibility of the participative form; routine, mechanical, and assembly operations tend toward the bureaucratic. Technology requiring special skills of different crafts, professions, and specialties tends toward the participative. Finally, automatic controls provide built-in coordination of machines and leave the human element greater freedom to employ participative techniques for coordination.

The External Environment

External environment
Consists of all those elements of a political, legal, social, and physical world outside the organization in which the manager operates.

A fourth factor on which structure is contingent is the external environment. **External environment,** in this sense, is defined as all factors in the setting outside the boundaries of the organization concerned.

The study of an organization's environment can be viewed as involving successively larger circles of factors as one proceeds from those immediately outside to the broader and more inclusive. We can classify this continuum in three degrees of scope: (1) the immediate environment that is most directly, closely associated with the organization, such as the local labor market, the size of the community, and the professional support services of bankers and lawyers; (2) the industrial environment, which includes the industry in which the organization competes and which provides services, supplies, and revenue to sustain the organization (also, in a regulated industry, regulatory bodies and legal structure); and (3) the societal and cultural environment, which includes the sociological, cultural, political, and economic elements underlying the broadest indirect factors. Figure 7-8 illustrates the differing scopes of external environments.

Paul Lawrence and Jay Lorsch have formulated a theory based on empirical studies that classify on the basis of characteristics of the industrial environment. They identify three types of this environment: market, technical-economic, and scientific (which, in general, correspond with sales, production, and research and development functions). Each of these environments may vary depending on (1) the rate of change experienced in the industry, (2) the degree of uncertainty of information about the situation, and (3) the length of the feedback time in which results become known.

Lawrence and Lorsch studied three industries: plastics, food, and containers. They first studied the plastics industry, because it represented a diverse and dynamic environment. The food and container industries were added at a second stage to provide a comparative approach with more stable industrial environments. They found not only that the environment resulted in different structures in the three industries but also that within the plastics industry, varying structural theories were employed. The production departments were more highly formalized for routine procedures; the sales departments were less formally organized because of the greater competitiveness and uncertainty experienced in the situation; the research and development departments used propositions from participative theory. Thus, environments not only affected the general organization pattern but also caused variations of organization structure within a given firm.

Increased attention to environment as a determinant of structure results in

Figure 7-8 Differing Scopes of External Environments

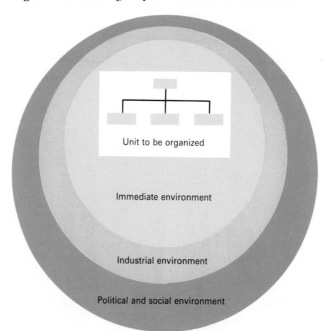

identification of four characteristics of environment that cause modifications of structure:

1. Environments can be stable or dynamic, ranging from that of an Indian village with age-old customs and habits to the fashion industry with its ever-changing demands. Dynamic environments experience unpredictable changes, which require organizations to maintain structures adaptable to unexpected, new conditions.

2. Environments have different degrees of complexity, from simple, homogeneous regional preferences for food and clothing to heterogeneous races, religions, languages, and customs in societies.

3. Markets served by an organization can range from a single customer of one product to a diverse international area involving many products and services.

4. Environments may range from very competitive and hostile to cooperative and friendly. Organizations facing extreme competition need structures that can respond rapidly.[12]

Modern organizations increasingly face dynamic, complex, diverse, and hostile environments. Thus, structures that can adjust quickly and adapt to many changes have become more common. The large multinational firms, such as oil, computers, mining, and arms manufacturers, have attempted new formal structures and participative techniques to meet the challenges from multiple environments. Comparative research of similarities and differences in the values, political systems, stages of growth, educational systems, and cultures of various nations uncovers new problems of structure for these multinationals.

Strategy and Personal Preferences of Managers

Finally, two organizations facing similar situations with regard to the four preceding factors may find different successful structures because of different

Managing in a changing environment is best illustrated in the fashion industry. This picture shows the autumn/winter 1991/1992 line modeled in Paris, March 1991.

strategies and personal preferences of top management. We saw in Chapter 6 that an organization's strategy is developed based on its goals, mission, strengths, and weaknesses, and top management's beliefs and viewpoints regarding the environment in which it operates. Since structure is a powerful means for implementing its strategy, any organization should use a structural form suited to its strategy and personal beliefs. For example, the top management of an oil company with a strategy of invading the established marketing area of another company with a large market share will seek a structure that will enable it to respond quickly and aggressively to actions of that competitor. The established company, seeking to retain its market share, will tend to use a bureaucratic structure; the aggressor will tend to adopt a participative structure that will enable its members to upset the stable conditions (that is, capture a part of the market share). The structure adopted by the strong, aggressive chief executive will differ from that of the executive of the established company. In fact, a great advantage of the invading company may be the adoption of new structures to fit its personal preferences and strategy.

Much of the research on structure has been designed to determine the effect of only one or two of the five groups of situational factors we have discussed. Results have been that one factor—say, technology—appears more important than another, such as size. In fact, in an actual situation, a practicing manager needs to consider all five factors and to tailor structure to all of them. Thus, the contingency approach makes the selection of a suitable structure a complex and difficult problem.[13] The choice of design is no longer a simple matter of selecting one of the basic forms and applying its principles and guidelines—but that is what makes design of structure interesting.[14]

SOME COMPOSITE ORGANIZATIONAL STRUCTURES

Matrix Structure

Matrix design The integration of both a product and functional structure for identifiable projects.

Modern organizations have increasingly experimented with new designs that seek to optimize their structural arrangements with respect to the two basic forms and the five situational factors. One approach is a **matrix design,** or grid structure, a device for integrating the tasks, types of authority, and situational factors.[15] For example, one matrix approach identifies four situations calling for different structures:

1. The routine-task situation that requires repetitive solutions by personnel with technical backgrounds. (Taylor and scientific management proposed functional specialists in the design for this situation.)
2. The engineering situation that requires nonrepetitive solutions by personnel who are professionally educated. (A professional staff usually appears in the structure to analyze and advise the line manager.)
3. The craft situation that deals with unique but repetitively processed outputs. (This situation requires a flexible and person-oriented structure.)
4. The uncertain situation that deals with unique and nonrepetitive tasks, with the output ill defined. (A flexible and participative design is called for in this situation.)

Management Application

Organizing Styles of the 1990s

Organization charts may go the way of the dinosaur. In many contemporary organizations, change occurs too rapidly for permanent relationships to be designed through the traditional principles of organizing. The "in" term is *adaptive,* and it describes an organization that creates new structures to get the job done. Informal teams of people form as the need arises and might include managers, customers, shop workers, and suppliers. To apply traditional concepts of authority to customers and suppliers would result in difficult relationships, and getting the job done takes priority over who has the authority to give commands.

The list of companies moving to an adaptive style of organization is small but growing (Levi Strauss, Xerox, Cypress Semiconductor, Becton Dickinson—maker of high-tech medical equipment—and AES). The adaptive organization creates interesting opportunities and challenges.

By forcing the decisions closer to the source of the problem, the adaptive system reduces bureaucracy and the formal involvement of many staff personnel. The constant changing of personnel from team to team requires people to become proficient at and comfortable in performing many roles. In one situation, an engineer may be the leader of the team; in another situation, that same person may assume the role of a follower.

The adaptive system puts a premium on coordination and information. Computer systems collect personnel inventories of skills, experience, and availability for team assignment. They also track the progress of the team and offer access to various data bases.

For managers accustomed to the traditional organization styles, adaptive styles create frustration and tension. They see the flexibility as chaos. Managers using adaptive organization say it unleashes employee creativity, reduces unnecessary paperwork, develops employee team skills, solves problems quickly, and prepares people for situations they will have to face.

Source: Adapted from Brian Dumaine, "The Bureaucracy Busters," *Fortune,* June 17, 1991, pp. 36–50.

This matrix approach, illustrated in Figure 7-9, encourages the adapting of organizational structure to the situation existing in different parts of an enterprise and can result in the use of different organizational designs, depending upon differences in environment, tasks, and personnel involved. For example, managers of machine shops would face the routine situation in departments having automatic equipment and semiskilled personnel but would face the engineering situation in the units that plan and design products; they would op-

	Few exceptions	Many exceptions
Unanalyzable	Craft	Nonroutine
Analyzable	Routine	Engineering

Figure 7-9 Matrix Structure

erate in the craft situation for die makers; they would experience uncertain situations in research and development units.

Project Organization

Project organization
An organizational design tailored to a particular mission or project, when the project is done, the group is disbanded.

Matrix thinking leads to another type of structure, uniquely adapted to special projects. **Project organization** is tailored to a particular mission or project, to coordinate actions toward the completion of the project while retaining the advantages of functional specialists. Whereas the classical approach is built around authority centers and the behavioral approach is built around people, project organization is designed to meet the demands of a particular job. A functional specialist can be lent out for a particular project and would answer to the project manager with line authority, but when the project is finished, he or she would return to the functional department and gain the advantage of relationships with others in the same specialty. This approach leads to the development of temporary structures that are tailored to the successful completion of a project, as illustrated in Figure 7-10.

The project type of organization was very effective in the space program, because it was capable of adjusting to the changing needs of the specific environment. When production involved high uncertainty of results and the application of new scientific knowledge, a project manager coordinated production by using line authority. Functional specialists (including specialized scientists) were borrowed by the project manager from functional departments for the length of time required by the project and returned to their functional departments afterwards.

Figure 7-10 Project Organization

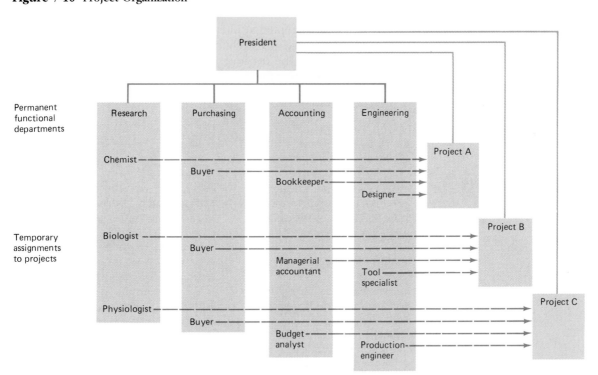

Project organization has been found to fit a number of widely differing situations, from building contractors and advertising agencies to accounting and consulting firms. The increasing complexity of projects requiring highly specialized experts and the rapid changes from one project to another that are needed in modern society often demand the flexibility provided by project organization. A project structure accommodates the formal ideas of classical thinking, together with the team and participative ideas of behavioral contributions.

The number of people actively engaged in organizational research has expanded greatly. Their output is certainly nontraditional. For example, Gareth Morgan, in his book *Images of Organizations,*[16] provides a number of metaphors to explain organizations. Some chapter titles describe organizations as machines; organisms; brains; cultures; political systems; psychic prisons; flux and transformation; and instruments of domination.[17]

SUMMARY

The design of structure is a powerful tool available to managers for affecting organizational behavior. The organizing function deals with designing the structure for coordinating the specialized parts of the organization. This coordination can be achieved by direct supervision, mutual adjustment, or standardizing the work content, results, or skills of specialists. Organization charts graphically show the flow of the three basic types of authority: line, staff, and functional. Two forms of structure, bureaucratic and organic, have received support from leading authorities as being universally applicable, but contingency approaches have attempted to integrate these two forms by considering such situational factors as age, size, technology, environment, and the strategies adopted by organizations. The dynamic changes in the environment suggest that the organizing function of managing will continue to evolve.

KEY TERMS

Organizing The function of determining the structure for allocating individual (specialized) tasks and coordinating activities toward the organizational structure.

Coordination A condition where departments, people, and tasks are designed or managed so that their activities merge into achieving a unified goal.

Authority The right to decide or act.

Line authority The direct and general authority over subordinates in an organization's most important activities.

Staff authority Advisory authority that provides expert specialists for line authority.

Functional authority Permits specialists in a given set of activities to enforce directives within a clearly defined scope of authority.

Unity of command No member of an organization should report to more than one superior on any single function.

Exception principle   The concept that recurring decisions should be delegated, allowing superiors time to make the most important, nonrepetitive decisions.

Span of control   The limit of the number of subordinates that one superior should supervise.

Scalar principle   The concept that holds that authority and responsibility should flow in a clear, unbroken line or chain of command from the highest to the lowest manager.

Departmentation   The manner in which activities should be divided and formed into specialized groups.

Centralization   A condition in an organization where authority and decision making is primarily positioned at the top of the structure.

Decentralization   The process of delegating authority to lower-level managers.

Mechanistic model   A model that suggests that the best way to organize a company is by planning rationally, objectively, and in advance; subjective and interpersonal adjustments are to be minimized.

Organic model   A structure that is flexible and adjusts through the interaction of its members; one that evolves from the needs and goals of members, where coordination is by mutual adjustment and where informal groups provide the cohesion; the community of interests should determine a network structure.

Linking pins   Structures should be organized so that groups will overlap both horizontally and vertically; there would be no tight chain of command.

Technology   The instruments, machines, control devices, and techniques needed in an organization to attain its objectives.

External environment   Consists of all those elements of a political, legal, social, and physical world outside the organization in which the manager operates.

Matrix design   The integration of both a product and functional structure for identifiable projects.

Project organization   An organizational design tailored to a particular mission or project, when the project is done, the group is disbanded.

STUDY ASSIGNMENTS

1. The organization and structural problems of the Price Construction Company are typical of many rapidly growing firms. In this type of company, what prevents managers from effectively organizing their firms? How can managers overcome the structural and operational problems created by poorly managed growth?

2. How can an organization's overall financial performance be enhanced as a result of managers applying the concepts that are the basis of the organizing function?

3. How does increased specializing contribute to optimum utilization of the organization's talents and resources? Are there limits to the amount of specializing that can be designed into an organization's structure?

4. What can an individual learn about the nature, purpose, and character of a company by analyzing the company's organization chart?

5. What is the distinction between line authority, staff authority, and functional authority?

6. Explain the six classical principles of organization. How can a manager utilize these principles in designing an organization's structure?

7. Why would two organizations who make essentially the same product or provide the same service have significantly different organizational structures? Identify some specific examples that illustrate this situation. (For instance, both Nucor and Bethlehem Steel manufacture steel products, but they have radically different organizational structures.)

8. What are some of the factors that a manager must consider in determining how activities are departmentalized?

9. What factors contribute to whether a firm is structured on a centralized or a decentralized basis?

10. What are the fundamental differences between the organic model and the mechanistic model of organizational design? When would an organic structure be appropriate? When would a mechanistic model be appropriate?

11. How would a manager apply Likert's "linking pin" concept in designing the organizational structure of a firm?

12. Discuss how the different factors of the contingency theory are used to shape and influence the design of an organization's structure.

13. How have technology and the increased rate of technological change influenced structural design in recent years?

14. According to Lawrence and Lorsch, how does the environment influence the design, nature, and adaptability of an organization's structure?

15. How are some of the bureaucratic, organic, and contingency concepts reflected in the design of matrix and project organizations?

Case for Discussion

THE BC GENERATOR CORPORATION

For Mike Johnson, the past few months have been exceptionally busy at the Maysville plant of the BC Generator Corporation. As personnel manager of the plant, he has been directly involved in the design and implementation of a new production method for manufacturing generators. The program is called Team Plus. Mike had expected that the program would improve productivity and enhance employee job satisfaction. Production employees would manufacture generators by working in teams, instead of working as individuals on an assembly line. But ever since the program became operational, it has been plagued with problems, and recently the vice president of operations began circulating a report that is highly critical of the program. Because he wants to respond to the report, Mike has begun his own review of the Team Plus program.

The Team Plus program was conceived by Bob Harding, the Maysville plant manager, and Mike. They developed the idea after attending a seminar on the use of quality circles in manufacturing plants. About six months ago, the two suggested to BC's president that if the Maysville employees were organized into teams, they would be more productive and could manufacture a higher-quality generator than employees at any other BC facility, where the more traditional assembly-line method was used. As it turned out, they presented their proposal at a time when the president was particularly concerned about BC's declining productivity, and its loss of sales in the face of competition from recently introduced foreign-made generators. Because of his concerns, BC's president was willing to try anything to strengthen BC's competitive position, and he immediately authorized Harding and Johnson to implement their Team Plus program.

Bob and Mike implemented the program within thirty days after the president had approved the proposal. The main reason the program was implemented so quickly was that the president had made his approval conditional. Bob and Mike would be able to implement the Team Plus program only if the cost of the program could be kept to a minimum and only if the reorganization could be accomplished without any alterations in the production schedules at the Maysville plant. As it turned out, the Maysville plant was scheduled for its annual two-week shutdown about three weeks after the president had approved the program. Thus, Bob and Mike had to act quickly so that the program would be operational the first day after the shutdown. Despite the time constraint, Bob and Mike were confident that the Team Plus program could be implemented with only a few problems and that the Maysville employees would respond positively to the changes created by the program.

However, after the program had been in effect for a few months, various staff sections at BC's headquarters began noticing that there were obvious declines in the production levels at the Maysville plant. In addition, the sales department had an unusually high number of customer complaints about new generators that had been manufactured at Maysville after the Team Plus program had been implemented. It was at that time that the vice president of operations directed his staff to prepare a report evaluating the Team Plus program.

Mike was quite disturbed at the findings and conclusions of the report. The report noted that in addition to declines in productivity and quality assurance, there had been increases in the absenteeism rate, grievances filed, and fights between employees at Maysville. The report also found that the Maysville production employees and their supervisors were extremely confused and frustrated with their new work assignments. Many employees were simply unhappy about the change in working conditions at the plant. In reading the report, Mike could not understand how such a good program could have received such a negative response from the employees, particularly since one of the principal objectives of the program was to improve job satisfaction for the employees.

Before the Team Plus program, the plant operated with two assembly lines, each of which had the capacity to produce seven types of generators. Under the assembly-line arrangement, the production employees were trained to work on only certain components of the generator, such as the engine housing, electrical controls, or transmission units. When the Team Plus program was initiated, the production layout of the plant was reorganized so that it was similar to a job shop operation. The new arrangement consisted of eight self-sufficient work areas or production centers, each of which could produce the entire generator. A specific team was then assigned to each of these work areas. Bob had intended that some of the teams would produce only one type of generator (the models that were in greatest demand) and that some of the other teams would produce a variety of models on an as-needed basis.

For the production employees, the Team Plus approach meant that they would no longer be trained in or be expected to perform a specialized assembly function. Rather, Mike wanted the employees to be trained to perform any task involved in the entire production of a generator. He also directed that the team determine who would perform what tasks on any given day. Mike envisioned that under the Team Plus program, supervisors would have fewer responsibilities than did supervisors on the assembly line. Essentially, Mike expected that the teams would be self-directed and that, as a result, supervisors would be needed to perform only administrative and control-type responsibilities. Furthermore, once the program became fully operational, Mike planned to reduce the number of supervisors over the next year by having one supervisor assume the responsibility for two teams.

Mike had hoped to develop a comprehensive selection process to ensure that the best possible mix of people would be achieved for each team. But the time constraint made the development of such a process an impossibility. As a result, Mike simply assigned production employees to the teams based solely on their assembly-line job assignment. By using this selection criteron, Mike hoped to end up with a team mix, in which at least one member of the team could perform any given task required to produce a generator. Then, once the team became operational, each team member would be cross-trained to perform a variety of tasks, and likewise that individual would train other team members to perform the specialized task that he or she performed on the assembly line.

The time constraint created another problem for Bob and Mike. They found that there was insufficient time to develop an adequate orientation program for both management and employees involved in the Team Plus program. They were able to schedule only two days for supervisory orientation during the shutdown period. Attendance was poor, since many supervisors had long-standing vacation plans. The orientation for the production employees was held on the day production resumed after the shutdown period. While attendance at this orientation was not a problem, the orientation hardly went off as planned. Many employees complained about their lack of involvement in developing and implementing the Team Plus program. Some employees asked what was wrong with the old system, and others were confused about their specific responsibility and job assignments under the new program. At that time, Bob and Mike dismissed their concerns, saying that many of the program's bugs would be worked out in time. They also stressed to the employees that the primary reason for instituting the Team Plus program was to allow management to redesign jobs so that employees would realize greater job satisfaction. The response to these comments was mixed, but for the most part, the employees were willing to give the program a try.

Beyond what both Bob and Mike considered a hasty and rough start, they thought the Team Plus program was progressing adequately. But in thinking about how he is going to reply to the report from the vice president of operations, Mike realizes that perhaps they made some significant mistakes in developing and implementing the program. He is concerned about his handling of the issue of job redesign, not only for the production employees, but for the supervisory personnel as well. He is also troubled by the selection process for placing employees into different groups, and the tendency of some members to continue doing the same types of tasks that they had performed on the assembly line. Finally, he is bewildered by the failure of the program to foster greater job satisfaction for the employees. Despite these problems, he believes that the Team Plus program can achieve the objective that he and Bob set forth in their original proposal, but he realizes that for the program to continue, he will have to propose some specific courses of action to correct some of the existing problems, and he will have to demonstrate that there are definite benefits in the program.

Chapter 8

Staffing and Managing Human Resources

Learning Objectives

1. **Describe** the two-step procedure for matching jobs and people.
2. **Identify** the most important legislation affecting the staffing of a firm's human resources.
3. **State** three reasons for the change in the scope of human resource managing.
4. **Describe** the significance of global competition on human resources.
5. **Identify** three significant changes coming in the U.S. labor force.

For much of the past fifty years, BMC has been the unchallenged leader of the automobile industry, dominating the industry in size, revenues, sales volume, technology, and profits. In addition, BMC has become a multinational corporation that not only manufactures automobiles but also is involved in electronics, consumer appliances, military equipment, locomotives, and financial services. However, over the past ten years, the firm's lackluster management, its involvement in diverse industries, and its weak response to increasing foreign competition have caused many observers of the auto industry to question whether BMC can retain its leadership position.

About a year ago, BMC's board of directors became so concerned about the firm's overall weakening position that it appointed a new chairman, George Appleman. After a year of assessing BMC's operations and considering the various alternatives that the firm could pursue in reversing its decline, Appleman announced that BMC would initiate the largest corporate reorganization in history. In speeches and press releases, he made it quite clear that he wanted to reestablish BMC as the unquestioned leader of the auto industry through the year 2000 and beyond and that the way to achieve this was by first reorganizing BMC into a more effective and efficient operation.

To "encourage" BMC's top management to move on the reorganization effort, Appleman held a retreat for the firm's 900 top executives in a secluded area of upstate New York. In his opening remarks to the group, he noted that the firm had lost the ability to respond quickly to changing environmental con-

ditions and to the activities of BMC's competition. He emphasized that both the board and the firm's senior executives felt that a leading factor in BMC's present condition was the firm's fragmented and cumbersome organizational structure. Simply, the firm had too many divisions, managerial levels, and managers. Appleman noted that BMC needed twelve levels of management to produce the same car that one of BMC's principal foreign competitors was producing with only seven levels of management.

Appleman also attributed the current condition to the firm's go-it-alone philosophy. He was critical of the practice that dictated that every aspect of any new product, new technology, or new idea had to be the result of a total in-house effort. To accommodate this philosophy, BMC had been staffed with individuals of every imaginable expertise so that the firm would be able to handle or solve any conceivable problem. However, the result of that practice was that BMC now had considerable personnel with little or nothing to do. This problem was compounded by the fact that each of BMC's seven auto and truck divisions independently followed the same philosophy. As a result, BMC had many individuals with the same expertise working independently of one another and, according to Appleman, duplicating "the effort of doing little or nothing."

In discussing the issue of excessive staffing, Appleman expressed amazement that BMC, despite all of its underutilized talent, could not effectively respond to changing conditions or develop viable new products. Even when there were attempts at collaboration in the design, development, and manufacturing of a new series of automobiles, divisional and staff rivalries generally resulted in products of marginal quality. As Appleman saw it, BMC had become an overly cautious, inefficient, and inflexible organization. In the closing moments of his speech, he told his managers that for BMC to reestablish itself as the unquestioned leader of the automobile industry, it must reorganize in a way that would encourage management to be both innovative and aggressive.

After the chairman's opening address, the executives spent the remainder of the retreat in various discussion groups, where they addressed the different issues raised by the chairman, discussed potential problems involved in the reorganization, and proposed ways to efficiently implement the reorganization. Although each group was supposed to work on a specific topic, they all began by discussing the issue that was foremost in their minds—that is, what impact the reorganization would have on the employees and managers of BMC.

Everyone realized that the size of BMC would be substantially reduced by the reorganization. Economic conditions and competition had already resulted in huge layoffs of hourly workers, most of whom would never be recalled regardless of how well BMC would do. In the managerial ranks, morale was extremely low. Many executives suggested that if 5,000 to 8,000 managers lost their jobs as a result of the reorganization, any semblance of morale would collapse altogether. In addition, a number of executives expressed concern over how they would handle firing individuals who had been their close associates for years, and others commented about the uncertainty of retaining their own positions. There was also concern that the reductions would go beyond simply meeting the requirements for downsizing the firm, and some executives suggested that the reorganization was merely an excuse to eliminate managers who were marginal performers. ∎

The situation at BMC is becoming more and more common in American firms. Dramatic events in the environment change more rapidly than the adjustments within the firm; the result is stress and pressure placed upon the human resources. Personal and job security is replaced with tension and anxiety; career plans are scrapped for frantic networking to find other managerial positions; many families find that the "second income," once a luxury, has now become a necessary protection against unplanned job uncertainty; "corporate loyalty" is a concept of the past, and "career flexibility and mobility" are the words of contemporary Americans. These changes in environment and structure demand changes in the understanding of basic managerial functions.

Traditionally, firms have been able to exist within fairly predictable time frames. Ten-year time horizons for strategic planning have now given way to five-, three-, and even one-year periods. Organizing the resources and designing the structure and jobs to meet strategic plans no longer can be viewed as having certainty and permanency. **Staffing**, the managerial function that creates the work force to implement the plans, shows little resemblance today to the same activity done years ago.

The staffing function during the infant days of the factory was a fairly simple process. Managerial and professional personnel frequently came from the "old-boy network." Friends and relatives were the primary source of replacements or new hires. Manual workers were easily found from the pool of unemployed men and women waiting outside the plants for jobs. All a foreman had to do was walk to the back lot, look over the applicants, and pick those that would meet expectations. Bribes of money, liquor, or other favors influenced the decision process. Physical strength often was an essential attribute for the

Staffing Selecting, training, and evaluating people and matching people with the requirements of organizational structure.

How was staffing done in the past?

heavy work and long hours. When labor unions became part of the industrial scene, the hiring of union members became part of the negotiated contract, so that people were selected at the union hiring halls. Most of those practices are things of the past.[1]

Today, the staffing function has the same objective as in the past—hiring the best people for the organization—but the process of achieving this human resource objective has vastly changed. In this chapter, we will first present a brief and simple overview of staffing and managing an organization's human resources and then move into some important issues that managers must address to maintain a viable firm.

AN OVERVIEW

Staffing and managing human resources is an obvious function of managers. They are constantly faced with fundamental human resource questions. How are my people performing? If they are doing well, will the organizational rewards ensure that satisfactory performance continues? If people are not meeting standards of performance, is there training to bring them up to standard? Do I need new positions and people to meet my unit's objectives? What type of person is needed? How do I find the best-qualified people? Should I seek a specialist for an immediate job or someone who will be receptive to training and development and thus be more flexible as our job demands change?

The foregoing questions give you an idea of the scope of the staffing function, and the types of questions have been deliberately selected to keep the scope simple. The last question (specialist vs. generalist) is the type that we will view in the second section of this chapter. For this section, four questions will be addressed: What is the objective of staffing? How is staffing accomplished in an organization? What is the method of performing the staffing function? What are some legal constraints all managers should be aware of? This first section will end with an example incorporating some elements of the staffing process.

Matching Jobs and People

Any organization contains a rich variety of jobs and people. It is a challenge to managers to match the person to the job. There are at least three approaches to staffing the organization with human resources: (1) design the jobs first and fit people into the positions; (2) hire people and build the organization around them; and (3) do the two simultaneously and develop a contingency approach whereby the organizing and staffing depend upon individual situations.

The first approach has been used by many larger firms, especially in the staffing of hourly jobs. It has the advantage of being implemented in a systematic manner and appeals to those in the organization who believe that the design of an organization, like the design of a machine, must come first. Some critics of this approach believe it depersonalizes the human resources by demanding routine, predictable job behavior. These critics prefer the second or third approach, in which "good" people are hired and there is an expectation

Interviewing is an important activity in organizations. Top job candidates may be interviewed by many people during a company visit. It's important for applicants to prepare for these interviews and to take them seriously—most employers take them very seriously.

that they will perform to fit the demands of ever-changing jobs. If you were to compare firms in a similar industry, you would probably see these differences. (IBM, Hewlett-Packard, and AT&T, for example, place more emphasis on formal job-design approaches than would the newer firm in the industry—Apple.)

The Structure for Staffing

How are organization structure and staffing related?

The organizational solution for matching people with jobs varies with the size of the firm. In extremely small firms, the owner-manager does the hiring, administering, training, performance appraising, rewarding, and firing of personnel.[2] In extremely large organizations, the staffing function may be divided between the local plant operation and headquarters. The plant manager is given the authority to hire local people for certain positions but must involve corporate staff when the position calls for more professional or managerial personnel. In medium and large firms, staffing may be a shared responsibility between the professional staff of the human resource or personnel department and the line managers of the organization.

The context in which staffing occurs has become extremely complex and in many instances calls for specialists.[3] An examination of Figure 8-1 will show you just how complex and specialized are the functions of departments responsible for staffing and managing the human resources of the firm. Notice in Figure 8-1 that the example describes only the activities in the area of employee relations (in the illustration there is no mention of industrial and labor relations).

In the overview section of a book on management, it is important to show the various locations where staffing and managing may occur. If you become a general manager, your role and responsibility will differ from those of a staff professional in human resources. Your role will also vary with the size of your

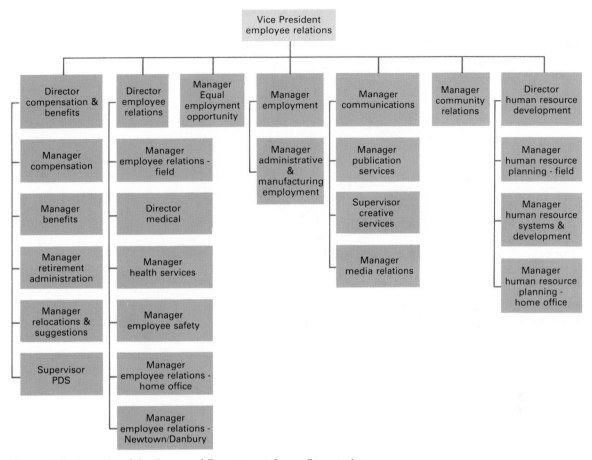

Figure 8-1 Example of the Personnel Department, Large Corporation

organization. The challenge of finding good people to perform responsibly in organizational positions, however, will remain a common denominator.

Methods of Matching

In most staffing situations, someone has a notion of why a new person is to be hired or a present employee is to be relocated through promotion or transfer or terminated from employment. Assume, however, that your company has received a recent contract with a relatively short completion date that calls for new positions at either the skilled, the semiskilled, the professional, or the managerial level. You do not have the time even for simple orientation training—informing new personnel about the rules, procedures, regulations, and work codes of the organization. You most likely will follow a two-step procedure.

Determining the Job Structure
The most likely approach to the staffing need would be through a process for determining the job structure. This process contains four steps, and each will be described briefly. (See Figure 8-2.)

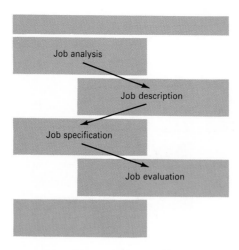

Figure 8-2 The Process for Determining Job Structure

Job analysis The orderly and systematic assembling of all the facts about a job.

Job Analysis. **Job analysis** is the orderly and systematic assembling of all the facts about a job. The purpose is to study the individual elements and duties that will make the formal organization structure meaningful and eliminate gaps in and overlaps of responsibilities of the total organization.

Job description A written statement that defines the duties, relationships, and results expected of anyone in the job.

Job Description. The **job description** is a written statement that defines the duties, relationships, and results expected of anyone in the job. It usually

Figure 8-3 Job Description in a Bank

DEPARTMENT: Trust
JOB TITLE: Supervisor, Trust Accounting
DATE:

The trust Accounting Supervisor is directly responsible to the Trust Department Head for duties and responsibilities as outlined herein:

Primary Responsibility

Perform diversified assignments to supervise the accounting activities of the Trust Department.

Typical Duties

Verify commissions taken on the trust accounts and approve for posting.
Verify and approve interest calculation on mortgage payments received.
Prepare purchase tickets on new mortgages.
Maintain an inventory of supplies and requisition additional supplies as needed.
Assist the Data Processing Department in programming and processing Trust Department systems.
Assist in the operation of the accounting function as work requires and time permits.
Perform such other duties as may be assigned by the Department Head.

General Information

The supervisor must possess a complete and thorough knowledge of procedures related to Trust and other departments, and must keep abreast of the latest developments in trust accounting systems.
The supervisor is responsible for training personnel assigned to this section and for employee evaluation in the section.

Prepared by:

includes a job title, the title of the immediate supervisor, signatures of those who prepared the description, a brief statement of the purpose of the job, and a list of duties and responsibilities. Figure 8-3 is a simple job description for a bank supervisor.

The job description is invaluable to a person immediately after accepting a position, because it offers at least a first overall picture of just what is supposed to be done. When new jobs are created or when reorganization takes place to keep in tune with the needs of the organization, the job description is basic for handling those changes. It is definite and explicit and thus can reduce frustrations. Even if no formal job descriptions are prepared (they seldom are in small firms), each person in a specific job will find it helpful to write down exactly what the job is, then check with the supervisor to determine if the description is correct. Unless there is common understanding, disagreements between the superior and the subordinate may cause unnecessary friction.

What kind of person does it take to do the job?

Job specification Statement of the requirements for a person to do a job.

Job Specification. The **job specification** sets forth clearly and specifically what kind of person it takes to do the job—it gives the qualification requirements. The specification includes the degree of education required, the desirable amount of previous experience in similar work, the skill required, and the physical (health) requirements. In applying for a job, it is very handy to have a clear job specification, so that one can estimate how one's own background fits the specifications desired by the employer.

Job evaluation The process of studying job descriptions and specifications to determine levels of responsibility and degree of difficulty for grading and pay purposes.

Job Evaluation. **Job evaluation** is the process of studying job descriptions and specifications to determine levels of responsibility and degree of difficulty for grading and pay purposes. Normally, the ingredients of the jobs can be measured by mental requirements, skill requirements, physical requirements, responsibility inherent in the job, and working conditions. In evaluating jobs, it is desirable to find ways in which these ingredients can be measured and handled objectively. For some ingredients, it may be useful to use a point system, in which points are given (say, 1 to 10) for each requirement; the points can then be totaled and compared with those of other jobs, and the totals ranked in order of the overall level for the job. It is at this stage that jobs are grouped into ranks and grades.

Determining People's Qualifications

How do you find the right people?

After the job needs of the organization are determined, company personnel must locate the suitable people. These people may be found through a search of internal sources (those currently employed in the organization) or through external sources. When seeking human resources, the organization must rely on its employment process of selection (the use of personal data sheets, testing, and interviewing).[4]

Personal Data Sheets. The personal data sheet (Figure 8-4) supplies the introductory information to the employer (either through the personnel department or to some designated member of management) so that the qualifications of applicants may be checked and tested for compatibility with the needs of the organization. The recruiting organization usually provides an application form that organizes the factual material about the applicant to guide the further investigation in the selection process.

JOHN W. McCABLE

Home Address:	3 High Street Centre City, NJ 07632	**Phone:** 201 592-7766
Birthplace:	Centre City, NJ	
Date of Birth:	February 4, 1956	
Marital Status:	Single	
Work Experience:	Nov. 1975 to present Centre City Memorial Hospital Admission Clerk with responsibility of scheduling rooms	
	1973-1975 United Parcel Service, Newark, NJ Parcel Delivery Driver (part-time, on night shift while attending school)	
Education:	Centre City High School, graduated with honors Centre City Community College, 1973-75	
References:	Dr. James Roe, Superintendent, Centre City Memorial Hospital Mr. John Franks, Manager, United Parcel Service, Newark, NJ Rev. Charles Rich, Centre City Community Church Dr. James Rosenberg, Asst. Professor, Centre City Community College	
Avocations:	Photography Citizens Band Radio	
Aspirations:	To complete my college education, possibly in night school To obtain experience in some health-delivery organization	
Comments:	My father died when I was 15 and I have partially supported myself in part-time jobs since his death	

Figure 8-4 A Personal Data Sheet

Testing. One source of additional information at this stage is the applicant's performance on standardized tests. Well-developed standardized tests are available for a number of purposes. These tests have been scientifically checked for validity (does it measure what it is supposed to), reliability (will the test give approximately the same results if repeated a number of times), and the establishment of norms (what standards of results for comparison and interpretation are available). Some examples of tests are given in Table 8-1.

When the recruiter has collected information about the most-suitable applicants, there is normally a check of references to determine how the selected applicants have performed in school and on other jobs. The most promising candidates are then asked in for interviews.[5]

Interviewing. The art of interviewing is important to a manager from two perspectives: as one who is being interviewed for a managerial position and as a manager who is staffing the organization.

From the former perspective, an applicant scheduled for an interview with a prospective employer can assume that the interviewer has studied the information obtained from the data sheet, application forms, and test scores and is seeking to supplement this information by personal contact. The applicant is understandably apprehensive. How best to prepare for the interview? How should one act? What should one say? Several generalizations are helpful: (1) Since the interviewer has shown interest in the applicant by obtaining in-

Table 8-1 Examples of Tests

TEST	DEFINITION OR EXPLANATION
Achievement	Measures past accomplishments
Aptitude	Designed to predict potentialities of a person, such as verbal, quantitative, and manual skills
Proficiency	Measures the attained skill in a task in which the applicant has past training or experience
Personality	Reveals characteristics of a personality that may affect a person's success in adjusting to work
Interest	Identifies what type of work is pleasing to the test taker
Assessment center	A two- to three-day experience during which a number of candidates (usually managerial) engage in a number of realistic management tasks (in-basket exercises, group tasks, leading discussion group, making formal presentation).

formation, the applicant can prepare for the interview by prior study about the company. This preparation will help indicate to the interviewer that the applicant is interested in the particular company and not just in landing a job. (2) The applicant's initial appearance and behavior will have a great effect on the interviewing process; therefore, a person should dress neatly and try to be at ease. (3) Natural behavior, as opposed to role playing, will create the proper setting for a successful interview. The recruiter is trying to match a person with the organization's needs, but the applicant is also trying to find out whether he or she will fit with the company. An honest exchange of comments will support the objectives of both parties. (4) The tone of the interview will be set by the interviewer, and the applicant should speak freely but refrain from "taking

Many of the gains in employment equality came from the efforts of Americans involved in the Civil Rights movement of the 1960s. In this classic picture are many of the leaders: Dr. and Mrs. Martin Luther King, Jr.; the Reverend Ralph Abernathy, Dr. Ralph Bunche, and the Reverend Hosea Williams.

Ethics Issue

Discrimination in the Workplace

Ten years ago, women in management were told to just wait, that their time to join the ranks of top management would come. They were told that they just needed more seasoning, more experience. Articles were written in *Business Week*, in *Fortune*, in the *Wall Street Journal*, in books and other publications about the "glass ceiling" that women were reaching and could not go beyond. This glass ceiling was a barrier—women could see, but never reach, positions in top management.

After ten years, the glass ceiling is still in place. Women represent less than one-half of one percent of top management in American corporations. (Their numbers are even smaller in European, Japanese, Chinese, Taiwanese, and other foreign companies.) Of the baby boomers who are now in their forties, the males are in senior-level management. The women are not.

It is generally acknowledged that women have the technical skills needed for top management; they have usually received the same education as their male counterparts. (Women now represent half of all college students, 37 percent of graduate students, and 40 percent of law students.) Many times, their work experience has been approximately the same.

Lack of education is not the cause of the glass ceiling. Lack of experience is not the cause of the glass ceiling. According to surveys done by *Catalyst* and by *Fortune*, stereotyping and preconceptions about what women should and should not do or should and should not be appear to be the cause. The stereotyping and preconceptions lead to unconscious discrimination. A male executive may claim that he is an equal-opportunity employer, but the bottom line is that he will choose a male for an executive position time after time.

One of the preconceptions is that women are undependable and unreliable, that women are the mothers of the world, and as such, will miss deadlines and quit work for their children.

"Don't Blame the Baby" is the name of a publication by Wick and Company, a management consulting firm in Delaware. They surveyed 110 executives and found that women did not quit work because of their children. They quit work to obtain more satisfying positions in other companies.

Some of those other companies may be U.S. West, Avon, Kelly Services, Gannett, and CBS. At U.S. West, women make up 21 percent of the top 1 percent of employees earning $68,000 or more. Sixteen percent (seven out of forty-three) of the top officers are women. The CEO views cultural pluralism as a business strategy. At Avon, 27 percent of the top officers are women, and there are two women on the board of directors. Avon has been a pioneer in on-site day-care centers and management development programs. At Kelly Services, 90 percent of the employees and 30 percent of top management are women. At Gannett, women hold 27 percent of the top jobs. At CBS, management has implemented policies on sexual harassment, discrimination, and career development. Approximately 25 percent of upper management are women. These companies have been leaders in creating a culture in which all have an equal opportunity to succeed in the workplace.

There have been many predictions of shortages of management in the near future as the work force shrinks—the baby boomers are heading toward retirement and there is a shortage of young people, particularly white males, to take their place. Companies will need to develop more diverse sources for top-level management. Until now, women and minorities have been severely underutilized. We hope that this will not be the case in the future.

References: Jaclyn Fierman, "Managing/Cover Story: Why Women Still Don't Hit the Top," *Fortune*, July 30, 1990, pp. 40–62; Walecia Konrad, "Cover Story: Welcome to the Woman-Friendly Company," *Business Week*, August 6, 1990, pp. 48–55.

over" the interview. Answering questions concisely and to the point will provide a favorable reaction by the interviewer. In addition, if the applicant asks pertinent questions, the interviewer will have additional material to use for evaluation.

From the perspective of the manager who is conducting the interview, the interviewing process offers many opportunities. Interviews in general may be either directed or nondirected. In the **directed interview**, which is generally suitable for employment interviews, the interviewer knows what to cover to obtain the necessary facts. The **nondirected interview** is more free-flowing, for the purpose of not only finding facts but also building confidence in the interviewee and permitting conversation to be about important matters. In both types, however, the interviewer must continually try to allow the interviewee to talk; the interviewer must be a good listener.

Some guides for the interviewer are these:

Directed interview The interviewer sets the purposes of an interview and then guides it to its conclusion.

Nondirected interview A more free-flowing interview that allows both parties an opportunity to pursue promising avenues.

1. Know the law and its relevant impact.
2. Before the interview, review the specific situation so that you have the basic facts in mind for the talk. The interviewer should receive the person being interviewed promptly at the appointed time, plan the physical layout (the location of chairs, for example) so that the person will be comfortable and at ease, and try to avoid interruptions by other visitors or the telephone.
3. Provide an informal, friendly opening to set the tone of the entire interview.
4. Use questions during the interview that clarify facts previously stated in writing (on the application form, in letters from the applicant's references, and so forth); however, get information from nonverbal sources, such as personal appearance, voice, general personality, and emotional characteristics of the applicant. Thus, observation is often as important as listening.
5. Jot down several words during the interview, and dictate or write down the important impressions and facts immediately afterward. If the interview is short, there may be little need to take notes while the applicant is present.
6. Face emotional overtones and evidence of resistance frankly; do not avoid them. A wealth of information may be available from unexpected reactions of the applicant if the interviewer allows free expression.
7. Plan the conclusion of the interview. The last few remarks by each party in an interview leave a lasting impression.

An interview is one method by which a manager adds to the information obtained from other sources. Throughout the manager's work, there will be numerous interviews, such as employment interviews, exit interviews (when a person leaves employment), counseling sessions, and the handling of grievances. A basic requirement of all interviews is that the interviewer show real interest in the matter, be candid, and encourage free expression from the one interviewed.

At various places in this overview, reference has been made to the legal environment for staffing and administering human resources. The first guideline in the interviewing materials you have just read is that you should "know the law and its relevant impact." The United States leads the world in the volume of laws and court cases that affect the management of human resources.[6] In the next section, we will introduce you to the scope of the law; for those who are interested in more detail about the legislation, we have added an Appendix at the end of this chapter that describes the Law or Executive Order for Union-Management Relations; Wages, Hours, and Working Conditions; and Employment Rights.

The Legal Base

We view the staffing and managing function broadly so that it includes the cycle of activities most personnel encounter in a lifetime of employment: selection and hiring, training and development, compensation, retirement, termination, safety and health, and labor relations. As can be seen in Table 8-2, managers need to know the legislation relating to a firm's human resources. The principal acts are these: the Civil Rights Act (1964) as amended by the Equal Employment Opportunity Act of 1972, the Equal Pay Act of 1963, the Age Discrimination in Employment Act of 1967, the Employee Retirement Income Security Act (ERISA) of 1974, the Occupational Safety and Health Act (OSHA) of 1970, and the National Labor Relations Act of 1935 (Wagner Act), amended in 1947 (Taft-Hartley Act) and 1959 (Landrum-Griffin Act).

In most companies, the complexities of the laws and court interpretations require staff specialists. Large firms have such people as full-time members of their human resource or personnel departments; medium and small companies will usually have access to these specialists through consulting or law firms, hired on a retainer basis. Knowledge of the law by management personnel, however, will frequently prevent violation of the law and subsequent costly litigation.[7]

As a summary of the staffing function in organizations, we now offer a description of the process used by one organization, the Eaton Corporation. Every firm will vary in its specific plan and procedures; every firm, however, does have similar processes.

The Eaton Example of Staffing

The Eaton Corporation has a well-developed two-tiered recruitment program. First, they recruit local people for their plants. Their first action in this regard is to post the jobs in the plant, so that all employees have a chance to bid on

The racial mix in the United States is changing. More Hispanic, Afro-Americans and Asians enter the work force and more will move into higher management positions. In addition, more foreign companies are operating businesses in America (depicted in the Nissan worker meeting picture). The result is greater diversity and increased need for understanding the importance of different cultures.

Table 8-2 The Legal Base for Staffing

STAFFING AREA	RELEVANT LEGISLATION	IMPACT
Selection and hiring	Title VII, Civil Rights Act (1964) as amended by Equal Employment Opportunity Act (1972)	Bars discrimination based on race, color, religion, sex, or national origin
Compensation	Equal Pay Act (1963)	Equal pay for equal work regardless of sex
Hiring and retirement	Age Discrimination in Employment Act (1967) as amended in 1978	Bars discrimination based on ages 40–70
	Employee Retirement Income Security Act (1974) (ERISA)	Identifies certain vesting rights for employees
Working conditions, health, safety	Occupational Safety and Health Act (1970)	Government-set safety and health standards for work environment
Unions, collective bargaining	National Labor Relations Act Wagner (1935) Taft-Hartley (1947) Landrum-Griffin (1959)	Specifies unfair labor and management practices Gives "bill of rights" for union members by requiring strong internal controls

the job. Where unionized labor is involved, they also notify the union that the job is open. Then they search their own files to see if there are any likely candidates who have applied previously. They will always place an ad in the local papers to assure that they meet Equal Employment Opportunity Commission (EEOC) requirements, in that everyone, regardless of race, religion, color, sex, national origin, or age, has equal access to the newspaper. In addition, they encourage employees to tell their friends about job openings and to make recommendations.

Almost always, that series of actions is enough to obtain a sufficient number of candidates from whom to select. The most likely candidates are then interviewed and sometimes tested; then, if they are still candidates, a background check and a reference check are conducted. If everything checks out satisfactorily, a candidate is hired. This process continues until all the job openings are filled.

The second tier of recruitment is for professional employees. The process here is quite elaborate, and several courses of action occur simultaneously. Let us take the recruitment of engineers as a specific example, because the recruitment strategy is generally applicable to most professional employees.

About a year before any actual recruitment takes place, a recruiting plan is developed. The plan, subject to modification, anticipates what will be the organization's needs for engineers. This determination is based on projected turnover, retirements, anticipated promotions, and future roles in the technical area. It is also based on what management views as desirable technical areas to penetrate or to strengthen and how much money the organization is willing to spend to accomplish those ends. Then an assessment of the desired mix of new engineers is made: What types of specialists? How much experience? What kinds of experience? Once the answers to these questions have been found, human resource managers run through scenarios of the "what if" variety. For example, what if we have to operate on a reduced budget? What if the projected market softens? What if we are able to hire more experienced people than we expected? On the basis of the answers to these questions and others, contingency plans are developed that may be invoked if necessary.

As an aid to the formal recruitment plan, the company often uses a simple but useful technique called a recruiting yield pyramid. (See Figure 8-5 for a pictorial demonstration.)

How does the yield pyramid work?

If our objective is to hire 100 engineers next year, the human resource staff checks their records and experiences and estimates how many offers they must make to yield 100 acceptances. If there is a high demand for engineers, that number might be 300. Again, to make 300 offers, the company's history may tell them to bring 400 men and women to the site for personal interviews and testing. It may be, however, that they must invite 500 candidates to have 400 accept the invitations. To generate a list of 500 generally acceptable candidates requires 1,500 leads. The concept of the yield pyramid is valuable as a planning device even though the specifics will vary from year to year and from job to job.

An advertising strategy is developed to attract experienced candidates. Advertisements are placed in the Sunday business section of the *New York Times* and in all newspapers in a metropolitan area where there is known to be an abundance of working engineers. Advertisements are also placed in professional journals. All advertisements are professionally designed and include the specialties required, as well as the possible locations of the job openings. If only a small number of highly skilled and experienced people are needed, private employment agencies may be used. Their mission is to ferret out skilled and experienced engineers who are currently employed and who can come in at a project engineering management level or higher.

Concurrently, plans are developed for college recruiting. The most promising colleges of engineering are identified, the number depending on the number of engineers who are needed and whether the company wants to maintain good relationships with any specific college. Once the colleges have been identified, the company chooses its recruiting staff.

Recruiters are often taken from the human resource staff, although when a big push in recruiting occurs, more people may be required to do the recruiting than exist among current human resource personnel. Consequently, people are selected from other functions, usually from those who will be employ-

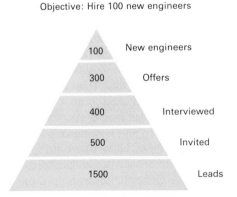

Objective: Hire 100 new engineers

Figure 8-5 Recruiting Yield Pyramid

ferret?

ing the new recruits. The recruiters must be personable, knowledgeable, enthusiastic about the company, and able to relate well to young professional people.

Plans for visiting the colleges are then made. Because the college recruiting job is arduous, requiring intensive interviewing and a great deal of traveling from campus to campus, the country is divided into geographic areas. Recruiters are assigned to those areas and then visit all target campuses within each area. Before visitations are made, the college placement office is notified so that arrangements for private interview space can be made. The students are notified by the college placement office that Eaton is coming to the campus, and they are encouraged to sign up for an interview during a specified time period.

After arriving on the campus, the recruiter is given the list of students who have signed up and the time allocated for each interview. The recruiters may interview as many as fifteen prospects during a day, although the preferred number is between eight and ten. Even so, the recruiters may see so many prospects that they all blend into each other. As a consequence, the recruiters must take copious notes and keep complete records for each interview, as well as writing brief summaries of each to highlight their impressions. Each candidate, therefore, has a reasonably complete file, protected to some extent from the dimmed impressions of recollection that might interfere with a proper assessment of his or her qualifications.

After the recruiters do their rounds, they write up a final brief on each candidate and make recommendations concerning who should be considered further for employment. These briefs, along with the students' records, are then processed by the human resource managers.

The complete file of students and the experienced people recruited through the process previously described are then analyzed to determine the potential pool of likely candidates. From this assessment, judgments are made to determine the best-qualified candidates, and job offers are made.[8]

Most of the materials in this overview have pertained to the staffing of human resources for the organization. It is essential to the long-run success of an organization that the human resources brought into the firm grow and develop. It is not enough to hire good people; they must be managed throughout their employment years. In the next few pages, therefore, we will review some of the other elements in the staffing and managing function of the human resources of an organization.

The Management of Human Assets

As mentioned, the staffing function includes not only the matching of the needs of the organization in recruiting new people but also the dynamic process of retaining the best people in the organization. This management of human assets uses many ideas discussed earlier in this book, but it will be helpful to discuss the following chief elements of the staffing function.[9]

Performance Appraisal

Performance appraisal
A system to rate people's performance in their jobs.

Job evaluation rates and ranks jobs; **performance appraisal** rates people's performance in their jobs. Systematic procedures for rating a person's performance are referred to under several headings (all meaning about the same thing), including efficiency rating, merit rating, merit review, progress appraisal, and performance appraisal. All ratings yield several returns to the company: they supply a control function for people (to be discussed in Chapter 11); they are closely related to motivation theory (discussed in Chapter 13); they encourage an objective basis for pay increases to people who continue in the same job; they enable the company to develop an inventory of people for promotion; and, most important, they provide each person with an answer to the recurring question: "How am I doing?" In short, merit ratings challenge people to do well.

Merit rating systems must be built carefully; if installed too soon, they can fail miserably. Here are some guidelines:

1. Good systems depend upon day-by-day measures of performance of both good and bad points; for example, if a system involves semiannual reviews, the supervisor should keep good records throughout the period and should not depend only on the performance at the time of review.

2. In any merit system, each subordinate should be told the truth. A person who is not performing properly should be told as soon as possible after it becomes clear that his or her performance is not measuring up. The human tendency is to avoid such difficult interviews and to let mistakes build up to an explosion point—at which time it might be too late to effect a change in performance.

3. Good systems encourage involvement by those being rated. Those being rated should know clearly the "rules of the game" and on what basis they are being rated.

4. Systems should rate the performance of the person and not the person himself or herself.

5. The system should be consistent with the training program; for example, a new supervisor should be allowed a learning period and should not be rated on the same basis as those who have had time to develop their skills.

6. Some clear method of describing levels of performance should be developed. Some systems use numbers for identifying quality of performance; others use such terms as *outstanding, satisfactory, improvement needed*, and *unsatisfactory*. See Figure 8-6.[10]

Personal data sheets and merit rating systems help determine the qualifications of people working in the formal job structure of an organization. With this knowledge of the people and their jobs, we can briefly explain how money payments to workers are administered.

Compensation

What is the basis for compensation?

The money paid to each participant in an organization is administered with attention to the three basic subjects illustrated in Figure 8-7 on page 208: the general (community) level of wages and salaries, the internal equity of pay scales, and incentive pay systems.

The general wage level is determined by economic forces. Productivity, collective bargaining, and rates paid by competitors for similar services are important factors treated by labor economists in explaining wage determination.[11] Each company must obtain factual information about wages currently paid in its labor market. From time to time, the company will make a "labor survey" to determine the supply of labor in its market and the going rates of pay.

The internal equity of a company's pay scales depends on relating the value of each person's contribution to that of every other person and to the needs of the company as a whole. An employee's satisfaction with a rate of pay

EMPLOYEE PERFORMANCE REVIEW

Employee Name:_____

Date:_____

Quality				
Factors	Poor-0	Fair-1	Good-2	Excellent-3	Rating points
Appearance of work	Work is generally sloppy and incomplete. Employee has little or no regard for appearance. Work must be redone often _____	Some work is sloppy and incomplete. employee tries to do acceptable work, but rework is required often enough to cause repeated reminders. _____	Work is generally neat and complete. Employee has pride in work. Rework seldom required. _____	Work is exceptionally neat, well.organized, and complete. Employee has exceptional pride in work. Rework rarely required _____	
Accuracy of work	Continuously makes errors. Makes no effort to check own work. Work must be checked 100 percent by others. _____	Frequently makes errors. Checks own work fairly often.Work must be checked 50 percent of the time by others. _____	Occasionally makes errors. Almost always checks own work for accuracy. Only spot checking required by others. _____	Rarely makes errors. Always checks own work. Little or no checking required by others. _____	
Supervision required	Constant direction required with little effect. _____	High degree of direction required to maintain level of quality. _____	Needs occasional direction to maintain a high level of quality. _____	Rarely required direction to maintain outstanding level of quality. _____	
_____ Has improved _____ Little or no change _____ Has regressed	Recommendations for improvement				

Quantity				
Factors	Poor-0	Fair-1	Good-2	Excellent-3	Rating points
Volume	Volume of work is below acceptable level.	Volume of work meets minimum acceptable level. _____	Volume of work meets that of average worker. _____	Volume is exceptional, exceeding average requirements._____	
Utilization of time	Frequently wastes time between assignments. _____	Occasionally wastes working time. _____	Wastes very little of available working time. _____	Utilizes working time to the fullest. _____	
Work pace	Work not organized; rarely meets deadlines. _____	Work is partially organized; frequently misses deadlines. _____	Work is well organized; occasionally misses deadlines. _____	Work is exceptionally well organized; rarely misses deadlines. _____	
Supervision required	Constant direction required to obtain quantity produced. _____	Frequent direction required to obtain quantity produced. _____	Occasional direction required to obtain quantity produced. _____	Rarely requires direction to obtain quantity produced. _____	
_____ Has improved _____ Little or no change _____ Has regressed	Recommendations for improvement				

Figure 8-6 Employee Performance Review

is determined greatly by how the pay relates to that of others. Even a person receiving a very generous wage will consider it unsatisfactory if others less deserving are receiving more. Thus, the manner in which job evaluation and merit rating are translated into money terms is very important in the development of a wage and salary structure that contributes to the long-range goals of the organization.

Systems for providing money incentives have the objective of relating money payments directly to productivity. **Piece-rate plans** are the simplest

Piece-rate plans
A method of compensation calculated by multiplying the quantity of goods produced by a worker by a money rate per piece.

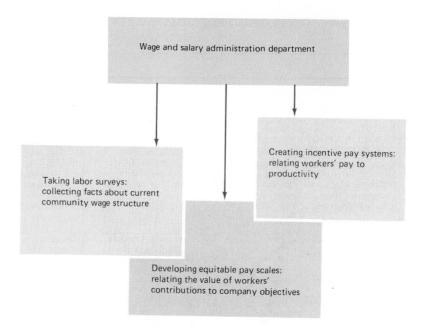

Figure 8-7 Duties of a Wage and Salary Administration Department

and oldest. In these plans, the worker's pay is calculated by multiplying the quantity of products produced by a money rate per piece. Hourly pay systems are often modified by the addition of an incentive element. Merit ratings can be translated into money terms for pay purposes. Many variations of incentive systems are available; however, each company tends to adapt the money-incentive concept to fit its own particular situation.

Training and Development

People never stop learning. Organizations never stop educating and training. Thus, the training function takes the present personnel as raw material and improves and develops them to their highest potential. The direct line supervisors continually serve as on-the-job instructors; however, the personnel department provides a number of training programs that support the improvement of personnel. Table 8-3 depicts a range of training and development experiences.

Training and development can be a costly business. In many cases, it may be difficult for you to see the direct benefit of the expense (especially true with management development activities). Many companies view the training and development of their employees as an investment in a valuable asset— their personnel. The return on that investment may come in one month or one year; it's important to realize that untrained or underdeveloped people will also be a cost to your firm.

This approach of looking into the indirect impact of human resource activities is also applicable to the area of grievances.

Handling Grievances

An organization that claims to have no complaints or grievances may be in worse shape than one with a record of complaints and their satisfactory resolution.[12] Subordinates generally have numerous questions and criticisms; if they

Table 8-3 Training and Development Experiences	
TYPE	EXPLANATION
Orientation sessions	Given to new personnel to explain objectives, policies, procedures of the firm, and specific details of job positions.
Worker training	Given to workers new to a job. They are taught the necessary skills to perform on the job.
Apprentice training	The learner is made an understudy of an experienced person. The apprenticeship usually lasts for a fixed period of time, after which the learner "solos," or goes it alone.
Supervisory training	For supervisors and first-line managers. Topics might include: spreadsheet analysis, dealing with the union, employee participation, quality circles, dealing with minorities, relevant legal developments, or a class in Oriental culture.
Mentorship	One or more junior people are assigned to a senior person (the Mentor). This Mentor serves in a nonthreatening way and provides counsel, guidance, and assistance in topics ranging from problems in work-related skills, to interpersonal problems with a boss, peer, or subordinate, to career questions.
Executive development	Taught to middle- and top-level people, either on-site or off-site. These sessions frequently use experts from outside the company; the programs may be conducted by an executive development consulting firm and may be from one day, to one weekend, to a thirteen-week program at the Harvard Business School; and the topics will range from Acquisition Evaluation to Defending against Hostile Takeovers, from Team Development to Rewarding Individuals, from dealing with local communities to preparing for the global opportunities in the next decade.

are not being expressed, they are being submerged and may cause bigger problems later. Therefore, any organization should maintain an appeals process, a complaint procedure, and means by which this information can flow to the person who can correct the situation.[13]

In companies with unions, the grievance procedure is included as part of the union contract. In general, the procedure is to have the person with the grievance attempt to resolve the matter with the immediate supervisor with the help of the union shop steward. If it cannot be resolved at a lower level, it is referred to higher levels in both union and management organizations. Figure 8-8 outlines this procedure.

Unions and Staffing

The staffing procedures of unionized firms differ from those of nonunionized firms because of the existence of the union's organization structure and the legal aspects of the union contract and collective bargaining. The subject of union–management relations is beyond the scope of this book, but perhaps we can give you some idea of the complexity of this area.

The question of union or nonunion labor is not one of all good or all bad.

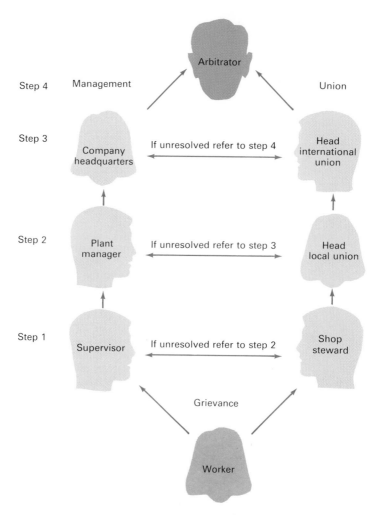

Figure 8-8 Grievance Procedure in a Unionized Company

The existence of a union organization can support company personnel practices and can provide the company with procedures and opportunities that could help management. The chief question is whether the labor-management relations are handled in a favorable climate—one of mutual respect and understanding.[14] The existence of a union can also help the company meet the continual changes that both union and management must face. Since the union is the official representative of all member employees, management need convince only the union officers of needed changes and leave to the union the problems of bringing the membership into line with the changes.

The material you have just read completes the brief overview of the staffing and managing of the human resources of an organization. The perspective was more general than specific, since this is a book on managing, not one on personnel or human resource management. People interested in the personnel or human resource field will find a plentiful supply of excellent books, articles, case studies, arbitrators' hearings and decisions, and research contributions from many different disciplines and areas. The field is a rich one and important for the continued success of most organizations facing change. The description just presented contained historical information about the activities of firms. What is now called for is a shift of focus from the past to the dynamic present and the uncertain future. In the remaining sections of this chapter, you will read of issues that shape both the staffing and the managing of the human resources of an organization. A few introductory paragraphs will prepare you for the context of the important issues.

Two events, 500 years apart, will be seen as having a similar impact upon the thinking of political and economic leaders worldwide. In 1492, Europe discovered that there were opportunities in the west—beyond the seas. Nordic seamen had known about the fishing opportunities in the lands to the west for years, but the news Christopher Columbus brought to Europe created visions of treasures other than fish. In 1992, America will discover there are opportunities in Europe when all trade barriers within the European Community (twelve countries) will be eliminated and a trading market of 320 million people will become a reality. In both instances, economic and material gain served as a motivating force.

The creation of a new economic marketplace in 1992 raises hopes that the powerful nations of the world seem willing to substitute international trade for international aggression as instruments of competition. During the twentieth century, there have been two major hot wars, an energy-draining cold war between the East (dominated by the USSR) and the West (dominated by the United States), two confusing military actions (Korea and Vietnam), two confusing military Russian actions (the suppression of Eastern Europe and Afghanistan), and the Gulf War of 1991 between Iraq and the allied forces of the world.

The United States tasted the impact of economic competition during the 1970s and 1980s when the Japanese and then the Koreans entered the American market in electronics, steel, and autos. There are signs already of the impact the creation of the "Common European Market" will have upon the rest of the industrial world. There are also positive signs of unlimited but difficult manufacturing and trade opportunities that may exist with the USSR and China.

These events do not mean that "world peace and harmony" exist and that basic political questions will fade away. On the contrary. The reunification of Germany will have a tremendous impact on world business; the call for independence from the Baltic countries and other republics of the Soviet Union carries with it the potential danger of local armed conflict. Difficult issues remain in the Middle East. But the possibility of the substitution of international trade for international aggression (and thus the concern for the economic, social, and political status of trading partners) does provide unlimited opportunities for all.

IMPORTANT ISSUES AFFECTING HUMAN RESOURCE MANAGEMENT

What are some contemporary issues in human resources?

A reading or viewing of news media events will convince any skeptic that change is upon us.

The real and potential changes just mentioned provide both threats to and opportunities for American organizations. The impact of these changes upon the staffing and managing of human resources will form the base for the re-

Management Application

The Need for a Change in Scope

Uncertain Economic Situations. International competition will continue; international corporate arrangements will become more common (for example, General Motors–Toyota; Honda Motors with a manufacturing plant in Marysville, Ohio); the shifting of factory work (off-shoring) to lower-cost geographic areas will grow (Mexico, the Pacific Basin, South America, Africa); benefits for economic recovery will not be equally shared, and there will be a trend toward greater polarization into the haves and the have-nots.

Technology Explosion. Automation, robotics, and computerization will grow geometrically; the American concept of work will undergo dramatic changes; organizations will face tension in trying to keep up with changes and the impact of those changes.

People. A part of the American work force will be more educated and will demand more meaningful work and a voice in decisions affecting their work and careers; organizations will have to develop a more flexible approach to all aspects of traditional employment: the job, hours, working conditions, and schedules. Another segment of the work force will be lacking in many basic skill areas, and the need for training will be apparent.

Government Involvement. Government involvement in worker relations is more the norm. The EEOC, OSHA, and EPA will continue to be concerned, although the intensity will ebb with the political climate. More-complex topics will be addressed by the courts: mandatory substance-abuse testing; corporate day-care centers; fetal protection for pregnant women working in plants using dangerous chemicals.

Unions. The unions are facing the greatest challenge to their survival since they won the right to collective bargaining (1935 National Labor Relations Act). The traditional blue-collar factory jobs are declining; companies are increasing their efforts to encourage workers either to decertify union elections or to remain nonunion; companies are using Chapter 11 bankruptcy laws (Continental and Eastern Airlines during the mid- to late 80s) and wage concession strategies to reduce the influence and power of unions; wage rates of many nonunion workers are increasing at a faster rate than those of union workers; and the union leadership is looking for new goals, objectives, approaches, and fields for membership growth.

CHANGE IN PEOPLE PROFILE

	Composition of Labor Force, 1985	New Entrants to Labor Force, 1985-2000
US born white males	47%	15%
US born white females	36%	42%
US born nonwhite males	5%	7%
US born nonwhite females	5%	13%
Immigrant males	4%	13%
Immigrant females	3%	10%

Source (art on p. 213): "Special Report: Where the Jobs Are Is Where the Skills Aren't," *Business Week,* September 19, 1988, pp. 104–105.

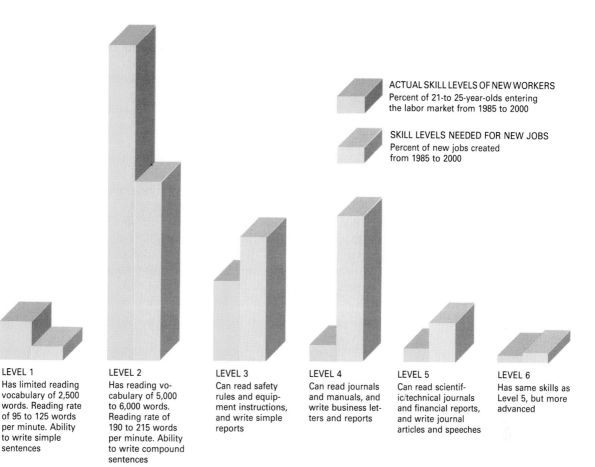

ACTUAL SKILL LEVELS OF NEW WORKERS
Percent of 21-to 25-year-olds entering
the labor market from 1985 to 2000

SKILL LEVELS NEEDED FOR NEW JOBS
Percent of new jobs created
from 1985 to 2000

LEVEL 1
Has limited reading
vocabulary of 2,500
words. Reading rate
of 95 to 125 words
per minute. Ability
to write simple
sentences

LEVEL 2
Has reading vo-
cabulary of 5,000
to 6,000 words.
Reading rate of
190 to 215 words
per minute. Ability
to write compound
sentences

LEVEL 3
Can read safety
rules and equip-
ment instructions,
and write simple
reports

LEVEL 4
Can read journals
and manuals, and
write business let-
ters and reports

LEVEL 5
Can read scientif-
ic/technical journals
and financial reports,
and write journal
articles and speeches

LEVEL 6
Has same skills as
Level 5, but more
advanced

mainder of this chapter. The issues addressed will be the impact of global competition; the need for human capital; and the impact of ideological changes.

The Impact of Global Competition

There are three time frames in the discussion of the impact of global competition upon American firms. The first covers the period of the 1970s and 1980s and resulted in American firms turning to the structural solutions of downsizing their work force or changing their organizational form through mergers and acquisitions. The second time frame, the period of the late 1980s and the 1990s, calls for American firms to select, train, and develop personnel for the coming cultural changes. The third covers the period during the twenty-first century when there may be more developments toward economic community. The "European Community Model" may be replicated in sections of the Soviet Union, the Pacific Basin, Scandinavia, the Northern Hemisphere, and Central and South America. The movement toward economic integration, best illustrated by the European Common Market, may become the model of the future. There will be obvious impact, but for this chapter, we will deal only with the first two time frames and discuss the implications of the solutions within each period.

Downsizing

How does downsizing affect personnel?

The first time frame alluded to earlier occurred shortly after the OPEC oil embargo against Western countries (1973) that led to the fuel crisis. Fuel-efficient automobiles were in high demand, and Japanese manufacturers were supplying them. The resultant decline in demand for "Detroit-type" autos rippled to the supporting industries of steel and rubber. The states of Michigan, Ohio, Indiana, and Illinois suffered as corporations, large and small, adjusted to the switch in consumer demand for cars with higher miles-per-gallon performance. Many solutions were tried as Detroit's Big Three (General Motors, Ford, and Chrysler) struggled to meet governmental standards for miles-per-gallon improvement. Manufacturers attempted to become price-competitive by reducing costs through wage and job rule concessions.

Downsizing of staff also became a common approach. The impact of downsizing, the deliberate reduction of the work force, varies by occupation and level in the organization. Some hourly workers, protected from termination and job transfer through union rules, were able to find new employment with the same firm. Many workers saw their long-run future in other areas and moved from the Midwest to other sections of the country for similar jobs or new careers.

Outplacement

Outplacement Service offered by firms to help their laid-off employees find work with other companies; includes career counseling and the use of firms' resources like telephones, word processors, and Xerox copiers.

Managerial and professional staffs suffered huge reductions as companies terminated 5,000–8,000 employees at a time. Many socially responsible organizations created a new service for people who were facing unemployment because of the economic recession brought about by increased global competition. This new service was called **outplacement** and emphasized the following techniques:

- Career counseling
- Résumé assistance
- Improving interviewing skills
- Improving communication with a prospective employer

When mergers and acquisitions occur, a similar impact is felt by personnel, especially those in professional and managerial positions. Frequently, the motivation behind the merger or acquisition is cost reduction through greater integration of resources: One plant operating at 60 percent of capacity now takes the unused capacity of a plant closed down or sold. Manpower costs are reduced and capacity efficiency is improved. Outplacement services will assist many to find new jobs or careers or to prepare themselves for earlier-than-expected retirement.

Transition Teams

Another approach to dealing with the organizational shifts caused by downsizing, mergers, or acquisitions is to develop a transition team to perform the planning for staff changes. Transition teams can help by doing the following:

- Prepare organizational members for coming changes with accurate and timely communication. Rumors adversely affect morale.
- Identify personnel who might prefer a new work status and allow those people to voluntarily make changes.
- Be an advocate for all affected personnel so that alternative plans may be developed. Flexible or reduced work schedules, voluntary reduction of wages, salaries,

or benefits, and job sharing are a few alternatives to wholesale termination, plant closing, or job transfer.

Cultural Training

This new scope of activity for managers is a direct reflection of the globalization of many aspects of running a business or an organization. The world has now become both larger and smaller. Manufacturing options are no longer concentrated in the Midwest; marketing options are no longer concentrated in New York, Atlanta, Chicago, and Los Angeles; and finance options are no longer concentrated on the East Coast. Locations the world over are becoming options for the manufacture, promotion and distribution, and financing of products and services. The world is larger.

From another point of view, the world is smaller. Communication technology links Semmering, Austria, to Chicago; Interlaken, Switzerland, to Rome, Georgia; and Freudenstadt, Germany, to Stow-on-the-Wold in England. An increasing number of top executives have national roots in Australia or Tokyo or Iceland. The domination and cultural oneness of Western or American managerial personnel is giving way to a much more diversified population.

How are managerial jobs changing?

Either dimension, large or small, demands that American corporations provide training for functioning in new cultures. This training goes beyond preparing people to be tourists in foreign lands; the training goes beyond learning a few foreign phrases ("Where is the rest room?" "How much is the bill?" "Where is the police station?" "Where is the train?" "Where is the American Embassy?"). Managerial personnel must know how to relate and interact with people of different cultures as bosses, peers, subordinates, customers, suppliers, or financial backers. They must learn how to negotiate and bargain with Chinese as well as Mexicans and must realize that an arrogant attitude toward global opportunities will be rejected. Expecting the rest of the world to become "Americanized" will result in "no sale." It is no longer enough to believe that the American perspective of the world is the only one that has validity. The career road for today's new managers will include international exposure.

The Need for Human Capital

The opportunities arising from developments in Europe, the USSR, and China are attractive, even though care must be taken to not be overly optimistic.[15] There are critics of U.S. governmental and corporate policy who fear that these opportunities may be snatched by others. Now that you have seen the explosive changes in jobs and people, the simple techniques may no longer guarantee success. So many American policies, practices, and procedures are based upon assumptions about jobs and people. These assumptions may need revision because of the changing demographics and technology.

- White males will play a smaller role in the U.S. labor force.
- Women and minorities will make up a greater percentage of the U.S. labor force.
- Perhaps 25 percent of the U.S. labor force may not have English as their first language.
- There is a mismatch between the skills demanded for knowledge-intensive jobs and the limited skills new workers possess.

Global Application

Solutions to Shortages of Qualified Workers and Managers

Japan and the United States face the same problem: an aging and shrinking work force. In the United States, the baby boomers are working their way to retirement while the birth rate has been falling for the past twenty years. In Japan, there are 143 jobs for every 100 job seekers. Corporate recruiters at Japanese college campuses offer trips to Hawaii, bonuses, and other incentives to attract qualified graduates to the corporations. Both countries are faced with a shortage of skilled laborers ready to work with new technology, including robotics and computers. Both countries are faced with a shortage of creative and flexible managers ready to compete in an international marketplace. The shortages are not just in the United States and Japan. The Soviet Union, facing a new future as a democratic, free-market society, also faces a shortage of managers trained to lead their companies into international competition. Both Taiwan and China have been growing very rapidly economically. This growth could be halted by a lack of managers.

All these countries are basically seeking the same solutions to the shortage of qualified workers and managers: (1) training and (2) changing societal and corporate cultures to bring in previously underutilized talent in women and minorities.

In the United States, Sears is helping to create a curriculum in a Chicago vocational school. The student studies regular academic subjects, such as English and history, for three hours a day, and electronics, electricity, and appliances for three hours a day. In addition, the student may opt to work twenty hours per week at a Sears store as an apprentice technician. Sears is attempting this program in an effort to relieve the shortage of technicians.

At Marshall and Grant high schools in Portland, Oregon, students obtain on-the-job training at twenty local employers, including IBM,

First Interstate Bank, and Providence Medical Center. The students must be from poverty-level families and maintain at least a 2.0 grade point average in academic subjects. They work in entry-level positions and are paid entry-level wages. After they graduate from high school, they are often employed by the company that supplied the on-the-job training.

Other U.S. companies are identifying promising students early in their academic careers, usually at the junior high school level. A special effort is made to target blacks and minorities, to encourage them to go on to college to help relieve the shortages in engineering and science.

Throughout the Soviet Union, new schools and training programs are springing up as businesses try to change attitudes. For decades, all Soviet decisions were made at the top, and the master plan was handed down to businesses to fulfill. The emphasis was on quantity, not quality. Now Soviet businesses must figure out how to improve quality and productivity and relieve shortages of everything from soap to steel. The Soviet managers are now taking crash courses in everything from quality to cash flow.

Asia may have even more problems than the Soviet Union. In Singapore, for example, only 6 percent of the population is college-educated as compared with 23 percent in the United States and 16 percent in Japan. The educational system is very elitist. The averages are not much higher for Korea and other countries in that region. New universities are springing up, and new MBA and management training programs are being offered.

Both societal and corporate cultures are being changed worldwide in response to the need for more creative and flexible workers and managers. In China, for example, promotions have traditionally been based on longevity—the people who stayed with the company the longest received the most pay, regardless of their abilities or what they contributed to the company. This is being changed so that companies now pay for ability and contributions and not longevity. In countries that had been run by dictators but are now moving more toward democracy, workers are demanding more freedom, more responsibility, and more participation in decision making. In all countries, women and minorities are being utilized more in the work force, and United States companies are looking to women and other minorities as the next source of management talent. Entire cultures are being changed, both inside and outside the corporations.

References: "Moscow Tackles Its Manager Gap," *U.S. News and World Report*, July 31, 1989, pp. 40–41; Ford S. Worthy, "Asia: You Can't Grow if You Can't Manage," *Fortune*, June 3, 1991, pp. 83–88; Nancy J. Perry, "Training: The Workers of the Future," *Fortune*, Special Issue: The New American Century (Spring-Summer, 1991), pp. 68–72; Robert Neff, "International Business: When in Japan, Recruit as the Japanese Do—Aggressively," *Business Week*, June 24, 1991, p. 58.

- Job growth will be in the high-skill occupations.
- Written and oral communication skills will be in high demand.

Other conclusions from employment projection and global education statistics paint a challenging picture. In the United States, there has been a decline in birth rates since 1960; Japan and Europe show greater "success statistics" in their educational systems. Japanese and European elementary and high school students spend more days in class, score higher on math and science tests, and have fewer dropouts. American corporations thus face a serious resource problem. There is a shortage of traditional work-force personnel, the new jobs call for a more highly educated work force, and many of the new entrants available in the labor pool do not have the job skills for employment in a competitive world.

Managerial jobs are also changing rapidly. The developments in computers and management information systems (to be discussed more fully in Chapter 17) have done away with many positions in middle management; more jobs are demanding skills in knowledge and information processing; managerial work is being redesigned for team, rather than individual, responsibility; mobility among all levels of management is increasing—you can no longer assume that a manager will spend his or her entire career with one company; more managers are having international experiences; more of the middle and top managers are not U.S.-born.

The need for human capital is a pressing one. Corporations no longer have the luxury of having the pick of the crop. Human resource and managerial personnel at every level will become more involved in staffing and managing people. All will have to be prepared and trained for the changes affecting U.S. organizations.

The Impact of Ideological Changes

The changes described in the previous sections are more than statistics; there are ideological changes coming into the American work force as well. It is obvious that new workers will have different needs (as mentioned in the previous section), will perhaps respond differently to supervision, will have a unique set of expectations and career aspirations, and may have no understanding or appreciation of the history of employment within your industry or

For the labor movement to survive in the United States, union leaders must accept the need for change in the mission and goals of the union. Some believe unions are no longer needed; some believe workers will always need representation from potential or real employer exploitation.

firm. We will review just two of the many changes that will affect the ideology of the workplace: the new role for labor unions and the notion that participation in decision making is a right of all workers.[16]

New Unions

In the United States, the history of labor–management relations is one of conflict, struggle, government involvement through the courts and legislation, and growth and decline of unions as a percentage of the labor force. Most of the relationships between labor and management could be described as adversarial, although some have had success at cooperative efforts.

Union leaders face difficult choices as companies seek cost reductions and threaten to close plants and move employment to lower-wage countries. Traditional manufacturing blue-collar jobs, the backbone of the labor movement, are in decline, and the growing service industry frequently does not lend itself to organization. Unionization among teachers, however, has achieved success and represents a significant portion of union growth.

A major complaint from management is that restrictive union rules and excessive wage rates put U.S. companies at a competitive disadvantage. Table 8-4 shows that changes are coming, however, from some of the unions.

The role union leaders will take in the changes brought on by increasing globalization is not clear. There seems to be potential for change; at the same time, there are those in management who feel that now is the time to deal the labor movement a severe setback. They believe that the American public supports management efforts to keep jobs within the United States; the climate seems favorable for a shift in power from labor to management. The American labor movement, however, is strongly supported by legislation and a political system that would question the possibility of drastic revision in prescribed relationships. A direct threat to the labor movement will bring a strong resistance to change. There are some who believe that management's best approach to

Table 8-4   Changes in Work Rules Being Generated by Unions

WORK AREA	MAJOR CHANGES IN WORK RULES	INDUSTRIES INVOLVED
Job assignments	Cutting size of crews; enlarging jobs by adding duties, eliminating unneeded jobs	Steel, autos, railroads, meat packing, airlines
Skilled maintenance and construction	Combining craft jobs such as millwright, welder, rigger, and boilermaker; allowing journeymen to perform helpers' duties; permitting equipment operators to run more than one machine	Autos, rubber, steel, petroleum, construction
Hours of work	Giving up relief and washup periods; allowing management more flexibility in scheduling daily and weekly hours; working more hours for the same pay	Autos, rubber, steel, meat packing, trucking, airlines (pilots), textile
Seniority	Restricting use of seniority in filing, "bumping" during layoffs, and picking shifts	Autos, rubber, meat packing, steel
Wages	Restricting pay to hours worked rather than miles traveled	Railroads, trucking
Incentive pay	Reducing incentives to reflect changing job conditions	Rubber, steel
Teamwork	Allowing team members to rotate jobs; permitting pay for knowledge instead of function, allowing management to change crew structure to cope with new technology	Autos, auto suppliers; steel, rubber

Source: John Douglas, Stuart M. Klein, and David Hunt, *The Strategic Managing of Human Resources,* New York: John Wiley, 1985.

reducing the importance of labor is through employee participation programs. But even with those programs, the picture is fuzzy.

Participation as a Right

Many of the new management approaches to human resource administration come from techniques of European or Japanese firms. Quality-control circles and employee participation programs seem to provide one way to give a voice to workers seeking involvement. Not everyone sees participation in the same light. For example, here are some different interpretations of employee participation.

- An opportunity to give workers a voice in decisions that affect them.
- A tactic to minimize the need for union personnel to represent people on the issues of hours, wages, and working conditions.
- A method for employees to feel a part of the company.
- A motivational fad that works only if there are productivity gains, reduction of costs, or improvement of quality. The involvement is conditional, not freely given.
- It may be illegal under Section 2(5) of the National Labor Relations Act as unlawful domination by management of a labor organization.

Table 8-5 Principles of Work Design	
AT THE INDIVIDUAL LEVEL	**AT THE GROUP LEVEL**
Optimum variety of tasks within the job	A necessary interdependence of jobs (for technical or psychological reasons).
A meaningful pattern of tasks that gives to each job a semblance of a single, overall task	Individual jobs entail a relatively high degree of stress.
Optimum length of the work cycle	Individual jobs do not make a perceivable contribution to the utility of the end product.
Some scope for setting standards of quantity and quality of production and a suitable feedback of knowledge of results	The linkages create some semblance of an overall task.
The inclusion in the job of some of the auxiliary and preparatory tasks	There is some scope for setting standards and receiving knowledge of results.
	Some control can be exercised over the "boundary tasks."
The inclusion of some degree of care, skill, knowledge, or effort that is worthy of respect in the community	
The inclusion of some perceivable contribution to the utility of the product for the consumer	Channels of communication are such that the minimum requirements of the workers can be fed into the design of new jobs at an early stage.
	Channels of promotion to supervisor rank exist that are sanctioned by the workers.

Source: Adapted from Andrew H. Van de Ven and William F. Joyce, eds., *Perspectives on Organization Design and Behavior* (New York: John Wiley & Sons, Inc., 1981), p. 43. Reproduced with permission.

Other efforts to provide meaningful work can be seen in Table 8-5. Many workers want more meaningful work, and a response to this need comes from being both flexible in work design and receptive to a search for new forms of job arrangements.

Ford Motor Company, Volvo (in Sweden), Kroger Company, U.S. Air Force Air Logistics Center (Ogden, Utah), and Smith-Kline Company (in Philadelphia), to name but a few companies, have implemented work-design principles and enrichment of jobs to achieve long-run productivity gains.

SOME CONCLUSIONS

This chapter is a good representation of the dynamic character of the field of managing. The need for sound staffing and managing of human resources is clearly seen from a historical perspective of the evolution of the workplace. The objective of matching jobs and people would rarely draw argumentation. Yet, a review of just a few issues facing the contemporary manager shows a set of changes unlike any of the past.

International competition highlighted the weaknesses in American industry. This same competition provides U.S. firms with unbelievable opportunities. A close look at the labor supply in America points to many, many difficulties in the next few decades. All factors point to critical changes coming in the culture of firms.

American managers must realize that their missions, objectives, procedures, policies, and practices reflect a value system that is a by-product of a culture created by a different set of players. Staffing an organization is the most direct way of creating a new culture or the reinforcement of the status quo. Some CEOs want subordinates who are exact images of themselves; some want new entrants for their image value ("we just hired twelve lawyers from the most prestigious Ivy League school"); some truly hire with an eye to supporting affirmative action goals; and some may staff with an expectation of finding the most flexible people possible, since the future cannot be predicted with any certainty.

Our objective was to show you as much of the turmoil as possible. Facing reality is one of the trademarks of a contemporary manager.

SUMMARY

The person who plans to be a manager in today's world needs to understand all dimensions of the environment and context within which an organization seeks to staff itself with human resources. We have seen in this chapter those elements that constitute some basics of staffing and managing human resources: determining the job structure and the qualifications of the people. The importance of the legal base was highlighted, and reference was made to the greater detail found in the Appendix of this chapter. The overview section of the chapter ended with a description of many factors used in managing human assets: performance appraisal, compensation, training and development, handling grievances and staffing when your people are part of a union arrangement.

The tone of the chapter changed when a few relevant issues were discussed, most stemming from the dramatic escalation of global competitiveness, the urgent need for human capital, and a thought-provoking insight into some ideological changes.

KEY TERMS

Staffing Selecting, training, and evaluating people and matching people with the requirements of organizational structure.

Job analysis The orderly and systematic assembling of all the facts about a job.

Job description A written statement that defines the duties, relationships, and results expected of anyone in the job.

Job specification Statement of the requirements for a person to do a job.

Job evaluation The process of studying job descriptions and specifications to determine levels of responsibility and degree of difficulty for grading and pay purposes.

Directed interview The interviewer sets the purposes of an interview and then guides it to its conclusion.

Nondirected interview A more free-flowing interview that allows both parties an opportunity to pursue promising avenues.

Performance appraisal A system to rate people's performance in their jobs.

Piece-rate plans A method of compensation calculated by multiplying the quantity of goods produced by a worker by a money rate per piece.

Outplacement Service offered by firms to help their laid-off employees find work with other companies; includes career counseling and the use of firms' resources like telephones, word processors, and Xerox copiers.

STUDY ASSIGNMENTS

1. The opening case concerning BMC's restructuring illustrated a situation faced by many U.S. corporations during the 1980s and the early 1990s. What are the human resource management issues and challenges raised when an organization undergoes downsizing or restructuring? How can the need for extensive restructuring be prevented through effective human resource management?

2. What are some of the reasons it is so difficult to match the right person to the right job?

3. Compare and contrast the staffing approach of designing the job first and fitting people to the position and the approach of first hiring the individual and then building the organization around the individual.

4. How do the staffing problems of a small firm compare with the staffing problems of a large Fortune 500 firm?

5. Describe the four-step process of determining the job structure. Why should line managers, not involved with the human resource function, need to know and understand the job structure process?

6. Compare and contrast the different approaches used to determine and evaluate the job qualifications of an individual. Which approach is most effective and why?

7. What are some of the strengths and weaknesses of the interview approach in the hiring and placement process?

8. With respect to human resource management, how have legal considerations, legislative acts, and labor agreements influenced the selection, hiring, placement, and promotion process?

9. Knowing what you know about the hiring and placement process, what would you do to improve your chances of getting a job? What would you do to ensure that you are applying for the right job for you?

10. Discuss some of the strengths and weaknesses of using performance appraisals in the management of an organization's human assets.

11. How can employee training and development be utilized to enhance the performance of an organization's human resources?

12. When it comes to employee compensation, why are organizations discovering that they must consider and offer their employees more than just wages or salaries? How does a manager determine the appropriate compensation for a particular employee performing a particular job?

13. What is your assessment of the current relationship between labor unions and management in the United States? How does that relationship affect the overall competitiveness of the United States? What do you think should be the role of unions in the future?

14. What do you believe will be the human resource management issues and challenges of the twenty-first century? What will managers and organizations have to do to prepare for these human resource management challenges?

APPENDIX

Selected Federal Legislation Affecting Human Resource Management and Labor Relations			
LAW OR EXECUTIVE ORDER	FOCUS	DESCRIPTION, PROVISIONS	SCOPE AND LIMITATIONS

I. Union–Management Relations Legislation

LAW OR EXECUTIVE ORDER	FOCUS	DESCRIPTION, PROVISIONS	SCOPE AND LIMITATIONS
Arbitration Act (1888)	Labor–management relations	Provides for the use of arbitration and investigative boards, especially in work stoppages.	Applied to railroad industry only.
Sherman Anti-Trust Act (1890)	Anti-monopoly	Relevant to labor relations because the act was applied to union boycotts of an employer; thus, all boycotts were held to be illegal under this act.	Clayton Act (1914) exempted unions from the provisions but did not protect unions from civil damage suits resulting from economic sanctions by unions.
Erdman Act (1898)	Labor–management relations	Encouraged railroad employers to add mediation and conciliation to the terms of the Arbitration Act (above).	Initially protected labor against dismissal or discrimination based on union membership, but this portion of the act was declared invalid by the U.S. Supreme Court.
Railway Labor Act (1926)	Labor–management relations	Required employers to bargain collectively and legitimized the right to organize: prohibits discrimination on the basis of union membership; also provides for settlement of railway labor disputes through mediation, voluntary arbitration, and fact-finding boards.	Established a mediation board. Early legislation focused on the railroad industry, because the U.S. government had clear regulatory power in this industry.
Norris-La Guardia (1932)	Labor–management relations	Severely restricts an employer's ability to obtain an injunction that forbids a union to engage in picketing or strike activity; also makes yellow-dog contracts (prehire agreement not to join a union) unenforceable.	
National Labor Relations Act (NLRA) or Wagner Act (1935)	Union–management relations	Established a national policy protecting the right of the worker to organize and bargain collectively; also defines unfair labor practices and provides for good-faith bargaining, representation election, etc.	Administered by the National Labor Relations Board (NLRB), also set up by the Wagner Act.

Selected Federal Legislation Affecting Human Resource Management and Labor Relations *(continued)*

LAW OR EXECUTIVE ORDER	FOCUS	DESCRIPTION, PROVISIONS	SCOPE AND LIMITATIONS
Labor-Management Relations Act or Taft-Hartley (1947)	Union practices	Defined unfair union practices, among them: coercion of employers in selecting the party to bargain in their behalf, refusal to bargain collectively with an employer, charging excessive initiation fees, featherbedding (requiring employer under a union rule to pay for more employees than needed; or to limit production), closed shops.	Amendment to the NLRA (1935); also modified conditions under which injunctions could be used to include strikes found to threaten the nation's health and safety by allowing for an 80-day "cooling off" period.
Labor-Management Reporting and Disclosure Act or Landrum-Griffin (1959)	Union reform	Designed to eliminate improper activities; provides standards on financial dealings and business practices of labor organizations; safeguards union election procedures, closes loopholes in earlier legislation protecting employers against secondary boycotts.	Amendment to the NLRA (1935).

II. Wages, Hours, and Working Conditions

Davis Bacon Act (1931)	Wages	Mandates payment of prevailing wage rates and fringe benefits, a standard 8-hour day, and overtime compensation.	Affects private contractors engaged in public-works construction involving more than $2,000 and public construction projects financed with $2,000 or more in federal funds.
Social Security Act (1935: amended approximately every two years)	Employee benefits	Established a federal tax placed on payrolls to provide for unemployment and retirement benefits, disability benefits, and old-age and survivors' insurance; automatically adjusted benefits tied to consumer price index.	Includes fully insured (worked in covered employment 10 years) individuals eligible for retirement benefits and currently insured (worked 18 months of last three years in covered employment) employees, eligible for unemployment and disability coverage only.
Walsh-Healey Act or Public Contract Act (1936)	Wages and safety	Required firms doing business with the government to pay at least the prevailing minimum wage rate for that industry; required overtime compensation for work in excess of 8 hours in a day or a 40-hour week; regulated safety and health issues and child labor.	Restricted to those doing business with the government in excess of $10,000 annually; exempts professional, executive, and administrative classes as well as solely office or custodial workers; thus, the classes "exempt" and "non-exempt"

Selected Federal Legislation Affecting Human Resource Management and Labor Relations *(continued)*

LAW OR EXECUTIVE ORDER	FOCUS	DESCRIPTION, PROVISIONS	SCOPE AND LIMITATIONS
Fair Labor Standards Act (1938; last amended in 1977)	Hours and wages	Extends minimum wage provision to include most workers in commerce, hospitals, educational institutions, all levels of government.	Exempts specific groups, notably specifying supervisors (who may not spend more than 20% of their time doing the same work as their subordinates and who must be salaried), thus identifying them as part of management.
Equal Pay Act (1963; amended by Education Act, 1972)	Discrimination in wages	Prohibits wage differential based on sex.	Includes only those employers subject to the Fair Labor Standards Act; administered by the Equal Employment Opportunity Commission since 1979.
Occupational Safety and Health Act or OSHA (1970)	Safety	Sets mandatory standards for safety and health.	Extended from private sector to federal agencies by Executive Order 12196 (1980).

III. Employment Rights

Immigration and Naturalization Act (1952; frequent amendments)	Employment discrimination	Covers the hiring of resident aliens and the hiring of new or prospective immigrants.	Some court cases have also used the Fourteenth Amendment to the Constitution, Section 1, to argue that it is "people," not "citizens," who are covered by constitutional rights.
Civil Rights Act (1964; last amended 1978)	Employment discrimination	Prohibits hiring, discharge, or discrimination due to race, color, religion, sex, or national origin.	Defines exceptions due to bona fide occupational qualifications; also exempts classes including employers with fewer than 15 employees, employment agencies, and training programs.
Executive Order 11246 (1965; amended by 11375, 1967)	Minority or protected classes	Prohibits discrimination on the basis of race, color, religion, sex, or national origin at any point in recruitment, transfer, promotion, or termination.	Administered by the Office of Personnel Management; established Office of Federal Contract Compliance Programs.
Age Discrimination in Employment Act (1967; last amended 1978)	Employees age 40–70	Prohibits discrimination against employees in the protected class (age 40–70) and defines need for bona fide occupational qualifications or need for good-	

Selected Federal Legislation Affecting Human Resource Management and Labor Relations *(continued)*

LAW OR EXECUTIVE ORDER	FOCUS	DESCRIPTION, PROVISIONS	SCOPE AND LIMITATIONS
Fair Credit Reporting Act (1971)	Consumer credit	cause dismissal to be applied to disqualify persons in this age group. Provides employees with the right to review and correct any information in their file, and to delete or omit obsolete information; requires users to notify consumers if they are using the credit information.	
Equal Employment Opportunity Act (1972)	Employment discrimination	Strengthens the enforcement powers of the Equal Employment Opportunity Commission (EEOC)	Extends the coverage of Title VII of the Civil Rights Act to government employees and those in higher education.
Rehabilitation Act (1973)	Employee rights	Mandates affirmative action programs for hiring, placing, and advancing handicapped persons.	Includes rehabilitated alcoholics and drug addicts; only exemptions are private-sector firms receiving less than $2,500 annually in federal contracts.
Comprehensive Employment and Training Act or CETA (1973)	Disadvantaged, underemployed, and unemployed	Provides for local direction and control of training programs.	
Vietnam Era Veterans Readjustment Assistance Act (1974)	Employment opportunity	Requires affirmative action to hire and advance Vietnam era veterans	Applies only to firms holding federal contracts or subcontracts of $50,000 or more.

Case for Discussion

JAMISON MANUFACTURING COMPANY

Ken Steinweg is in charge of the employment office of the Jamison Manufacturing Company. His office recruits and hires individuals for hourly and salaried positions and then places the new employees in entry-level positions. Despite a good economy, business has slowed somewhat for the company. Because of this decline, Ken began a comprehensive review of the recruiting and hiring policies and procedures, to evaluate their impact on the operations of the company.

Jamison Manufacturing is a nonunion firm and has an excellent reputation with regard to employment practices. The company has never experienced a strike, and there has been only one, unsuccessful attempt to organize the work force. The company has very low turnover rates, low absenteeism, and few filed grievances.

Two policies serve as Ken's guidelines for recruiting and hiring hourly and salaried employees. The first policy is that individuals will be recruited and hired to fill entry-level positions only. The second policy is that only individuals who have no prior working experience are to be considered for employment. These policies have been a part of the company's employment practices for over fifty years. With few exceptions, the company has filled its vacant nonentry-level positions by internal placement or promotion.

Most managers believe that these two policies have served the company well, particularly since Jamison Manufacturing has been considered a leader in its field for a number of years.

For an entry-level machine operator's position, Ken's staff would rather recruit and hire a 48-year-old housewife who has no working experience than to recruit and hire a highly trained and experienced 25-year-old male machinist. Management has come to believe that it is easier to train an inexperienced individual to adopt what management considers are desirable attitudes and work habits than it is to correct inappropriate attitudes and work habits of an experienced individual, particularly if that individual has been a union member or has worked in a union shop. So although training an inexperienced individual may require more time in the short run, in the long run the employee will perform better and will have a greater commitment to the goals and objectives of the company.

Jamison Manufacturing has been making essentially the same products for over fifty years. However, in recent years, high technology has had a significant impact on the industry in which the company operates. Jamison's reputation for quality gave the company a competitive edge for years, but that edge was lost as Jamison's competitors adapted high technology to their products.

Many of the company's managers have argued that if the company is to maintain its leadership position, it will have to establish operations to produce high-tech components and products. However, it will be extremely difficult for Jamison Manufacturing to fill middle-management and senior engineering positions in newly established high-tech operations by internal placement or promotion. Although the managers and engineers that Jamison hires directly out of the universities have been exposed to the latest managerial practices or new technology, these individuals simply do not have the experience necessary to succeed in middle management and senior engineering positions.

Like most managers, Ken believes that although the recruiting and hiring practices have influenced the success of the company, now is the time to adjust the hiring and recruiting policies. Ken and other managers have begun to argue that if Jamison Manufacturing Company is to regain its leadership position, it must change those policies and practices that prevent the company from being able to respond effectively to changing conditions.

Chapter 9

Directing: The Leadership Function

Learning Objectives

1. **Define** the term leadership.
2. **State** some reasons why organizations need leaders.
3. **Explain** how leaders differ at each level of management.
4. **Define** the basic two-factor theory of leadership.
5. **State** some limitations of the two-factor theory.
6. **Compare** the two-factor theory with three contemporary themes.
7. **Explain** why the situational theory emerged.
8. **Describe** two nontraditional leadership themes.
9. **Present** a summary statement on the status of leadership today.

I N 1984, Texas billionaire H. Ross Perot sold his computer service company, EDS, to General Motors. As a result of the sale, Perot became GM's largest stockholder, and he assumed a position on GM's Board of Directors. Perot's reason for selling went far beyond money. It represented Perot's personal commitment and mission to restore, wherever he could, America's competitive edge. In this instance, the sale gave him an opportunity to help rebuild the image and competitive ability of the recognized symbol of American business, General Motors.

When he joined GM, he found it hard to believe that with all its resources, the corporation was unable to produce quality products and effectively respond to the Japanese threat. During his first few months at GM, he talked with hundreds of GM's employees, managers, and customers about what was wrong with the corporation. He concluded that the decline of GM could be attributed specifically to a lack of leadership on the part of GM's management. He decided to bring to GM the type of managerial leadership that he had created at EDS, leadership that had made EDS's performance and commitment to its employees second to none.

Perot's record at EDS was legendary. From a $1,000 investment, Perot built EDS into a billion-dollar organization in less than a decade. He achieved this phenomenal success by emphasizing customer service and by instilling in his employees a commitment to being the best. He had a tremendous ability to inspire and challenge his employees. His unbounded enthusiasm and a "can do"

approach served as a role model for his employees. At EDS, he demonstrated his belief that a manager must earn the trust and respect of his employees before he or she can lead them. One of the most noted examples of how Perot accomplished this was the commando raid he mounted in 1980 to free two employees jailed in Iran during the Iranian hostage crisis. The results of Perot's unique approach to managerial leadership was quite evident. The employees of EDS were extremely loyal, its customers promoted EDS's reputation for quality and service, the firm was recognized as the industry leader by both observers and competitors, and the shareholders were extremely pleased with the return they received on their investment.

At GM, however, things were "different." Perot found that GM's managers viewed customers, shareholders, and labor as adversaries. He also discovered that GM's management consistently relied on money to solve problems, even when the situation only required effective leadership. Ironically, GM's senior

A forceful and dynamic
H. Ross Perot.

Leadership The ability to
influence people, to direct
their activities toward a
goal. Includes the people,
the organizational positions
and levels, and the situations surrounding the
leadership event; includes
concern for task, concern
for people, and other
factors.

management followed the same kind of thinking in dealing with Perot. Perot's efforts to revamp GM's bureaucratic management style became a problem for GM's top management. His energy, commitment to the customer, and zeal in advocating leadership over technology to influence organizational perfor-mance were too much for GM's management to stomach. In the end, their so-lution was to eliminate Perot as a problem by using $700 million, twice the market value of his holdings in GM, to buy him out.

But Perot was not finished with his mission. After leaving GM, he contin-ued to advocate his view that GM needed a heavy dose of leadership to turn its adverse situation around. Many interested parties listened to what Perot had to say, particularly when GM's fortunes continued to decline during the late 1980s. He argued both publicly and privately that GM needed to break away from the traditions of the past. He suggested that if GM wanted to regain its former position in the marketplace, it would need to radically overhaul the way it does business, and its employees would have to make a total commit-ment to working together as a team. Such a commitment, according to Perot, required inspired managerial leadership, starting from the top of the organiza-tion. Unfortunately for GM, H. Ross Perot was no longer in a position to provide the type of managerial leadership needed to reestablish General Mo-tors as the unquestioned leader of the automobile industry. ■

The term **leadership** has as many meanings and interpretations as there are people discussing the topic. To some, it brings to mind outstanding per-sonalities. Few would argue that John Fitzgerald Kennedy, Martin Luther King, Jr., and most recently, former British Prime Minister Margaret Thatcher were people of unusual force and persuasion. The biographies of many great people are filled with early indications of leadership ability, suggesting that these peo-ple were special and that fulfillment of their destiny was just a matter of time. There are other great people whose destiny seemed matched to particular events in time. Would Fidel Castro be as well remembered if his leadership skills had been confined to his original legal career, if there had been no Cuban revolution? Would Susan B. Anthony have displayed leadership skills if she had stayed at home "in her place"? Winston Churchill was a fading politi-cian until events in Central Europe exploded into World War II. There are some historians who believe that without Churchill, the British effort might have failed. For these people, the situations seemed to be ready for them, or events brought them the attention needed to get started.

To others, the term *leadership* has no overtones of greatness; people are leaders because the organization defines their job in that way. Take, for exam-ple, the traditional infantry army sergeants; they are leaders because they have the authority to be leaders, to issue orders. To us, the term describes an act that influences the direction of the behavior of other people.

Your future in management as a leader would certainly be limited if the only two options were as an outstanding personality (a rare event) and as a stamped-out replica of a tin soldier (a depressing event). You might feel that the materials presented so far in this book should be sufficient for managing an organization. At this point, you know something about planning, setting ob-jectives, organizing the workplace and the work force, staffing the unit, and de-cision making. Isn't that enough? What would happen in organizations if there were no leaders? Wouldn't the work still continue? Do leaders make any differ-ence?

Global Application

Leading and Managing the Stateless Corporation

Evolving from the multinational corporations are the stateless or global corporations. The stateless corporation knows no national boundaries and has no home country. The stateless corporation takes full advantage of global opportunities, creating global products that will satisfy wants and needs all around the world, and not just in a few countries; locating labs and research facilities where they will accomplish the most, regardless of national boundaries; and placing manufacturing facilities where they will make the most effective use of resources and provide the best service to customers, regardless of the impact on individual countries. A global manager must be

■ A global strategist. The global manager should feel equally at home in Singapore, Chicago, Paris, and Rio de Janeiro, should be able to design products with all those locations in mind, and should be able to make deals effectively everywhere in the world.

■ A master of technology. The global manager must be computer- and technology-literate and be able to accept and process information quickly. The global manager often has a jet plane for an office: he or she flies between numerous work sites throughout the world, receiving information from fax machines and satellites and processing it on a laptop computer to make sharp decisions. In addition, the global manager must know how to harness technology to create innovative products and services.

■ A politician par excellence. The global manager must be able to balance the global corporation's economic interests with those of the local cul-

ture. The global manger must keep a global outlook yet act like a local citizen, whether that citizenry be in Brazil, the United States, Japan, or Germany. The global manager is a native no matter where he or she is at a particular moment.

■ A leader/motivator. The global manager must be a leader/motivator both inside and outside the global corporation. This may require twice as much charisma and twice as much nerve as a traditional manager.

Percy Barnevik is a global leader. He is the CEO of ASEA Brown Boveri; he is Swedish. In 1987, Barnevik merged Sweden's ASEA with another electrical engineering company, Switzerland's Brown Boveri. In 1989, he purchased Combustion Engineering, Inc., of the United States. Now, top management—which includes Swedish, Swiss, and German executives—works out of an office in Zurich while research, development, manufacturing, and marketing firms are located throughout the world, without regard for national boundaries. The books and records are kept in English, and business transactions are handled in U.S. dollars. Barnevik spends much of his time in a jet plane, traveling throughout the world.

References: William Holstein, Snaley Reed, Jonathan Kapstein, Todd Vogel, Joseph Weber, "Cover Story: The Stateless Corporation," *Business Week,* May 14, 1990, pp. 98–105; Clemons P. Work, Beth Brophy, Andrea Gabor, Robert F. Black, Mike Tharp, Alice Cueno, "The 21st Century Executive," *U.S. News and World Report,* March 7, 1988, pp. 48–51; Jeremy Main, "How to Go Global and Why," *Fortune,* August 28, 1989, pp. 70–76.

Studies have shown that women have a different style of leadership than men. Some believe that this is a result of cultural differences between men and women. Women were traditionally raised to nurture those around them; men were traditionally raised to compete with those around them. Some believe that women are better managers.

THE DEMAND FOR LEADERSHIP

Is leadership necessary?

According to authors Daniel Katz and Robert L. Kahn, there are at least four inescapable facts of organizational life that demand leadership.[1]

- No matter how superior the planning, charts, procedures, scheduling, and design, there is a fundamental *incompleteness* in organizations. Gaps appear, overlaps emerge, and the segments would come apart if it were not for someone functioning as a leader.

- A fact of life is *environmental change.* Few firms can isolate themselves from the external environment, and your own life experiences attest to the almost frantic types and rates of change. Organizations need people to interpret these changes—people who can then transmit the character or urgency of the new approaches demanded.

- The *internal dynamics* of organizations represent a third fact that requires someone in leadership. Organizations are composed of many parts or subsystems. The value, strength, vitality, purpose, and power of each subsystem is in constant interaction with those of other subsystems in the organization. If left to their own movements and energy, subunits might never become functional for the whole organization. If each wheel of an automobile were to operate totally independently, there's no telling what kind of ride would result.

- The last fact of life should be apparent to you: *The nature of human membership in organizations is somewhat unpredictable,* at least in the specific sense. Human behavior and subsequent responses vary so greatly that individual leadership is needed for adjustment and adaptation.

The conclusion from these observations is clear: Organizations and their members need direction. The history of successful and unsuccessful firms and their people suggests that directing the resources, especially the human resources, is not as easy as it may seem. The basic objective of this chapter, therefore, is the study of the directing function of management. In particular, we want to know what leadership is, what conditions make for effective leadership, and what you might do to become an effective leader.

A word of caution must be given early in this study of leadership. *There is no one leadership or management style for all people and situations.* Recall the opening case and ask yourself why H. Ross Perot was effective as president of the computer service company, EDS, and not as effective in his efforts with General Motors. You cannot pick up a book or manual and simply read the directions for being a good manager; you cannot simply follow a set of rules and procedures and hope that all will work out as expected. Does that mean that there is no way of understanding how to manage or how to improve your leadership skills? Of course not, and the following materials will give you a basis for your pursuit of effectiveness as a manager and a leader.

LEADERSHIP HISTORY

The informal interest in and the formal study of leadership parallel the history of management discussed in Chapter 2.

The Focus of Leadership Study—by Levels

In the early 1900s, leadership concern and training related to the area of greatest need: training for first-level supervisors in manufacturing plants throughout industrial America (primarily in the East and the Midwest). The factory system of the late 1800s was expanding, engineering principles were becoming a part of the work environment, and the pressing problem of industry was solving manufacturing issues and matching personnel and work methods with mechanical production lines. First-level managers faced serious operational problems requiring technical expertise, and thus much of the training of foremen took on an engineering flavor. The country had a surplus of unskilled labor, and the Industrial Revolution had transferred worker skill to the machines. F. W. Taylor and others tried to improve worker productivity by trying to simplify and routinize work methods. This emphasis on task-oriented supervision at the first level of management continued in most industries and firms until the end of the Second World War. During the war, the focus on task and worker productivity received high priority because of the military demand for high industrial output.

The need for productivity during the war years was not limited to the industrial environment. The military faced new situations that required different approaches to the selection and training of personnel for leadership positions. Combat frequently broke the will of some people but brought forth heroic behavior from others. Morale and battle fatigue raised puzzling questions, as did the need for productivity and cooperation in bomber crews in a new U.S. Air Force. After the war, the insights from those military experiences, the pent-up demand for industrial goods, and the new returning American work force changed the corporate environment dramatically.

The assumptions about the motivations and reasons for work, especially the belief that the economic man model best described the American worker, came under challenge and attack. More interest developed in the area of worker motivation, greater attention was given to work-group productivity, and

First-line supervisors played an essential leadership role in the development of the early factories during the Industrial Revolution. This particular picture shows an early factory in France, although the same type factory could just as easily have been found in the United States, Great Britain, or any other industrializing country at that time.

leadership training expanded to all levels of management, particularly the middle levels. The size, complexity, and urgency of many military problems had created a need for administrative staff and a higher number of personnel providing support functions. Thus, the expansion of corporate America in the 1950s began to take on many of the characteristics of military organizations, where more attention was given to those people who had responsibility for first- and second-level personnel.

American industry continued to emphasize the importance of technical and operational supervisory training but added leadership training for the expanding number of personnel in the middle levels. At those levels, the problems seemed to be of a different nature: obtaining the cooperation of other managers, coordinating the work of unrelated units, and addressing interpersonal and human relationships. Administrative and nontechnical problems became the primary topics in leadership training throughout the corporate, university, and training consultant worlds.

The evolution of leadership training and focus has taken another step in the 1990s. In addition to technical, operational, administrative, human-relations, and organizational behavior training, there has been a movement to address the strategic needs of the top levels of organizations. Top-level training programs now contain topics related to stakeholder interests, values and ethics, governmental relations, infusing quality concepts throughout all levels of personnel, and surviving global competition.

With this background in mind, we present two simple models of leadership and then proceed to an in-depth study of leadership themes.

Conceptual Models

The Two-Factor Model

Why just two factors?

Figure 9-1 shows the terms and concepts used to describe leaders or leader behavior during the past years. One of the first sets of bipolar concepts was the

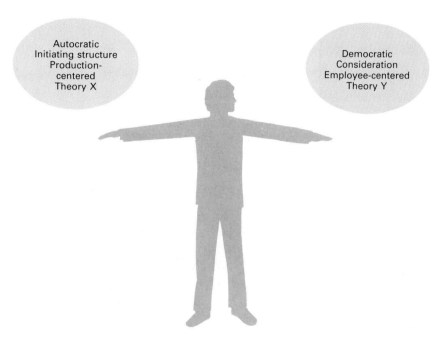

FIGURE 9-1 Two-factor Model of Leadership

Autocratic leadership
The leader makes all decisions, assumes total authority over as many areas as possible, rarely delegates to anyone, and maintains centralized control.

Democratic leadership
The leader delegates authority to subordinates, encourages participation in decision making, and shares in information with others in the organization.

idea of **autocratic** or **democratic** leadership. The autocratic leader made all decisions, assumed total authority over as many areas as possible, rarely delegated to anyone, and maintained centralized control. The democratic leader, on the other hand, delegated authority to subordinates, encouraged participation in decision making, and shared information with others in the organization.

Later, other terms were added to this either/or model. Leaders were either *task oriented* (concerned primarily with the work at hand) or *social emotionally oriented* (concerned primarily about the welfare of the workers). In a study by researchers at The Ohio State University (to be developed later), the terms used were *initiating structure* and *consideration*.

The Multifactor Model

The two-factor theory was tested in a variety of settings and situations, and weaknesses emerged. As researchers looked at the components of leadership, they uncovered many factors and conditions that seemed to support different styles of leadership. In Figure 9-2, some of those factors are identified, and it should be noted that this model is probably an open-ended one, for new studies are being conducted and new insights coming to light. The simple focus upon one individual exercising leadership of others (usually a group of subordinates) gave way to a series of additional questions about the total leadership relationship. The effectiveness of a leader, thus, depends on

- ■ WHO is involved
- ■ WHERE the leadership is taking place
- ■ WHAT task is being performed
- ■ WHEN it is occurring (the time dimension)

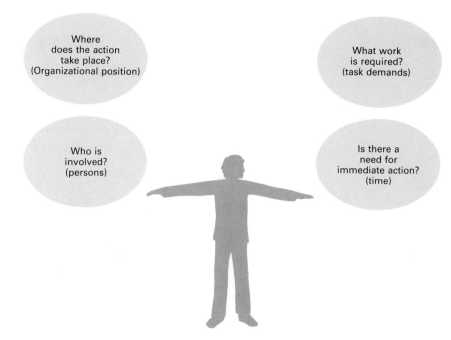

FIGURE 9-2 Multifactor Model of Leadership

In the next section, you will see the research data to support both the early two-factor and the multiple-factor theories.

LEADERSHIP THEMES

Are leaders born or made?

King Robert Bruce of Scotland led his people to many victories on the battlefield. Today's battlefields are in the factories and market places of the world.

The themes presented shortly will span a broad horizon of type and time. Some come from the early 1900s and some from the early 1990s; some are insights from biographies and some are products of rigorous research. The order of presentation will be historical, with the first theme taken from the early years of America's industrial experience.

Trait Theory

This leadership concept had its roots in the notion that leaders were born and not made. Centuries ago, people believed that kings and nobles had a divine right to rule, and thus leadership was assumed to be a hereditary feature. Wars and political conflicts arose from a king's desire to find a male heir so that the power of the throne would be passed down the line. As monarchy gave way to other forms of government, the search for "kinglike" qualities became popular and people looked for qualities or traits in successful leaders—qualities that, they hoped, could be learned. This search was labeled the Great Man Theory.

Even though monarchy remains in only a few countries in the twentieth century, the notion survives in a "great man" theory of leadership. Any "great person" theory, although interesting, is not very useful for those of us who

"Great Woman" Theory

Leadership greatness has not always been a monopoly of the male sex. In a recent book by Antonia Fraser, *The Warrior Queens,* the female sex displays those qualities and characteristics usually attributed to men (and thus the source for the Great Man Theory). For example:

■ Boadicea (b. ca. A.D. 26), Celtic queen of the Iceni people, led the uprising against the Romans in Britain. She died while personally waging battle.

■ Jinga Mbandi (1580–1663) was queen of Angola. She became queen in 1624 and negotiated peace with the Portuguese government. When the Portuguese declared war later, she led the resistance against them.

■ Golda Meir (1898–1978) served as Israeli minister of foreign affairs from 1956 to 1965 and as prime minister of Israel from 1969 to 1974. She was a compelling speaker and an esteemed leader during the Arab–Israeli War of 1973.

The shortage of executive talent around the globe suggests that more women should be in the higher ranks of management; yet, that is not the case.

Study after study shows similar results. In 1990, there were only 19 women in the list of the top 4,000 officers and directors of the publicly held *Fortune 500* service and industrial companies; and in the 1991 *Business Week* list of 1,000 CEOs, only 2 were women. There is hardly any evidence to suggest that women cannot be effective executives. There is evidence to validate their abilities as doctors, lawyers, educators, researchers, law enforcement personnel, military officers, and politicians.

Must a woman be a Boadicea, a Jinga Mbandi, or a Golda Meir to be accepted in the CEO club of American or global corporations? Perhaps the twenty-first century will be a time when top management contains more and more personnel who achieve their rank because of their leadership and managerial effectiveness rather than because of their sex, race, or age.

References: Antonia Fraser, *The Warrior Queens* (New York: Knopf, 1989); "Why Women Still Don't Hit the Top," *Fortune,* July 30, 1990, pp. 40–62; "CEO Disease," *Business Week,* April 1, 1991, pp. 52–60.

have more common talents and characteristics. However, our personal experiences suggest to us that there are individual characteristics that work for or against people as leaders. Most organizations have been looking for the secret formula for identifying traits that make successful leaders. Are there traits that can be learned so that managers can improve their leadership? Or are there traits that can be identified as preferable for effective leadership so that you might be able to staff the appropriate subordinate managerial positions?

Research studies done on leaders and nonleaders suggest that leaders tend to be brighter, to be better adjusted psychologically, to display better judgment, to interact more, to give more information, to ask for more information, and to take the lead in interpreting a situation. As Paul Hare says, "There are indications that certain traits, such as intelligence, enthusiasm, dominance, self-confidence, and social participation, are frequently found to characterize leaders."[2] The industrial psychologist William Henry, doing research in the late 1940s, found a definite personality pattern in a study of more than 100 successful business executives; he found the following traits:

■ Powerful work motivations and desire for achievement
■ Warm feelings for superiors (with whom they identified)

- Detached attitudes toward subordinates
- Stable and well-defined self-concept
- Ability to see relationships and make decisions
- A high degree of activity and aggressiveness
- Interest in practical realities here and now
- Smooth relationships with superiors
- A certain insecurity about their abilities to achieve[3]

In a later work, Edwin E. Ghiselli continued the examination of managerial leadership traits.[4] Among two groups of 105 people each, Ghiselli found that the traits of supervisory ability, intelligence, and initiative related to success in managerial positions. Of these three abilities, Ghiselli says that supervisory ability and intelligence are the most important aspects of managerial success.

There are certain personal characteristics that cannot be altered—physical build, facial characteristics, perhaps voice, and other aspects of the biological makeup. Measurement of intelligence seems subject to change, for we know that scores on intelligence tests can be improved through training. In spite of an early interest in trait theory, few see it today as meaningful in the training and development of leaders. The primary emphasis in research during the past fifty years has been on the behaviors of leaders and under what conditions one leadership style or practice produces more effective results.

Two-factor Behavioral Model

The Ohio State Studies

The Ohio State Studies began with an interest in describing what leaders did on the job rather than what traits or characteristics they possessed.[5] Researchers had subordinates respond to a Leader Behavior Description Questionnaire and found two independent factors in the responses:

- **Consideration.** Leaders engaged in social behavior by showing concern for their subordinates. These leaders listened, took time to explain, helped others with personal problems, and generally showed respect for their subordinates' ideas and feelings.
- **Initiating structure.** The leader's behavior emphasized structuring the work, scheduling, work organization, and goal attainment. These leaders placed performance and production higher than other aspects of the job and sought to achieve high levels of output.

Two conclusions emerged from The Ohio State Studies on leadership.[6] First, there were employees who responded very well when their leaders were high on both consideration and initiating structure. Second, there were situations in which the relation between the leader behavior and effective performance was not clear and was often contradictory. In other words, the two-dimension description was a contribution to leadership understanding, but it was not the last word.

The University of Michigan's Survey Research Center

The researchers at this center also developed a two-dimension description of leader behavior during the same time as the work at The Ohio State University. They compared the behavior of effective and ineffective supervisors and used

Why the focus on leadership behavior?

Consideration
A leadership style that shows concern for the ideas and feelings of subordinates.

Initiating structure
Leader's behavior emphasizes structuring the work, scheduling, work organization, and goal attainment.

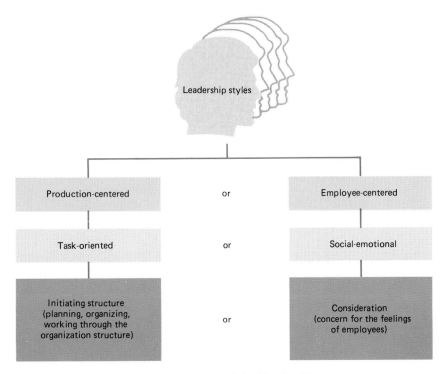

Leadership styles

| Production-centered | or | Employee-centered |

| Task-oriented | or | Social-emotional |

| Initiating structure (planning, organizing, working through the organization structure) | or | Consideration (concern for the feelings of employees) |

FIGURE 9-3 A Combined Two-factor Model of Leadership

Employee-centered The manager puts emphasis on development of work teams and interpersonal relations.

Production-centered Also known as job-centered. Manager puts emphasis on the work performed, meeting schedules, and achieving low costs.

different labels for their description: **employee-centered** and **production-** (job-) **centered.** The job-centered supervisor paid attention to the work performed, meeting schedules, and achieving low costs; the employee-centered leader put emphasis upon the development of work teams and interpersonal relations. Figure 9-3 depicts the terms from both these early studies.

A number of research findings supported the idea that employee-centered supervision contributed more to higher production than did job-centered supervision.[7] But again, as more research came forth testing the various populations studied (blue-collar, white-collar, insurance personnel, factory workers, and so on), the nature of the work, and other conditions, mixed results appeared. The two-dimension, leader-behavior model did not adequately explain all leadership situations.[8]

Today, there is a more balanced position regarding leadership theory and training. Effective leadership is more than emphasizing the production side or the people side of the workplace. Leadership includes the people, the organizational positions and levels, and the situations surrounding the leadership event; it includes concern for the task, concern for people, and other factors. Most of the leadership research since the 1970s has looked at many more factors that influence the effectiveness of leadership. Concern for the situation surrounding the leadership event is the topic of our next section.

The Situational Theme

In this section, we look at four contributions to our understanding of leadership. The previous Great Man or Great Woman explanation had limitations, as did the notion of traits. The two-factor theories of leader behavior developed in the 1940s also appeared too simplistic to explain what made for effective leadership or why some leaders were successful and some unsuccessful. One of the first researchers to study the impact of the leader, the subordinates, the task, and the power position of the leader was Fred Fiedler.

Fred Fiedler

The Fiedler Contingency Model[9]

Is one leadership style better than another?

Fiedler Contingency.

After years of research, Fred Fiedler proposed that effective group performance depends upon the proper matching of a personality variable in the leader with three contingency dimensions:

1. The leader–member relations: a measure of the acceptance of the leader by subordinates (the most influential dimension).

2. The task structure: How structured or unstructured is the work to be done (the second most influential dimension)?

3. The leader's power position: How much influence over critical power factors does the position have? Is the leader allowed to hire, fire, reward, and discipline?

Fiedler believes that the effectiveness of either a production-oriented or an employee-oriented style depends on the answers to the three contingency dimensions. Being task-centered all the time will not result in effectiveness. Spending a large share of your leadership efforts on the social-emotional needs of your subordinates will also not result in effectiveness. But if you and your subordinates have mutual respect and trust, if your organizational position gives you power, and if the job is structured, then task-motivated behavior will result in better group performance.

Not all researchers are satisfied that the Fiedler model represents all there is to know about leadership. There is little question, however, that the contingency type of thinking has opened up the area. Effective leader behavior is a far more complex topic, but perhaps a more valuable one, as managers become free of "principles" that had limited usefulness and application. You can see other opportunities to improve overall leadership effectiveness by using a form of the Fiedler model. You have the authority to select people who may produce more positive leader–member relations.[10] You also have the authority to redesign the task, making it more structured or more unstructured. And you have the power to change the power position of your own job or that of subordinate managers, thus affecting their effectiveness. Effectiveness in leadership is no longer limited to personality or leader-behavior characteristics.

Hersey and Blanchard's Situational Theory

Hersey Blanchard

This theory is a contingency approach to leadership.[11] It focuses more attention on the followers and what they do than it does on the leader. Currently, situational leadership theory is receiving support from many corporations; it is being used as a training device in a number of Fortune 500 companies, including BankAmerica, Caterpillar, IBM, Mobil Oil, and Xerox, and in many branches of the U.S. military.

Hersey and Blanchard argue that successful leadership stems from matching the leader's style with the maturity of the followers. Two important elements of their theory deserve a brief discussion.

First, concern for the role of the followers is necessary, according to Hersey and Blanchard, because it is they who either accept or reject the leader. (You may recall that Chester I. Barnard called this the "acceptance" concept of authority.) In this regard, Hersey and Blanchard stress that effectiveness depends more on what the followers do than on what the leader does. Traditionally, the role of the followers in leadership theories has been overlooked. Second, maturity is the extent to which subordinates display both the willingness and the ability to take responsibility for directing their own behavior. Maturity has two components—job maturity and psychological maturity. Job maturity is the extent to which workers possess the knowledge, ability, and experience to perform their tasks without direction or assistance from others. Psychological maturity is the extent to which workers are intrinsically motivated or willing to perform their tasks without external rewards or encouragement.

Situational leadership is much like Fiedler's contingency approach because it also focuses on task and relational dimensions of leadership. Hersey and Blanchard, however, extend these dimensions by noting that each can be either high or low, and then they combine them into four specific leadership styles: telling, selling, participating, and delegating.

In the _telling style_ (high task–low relationship), the leader specifies the roles and tells people where, when, what, and how to perform various tasks. This style emphasizes the traditional concept of directing. The _selling style_ (high task–high relationship) involves the leader in both directive and supportive behavior. In the _participating style_ (low task–high relationship), the leader and the followers share in the decision-making process. The main roles for the leader using this style are facilitating and communicating. Finally, in the _delegating style_ (low task–low relationship), the leader takes a relatively laissez-faire, laid-back approach. That is, the leader provides little in the way of either direction or support for the followers.[12]

The other component of situational leadership theory is the identification of the four stages of follower maturity. In stage _M1_ (see Figure 9-4), followers are neither able nor willing to take responsibility for their tasks. According to Hersey and Blanchard they are neither competent nor confident. In stage _M2,_ the followers are willing but unable to perform the necessary job-related tasks. In this stage, the followers are motivated, but they lack the appropriate skills. In stage _M3,_ the followers are able but unwilling to perform what the leader wants them to do. The followers are lacking in motivation, not in skills. Finally, in stage _M4,_ the followers are both able and willing to perform what is asked of them.

If you look at Figure 9-4, you can see the application of this theory to the study of leadership. As followers attain higher levels of maturity, the leader should respond by decreasing both control and relationship behaviors. For example, at stage _M1,_ followers will require clear and specific directions. At stage _M2,_ both high task and relational behaviors are needed. Here, followers need direction to make up for their lack of ability and relational behavior to motivate them to accept the leader's goals. Stage _M3_ requires more support behavior than direction because the followers know what to do; they just don't want to. Hence, the leader should be more concerned with gaining their participation and support than with telling them what to do. Finally, in stage M4, the leader does not have much to do because the employees are both willing and able to perform their tasks.

The focus of concern has moved from individual leader behavior to the followers' behavior and the nature of the task. We turn now to another situational theory that uses some of the ideas already presented but adds some new twists.

Situational leadership A contingency approach; the type of leadership needed is determined by the nature of the situation, including who the followers are. Focuses more attention on the followers and less on the leader.

Can managers change their styles?

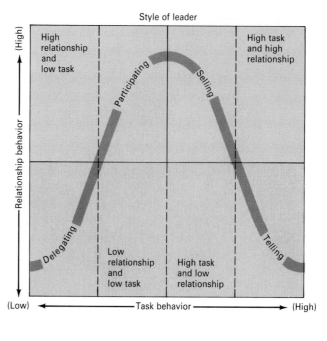

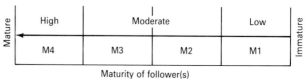

FIGURE 9-4 A Hersey-Blanchard Situational Leadership Model
Source: Adapted from P. Hersey and K. Blanchard, *Management of Organizational Behavior: Utilizing Human Resources,* 4th ed. © 1982, p. 152. Reprinted by permission of Prentice-Hall, Inc., Englewood Cliffs, N.J.

Does path-goal apply to all workers?

Path-Goal Theory The concept that people will select the behavior that they believe to have the best chance to reach personal goals.

The Path-Goal Theory

The **Path-Goal Theory** uses the ideas of leaders' positional power to design structure and influence the sanctions in a work unit plus some concepts from a motivational theory that will be more fully developed in a later chapter. The motivational theory is that of Victor Vroom,[13] and it states that people will select the behavior (or be motivated to do things) that they believe (perceive) has the best chance of enabling them to reach personal goals (things that are valued). In other words, people behave in accordance with their expectations.

Martin G. Evans and Robert J. House have performed interesting research and developed a line of thinking to answer the question of the relationship between leader behavior and workers' motivational expectations.[14] These men believe that managers should use their authority in the initiating structure and consideration areas to clarify both the goals and the paths that lead to goal satisfaction. They identify four leadership styles to focus on both goals and goal paths:

- *Directive.* Similar to initiating structure style.
- *Supportive.* Similar to consideration style.

- *Participative.* Leader shares and involves members.
- *Achievement oriented.* Leader sets high goals, has confidence that subordinates will reach them, and helps them learn how to reach high goals.

Figure 9-5 shows four different situations that followers might face, the preferred leadership behavior to fit each situation, the impact of the leader's behavior on the followers, and the expected outcome in each situation. The fundamental task of the leader is (1) to increase the followers' motivations to achieve by seeing that the goals and the paths to those goals are clear, and (2) managing the rewards that they value to get them on the path that leads to desired goals.

The last situational or contingency model shifts to a different set of managerial behaviors: decision making. Notice in this theory how some of the concepts in Chapter 5 have been expanded and become more complex. As you are now seeing, the reality of the manager's world is complex.

The Vroom-Yetton Decision Model[15]

Victor H. Vroom and Philip W. Yetton believe that the leader is capable of flexible behavior, and, thus, the leader needs to know the dynamics of the situation to determine the appropriate decision style. They identify five decision styles in a given situation:

1. Managers decide with the information they have.
2. Managers decide after getting information from their subordinates.
3. Managers share the problem with certain subordinates individually and then make the decision.
4. Managers share the problem with the group and then decide.
5. Managers share the problem with the group and then develop a decision by consensus.

FIGURE 9-5 A Path-Goal Situations Model

Path-goal situations and preferred leader behaviors

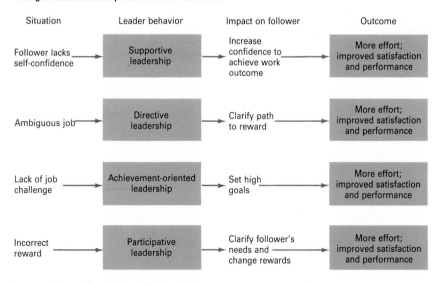

Situation	Leader behavior	Impact on follower	Outcome
Follower lacks self-confidence	Supportive leadership	Increase confidence to achieve work outcome	More effort; improved satisfaction and performance
Ambiguous job	Directive leadership	Clarify path to reward	More effort; improved satisfaction and performance
Lack of job challenge	Achievement-oriented leadership	Set high goals	More effort; improved satisfaction and performance
Incorrect reward	Participative leadership	Clarify follower's needs and change rewards	More effort; improved satisfaction and performance

Source: Adapted from Gary A. Yuki, *Leadership in Organizations* (Englewood Cliffs, N.J.: Prentice-Hall, 1981), pp. 146–152.

To implement this theory, you would ask a series of questions about the nature of the situation requiring the decision and select a decision style based on the answers to those questions. Some sample questions are: Do I have sufficient information to make a quality decision? Is it important for followers to accept the decision, and will they have to implement it? What will happen if I make the decision myself? What kind of climate exists in the work unit—will subordinates seek organizational goals or just look out for their own interests?

You can see that the answers to your questions might suggest a particular decision style, and that idea is the basis of the Vroom-Yetton model.

We will make another shift now to get a better view of the totality of the leadership function in management. This approach picks up the ideas of Vroom and the Path-Goal Theory and focuses on the role that expectations play in determining the effectiveness of any leader or any leadership style.

Role Theory

The Role of Expectations

How do roles relate to styles?

This theory explains how an individual who has been successful in one environment may become less successful in another environment. The evaluation of effectiveness showed different results for Dwight Eisenhower as he changed careers from the military (General of the Army) to education (president of Columbia University) to government (president of the United States). The same could be said about World War I flying ace Eddie Rickenbacker, who became president of Eastern Airlines; or about Steven Jobs of Apple Computer, and H. Ross Perot, president of EDS.

Personal Expectations

Personal expectations are the ways in which people expect the leader to behave. In Figure 9-6, we repeat the range of managerial roles that Henry Mintzberg found in organizations and that was discussed in an earlier chapter. Organizational members expect managers to perform an interpersonal role, an informational role, and a decisional role. There are other insights that relate to the concept of personal expectations.

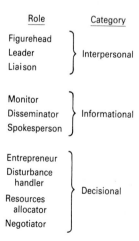

FIGURE 9-6 Mintzberg's Managerial Roles

In every group, there is a pattern of expectations—the group expects the leader to do certain things and to refrain from doing certain things. For example:

- The group expects certain patterns of behavior from its formal leader.
- The role the leader plays depends upon the role expectations of the followers.
- The leader tends to be selected by the nature of the role; that is, certain roles attract certain people. Foremen in foundries are usually rough, tough, and physically strong men. Nurses in hospitals are usually emotionally tough, reality oriented, and frequently physically strong women.
- All members of a group have roles and these roles are related to one other. One member, for example, may assume the role of the "joker" so that group tensions and frustrations are released.
- Roles are related to the people in them. Certain professional quarterbacks influence the style of play of the whole team.
- Roles are related to the situations in which they are played. The behavior of a union steward may depend on whether the company is near a strike.

Organizational Expectations

Many companies have definite and specific expectations about the behavior of their managers and leaders. These expectations are frequently written into formal position guides or job descriptions. As we mentioned earlier, most jobs have some heritage within an organization, so that the previous person in the job helped develop the expectations that people have for the job now. In addition, there are both technical and nontechnical organizational expectations. The job behavior of a manager of a live TV production would be quite different organizationally from the job behavior of a manager of a taped program, which has a different time dimension. Nontechnical organizational expectations also differ in what is allowed in personal habits, status, group relationships, coffee breaks, and the place you park your car.

Cultural Expectations

In addition to the specific personal and organizational patterns of role expectations that contribute to the shaping of the leadership role, there are other cultural expectations of many types. One of these is the industry culture. The banker and the CPA are expected to be serious, conservative, and cautious. The advertising executive is expected to be creative. The politician is expected to shake hands, kiss babies, secure appropriations for his or her home state, and make extravagant promises that are reassuring but not taken too seriously. The tax collector is expected to be rather suspicious and perhaps hostile. And the military leader is expected to be gallant, fearless, and conscious of his or her status.

In the late 1970s and continuing into the 1990s, the cultural expectations affecting many managers dealt with women as members of management. Traditional roles and stereotypes placed women in less than equal positions in organizations. In some instances, women managers were expected to get the coffee, take notes at meetings, and be pleased when men held doors open for them. Language was cleaned up, or softened, if women were present. These expectations and many more made life difficult for career-oriented women. These women were effectively excluded from the "old-boy network," the informal mechanism of gossip, and executive opportunities for informal influence.

Today, men and women are changing, as research data and experience dispel the stereotypes. Many recent books and new consulting groups exist for helping women and organizations cope with the conflicts of outdated role expectations.[16]

Cultural expectations have a profound impact upon leadership effectiveness. Hulin and Blood found, for example, that some workers prefer routine work, or show less interest in high-quality work or learning more about their jobs, and really prefer money as an incentive.[17] The reason for this preference is not the leadership style or the climate in the organization; the contributing factor is where the workers live, or where they lived as children.

We have come almost full circle in discussing leadership themes—from trait theory through role theory. Although the interest in trait theory remains dormant, there is an acknowledgment that certain top leaders influence organizational members in a special way. American audiences were amazed at the influence that Saddam Hussein had over his followers, and allied coalition forces might also have demonstrated a strong admiration for one of their leaders, U.S. General Norman Schwarzkopf.

Charismatic Leadership Theory

Can anyone be a charismatic leader?

Charismatic leadership Leaders are viewed by followers as heroic and extraordinary. Leaders are described as being inspirational, revolutionary, visionary, spellbinding. Also called transformational leadership.

Charismatic leadership theories are based on the notion that followers look up to leaders (usually at the top levels of the organization) whom they believe to be heroic or extraordinary in some way. Some terms used to describe these people include spellbinder, inspirational leader, changemaster, empowering leader, charismatic leader, heroic leader, pathfinder, revolutionary leader, and transforming leader.

Whatever term is used, it describes a leader who inspires his or her fol-

Norman Schwarzkopf is regarded as a very charismatic leader. Although he is recognized as being very intelligent and a great strategist, particularly in leading the allied forces to victory in the Gulf War, he is also seen as being very human. He has a genuine concern for the well-being of people, particularly caring for the troops who served under him. Although Schwarzkopf has since retired from the military, people are looking to him to assume other leadership roles, perhaps in government, in a major corporation, or in an activist group trying to save the environment.

lowers to transcend their own interests and work exceptionally hard for the goal, cause, or mission. To achieve such high levels of compliance and commitment, these leaders must pay special attention to meeting the development needs of their followers. In the end, charismatic or transformational leaders have a profound impact on their followers because they encourage and inspire them to do such things as look at old problems in new ways, extend extra effort, and develop new ideas and procedures.

For the most part, the authors who write in this area spend most of their time trying to identify the factors that differentiate charismatic leaders from noncharismatic leaders. A few examples of their speculations and research deserve mention.

Management Application

CEO Disease

The search for the key to executive effectiveness is relevant in this period of corporate unrest and upheaval. Each week, the headlines of the business media contain another casualty of hostile takeovers, Chapter 11 bankruptcies, global mergers, and scandals.

Such a state of affairs brings an expected response from authors and researchers. Books and articles flood the market with either the juicy details of the latest scandal or new problems or insights.

A slightly different twist to understanding the behavior of those in leadership positions appeared in a *Business Week* cover story on the "CEO Disease." The purpose of this article was to describe the behavior of a new group of CEOs, who contribute to the ineffectiveness of the organization. In other words, the effectiveness of organizations might be improved if this CEO disease can be addressed.

The CEO disease begins with the egotism of the top executive. This person may show some of the following signs of the disease. Such people

- Rarely concede that they make any mistakes
- Always seek to have more company perks than CEOs in other companies
- Have an unrealistic sense of self-importance

- Consider themselves indispensable and stay in their jobs forever
- Are reluctant to share authority with or delegate it to others
- Believe they have earned special rights within the organization, rights not given to others, and expect to be treated as if they were royalty

The damage to the corporation can be immense: millions of dollars can be spent on corporate jets, vacation homes, yachts, cars, and other "required" perks of the office; decisions that require group participation can become private and personal decisions because of egotism; subordinate managers' morale can suffer severely, since they don't feel free to say anything but yes on all issues of potential conflict with their boss; and secret deals conducted by CEOs can lead companies to the edge of bankruptcy.

It has been suggested that one cure for this disease is an alert board of corporate directors who view themselves as responsible for many stakeholders and not just as a sounding board or a rubber stamp for the CEO.

References: "CEO Disease," *Business Week,* April 1, 1991, pp. 52–60; "The Rx for CEO Disease: An Alert Board," *Business Week,* April 1, 1991, p. 92.

Warren Bennis,[18] who studied ninety of America's most successful leaders, found they had four skills in common: they had a *compelling vision* or sense of purpose; they could *communicate clearly and concisely* this vision to their subordinates or followers; they were *vigilant and consistent* in the pursuit of their vision; and they *capitalized on their respective strengths.* Professor Robert House found that such leaders had extremely *high confidence, dominance, and strong convictions* in their vision.[19] Conger and Kanungo found that charismatic leaders have an *idealistic goal* they want to achieve, have a *strong personal commitment* to their goal, are perceived as somewhat *unconventional,* and are viewed as *inspirers of radical change,* not proponents of the status quo (see Table 9-1).

The themes just presented represent the viewpoint of many mainstream researchers in educational and industrial institutions. Another set will be offered to suggest to you that the last word on leadership has not yet been made.

Nontraditional Leadership Themes

How can you manage without authority?

Professor Leonard Sayles is interested in what managers do.[20] He has reviewed the empirical studies of managerial behavior and has found that there is a discrepancy between what many people say managers should do and what some researchers find managers doing. Sayles's summary of his findings shows the following:

1. Management means working with and through people. Approximately 80 percent of a manager's time is spent in contact with other people.

2. The manager has a wide variety of contacts. Some of these contacts last a short time; others extend for large portions of time (an hour or longer).

TABLE 9-1   Key Characteristics of Charismatic Leaders

1. *Self-confidence.* They have complete confidence in their judgment and ability.
2. *A vision.* This is an idealized goal that proposes a future better than the status quo. The greater the disparity between this idealized goal and the status quo, the more likely that followers will attribute extraordinary vision to the leader.
3. *Ability to articulate the vision.* They are able to clarify and state the vision in terms that are understandable to others. This articulation demonstrates an understanding of the followers' needs and, hence, acts as a motivating force.
4. *Strong convictions about the vision.* Charismatic leaders are perceived as being strongly committed, and willing to take on high personal risk, incur high costs, and engage in self-sacrifice to achieve their vision.
5. *Behavior that is out of the ordinary.* Those with charisma engage in behavior that is perceived as being novel, unconventional, and counter to norms. When successful, these behaviors evoke surprise and admiration in followers.
6. *Is perceived as being a change agent.* Charismatic leaders are perceived as agents of radical change rather than as caretakers of the status quo.
7. *Environment sensitivity.* These leaders are able to make realistic assessments of the environmental constraints and resources needed to bring about change.

Based on J. A. Conger and R. N. Kanungo, "Behavioral Dimensions of Charismatic Leadership," in J. A. Conger and R. N. Kanungo, *Charismatic Leadership* (San Francisco: Jossey-Bass, 1988), p. 91.

Sayle 1.

3. The manager has breadth in the range of his or her contacts. In most studies, the supervisor is not dealing primarily with subordinates; contacts include people who are not subordinates.

After his review of the literature, Sayles describes what managers really do when operating in situations where position authority does not apply. They participate in external work flows. This means that they spend a great deal of time in nonauthority relationships with other people.

Sayles believes that a large portion of the manager's and leader's workday behavior should be called lateral, horizontal, or work-flow behavior. It takes a different form from the behavior between managers and subordinates, because there is no authority relationship between the two or more parties; indeed, Sayles is describing a relationship based on exchange and power. He talks about trading, work-flow, service, advisory, auditing, stabilizing, and innovative types of relationships. Managing subordinates when the leader has authority and the right to administer sanctions and rewards represents a small percentage of the total managerial workday. Potential managers and leaders must realize the importance of the soft areas of directing the efforts of people in organizations. Power, politics, tactics, and operating in nonauthority relationships should not be viewed as interruptions in effective management; rather they should be viewed as critical dimensions of effective management. We consider Sayles's statements to contain much truth and have written a separate chapter on the topic of power, politics, and tactics (Chapter 15).

A second nontraditional approach to the topic of leadership deals with the idea of substitutes for leaders or the no-leaders approach.

Leadership has been the topic of study for literally hundreds of years. In spite of all these studies, we have yet to (1) agree on a single operational or conceptual definition of leadership, (2) differentiate behaviors or personality characteristics that belong just to leaders, (3) consistently account for why leaders who are successful in one setting fail to achieve the same prominence in other settings, and (4) account for how and why some societies and organizations grow and thrive without the presence of any leaders. Therefore, some authors are beginning to argue that leadership may not be the important concept or variable we once thought it to be.

Kerr

Substitutes for Leadership Theory The theory that some organizational characteristics or conditions actually reduce the need for leadership function in an organization.

Are leaders needed?

One such author is Steven Kerr,[21] whose **Substitutes for Leadership Theory** argues that some organizational characteristics may actually mediate or reduce the need for leadership functions in a business. A key element in Kerr's theory is the idea that there are conditions in the subordinate, task, or aspects of the organization that may serve as *leadership substitutes* and actually neutralize the effectiveness of leadership. Leadership in a scientific laboratory, for example, may not be necessary because of the expertise of the personnel and the desire of many professionals to do their own planning and organizing of projects. Productivity might even be hampered by efforts at directing their work or even being concerned for their social needs.

Kerr's Substitutes for Leadership Theory raises a number of interesting questions regarding the importance of leadership in organizational settings. For example, do we place too much value on leadership? Do we expect too much from our leaders? Will we ever be able to predict who can or will become effective leaders? Does too much emphasis on leadership rob followers of taking the lead themselves?

SUMMARY

Directing the resources of the firm was the topic of this chapter. The primary focus was leadership. The chapter began with the example of H. Ross Perot and went on to summarize the history of the study of leadership. Leadership themes followed to give you a view of the spectrum of the leadership act in most organizations. The chapter ended with a brief view of some nontraditional themes of leadership. The topic is complex but, as you have read, extremely important.

KEY TERMS

Leadership The ability to influence people, to direct their activities toward a goal. Includes the people, the organizational positions and levels, and the situations surrounding the leadership event; includes concern for task, concern for people, and other factors.

Autocratic leadership The leader makes all decisions, assumes total authority over as many areas as possible, rarely delegates to anyone, maintains centralized control.

Democratic leadership The leader delegates authority to subordinates, encourages participation shares in decision making, and shares information with others in the organization.

Consideration A leadership style that shows concern for the ideas and feelings of subordinates.

Initiating structure Leader's behavior emphasizes structuring the work, scheduling, work organization, and goal attainment.

Employee-centered The manager puts emphasis on development of work teams and interpersonal relations.

Production-centered Also known as job-centered. Manager puts emphasis on the work performed, meeting schedules, and achieving low costs.

Situational leadership A contingency approach; the type of leadership needed is determined by the nature of the situation, including who the followers are. Focuses more attention on the followers and less on the leader.

Path-Goal Theory The concept that people will select the behavior that they believe to have the best chance to reach personal goals.

Charismatic leadership Leaders are viewed by followers as heroic and extraordinary. Leaders are described as being inspirational, revolutionary, visionary, spellbinding.

Substitutes for Leadership Theory The theory that some organizational characteristics or conditions actually reduce the need for leadership function in an organization.

Transformational leadership Synonym for Charismatic Leadership.

STUDY ASSIGNMENTS

1. Do all organizations have the same needs for leaders? What differences exist in leadership within different industries and levels of management?
2. Why did the early study of leadership focus on the trait theory?
3. Think of a leader you admire. What leadership characteristics does that person have? In what ways could you adopt that person's leadership style?

4. "The most popular person is not always the best leader." "The best leader may never be able to win an election." Explain.

5. Can leadership ability be identified early in a person's career? What would you look for?

6. What would be the topics of a leadership training course for managers? Would there be any difference in topics if all were middle managers, supervisors, or top management?

7. Give reasons to support this statement: Directive managers can be trained to be supportive leaders. Give reasons to refute the statement.

8. How many charismatic leaders can one organization have? Explain.

9. Why do you think some effective leaders from one organization are not effective in another organization? Is there anything an organization can do to improve the effectiveness of new managers?

10. Which of the various leadership themes appeals most to you? Explain.

Case for Discussion

THE GUP CORPORATION

For the past five years, Jerry Runte has been vice president of human resources at the GUP Corporation. He enjoys his job and the opportunity to be a part of an organization that was experiencing substantial growth. However, he knows that today will not be very enjoyable, for today he has to make one of the most difficult decisions he has ever had to make since coming to GUP. He must decide whether or not to fire Ted Martin, the head of plant maintenance.

Recently, a number of supervisors and production managers have begun demanding that the firm fire Ted. They believe that the increasing frequency of equipment breakdowns and excessive production-line downtime is a result of Ted's inability to supervise his subordinates and to ensure the proper maintenance of production equipment. Production scheduling has become totally disruptive, causing delays in various projects. On a couple of occasions, equipment failures have caused the company to miss delivery dates. Concern about this situation has spread to top management, and Jerry is under pressure to resolve the problem about Ted.

Ted has been with the company for over ten years. When he was hired, the company had only fifty employees. Initially, Ted was the only maintenance man that the company had, and he developed a good reputation as a loyal and conscientious employee. Ted displayed considerable competence in the repair and maintenance of the company's equipment. He was one of the most well liked individuals at GUP. Jerry particularly appreciated Ted, because Ted went out of his way to help Jerry orient himself to the firm when Jerry was hired to head up the newly created human resources department about five years ago.

As the size and scope of GUP's operations expanded over the years, so did Ted's responsibilities. At first, he was able to meet new demands simply by working longer hours. About six years ago, the plant manager pressured Ted into hiring two assistants. Ted had these individuals perform only simple maintenance procedures, left them largely unsupervised, did not train them in how to repair equipment, and did not involve them in any comprehensive plant-maintenance program. Thus, even with the new assistants, Ted continued to perform almost all the repair and maintenance work himself. At the time, however, he was still able to ensure that the equipment and production lines were able to operate without any mechanical problem.

However, in the past two years, GUP again expanded the size of its production facilities. Today, the company employs about 1,000 people in the production area alone. During this last expansion, Ted was given a substantial raise, the title of plant-maintenance manager, and a greater area of responsibility. In addition, the plant manager expanded the maintenance crew to a total of 10 employees. When all this occurred, the plant manager informed Ted that he expected Ted to function primarily as a supervisor and that Ted no longer needed to "get his hands dirty." However, as before, Ted attempted to do all the maintenance work himself. He did little or nothing in the way of supervising or training his crew. In fact, he repeatedly complained that he did not need all those people hanging around with nothing to do. Ted also mentioned that he believed that the reason he was so far behind in repair and maintenance work was that so much of his time was diverted to performing unimportant supervisory activities.

Jerry is not sure what is wrong with Ted or the maintenance department. Jerry, like almost everyone else, had believed that Ted could handle increased responsibilities. At this point, however, Jerry knows that the maintenance department is no longer functioning effectively and that he must act to correct the situation.

Chapter 10

Communicating

Learning Objectives

1. **List** and explain the six myths that hamper our understanding of the communication process.
2. **Explain** what is meant by this statement: "Poor communication is usually a symptom of a problem, not a problem itself."
3. **List** and explain the five characteristics of communication.
4. **Explain** the term "mutual meaning creation," and discuss why it is important for managers to understand.
5. **Diagram** and explain the "parts" that constitute our transactional model of communication.
6. **Discuss** how self-disclosure works to promote mutual meaning creation.

"M
R. Perry, I'm afraid we have a bad situation developing between some people in your marketing division and the personnel department. We in personnel try to do the best job we can for the company. We also consider ourselves professionals and will do only what we feel falls within our duty to our profession and the company."

"Wait a minute, Mr. Lumous. I don't know what you're talking about. Obviously, you're upset about something. Just what is it?"

"Do you have a Mr. Harold Martin working for you?"

"Yes, I do."

"Mrs. Anne Taylor of your division called us last Friday and asked for an investigation of Mr. Martin, and I want to tell you right now that my department does not perform private detective services for anyone in this company. If you have some reason to investigate Mr. Martin, you should—"

"Whoa, Mr. Lumous! Just hold on a minute. There's obviously a misunderstanding between my request and your response. Did Mrs. Taylor tell you what our problem was and why we need additional information on Mr. Martin?"

"No, Mrs. Taylor did not give us any information other than a bare request that we perform the investigation."

"We are considering Mr. Martin for a promotion and transfer to a new area where he would work with U.S. government contracts and the contracts of other national governments. To comply with government regulations, we must file certain documents about Mr. Martin. I cleared all this with Mr. Martin first, and then told Taylor to contact you. I didn't use the term *investigation*. I told

Taylor to ask you to help gather additional data to help us comply with regulations and help Martin get the promotion and transfer. Now, I don't see how this violates company policy, do you?"

"Mr. Perry, I owe you an apology. Your request, as you've just stated it to me, is a legitimate one and one that we will get to right away. Thank you."

"Ginnie, have Anne Taylor come in to see me. . . ." ∎

Trol Jorden, Inc.

Every first Monday of the month, the executive staff has a luncheon meeting. Today, we were to discuss whether to go with the new product line. The discussion started rather quietly, as the executive VP outlined our present financial position and problems. I then talked about our market analysis and projections for the success of the new product. Ed, our production VP, spoke about the production problems of the project, and as he spoke, I could see that Milt, from Product Development, was beginning to appear tense and anxious—he was breathing harder, his face was turning red, and he was chain-smoking. I tried to be as objective as possible and not say anything be interpreted personally by Milt, but Ed was going way beyond me. Now he was commenting that this was the third new product idea in the last three months from Milt's people, that all three had cost everybody time and money, and that in every case the decision had been the same, no go. I could see Milt looking daggers at Ed, and I waited for Milt to explode.

"I'm getting tired of having to defend our proposals every time," said Milt. "Six months ago, the president asked all of us to make that extra effort to overcome the crisis our company faced. We in Product Development have done all that we have been asked to do." Milt's voice had started out in a low tone, but it now reached a higher pitch. His speech had become more rapid-fire, and everything was coming in short bursts.

"It's not my job," continued Milt, as he looked directly at Ed, "to point an accusing finger at anyone. As members of the executive staff, you have the power to do as you will. I no longer care if the project goes or dies. It certainly doesn't matter to me. If you'll all excuse me, I have another important meeting to attend."

I looked at Ed—he now knew that it mattered a great deal. ∎

TMA Star, Inc.

It had been a rather full day, but I thought I'd stop back at the office before leaving. It was now 4:30—I was just in time to pick up the mail. There in the pile was this memorandum that made me pause:

MEMORANDUM

DATE: February 11, 1991
   TO: Division Vice Presidents, TMA Star, Inc.
FROM: Art Moss, Controller

According to the instructions from the Corporate Headquarters Financial Staff, the printouts you recently received from them should be returned with corrections and comments. Each division should check that the printout data correspond with the previously published budget data.

AEM: gg

P.S.   THE DEADLINE FOR THESE PRINTOUTS TO BE TURNED BACK TO US IS FEBRUARY 11, 1991.

Art Moss wanted the information back the same day he requested it! It was 4:30 now, so I couldn't possibly meet this request. I wondered if Art really meant for us to respond by February 14. Art had done this before, and his "emergency memos" usually meant that we added three workdays to his deadline. Since today was Tuesday, I had until Friday, and even though I had to fly to Chicago tomorrow, the checking could get done. I dictated a memo to Miss Johnson to have all the reports on my desk by Thursday. That way, I was sure they'd be on my desk by Friday. Just think of the confusion Art's memo caused. Why can't people say what they really mean? ∎

INTRODUCTION: MYTHS ABOUT COMMUNICATION

Communication Complex dynamic process of mutual meaning creation.

Communication is essential to management. At the heart of all managerial functions or roles is the act of communicating.[1] For example, Henry Mintzberg revealed that managers spend from 66 to 80 percent of their time communicating with superiors, subordinates, peers, and outside constituents.[2] Furthermore, research conducted by W. Charles Redding at Purdue University indicates that communication skills are the manager's most important asset or biggest liability. Stop and think about the importance of managerial communication for a moment. If managers do not understand the processes involved in communicating with their superiors, peers, and subordinates, their best-laid plans can still fail. Thus, when managers fail to understand the dynamic and complex nature of communication, effectiveness and efficiency are limited.

The opening case should have served to trigger some questions that managers frequently ask regarding communication. For example, you may have wondered: Why can't people say what they really mean? Why is interpersonal communication so difficult? Did Milt and Ed really communicate with each other? Doesn't Art see the confusion of his February 11 date? What can a manager do to improve communication? To the extent that we are successful in conveying meaning in this chapter, you will have the answer to these and many more questions about communication.

Our discussion of communication in this chapter will have two focal points. The first half of the chapter will examine interpersonal communication. That is, we will examine the processes that influence how managers interact with their superiors, subordinates, peers, and outside constituents. The second half of the chapter will examine organizational communication. In this area, we take a larger perspective that views communication as an element of the organization's structure.

As we noted earlier, managers spend a significant amount of their time "communicating." Is this time well spent? The answer to this question is both yes and no. Yes, because the act of communicating is a vital component in the managerial process. No, because managers may believe myths that prevent them from understanding the very nature of the communication process. In a lively and well-written article entitled "The Nature of Communication,"[3] Professor Stephen King presents widely believed myths that prevent people from fully understanding the communication process.

A typical picture of a contemporary manager shows people communicating with each other. Managers write memos, letters, reports; they explain to others, attempt to persuade others, and even argue with others. They communicate with one person or with a small group or to a large audience. Communicating is a critical factor in managing.

What are some myths about communication?

Myth One: I understand communication because I have done it for years. This myth is analogous to breathing. Since birth, we have been breathing to stay alive. The truth, however, is that most of us breathe incorrectly. When we inhale, we expand our lungs, not our stomach and diaphragm. As a result, we do not get the full advantage of breathing. Similarly, you may know or have worked for a person who has been in management for many years and yet is not what you would call a "good manager." Dispelling this myth should help you to realize that communicating is no different from breathing or managing. Even though we have "communicated" for a long time, that does not mean we know how to do it correctly.

Myth Two: Communication can be improved by improving communication-related skills. Every day, literally hundreds of seminars and workshops are conducted to provide managers with "communication" skills. Frequently, the focus of these workshops is on message creation or how to be a better speaker or writer. Although message creation and public speaking are parts of the communication process and the manager's role, they are far from being the whole communication or managerial process. Focusing on the message creator also makes two erroneous assumptions. First, it assumes that some set of universal laws exists that, if adhered to, will guarantee the manager success in conveying a message. Communication is much too complex a phenomenon for that to be the case. Furthermore, if such laws did exist, we could teach them to you early in your career, and there would be little need for the material contained in this chapter. Second, focusing attention on the speaker places the emphasis on the wrong person in an interaction. The attention should be on the "receiver," not the sender, when a message is transmitted. This myth is important for you, as a manager, to remember, because frequently your subordinates will not act on what you say but will base their attitudes and behaviors on what they think you mean! Thus, you could spend hours trying to devise the "perfect way" to say something and still find your subordinates responding in a way that is contrary to your expectations or desires.

Myth Three: I didn't misunderstand them; they misunderstood me. This myth is rooted in our natural human tendency to assume we are right and others are wrong when things go awry. As a manager, you have to accept the fact that communication is a two-way process. Sometimes, mixed messages or communication confusion is the other person's fault, but it is equally likely to be your fault. This myth should indicate that you need to take attention away from message creation and work on those practices that facilitate your understanding of the needs and perspectives of those with whom you are interacting.

Myth Four: Most problems stem from communication breakdowns. In the movie *Cool Hand Luke,* a wiley Southern sheriff said to a rebellious Paul Newman, in an attempt to explain the "problem/tension" that was occurring between them, "What we have here is a failure to communicate." Likewise, "communication gap," "communication breakdown," and "communication problem" are phrases uttered every day by managers who are attempting to identify and explain a wide range of dysfunctions in their work groups and organizations. In fact, "we have a communication problem" is one of the most commonly stated phrases in all our vocabularies, and we are all too quick to use it when we are experiencing problems in our families, love lives, schools, and communities. The reality is that poor communication usually is a symptom of a much deeper psychological, economic, political, or physical problem. For example, just as a cough (the symptom) might indicate the presence of a cold, an allergy, or a disease (the problem), poor communication (the symptom) usually stems from some underlying situation (the problem) that is causing the communication to be bad. Additionally, because communication is a dynamic process and not a static entity, the statement "we have a communication problem" really says nothing and offers you few, if any, concrete ideas as to where the real or underlying problem might lie. When you hear the phrase "communication problem," you should realize the bad or poor communication is usually resulting from an underlying issue that deserves your attention or examination.

Myth Five: Communication attempts to achieve perfect understanding. King suggests that this myth is dangerous because it assumes that perfect understanding is possible and it denies that sometimes the goal of communication is to be misunderstood. The simple statement "you are doing a good job here" may mean any number of different things to a manager and an employee. For example, the boss might mean it as a compliment, and the subordinate could take it to mean that this is the only place or task in which his or her work is good. Likewise, "good" could also be taken in a negative sense if the worker thought the performance was outstanding. The simplest statements can mean literally hundreds of things to different people, so perfect understanding is rarely, if ever, possible. As noted in Myth One, we often assume that if we develop the skill to phrase our comments just right, our employees will know exactly what we mean. That simply is not true. Additionally, sometimes we don't want our communication to be perfectly understood. Have you ever been purposefully vague in the hopes that the person you are interacting with will not know your true feelings or intentions? Have you ever "rambled" through an essay hoping the instructor will not know you don't know what you're talking about? In either case, your intent was not to be "perfectly understood." Rather, you used communication to hide your feelings or lack of knowledge. The point is that being perfectly understood is a rare occurrence, and you should not think of this as some goal that you must attain to be an effective "communicator/manager." To King's myths, we add one more that may inhibit your ability to understand the communication process.

Myth Six: More communication equals better communication. We live in a society in which more is usually preferred to less. We tend to think the same about communication. Consider this phrase; "Missiles of ligneous or petrous consistency have the potential of fracturing my osseous structure but appellations will eternally be benign." Do you know what it says? We could have made it simple and just written, "Sticks and stones may break my bones but words will never hurt me." As you can see, more words probably kept us from making our point and prevented you from understanding what we meant. When it comes to the practice of management, more communication does not always equal better communication. For example, consider the firm that has recently installed computers and an electronic mail ("E-mail") system in the offices of each of its managers. Soon after the installation, the managers who once hated preparing and sending memos were now routing their memos through the E-mail system to anyone who might have even a remote interest in what they had to say. As one manager put it, "It was not uncommon to come back from lunch and find ten to thirty messages on your computer screen, indicating the arrival of E-mails during the lunch hour." Because there was no way to prioritize these documents, the managers wasted precious hours sorting through their messages to find the one or two documents they needed or had requested.

More communication was not better communication for these managers. It wasted both their time and their energy.[4]

We have presented these myths because they represent some widely held beliefs in both managerial circles and life in general regarding communication. Unfortunately, these myths distort and inhibit our understanding of the communication process. They also cause us to view communication as a sender-oriented phenomenon when we should be striving to adopt a receiver-oriented view. Finally, they tempt us to believe that many problems are the result of poor communication when, in reality, poor communication is generally a symptom of a much deeper problem. To the extent that you can remove these myths from your thinking about communication, you should find that you become both a better communicator and a better manager.

THE TRANSACTIONAL NATURE OF COMMUNICATION

You might now be wondering, "What is communication?" Like love, communication is difficult to define and it has been defined in numerous ways. For our purposes, we will define communication as a complex dynamic process of mutual meaning creation. In this regard, communication is not a thing unto itself. Rather, communication is a constantly evolving system of "characteristics" that form a larger whole known as the communication process. We will discuss the two parts of our communication definition—complex dynamic process and mutual meaning creation—in the following sections.

A Complex Dynamic Process

What are the five basic characteristics of communication?

To begin, we will briefly examine five basic characteristics of communication that make it "a complex dynamic process." First, communication is a process in which senders, messages, channels, and receivers do not remain constant or static. These parts change and evolve over time, and they cause changes in the other parts of the system. For example, if a new member joins a work group, the patterns of interaction among all the other members will change.

Second, communication is complex. Stephen King,[5] David Berlo,[6] Dean Barnlund,[7] and many other communication theorists suggest that even in a simple two-person interaction, at least six people are present: the person you think you are; the person your partner thinks you are; the person you believe your partner thinks you are; plus the equivalent "persons" at the other end of the interaction. If four people, such as in a quality-control circle, were interacting, then at least fifty "persons" would be engaging in the interaction. Not only are these "people" present, but there is also a host of other variables, such as the setting, experiences each person has had, and the nature of the task, that influence the interaction. In a nutshell, there are many things to consider when we say people are communicating, any number of which affect the efficiency and effectiveness of the process.

Third, communication is symbolic. We use a variety of arbitrary words and signs to convey meaning to those with whom we are interacting. Although

Ethics Issue

Truth in Advertising

Advertising is one way that sellers communicate to buyers the availability and quality of their products. Advertising includes television and radio commercials, newspaper and magazine print ads, flyers, brochures, and package labeling. Truth in advertising is mandated by federal and state law, but truth in advertising is not always easy to achieve.

Cadillac won the Malcolm Baldridge National Quality Award in 1990, which surprised many critics because Cadillac's reputation for quality automobiles had not been very good in recent years. What surprised critics even more was the advertisement that Cadillac published to describe this achievement. First, it said that it was one of 167,000 companies that "applied for consideration." Actually, 167,000 applications were mailed out to companies by the U.S. Commerce Department. Only 97 completed the application. (The application requires companies to complete seventy-five pages describing quality control and processes, personnel policies, leadership, customer relations, training, and so on.) The Baldridge award praises the process of quality control, not the product itself. When it awarded Cadillac the award, it was in recognition of Cadillac's quality-control team, not the quality of the car. Cadillac stated that the Commerce Department was praising the car itself, particularly the 4.9-litre V-8 engine. The Attorney General's office in Texas threatened to press charges of false advertising. After the discrepancies were pointed out to Cadillac, the company changed its advertisement.

The U.S. Food and Drug Administration (FDA) tries to help manufacturers to remain ethical and truthful in their advertisements. For example, the FDA seized shipments of Procter & Gamble's Citrus Hill Fresh Choice orange juice. The FDA felt that P & G should not have used the word *fresh* on the label because the juice was made from concentrate. P & G had to scramble to produce new cartons with new labeling to keep selling the product. The FDA then ordered P & G and two other food companies, Great Foods of America and CPC International, to remove the words *No Cholesterol* from their labels on vegetable oil. The labels were truthful—vegetable oil does not have cholesterol. The FDA felt, however, that leaving "no cholesterol" on the label would be confusing to consumers, since surveys showed that consumers assumed that "no cholesterol" meant "no fat." Vegetable oil is 100 percent fat. The FDA is now planning to target other companies using *no cholesterol* on their products, and then move on to making sure labeling is correct on products marked *light* and *high fiber*.

In November 1990, Congress passed legislation that required the FDA to issue new food-labeling regulations by 1993. It is expected that the FDA will take on even more corporations at that time.

References: John Carey and Zachary Schiller, "The FDA Is Swinging 'a Sufficiently Large Two-by-Four'," *Business Week,* May 27, 1991, p. 44; Jeremy Main, "Is the Baldridge Overblown?" *Fortune,* July 1, 1991, pp. 62–65.

there is much agreement about the meaning of most of our words and signs, there is not perfect agreement on those meanings, and the meanings may change over time. For example, holding up two fingers signified "V" for victory in the 1940s and signified "peace" in the 1960s. That human communication is symbolic also means that it may sometimes be indirect and is always open to interpretation. For example, bosses who keep their doors open may be symbolically saying to their workers that they can come to see them whenever they want. On the other hand, they may be saying that they are keeping an eye on them. We must keep in mind that thoughts, meanings, and intentions are not transferred—messages are—and the way we transmit messages is through the signs and words we use. These signs and words may have similar or different meanings for the people using them.

(4) Fourth, communication is transitory. This means that communication is spontaneous and evolutionary, not static or mechanistic. Communication always moves forward and is unrepeatable. To demonstrate the ever-forward movement of communication, we ask if you have ever said something mean to another person and later said, "Forget it, I didn't mean it." Because of the transitory nature of communication, that is not possible. Once stated, a message will not be forgotten—forgiven maybe, but not forgotten. To demonstrate repeatability, think about a good joke. The first time you heard it, you probably laughed long and loud. Each repetition, however, probably produces a less emotional response. Managerially speaking, knowing the transitory nature of communication should make you aware that virtually all of what you say and do will, in some way or another, leave indelible marks on those with whom you have interacted. In time, those marks may come back to help or haunt you.

(5) Fifth, communication is a receiver-oriented phenomenon. You may remember that earlier in this chapter, we stated that improving message-creation skills to improve communication is a myth. It is a myth because, as this fifth point suggests, meaning always occurs or lies in the mind of the receiver. As a result, the intention of the sender is almost irrelevant. For example, in a previous paragraph, we talked about a manager's having an open-door policy. Regardless of what the manager means by that, the employees' responses to the open door are dictated by what they understand it to mean, not what the manager intends it to mean. Hence, try as you may to create the "perfect" message, the meaning lies in the head of the receiver, not in your intentions. That is, the receiver, not you, gives the message meaning.

Typically, communication is presented as a static and linear phenomenon such as that displayed in Figure 10-1. We believe this model of communication is incorrect. It does not capture the dynamic nature of communication, and because of its left-to-right orientation, it focuses attention on the sender and on his or her message. This is bad because it perpetuates the myths we presented earlier in this chapter.

Therefore, we have presented the characteristics of communication to help you see that communication is not the static and linear entity pictured in Figure 10-1. Instead, you should think of it as a complex set of communicators, receivers, messages, and effects that are dynamic and moving perpetually forward. Our model of communication will appear later in the chapter in Figure 10-4.

FIGURE 10-1 Typical Model of Communication

Mutual Meaning Creation

What is mutual meaning creation?

Now we will turn our attention to the second half of our communication definition—"mutual meaning creation." What we mean by mutual meaning creation is perhaps best portrayed in Figure 10-2.

As you can see, when two or more people interact with each other, each comes to that interaction with a uniquely individual past. Some of the elements that make up that past include values, experiences, culture, and personality traits and dispositions. In a sense, we bring our past and our beliefs about the present and the future with us to any interaction. Think about it for a minute. What do you bring to an interaction? Given similarities in background, most people probably share some degree of understanding of the "meaning" of various words and signs. For example, most of us would agree that "NFL" stands for National Football League. There is some degree of overlap. However, there are probably many words and signs whose meanings are not interpreted the same way by all people. For example, as many unfortunate motorists have found out, a red sign that says STOP may be interpreted to mean a slow, rolling pause. As a result, sometimes we get tickets from police officers who interpret it to mean a complete STOP! Thus, as Figure 10-2 notes, at the start of an interaction, there is usually not much mutual meaning regarding words and signs. There is very little overlap in the two circles.

Communication is the process that allows us to bring our two circles together, or to create mutual meaning. However, it is important to note that mutual meaning creation does not imply "agreement." Two people can disagree on the meaning of a word or a sign. As long as they share a definition of the

FIGURE 10-2 Mutual Meaning Creation

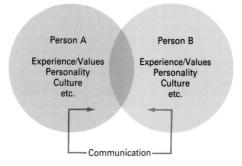

word or the sign, even if they disagree on the meaning, they are still closer to-gether because each is aware of what the other believes the word or the sign means. How much meaning there is between people is indicated by how much the circles overlap. Perhaps the easiest way to understand how communication works in the creation of mutual meanings is to consider your first days on a job. At first, you and your boss probably share some, but relatively little, under-standing of the meanings you attach to various words or signs. As time passes, however, you indicate to each other by verbal and nonverbal cues how you "see the world" and what meanings you attach to various words or signs. As you share these definitions, your circles move closer together. You create more mutual meaning than you had during your first days on the job. Eventu-ally, say by the time you celebrate your tenth anniversary of working together, the two original circles probably resemble one circle. They overlap a great deal. You have created a significant degree of mutual meaning. Thus, the cre-ation of mutual meaning is how one person can come to know exactly what another person is thinking or feeling without saying a word. Thus, communica-tion is the process that enables the two circles to move closer together or al-lows two or more people to create mutual meaning.[8]

Mutual meaning creation is an important element of our definition of com-munication, and it has a significant impact on the practice of management. We will provide three examples of how mutual meaning creation plays a role in management. First, the work world uses a number of techniques to create mu-tual meanings. Many professions use acronyms, lingo, or technical terms so that workers can convey meanings to each other quickly and concisely.[9] For example, instead of detailing the method used to account for inventory, a se-nior accountant might tell junior partners to use "FIFO." Little else would have to be said. The junior accountant would know to use the "first-in, first-out" method. On the other hand, lingo is often confusing or may not be understood by those who are not in the profession. When the marketing, accounting, and finance managers meet, they may have great difficulty understanding each other if they use the lingo of their professions. Second, performance evalua-tion reviews also rely on mutual meaning creation. In this case, you will want to make certain that your subordinates attach the same meaning to your com-ments as you do. If there is any doubt, ask them what they think you mean. Third, mutual meaning creation is the foundation for organizational culture. Companies with strong cultures exhibit a remarkable degree of overlap re-garding the meaning of various organizationally relevant words, events, and practices. Ultimately, then, when you think of our definition of communication as the complex dynamic process of mutual meaning creation, you will see that your job as a manager is not to create "perfect" messages. Rather, your job is to engage in a variety of practices that will help develop for you and your subor-dinates enough mutual meaning so that your tasks can be completed efficiently and effectively. In the next section, we will discuss one way in which people can come to develop mutual meaning—self-disclosure.

Self-Disclosure and Mutual Meaning Creation

The creation of mutual meaning is one of the most important ways for people to establish and maintain trusting relationships. However, you might be won-dering how, aside from "communication" or "interaction" with others, you can

	Known to self	Known to others
Known to others	Arena/Open area	Blind spot
Known to self	Facade/Hidden area	Unknown

self disclosure.
Johari Window

Self-disclosure Deliberate sharing of information about oneself with others.

create mutual meaning. One way is through a process known as **self-disclosure.** Self-disclosure can be defined as the deliberate sharing of information about oneself with others. A theoretical description of the self-disclosure process can be depicted by a diagram known as the Johari Window, shown in Figure 10-3. The Johari Window is named after its founders, Joseph Luft and Harry Ingram.[10] Each element of the window will be described in the following paragraphs.

How does the Johari Window work?

The arena or open area refers to information others know about us and we know about ourselves. It represents shared perceptions of "who we are." The blind spot refers to information that other people know about us but that we do not know. These are things others perceive in us but we do not see in ourselves. For example, we might think many of our comments in a meeting are witty or humorous. However, others in the meeting might perceive them as sarcastic or contentious. Thus, we see ourselves as "easygoing" while others see us as "bitter." In this regard, we are "blind" to their perceptions. The facade or hidden area refers to information we know about ourselves but do not share with others. Also included in this cell are thoughts and feelings we have about others that we do not share with them. For example, we might believe we can't perform a task that has been assigned to us, but we don't share those fears with anyone. Or, we might think one of our colleagues is a lazy worker, but we don't share that feeling with our coworker. In either case, we keep the information to ourselves. This often causes us to act in ways that may be the opposite of our true feelings. In this sense, we are keeping things hidden by putting up a facade. Finally, the unknown area refers to information that is known neither to us nor to others. However, don't assume that because this area is not consciously known to us it won't affect our attitudes and behaviors—it will. Though it is not our intent to explore this area in depth, you should realize that the unknown area is largely the domain of and basis for Freudian or psychoanalytic psychology. That is, it suggests that much of who we are and how we behave is driven by factors about which we are unaware, such as family influences, socialization, and significant or traumatic life experiences. The point is, one way or another, the material contained in this cell will emerge and influence our thoughts, words, and deeds even though we are unaware of it.

When we self-disclose to others, we are expanding our open area and reducing our hidden area. When others self-disclose to us, their hidden area is reduced and their open area expands. Thus, self-disclosure is largely a process of expanding the known area or creating mutual meaning between two or more people. Aside from assisting in the creation of mutual meaning, the process of self-disclosure has some managerial implications, which we will briefly explore.

First, when we self-disclose, we open ourselves to the possibility that others may reject us or use this information against us. As Powell notes, we hesitate to self-disclose because "if I tell you who I am, you may not like who I am, and it's all I have."[11] Second, many managers suffer from large hidden and blind areas. When managers fail to stay visible and interested and actively involved in the work, thoughts, and feelings of their subordinates, they lose touch with the factors that inhibit or promote employee performance. Third, the more accurately we know ourselves and the more we know about how others perceive us, the better our chances to establish open and authentic relationships. Fourth, managers must remember that the hidden and blind areas are often the breeding ground for covert attitudes and actions that may hinder performance. Finally, it takes a lot of energy to keep things hidden or to put up a facade—so much energy that it may hinder role performance. If social trends continue, we can assume that workers in the 1990s and beyond will desire meaningful and authentic work relationships with their peers, superiors, and subordinates: relationships free from hidden assumptions and covert agendas, relationships in which significant mutual meaning is created and shared. Self-disclosure, then, is one method managers can employ to facilitate the creation of such trusting and genuine work relationships.

A COMMUNICATION MODEL

Having exposed the myths that hinder our understanding of communication and having given our explanation of the characteristics and definition of communication, we would like to present you with our model of the communication process. The model is based on our definition of communication. Figure 10-4 shows how we diagram the communication process. A brief explanation of the components and managerial relevance of our model follows.

First, you should note that the model is enclosed in a box labeled **social context,** which can be defined as the setting in which an interaction takes place. The setting in which an interaction takes place has a profound impact on both the people and the process of communication. For example, an inter-

Social context The setting in which a communication interaction takes place.

FIGURE 10-4 Transactional Model of Communication

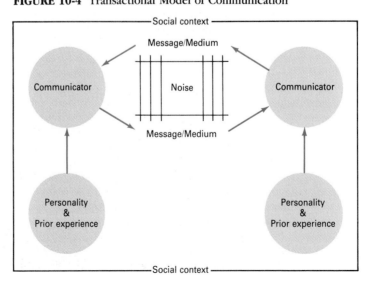

action between a boss and a subordinate in the boss's office will likely be
more formal and stilted than if it occurred at a local tavern. Furthermore, social context is increasing in importance, especially in light of the international
nature of modern business. For example, did you know that it is considered
the height of rudeness to allow someone of Arabic descent to see the soles of
your shoes? We know a salesperson who didn't know that. One day, while he
was sitting with his feet propped on his desk, as we are prone to do when we
relax in America, a Saudi customer entered his office and saw this display. The
client left, offended, vowing never to do business with that salesperson or his
firm again! Therefore, you should strive to remember that the setting in which
an interaction occurs will have a significant impact on the nature of the interaction. If you ignore or don't account for this component of the communication
model, your understanding of what, why, and how interactions take the tone
they do will be hindered.

Second, you should note that we no longer use the terms *sender, receiver,*
and *feedback.* We also place *message* and *medium* in the circle that connects
the two communicators. This is our attempt to reflect the transactional, fluid,
or dynamic nature of the communication process. What we are trying to show
you is that communicators send messages continuously and simultaneously.
Communication is not a perfectly linear sender $\longrightarrow$ message $\longrightarrow$ receiver $\longrightarrow$ feedback phenomenon. Rather, whenever people interact, they are
continually offering definitions of themselves and responding to the definitions
of the others with whom they are engaged. They do this both verbally and non-
verbally as well as intentionally and unintentionally. For example, in the course
of a meeting, managers may take off their coats and roll up their sleeves.
Though they have not intentionally said a word, they are sending a message
that could be interpreted as, "It is time to get down to serious work." Managers
must be aware of the circular and dynamic process of communication. As this
element shows, you are sending signals to your employees even when you are

Not all business is con-
ducted in formal settings.
Frequently a picnic or social event opens up opportunities for very effective
communication.

What is meant by "levels of meaning"?

Cntent vs pncess

Content level of a message The thinking or "face value" meaning of the message; the rational, concrete, objective, or quantifiable aspect of the message.

Process level of a message The feeling, emotional, or underlying meaning of the message.

not aware of it—signals they will interpret and act upon in a manner that is consistent with the meaning they attach to them. For example, professors usually know when the class period is about to end by the way students "pack up" and get ready to leave. Even if a professor is completely engrossed in making a point, the students are simultaneously sending signals to wind things up.

Before we leave this element of the model, one other comment regarding the nature of messages is in order. Any message has two components or levels of meaning—content and process. The **content level of a message** is the thinking or "face-value" meaning of the message. It is the rational, concrete, objective, or quantifiable aspect of the message. For example, if a manager said, "You did a good job on this report," that statement simply indicates the value of your work on a particular project. The **process level of a message** is the feeling, emotional, or underlying meaning of the message. The same "you did a good job on this report" may mean that the manager is impressed by your work, is proud of you, or is wondering how you finally managed to do something well. We must strive to be sensitive to both levels, or we may be missing "half the meaning" of any interaction.

The third element in the model is the medium or technology used to send the message or give feedback. As we pointed out in the "E-mail" example, the choice of medium has a significant impact on the communication process. For example, fax machines have made it possible to send and receive written messages thousands of times faster than was possible a few years ago. As the "E-mail" example should have shown, the medium used for interaction can hinder as well as help the communication process.

Fourth, you will see that each communicator is influenced by both prior experience and personality. Although many factors influence communicators, we think these two are very important. Past experience includes all the things you bring with you to an interaction, such as your history or emotional bag-

Technological advancements in the communication field have reduced the size of the globe. This picture shows the 235-ton Radio Telescope located in New Mexico.

Personality Any of the social psychological variables such as intelligence, which shape who you are and how you behave.

Noise Any of the mental, physical, and perceptual stimuli that cause distortion in the sending and receiving of messages.

gage, familiarity with the other person, experience in the context, experience with the message, and experience with the medium. All of these things will affect the communication process. For example, when you first start to manage others, you may find it hard to delegate authority to your subordinates because you have never done it before. As a result of "lacking experience" in this context or with this type of message, you will probably find that your first attempts at delegation will not be as effective as you desire. As you gain experience with delegation messages, you should get better.

Personality is any of the social psychological variables, such as intelligence, that shape who you are and how you behave. Like prior experience, these factors will also significantly shape the way in which you send and receive messages. For example, psychologist David McClelland has found that all people have needs for achievement, affiliation, and power.[12] Given what we know about these needs, those with a high need for affiliation are more likely to be empathetic and responsive listeners than those with a high need for power. As a result of their personalities, then, these people will probably have markedly different communication styles. The point is, your personality will significantly influence how you interact with people.

Finally, **noise** is any of the mental, physical, and perceptual stimuli that cause distortion in the sending and receiving of messages. Although you cannot escape noise, you should strive to minimize it whenever and wherever possible. For example, as a manager, you should try not to accept or receive phone calls when holding meetings with your employees. Taking a call will create noise that distracts your attention and the attention of your subordinate and will alter the course and flow of your interaction.

This discussion has shown you that communication is a complex dynamic process, a process with many ties to the practice of management. In the end, what we have tried to explain to you is that because of its very complexity, you must work very hard at understanding communication. You cannot and should not assume that because you have "communicated" for quite some time or even taken a public speaking class, you understand communication. As we stated near the outset of this chapter, "we have a communication problem" is one of the most-uttered phrases in America. In reality, communication is a nebulous term that refers to a process. To say you have a communication problem usually says nothing, nor does it offer you a guide to correcting the problem. This section should help you see the complex nature of communication and increase your willingness and desire to promote greater specificity than simply saying you have a "communication problem."

In the next sections, you will move beyond the description of communication as a process and focus on the types of organizational roles managers must play, the channels and networks managers use, and some suggestions for overcoming barriers to effective communication.

ORGANIZATIONAL ROLES AND MANAGERIAL COMMUNICATION

Organizational life requires managers to behave and communicate in a number of varied roles (see Figure 10-5). We will discuss four important roles.

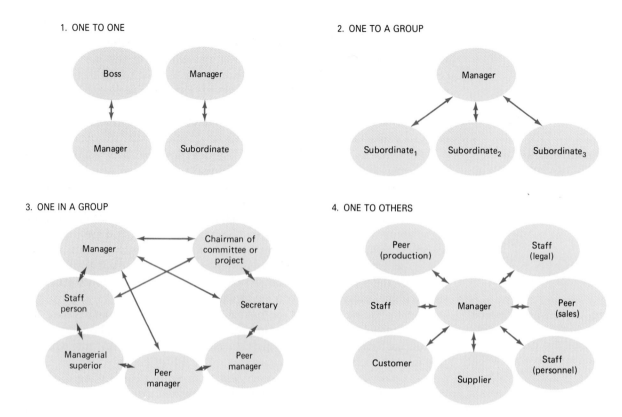

FIGURE 10-5 Organizational Roles in Managerial Communication

A manager engages in communication with a boss and individual subordinates in a one-to-one relationship. Managers also communicate with subordinates as a group. Managers frequently find themselves members of groups or committees. And managers spend many hours in lateral or diagonal relations with peers or people outside their immediate departments, dealing with external work flows.

The differences in roles add variations to the communication processes for managers. For example, in the first two situations, the communicators share a work environment and experience that probably create some common elements in their perceptual fields. Greater communication is more difficult because of the differences in the use of words (staff personnel frequently use more technical and sophisticated language), perceptual fields, goals and objectives, and climate for feedback. The meaning given a message will also differ according to whether a communicator is alone (as in the first role) or is subject to the interpersonal pressures of the group (as in the second and third roles).

You can see that the interpersonal roles a manager faces in organizations call for different communication skills and approaches.[13] The specific approach should be related to the communication channels and networks existing in the organization.

ORGANIZATIONAL COMMUNICATION CHANNELS AND NETWORKS

Communication permeates every organization. Some messages are sent and received clearly and effectively; others cause confusion and errors. In addition, some messages that are sent throughout the organization contain misinformation or secret information that may impede organizational processes.[14] In this section, we describe the networks that carry messages to all parts of the organization. The channels can be categorized as either formal or informal. **Formal communication networks** are those designed by the organization and known by all. In most instances, legitimate organizational means are used to transmit messages along formal lines—direct mail, closed-circuit television, called meetings, telephone, and so on.

Informal communication networks arise to fill needs not met by the formal channels; they are networks often unknown to corporate officials or used by all managers or employees. They are those channels developed to transmit sensitive or personal information. The messages are usually oral, rarely written. These two forms require elaboration to show their importance for organizational communication.

Formal communication networks Those communication networks designed by the organization and known by all.

Informal communication networks Communication channels developed to transmit sensitive or personal information; usually only oral messages; network not officially recognized or sanctioned by the organization.

Formal Communication Networks

One way to view communication in organizations is to examine the nature and direction in which it flows—downward, upward, or horizontally (see Figure 10-6). Specific types of communication are often associated with directional flow.

Communication that flows down from managers to subordinates can usually be classified according to one of the following five types: (1) job instruc-

FIGURE 10-6 Formal Communication Networks

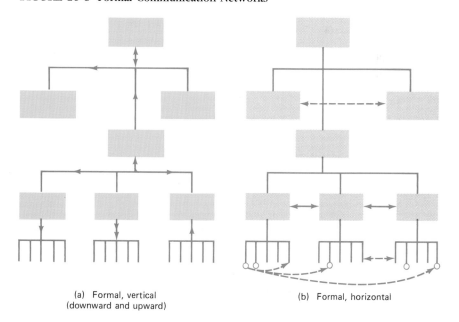

(a) Formal, vertical
(downward and upward)

(b) Formal, horizontal

tions; (2) job rationale; (3) organizational policies, procedures, and practices; (4) performance feedback; and (5) indoctrination of corporate mission designed to create organization commitment. These types of messages are frequently sent to several organizational levels through written channels such as published manuals, booklets, or memos.

Unfortunately, research findings show a tendency for messages not to filter down to the lower organizational levels and for managers to wrongly believe that those messages have been absorbed by their subordinates. There are several reasons for this. First, managers may rely too heavily on written channels.[15] An avalanche of written material may cause the overloaded subordinate to ignore some messages. Second, the oral face-to-face channel, which can command more attention and provide immediate feedback, is often underutilized. Finally, many downward messages may be perceived by subordinates as irrelevant or obsolete by the time they are received.

Upward communication, from subordinates to managers, can usually be classified according to one of the following four types: (1) personal reports of performance, problems, or concerns; (2) reports of others and their performance, problems, or concerns; (3) reactions to organizational policies and practices; and (4) suggestions about what tasks need to be done and how they can be accomplished. These types of communication are frequently sent up only one level in the organization to the immediate supervisor. The supervisor may send some of the information to the next higher level, but usually in a modified form. Both written and oral channels may be used in these instances.

Upward communication is beneficial to both the manager and the subordinate. For the manager, it provides feedback and an indication of the subordinate's receptiveness to messages sent downward. For the subordinate, it may provide a release of tensions and a sense of personal worth, which may lead to a feeling of commitment to the organization. The key to successful upward communication is a trusting relationship between the communicators. Trust, however, cannot be mandated by policy or directive; it must be earned by the manager through credible behavior and communication. One example demonstrates the value of rewarding upward communication.

Horizontal communication provides a means for members on the same level of an organization to share information without directly involving their superiors. Examples include the communication that may occur between members of different departments of an organization and between coworkers in the same department. Horizontal communication can usually be classified according to one of the following five types: (1) task coordination; (2) problem solving; (3) information sharing; (4) conflict resolution; and (5) social support. Through horizontal networks, peers can avoid delay and act to solve a task or relationship problem while relieving overloaded superiors of involvement. In addition, many workers find social and emotional support through peer communication. Both written and oral channels may be used for these efforts. It should be noted, however, that horizontal communication networks can be dysfunctional if they are indiscriminately substituted for upward and downward communication. (See Figure 10-6.)

Informal Communication Networks

To meet needs not fulfilled by the formal communication networks, supplemental or informal networks are likely to emerge. These emergent networks

Management Application

GE Listens

Encouraging upward communication can be rewarding for both top management and subordinates. At General Electric, listening to employee suggestions paid off in significant production cost savings. Employees also receive financial and psychological rewards for communicating their ideas. For example, one employee was reported to have received personal satisfaction for coming up with an idea that saved the company $120,000 in materials for just one year. He also received almost $12,000 as a reward. The manager of employee communications at one GE plant reports adopting 3,900 employee suggestions in one year. The average reward for an idea that is implemented is $200. It pays to communicate!

generally develop among organizational members who have friendly relationships. People who consider themselves friends are likely to interact more than those who do not. This is a natural development for those who come into contact for job-related reasons and discover that they have other things in common and therefore begin to share social information. This discovery creates an informal channel by adding a new message dimension to a formal channel.

Informal communication can often be classified into one or more of the following five types: (1) confirming formal communication; (2) contradicting formal communication; (3) expediting the delivery of messages faster than formal channels; (4) supplementing incomplete formal communication; and (5) maintaining social relationships. An example of type 4 follows.

Suppose you discover a problem in a project you are responsible for. Your boss has been putting the pressure on you for early completion, and you run into a snag. You do not feel free to go to your boss for help, so you call a fellow manager in another department or company who is your friend. She gives you suggestions that help to solve your problem and meet the deadline. The communication network between the two of you was not formally sanctioned by the organization; rather, it emerged informally to supplement the information you needed to resolve your work problem. Most likely your friend will view your relationship as reciprocal and feel free to call you in similar circumstances.

Another type of informal communication network is called the grapevine. The term was first used during the Civil War when intelligence telegraph lines were strung on tree branches in a manner resembling a grapevine. Messages coming through these channels were often distorted—a characteristic also associated with the human counterpart. Today, the grapevine spontaneously emerges to disseminate information from the point of origin to other points throughout the organization. (See Figure 10-7.)

Items on the grapevine may appear random—whatever seems to sound like something someone would want to know.[16] In some instances, the infor-

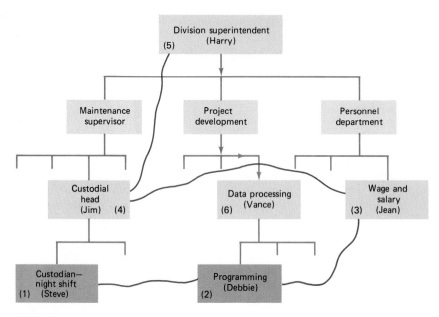

FIGURE 10-7 An Example of Grapevine Communication

mation is factual; in some, it is partially factual and partially fabricated; and in some, the information is totally "created"—simply what people want to hear. Examples of grapevine communication range from overheard comments from the president on the elevator or in the washroom to the names of workers on the promotion list spied from a secretary's word processor. Examples of "created" information include rumors about company mergers, stories of improper social behavior on the part of executives, and speculation about coming salary increments.

Much of a manager's time may be spent in relationships outside the formal work scene, as illustrated in the foregoing examples. In these informal relationships, you face entirely different situations from those in formal ones. You might have little or no direct authority over the other person. People cannot be forced into giving information or cooperating. Terms like *trading, mutual,* and *reciprocal* replace terms like *procedures, rules,* and *policies.* Communication guidelines, effective when using formal channels with superiors or subordinates, may no longer prove effective.[17]

Managers interested in being effective will be aware of all the communication networks and channels. Managers must be aware of the differences in these channels and adapt their behavior to the situation and improve communication throughout the organization. They will participate in formal and informal networks in an effort to avoid or correct misunderstandings. They will manage the grapevine to their advantage by strategically providing it with information and not being threatened by its existence.[18]

Throughout the discussion of the communication process and organizational channels and networks, you have read examples of communication failures. It would seem important to our educational objective of understanding how to be an effective managerial communicator to address why failure occurs in organizational communication.

OVERCOMING BARRIERS TO EFFECTIVE COMMUNICATION

What are some barriers to effective organizational communication?

A number of factors interfere with the communication process. These factors can be viewed as opportunities to enhance organizational effectiveness or as barriers that can lead to organizational breakdowns and misunderstandings. In this section, we describe five phenomena (uncertainty absorption, distortion, message competition, message conflict, and grapevine) present in organizations that elicit possible manager responses. Table 10-1 summarizes how you as a manager might be influenced by these factors in organizational communication.

Uncertainty absorption Increasing omission of information in the message as it progressively moves from the source; the tendency of details to be lost as one person processes a message and passes it on to the next person.

The first factor, **uncertainty absorption,** refers to the increasing omission of information in the message as it progressively moves further away from

TABLE 10-1   Manager Responses to Effective Organizational Communication Threats

THREAT	UNCERTAINTY ABSORPTION	DISTORTION	MESSAGE COMPETITION	MESSAGE CONFLICT	GRAPEVINE
Range of Managerial Responses	1. Ignore it.	1. Ignore it.	1. Ignore it.	1. Ignore it.	1. Ignore it.
	2. Keep message short and simple.	2. Always verify second-party information before acting upon it.	2. Code formal messages with priority level.	2. Communicate rather than suppress bad news.	2. Rely on it for information.
	3. Recognize information from lower levels probably omits nuances and uncertainties of the original message.	3. Use message redundancy (use several channels or repetition in same channel).	3. Indicate when response is expected.	3. Give concrete rationale for countermanding previous messages.	3. Attempt to suppress it by refutation of its accuracy.
		4. Keep message short and simple.	4. Limit message distribution to those who really need it.	4. Seek independent sources to resolve conflict.	4. Participate in it by planting strategic messages at different organizational levels.
		5. Minimize number of organization levels through which a message must pass.	5. Distinquish between informative messages and those requiring action or problem solving.		

Message distortion
Changes to the message
as a result of additions,
deletions, or differences
in the perception.

the source. There is a tendency for some message details to be "lost" as each person processes the message and sends it on.

The second factor is **message distortion,** and there are three principal types of message distortion likely to be found in organizations. The first type is characterized by a communicator adding spurious information to a message. In the second type, the communicator inadvertently deletes or loses information from the message. Finally, the information may be transformed according to personal perceptual filters and idiosyncracies.

Global Application

Even the Japanese Have Difficulty Understanding Cultural Differences

The success of Japanese products in the U.S. market has been attributed to Japanese efforts to develop a good understanding of the American culture and to learn how to effectively get their message across to the American consumer. Even in the realm of American politics, the Japanese have learned how to successfully advocate and protect their interests. As a result, the Japanese have gained a reputation for being competent and formidable lobbyists.

In Washington, Japanese lobbyists have learned to work behind the scenes, using discussions, political contributions, and gifts to influence the decision makers. The Japanese are quite comfortable with this kind of low-profile lobbying effort because they are characteristically not skilled or adept at publicly expressing their ideas, feelings, or positions.

But the Japanese have had difficulty transporting their successful U.S. formula to the European continent. They mistakenly assumed that the way of communicating, selling, influencing, and doing business is the same in all Western cultures. Their initial lobbying efforts in the political bodies and agencies of the European Community (EC) were unsuccessful. They made campaign contributions of millions of yen to members of the European Parliament, only to discover that the Parliament was only an advisory body and that the real decision making rested with the various commissions that make up the EC. Their efforts to offer drafts of specific legislative proposals to European officials and governmental leaders, a common practice of lobbyists in the U.S., were taken as an insult and considered bad form.

The Japanese have come to realize that they must use a different approach in dealing with the European market. Now they are taking a high-profile approach to influencing European decisions and decision makers and are learning to be more aggressive and more public in advocating their interests. As a result, the Japanese ability to assess and interpret political and popular European trends has improved, and they are succeeding in stopping the implementation of proposals that would seriously restrict their ability to operate in the EC.

The change in Japanese lobbying efforts in Europe demonstrates the importance of recognizing and understanding the nature of cultural diversity. To be successful on the global scale, businesses and organizations have to be flexible and adaptive in the way they communicate their interests and conduct business in foreign markets.

Source: Patrick Oster, "Lobbying European-Style: Japan Inc. Catches On." *Business Week.* June 3. 1991, p. 50.

Message competition
Messages compete for attention and processing; some messages are processed more quickly than others depending upon communicator's perception of what is important.

Message conflict Two messages contain contradictory directives, claims, or positions.

Grapevine A communication network that spontaneously emerges to disseminate information throughout an organization.

The third factor, **message competition,** results from difficulties in assigning message priorities. Without clear guidelines, individuals may process messages in a random manner. Thus, communicators may differ in the importance they attach to any message. Usually, messages sent downward in the formal network carry the highest and clearest priority. Messages communicated upward and horizontally typically do not have clear or shared priority levels. Consequently, messages compete for attention and processing.

Fourth, **message conflict** occurs when two messages contain contradictory directives, claims, or positions. The conflicting messages may come from the same or different sources. Another type of message conflict occurs when a message is received that does not match the expectations of the receiver (for example, "I never expected to have to work weekends but was told by my boss to be here Saturday").

The **grapevine,** as has been mentioned, typically involves small clusters of people who exchange information through unsanctioned organizational channels and networks. The information in this informal network is usually unverified and often includes rumors. To some extent, the grapevine is always present in any organization.

Organizations may be viewed as complex information-processing machines. Just like other machines, organizational communication systems must be maintained properly or face the possibility of breaking down. How you, as a manager, handle these ever-present phenomena and challenges will determine the communication effectiveness of your organization.

SUMMARY

Communication is integral to most management functions. Reviewing the elements of the communication process that were presented in this chapter can help you plan for more effective communication and help you diagnose the cause of misunderstandings when communication breakdowns occur. This chapter also discussed interpersonal communication issues and the role of different types of communication networks in the organization. It concluded with a look at ways of overcoming communication barriers.

KEY TERMS

Communication Complex dynamic process of mutual meaning creation.

Self-disclosure Deliberate sharing of information about oneself to others.

Social context The setting in which a communication interaction takes place.

Content level of a message The thinking or "face value" meaning of the message; the rational, concrete, objective, or quantifiable aspect of message.

Process level of a message The feeling, emotional, or underlying meaning of the message.

Personality Any of the social psychological variables such as intelligence, which shape who you are and how you behave.

Noise Any of the mental, physical, and perceptual stimuli that cause distortion in the sending and receiving of messages.

Formal communication networks Those communication networks designed by the organization and known by all.

Informal communication networks
Communication channels developed to transmit sensitive or personal information; usually only oral messages; network not officially recognized or sanctioned by the organization.

Uncertainty absorption Increasing omission of information in the message as it progressively moves from source; the tendency of details to be lost as one person processes a message and passes it on to the next person.

Message competition Messages compete for attention and processing; some messages are processed more quickly than others depending upon communicator's perception of what is important.

Message conflict Two messages contain contradictory directives, claims, or positions.

Message distortion Changes to the message as a result of additions, deletions, or differences in the perception.

Grapevine A communication network that spontaneously emerges to disseminate information throughout an organization.

STUDY ASSIGNMENTS

1. In the opening case, you read three communication problems. What were the three problems? What were the reasons for these problems? With respect to managerial communications, what could have been done to prevent these problems from occurring?

2. What lessons can managers learn about the communication process from reading Professor King's observations concerning the six myths of communication?

3. What are the five basic characteristics of communication, and how do they contribute to making communication a "complex, dynamic process"?

4. Why is it important for a manager to understand that communication is not a static and linear phenomenon but a dynamic concept?

5. What is meant by the statement that communication is the process of "mutual meaning creation"?

6. What impact has "mutual meaning creation" had on the practice of management?

7. How does self-disclosure in the communication process facilitate a manager's ability to create trust and establish genuine work relations with subordinates?

8. How does the setting of an interaction influence the communication process?

9. Explain how the transactional model of communication is different from the typical model of communications. How is it different from the "mutual meaning creation" model?

10. Describe the four roles that managers assume in the communication process. How are the roles different? Which role do you think is the most important? Why?

11. Compare and contrast the informal communications network and the formal communications network of an organization that you know of or of a business where you have worked.

12. When it comes to providing direction to others, why do some managers rely more heavily on written channels of communication and less on the oral face-to-face form of communication?

13. In the workplace, how should managers handle the existence of the informal communication network known as the grapevine? What benefit, if any, can the grapevine provide to a manager?

14. What actions can managers take to overcome the various barriers to effective communication?

Case for Discussion

NORTHRIDGE ELECTRIC, INC.

In the spring of 1975, Northridge Electric lured R. Henry Springer away from Elmhurst Community College to become director of the firm's newly formed Manpower Planning and Development Department. In his new role, Dr. Springer was responsible for comprehensive, long-range plans and programs for securing and developing necessary manpower to meet the firm's needs. His boss, Mr. Jenkins, Vice President of Human Resources, gave Dr. Springer wide latitude in his new assignment. As Jenkins put it, Dr. Springer was "to do whatever needs doing to ensure that the necessary manpower requirements for Northridge are met."

Northridge Electric had annual sales in excess of $100 million. It was composed of four principal divisions of approximately equal size. The heads of these four divisions reported to Mr. Gray, Executive Vice President of Operations. Each of the four divisions had from eight to twelve production plants, located mostly in the East and ranging in size from 350 to 750 employees.

Upon Dr. Springer's arrival at Northridge, the firm's communications department sent the following announcement to all the corporation's departments and to each of the plant managers of the four divisions:

> We are pleased to announce the addition to our staff of Henry Springer, Ph.D. Dr. Springer will head the new Department of Manpower Planning and Development. Dr. Springer has a fine academic background in the fields of personnel and organizational behavior.
>
> R.T. Jenkins
> Vice President—Human Resources

Dr. Springer spent the first few weeks orienting himself to his new surroundings and laying out on paper some of his thoughts about what he should be doing. It seemed to him that as a first step, he should get everyone "onstream" with a sound manpower plan. The place to start, as he saw it, was the collection of information on all the firm's executives, middle managers, and supervisory personnel. This would form a data base from which his planning could begin.

He discussed this approach with Mr. Jenkins, who agreed that it sounded logical. Jenkins suggested that he might want to talk with several of the firm's personnel managers at the various plants to see how available were the information requirements for which Dr. Springer asked. Dr. Springer was most eager to get on with his project, so he telephoned two or three plant personnel managers in the area to talk about his needs. They seemed to go along with his thinking but raised concerns that Dr. Springer dismissed. In early July, Dr. Springer prepared and sent the following memo to each of Northridge's plant personnel managers:

> For a long time, Northridge has been seriously lacking in manpower planning and development. To solve this problem, I am initiating a comprehensive plan that will enable our firm to have the necessary manpower to fulfill our needs in the future. I'm sure you understand the importance of this. I ask each of you to fill

out the enclosed information forms on each of your operation's key managers and supervisors. Please return the forms to me by the end of this month.

Sincerely,

Henry Springer, Ph.D

Director, Manpower Planning and Development

By the close of the first week of August, Dr. Springer had received only a handful of responses to his request, and most of those were so poorly prepared that they needed to be redone. During the second week of August, he called on several of the plant personnel managers who had tried to comply with his request. He found that his reception was pretty much the same in all places—chilly.

Those who did agree to talk with him held their meetings to as short a time as possible, claiming that they had other pressing matters that needed their immediate attention.

Chapter 11

Controlling

Learning Objectives

1. **Define** the word control when used as a managerial function.
2. **Show** how planning and controlling are interrelated and how they are the two main functions of management.
3. **Describe** the four components of an effective control system.
4. **Explain** the characteristics of setting sound objectives.
5. **Define and illustrate** the terms feedback, preventive control, concurrent control, and strategic point control.
6. **Illustrate** the procedure for establishing budgetary control.
7. **Demonstrate** why budgets are a critical element in the control process.
8. **Characterize** what factors are used to determine an effective performance measure.
9. **Identify** some of the different types of control systems.
10. **Explain** the term management by exception.
11. **Describe** how the human element influences the controlling process.

T OM BECKER carried three grocery bags filled with receipts and cancelled checks into his new accountant's office. "I'm sorry to be so late with this," he said. "I know our taxes are due in less than two weeks, but I've been busy. Business has been great. By the way, after you sort through all this stuff, can you give me a call and let me know if we made any money last year? I thought we did—we almost had more work than we could handle—but I probably put about $40,000 of my own money into our checking account during the year. You'll see when you start looking at the deposit slips—I tried to mark the ones that came out of my savings, but I may have missed a few."

Tom Becker was one of two owners of B & L Construction Company. The other owner was Jeff Lackman. Each man had started his own business out of his garage. The two of them had merged just two years ago, incorporated, and opened an office. Now they had the additional expense of the office and the office manager.

The office manager was supposed to keep track of income and expenses, but somehow the information she fed into their computer came out very strange. The computer printouts made no sense at all and were totally useless to anyone. Although the office manager was not very good at using the computer, she did a good job of answering the telephone and keeping track of where all the employees were. Besides, according to both Jeff and Tom, Helen loved them "like a mother would."

Within the last two years, B & L had grown large enough to hire ten full-time employees, who were all paid on an hourly basis. They were able to keep most of their employees working year-round, which was unusual in the area, since snow generally covered the ground from the end of November until the first of March.

They did all kinds of work—from repairing roofs and replacing downspouts to building $350,000 homes. They considered no job too small or too big. However, they had been unable to obtain many large jobs because they had been unable to obtain bonding. The bonding company said that B & L was not strong enough financially to qualify for bonding.

They also employed many subcontractors, people who were paid by the job instead of by the hour. The subcontractors were considered independents rather than employees; B & L did not withhold income tax or Social Security from their checks. Employees were always paid first, before any other bills, and B & L had always been able to meet payroll. Subcontractors were paid second. Other bills were paid as money became available.

B & L had been building a good, solid reputation for doing excellent, high-quality work. They had done remodeling on quite a few of the businesses in the downtown area, and people were generally impressed with their work.

B & L was pleased to find a new accountant. They had been taking their work to another accountant for the past two years but had not been satisfied. Although he seemed to do a very good job preparing the tax returns, his lateness on the corporate, individual, and payroll tax returns, plus, as they saw it, his failure to tell them when to make Federal Tax Deposits (FTDs) had cost them close to $5,000 in IRS penalties.

"We seem to bring in a lot of money. I would estimate that we had over $500,000 in gross receipts last year," Tom continued, "but I have no idea where it's all going. I don't have any experience in accounting or business. I am a very good builder, not an accountant. We have several things we would like for you to do after you finish the tax return. First, we need to find out where our money is going. Second, we are competing with people who are still operating out of their garages. We have much higher overhead than they do. We're finding it difficult to make competitive bids and still support an office with an office manager. Third, we are not sure how to do our bids to cover all of our costs. Fourth, both Jeff and I would like to give ourselves raises. We've taken very little out of the business, but we both seem to be putting in a lot of time and money. Fifth, we would like to reduce our tax liability. Sixth, we want to figure out what's wrong with our computer system. We paid a small fortune for a genuine IBM system and it gives us garbage. Seventh, we would really like to be able to obtain bonding. Can you help us?" ■

Although the owners of B & L excelled at construction work, they were lost when it came to the control function of management. They had planned, for example, to make a profit. Even though they were working on many projects and bringing in money, they had no idea where that money was being spent. They had hired someone to keep track of their revenue and expenses and acquired an IBM computer to record the information, to no avail. Apparently, it was a case of "garbage in, garbage out" for the computer. So, although Tom and Jeff were trying to do everything right, everything was not going as planned.

Managing an organization requires many skills and abilities. We have already discussed six of the seven management functions: decision making, planning, organizing, staffing, directing, and communicating. We turn now to the function many consider the most basic and critical—controlling. **Controlling** is making sure that actual performance matches expected performance. Controlling is the function of management that compares actual results with planned results and takes corrective action as needed to make sure the actual more closely matches the plan.

Controlling Activity that measures performance and guides actions toward some predetermined target.

The control function of management relates to all other management functions, particularly planning, and most of the other functions cannot be completed effectively without the control function.[1] In this chapter, we will first take a brief look at some relationships between controlling and the other management functions to show the vital role that control plays. Then, we will continue our discussion of controlling by answering two basic questions: What are the essential steps in controlling? What are some of the basic concepts applicable to control systems? We conclude the chapter by looking into the human factors in controlling.

THE RELATIONSHIP OF CONTROLLING TO THE OTHER MANAGEMENT FUNCTIONS

How can I find out what's going on?

Recall for a moment the other management functions: Managers decide, plan, organize, staff, communicate with others, and lead through the process of directing and supervising. Those functions usually involve the managers and others—bosses, peers, or subordinates. What controlling does is to provide the means to know what is going on and to evaluate performance. When control exists in an organization, people know what goals they are trying to achieve; they know how they are doing in relation to those goals; and they know what changes, if any, are needed to maintain the performance at a satisfactory level.[2]

Planning and controlling are so interdependent that doing one implies the performance of the other. Planning, as we saw in Chapter 6, results in statements of what we expect to do in the future. Controlling uses those statements as the basis for determining whether actual performance is meeting expected performance. Thus, planning is necessary for controlling, and a good plan is ineffective if control is not maintained.

In organizing, the flow of authority is channeled to departments with responsibility for performance.

Accountability is the control element in the structure that requires reporting of whether subordinates have actually fulfilled their responsibility.

Leadership is effective if the results meet the objectives of the organization. Controlling is the function that continually tests, measures, and evaluates that effectiveness.

As for communicating, you learned about its role in informing individuals about the meaning and intent of an organization's plans and objectives, as well as conveying directions for implementing those plans. With respect to controlling, the feedback dimension of communication is an essential element of the control process. Communication feedback provides a means to evaluate and compare actual performance with expected performance, and it helps identify potential problem areas that need managerial attention and corrective action.

Control should be pervasive throughout the organization. A lack of control, insufficient control, or a defective control system could result in lost opportunities or cost the organization thousands of dollars. Many businesses experience financial, marketing, sales, operational, organizational, and staffing problems because they have an inadequate control system. In some cases, inadequate control systems may even lead to business failure.

THE ESSENTIALS OF CONTROLLING

Controlling is the activity that measures performance and guides actions toward some predetermined target.[3] There are four steps to successful controlling:

1. Set a target.
2. Measure performance.
3. Compare the target with actual results.
4. Take corrective action (if necessary).

Set a Target

Why set targets?

The first step is the foundation upon which the entire process is built: You must determine what the results should be or what results can be expected.

(Many people consider this first step to be part of the planning process, so that controlling does not begin until step 2. Either way you look at it, controlling needs planning, and planning is pointless without controlling.)

Setting a target demands a look into the future and a prediction of a definite, feasible, and appropriate target. Typically, the target is expressed as an objective.

Objectives

Objectives Specific statements of what an organization hopes to achieve.

Objectives are specific statements of what an organization hopes to achieve. Objectives in an organization form a hierarchy. At the top, the entire organization aims in a given direction; each department in turn directs its efforts toward its own objectives; each division of each department has its own meaningful aims; and finally, each individual can be assigned definite objectives, which can clarify the role of the person who fills that position. Figure 11-1 illustrates this hierarchy for a middle-sized company.

FIGURE 11-1 Sample of a Hierarchy of Objectives in a Middle-sized Company

TOP MANAGEMENT
1. Represent stockholders, interests—net profits of 10% or more
2. Provide service to consumers—provide reliable products to clear specifications
3. Maintain growth of users and sales—double each decade
4. Provide continuity of employment for company personnel—no involuntary layoffs
5. Develop favorable image with public

PRODUCTION DEPARTMENT	SALES DEPARTMENT	FINANCE & ACCOUNTING DEPT.
1. Keep cost of goods no more than 50% of sales	1. Introduce new products, so that over a 10-year period, 70% will be new	1. Borrowing should not exceed 50% of assets
2. Increase productivity of labor by 3% per year	2. Maintain a market share of 15%	2. Maximize tax writeoffs
3. Maintain rejects at less than 2%	3. Seek new market areas, so that sales will grow at a 15% annual rate	3. Provide monthly statements to operating depts. by 15th of following month
4. Maintain inventory at 6 months of sales	4. Maintain advertising costs at 4%	4. Pay dividends at rate of 50% of net earnings
5. Keep production rate stable, with no more than 20% variability from yearly average		

SUPERVISORS	DISTRICT SALES MANAGERS	OFFICE MANAGERS
1. Handle employee grievances within 24 hours	1. Meet weekly sales quotas	1. Maintain cycle billing within 3 days of target date
2. Maintain production to standard or above	2. Visit each large customer area each month	2. Prepare special reports within a week of request
3. Keep scrappage to 2% of materials usage	3. Provide salespeople with immediate follow-up support	

Each individual in the organization must have a clear understanding of what he or she is trying to accomplish and must see how those objectives interrelate with the broader and longer-run goals of the larger group. In other words, we are focusing on a pyramid or hierarchy in which the top is supported by the individual building blocks (individual's objectives) used by each member of the organization. The hierarchy of objectives provides a structure by which each member in a group effort can concentrate on interrelating his or her own output with the total effort and on clarifying each contribution to the broad, long-run goals. One method that has been used to clarify goals and objectives for each individual is Management by Objectives (**MBO**).

Management by Objectives (MBO)
Management approach involving planning, motivating, and controlling consisting of joint planning sessions by superior and subordinate to establish attainable goals for the subordinate and joint evaluations after performance to check attainment of objectives.

Management by Objectives. The basic idea of MBO is the joint participation of subordinates and their superiors in establishing clear and definite objectives for each individual and unit (as illustrated in Figure 11-2). The usual approach is for the managers to meet with each subordinate at the beginning of a period and discuss the objectives of each until they reach an agreement. In this discussion, the subordinate has the opportunity to participate in setting objectives. Together, superiors and subordinates work to set priorities and to clarify any differences in objectives. It is very important that these differences be brought to light, because all concerned can then adjust their expectations and understanding of the targets.

MBO is also called managing by results. It involves setting yardsticks of effectiveness for each managerial position and a periodic conversion of those yardsticks into usable objectives. Many advantages are claimed by proponents of MBO.[4]

1. A subordinate learns at the beginning of a period what the performance expectations are, thus reducing any misunderstandings of what behavior is expected.
2. A subordinate agrees on a clear method of measuring performance and therefore feels a sense of participation and fairness.

FIGURE 11-2 MBO Model

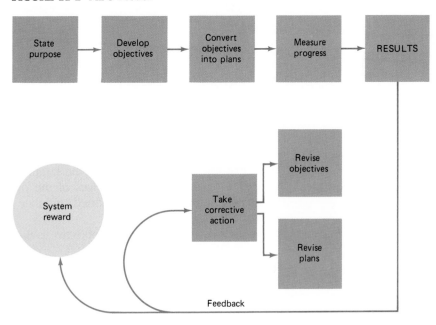

3. Because managers have helped set their own achievable objectives, they are motivated to hit their targets.

4. Superiors feel more security in forecasting results and in planning future activities.

At first glance, one would expect that given the fundamental ideas and concepts behind MBO, it should have been widely accepted by managers. However, managerial response to MBO has generally been negative, and only a few organizations have been able to successfully implement an MBO program. As a result, many managers and observers have dismissed MBO as a fad.

The failure or the termination of a large number of MBO programs can be attributed to a wide range of factors. Foremost, MBO requires a great amount of time and effort on the part of managers and subordinates and necessitates the commitment of costly clerical resources. Some MBO programs have been initiated without the complete support of top management. That has made it difficult to achieve the needed changes in organizational culture, leadership, behavior, and structure, thereby making it next to impossible to implement an effective MBO program. In addition, managers have discovered that MBO is appropriate for only certain segments of the organization. For instance, it is easy to use MBO for salespeople and production workers, but it is more difficult to use it for research scientists or people doing public relations. What has happened to MBO illustrates the difficulty of developing objectives that are realistic, achievable, appropriate, and representative of priorities, interests, values, and concerns of different groups.

Characteristics of sound objectives. We may agree that a focus on results, participation in setting objectives, and the availability of yardsticks all sound good, but how can sound objectives be set for each individual and unit in an organization? Take the following three statements of objectives: Improve performance, work harder, and improve the motivation of workers. All are commendable goals, but none satisfies the criterion of sound objectives for individuals or units. They do not satisfy the basic requirements for sound objectives:

1. Be measurable and usually quantitative.
2. Be specific.
3. Identify expected results.
4. Fall within the power of the individual manager or unit.
5. Be realistic and obtainable.
6. Clearly state time limits for completion.

Other characteristics of sound objectives have been proposed: Objectives should make people reach a bit, should allow for creative methods, and should not prescribe the means for achieving them; they should be known to all workers so that the workers understand the targets for their own work and how they relate to the broader objectives of the organization; periodically, they should be reconsidered and redefined; and they should not be too numerous or complex.

Another example of target or objective is the budget.

Budgets Financial statements by which a manager formalizes and expresses targets in terms of revenues and costs.

Budgets

One way to set, define, and clarify a target is to use a budget. A **budget** is a plan that expresses the organization's goals and objectives in dollar terms. Often, budgeting is discussed as a planning tool, but too often, the manager uses it for planning only. Like other types of plans, budgets are effective only when managers utilize them throughout the implementation process as feedback or as an indicator of whether the organization is still adhering to the intended course of action. Budgets provide the financial targets; accounting data supply the actual costs and revenue as measures of performance. With budgetary targets and financial measures of performance, the manager can compare the two and take corrective action if necessary.

Everyone who will be affected by the budget should be involved in the preparation of the budget. Some organizations try to involve everyone in the budgeting process, from the bottom of the organization to the top. When people are involved in the budgeting process, they are more likely to work with and adhere to the budget. In addition, as we discussed in Chapter 5, employee morale tends to be higher when the employees are a part of the decision-making process. The actual completion of the budget is usually handled by a budget committee composed of key operating-unit managers. Thus, the budget preparation process involves all levels of the organization and is a planning device that permits participation by all managers involved.

Within this ideal framework, the actual process faces typical organizational problems. Subordinates will usually seek as large a budget as they feel their superior will approve. The superior, in an effort to hold down costs, will press subordinates to reduce their budgets. In reality, the budget process can be quite a political exercise, with various factions of the organization using the budget to set priorities and to fight over the organization's limited resources.

Budgets are based on forecasts of future conditions. To compensate for the uncertainty of the future, budgets can be made more useful by (1) frequent revision or (2) preparing several budgets under different volume assumptions.

Moving budgets. The periodic method of revising budgets is called a moving or perpetual budget; the revisions may be made each month or quarter. Each revision extends the budget an additional month or quarter into the future. The budget contains the traditional twelve months, but the twelve months "move" into the future with each revision.

Flexible budgets. A flexible budget shows expected cost of production at various levels of volume. Flexible budgets have many benefits: (1) They indicate cost variations resulting from output changes; (2) the segregation of fixed and variable costs is useful for other management functions; and (3) standard costing is more easily implemented. Table 11-1 illustrates a flexible budget.

The prerequisite for flexible budgeting is the separation of fixed and variable costs. A **fixed cost** is one that remains the same no matter what the level of production is. Examples include mortgage payments on the building, executive salaries, and property taxes. The fixed expenses must be paid when there is no production and when there is full production. **Variable costs** are those that vary with different levels of production. Examples of variable costs are raw materials, electricity to run the machinery, and the wages of hourly production employees. Variable costs are zero when there is no production and increase as production increases. Figure 11-3 is a graph showing fixed and variable costs at different levels of production. Fixed and variable costs together are known as total costs. It is also interesting to note that where total costs equal total revenues, the firm is breaking even; it is not making a profit, nor is it

Fixed costs Those costs that remain fixed regardless of the rate of production.

Variable costs Those costs that vary with the rate of operations and that can be changed in the short run.

TABLE 11-1   Flexible Budget

TYPES OF COSTS	RATE OF OPERATIONS (OUTPUT; 000 OMITTED)			
	700 UNITS	800 UNITS	900 UNITS	1,000 UNITS
Manufacturing costs				
Direct labor	$ 350	$ 400	$ 448	$ 497
Raw materials	700	800	900	1,000
Overhead	400	415	425	435
Selling costs				
Salespeople (on commission)	700	800	900	1,000
Advertising	200	200	200	200
Administrative costs				
Fixed	200	200	200	200
Variable	50	55	58	60
Total	$2,600	$2,870	$3,131	$3,392

showing a loss. The point where total costs equal total revenues is known as the break-even point. Although fixed and variable costs are explained here using a manufacturing facility, the concepts also apply to service and other organizations. The concepts of fixed and variable can be used in all budgets involving costs.

Budgets should not merely be prepared and put into the bottom desk drawer. They should be compared with actual performance on a continuous or near-continuous basis. Budgetary control is a powerful tool for managers only if the budgets are realistic and accepted as operational. But good planning is not enough; the strength of the process is in controlling.

Standards

Objectives and budgets are overall targets for the entire organization. A **standard** could be considered as a budget for one unit of product—for example,

FIGURE 11-3 Fixed Costs, Variable Costs, Total Costs, and Total Revenues

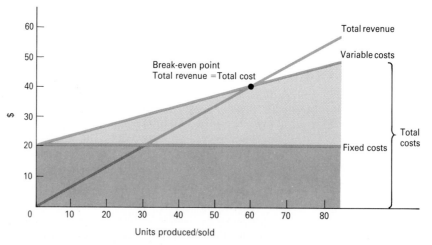

Variable costs + fixed costs = total costs. The area shaded in gray is fixed costs, which remain the same no matter how many units are produced. Variable costs are 0, when 0 units are being produced. The area shaded in blue is variable costs.

TABLE 11-2   Standards

STANDARDS EXPRESSED IN TERMS OF TIME

An accountant should be able to complete a tax return for a person with an income level of under $40,000 in less than forty-five minutes.
A laborer should be able to install eight seats in a school bus in one hour.
A mechanic should be able to tune up an eight-cylinder car in less than 1.2 hours.
An assembly plant should be able to produce 120 cars per day.
A copier should make at least four copies per second.

STANDARDS EXPRESSED IN TERMS OF COST

The flour for a bakery should not cost any more than $2.00 per pound.
The steel to make a bicycle should not cost any more than $6.50 per pound.

STANDARDS EXPRESSED IN TERMS OF QUANTITY

Manufacturing a clock radio should not require more than ten ounces of raw plastic.

STANDARDS EXPRESSED IN TERMS OF QUALITY

There will be no defects allowed in the entire Space Shuttle program.
Ninety-five percent of all flights scheduled by the airline should depart and arrive on time.

---

how much one unit should cost. Standards are more specific targets for individuals within the organization. A standard is a model—an expected or desired level of activity, performance, or expense. A standard could be stated in terms of the time, quantity, quality, or cost. Standards can be developed in several ways. They can be based on past experience, or they can be based on what "experts" (industrial engineers, accountants, and others) say can be done. They can also be based on what competitors are able to do. See Table 11-2 for examples of standards.

Measure Performance

How do you measure performance?

The second step in the control process is the measurement of actual performance. This measurement could be something as simple as a cash register keeping a tally of the daily sales, or a monitor that measures the consistency of oven temperatures while baking bread at a large bakery, or a counter on a turnstile noting the number of people entering a stadium. The second step of the control process involves looking at and noting performance, measuring results without interpretation or evaluation. It is the task of collecting performance data.

But measuring performance may not always be an easy task. It is one thing to measure the number of televisions produced at a Sony plant. Sony simply uses a computer to count the number of televisions coming off the assembly line. It is another thing for Sony to measure how well their televisions perform when it comes to achieving customer satisfaction. With respect to the control process, Sony's management is interested in measuring production levels so

Management Application

Perspectives on Measuring White-Collar Productivity

For the most part, the measurement of organizational productivity has focused on the people and equipment directly involved in creating the organization's output. Measuring the productivity of a line worker or a piece of equipment is usually a rather straightforward exercise. The output is tangible, and the input resources are easily determined. But what about the measurement of managerial, "white-collar," productivity? Only a handful of organizations have made any real effort to evaluate white-collar productivity. Unfortunately, the results and the value of such efforts have been very questionable.

Typically, management is not exactly sure of what kind of performance or value added it should be getting from its white-collar employees, but it does know when it is not getting the desired performance. Therefore, some researchers and management observers have suggested that because the measurement of white-collar performance is so difficult, a better approach might be to measure how much some "on-the-job" factors detract from the productivity of a white-collar employee.

One comparative study of how engineers spend their time revealed that American engineers spend only 10 to 20 percent of their work hours in engineering tasks. The remainder of the time they spend doing paperwork, performing administrative tasks, and attending meetings. In contrast, Japanese engineers were found to spend more than 40 percent of their time performing engineering tasks. The study concluded that because the Japanese engineers had more time to devote to engineering activities, they were able to be more productive than their American counterparts.

Another study examined the amount of time white-collar employees spent doing high-priority projects and activities as opposed to how much time they spent on doing low-priority projects. The study found that white-collar employees devoted more than 40 percent of their time to performing low-priority activities, thereby reducing productivity.

Some studies of white-collar productivity suggest that most organizations fail to recognize and evaluate their white-collar employees as intellectual capital. As a result, organizations typically make the mistake of misapplying and underutilizing their intellectual capital, which is primarily composed of white-collar employees.

Today's organizations and managers are beginning to understand that they must eliminate or control the factors that diminish white-collar performance. For most organizations, the productivity of white-collar employees will be incidental until those employees can play a significant role or have a direct impact in creating the organization's output.

References: Thomas Stewart, "Brain Power, How Intellectual Capital Is Becoming America's Most Valuable Asset," *Fortune,* June 3, 1991; P. R. Nayak, "Productivity and the White Collar," *New York Times,* July 7, 1991.

that it can later compare actual production with planned production. Likewise, Sony's management is interested in measuring how customers actually feel about Sony televisions, so that management can determine whether they are producing televisions that are meeting their targeted standards for customer satisfaction.

Determining what, how, when, and where to measure is difficult, but it is a critical decision, one that will influence the effectiveness of the control process. Using a wooden yardstick to measure a building's foundation to see if it has been laid out correctly would be inappropriate and very inaccurate. Similarly, using highly sensitive laboratory scales and laboratory technicians to determine whether all twelve-ounce bags of potato chips are uniform in weight would be expensive and an inappropriate use of resources. Therefore, the type of measure made and the means of measurement used will depend on the nature of the product or service being measured and on the time, effort, and money management is willing to commit to obtain specific performance results.[5] However, it should be noted that with the advent of the computer, it has become considerably easier and more cost-effective to measure performance.

Factors Determining Performance Measures

There are a number of factors that determine the nature and character of performance measures.[6] One of the most significant of these factors is whether the measurement is going to be qualitative or quantitative. There are no fixed rules or criteria governing when to use which type of measure: It may depend on the situation, the object being measured, or simply managerial preferences. Quite often, the object under consideration can be measured both qualitatively by taste and quantitatively by production or sales volume. Managers can measure employee performance quantitatively by production output and qualitatively through the performance appraisal process.

Timing is another factor that can define the nature and character of a performance measure. The first-time start of an automobile when it hits the end of the assembly line is an example of immediate performance measure (this is often referred to as a go/no-go performance measure). In contrast, automobile companies have used warranty repair records as another means to measure manufacturing and quality performance. However, what good does it do to discover that over a two-year period, the record of warranty repairs of a certain type of transmission produced at a particular plant was extremely high? Although it is a little late to correct problems that occurred years ago, these kinds of performance results may provide insights into assembly practices, the durability of materials, and adherence to design expectations, which makes this a valuable long-term performance measure.

The type of performance measure used can be influenced by whether the performance result being measured is an attribute or a variance. For instance, customer satisfaction in a restaurant can be measured by an attribute such as the number of customer complaints about poor service or poor food. Likewise, a restaurant can measure performance by the variance in customer-service times. If the restaurant promises to serve a lunch within ten minutes of the customer's placing the order, service-time results would indicate how often and by how much customers failed to receive their lunches within that time. Based on such performance results, managers can determine to initiate corrective action that could adjust the target or make adjustments in servicing practices.

Financial Statements

Some of the most commonly used performance measures are the organization's financial records and statements.[7] At certain intervals, sales, production, inventory, materials, taxes, and research records are compiled into financial statements—the Income Statement, the Balance Sheet, and the Statement of Cash Flows. Although these statements are frequently used by "outside" users, such as creditors and investors, they are also used by managers as a means to control. Managers use financial statements to compare the actual results with the planned results. (Financial statements used by managers can be developed to meet the needs of managers, showing them specifically what they need to know to make decisions. Managers also use financial statements to plan for the future and to compare their company with other companies in the same industry.)

The Income Statement summarizes the revenue and related expenses for a particular time period—a day, a month, a year. The Balance Sheet shows the organization's financial position at a particular time; it shows the organization's assets, liabilities, and owners' equity. The Statement of Cash Flows shows how the firm obtained its cash and how it used its cash. See Table 11-3 for abbreviated examples of each.

Compare the Target with the Actual

Why compare?

Once the actual results of operations have been assembled into financial statements or production or other reports, they can be compared with the plans, objectives, and standards that the managers have developed.

The manager should compare the actual results (as shown on the financial statements and other reports) with the expected results planned in the budgets. For example, the Income Statement can be compared with the sales and other budgets to see if the results match what was planned. The production reports can be compared with the production budget. The actual results can be compared with the established standards.

This step adds meaning to the data. Some variation in performance can be expected in all activity; therefore, the manager must determine what amount of variation is significant and requires attention. For this reason, the technique for comparison should indicate clearly and quickly the size of the variation. (The difference between planned and actual results is normally termed "variance.") One of the simplest techniques is to record the target and actual performance on a graph as shown in Figure 11-4. (The computer can be used to do this, too.)

In addition to comparing the actual results with targets, goals, budgets, and standards, managers will want to compare their actual results with the actual results of other organizations within their industry. This comparison will help them to determine how well they are doing as compared with other firms. In a sense, the actual results of the other firms become a standard for the company.

FIGURE 11-4 Actual Results Compared with Targeted Performance

TABLE 11-3   The Financial Statements

AN INCOME STATEMENT (SIMPLIFIED)

William Patrick Healey, M.D., Inc.
Income Statement
For the Year Ending 12/31/91

Fees Earned		$350,000
Operating Expenses:		
Wages Expense	$75,000	
Rent Expense	24,000	
Supplies Expense	15,000	
Utilities Expense	20,000	
Miscellaneous Expense	2,000	
Total Operating Expense		$136,000
Net Income		$214,000

A STATEMENT OF CASH FLOWS (PARTIAL, SIMPLIFIED)

William Patrick Healey, M.D., Inc.
Statement of Cash Flows
For the Year Ended 12/31/91

Cash Received from Operating Activities:		
Cash Received from Patients	$350,000	
Cash Paid to Suppliers and Employees	($136,000)	
Net Cash Flow from Operating Activities		$214,000

A BALANCE SHEET (SIMPLIFIED)

William Patrick Healey, M.D., Inc.
Balance Sheet
At 12/31/91

Assets		
Cash		$100,000
Supplies		50,000
Total Assets		$150,000
Liabilities		
Accounts Payable		4,000
Owners' Equity		
Capital Stock	$90,000	
Retained Earnings	$56,000	
Total Owners' Equity		146,000
Total Liabilities and Owners' Equity		$150,000

The company's financial statements are compared with those of other firms. This can be done in two ways. First, the company can obtain financial statements directly from the other companies (usually in the form of annual reports). Second, the company can obtain the information from published sources such as *Standard and Poor's* and *Moody's*.

Both *Standard and Poor's* and *Moody's* obtain information on actual results (usually in the form of financial statements from organizations within each industry). These two publishers then compile the information and form "industry averages." The industry average is a composite view of each industry. It is an average based on all the companies who sent information to the publishers.

It is difficult to compare one company with another on a dollar-by-dollar basis because companies differ in size and in amount of sales and production. Two methods are widely used to compare the financial statements of different companies: common-size financial statements and ratios.

Common-size Financial Statements

Common-size financial statements use percentages instead of dollars. Sales are always expressed as 100 percent. The various expenses are listed as a percentage of sales. Figure 11-5 shows an actual financial statement converted into a common-size financial statement. Once the common-size statements have been developed, the percentage of sales used for cost of goods sold in one company can be compared with the percentage of sales used for cost of goods sold in another company. The company will also want to compare its common-size statements for the current year with common-size statements of past years. This will give the company an indication of where costs are improving or increasing, where it can be saving money, and where it is losing money.

Ratios

The second method used to compare the financial statements of one company with the financial statements of a second company is **ratios.** Ratios express the results of operations as a fraction or a percentage. Ratios by themselves are meaningless. Ratios must be compared with other ratios—either the ratios from industry averages as reported in *Standard and Poor's* or *Moody's* or prior-year ratios for the same company. Ratios can be used to analyze a company's liquidity, leverage, activity levels, and profitability. See Table 11-4 for a listing of useful financial ratios.

Common-size financial statements Financial statements expressed in terms of percentages of a base amount rather than in dollars. The normal base is sales; cost of goods sold and other expenses are expressed as a percentage of sales.

Ratios Comparison of one item on the financial statements to another; expressed in terms of a fraction or percentage. For example, the ratio of current assets to current liabilities could be 2 : 1.

FIGURE 11-5 Actual Financial Statement Converted into Common-size Financial Statement

AN INCOME STATEMENT (SIMPLIFIED)

William Patrick Healey, M.D., Inc. Income Statement For the Year Ending 12/31/91		Common Size
Fees Earned $350,000		100%
Operating Expenses:		
Wages Expense $75,000		21%
Rent Expense............................. 24,000		7%
Supplies Expense 15,000		4%
Utilities Expense 20,000		6%
Miscellaneous Expense 2,000		1%
Total Operating Expense	$136,000	39%
Net Income	$214,000	61%

TABLE 11-4   Useful Financial Ratios

NAME OF RATIO	FORMULA	INDUSTRY NORM (ASSUMED MERELY AS ILLUSTRATION)
1. *Liquidity Ratios* (measuring the ability of the firm to meet its maturing obligations)		
Current ratio	$\dfrac{\text{Current assets}}{\text{Current liabilities}}$	2.6
Acid-test ratio	$\dfrac{\text{Cash and equivalent}}{\text{Current liability}}$	1.0
2. *Leverage Ratios* (measuring the contributions of financing by owners compared with financing provided by creditors)		
Debt to equity	$\dfrac{\text{Total debt}}{\text{Equity}}$	56%
Coverage of fixed charges	$\dfrac{\text{Net profit before fixed charges}}{\text{Fixed charges}}$	6 times
3. *Activities Ratios* (measuring the effectiveness of the employment of resources)		
Inventory turnover	$\dfrac{\text{Sales}}{\text{Inventory}}$	7 times
Net working-capital turnover	$\dfrac{\text{Sales}}{\text{Net working capital}}$	5 times
Fixed-assets turnover	$\dfrac{\text{Sales}}{\text{Fixed assets}}$	6 times
Average collection period	$\dfrac{\text{Receivables}}{\text{Average sales per day}}$	20 days
4. *Profitability Ratios* (indicating degree of success in achieving desired profit levels)		
Gross operating margin	$\dfrac{\text{Gross operating profit}}{\text{Sales}}$	30%
Net operating margin	$\dfrac{\text{Net operating profit}}{\text{Sales}}$	6.5%
Sales margin	$\dfrac{\text{Net profit after taxes}}{\text{Sales}}$	3.2%
Productivity of assets	$\dfrac{\text{Gross income less taxes}}{\text{Total Assets}}$	10%
Return on capital	$\dfrac{\text{Net profit after taxes}}{\text{Net worth}}$	7.5%

The process of comparing the actual results with planned results provides managers with valuable information about and insights into individual, group, and organizational performance. With this information and insight, managers can decide if employees are moving in the right direction, if the control system is functioning appropriately, and if corrective action is needed. When it is determined that corrective action is necessary and appropriate, managers take the fourth step of the control process.

Take Corrective Action (if Necessary)

Management by Exception

The idea of taking corrective action only where necessary has led to the concept of Management by Exception and the **Exception Principle.** The manager concentrates only on those areas where the actual performance deviated or varied from the targeted or standard performance by a material or significant amount. (The difference between actual and standard is normally called variance or deviance.) In other words, the manager will generally ignore those areas where the standards are being met and will focus instead on the "exceptions"—those areas where the actual is not meeting the standard. The manager can thus take corrective action only in those areas that need it.

Involve the Other Functions of Management

This step could involve one or all of the other functions of management. For example, the manager may want to revise the original plan, reorganize the projects or departments involved, and communicate to employees and supervisors exactly what is expected of them to meet the organization's objectives.

This step may be the most time-consuming and the most difficult to complete. Often, the variances from standards may indicate only the existence of a problem. The manager will need to investigate what the problem is and then use problem-solving skills to resolve the difference between what was planned and what actually happened. The manager may also want to take a look at changing the control system itself, evaluating the situation to see if the control system needs improvement or modification or possibly needs to be replaced by an alternative approach.

CONTROL SYSTEMS AND APPROACHES

Controls and the types of control systems used should be tailored to fit the organization. Managers need to develop and implement control systems that are unique and reflective of their organization's mission, markets, operations, and culture. Managers can choose from a variety of control systems and approaches to control. In some instances, managers can use a combination of control systems to accomplish the control function.

However, control systems by themselves are never enough. As Peter Drucker observed, self-control by each member of an organization is absolutely essential to ensure that all parts of the organization operate effectively. In addition, control systems should be dynamic, flexible, and responsive to changing conditions.

In his book *The Renewal Factor,* Robert Waterman devotes an entire chapter to "Friendly Facts, Congenial Controls." According to Waterman, all facts are friendly.[8] Facts that affirm that the company is doing things right are friendly

---

Exception Principle The concept that recurring decisions should be delegated, allowing superiors time to make the most important, nonrepetitive decisions.

What are congenial controls?

because they are good for morale and self-confidence. Facts that warn that there are problems in the organization are "equally friendly" because they give the business an opportunity to respond to problems, to change where needed, and to allocate resources in the most efficient ways possible. Facts should always be welcomed and should be treated as the "kind of best friends who will tell you what you need to know." Controls should be congenial; they should not strangle or choke a business and its employees. Controls should "reflect the realities of running a business and serve—not entangle—the people doing the job." Controls are congenial because they keep the business healthy. A healthy business has the finances available to invest in new and exciting projects. In other words, controls can set the business free to invest in new projects, to be innovative. Controls give employees the opportunity to be creative. Waterman recommends the following steps to keep facts friendly and controls congenial:

1. Figure out where you can cut costs without lowering quality. Once the excess costs have been identified (through facts), use your system of controls to get rid of them.
2. Reward the messenger. Let everyone know you welcome facts, even when they come in the form of bad news. Bad news provides an opportunity to react, to respond to problems, to change.
3. Communicate. Let everyone know the facts so that all people involved can better understand what management is trying to do.
4. Use the facts as a common language for communication.
5. Treat financial control as liberating.
6. Go for simplicity in a complex world. Ask basic questions, like "Where's the cash?" Fight clutter.
7. Push for better and better cost information.
8. Assume that no matter how good the facts and the controls are, they could always be better. Keep trying to make them better.
9. Insist on comparisons. Information is contained in comparisons and can be presented in the form of differences—difference from what is expected, from history, from competitors, from customer needs.
10. Make friends with your electronic spreadsheets. Use "what-if" analysis.

There is a variety of control systems and approaches that managers can utilize. Each approach offers distinctive benefits and each assumes a unique orientation to how control is implemented in the organization. Let us review some of these different control systems and approaches to control.[9]

Preventative Control

Preventative control
Also known as feedforward control. Assuring that inputs to an organization (raw materials, labor) are of sufficient quality to prevent problems occurring.

Preventative control is also known as feedforward control. Its purpose is to make sure that the inputs to the organization are of sufficient quality to prevent problems from occurring. In other words, the organization is attempting to take preventive action, rather than corrective action, to make sure that the actual results will meet the planned results. Preventative control anticipates where there might be variances and then tries to prevent those variances from happening. Some examples of preventative control are hiring graduates of top-ranked universities only, purchasing the highest-quality materials, and maintaining equipment at peak operating condition.

Concurrent Control

Concurrent control
Monitoring activities on a step-by-step basis (using checkpoints) to make sure they are consistent with planned standards for each step and taking corrective action as needed.

Concurrent control monitors activities to make sure that they are consistent with planned standards. The manager may have a series of checkpoints to look at an employee's work as a project or production line progresses, or to look at the product as it reaches certain points on an assembly line. Corrections are made at the checkpoints to make sure that the actual results will be the same as the planned results.

An example of concurrent control can be seen in a baseball game. If a pitcher is allowing too many hits, he may be replaced by another player.

Direct Control

Direct control Personal observation and inspection by the manager as the work is in process, taking corrective action as needed.

Direct control may be the simplest and most easily implemented method of control. With direct control, the manager simply observes the employee and the employee's work and takes corrective action as needed. An example is the manager's walking through the word-processing pool at frequent intervals to make sure all employees are working, or walking past the assembly line to make sure the employees are manufacturing the product correctly and efficiently. The manager could also personally check the raw materials and other inputs for quality.

Strategic Point Control

Strategic point control
Actual performance is measured at critical, key, or limiting points and corrective action taken as needed to meet planned performance.

In **strategic point control,** all critical, key, or limiting points are identified. Actual performance is checked at those key points, and if actual performance is not as planned, corrective action is taken. One strategic point in a manufacturing firm, for example, could be the point at which the raw material passes from one department to the next department for further processing. The manager should require a production report at that point to make sure that all the raw materials that had been transferred into Department One are now being transferred into Department Two. If any raw materials are missing, the manager will want to check to see what the problem is. Some of the raw material could have been wasted, or an employee could have taken some of it home. Discovering the shortage of raw materials at this strategic point would prevent even more problems later.[10] Focusing on strategic points allows an organization to have an effective control system without having to control all the details.[11]

Total Quality Control

Total quality control (TCQ) Everyone in the organization is committed to high standards of quality; all employees are involved in decision making and problem solving.

This approach to control was originally introduced in a book written by an American: *Total Quality Control* by A. V. Feigenbaum.[12] His ideas were originally implemented in Japan and then used in the rest of the world.

Total Quality Control (TQC) involves all employees, not just the managers. Everyone is responsible for making sure that high standards of quality are achieved—both in goods and in services. TQC becomes part of everyday business life as everyone strives for high quality.

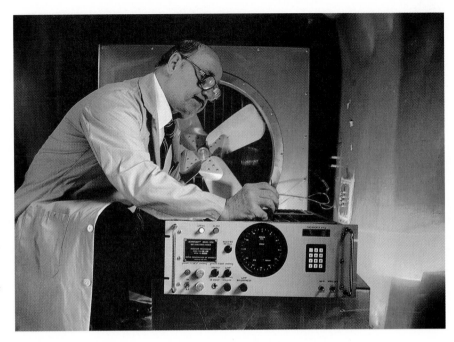

Measuring performance is an important part of the controlling process. Measuring the performance of machines and engines is sometimes easier than measuring the performance of a product in terms of customer satisfaction and company reputation.

TQC stresses employee involvement through involvement of the employees in decision making. Sometimes, employees are also involved in this process through Quality-control Circles. Employees work together in teams to first identify quality problems and then develop and implement corrective actions to resolve the problem.

TQC requires that employees be trained in preventative and concurrent control. They must also be given the responsibility for correcting their own mistakes, and they must be encouraged to report poor quality in materials or in workmanship.

Statistical Process Control

Statistical Process Control A method used to monitor and adjust production to prevent variations in the manufacturing process; the goal is to maintain high quality, the control function.

Statistical Process Control incorporates the use of statistics to facilitate the control function.[13] Collected data are put into a form that allows the statistical analysis of quality and productivity. The use of statistics can help to make the control function more accurate. Statistical analysis can be done on a computer, and the computer can also create bar graphs and charts to allow for the visualization of the variances between actual results and planned results.[14]

Internal Control

Internal control The organization's system of procedures and processes that are designed to safeguard the firm's assets and ensure that the firm's financial records are accurately maintained.

Internal control is the organization's system of procedures and processes that are designed to safeguard the firm's assets and to ensure that the firm's financial records are accurately maintained. Internal control aids the organization in retaining its assets and enables management, owners, investors, and creditors to rely on the organization's financial statements. Table 11-5 notes some of the things that management can do to help ensure internal control.

TABLE 11-5   Some Steps to Achieving Internal Control
1. Hire competent, qualified, and trustworthy employees.
2. Make it difficult for the employees to commit fraud, embezzlement, or theft. Separate employee functions; that is, separate record keeping from custodianship from authorization from operations. For example, do not have one employee authorizing transactions, collecting cash, depositing cash, and recording cash. If one employee were to do all of that, it would make it very easy for him or her to embezzle the cash. In addition, make sure that employees take vacations and alternate doing various functions. Keeping one person in one function for an indefinite length of time would give that person an excellent opportunity to embezzle. Make sure the employees are supervised.
3. Require management authorization of transactions. Managers should approve credit sales, sales returns, and the like.
4. Control access to assets. Lock doors. If there is a computer system, limit access to the computer through the use of passwords.
5. Establish standard procedures for recording transactions. Investigate any problems.
6. Compare physical assets with what accounting records say should be there. Take inventory counts on a regular basis.

HUMAN FACTORS IN CONTROLLING

How can controls backfire?

The human element is central to the effectiveness of any control system, for human beings design, create, and implement the systems, respond to the systems, and frequently resist the systems.

So far, most of our descriptions of controlling have answered the questions of what is to be controlled and how a manager uses control. We have talked of a control process and its essentials without locating the control function in the organization and without reference to the specific person exercising the control. The literature in the behavioral science field is full of examples of employee and subordinate reaction to control. Much of the criticism directed at managers is due to the misuse of control. Where in the control process should managers look for signs of misuse? What are the points of potential conflict that result from implementing a control system? Answers to these questions dealing with the human elements in control form the subject matter of this last section.

Misuse of Control

When the control process is used to create power for the purpose of coercion, the misuse is obvious and the reactions fairly predictable. This concept of control has no place in our definition or presentation. Our premise is that exercising control over work in an organization improves the relationships, reduces the uncertainty, and results in benefits to both the organization and its members. Our concept of managerial control is a positive one and is as natural in its behavioral implications as the other management functions. One example of misuse will illustrate the potential dangers for managers.

Global Application

Quality Control and W. Edwards Deming

If you were to believe the advertising slogans about quality, you might think that attention to quality in products and services had been a top priority of American firms for years. Such is not the case in the majority of most American firms. Quantity production and bottom-line profits have assumed the top spot in corporate boardrooms. The critical nature of quality in manufacturing was realized by the Japanese because of the teachings of American advocates, primarily W. Edwards Deming and Joseph Juran. If F. W. Taylor could be called the Father of Scientific Management, Deming could be called the Father of Statistical Quality Control.

During World War I, Deming was part of a small "think tank" at Stanford University in California, where Walter Shwehart's ideas about the use of statistics in production were being applied to industrial problems. Deming became an expert in the application of statistics, and this work seemed to fit his personal values of making quality products and reducing waste.

After the war, Deming's ideas about quality fell on deaf ears, because the American industrial system had turned its attention to meeting the pent-up demand for consumer products. The expansion of production became the top priority, with little time left for implementing quality-control standards. Frustrated, Deming became a statistician at the U.S. Bureau of the Census and in 1946 and 1948, was sent to Japan to work on census problems. While there, he met with Japanese engineers and started to introduce them to the ideas of quality control, particularly statistical quality control.

Japan was recovering from World War II and was in the process of rebuilding its industrial base. Deming explained to executives and engineers that his techniques, if applied as a philosophy throughout every level in the organization, would enable the Japanese to overtake the American industrial giant. By 1951, Deming was recognized as a guru, idolized along with Douglas MacArthur, and honored by having a medal named for him to be given to companies that achieved the highest level of quality. In 1960, the Deming prize went to Nissan, and Deming's predictions became a reality, at least in the automobile industry.

References: David Halberstam, *The Reckoning,* New York: Avon Books, 1986, pp. 312–20; W. Edwards Deming, *Quality, Productivity and Competitive Position,* Cambridge, Mass.: MIT, 1982.

An organization was experiencing difficulties with mailing costs. Each month, costs were increasing. The investigating manager, having authority over the secretaries of the departments, instructed all secretaries to log in the mail of the department managers. He felt that some managers used the company mails for personal correspondence.

The reaction was predictable. The secretaries were agitated because of the increased burden placed upon them. The department managers became furious, since most knew that the culprits were few and possibly were not aware of policy restrictions on use of the mail. In this situation, the improper implementation of control resulted in lost productivity, employee conflict, and inappropriate use of resources.

Potential Conflicts

Why do controls create conflicts?

The primary source of conflict is the question of who controls. Real and legitimate differences of opinion may exist on such questions as the following: Who sets the target? Who determines what unit is to be measured? Who decides what is to be compared and how and when it is compared, and who does the comparison? Who participates in determining when and what kind of corrective action should take place? For every question, there may be at least three views to consider: the line manager, the staff manager, and the worker.

Illustrations abound of conflicts that may arise from the different answers individuals or groups give to these questions. For example, some managers, fearing failure, might set their targets too low, thus ensuring that they always reach the goal. Other managers enjoy overreaching and setting goals very high. The second group might outperform the first but might not be rewarded if some boss worships "reaching the goal."

Conflict may arise between line and staff over the authority in the control process. If staff personnel set the targets, do the measuring and comparing, and expect the line managers to take corrective action, conflict is almost inevitable.

Corrective action is the crucial last step in controlling. Whether it is taken by the manager as boss or by the worker as subordinate, certain options are open and some may create conflicts. When data are compared, the decision maker has two options—to make some change or to make no change. Assume that some change is required. Now the options expand: The target or standard may need revision, the measuring process may need reviewing and change, the work pace or method may have to be completely changed, or the worker's effort may need correction. At every point just mentioned, there is the potential for change and thus resistance to change.

As a manager, you must expect the problems just mentioned. Some of the leadership approaches in Chapter 9 may appeal to you, especially those based on contingency thinking. You must identify the conditions in the situation that will aid you in deciding the questions of who is controlling, what the standards are, and how the control is being applied. One idea from Chapter 9, dealing with rewards, incentives, and quality, may prove successful for companies and country alike.

Quality affects the competitiveness of individual firms and the competitiveness of our country. If we can't produce a quality product, we have problems selling that product, and those that we do sell cost us more because we have had to spend extra money on waste and inefficiencies in the system. So how do we improve the quality of our products and services?

Several ideas have already been put forth in this chapter and text but an additional incentive was set up by Congress in 1987. They established the Malcolm Baldridge National Quality Award, which has since become the standard of excellence for U.S. firms.[15] Few American companies can now meet the high standards required by the award. To date, there have been eight winners.

Many CEOs want to have this prestigious award—the Malcolm Baldridge National Quality Award—sitting on their desks. This award was established by the U.S. Congress in 1987 to recognize quality in American companies. It is the standard of excellence for U.S. firms.

- The 1988 winners: Motorola
                     The Nuclear Fuel Division of Westinghouse
                     Globe Metallurgical of Cleveland
- The 1989 winners: Milliken and Company
                     Xerox Business Products Division

Ethics Issue

Is It Business Research or Corporate Spying?

The loss of critical proprietary, promotional, and operational information to a competitor can adversely affect the market, financial, and competitive position of any organization. In recent years, this has become a problem for many businesses, primarily because of a growing acceptance of industrial espionage—"spying"—as a necessary business activity. Many firms argue that they must engage in "business research" to counter their competitors' spying activities, to maintain a competitive position, and to assess changes in the business environment.

Most firms become involved in industrial espionage in an effort to control the release of critical information from their own operations. This usually occurs after the firm has been "burned" in the marketplace by a competitor who has obtained information and has initiated a preemptive promotional or new-product campaign against the firm. Firms think of their action as more of a counterspying activity to determine how much the competition knows about their operations.

The introduction of the disposable camera is an example of how business intelligence works. Fuji Film was monitoring Kodak's operations and learned, mostly through information that was publicly available, that Kodak had the ability to produce and market a disposable camera. Fuji moved quickly to develop its own version of the camera and introduced the product in Japan before Kodak could even consider producing the camera. Kodak, in turn, monitored Fuji. When Kodak found out that Fuji intended to sell its disposable camera in the U.S. market, Kodak responded by introducing its own version of the disposable camera a day before Fuji announced its plans to market the camera in the United States. When Kodak's management was asked how they learned about Fuji's intentions, they responded, "We just had a gut feeling about it."

A common "business research" approach used by corporate raiders was to have their researchers pose as students. The "student researchers" would call targeted firms and ask for help on a class project. Managers who were eager to talk to an interested student about what they did would unintentionally provide inside information to a party that would eventually use the material for a hostile-takeover attempt. Raiders found this technique particularly helpful when targeting privately held firms from which little public information was available.

The dilemma facing many firms is how to ethically control unauthorized access to critical internal information. Although it is generally accepted that one can purchase a competitor's product to do a little "reverse engineering" and learn what the competitor can do, it may be another matter to hire former CIA agents to "plug leaks" and to "analyze" the products and the competitive capabilities of the competition. The practice of business intelligence gathering is growing, particularly as more and more managers accept the notion that, ultimately, competition is really economic warfare.

References: Eduardo Lachica, "U.S. Firms Turn to Former Spies for Intelligence," *Wall Street Journal,* August 8, 1991, p. B1; Kevin Kelly, "When a Rival's Trade Secret Crosses Your Desk," *Business Week,* May 20, 1991, p. 48.

■ The 1990 winners: Cadillac Division of General Motors
                      IBM in Rochester, Minnesota
                      Federal Express

Throughout this chapter, we have emphasized that the purpose of the control function is to enhance individual and organizational performance. Control is an extension, the follow-through of planning. It is a means to move the individual and the organization in a positive way toward a target and an expected level of performance. Effective control occurs when objectives are clearly stated, performance is appropriately measured, actual results are compared with an acceptable standard, and corrective action is taken in a constructive manner. But most important, control works when all members of the organization are involved in the design and implementation of the control system and when they are mutually committed to the objectives of the control system.

SUMMARY

This chapter focused on the last function of managing—control. We showed how control is an indispensable part of all functions of management that ultimately lead to performance. For controlling to be effective, all other functions of management must be working properly.

The integral nature of control—its relationship with other management functions—was stressed in the initial section of the chapter. There, the essential stages of controlling were considered. After discussing the ideas of control, we illustrated the dynamics of control through management by objective (MBO) and budgets. The central position of the human element in the effectiveness of any control system was the subject of our concluding section.

KEY TERMS

Controlling Activity that measures performance and guides actions toward some predetermined target.

Objectives Specific statements of what an organization hopes to achieve.

Management by Objectives (MBO) Management approach involving planning, motivating, and controlling consisting of joint planning sessions by superior and subordinate to establish attainable goals for the subordinate and joint evaluations after performance to check attainment of objectives.

Budget Financial statements by which a manager formalizes and expresses targets in terms of revenues and costs.

Variable costs Those costs that vary with the rate of operations and that can be changed in the short run.

Standard Expected or desired level of activity, performance, or expense; an objective put in terms of one unit of production.

Fixed costs Those costs that remain fixed regardless of the rate of production.

Common-size financial statements Financial statements expressed in terms of percentages of a base amount rather than in dollars. The normal base is sales; cost of goods sold and other expenses are expressed as a percentage of sales.

Ratios Comparison of one item on the financial statements to another; expressed in terms of a fraction or percentage. For example, the ratio of current assets to current liabilities could be 2:1.

Exception Principle The concept that recurring decisions should be delegated, allowing superiors time to make the most important, nonrepetitive decisions.

Preventative control Also known as feedforward control. Assuring that inputs to an organization (raw materials, labor) are of sufficient quality to prevent problems occurring.

Concurrent control Monitoring activities on a step-by-step basis (using checkpoints) to make sure they are consistent with planned standards for each step and taking corrective action as needed.

Direct control Personal observation and inspection by the manager as the work is in process, taking corrective action as needed.

Strategic point control Actual performance is measured at critical, key, or limiting points and corrective action taken as needed to meet planned performance.

Total quality control Everyone in the organization is committed to high standards of quality; all employees are involved in decision making and problem solving.

Statistical process control A method used to monitor and adjust production to prevent variations in the manufacturing process; the goal is to maintain high quality, the control function.

Internal control The organization's system of procedures and processes that are designed to safeguard the firm's assets and ensure that the firm's financial records are accurately maintained.

STUDY ASSIGNMENTS

1. How could Tom Becker have applied the concepts of the control function to improve the performance of B & L Construction Company? What kind of control system should he have implemented for the firm?

2. What is the relationship between the planning function and the control function? Why is the argument made that plans can succeed only when supported with an effective control system?

3. What are some of the problems associated with the "Set a Target" step of the controlling process?

4. What are some of the reasons that MBO has had such limited acceptance and success?

5. Why in most organizations are budgets such a central part of the controlling process? What is the relationship between a firm's budget and its financial statements?

6. What makes standards different from objectives and budgets?

7. What are some of the reasons that employees might be sensitive about organizations using computers as a part of the control process?

8. What role do financial statements play in the controlling function?

9. Explain the fundamental characteristics and concepts of the Management by Exception approach to taking corrective action as a part of the control process.

10. Compare and contrast some of the different control systems and approaches. Why would a manager choose one system over another?

11. What are some of the "human factors" that influence the control process?

Case for Discussion

I. CONTEMPORARY OFFICE SUPPLY

For Tom Soxman, it had been a difficult and chaotic day. Somehow, he had expected that after a year of his being the operations manager of the Contemporary Office Supply Company (COS), the business would be better managed by now. Instead, he was spending most of his time trying to "put out fires." This continuing chaos made him realize that the operating conditions of COS were deteriorating rapidly. But what frustrated Tom the most was his inability to convince anyone of the seriousness of the situation. When he talked about the situation, his observations were dismissed because things appeared to be going well, particularly since last year's revenues jumped 42 percent and there were new retail stores "opening all the time." Soon, Tom began to realize that COS's expansion was not based on a sound business plan or strategy—COS was merely "muddling along" as a highly inefficient business plagued with numerous problems.

Tom began working at COS a little more than a year ago. A long-time acquaintance of his—John Sarver, owner of COS—offered him the number two position in the company and a share of the business.

Shortly, Tom discovered that the most difficult part of his job was getting John to address the problems Tom had identified. Tonight, he thought he would try one more time to show John the lack of control within the company. This time, Tom wanted to put his concerns in writing.

Six years ago, John Sarver bought the Central Office Supply Company. It consisted of one retail store serving downtown businesses and a commercial supply operation with a warehouse located next to the downtown store. It had been a family-owned business for about thirty years and was moderately profitable. The previous owners had left the running of the store to the general manager, Ben Cross. The retail store had five full-time employees, the commercial supply operation had two full-time sales representatives, and the warehouse operation had three full-time employees who prepared and delivered orders to commercial customers as well as maintained the inventory of the retail store. In addition, the company employed a secretary, a bookkeeper, an order clerk (Mrs. Helen Cross, Ben's wife, who was also responsible for the purchasing operations), and an administrative assistant (who primarily handled personnel and marketing functions). The employees worked well together and liked working for the company. Overall, the company operated rather smoothly.

During his first year of ownership, John Sarver did nothing to change the organization. Ben Cross continued to be manager. Then, John announced that he was reorganizing COS. He said that he was making himself the general manager and demoting Ben Cross to operations manager. In addition, John changed the name of the company from Central to Contemporary Office Supply and announced an ambitious expansion program. Shortly, John closed the downtown retail store completely, relocating it to a suburban mall. In addition, he relocated the commercial supply operations and warehouse in a new office development near the mall. In the process of relocating, COS lost four of its retail-store employees, one commercial supply sales representative, one of its warehouse employees, and the company's secretary. Most of the employees who left COS stated they had problems commuting to the new location. Tom later found out that the transportation problems really applied only to the warehouse employee and that all the others had used the relocation as an excuse to quit.

Tom learned later that none of those five employees could stand to work for John. They felt that he was constantly pressuring them to work harder or sell more and had shifted more and more of their earnings to a commission basis. The company hired more employees, and more employees, particularly sales representatives, quit. The sales reps usually took jobs with competing office-supply stores and generally took their customers with them to the new supplier. Ben continued to hire new sales representatives (many of them college students working part-time), but because John did not want to pay his employees very much, the employees Ben hired were inexperienced. Ben felt that the company could not build a client base without experienced, full-time sales representatives.

Within a year of the closing of the downtown store, COS had lost all the downtown commercial customers. However, the sales representatives were able to bring in new customers from the suburban office complexes.

In the new retail store, John made the one remaining employee from the old store assistant manager. This employee had worked as a clerk in the old store and had no experience in management. After six months, the employee quit. John hired another assistant manager. That one lasted four months. John hired another, and another. The turnover rate was even higher for clerks in the store. In spite of the difficulties and problems of the retail store, John was determined to open a second store at another major area mall.

While John was preoccupied with the opening of the second store, Ben Cross was preoccupied with the problem of sales reps. When the top three sales reps left the company, Ben confronted John and demanded that the compensation package be changed and that the sales reps be given more support. Soon after John hired Tom, he fired Ben.

When Tom started working at COS, the company operated three retail stores (one store had opened a month before Tom joined COS) and the commercial office-supply operation. Tom was directly responsible for the sales representatives (three out of five had been with the company for less than one year) and "sort of" responsible for the office staff and warehouse personnel.

Tom began socializing with the sales reps to find out more about them. While talking with them, he learned that they actually had a great deal of contact with the retail stores, picking up orders for customers, and checking out products. They told him that they had a low opinion of how the retail stores were operated. Frequently, customers would leave the stores without having been helped by a clerk. The sales clerks appeared to be ignorant about office supplies, particularly about the profitable items like the electronic typewriters and personal computers. Tom observed some of the clerks in the stores and found what the sales reps were saying to be true: The sales clerks did not know what they were doing. When Tom brought this problem to John's attention, John dismissed Tom's observations as isolated incidents.

Tom also experienced increasing difficulties with Helen Cross, who apparently was deliberately billing customers for supplies they never ordered or received and sending customers the wrong orders. In addition, she was ignoring and losing orders for inventory from the retail stores so that the stores were often left with empty shelves. Although Helen was technically an order clerk, she had assumed control of the office and the warehouse, and other employees said that they were afraid of her. It was clear that she was in charge of the entire area. Some of the other employees stated that the problem with Helen had started when her husband, Ben, was fired. The employees felt that Helen was doing all she could to drive away customers, to put the company out of business as some sort of retaliation for what had happened to her husband.

Three months ago, Tom had another meeting with John, but John again dismissed Tom's concerns. Since then, the problem with Helen Cross had increased to the point where the sales reps were walking their orders through her department to make sure they were filled and billed correctly. And more sales reps had quit, taking customers with them. And John had opened yet another store.

II. DUTCHER MANUFACTURING COMPANY

Robert Turner groaned to himself as he reviewed his company's income statements for the past four years. He knew that the firm's board of directors would be asking him, as the president of the Dutcher Manufacturing Co., a great many tough and embarrassing questions at its meeting at the end of the week. Since assuming the presidency of Dutcher Manufacturing six years ago, Mr. Turner has struggled with many problems, which include such things as

- Inflation rate, which has averaged slightly above 9-1/2 percent during each of the past five years
- Managing a rapidly growing organization
- The introduction of seven new products
- The expansion of sales territory into twenty-eight new states

The Dutcher Manufacturing Co. makes and sells temperature control systems. Its customers are primarily industrial firms. During the past three years, however, some business has been generated by the sales of units to municipal governments. The prospects for continued sales growth appear bright, and Mr. Turner wondered if it would be wise to add personnel to the sales force. He also wondered about the wisdom of introducing too many new products to stay ahead of competitors. It is so tempting to grow where the possibilities appear favorable. But the problems associated with growth are overwhelmingly difficult to manage.

Chapter 12

Individual Behavior

Learning Objectives

1. **Define** perception.
2. **Describe** the relationship between motivation, perception, and behavior.
3. **Describe** the four components of the self-concept.
4. **Describe** the four factors that affect an individual's perception process.
5. **Describe** three examples of predictable perception responses.
6. **Identify** three sources of attitudes and opinions.
7. **Describe** and give an example of a defense mechanism.

I N the fall of 1987, the community of Clark, New Jersey, was experiencing an all-too-familiar story. Hyatt Clark, a local ball-bearing manufacturer, was going bankrupt as a result of declining sales, foreign competition, obsolete technology, and ongoing labor–management conflict. Although Hyatt Clark had much in common with other firms in similar circumstances, there was something about Hyatt Clark that made its situation different and that made Hyatt Clark's failure a surprise to many observers.

In 1981, the employees of Hyatt Clark purchased the firm from General Motors. At the time of the sale, most of the firm's equipment and facilities were outdated, and labor–management relations were characterized as adversarial. Therefore, many employees were apprehensive about the firm's future, and they did not trust management to act in the workers' best interest. On the other hand, many outside observers believed that Hyatt Clark would become the model of employee ownership and that this experiment in employee participation would demonstrate how productivity can improve when workers have a vested interest in the success of the firm.

During the first few years of operation as an employee-owned firm, Hyatt Clark was profitable, and as a result, most observers felt that the firm was going to be an unqualified success. However, most employees thought that the firm had become profitable primarily because they had taken a 25 percent wage cut. Employees also felt that although the firm's financial condition had improved, little else actually had changed. Even with employee representatives on Hyatt Clark's board of directors, management was unwilling to share power and to involve the workers in the decision-making process.

In 1985, labor–management relations began to deteriorate drastically. The board had decided to fore go distributing any dividends or granting any bonuses or pay increases to the employees, and instead reinvested the profits in new equipment and provided bonuses to senior managers. The employees were shocked by the action. They felt that both the board and management had failed to recognize and reward their efforts in improving Hyatt Clark's performance and profitability.

In the wake of the board's decision, the employees felt betrayed and powerless to exercise any control or influence over the business they owned. In response, they initiated a number of walkouts and slowdowns and, in most instances, simply quit caring. As a result, Hyatt Clark's output sharply declined.

While the internal conflict was escalating at Hyatt Clark, a price war broke out between ball-bearing producers. Management and labor soon realized that their inability to change attitudes and their unwillingness to work together prevented the firm from matching any of the industry price cuts. When Hyatt Clark lost its contract with GM, most observers concluded that it was only a matter of time before the firm was finished. In the remaining months of operation, the attitude among Hyatt Clark's employees was one of resignation. There was little interest in saving the firm, and in the fall of 1987, Hyatt Clark went bankrupt. ■

We may never really know the answers to most behavior questions because people are very complex and do not lend themselves very well to scientific investigation. However, even though we may develop only partial answers, we must remember that managers need all the help they can get when dealing in the behavioral area.

What are some of the factors we should examine to gain a better understanding of behavior? Of the many possible ones, we have chosen three to discuss at this point: perception, attitudes, and defense mechanisms.

These three concepts are very personal and highly individualized. No two people perceive the world the same way; no two have identical attitudes about or preferences for the objects in their work world; no two people react the same way to the consequences of their behavior—each individual has defense mechanisms. However, it is important to realize that managers can play a large role in influencing the perception, attitudes, and defense mechanisms of those who work for them.

PERCEPTION: A CONCEPT FUNDAMENTAL TO BEHAVIOR ANALYSIS

The treatment of perception in this chapter is oriented to the manager's use of the concept. Frequently, psychology texts describe the perception process in very sophisticated and scientific language. That is not our intent. Rather, we hope to offer a condensed and useful presentation of perception.[1]

Perception The process by which people interpret the experiences around them.

Perception can be defined as the way people experience the universe: the process by which they interpret the world around them. All kinds of sensations and stimuli exist around us, but we take in or see only certain elements in every situation. Some illustrations might help to highlight our common-sense definition of perception.

First, although people may share the same event, their perceptions of the event will be different. For example, you may have read two newspaper accounts of the stock market crash in October 1987 and been amazed at how different they were. The sales and production managers of the same company will perceive the weekly printout data very differently. Would you expect the presidents of the United Auto Workers (UAW) and General Motors (GM) to agree on the distribution of corporate profits? The announcement of promotions or staff reductions will be "interpreted" in a unique way by those who are young or old, single or married, job-mobile or restricted in mobility. In many different ways, the truth about perception comes through. Individuals are just that—each person experiences the world in a unique and very personal manner.

Second, we experience the world subjectively; that is, we interpret it. There is a difference between what is sent out and what is received. You will be a naive and ineffective manager if you believe that the information you send to bosses, peers, and subordinates is "objective." What is, is what people believe it to be; the same event is not "read" the same way by two different people.

As a manager, you must accept the complexity of perception without feeling discouraged or overwhelmed. If you want to be a part of the challenging field of managing, understanding some factors that make up the perception process is a good first step.

Factors Affecting the Perceptual Process

A number of factors influence the perception process.[2] The factors shown in Figure 12-1 were chosen to give you a sample of some of the significant factors that affect the perception process. You may be able to add some of your own to this list because all of us are constantly involved in the act of perception. Each of the factors in Figure 12-1 will be briefly explained.

Inner Needs

How do inner needs relate to perception?

What you see in the universe depends partly on your inner needs. When you are hungry, for example, you sense the aroma of a hamburger or bakery goods far more quickly than when you have just finished a pepperoni pizza. Your basic needs affect whether you perceive objects as desirable or repugnant.

A manager must be aware, therefore, that the inner needs of a person have an impact upon what that person sees in or takes away from any situation. Since all people have different needs and are at different need levels, all people perceive similar situations differently.

Mental Set

Mental set The tendency to act or react in a certain way to a given stimulus; one tends to "see" what one expects to see.

How do you use mental set?

Mental set means the tendency you have to react in a certain way to a given stimulus. For example, suppose you are a contestant in a track meet and are positioning yourself in your starting blocks as you hear the preparatory commands "Get ready! Get set!" When you hear the command "Go!" you take off at once, since you are already set and ready to react to this command. This is a very simple illustration of what is meant by mental set. Mental set has three components—expectations, stereotyping, and halo effect.

You have been aware of the mental-set feature of perception, although you

Figure 12-1 Some Factors in Perception

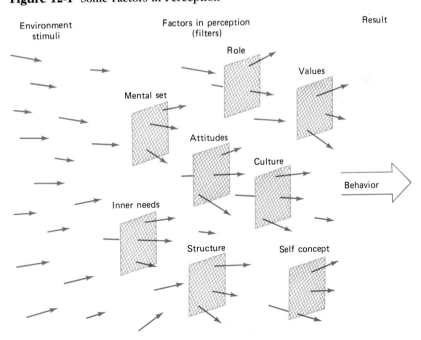

may not have used this language. You may have talked of expectation. When we use the term *expectation,* we mean that people tend to perceive what they expect. For example, your parents may expect you to be smarter when you return home for vacation after the first term. Production managers may erroneously anticipate that marketing managers will know little about statistics and work only with ideas. There are those who expect professors to speak "intelligently," women "softly," and union officials "roughly." Many of these examples of mental set are changed soon after direct contact, and the perception process does not remain distorted. But a mental set about ideas, beliefs, and values filters perception and may be lasting and difficult to change.

Stereotyping   The tendency to have a mental set about a person's behavior based upon some previous classification of that person, e.g., "People with glasses are intelligent."

Another aspect of the mental set is **stereotyping,** the tendency to have a mental set about a person's behavior based upon some previous classification of that person. There are many classic stereotypes: the redhead with a fiery temper, the jolly fat man, the absent-minded professor.

Stereotyping is a principal source of distortion in perception. It is very pronounced in organizations with many different natural groupings. In addition to the traditional male–female stereotyping that occurs, managers in organizations are faced with the stereotypes of education, age, race, management level, membership affiliation (as with the union member), and function (such as production, engineering, or marketing personnel). To each of these classifications, people give their own perceptual interpretations and then tend to perceive what they expect to perceive.

Halo effect   The tendency to believe that a person with one good or bad trait must have certain other good or bad traits.

Very closely related to the idea of stereotyping is the **halo effect.** The halo effect is the belief that a person with one good or bad trait must have certain other good or bad traits. For instance, someone who speaks with rough tones will be perceived as cold, domineering, and bossy. One who is well liked may be judged to be more intelligent than one who is not liked.

In both stereotyping and halo effect, the perceiver makes a judgment, which then creates an expectation that helps filter the environment so that the perception agrees with the expectation or mental set. The mental-set factor is fundamental in perception and is obviously very important in the perceptual process.

Since the mental set or the expectation is developed primarily from past experiences, the manager of an organization does have the potential of influencing the experiences of others and thus influencing the mental set or expectation.

You can influence the perception of a group, for example, by introducing a friend with very appropriate and descriptive titles. The common-sense language of this effort is called "impressing others," and what is obviously happening is the development of a mental set or expectation that may or may not prove true through later experience. Do not misinterpret our intention here. Our illustrations only point to the importance of mental set and expectation in the perception process, and also to the way in which the perception process can be influenced.

Why is self-concept important?

Self-Concept

Self-concept   The expectations that a person has of himself or herself; the self-concept filters the experiences a person has.

The way people view the world depends a great deal on the concept or image they have about themselves.[3] **Self-concept** is the expectation or belief a person has about his or her personal worth or value. Much of the filtering of a person's experiences is done to meet his or her self-concept. Self-concept comprises a number of components, depicted in Figure 12-2. Each of the components will be described in the following paragraphs.

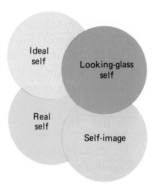

Self-image—The way you see
 yourself
Ideal self—The way you'd
 like to be
Looking-glass self—The way
 you think others regard you
Real self—You as you are

Figure 12-2 Components of Self-Concept

Self-image The way you
see yourself.

Ideal self The way you
would like to be.

Looking-glass self The
way you think others see
you.

First, there is the **self-image**—the way you see yourself. For example, you might consider yourself to be well liked by others, a forceful person, honest, sincere, and responsible. Or you may feel that you are incompetent in competitive situations.[4] You can recall many situations where you failed when the competition became tough and have concluded that you can't handle the stress. Second, there is the **ideal self**—the way you'd like to be. Perhaps you would like to be brave or tough or strong or respected or confident in stressful situations. All of us have images of the person we'd like to be. Third, there is the **looking-glass self**—the way you think others see you. The emphasis here is still on your perception of others' perceptions, for this is not the way people actually see you but, rather, the way that you think they see you. You may believe that production people don't trust you because you're in sales, that noncollege graduates resist your suggestions because they view college graduates, like you, as "know-it-alls," that your youngish looks make respect difficult to get.

These three components are all a function of individual perception, and they may be the same as, or different from, the last component, the real self, or the way you really are.

The key to much of your behavior is your self-concept. Establishing a mental picture of yourself—your pluses and minuses—is essential for mental health. This process continues as you change and adjust your concept throughout your life. The urge to preserve a relatively stable, somewhat flattering, and steadily more satisfying self-concept is the driving and organizing force behind a large portion of human activity. Each of these components is an important feature in the development of a healthy, mature individual.[5] For example, you might be said to be somewhat disoriented if your self-image, your ideal self, and your looking-glass self are the opposite of your real self. You may undergo a great deal of stress and frustration and may have to resort to a kind of personality fantasy to maintain this self-concept. There are people in mental hospitals who think they are famous personalities of past ages: Napoleon, George Washington, Sitting Bull. In one view, their personality disorders result from the difference between the components of the self-concept.

The healthy, developing, maturing type of concept might be one in which the similarity among all these components is great. This would mean that you have a pretty good picture of the real world and are not trying to escape from the reality of interpersonal feedback. If you feel an urge for power and some form of domination, and people see you behaving in that way, then there is a match between the two components, and, most likely, adjustments and accommodations will not have to be made in perception or in behavior.

You have probably experienced changes in your personal search for identity, since the self-concept you had as a child was probably revised throughout the stages of your growth. This concept is under constant rearrangement; we frequently express this by saying that a person "finds" himself or "really knows who she is." This means there is a form of agreement in the components of self-concept.

What is important here is to realize that your self-concept influences the perception process. You tend to screen and filter the world around you so as to meet your personal goals of self-image and ideal self. You may even accuse others of prejudice and bigotry if the looking-glass self differs from the ideal self and the self-image. In short, the self-concept is a pivotal factor affecting the perception process.

Structural Factors

What else affects perception?

Structural factors relate to the objective world that exists in concrete form. For instance, if you are reading this chapter in a room, the objects in the room constitute structural factors in perception. There may be a radio, a number of chairs, a desk, several books, and perhaps some dirty clothes around the room. These are objective structural factors. When someone walks into the room and assigns meaning to these structural factors, then individual perception is occurring. If the dirty clothes, for example, are on the floor near a laundry basket, someone might perceive that you couldn't throw dirty clothes into a basket. If the dirty clothes are all around the room, a different interpretation might be made.

Two illustrations in housing projects demonstrate the importance of structural factors. In one housing project, there were a number of bicycle racks that were not being used; yet, bicycles were being dropped on the ground. Letters to parents and threat of punishment did little to change the behavior of most of the children; the problem was solved only when the manager put the bicycle racks where most of the youths were dropping their bikes.

In another situation, the large dumpster trash cans were moved to a different location; yet, the tenants still dumped trash at the old spot. Efforts had to be made to change the behavior and perception of the tenants to get the trash into the trash cans. The cycle racks and the dumpsters are the structural factors in these examples.

Although the structural factors may be easy to change, there is often a tendency to ignore them. Managers need to realize the power of structural factors in affecting perception.

Role Demands

The term *role* refers to the behavior associated with a particular position. All positions in organizations have a written or an unwritten expectation of behavior. It helps, for example, if you know the "legitimate," accepted behavior possibilities of your boss, your peers, and yourself.

Ethics Issue

Employee Exposure of Secrets and Wrongdoing

Many managers fear that an employee will pass proprietary information, internal secrets, or information about the firm's practices, products, and activities to someone outside the firm. That someone could be the competition, the media, an unwanted investor, or a governmental agency. Unauthorized or unintended access to such information can have disastrous effects on any firm's operations, financial performance, and reputation.

The reasons employees pass information range from simple greed (doing it for the money), to revenge, to internal politics, to moral convictions. Whatever the reason, the behavior is a reflection of their personal needs, concerns, values, and attitudes. An organization's or a manager's ability to prevent or even predict this kind of employee behavior is extremely limited. Typically, employees act without regard to the potential job, family, career, or financial consequences of their action, and in some cases, they do so expecting to be rewarded for their action.

A 3M contract employee sent a new type of bone casting tape to some of 3M's competitors. Many attributed the employee's action to greed and perhaps a feeling of being slighted. He had helped develop the product and wanted to benefit from it. Ironically, he offered to sell the technology, which had a potential market value in excess of $100 million, for a mere $20,000. In the end, the employee was convicted of mail fraud and served twenty-two months in prison.

"Whistleblowers" pass on information about organizational wrongdoing from a sense of moral outrage or, in some instances, out of conviction that they have an obligation to report corporate misconduct. These individuals believe that they are doing what is right. A medical office worker was fired after she reported to senior management that the firm's accounting operation was billing insurance companies for services that the medical office did not deliver. An employee of MCA notified his supervisors that executives were arranging shipments of free record albums to individuals unauthorized to receive them. He expected to be rewarded for exposing a possible kickback scheme, but, instead, he was fired.

Responding to an employee's passing of organizational secrets or whistleblowing poses an ethical dilemma for both the organization and the individual. Neither side seems to benefit by firings or wrongful-termination suits. If the organization can expect loyalty from the employee, then the employee can expect that the organization operates with integrity. Thus, the challenge facing both sides is what to do when the behavior of the other does not meet those expectations. Is there a better way for employees to resolve their grievances or moral conflicts than to expose their employer's internal secrets?

References: Joan Hamilton, "Blowing the Whistle without Paying the Piper," *Business Week,* June 3, 1991, p. 138; Kevin Kelly, "When a Rival's Trade Secret Crosses Your Desk," *Business Week,* May 20, 1991, p. 48.

In addition to the formal demands of role behavior made by the organization, there are informal role demands. For instance, you may learn that even though there is nothing in any formal policy statement about manager involvement in community affairs, such involvement is expected of managers who want to move up in the organization.

Role demands can create perception problems when there is role conflict. Role conflict exists when the demands from two roles are incompatible within one situation. Suppose you were brought up in a steel town. Your father has worked for years as an hourly employee. You are hired into the company as a management trainee and soon become a supervisor over hourly employees. It may be the company's expectation that supervisors will be "tough" with the hourly workers. From what your father has said, you see much of their "playing-around" behavior as a natural release from the tensions and pressures of the job and believe it is all done in fun. Your management peers and your boss perceive the same behavior as "goldbricking" or "slowdown tactics" and insist you tighten up your management methods. Thus, your role as manager conflicts with your role as your father's child.

We need not expand the illustration for you to see the implications and perceptual complications arising from role conflict. It is obvious that an organization will try to minimize role-conflict situations in both the formal and the informal settings.[6]

Culture

> **Culture** Those acquired and learned behaviors which have persisted in human groups through traditions.

Culture, which is defined as everything that is learned and passed on from one generation to the next, affects every aspect of the perception process. Culture includes such things as language, value system, religious beliefs, and other patterns of behavior. Societies have a culture, organizations have a culture, and groups have a culture. The individual, as a participant in all these areas, is thus a composite of many cultural elements. If we look at particular cultures within organizations, groups, or societies, we are looking at the image, the character, or the personality of the unit. In what ways does the culture of a unit affect the perception processes?

Think for a moment of the culture most familiar to you. The United States of America has a culture that may include such terms as *strong, powerful, invincible, independent,* and *competitive.* (The terms you use depend upon who you are—people of other nations might offer a different set of terms to describe U.S. culture.) If an American accepts these terms and the meanings behind them, you can understand how difficult it would be for him or her to interpret government action as weak, unresponsive, exploitive, and so on. There will be a tendency, therefore, for people to perceive events and defend actions in terms of their cultural positions.

What is true for corporations is true for smaller groups or classes. The culture of the production department differs from that of the personnel department, which differs from that of the marketing department. The union membership differs from the management membership.

The cultures of organizations are developed and maintained through the transmission of language and values. Each group or class has its own language and values. These are communicated and reinforced through rewards and punishment of the unit. What a company values, for example, is communicated to its managers through the qualities that are rewarded by salary increases or promotions. Deviants from the organizational ethos are either removed or not rewarded, thus reducing their effectiveness. Organizations, through language and value efforts, try to ensure common perceptions for their members.[7]

Culture operates in another behavioral process when it becomes the standard for evaluating environment responses. Managers frequently "explain away" reactions to the environment (competitors, customers, or the government) by appealing to the established ethos or the culture of the organization.

Culture affects perception and thus behavior. Cultures are developed and maintained through language, values, and customs. A custom common in the United States and other countries is a handshake, both as a greeting and as a symbol of agreement and acceptance on a "business deal." In Japan, business people bow to each other as a sign of respect. In Russia, the greeting may be in the form of a hug.

So in both the perceptions leading to behavior and the explanations for environment feedback, culture and ethos play an important part.

We have seen that many other factors affect the perceptual process. As we stated earlier, the factors explained in this chapter do not represent all possible factors affecting perception. Being selective, we have identified those most critical to organizations and those having the potential of being influenced by managers.

Predicting Perceptual Responses

How do you predict behavior?

Sometimes, it is possible to predict the perceptions people hold and then predict their behavior or responses. For example, it would not be difficult to predict that the residents of Kentucky would respond with "University of Kentucky" to the stimulus initials UK, whereas residents of England would more readily respond with the words "United Kingdom." It similarly follows that the capital letters SEC would generate different responses in different parts of the world. To people on the East Coast, SEC might mean Securities and Exchange Commission. To the followers of athletic activities in the Midsouth, it stands for Southeastern Conference. And to Australians, it would mean State Electric Commission.

The examples just given to illustrate the connection between behavior and perception are oversimplified ones. The ease in predicting word associations does not mean that it is easy to predict an employee's behavior when told of a change in work procedure. Even though the problem is more difficult, it does not mean the attempt at prediction should be discarded. Prediction of behavior from knowledge of others' perceptions is possible and has the potential of improving a manager's understanding of a situation. In the following paragraphs, we will describe how such predictions are possible and why they are useful.

ATTITUDES

The formulation of attitudes relates to perception and our predictions of behavior.[8] Attitude may be seen as a moderating concept or variable. For instance, if you see two people arguing and you stand at a distance so you cannot hear what is said, your perception of that event will be affected by attitudes that you have if one of the people is from a different race or sex. If we tell you that one of them is from Italy and you have an attitude about Italians, your perception of the event will be moderated or affected by that attitude. Thus, to understand perception and the behavior, we need to understand attitudes.

Just as the factors described in the perception process make each person unique in the way he or she relates to his or her world, the attitudes that people have contribute to the uniqueness of and the differences among people.

Clarification of Terms

Three terms usually cover this area of study: *opinions, attitudes,* and *values.* (See Table 12-1.) In each case, the term represents your preference, your position, your bias for or against something. A distinction is usually made between

TABLE 12-1	Personal Preferences Classification		
TERM	**DEFINITION**	**QUALITY**	**EXAMPLE**
Opinion	Preference on a topic or subject	Short duration, changeable	U.S. involvement in foreign affairs
Attitude	Preference about an object	Mixed duration, somewhat difficult to change	Conservative, protective, liberal
Value	Preference on belief	Long duration, very resistant to change	Loyalty, honesty, responsibility

Opinions Your short-term preference, position, or bias for or against something. Tends to change frequently.

Attitudes A preference for objects; usually lasts a long time and is difficult to change.

Values Preferences about beliefs; deal with deeper, more philosophical subjects.

the first two terms and the last. Opinions and attitudes are similar in that they deal with the learned preferences you have about an object.[9]

Opinions on topics or subjects usually take some thought but are not necessarily long-lasting—they change rather frequently. **Attitudes** are also preference, not necessarily for subjects but rather for objects; they are of longer duration and usually more resistant to change. **Values** deal with deeper, perhaps more philosophical subjects and are usually the most enduring of the three.

It is important to understand how opinions and attitudes are formed and what effect they have on perception and ultimately on behavior. At the present stage of understanding in the field, it is not possible to say that attitudes are necessarily the direct cause of behavior. In other words, knowing a person's attitude is no guarantee that you can predict his or her behavior. At this time, we are not really interested in whether behavior affects attitude or attitude affects behavior; probably, each has an effect on the other. We might start this discussion of opinions and attitudes by looking into some of the sources of attitudes. (See Figure 12-3.)

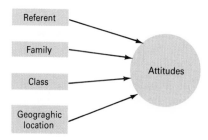

Figure 12-3 Some Attitude and Opinion Sources

Sources of Attitudes

What does attitude come from?

The family is probably the earliest source for the development of opinions and attitudes. Your opinions and beliefs about religion, fairness in play, and honesty and cheating are usually similar to those held by your parents. Similarly, people's voting patterns and career choices are very closely linked with those of their parents.

A second important source is class. Each of you is a member of a class that has a defined status. For example, a person may be affiliated with the working class, the middle-income class, the upper class, the educated class, or the

A person's family is the first and earliest source of opinions and attitudes. Your opinions and beliefs are probably very similar to what your parents think and believe. Values are developed at the Thanksgiving dinner table, at Church, at the playground, on vacation, at family reunions, and through other occurrences in everyday life.

young-generation class. Each class is measured by various criteria, including income, occupation, and education, or by some combination thereof. People within classes tend to share similar attitudes, perceptions, and behaviors.[10]

A person's geographic location can also be a subtle source of attitudes and opinions. For example, people from the same region tend to hold similar, although not necessarily identical, opinions. Residents of large cities tend to be more like one another in their attitudes than people who come from either rural or suburban areas.

Most of the sources of attitudes and opinions mentioned are part of a person's given set of characteristics; you have little choice in being born into a family with a specific culture, a set of norms that belongs to an economic class living in California, Iowa, or New Jersey. To look to the family or peers as a source of attitudes and opinions is a natural behavior process. A good deal of behavior depends on identifying with others. When we analyze behavior in terms of the influence of others, we are using a theory or an explanation called **reference theory**—with whom you identify or to whom you refer when making behavioral decisions.

Reference theory
Analysis of behavior in terms of the influence of others.

In some cases, the referent is a person you know and probably admire. Examples include one or both of your parents, a successful aunt or uncle, an older brother or sister, a revered teacher or athletic coach, an older employee, a union official, your boss, and a successful manager of a technical unit. You may seek out this person's advice or help when faced with problems, and your attitudes and opinions will most likely be shaped by those of this other person.

In other instances, you may never come in contact with the other person, or that person may not be living. Martin Luther King's life stands as a model for many, young and old; U.S. presidents serve as referents, as do professional athletes; the same is true of organizational officials. In all illustrations, you can see the value of knowing a person's referent—the values, attitudes, and opinions of one help you understand the values, attitudes, and opinions of the other.

The referent can easily be a group (classmates or peers at work), as well as a person, and the influence on behavior can be as important. The group reference is a topic more fully developed in Chapter 14.

Attitudes and opinions play an important role in behavior. Managers are one step closer to effective managing if they have insight into the sources of their own and others' attitudes and opinions. They are better able to anticipate the consequences of organizational action if they have some knowledge of the factors affecting behavior. There is another concept that helps managers to either "explain" behavior or anticipate behavioral responses to organizational decisions and actions. This concept is called defense mechanisms.

Management Application

Managers and the "Working Vacation"

Many American managers have long been accused of being workaholics by their associates and families. Psychologists and management consultants have argued that this kind of managerial behavior is unhealthy and counterproductive. They reason that managers need periodic rest and relaxation to maintain high levels of performance. However, in the age of the fax, cellular phones, and laptop computers, a carefree, family-oriented, and fun-filled vacation may be only a dream, a thing of the past, or a part of Hollywood fiction.

Although today's managers are receiving considerable incentives and encouragement to take time away from work, studies have found that they are being urged to do so only if they can "keep in touch." Some managers find that they are expected to provide detailed itineraries of their travel, with hotel addresses that include fax and phone numbers. Clients likewise demand that managers and sales personnel continue to be accessible and available to meet their needs, regardless of where the manager or salesperson intends to take vacation.

Dual-career couples find scheduling vacation time even more complicated. Those who do manage to coordinate their schedules often discover that instead of enjoying a romantic weekend, they are stuck in their motel rooms trying to complete the heavy workload that they brought with them.

Researchers for the travel industry have found that there is a growing trend for managers to take shorter vacations. These vacations are more like extended weekends that combine business with pleasure. Researchers also have found that managers are often taking their families with them. This is growing in popularity, particularly when the business travel is distant and long-term. Surprisingly, many firms not only encourage their managers to take the family along for all or part of the trip but also help in making travel arrangements. The firms feel that they benefit from such an arrangement because it eliminates major stress factors of travel—being away from home and family—and eliminates worries. Managers find themselves more relaxed and better able to concentrate on doing business.

What is emerging is a whole new notion of the working vacation: Managers can get a break from the stress and turmoil of the workplace while still maintaining contact and continuing to get the job done. Even with this new arrangement, however, some managers and their families still long for the real getaway vacation, a time when the manager's secretary diligently maintains the secret of where they really are.

References: Marita Thomas, "All Work and No Play," *World Trade* (June-July 1991), p. 65; L. A. Winokur, "Vacations Are Becoming Part of the Job," *Wall Street Journal,* July 9, 1991, p. B1.

DEFENSE MECHANISMS

How do you behave if you
don't like the feedback?

Defense mechanisms
A behavioral process that
allows a person to main-
tain a balance with the
self-concept.

Once you have acted, there is likely to be some consequence or result. The
consequence may be good or bad, rewarding or punishing, effective or ineffective, or even confusing. Consequences of your initial behavior invariably lead
to some further behavior. You can either accept the consequences for what
they are or reject the consequences and go through a behavioral process to
maintain a balance or congruity with your self-concept. This behavior response
to a threat to self (when the feedback of your behavior does not match your
expectations) is called a defense reaction. **Defense mechanisms** are the ways
people defend themselves against threat.[11]

Defense mechanisms are based on the assumption that when confronted
with an experience of anxiety, conflict, frustration, or failure, you would rather
be psychologically comfortable than psychologically uncomfortable. It is natural for you to dislike personal embarrassment, rejection, or attack. The healthy
person strives for a balance in his or her personal life so that there is psychological comfort. When discomfort occurs, when stress and tension arise out of
the conflict between what you want and what is happening, you may resort to a
defense mechanism—a process that the organism uses to protect itself and
maintain the balance. (See Figure 12-4.)

Suppose a young man believes he has the ability to be an outstanding basketball player but fails to make the team. He is faced with two options. First, he
can accept the judgment of the basketball coach and decide that he will get en-
joyment from playing basketball as a hobby even though he is not good
enough for the school team. Or he may use a defense mechanism by deciding
that the coach was prejudiced against him and thus he was not given a fair
chance to show his ability.

You can see how defense mechanisms relate to the self-concept. When
feedback from a person's environment does not correspond with the self-

Figure 12-4 Defense Mechanisms as Behavior Processes

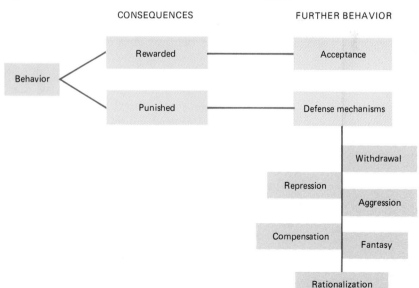

concept, protective behavior comes into play. You may know people who simply withdraw when placed in a situation that is uncomfortable to them. Or you know people who compensate (or overcompensate) because of unacceptable information from peers or authority. There are many stories in the sports field of men and women who, when told by a coach, a parent, or peers that they'd never perform well in some activity, took that information as a challenge and displayed very aggressive behavior, resulting in success. Thus, defense mechanisms are not necessarily harmful.

There are two other dimensions of defense mechanisms that improve a manager's understanding of individual behavior processes—the theory of cognitive dissonance and the theory of equity. Simply stated, the **theory of cognitive dissonance** says that you will be motivated to match up two elements of knowledge if those two elements are "objectively" in disagreement with each other.[12] For example, if you want to buy a small sports car but are worried about accident statistics, you may resolve the disagreement by believing that the small car gives you greater maneuverability and thus reduces the likelihood of accidents. Or if you enjoy smoking, you will do a kind of psychological manipulation with the facts and statistics showing the relationship between smoking and cancer. Cognitive dissonance is helpful in understanding behavior, for it assumes that people cannot tolerate inconsistency and thus will use some defense mechanism to bring elements back into agreement.

Another way to understand defensive behavior is to use the **theory of equity.** People frequently evaluate their possible behavior according to perceived fairness when compared with those considered their equals.[13] An example will best demonstrate this useful theory.

Jason is one of many product managers in a large multinational firm. All the managers at his level recently completed their performance reviews. Jason was pleased with his review and the salary increase that resulted from it—until he compared his increase with the increase given to Jennifer, one of his peers. Faced with this inequity between perceived performance and salary increase, Jason moves to create balance and restore equity. Figure 12-5 shows the states of the relationship. At first, Jason is pleased; then he is displeased. To get balance, he may reduce his inputs in relation to the outcomes (that is, work less for the same pay so that he feels he's earning more). He may even resort to rationalization (a defense mechanism) by believing that Jennifer received her larger increase because she lives in the same neighborhood as her boss and their children attend the same schools.

The example of Jason and Jennifer dealt with pay, and most research on this theory has focused on pay as the basic outcome. In many instances, the theory has been used to explain behavior in response to a managerial decision. The next example will show you the power of equity theory by (1) applying the concept to a nonpay area and (2) applying the concept in a preventive way.

The manager in this instance was the chairperson of an academic department in a university. She was surprised one morning when a delegation of three students handed her a petition signed by fifteen students complaining about the teaching of a faculty member who taught one of the sections of a basic required course. In the petition, the students described the teacher as "unfair," "caustic," and "too demanding." The chairperson accepted the petition, set up a meeting with the faculty member and a spokesperson for the students, and wondered if she might have to file charges.

Theory of cognitive dissonance A person "matches" elements if those elements are "objectively" in disagreement with each other.

Theory of equity The behavorial process that gives meaning to a situation in terms of the effect and value given to other people.

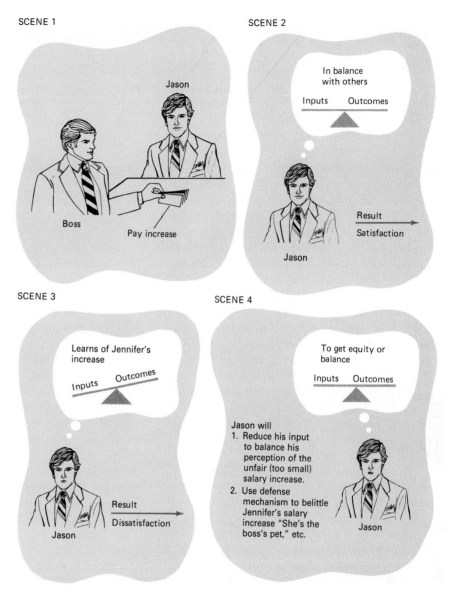

Figure 12-5 Equity

At the meeting, the chairperson asked the faculty member to describe the course—the outline, the exams, and the standards for grading. She then encouraged the student to respond. After more probing by the chairperson the student stated the real issue. Fellow students in other sections did less reading and less exam preparation; yet, they received higher grades. The issue was one of perceived inequity. One set of students had greater perceived inputs but received lower outcomes (grades) and thus did what they thought would bring back balance—contacted the department chairperson with the intention of filing a grievance.

This illustration points to some important benefits to using theory (that is, possible explanations) before taking managerial action or jumping to false conclusions. If students (or managers, secretaries, machine operators, or what-

Global Application

Volvo Tries to Humanize the Automobile Plant

Automobile manufacturing plants have long been characterized as places where the work is repetitive, tedious, and boring. The assembly-line environment has afforded workers little in the way of personal dignity or job satisfaction. Consequently, automobile manufacturers have faced a variety of employee-related problems, such as low productivity, high absenteeism, high turnover, and poor quality.

Like its counterparts, Volvo has had to contend with high levels of absenteeism and turnover, problems compounded by the Swedish social system, which provides financial protection for absentee workers and for workers who quit. Volvo has been forced to look beyond financial incentives as a means to get people to come to work. It has had to find a way to make work a desirable and rewarding activity.

During the past twenty years, Volvo has implemented a humanistically based manufacturing philosophy. The Kalmar and Uddevalla plants reflect that philosophy and the efforts of Volvo's management to create a worker-friendly environment that promotes individual dignity and encourages personal development.

In the Kalmar plant, opened in 1973, individual cars are built on pallets that move through the plant to various work stations. At the stations, teams of workers take about thirty minutes to conduct a variety of assembly activities. Workers perform multiple tasks, and they determine their own work assignments.

At the Uddevalla plant, opened in 1988, Volvo initiated its most radical manufacturing reforms. It eliminated the assembly line. Teams of eight to ten workers take two or three hours to build an entire car. There are no supervisors or foremen at Uddevalla. Instead, the workers have complete control over and responsibility for their work area. They determine their work assignments, schedules, and procedures, and they have the opportunity to develop and exercise individual skills.

The results of these humanistic manufacturing practices at Uddevalla have been striking. Workers have expressed greater job satisfaction, quality has been up, and absenteeism rates have dropped significantly. But the happy work force has not proven to be a productive work force. Turnover remains high, and productivity has been extremely poor. It takes fifty man-hours to complete a car at Uddevalla, compared with thirty-seven hours at Kalmar and twenty-five hours at Ghent (one of Volvo's traditional assembly-line plants). In contrast, Japanese plants take about seventeen man-hours to build a car. Uddevalla was to produce 40,000 cars a year using forty-eight teams. But in 1990, the forty-eight teams were able to produce only 16,000 cars.

Volvo's efforts to introduce a more humanistic way to manufacture demonstrate the difficulty of trying to meet employee needs while also trying to meet the organization's need to remain competitive in a hostile environment.

References: P. G. Gyllenhammer, "How Volvo Adapts Work to People," *Harvard Business Review* (July-August 1977), pp. 102–13; S. Prokesch, "Edges Fray on Volvo's Brave New Humanistic World," *New York Times,* July 7, 1991, p. F5.

ever) perceive inequity in a situation, frustration is likely, and the subsequent reactions to frustration may cause additional organizational problems.[14] Personal output may suffer; negative feelings may be generated—first toward the initiator (such as the faculty member), then toward the organization (the chairperson, college, and university), and finally toward the other members of the society (fellow students). Inequity is almost inevitable because of the normal errors in any organization and the differing perceptions occurring daily.[15] Managers can use the equity model to gain a better understanding of behavior by individuals within and between groups.

Understanding of the processes for individual behavior has been a primary objective of this first chapter of Part III, The People Factors in Managing. As a potential or practicing manager, however, you might want a proactive technique that will directly affect the behavior processes of your people. You know that the longer people stay with your organization, the greater the influence of the corporate culture upon shared values, beliefs, and meaning. You also know that training and development experiences may also have an impact upon behavior process. There is one more technique that should be explored briefly, a technique most applicable for those persons who are new to the organization. This technique is called organizational socialization.

ORGANIZATIONAL SOCIALIZATION

Organizational socialization The way a firm designs the experiences for people so that they learn the values, norms, rules, and procedures of the organization.

Organizational socialization is the way a firm designs the experiences for people so that they learn the values, norms, rules, and procedures.[16] Although the experiences may occur throughout your career, you will be most aware of socialization during the early days in a new company or position. Many organizations conduct formal orientation programs that last from a few days to eighteen months. You may be given company manuals so that you learn the goals, objectives, and expected procedures to follow. You may receive visits from executives who describe their responsibilities. You may even be assigned to a mentor who will help in your development. What you learn from these sessions ranges widely.

You need to know what the accepted dress code is, how to address senior executives, the expected length of coffee and lunch breaks, the appropriate car, and perhaps the appropriate role a spouse plays in the organization. The important point is that new people will learn the ropes—who should do the teaching? Managers can influence behavior by giving care to the way new members are socialized.

SUMMARY

This chapter discussed three concepts relating to the individual's process of selecting behavior. Perception, attitudes, and defense mechanisms are all basic to the "why" of behavior; they explain, in part, why the same set of circumstances can affect everyone differently. Every person differs; yet, every person uses similar processes. Managers who want to take advantage of this process information will not jump to quick conclusions about the behavior of others. They will not attribute all kinds of bizarre motives to behavior that has just occurred; rather, they will attempt to analyze the context of attitudes and perceptions and see the cycle by which every individual processes behavioral decisions. They will recognize the variety of factors possibly affecting people's perceptions and will use this knowledge to guide and influence others' work behavior toward unit goals.

KEY TERMS

Perception   The process by which people interpret the experiences around them.

Mental set   The tendency to act or react in a certain way to a given stimulus; one tends to "see" what one expects to see.

Stereotyping   The tendency to have a mental set about a person's behavior based upon some previous classification of that person, e.g., "People with glasses are intelligent."

Halo effect   The tendency to believe that a person with one good or bad trait must have certain other good or bad traits.

Self-concept   The expectations that a person has of himself or herself; the self-concept filters the experiences a person has.

Self-image   The way you see yourself.

Ideal self   The way you would like to be.

Looking-glass self   The way you think others see you.

Culture   Those acquired and learned behaviors which have persisted in human groups through traditions.

Opinions   Your short-term preference, position, or bias for or against something. Tends to change frequently.

Attitudes   A preference for objects; usually lasts a long time and is difficult to change.

Values   Preferences about beliefs; deal with deeper, more philosophical subjects.

Defense mechanisms   A behavioral process that allows a person to maintain a balance with the self-concept.

Theory of cognitive dissonance   A person "matches" elements if those elements are "objectively" in disagreement with each other.

Theory of equity   The behavorial process that gives meaning to a situation in terms of the effect and value given to other people.

Reference theory   Analysis of behavior in terms of the influence of others.

Organizational socialization   The way a firm designs the experiences for people so that they learn the values, norms, rules, and procedures of the organization.

STUDY ASSIGNMENTS

1. What were some of the reasons the employees of Hyatt Clark were unable to resolve the adversarial conflict between management and labor? What is your opinion about employee ownership and its role in influencing the job performance of individual employees?

2. What are some of the reasons that people perceive shared experiences or events so differently?

3. How do the various factors of the perceptual process shape and influence individual behavior?

4. How does an individual's self-concept influence his or her work and performance? How would you apply the notion of self-confidence to your own performance in school or at work?

5. How do structural factors (role demands) influence the performance and behavior of employees?

6. What role does culture play in shaping individual behavior and performance? How does your own cultural background and experience shape your behavior and performance?

7. First define the concepts of opinions, attitudes, and values, and then explain the differences among them.

8. What are some of the sources of attitudes? How do attitudes influence individual behavior? How can managers change attitudes that adversely affect an individual's work performance?

9. How do defense mechanisms influence individual behavior? Give some examples of individual defense mechanisms.

10. Why would an understanding of individual behavior enhance a manager's ability to influence an employee's performance? What do you think about the notion that managers should "manage the behavior" of their subordinates to enhance performance?

Case for Discussion

APPRAISAL AT PEMBROKE, SMOTHERS, AND PHELPS

Kelly Cushman felt irritated and upset as she got into her car and started the 25-minute drive home from her office. It was a steamy, hot, Friday afternoon in July. Kelly's anger was about as hot as the temperature inside her car, which had been parked outside in the sun all day. As the car's air-conditioning started to send forth cool air and began to make things bearable, Kelly downshifted as she neared the on-ramp to the interstate that led her home. "I'm glad to be getting away from work, and I'm really going to let loose and enjoy myself this weekend," she thought.

Kelly graduated from the State University with honors in accounting a little more than a year ago. She was one of the first of her class to find employment, which gave her an added sense of security during the second semester of her senior year at college; this is not to mention the added sense of superiority she enjoyed from having a job when others didn't. Her outstanding grade point average enabled her to land a job with Pembroke, Smothers, and Phelps, which many consider to be the most prestigious of the large public accounting firms.

As her small car moved on to the interstate, Kelly floored the accelerator. The sense of the car's advancing speed seemed to give a release to her feelings of anger and frustration over what had occurred less than an hour ago during the performance appraisal with her boss, Nancy Miller. Nancy was about fifteen years older than Kelly and had been in public accounting for over ten years. She had worked days and gone to school in the evenings for seven and a half years to earn a degree in accounting. She had been with Pembroke, Smothers, and Phelps for eight years. Nancy was known for her professionalism and attention to details. She was a stickler for meeting deadlines and getting things done along the lines established both formally and informally by the firm.

Many called her a perfectionist. Nancy was known to spare few words when it came to calling errors to the attention of those who worked under her and seeing to it that her people performed and presented the right impression to higher-ups in the firm. As she drove home, Kelly continued to feel angry with her boss but then started to blame herself and feel stupid and ashamed. A strong sense of failure crept over her. What would her parents say when she saw them for dinner on Sunday? What would she tell her friends?

Kelly reviewed in her mind for the third time what had gone on in her first performance appraisal. Her boss had told her that her overall performance for the year was average and that she needed to improve in several specific ways. In her mind, Kelly relived in detail what Nancy had said.

"Kelly, you are just too concerned with your personal life and not enough with your career. You need to pay more attention to the interests of our clients and the reputation of our firm. For example, three months ago you took off three hours early on a Friday afternoon without requesting permission or asking for a half-day of vacation time so you could catch a flight to attend your old roommate's wedding. Also, you have twice asked for a one-day extension on deadlines of assignments I gave you. Later on, I found out that you used this extra time just to check your work. It was already finished and you told me it wasn't. You can't be slow in getting work turned in."

Kelly tried to argue that she wanted to turn in error-free work, but Nancy didn't seem to be very receptive to her rebuttal.

Kelly thought about the more than two dozen Saturdays she had spent in the office working so she could be seen as a dedicated employee by others, especially one of the partners. "It's not fair," Kelly thought. "I put in all that extra time and ended up being evaluated as average." She really expected an "outstanding" performance rating or, at the very least, an "above average" one—but "average"? Kelly thought to herself, "I'll be darned if I'm going to give them any of my time tomorrow. In fact, I may even call in sick on Monday . . . well, no, I guess that would be going too far."

Kelly eased her foot off the accelerator as she signaled to move into the exit lane. It was lucky she didn't get picked up for speeding. Her thoughts turned to the Wolf's Den Lounge and the friends she could see there. It was just a few blocks away. The Wolf's Den was a place many young, single professionals frequented on Friday afternoons and evenings after work.

As she drove into the parking lot in front of the Den, Kelly remembered how guilty she had felt about padding her first travel expense report and several subsequent ones. She did this largely because she had been taken aside by some of the other, more experienced people she worked with, and encouraged to do as they did. As she thought about the "average" performance evaluation Ms. Miller had given her, her sense of guilt about her "padded" expense reports eased a bit.

Kelly shut off her car's engine and stepped into the hot afternoon sunshine. Across the parking lot, she could see her friend Ben as he slowly extricated his lean 6′3″ frame from his low-slung sports car. Seeing Kelly, he called out, "Kelly! How's it going, kid?"

"Awful. Simply awful! Let me tell you what my boss laid on me this afternoon. She's so off the wall, it's ridiculous."

The two walked toward the Wolf's Den.

Chapter 13

Motivation

"Prof, you got a minute?"

I turned to the door and saw Sue, one of the stay-awake students of my organizational behavior class at Wayne State University in Detroit, Michigan. She was married to a graduate student and was the mother of a small boy, and she always seemed prepared, rarely asked stupid questions, and stayed with you when you tried to develop a point. She had a good attention span and a good mind.

"Come on in and sit down, Sue," I said, moving the pile of unread *Wall Street Journal*s from the big chair to the floor. "What can I do for you?"

"I'm sorry I missed class this morning. The flu bug hit our family last night, and I had to be sure my son would be all right before I came to school."

"Is he okay now?"

"Yes, it must have been the twenty-four hour variety. I tried to get notes from the other students, but you know how some students keep notes. Fortunately, I've had some courses in psychology and sociology, and I'm familiar with Maslow's theory, but not Herzberg's or Vroom's. Would you have time to give me the highlights or a summary of your lecture on motivation? That way, I can take my own notes."

I had some time before Stu, my faculty colleague, and I were to go for coffee, and Sue was a good student.

"Well, let me run through the illustration I gave on car buying so that some characteristics of motivation might show up. You remember, I set up the

example in the form of a student in a marketing-research class whose job it is to find out why people buy automobiles, a rather common purchase here in Detroit. When the student reported back to the class, he told the students and the professor that he was confused. He had gone back to his hometown after the class assignment, had developed a good sample, and had put together a good interview schedule. It was the answers to his questions that had confused him. He remembered that the marketing professor had told him to probe after a person gives the first answer; that frequently the first answer is not the one the respondent really believes but is more of a convenience answer, or an answer that is expected."

"I know what you mean," Sue said. "I know people who live at the housing complex who'll give any answer just to get rid of an interviewer."

"Exactly. Well, when the student probed, he found people giving some strange reasons for the purchase of their last car or an anticipated one. One manager of a paint company said that his type of car was part of the total management fringe package of the company. Since it was a supplier to GM, the different levels in the company received different types of cars. Some drove Pontiacs, some Oldsmobiles or Buicks; he drove a Chevy and would continue to do so until he moved up in the company.

"Another respondent was concerned with the economy of the car. This person said she checked *Consumer Reports* and other journals comparing cars and usually picked the car recommended by these groups."

"Isn't that interesting?" commented Sue. "My husband, Tom, is just like that. He won't let me buy just any toothpaste; it has to be the one that's been rated best."

"Sue, I gave another example, of a woman with three children, who said her family belonged to a very active church group, all in their thirties, and that they liked to camp in the Upper Peninsula, so they needed a wagon. Most of the other families drove Ford, Chevy, or Plymouth wagons. This young mother felt that the kind of car you drive or park in front of your house tells a lot about the people who live inside. If you drive an old, beat-up clunker, you're probably a kind of messy person who walks around in a fog. 'You definitely don't work for anyone connected with the automobile industry if you drive a piece of junk.'

"Another young man said that ever since he was a struggling kid in graduate school, he had promised himself that one of the first luxury purchases he'd make would be a sports car. If he's depressed, a spin gives him a lift.

"Now, Sue, why do you think I gave all those examples to my class? What do you think was my intention and my main point?"

"You asked me before I got a chance to ask you. I guess I really don't know what your point would have been. I know if I had been in class, this is the place where I would have raised my hand. . . . I thought the purpose of studying motivation was so that managers of organizations could know why people behave as they do. If managers know why the people around them do what they do, then they can predict their behavior—get away from the 'art' in management and become more 'scientific.' If every answer is different, how can you possibly predict responses?"

"I gave those examples to show that the specific reason or motive for purchase behavior is very difficult to isolate. Look at all the motives that seemed expressed through car purchases: to appear younger and attractive; to appear respectable; to gain acceptance from others; to maintain the acceptance already gained through similar income levels and church affiliation; to satisfy economic values; to reinforce company-created status differentials. Motives can't be accurately inferred from behavior, since the same behavior may be used to fulfill different individual motives. An understanding of the field of motivation may help us interpret behavior and give us possible insight into the reasons people do what they do. We are a long way from being able to predict scientifically why specific people will select specific bits of behavior." ■

SIX GENERALIZATIONS ABOUT MOTIVATION

Basic to any discussion of motivation is the assumption that most of our behavior occurs for some reason.[1] Behavior is purposive. Larry shouts at Joe. Gail gets up from her desk and paces the floor. Vic steps between two of his subordinates to change the subject in a heated argument. In each instance, the person acts for some reason. Managers are usually interested in the reasons for behavior so that they can influence people. For example, the plant manager of Belden Corporation wants to know how to motivate first-level supervisors. A research director of Bell Labs seeks help from the human resource department, and the request focuses on the motivation of certain task groups. The head nurse at Massachusetts General searches for the best reward for nurses in

Elementary-school teacher
using motivational
techniques on her students

the renal intensive care unit. Teachers see students who appear lazy and apathetic and wonder how to motivate and excite them. Athletic coaches remark that motivation and the desire to perform at high levels frequently are more important than ability. The study of motivation, therefore, has strong appeal to managers.

The opening case illustrates a very basic characteristic of motivation. At first glance, the more you know, the more confused you become; the student who wanted to generalize on the motives for buying cars came back from his interviews more confused than before he started. But at second glance, we can see that our student learned two things: First, he learned that motives are widely varied; and second, he did learn about some specific motives that culminated in car purchases. Although our student could not report a neat, concise formula as the answer to his question, he knew more than he did before and would have a more valid basis for designing an advertising campaign.

There is a very pragmatic reason for you to understand motivation. It relates to organizational performance, and as we stated earlier, the performance of a firm's members is a primary responsibility of management. Motivation, that inner state that energizes or moves behavior toward activity, is not the only factor relating to performance. You may know of highly motivated people who do not have the *ability* to perform well or who may not be in a *work environment* that allows for effective performance (they may have faulty equipment, poor raw materials, hot or noisy conditions, inaccurate instructions, or a work group who puts a limit on the output).

Lack of ability may be remedied by training, and a poor work environment can be improved by a manager's actions. The question in this chapter is: What can a manager do about the motivation of an employee? We begin by looking at some useful generalizations about motivation.[2]

First, motives are the energizing forces within us. These forces are invisible and impossible to measure. Because all of us are different, the motives energizing us at any moment differ. All that is possible is to observe and measure the behavior we choose and, from that behavior, make a kind of backward causation statement to the possible motive. Observing someone's behavior may show that a certain need is present in that person, motivating him or her onward.

Second, one motive may result in many different behaviors. The desire for prestige may lead a person to run for political office, give money away, get additional educational training, steal, join groups, grow a mustache and sideburns, or shave off facial hair. The same behavior in different people may come from many different motives. In the opening case, the illustration about car buying supports this generalization. You may remember that the same behavior (purchasing a car) could be seen as coming from a number of different motives. Recall the motives that seemed expressed through car purchases: to appear younger and attractive; to appear respectable; to gain acceptance from others; to maintain the acceptance already gained through a similar income level and church affiliation; to satisfy economic values; and to reinforce company-created status differentials. Managers would commit a bad mistake if they tried to attribute the same behavior in different people to the same motive. People join unions, get married, attend class, and laugh at professors' jokes for many different reasons (motives). Thus, a motive cannot always be identified from the specific behavior.

Third, behavior can be used only as an estimate of a person's motive. This statement may seem to be in direct opposition to the preceding generalization, but there is an important difference. There, we said that the same behavior does not always follow the same motive. Here, we are saying that it is possible, after repeated observations of one person's behavior, to make an estimate of the cause of that behavior. For example, there is truth in the statement that some people always seem to feel insecure and thus always behave in a manner reflecting that insecure feeling. You know other people whose behavior radiates confidence. They are confident in many different social settings, so that what you see is a constant and repeated behavior, behavior from which people probably estimate the motive of the person. Obviously, if a person is in a state of near starvation, most of his or her behavior will be related to the need for food. Although it is dangerous to categorize people, it is also wrong to believe that individual behavior, when looked at from some time perspective, cannot be used as an estimate for motivation.

Fourth, motives may operate in harmony or in conflict. Behavior is frequently the result of the interplay of several motives. These motives may push a person in one direction or in a number of directions. For example, a girl may want to get high grades in school while also wanting to appear "dumb" to her boyfriend. An athlete may desire an outstanding performance but may also be sensitive to being shunned by teammates if the performance is too outstanding. Behavior, therefore, is the result of many forces differing in direction and intent.

Fifth, motives come and go. It is very rare that a motive has the same energy potential over a long period of time. The boy or girl who buys a paper route in the spring to get money may sell the route during the basketball season because the monetary need takes second place to the need to play basketball. People who are extremely concerned about hair and clothes during adolescence may turn their attention to other things once they grow up. Because human beings are constantly growing, their motives at one time will not be as intense as at another.

Sixth, the environment influences motives. The situation at a particular time may trigger or suppress the action of a motive. There have probably been times when you did not realize how hungry you were until your sense of smell picked up the odor of food cooking. Similarly, many of your sociological needs become stimulated when you are in a situation filled with the sociological factors. Thus, needs that are latent can quickly be stimulated by the environmental situation.

We have now identified a number of generalizations that are useful in understanding the concept of motivation. Notice the similarity in the generalizations. Few of them are simple statements: "One motive may result in many behaviors." "Motives may operate in harmony or in conflict." "Motives come and go." You may feel as confused as the marketing-research student in the opening case. Yet managers cannot escape a complex world.

One way to cope with the complexity of understanding management is to study analytical models. Rarely is a model (a simpler-than-real-life representation) thought to be complete or totally accurate. Rather, it is a depiction that shows how someone believes something works. Although crude and rough, models form one starting point for a manager's search for the answer to the "why" question of behavior.

MOTIVATIONAL THEORIES

Motivation The inner state that energizes or moves behavior toward activity.

Motivation is that inner state that energizes or moves behavior toward activity. There are several theories that have received a great deal of discussion in business literature, and it is to these theories that we now turn our attention. The theories selected for review can be classified as those built upon assumptions of man's basic nature, those focusing upon man's environment, and one containing parts of both. The first description, therefore, is of those theories whose authors suggest the universal application of their ideas, since they are developed from assumptions basic to all people.

Universal Theories

Abraham H. Maslow's Hierarchy of Needs

Hierarchy Needs are in a specific order so that one level of need satisfaction must be met before a person progresses to the satisfaction of a higher level of need.

In 1954, Maslow published a basic theoretical work built upon his interpretation of man's basic needs, and many find his work meaningful today.[3] These needs are in a specific order, or **hierarchy,** so that one level of need satisfaction must be met before a person progresses to the satisfaction of a higher level of need. (See Figure 13-1.)

The following nine points summarize the basic ideas of Maslow, together with some application to management practices.

1. Man has at least five sets of basic needs.
   a. Physiological—hunger, thirst, sex, and so on
   b. Safety—protection against danger, threat, deprivation, and so on
   c. Social—belonging, association, acceptance by others, giving and receiving friendship and love

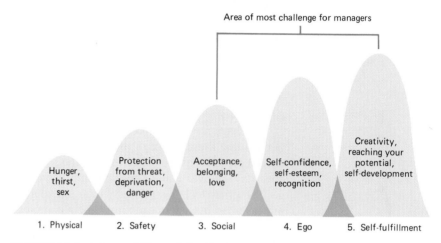

FIGURE 13-1 A General View of the Maslow Needs Hierarchy

d. Ego—self-esteem (self-confidence, independence, achievement, competence, knowledge) and personal reputation (status, recognition, appreciation, respect)
e. Self-fulfillment—realizing one's own potential, continued self-development, creativity

2. These needs exist in an order, or hierarchy, with the physiological being the most basic.
3. The needs at any level emerge only when the more basic needs have been gratified.
4. One hundred percent satisfaction is not required for a need to no longer be dominant.
5. Most people in organizations are past the physiological-need level.
6. The challenge to managers is in dealing with the social, egoistic, and self-fulfillment needs.
7. People operating at the higher need levels are healthier people.
8. The irresponsible behavior of some people in organizations is a symptom of illness—of deprivation of social and egoistic needs. The negative behavior observed is the result of poor management.
9. There are management techniques that result in the satisfaction of physiological and safety needs and many of the social needs. Managers in organizations can perform in a way that enables others to function in the higher and healthier areas of behavior.

Meeting the ego/self-esteem and social/belonging needs described by Maslow in his hierarchy of needs can be shown in the support the Desert Storm troops received back home. This rally in a Texas stadium was just one of many held for the troops in recognition and appreciation of their service in the Gulf War. This show of respect for the troops helped them to meet their ego/self-esteem need.

These statements by Maslow are very positive. They envision a person who wants to be healthy, who wants to be responsible, who wants to make a contribution to others. Therefore, it is a mismanaged organization that causes negative and unhealthy behavior in its participants. What we need is a new management approach that unleashes the human potentialities of organizations' participants.

The Maslow model has found great favor and use among many practicing managers, although care must be taken not to overgeneralize from it. We elaborate on this model in Figures 13-2 and 13-3. Figure 13-1 diagrams a needs hierarchy and indicates the normal movement from the basic (1, on the left) to the highest (5, on the right) needs. Note that there is overlap in each need area, for it would be far too simplistic to think that each area has an abrupt

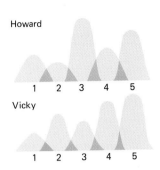

Howard

Vicky

FIGURE 13-2 Real-World Needs of Howard and Vicky. **The curve height represents the minimum amount of need in each area that must be gratified before the next area becomes dominant. The numbers correspond to the five basic needs of Figure 13-1.**

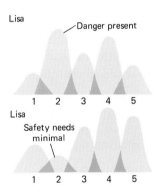

Lisa

Danger present

Lisa

Safety needs minimal

FIGURE 13-3 The Effect of a Situation on a Person's Needs Hierarchy

starting and stopping point. Figure 13-2 compares the needs hierarchies of two people, Howard and Vicky, who vary substantially in the amounts of need in different areas that each must satisfy before the complete set of needs can be brought into harmony. As the figure emphasizes, Howard will have to expend much more energy and time than Vicky to have his dominant social or "belongingness" need (level 3) gratified before he can move on to satisfying higher needs. Vicky, in contrast, will probably be searching for opportunities to satisfy her ego or self-esteem need (level 5) much sooner than Howard will.

Figure 13-3 illustrates the situational character of the Maslow model. A person may be fulfilling his or her ego needs (level 4) when a fire suddenly breaks out. The safety need (level 2) may then become dominant, and behavior will be directed toward that goal until the safety need is gratified.

Achievement The need to get things done.

Affiliation The need to have relationships with others.

Power The need for control or influence, either directly over others or over the means of influencing others.

David C. McClelland— Achievement, Affiliation, Power

Several motives have been identified and studied by McClelland.[4] Three have particular relevance to organizations. The individual personality is assumed to be composed of a network of three basic motives, as outlined in Table 13-1. Given that people have the need for **achievement** (*n Ach*), the need for **affiliation** (*n Aff*), and the need for **power** (*n Pow*), it is possible to think of specific types of behavior that are likely to be associated with each kind of motive.

TABLE 13-1	The McClelland Three-Motive Table	
CONCEPT	**SYMBOL**	**DEFINITION**
The need for achievement	*n Ach*	The need for success as measured against some internalized standard of excellence
The need for affiliation	*n Aff*	The need for close interpersonal relationships and friendships with other people
The need for power	*n Pow*	The need for control or influence either directly over others or over the means of influencing others

McClelland found that *n Ach* people:

■ Choose goals that are both challenging and attainable.
■ Are not gamblers. They prefer to work in situations where they can directly influence the outcomes.
■ Tend to value achievement of the goal more than the rewards.
■ Have a strong desire for specific performance feedback.
■ Spend time thinking about performing high-level accomplishments.

People with affiliation needs, on the other hand, seek to find warm relationships and friendships. They are not as concerned as the higher achievers with getting ahead; rather, they enjoy jobs that have many interactions with other people. Some insights about *n Aff* people follow:

■ The ability to satisfy this need is influenced by both the person's environment and his or her interpersonal skills. Unfortunately, those who have great amounts of this need frequently have very poor interpersonal skills.
■ This need is often best satisfied by the grapevine and employee contact periods such as lunch and coffee breaks.
■ High *n Aff*s rate social relationships over task accomplishment. This can be bad for leadership and lead to blind conformity.
■ When *n Aff* is satisfied on the job, there is usually a decrease in turnover and absenteeism.

People who seek power also seek positions of power, influence over other people, and control of the environment. These are people who enjoy jobs that entail authority and power. In addition:

■ *n Pow* can be satisfied in a variety of ways (control of resources, information, or people).
■ *n Pow* is basically value-free—it is what people do with their power that is important.
■ *n Pow*s can frequently be counted on to take on extra work.
■ In organizational settings, *n Pow* is often divided into either *n* for personal power or *n* for institutional power. Personal power is dangerous because these people try to dominate. Institutional power is good because these people strive to develop effective organizational groups, work in an orderly way, believe in equitable rewards, and sacrifice for the good of the organization.

Frankl.

Victor E. Frankl

In what ways are Frankl's thoughts a theory of motivation?

The first two analytical motivation models dealt with motives and the type of motivated behavior that a manager may apply to other people. Frankl, in his

McClelland identified and studied motives, including the need for achievement. The Olympic athletes have a strong need for achievement and will spend hours and hours each day developing their athletic strengths and capabilities, practicing over and over again, until they become world champions.

Frankl — Man's search for Meaning

book *Man's Search for Meaning*[5] writes more directly to the individual person and his or her own motivation. Frankl believes, for example, that a great deal of a person's basic frustration derives from the inability to find what Frankl calls the "will to meaning." He believes that people have a basic need to do meaningful things, and, thus, when put into an environment that does not allow for meaning, people become frustrated and develop neurotic behavior. In this sense, Frankl is similar to Maslow, who feels that unsatisfied needs result in unhealthy behavior. Frankl urges his readers to search for the why of life, for if people can find a why, they can bear with almost any type of situation that confronts them. His theory of finding meaning rests on the values that pull, rather than the needs and drives that push, a person.

Frankl speaks from a very difficult personal experience; he was imprisoned in a Nazi concentration camp and had to suffer the inhumane German treatment of Jews during World War II. His insights come from experiencing personal trauma and observing men, women, and children under conditions that tested the question, Why go on living, why survive? Yet, Frankl believes that to most—not all—people, "the striving to find a meaning in one's life is the primary motivational force in man."

Most managers and organizational employees never face the intense hardships of life in a concentration camp. Yet, because the work world makes up a large percentage of adult life, is it not appropriate for managers to apply the insights from Frankl's "logotherapy" (search for meaning) to their jobs and employment relationships? Many recent developments in job engineering (enlarging a job, enriching a job, redesigning a job to match personal qualities) aim to generate more meaning in the job.[6] Even with these developments, Frankl's insights help, for he believes that you possess "the last of the human freedoms—the ability to choose one's attitude in a given set of circumstances." You ultimately determine the meaning of work. Managers should not be amazed, therefore, when "meaningfully developed jobs" are not viewed as meaningful by all workers.

Managers today are not as familiar with Frankl's ideas as they are with Maslow's and McClelland's. But Victor Frankl's concept of ultimate choice, a search for meaning and values, forms much of the conceptual framework for this book.

Environmental Motivation Theories

In the universal theories that we have been discussing, the emphasis has been on people, particularly on their inner states. In the environmental motivation theories, there is a shift in emphasis: Factors or conditions in the environment are viewed as contributing to a person's behavior, and the analysis, or diagnosis, thus moves away from individual needs. Two examples are the "two-factor" theory of Frederick Herzberg and the "conditioning and reinforcement" theory of B. F. Skinner.

Frederick Herzberg—Two-Factor Theory

Does the two-factor theory make sense to you?

At the time of Herzberg's work, many people (especially managers) believed that the satisfaction or dissatisfaction of a worker affected output.[7] "If we can make people satisfied, we'll increase their productivity" might have been the motivational strategy of many managers. When Herzberg asked people what factors made them satisfied and highly motivated or dissatisfied and bored on the job, he found two different sets of responses. For example, when people talked about a satisfying job, it contained an opportunity for

- Achievement
- Recognition
- The possibility of growth
- Advancement
- Responsibility
- The work itself

Motivating factors (Herzberg) Job conditions that lead to job satisfaction and high levels of motivation, i.e., achievement, recognition, the possibility of growth, advancement, responsibility, and the work itself; if absent, their lack will not lead to employee dissatisfaction.

Herzberg called such satisfiers the **motivating factors** of the work content.

The factors that people believe contributed to their dissatisfaction were very different:

- Pay and security
- Working conditions
- Interpersonal relations with supervisors, peers, and subordinates
- Company policies

Hygiene factors (Herzberg) Job conditions like salary; working conditions; interpersonal relationships with supervisors, peers, and subordinates; job security; and company policy. If present, they will not lead to employee satisfaction—they will just prevent dissatisfaction; if not present, their lack will lead to employee dissatisfaction.

These dissatisfiers Herzberg called **hygiene factors** and are located in the job context or environment.

The first set of factors in the two-factor theory, the motivators, are those job conditions that, when present, lead to job satisfaction and high levels of motivation and performance. If absent, however, their lack will not lead to employee dissatisfaction but to a neutral state of motivation.

The second set of factors, if present, will not lead to employee satisfaction; they will just prevent dissatisfaction. If not present, their lack will lead to employee dissatisfaction. The maintenance–hygiene factors are thus not motivators that would lead to high performance.

Global Application

Workers' Needs: The Same around the World

From Zambia to Finland, researchers are discovering that employees all over the world have more in common than anyone ever imagined. People have always assumed that the Japanese employee is different from the American employee and the American employee is different from the South African employee. Research is proving that there are many more commonalities than differences.

Herzberg did his original research into motivation in the early and mid-1950s using mainly American employees. His study showed that job satisfaction was achieved through motivators—the intrinsic elements of the job including achievement, recognition, the work itself, responsibility, advancement, and growth. Job dissatisfaction was the result of what Herzberg called Hygiene factors—the job's extrinsic elements including working conditions, salary, job security, company policy, supervisors. In general, what Herzberg found was that managers did not motivate their employees by giving them higher wages and more benefits. Employees are motivated by their own inherent need to be successful at challenging work. Herzberg stated, as a conclusion, that managers should not motivate employees to achieve, but rather give them opportunities for achievement so that they will be motivated.

Studies similar to Herzberg's were conducted throughout the world during the 1980s. The studies have shown that the Japanese workers are very similar to the American workers—they achieve job satisfaction through the motivators and job dissatisfaction through the hygiene factors. Studies done in Finland, Hun-

gary, Zambia, and Italy proved that workers in those countries are also very similar to American workers.

It is interesting to note that studies done in South Africa and India show that the managers in those countries are very similar to American workers, but the laborers are not. The laborers in South Africa and India derive job satisfaction from the hygiene factors. In South Africa, researchers studied 789 unskilled blacks from various tribes who were employed in various companies. The researchers theorized from their results that the workers were at such low levels and doing such demeaning work that there were no motivating or intrinsic elements to their jobs and thus the workers had to be dependent on hygiene factors for job satisfaction. If the workers had motivating factors in their jobs, the researchers felt that their results would have been similar to the American study. The researchers came to similar conclusions with the study conducted on 300 textile-mill workers in Bombay, India. The fact that the workers were in South Africa and India was not relevant. The relevant fact was that workers in both countries were in impoverished jobs. Workers in any country in impoverished jobs would have responded the same way.

If the workers in South Africa and India would have had motivating factors within their jobs, they too would have responded the same as the workers in America, Japan, Finland, Hungary, Zambia, and Italy.

Source: Frederick Herzberg, "Workers' Needs: The Same around the World," *Industry Week,* September 21, 1987, pp. 29–31.

In sum, satisfaction is not the opposite of dissatisfaction. The scale ranges from no satisfaction to satisfaction and from no dissatisfaction to dissatisfaction (see Table 13-2). Much of what we typically think of as satisfying simply has no effect or only works to eliminate dissatisfaction. The bottom line is that it takes meaningful and challenging work to truly satisfy and motivate employees.

TABLE 13-2	Relationships in the Two-Factor Theory		
FACTOR	STATE		MOTIVATIONAL FORCE
Maintenance or hygiene (extrinsic)	If present	$\longrightarrow$	0
	If absent	$\longrightarrow$	Dissatisfaction
Motivational (intrinsic)	If present	$\longrightarrow$	Satisfaction
	If absent	$\longrightarrow$	0

Behaviorist   *Pavlov.*

B. F. Skinner—Reinforcement Theory

Skinner is best known as an experimental psychologist whose interest is in the effect of an organism's behavior on the environment.[8] Skinner's explanation of man's behavior differs from those of Maslow, McClelland, and Frankl. Absent from Skinner's approach are concepts such as needs, values, drives, power, achievement, or affiliation. Present are terms like *operant learning, stimulus, response,* and *reinforcement.* To understand the contribution of Skinner to the managerial knowledge base of motivation, we need a very brief review of the history of behaviorism.

What is a behaviorist?

Behaviorists of the early 1900s were greatly influenced by the work of Ivan Pavlov. Behavior, to the classical conditioning scientists, was a reflex to a previous stimulus. Thus, to get the desired response, attention was directed at generating the right stimulus. It is easy to see how managers and supervisors would receive support from the scientific community when they assumed that money or some other stimulus brought about the desired performance (a response). Philosophers had said that man was an economic animal, behaviorists supplied a stimulus-response model with experimental findings, and organizational practitioners managed people under these assumptions.

Figures 13.4 and 13.5, on the other hand, show the Skinnerian basic model, as well as the application of the concepts to a management setting. Skinner is less concerned with the stimulus and possible internal states of man. He rejects the traditional S-R theory and places emphasis on **operant behavior**—that is, behavior that is voluntary, learned, and a function of its consequences. The behavioral focus is now the response and subsequent interaction with its environment. In the work world, managers have great influence over that environment.

Operant behavior
Behavior that is voluntary, learned, and a function of its consequences.

Reinforcement The consequences that follow a response; may be positive, negative, or do-nothing (extinction).

Positive reinforcement
Responding in a positive manner to a person's behavior through rewards.

Managers influence the environment through managing the reinforcement factors. By **reinforcement** we mean the consequences that follow a response. Managers may give **positive reinforcement** through reward sanctions (praise, money, more responsibility) and thus increase the probability that the behavior will be repeated. Or they may give negative reinforcement, an act that increases the probability that the desired behavior will occur by presenting an unfavorable consequence if it does not. For example, an employee may change her behavior to keep her shouting boss quiet. Punishment, a third intervention strategy, decreases the probability of the behavior recurring. Some managers favor a do-nothing approach, thinking that little harm will come from the situa-

$R_1 \longrightarrow R_{S_1} \longrightarrow R_1$
(Response) (Reinforcing (Response)
stimuli)

FIGURE 13-4 The Operant Conditioning (R-Type)

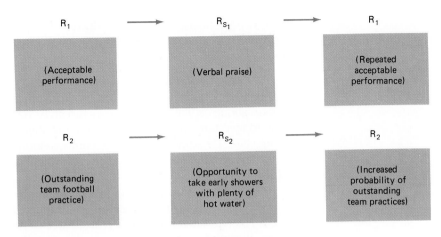

FIGURE 13-5 Example of R-Type Conditioning

Extinction Behavior not reinforced will eventually disappear.

tion. This approach, called **extinction**, does have an impact upon subsequent behavior. Responses not reinforced will eventually disappear.

Skinner believes positive reinforcement is the most effective long-run strategy. We have spent quite a bit of time and space explaining Skinner's behaviorism because we feel the ideas have direct application to the managerial world. You have experienced many events that you can recall now as illustrations of behaviorism: at home with your parents, in the classroom with your teacher, on the athletic field with your coach, or even in the work situation with your boss.

The use of rewards has become popular as a way of changing the behavior of others, and the following example shows that the idea of positive reinforcement can be developed into the greatest management principle in the world.

According to teacher and writer Michael LeBoeuf, the Greatest Management Principle in the World is "The things that get rewarded get done."[9] Or, in other words, "Managers who reward people for the right behavior get the right results."

Many critics blame the problems in today's economy on management's inability to focus on the long term. Managers have traditionally directed their attention to the short term, to maintaining an immediate cash flow, to showing a profit in this quarter, to getting a quick return on investment, to projecting a favorable image to Wall Street.

Investing in long-term projects (for example, plant and equipment) that would not show a return on investment for several quarters has been given low priority.

American factories have used old, high-maintenance-cost equipment while the Japanese have constructed totally new factories. In addition, American workers on the factory floor have been given little incentive to work. They are paid by the hour instead of by production; they are given little or no job security; and they receive pay increases only after strikes or grievances. American productivity has fallen.

LeBoeuf sees the subsequent decline in productivity as a direct result of the reward system used to motivate both managers and workers. Managers have been given bonuses based on short-term profits while workers have been paid to look busy, not to be productive. LeBoeuf thinks that all this can be changed by changing the reward system, and he makes the following suggestions:

1. *Reward solid solutions instead of quick fixes*. Evaluate people over longer time periods. Identify long-term goals. Invest in the future. Evaluate decisions about capital investment in research, new products, and new plants over longer time periods instead of tying them to quarterly budgets. Make money talk. Tie some of employee compensation to long-term profits.

2. *Reward risk taking* instead of risk avoidance. Encourage smart risks, not foolish chances.

3. *Reward applied creativity* instead of mindless conformity. The most important capital asset in any business isn't money, buildings, or equipment; it's ideas. Tolerate failure. Create a relaxed work environment to encourage creativity. Pay royalties. In most companies, employees must sign agreements that give patent rights for their innovations to the company. When the innovation is successful in the marketplace, the employee gets a pat on the back and management gets large bonuses.

4. *Reward decisive action*, not paralysis by analysis. Make quick decisions a habit. Weed away excess issues. Set a deadline for gathering and analyzing information. Brainstorm.

5. *Reward smart work* instead of busy work. Get the right person for the job. Give people the tools they need. Tell people why their jobs are important to the company. Beware of procedurocrats—people who don't care what is done but, rather, how it is done. Be flexible. If people have finished their work, let them go home. If they can do their work better at home, let them take it home. Results matter more than attendance.

6. *Reward simplification* instead of needless complication. Simplify structure. Simplify procedures. Simplify communications. Reward the simplifiers.

7. *Reward the quiet effective people* instead of squeaky wheels. Seek out the quiet heroes—the ones who do the best work. Tell them you appreciate their work. Take a sincere interest in your top performers as people, not just employees. This should help to create trust, which is necessary for the best teamwork. Ignore the complainers.

8. *Reward quality work* instead of fast work. Train everybody. Reward quality. Ask the person who does the job how to improve it.

9. *Reward loyalty* instead of turnover. Provide job security. Keep communication lines open. Promote from within. Invest in people's long-term growth. Offer fair pay and benefits.

Victor H. Vroom—Expectancy Theory

How does Vroom differ from others?

The Vroom model of motivation takes a different approach.[10] Victor Vroom developed his thoughts and published them in an important work in 1964. To Vroom, motivation is a process governing choices. For example, let us say that you have a desired goal. To get to that goal, you must perform some behavior. According to Vroom, you weigh the likelihood that the behavior or performance will enable you to reach the goal successfully. If you think or expect that a particular act will be successful, you are likely to select that type of behavior. Thus, this theory of motivation has been labeled the **expectancy model.**

Expectancy model If you think that a certain behavior or performance will allow you to reach your goal, you will select that behavior to act upon.

An example of career selection may illustrate the thinking of Vroom. There are many reasons why you might select one career over another. One could be that your parent is a very successful businessperson and steers you into that type of career or even offers you employment in the "family business." (Of course, your parent's occupation could also steer you away from the career—very few children whose parents are members of the clergy select the clergy as a career.) If your goal is to achieve success in business quickly, then the likelihood of your reaching that goal is much improved, as you might expect, if you work in your parent's firm rather than elsewhere.

Another idea in this motivational model is that people differ in how they see the desirability of certain organizational behavior. Not all workers in an organization place the same value on job security, or promotion, or high pay, or pleasant working conditions. Vroom believes that what is important is the perception and the value that the individual places upon the organizational behavior. Suppose a person wants to be promoted from his or her present job and feels that high performance is the best way of reaching that goal. It follows that the person will then perform in a superior way to get the promotion. But also assume that this worker knows of others who have performed in a superior way but have not received promotions. In fact, it appears to the worker that political behavior is more important than performance. Obviously, if promotion is important to this person, superior performance will not necessarily be the avenue chosen to achieve the promotion. Thus, Vroom highlights the importance of individual perceptions and assessments of organizational behavior. What the individual perceives as the consequences of the behavior is far more critical than what the manager thinks he or she should perceive. Vroom's model explains how people's goals influence their effort and that the behavior selected depends upon the person's assessment of its probable success in leading to the goal.

Research and study continue in the area of the expectancy theory of motivation. Social and behavioral scientists today believe that performance is a function of three things: the motivational levels of people, their abilities and traits, and their role perceptions—thus, the formula $P = f(M, A, R)$. From the material already presented about Vroom, we see that a person must want to perform; that is, a person must expect something worthwhile to come from performance. Vroom, Porter, and Lawler added that desire alone is not sufficient to explain performance; ability and capacity to perform must also be considered.[11] In addition, Porter and Lawler expanded the theory to include role perceptions, the person's idea of what he or she is supposed to do on the job. Examples will summarize this theory. (See also Figure 13.6.)

Charlie may have the motivation force (desire) to perform but not the abil-

FIGURE 13-6 Performance Factors–Expectancy Theory

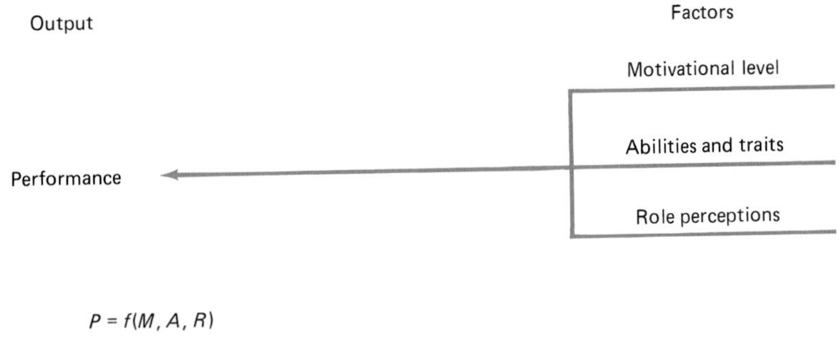

Output	Factors
	Motivational level
Performance ←	Abilities and traits
	Role perceptions

$P = f(M, A, R)$

Ethics Issue

How Much Time?

Overscheduling was a way of life in the 1980s as people tried to do more in less time. After downsizing, pressure to do more with a smaller staff was tremendous; the work was still there to do, but the managers who used to do the work were gone. Global competition and recessions added more pressure. There were other reasons for overscheduling: (1) It gave people a feeling of importance, a sense of self-worth, to be always busy, always in demand; (2) it made it easier to avoid problems at home, such as teenagers who think that their parents are dorks; (3) it allowed people to earn more money, to have a higher standard of living; (4) it allowed high achievers or overachievers the opportunity to be involved with everything; (5) it let managers keep work that they did not want to delegate to subordinates.

In the 1980s, calenders were filled to overflowing. People cut back on sleep, cut back on time spent with family, and often eliminated friends from their already-overbooked schedules. With the advent of car telephones, fax machines, and satelite communications, managers had no rest. The work followed them everywhere, day and night.

Experts feel the 1990s should turn out to be the decade of balance—balance between career, family, home, self. People are saying to themselves, "This is crazy," and are discovering that their children are growing up without them. People are heeding the warnings from experts in articles written in *Fortune, Business Week,* the *Wall Street Journal,* and so on, that their careers are hurting their children. People are realizing that there is more to life than working long hours at the office and then bringing more work home. (No one on his or her deathbed has ever said, "I wish I had spent more time at the office.") People are turning down promotions, turning down transfers, and looking for positions with flexible schedules so that they can spend time with family and friends and have some time for themselves. People are also looking for ways to give something back to society, to help solve the problems of homelessness and illiteracy.

People are giving up the extra money from working long hours to have more time to enjoy life. Others are purposefully scheduling more free time for themselves, more time with their families. Some are realizing that money is perhaps not the source of happiness, that perhaps family and friends are. Some are finding that a person does not need to drive a BMW to find true happiness; sometimes, a station wagon will do just as well.

Someone once said that if there is no time to sleep, there is no time to dream, no time to imagine, no time to create. How should time be used? How much time does a manager owe an organization? How much time should managers spend with their families? How much time should managers have for themselves?

Reference: Carol Hymowitz, "Trading Fat Paychecks for Free Time," *Wall Street Journal,* August 5, 1991, p. B1; Walter Kiechel III and Rebecca Lewin, "Overscheduled and Not Loving It," *Fortune,* April 8, 1991, pp. 105–7; Kenneth Labich, "Can Your Career Hurt Your Kids?" *Fortune,* May 20, 1991, pp. 38–56.

ity, whereas Susan has the desire and the ability but is confused about her role. Effective performance would seem to require the motivation, the ability and traits, and the clear understanding of the job demands. Proper organization, screening and training of employees, and communication of work demands all fall under the responsibility of the manager.

Some Nontraditional Theories

Fear

Fear is one motive for the behavior of many employees. This could be fear of losing a job and income; fear of punishment; fear of failure; or even fear of success. On a basic level, fear is beneficial—it keeps people from taking unnecessary risks and endangering their safety. Using fear as a motivator, however, could be destructive. For example, if a manager tries to use fear as a motivator, subordinates may build up hostility toward the manager and the organization. They may express this hostility in a variety of ways, including poor performance, disruption of production, insubordination, or destruction of company property.

Money

Money is another motive for behavior.[12] To low-income employees, money may represent the satisfaction of their basic needs for food, clothing, and shelter. For most employees, money represents security, power, independence, and prestige. For a few employees, money is more or less irrelevant. They have reached a level of comfort where additional money is not important. In addition, people's needs change over time. A tax accountant, for example, may decide to take a Sunday off during tax season to spend time with the family, even though he or she could earn more money by being at the office. Money, therefore, may be a strong motivator for some, and not a motivator at all for others.

Competition

Competition is a third motive for employees, particularly in the United States. Competition could be considered a national policy in the United States. At the very least, it is a strong part of the U.S. culture. In business, people compete for jobs, for job promotions, for recognition, in contests (particularly in sales), for bonuses, for awards.

These multiple explanations of behavior (from Maslow to fear) suggest that our present state of understanding possibly contains some limitations.

SOME LIMITATIONS OF THE MOTIVATIONAL MODELS

What are some limitations?

There are few "laws of motivation." Human subjects are difficult to research. Unlike animals, which are more amenable to experimentation and observation (because they have no choice), human beings are themselves an obstacle to rigorous scientific investigation. What we call knowledge, then, consists of observations that have been found to be in agreement by a number of researchers and scientists.

Answers to questions of behavior come from many sources. The work of Maslow has not had a great deal of empirical support and is viewed by some as a philosophical statement. Frankl's work comes from his own introspection and experiences and may or may not be applicable to all people. Nevertheless, the explanations of motivation that these two men offer can have strong valid-

Management Application

Incentives

Recent research suggests that incentives may actually be bad for business. Incentives tend to cause people to focus on the reward and not the task itself. The incentive becomes the goal and people work quickly to get the incentive, a reward that is external to the job—an extrinsic factor. When extrinsic factors (incentives) are stressed, people

- May feel controlled by the reward and believe they have lost autonomy
- May be less creative
- Tend to take fewer risks

On the other hand, when workers can determine for themselves many aspects of the job, intrinsic factors in the job (the work itself, achievement, responsibility) become more dominant, and the likelihood of satisfaction is enhanced.

In sum, if people perceive incentives as extrinsic factors, performance may suffer along with quality. Incentives should be used with caution. Unfortunately, many managers use rewards and bonuses to stimulate employees to achieve greater sales or profit goals.

Source: Alfie Kohn, "Incentives Can Be Bad for Business," *Inc.* (January 1988), pp. 93–94.

---

ity and practical usefulness as we attempt both to understand ourselves better and to practice explaining the behavior of others. The models described by Vroom and Skinner have had considerable research in support of the theory; Herzberg has performed a number of studies in support of his theory; and even though there is some question about the applicability of the research to other populations, the contributions from all these sources add insight into this most complex and difficult topic.

Managers should not assume that all things mean the same to all people. The behavior a person selects is dependent upon the behavior that is available. Thus, the environment is a very critical factor in motivation. And one of the most important facts for contemporary managers is that the environment of the 1990s is significantly different from that of any other period. As we mentioned in Chapter 1, the government assumed a new role in the 1970s in the field of equal employment opportunity, and it is likely that more equality will be the theme of groups previously denied acceptable options.

The number of women becoming managers increases daily. These women come into an environment that contains stereotypes and prejudices aimed only at them.[13] The behavioral alternatives for women are not the same as those for men—the workplace has certain acceptable and unacceptable expectations for men and for women managers. Eventually, these expectations will change, but today's manager must realize that people once barred from occupational positions may respond differently to the work environment. The theories of Maslow, Skinner, and Vroom place emphasis upon either the individual perceptions or the consequences of behavior. Although women may respond with the same motivational processes, the environment for their behavior must be understood. The behavior available in the environment also depends upon the individual's perception of the value of that behavior, or the relation that the behavior has to the goal that is to be achieved. The topic of motivation, therefore, is an interrelationship type of topic, in that the worker and the job environment are continually in interplay, one with the other.

Not all people consider work their central life interest. There is a temptation, when talking about the management of motivated behavior, to assume that the work world is the dominant place for motivation. For a great many, their work is their life (some have even been called "workaholics"). For some, work or their job is only a means toward some more important goal.[14] Some workers prefer a more routine, dull job if the pay for that work is high. For others, however, their sense of growth and satisfaction comes from associations and activities outside their workplace. If a majority of the rising generation of workers and managers should fall into this last group, the notion of "motivation at work" will be difficult to translate into action.

SUMMARY

We began this chapter by explaining why a manager must be concerned with the motivation of subordinates: The manager must acquire the direct efforts of workers to reach personal or organizational goals.

With that necessity in mind, we considered a basic question: Can the motivation of people be managed, and can managers know and control themselves sufficiently to get desired results from others? We hope that this discussion stimulated you to find out something more about motivation and that our six generalizations about what is known or assumed in this area will be of value to you.

Following that section, we summarized six theoretical models and considered some of their limitations. The various approaches to the concept of motivation were included for two reasons: First, these theories illustrate that no one theory of motivation exists. These theoretical models, all of which have merits and limitations, are current attempts to sort out and order the complex elements inherent in the concept of motivation. They illustrate the kinds of analyzing processes others have used in dealing with motivational problems.

Second, these models give practicing managers a place to begin their own diagnoses of particular problems. Since the manager deals in a changing environment, no one model could work even if it were completely true at the time of its creation. The manager must literally contrive relevant models. The motivational material provided in this chapter provides a basis on which to begin.

KEY TERMS	**Motivation** The inner state that energizes or moves behavior toward activity. **Hierarchy** Needs are in a specific order so that one level of need satisfaction must be met before a person progresses to the satisfaction of a higher level of need.	**Achievement** The need to get things done. **Affiliation** The need to have relationships with others. **Power** The need for control or influence, either directly over others or over the means of influencing others.

Motivating factors (Herzberg) Job conditions that lead to job satisfaction and high levels of motivation, i.e., achievement, recognition, the possibility of growth, advancement, responsibility, and the work itself; if absent, their lack will not lead to employee dissatisfaction.

Hygiene factors (Herzberg) Job conditions like salary; working conditions; interpersonal relationships with supervisors; peers, and subordinates; job security; and company policy. If present, they will not lead to employee satisfaction—they will just prevent dissatisfaction; if not present, their lack will lead to employee dissatisfaction.

Operant behavior Behavior that is voluntary, learned, and a function of its consequences.

Reinforcement The consequences that follow a response; may be positive, negative, or do-nothing (extinction).

Positive Reinforcement Responding in a positive manner to a person's behavior through rewards

Extinction Behavior not reinforced will eventually disappear.

Expectancy model If you think that a certain behavior or performance will allow you to reach your goal, you will select that behavior to act upon.

STUDY ASSIGNMENTS

1. What lessons about motivation can be learned from the opening case?

2. If behavior is so unpredictable, why would the study of motivation be beneficial for a manager?

3. From a managerial perspective, what is the relationship between motivation and performance?

4. What are some of the generalizations about motivation? Why is it important to have an understanding of these generalizations before studying the various motivational models?

5. Compare and contrast Maslow's Needs Hierarchy and Herzberg's Two-Factor Theory.

6. According to Frankl, why is it important for people to find meaning in their work? What does work mean to you? What motivates you to work?

7. How does B. F. Skinner's approach to motivating behavior and performance differ from the approaches suggested by McClelland and Frankl?

8. Discuss how a manager might utilize Vroom's concept of motivation to influence work behavior.

9. What is Expectancy Theory? Give an example of how Expectancy Theory has worked in your own life.

10. What are some of the limitations of the various models of motivation? Why have managers chosen to use some nontraditional motivational approaches to influence individual job performance?

Cases for Discussion

I. WORKING IN THE SILICON VALLEY

In the early 1980s, the Silicon Valley region of California had developed a reputation as one of the principal centers for high-technology research and production. It was populated with hundreds of new entrepreneurial and established firms that were involved in electronics, computers, software, and biotechnology. There were the established high-tech firms of Hewlett-Packard and Honeywell, as well as the young growth companies of Apple, Intel, Microsoft, and Genentech. In addition, there were hundreds of other venture-capital firms that appeared and disappeared overnight. These firms operated in an environment that was dynamic, highly competitive, and hostile.

Because of this high-tech reputation, the region had attracted a unique group of individuals who demonstrated an ability to be adaptive and extremely productive in this demanding environment. In the early years of the valley's development, these individuals were driven to incredible performance levels because of the desire to achieve success and wealth. But many observers noted that the real motivator for most of these individuals was the work itself.

Although these individuals may have had different occupational orientations ranging from venture capitalists to technological junkies to computer wizards to marketing geniuses, they did have a great deal of commonality in their values, experiences, and life styles. Typically, they were workaholics, who were motivated by their own self-interest. They were committed to working long hours just for the "fun of it," and they subordinated family and life in general to the pursuit of work-related goals and rewards.

There were substantial rewards in the form of money, fame, and material possessions, but as one marketing executive noted about her experience, "The reality for most of the individuals working in the valley is that they have no real life or activities outside their work. Their identities are based on where they work and their titles." The life style of the individuals working in the valley was typically narrow in focus. There was work and more work, with the only accepted alternative being drugs, exercise, or more work. They had but one fear, that of falling behind. In the long run, there was a personal cost as the pressures caused countless business failures, high turnover rates, divorces, drug abuse, and "burnout." And to top it all off, in 1984, the bubble burst for the Silicon Valley.

By 1984, many firms in the valley discovered that they had lost their competitive edge. The firms were taking a beating in the marketplace, and as a consequence, 34,000 individuals working in the Silicon Valley lost their jobs over the next two years. But for most people, there was a problem that went beyond lost jobs. The pace and the commitment demanded of the people had finally taken its toll. After years of struggling for material and technological success, much of the valley's population was exhausted. Many began asking that old question: "Is that all there is?"

Employers in the valley soon found that many of their personnel were working at a slower pace or simply dropping out. For instance, one highly successful entrepreneur gave up on the microchip business and started a toy store. By the late 1980s, success and work were no longer central concerns or motivating factors for many working in the valley. Rather, they were becoming concerned about improving the quality of their lives.

For businesses operating in the valley, this situation represented a serious problem. They realized that if they were to meet the competitive challenges from the Japanese, they needed to find some new means to motivate the performance and creativity of their employees. They knew that the old carrots of wealth and success were not working any more.

II. CONTRASTING APPROACHES—MERCK AND GENENTECH

Typically, firms operating in the pharmaceutical industry devote considerable resources and efforts to the development of new drugs. Research in this industry is a costly activity. It requires considerable managerial attention, particularly with respect to the complex task of motivating and sustaining the performance of highly skilled individuals.

In the research environment, performance is often difficult to manage because of the nature of the development process. Usually, the successful introduction of a new drug is the result of years of effort and research. The people involved in such an effort constantly live with uncertainty, experience numerous failures, must continually deal with government red tape, and face the ever-present possibility that the competition will make the critical discovery before they do. They also realize that in the end, their success will be only temporary. They know that they will move on to another project while others assume the ultimate responsibility for introducing "their" drug into the marketplace.

Merck is one of the premier pharmaceutical companies, and its management addresses this motivational problem by making a concerted effort to continually acknowledge the contribution of its researchers to the long-term success of the firm. For instance, researchers are even allowed and encouraged to conduct "underground and unofficial" research. This emphasis is not surprising, given that most of Merck's top management positions, including the CEO's position, are filled by former researchers.

Merck uses a variety of motivational approaches that go beyond merely ensuring that its researchers receive the best pay in the industry. Since Merck recruits most of its researchers from universities, its research facilities not only look like campuses but also are operated with the seriousness and atmosphere of an academic environment. This approach has enabled Merck to become one of the most admired corporations in the United States and has resulted in a turnover rate of less than 5 percent a year among Merck's researchers.

In contrast, Genentech is a relatively new business whose survival has depended on venture capital and major pharmaceutical breakthroughs by its researchers. The firm lacks the product depth, finances, and resources of established firms, such as Merck. But like Merck, it faces the problem of influencing the performance of its researchers.

To attract and motivate researchers, Genentech's management has attempted to create an environment in which it is "fun" to work. Managers use spontaneous and highly visible rewards such as the "Genen-Checks" (on-the-spot cash rewards for exceptional performance). When Genentech received FDA approval for its clot-dissolving drug Activase, the firm held a large party, complete with fireworks, toasts, "Clot-Buster" T-shirts, and an option of 100 shares of stock for every employee.

Despite those efforts, Genentech found that it could not be as effective as Merck in retaining research personnel. Ironically, many of Genentech's researchers have chosen to use the firm's first major success, Activase, as a springboard for new career and employment opportunities.

Chapter 14

Groups

Learning Objectives

1. **Describe** how groups form, and state three of their functions.
2. **Name** two types of groups, and give personal examples of each.
3. **Identify** four characteristics of all groups.
4. **Explain** how individual behavior can be changed in the context of a group.
5. **Describe** three ways of analyzing groups.
6. **Give** three properties that an ideal, highly effective work group possesses.
7. **Give** three ways a manager uses the organizational authority to influence group behavior.

"I WISH you the best of luck in this job. It about got me down. Perhaps a younger man will have more patience, or whatever it takes." Tony Risso was headed back to Detroit, still in personnel work, but with a new company. The Adam-Carey Company had denied his request for transfer, so Tony had contacted some of his friends in Detroit to find a new job. Harv Bell was his replacement.

"I think my problems began even before we opened our plant here. The company spent a bundle planning the new plant and making this move—we wanted to find a locale free of the labor problems we were having in Warren, Michigan. We wanted a town where the tax base was suitable and rail transportation was good, and we wanted an inexpensive supply of untrained people. The industrial development people and the Chamber of Commerce really put on a show. You'll soon realize that this section of Kentucky is a recreational area that's expected to grow. We became the major employer in the area, and with a brand-new plant, you'd think we wouldn't have had the problems we had."

"Tony, why don't you spell out some of those problems and give me some idea of what I'm walking into."

"Well, the first problem was housing—they had some bad weather down here, and it delayed construction on our houses. Most of us left our wives and families in Detroit and rented motel rooms. Then, when the weather got better, you'd expect the construction people to get busy, right? When the weather

got better, the construction foreman had trouble getting workmen because the fish were biting! That should have been my first clue that the so-called available nonunion labor in the area might not be available on our terms.

"The next problem was the trouble with the wilderness weirdos—you know, the hairy ones who complained about our proposed source of water and the possible pollution to the water and their damn fish. Well, all that trouble with the scenic bunch cost us two and a half months in delays for getting the plant ready to go.

"So, we finally get open with a big parade, the kids from the consolidated school band, a talk by the mayor and the industrial development guy from the governor. We had an open house for everyone in the area, and I thought that things were looking up and that everything might work out, right? Harv, what happened to me shouldn't have happened to anyone! I mean, I've been in the business a long time. I've attended courses at Wayne State in collective bargaining, labor relations, and all the rest. How come no one told me that the first big labor action I was going to get here was a wildcat strike? And this so-called nonunion, available, semiskilled work force not only didn't know what a wildcat strike was—they didn't even care! A small group of them got sore, and before I could get to the problem, they walk off the job to go fishing or whatever they do around here when they walk off a job. To make a short story long, Harv, the labor situation is touch and go.

"Well, after we got the labor situation toned down, I conducted a survey among our fifty-six first- and second-level managers to see what kind of development they needed. Most of those men are from around this area: southern Ohio, West Virginia, Tennessee, and, of course, Kentucky. There's a mixture of college and noncollege, and some of the younger men have two-year associate degrees from the community college. What the company needed, so these guys thought, were management training courses. I checked with Detroit, and they said to go ahead and use local talent if I could find any. And I did find some capable guys at the state university, in their business school. These profs came down and put on a two-day program for supervisors on both shifts for six weeks.

"I really enjoyed those guys. Yes, sir, they did a good job. Even though only one of the profs was from Kentucky, our first- and second-level supervisors really got to know them, enjoyed meeting with them for two hours at a stretch, and even looked forward to their visits each week. When the training was over, I invited the profs to dinner and asked them to give me all the feedback they could.

"They said that the plant contained two different cultures. One was an industrial culture (primarily the men from Detroit) where the emphasis was on performance, efficiency, hard work, monetary rewards, status, position, argumentation, directness, and openness. Most of the workers and many of the first- and second-line managers, on the other hand, were of a different culture—one where fishing, tobacco, and politics were more important than the Detroit Tigers; where Baptists and religious principles are a primary force in the development of attitudes and values; and where, on a bright, sunny, clear day in early spring, they will go fishing. These people don't like to be yelled at, and they don't like the abrasive character of the Detroit managers. The profs said that we were going to continue to have trouble and resistance to our efforts at productivity because we were dealing with a nonindustrial culture.

"And for what it's worth, Harv, I will pass on one bit of information that your friends in Cleveland won't believe. Bourbon County, Kentucky, is a dry county. No alcohol can be sold here. Harv, you have my blessings. I'll think of you when I'm in Detroit." ∎

Tony Risso, personnel manager, wanted to be a good manager. He had probably been effective in Detroit; yet, his experience in Kentucky overwhelmed him, and resignation from the Adam-Carey Company seemed the only way to cope—a very expensive way, since he would sacrifice seniority, pension rights, and other fringe benefits to keep his sanity, emotional stability, and self-respect. Could Tony have avoided such a problem?

The professors from the state university described an aspect of organizational life foreign to Tony. They talked of different cultures in the plant, cultures that might explain why the workers responded in unpredictable ways. Perhaps worker behavior seemed unpredictable only because of management's erroneous concept of what people's behavior should be. If the plant management had a better understanding of how individual behavior is modified and influenced by groups, intragroup processes, and group culture, many of the frustrations and conflicts might have disappeared.[1]

In this chapter, we first define what a group is. Second, we discuss how groups function. After the concept of "group" is established, we consider some ways of understanding group behavior. Finally, we turn from the analysis of groups to the possibilities open to managers for solving problems resulting from group activity.

A DESCRIPTION OF GROUPS

Like individuals, groups come in many sizes, shapes, and forms. A few examples will illustrate this point. You might be in a car pool with others who live in your neighborhood; you might be on a bowling team or spend lunch hours with an exercise group. You might be part of the 3rd district crime squad in the police department, the defensive secondary of a football team, the renal intensive care group in a hospital, or the executive committee of the plant. In

Ethics Issue

Go, Team, Go!

Graduate business programs in the United States have caught the spirit. The latest innovation in education is teamwork, and the business deans say they are reflecting the changing demands from corporations. More and more firms want their managerial recruits to be team players, to understand the bigger picture, and to be willing to give and take with their ideas when involved with group projects. Narrow specialization is giving way to understanding the broader aspects of leadership and managing a business. The concept of interdependence and overlapping among all the parts and units is now very popular.

Stephen R. Covey, in his book *The 7 Habits of Highly Effective People,* speaks of the importance of his Maturity Continuum. To improve their personal and interpersonal effectiveness, people need to move from a childlike state of dependence to a healthier state of independence and, finally, to a mature state of interdependence. Team participation is one of the ways for people to learn the value of interdependence. There is a point, however, that needs to be addressed before all organizations subscribe to total team management. Not all people are good at team playing, nor do all people want to become team members.

In many college classes, the instructor will assign students to task, project, or work groups or teams. These teams are usually leaderless—

no one person is given the authority to organize or direct the team toward its mission. The teams may have to write a project paper, and the grade may be a group grade rather than an individual one.

In a particular case course in business policy, an accounting major came to the professor and asked that she be allowed to do the case writeup on her own. She was seeking admission to a prestigious graduate school and felt that a high grade point average would help her application. From experiences in past classes, she knew that other students did not approach team projects as she did; some of them did not attend meetings, did not do work assigned to them, and openly stated that they would be glad to receive a passing grade of C.

The instructor faced a dilemma. Should she insist that the accounting major be on a team so as to learn the value of team play and risk receiving a lower grade on the paper, or should the student be allowed to do the project on her own and probably receive a higher grade?

Is the dilemma of the faculty member potentially a dilemma for organizations?

References: Stephen R. Covey, *The 7 Habits of Highly Effective People* (New York: Simon & Schuster, 1989), p. 51; "Hey, I Hear You Made Variety in LBOs," *Business Week,* August 19, 1991, p. 113; Alan Deutschman, "The Trouble with MBAs," *Fortune,* July 29, 1991, pp. 67–79.

Group   A unit of two or more people who work together to achieve a common purpose or goal.

Formal groups   A group given structure, a mission, authority, and legitimacy by an organization.

Informal groups   A work group that emerges from the formal group. It has no legitimacy, no authority, but has structure and mission; it fills the gap of the formal work.

What is a formal work group?

some cases, you're in a group as part of your job—it is your assignment; in some instances, you belong to a group for friendship or social reasons. For our purposes, we will focus primarily on work groups, and thus our definition of a **group** is: a unit of two or more people who work with one another to achieve a common purpose or goal.[2] In most organizations, you will find two general types of groups: **Formal groups** are those created by the organization to accomplish the goal of the firm, and **informal groups** are those created by the people themselves to meet their mutual needs and interests. A few examples will add meaning to these definitions.

Illustrations of Group Types

Formal Work Group[3]

Assume that you are part of a formal work group of five members, all of whom are charged with the responsibility of developing a feasibility study for a housing development corporation in a rapidly growing metropolitan area. The group is formed in September and has a December 30 deadline for the study report.

In this work group are five different people: Tom is on loan from the city commissioner's office and has expertise in budgets. Katharine, who has just completed a two-month scholarship training program in Washington sponsored by HUD (Department of Housing and Urban Development), is an assistant director of a housing corporation in the city. Jerry is on loan from the county planning commissioner. Carol, a volunteer worker and homemaker, has a great deal of knowledge and experience in developing feasibility studies for funding purposes. And Paul is a volunteer representative from the university, whose primary interest is housing. Of the five, therefore, you have three paid workers and two volunteers on this temporary formal work group committee with the responsibility to produce the study report. The project group is to report to the director of the local OEO (Office of Economic Opportunity) unit, and the work group's first organizational meeting is supposed to develop its structure.

One of the hired employees of the city is designated as chairperson of the group and conducts the first meeting. (The agenda items he develops deal with the description of the task at hand, the assignment of specific duties, and the planning of work to meet the deadline.) When the group meets for the first time, the two women already know each other from previous associations on other committees, as do the men from the planning commission and the budget section. Only the volunteer from the university is unknown to the other four. The agenda is discussed, the issues and missions of the committee are clarified, the resources necessary to get the job done are identified and committed, the work is allocated and the responsibilities are assumed, and an overall plan is generated, with early checkpoint dates for feedback and correction if necessary. This sounds like a well-oiled and fundamentally effective work group. The people are committed; they sense the importance of the feasibility study for housing; they recognize the need for a leader; the leader has been able to emphasize the importance of the mission; and on paper it appears that all will run smoothly. This is a formal group. It has structure, a mission, authority from the OEO, organizational legitimacy, a leader, and people willing to work toward goals and objectives.

Formal work groups exist in all organizations. The formal work group may be a team that puts together a special project; a team that assembles refrigerators; or a group of employees who work together to plan work flow.

Informal Work Group[4]

What is an informal work group?

Three teams, of three men each, are working in the pasteurizing section of a large brewery. These three teams are organized on the basis of the technology of the company: The cans of beer come out of the pasteurizer, are inspected, go to one station for weighing, and go to another station for packing and shipping. Every thirty minutes, the men at these stations rotate, so that no particular group is overcome by the boredom and routine of the operation. Charlie is a junior-college student who has come in for the summer months and apparently was very eager to find the job. He received instructions about work methods from the foreman who is responsible for the three stations on the pasteurizer and the other stations up and down the assembly line. So far, we have described a formal work group.

At first, Charlie works very rapidly, perhaps trying to prove to the foreman that he is worthy of the job. But Charlie's efforts are somewhat embarrassing to the other men on the merry-go-round operation, for Charlie weighs cans far too fast and creates a backlog for Hal; then Charlie packs cans too fast and creates a backlog for Sam; and so on. During the second break period, Rick, who has worked in the brewery for years and was once a union officer in the Teamsters, gets Charlie off to the side and gives him some of the "unofficial rules" of the work team. Rick explains to Charlie that the rest of the guys have to work there for months and years, whereas Charlie may be working there only for the summer. They do not want Charlie to work at his own rate. As Rick says to Charlie, "It's a good job and a good deal, and the union protects us and gives us this good deal. You owe it to us to do it our way." If Charlie agrees to go along with Rick's suggestions and gets accepted by the other members, he is thus a member of both the formal and the informal work group. This is an informal group. It has structure, a mission, no authority from the formal organization, no legitimacy from management, a leader, and people willing to accept unofficial norms of behavior.

Characteristics of Groups

We could go on with many other illustrations of formal and informal groups—family, fraternity, Girl Scout troop, bridge club. You would find, however, certain characteristics basic to all groups. These are listed here for clarification. In general, all groups have

- Leaders
- Followers
- A desire to get some "work" done

Specifically:

- Most formal groups will also contain informal groups.
- Some informal groups may contain members from different formal groups.

Having given a brief description of formal and informal groups, we now ask, What needs (or functions) do groups meet? At least two will be mentioned.

- Groups satisfy individual needs.
- Groups set norms.

Satisfying the Individual's Needs

Groups can meet a range of needs for individuals. You may not realize the array of needs met by groups when you hire into an organization. If you hire in as an hourly worker, for example, one group you may choose to join is the union. You can see from Figure 14-1 the many personal needs that might be met by group affiliation: political, economic, social.[5] Some of these reasons may sound familiar to you; in fact, they can be viewed as extensions of the motivational models from the previous chapter. Groups can meet your physical safety, social, esteem, or actualizing needs or your achievement, affiliation, or power needs. To say that groups may satisfy an individual's needs and expectations is to state the obvious. Three statements, therefore, may serve as a brief summary of the ideas just presented:

- Individuals want the group to help them produce some kind of measurable product.
- Individuals want the group to help them achieve satisfaction in what they do.
- Individuals have a need to grow. They expect that the group will facilitate this desire.

FIGURE 14-1   Reasons People Join Unions

POLITICAL	ECONOMIC	SOCIOPSYCHOLOGICAL
Power To offset the power of management and provide countervailing power to the workers	**Wages** To gain better wages; to ensure equity among all who perform similar work	**Alienation** To provide a sense of completeness to workers who feel separated from their tools and craft (unions fill the gap and give a link to the past)
Decision Making To provide an avenue for communicating ideas and inputs into the decision-making process	**Living** To improve a worker's standard and quality of living through some control and input on issues of wages and working conditions	**Belongingness** To give workers a group to identify with; to give them a sense of group solidarity
Class Struggle To offer the working class a way to redistribute the wealth of the capitalistic system	**Security** To ensure that job movement (upward, transfers, or layoffs) follows some procedure that is fair to all workers; to protect older, senior workers from arbitrary dismissal	**Inner Peace** To protect workers from arbitrary management actions and produce a sense of inner peace by reducing stress and fears
Justice To provide for due process so that justice prevails over worker disputes		**Fulfillment** To allow some to move into union leadership roles; these new roles might give people a sense of personal fulfillment
Protection To create through collective power protection from arbitrary management decisions		
Ideological To be part of an international movement		

Management Application

When Labor Acts Like Management

There was a time when managers would say, "Jump," and labor's response would be, "How high?" The roles each played in the workplace were quite clear—managers made decisions and labor did the work. But in the 1990s, the role of labor is evolving into something more than what it has been in the past. Labor is playing a bigger role in decision making and in determining how things get done. More significantly, labor is slowly acquiring a larger and larger ownership position in the business.

Employees currently own about $150 billion worth of the firms they work for (the ownership stake is higher if employee pension funds are counted). Employee equity holdings in some firms are high enough that the firms are beginning to consider placing employee/shareholder representatives on the firm's board of directors. However, few executives and directors have thought about the impact an employee/shareholder board member would have on the organization's decision-making and operating processes.

When employees have a financial stake in a firm, they expect to be included in managerial decision making. The easiest way for management to respond to this expectation is to utilize the team concept and to push for greater overall employee involvement. Employees hold about 40 percent of the struggling America West airline. To keep America West in the air, the employees have taken pay cuts, worked more free hours, and participated in decision making. Not every decision made is collaborative, however, and decision-making conflicts continue.

Some observers note that the owner/employees of firms at risk, like America West, are more inclined to endure hardships so that they may see their investment in the firm grow in the long run. As one America West employee explained, "It's like a marriage—you just don't walk out at every provocation or conflict."

Even when employee ownership is not a factor, employees will participate in the decision-making and implementation process when given the opportunity. At AT&T Credit, morale and operating costs were so bad in 1989 that management was willing to do anything to turn the operation around. A group of employees was chosen to develop and implement a restructuring plan. Observers note that when employees are empowered with decision-making responsibility, they show a greater commitment to and appreciation for what needs to be done. AT&T Credit found that by involving a group of workers in the restructuring process and minimizing management involvement in implementing the plan, operating costs were drastically reduced and productivity rose.

This is a significant trend in labor management practice and a change in the way groups operate in the workplace. Labor and management are striving to eliminate their adversarial relationship and are moving toward creating a working partnership committed to the success and competitiveness of the firm.

References: Claudia Deutsch, "Where the Cadre Sets the Pattern," *New York Times,* June 30, 1991, p. F23; Eric Schine, "America West Is Running Out of Other People's Money," *Business Week,* June 24, 1991, p. 48.

Setting Group Norms

Just as individuals have "expectations" regarding what the group will provide him or her, the group also has expectations regarding the individual's behavior.[6]

1. The group expects the individual to obey the "house rules." Each group has some idea of what should or should not be done by its members. It has an idea of the range of acceptable behavior (norms) for its members.[7] There are definite house rules or norms, and for a group to maintain its character, the behavior of its members must conform to certain expectations. The group has an expectation of the allowable behavior for a newcomer. Whereas a long-time member of a group is allowed to deviate from the group norms in personal behavior, a newcomer must conform. If there is deviation, the group will probably respond with negative sanctions—punishment.

2. The group expects individuals to support its sanctions. There are various kinds of sanctions in a group, ranging from violent physical sanctions (such as punching) to subtle social sanctions (such as cooling out). Members must accept the value of even extreme sanctions, for they are expected to realize the importance sanctions play in maintaining the character of the group.

If a group of secretaries, for example, is part of a work group and has established some informal and unofficial house rules, the secretaries might treat a "rate buster" as a social outcast; this outcast will be unable to find anyone to talk to at lunch. In many, many ways, the group will accept and implement the sanctions that have been created to maintain the character and integrity of the group.

3. The group expects the individual to give up some individual rights to be a member. People voluntarily give up many individual rights to affiliate with a group. They agree to come in on time, to follow the rules and regulations of the group, to work within the structure of the group, and to conduct themselves with some degree of responsibility and honesty. If they violate any of these rules and regulations, they are apt to find themselves ostracized by the group.

A popular, contemporary organizational expansion of the concepts about groups leads us to a discussion of culture, particularly corporate culture. You were introduced to groups and culture in the opening case. Recall that the university professors talked about two different cultures within the plant—cultures that conflicted with one another.

Culture Those acquired and learned behaviors which have persisted in human groups through traditions.

Culture is that set of shared beliefs, norms, customs, key values, and meaning that people accept and act out.[8] Organizations have a culture that is unique to them: The set of beliefs, customs, and rituals of IBM, Avon, Delta, and your local bank differ from each other. This unique organizational culture, called corporate culture, is a product of both the shared meanings that emerge from the social interactions of people and the managerial efforts to create desired patterns of meaning.[9] Managers influence these patterns through rules, procedures, policy statements, and personal behavior. As role models, they serve as symbols to others. For example, Eddie Rickenbacker, famous World War I ace pilot, shaped the corporate culture of Eastern Airlines; so, too, with Walt Disney and Henry Ford.

With this introductory description of groups (types, characteristics, and functions), we now turn to a deeper look at groups.

Homan-Whyte AIS

THE ANALYSIS OF GROUPS

In most of the illustrations given so far in this chapter, you have been asked to assume the role of an individual going into a group or of a member of the group. Suppose, however, you are a manager in an organization and are interested in analyzing or understanding the groups that report to you. What kinds of insights are available to help you understand what groups are, how they operate, and how they can be managed?

We have already spoken of the two principal components of the behavior of any work group. Repeated in simpler form, these are (1) the behavior that is required by the formal structure to get the job done and (2) the behavior that emerges above and beyond this required behavior. In the first case, required behavior is set by the organization and is usually known. It is the emergent or informal behavior that is most puzzling to the manager. Here are some models for analysis that might help solve the puzzle.

A-I-S Method

Homan Whyte

Both George C. Homans[10] and William F. Whyte[11] have written extensively about the elements of group behavior, especially the element of emerging group behavior. They have identified three basic ingredients for this emerging behavior: activities, interactions, and sentiments.

Activity Something that a group or individual does.

Interaction Communication between people.

An **activity** is just that—something that the group or the individual does. An **interaction** is a communication between people. There are verbal and nonverbal (for example, body language) communications and interactions. You have frequently had someone speak to you or tell you of an event and, without your giving any verbal response, seen that the other person is able to "read" your reaction. Your reaction might be a frown, a raised eyebrow, a snarl, a laugh, or a smile. What is important is that you are giving feedback to the other person and he or she is interpreting and reading that feedback. Thus, interactions are either verbal or nonverbal communications.

Sentiment An idea, a belief, or a feeling about something.

The last element is the **sentiment;** this is an idea, a belief, or a feeling that you have about something. A synonym for sentiment might be attitude or opinion—it is a liking or a preference you have.

In all groups, individuals perform activities, some required and some not required (emergent). Simultaneously, they are communicating with one another (interactions) about their sentiments toward the activities. Homans and Whyte suggest that there is a mutual dependence among these three elements (Figure 14-2) and that it might work in the following way.

Assume that the sentiments people have can be classified as either positive or negative. For example, one person might have a very positive attitude toward baseball, whereas another might have a very negative attitude toward baseball. (This illustration could also apply to attitudes toward communism, politics, religion, children, abortion, alcohol, smoking, AIDS, or anything else.) Now if these two people, one with a positive and one with a negative attitude, are put into a work situation where they are performing similar activities, you may find that the interactions they have are kept to a bare minimum because of

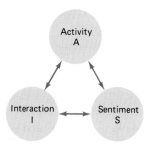

FIGURE 14-2 The Mutual Dependence among Activity, Interaction, and Sentiment

the differences in their sentiments. If, on the other hand, you put two people together who start out with neutral sentiments, it follows that the association in similar activities will probably result in increased interactions, which then may develop into a positive sharing of sentiments. It is a two-way street. The activities of two people affect their interactions, and the interactions affect the activities and the sentiments that each person holds.

Exchange Theory

What is exchange theory?

Another model for analyzing groups is given by Homans; it has been classified as a kind of exchange theory.[12] Homans sees groups as always having a purpose; they exist to satisfy certain needs. He believes that it is possible to describe behavior using economic terms, such as value, cost, profit, and marginal utility—that is, it is possible to think of behavior between two people as consisting of activities that are valued but are achieved at a cost. Each group enters into exchange relationships to achieve what is wanted.

For example, assume that we are thinking of two people in a workplace, Harry and Wanda. Assume further that Harry is the manager and boss of Wanda. Harry will reward Wanda for performing according to the standards of the organization, but the reward obviously costs money. Wanda will reward Harry for the compensation by producing so many units per hour, or so many sales per day, or whatever the productive unit is. But as we mentioned earlier, there are many nonmonetary and social rewards, such as acceptance, recognition, and pride. Harry can now reward Wanda by being more pleasant to her—in other words, by giving her a feeling of approval and acceptance. This effort costs Harry time and thought, but Wanda may respond well and reward Harry for the effort by showing greater loyalty to the company and greater cooperation and interest in what she is doing. Obviously, this costs Wanda effort. If the reward outweighs the efforts, each has a psychic profit. This same kind of scheme can be used in a nonboss-subordinate relationship; it can be used between individuals.

Although the example of exchange theory described two individuals (Harry and Wanda), the concept can be used to analyze behavior within a group. If your own work group is not performing as expected, you might look at the behavior of individual members to find out what each values and what costs and profits each sees in the interpersonal relationships. A particular work group may not value certain organization goals and may thus view any extra effort on their part as too costly.

Thus, the activity-interaction-sentiment model plus the exchange theory gives the manager some insight into the way groups tend to behave.

Formal and Informal Leader Relationships

How do the formal and informal leaders relate?

Another way of analyzing groups is to identify the objectives or goals common to most groups. In one way or another, the individuals in groups want to perform some kind of task, want to have some kind of social satisfaction, and want to feel some sense of contribution and growth. This language may sound very familiar to you, because it sounds like the theories of motivation describing needs for achievement, power, and affiliation. We also know that in most work groups, there is a formally designated leader, appointed by the organization.[13] This formal leader usually focuses on one or more of the group objectives. This person may attempt to be a task-oriented manager, placing most emphasis, behavior, and sanctions on meeting the achievement need. If the group has the same kind of achievement need, there may be a perfect match in the productivity of the group; but in most instances, the needs of the formal leader are not perfectly matched with the needs of the group. What will probably happen is that the group will develop emergent or informal behavior to compensate for the deviation. The group will even develop an emergent or **informal leader** (someone not officially appointed). This leader will be someone in the group to give it direction, to identify the appropriate sanctions, or perhaps to help in the creation of group norms.

Informal leader
A person in a group who is not officially appointed as leader yet assumes the leadership role to give the group direction and establish group norms.

Harmony will probably result in a work group if the formal leader is emphasizing behavior for one basic need while the informal leader is stressing behavior for another need. Confusion may exist if both leaders are vying for the same kind of objective. For example, if the formal leader is task oriented and the informal leader is oriented to the social needs of the group, a balance exists and harmony probably results. But if the formal leader is giving orders and directions for productivity and the informal leader is giving direction for productivity, the possibility of a conflict between the two leaders is very pronounced. Similarly, if both the formal and the informal leaders are too concerned about the social needs of the group at the expense of getting the task done, no balance exists and dissatisfaction is likely to follow.

The preceding pages have pointed to a number of ways a manager can approach group behavior. Managers are fools if they think that they can perfectly control and predict the informal and emerging behavior of a group, that groups should not be allowed to have an existence of their own, and that "unofficial" or "informal" is a dirty word, not to be allowed in the department. The informal, unofficial, emerging aspects of group behavior are very valuable and sound features of any work group.

After recognizing these groups and analyzing behavioral situations, managers must turn their attention to using the tools available to them to solve problems. What can be done to cope with situations that need changing?

THE MANAGEMENT OF GROUPS

Managers make at least two decisions that affect the behavior of work groups. One concerns the use of the authority system—who is to have the authority over whom, who is to do what, who is to receive rewards and punishments, how these sanctions are to be administered, and what the house rules are for employees. Another decision deals with the design of the work flow—the technology of the organization. Each of these decisions will be expanded in this section.

Leadership Techniques—Authority

Likert

The first method we explore for changing group behavior emphasizes leadership technique—in particular, the authority that managers have to influence the behavior and performance of work groups that report to them.

As a manager, you have the freedom to select people and assign them to positions and tasks. You may even have insight into the sentiments that people bring with them to the workplace. If you want to create conflict and disruption, you can probably do so by taking two people with extreme and incompatible attitudes on a topic and forcing them to work together. You may find greater success by matching sentiments of people and work assignments, or by staffing the unit with people whose sentiments are not as extreme. The field of the control of work groups is still in its infancy, and we do not want to suggest that it is simply a matter of putting round pegs in round holes. But the manager does make structure and staffing decisions, and the knowledge of the relationship between interactions, activities, and sentiments could prove invaluable.

As a manager, you may recognize the limitations upon yourself and perhaps understand that as a formally designated manager, you cannot satisfy all the needs of the work group. If you do, you might encourage the development of informal and emergent leadership, so that the balance exists between the formal and the informal leaders.

Another leadership approach is to use the criteria of effective work groups as the manager's leadership goal. A great deal of research has been done on the topic of work-group behavior and the methods to achieve the most effective work groups. Rensis Likert, of the University of Michigan, identified the "nature" of highly effective groups. He identified at least twenty-four properties and performance characteristics of the ideal group. It is possible to summarize these properties through a few generalizations.[14]

What are some features of highly effective work groups?

Highly effective work groups produce a supportive atmosphere and relationship. There is a great deal of confidence and trust between the formally designated leader and the members of the group, so that the concept of "our group" rather than that of "my group" predominates. Fear and distrust are removed, so that there is very open and frank communication by all members of the group. The values of each person, the values of the group, and the values of the leader are all moving toward a balance and an agreement.

This model by Likert is, of course, ideal, but it is the kind of model that a manager might seek.

A fourth approach to using authority is to recognize that managers of organizations have the authority to design the role positions as well as give the rewards and punishments for certain kinds of attributes. One attribute that tends to give a person status, for example, is age. If a company does not want age to be given status, it will have promotion and reward policies that favor youth and work against age. Status and status symbols are important management factors of organizational life that affect the behavior of individuals and groups, and we should look at what status can and cannot do for an organization.

You may receive status from one of two sources: from the organization or from others. For you to have status, others must value your attributes. These may be education, age, sex, training, experience, or seniority. As a manager in an organization, you can definitely affect the status of a person in regard to the job, or you can affect the perceptions that others have toward his or her personal attributes. The way in which you do both of these is through the use of status symbols. A **status symbol** is a visible sign of one's social position, and you can think of many kinds of status symbols. The insignia on a person's military uniform is a status symbol. The insignia on the shoulder is for an officer—a captain; on the sleeve, it is for a noncommissioned officer—a sergeant. Other status symbols include the type of furniture in your office, the number of square feet in your reception room, whether you have a personal secretary, the type of car the company gives you to drive, the proximity of your office to that of the head of the company, your privacy, and even the location of your parking space.

Status symbol A visible sign of one's social position, e.g., the corner office or the Mercedes.

Techniques for Using Organizational Structure

Leonard Sayles has made some important observations on certain group behavior based upon the technology of the organization.[15] Sayles looked at factories that frequently experienced strikes and work stoppages. He found that the troubles and problems seemed to come from the same departments, even though the personnel in both the leader and the follower roles changed. He concluded that there must be some other factor causing the similar and persistent type of behavior. This factor he found to be the structure or the technology of the work flow.

The workers studied performed different tasks and thus were members of different groups. Sayles found that the groups doing certain kinds of jobs tended to show very similar behavior, which Sayles was able to classify into four different groups. He classified the workers into the four categories of apathetic, erratic, strategic, or conservative according to the behavior that emerged from the structural features of the technology.

This finding is significant to the study of work groups, because what Sayles suggests is that the behavior of a work group does not depend upon the leadership style or even the individual personalities of the workers—rather, the type of job or technology of the workplace determines much of the behavior. Thus, if you were a manager in one of these factories, your effectiveness as a leader would depend more on which of these four groups you were managing than on any particular style you used. Therefore, the manager must be aware that the technology and the flow of work have an impact upon the behavior of a group.

SPECIAL GROUP TECHNIQUES

Quality Circles

Quality circles have been a hot management topic in the 1990s. As a technique in participative management and decision making, these groups meet regularly to discuss problems and make recommendations for the improvement of qual-

Global Application

Quality Circles

Organizations all over the world have attempted to use quality circles, and in many cases, those attempts have failed. Different reasons are given for the failures: "Not enough commitment from management." "Not enough commitment from the unions." "We didn't follow Japanese procedures closely enough." "Engineers don't need quality circles anyway—they use their intellect at work. It's the production people we need to motivate." A change in continents reflects similar reasons for failure.

One Australian researcher studied companies in his country that had tried quality circles; he came up with the following list of reasons for their failure:

- The circles ran out of ideas for new projects.
- The pressure of production made it difficult for supervisors and workers to make time for the QC meetings.
- Approved projects were not being completed because implementation was usually dependent upon the engineers who had to fit this work in with their "normal" assignments.
- The supervisors resigned en masse as circle leaders. They were feeling the effect of production pressures and were uncomfortable in a role that required them to act as "progress chasers."
- The facilitator was not provided with sufficient resources to deal simultaneously with all the quality circles within the plant.

It seems as though quality circles have a life cycle. There is a beginning period when everyone is enthusiastic with the idea of QCs and is willing to put out the extra effort to make them work. Some writers have referred to this as the honeymoon period. Some honeymoons last weeks; others, months; and a very few, years. After the honeymoon, the QCs fall apart.

Some critics have suggested that QCs are merely another management fad, a quick fix to the long-term problems faced by business. And since they are a fad, their failure is only natural.

Others have suggested that the failure of QCs is not so bad. These people feel that QCs are supposed to be short-term, that QCs are the transition into bigger and better things—spontaneous open communication between management and employees; active problem solving by employees; and, perhaps, more trust between management and the line workers.

Do all QCs fail? Of course not. As a matter of fact, they do excel in some places. They still excel in Japan. Some purists believe that Japan has the only true quality circles. In Japan, the QCs are made up of volunteer workers, who meet regularly to analyze the problems of the workplace, develop solutions to those problems, and then make recommendations to management. Management is not in the actual quality circle itself.

France is considered a leader in quality circles, particularly among the European nations. In a typical French quality circle, however, the manager is the discussion leader and actively participates in the problem solving. Over 2,500 companies in France, including auto manufacturers Renault and Peugeot, aerospace specialist Aerospatiale, glass manufacturer Saint-Gobain, and aluminum producer Pechiney, have established QCs. Total QCs in France number over 25,000; all of them were started in the 1980s.

References: Richard Dunford and Peter McGraw, "Abandoning Simple Recipes and Benefitting from Quality Circles: An Australian Study," *Work and People* 12, no. 2 (1986) 22–25, Linda Bernier, "Corporate Culture: French Circles Multiply, but with a Difference, *International Management,* 41 (December 1986) 30–32.

These Westinghouse employees work on problems together in quality circles. It is estimated that over 500 companies in the United States are using quality circles to solve problems within organizations. Quality circles are made up of employees from all levels of the organization.

ity. Managers from the Lockheed Missile and Space Company are usually credited with importing the concept of quality circles from Japan and applying it to their company in 1974. Their experiment with QCs was successful, and other U.S. companies adopted the idea. Recent estimates have stated that at least 500 U.S. companies use quality circles. Originally, QCs were used only in manufacturing areas and generally involved only people from the "shop floor." The theory behind this idea was that the people actually doing the production work should be the best people to come up with ideas and suggestions to solve the related production problems. They were, after all, the people most familiar with the job. In recent years, quality circles have moved into other areas, including service departments and industries, and salaried personnel issues. The potential for their use in all areas is unlimited. However, quality circles are not always successful.[16]

Decision Making

In Chapter 5, reference was made to involving groups in the decision-making process. It has been suggested that groups are good at setting objectives, evaluating options, and participating when they will be involved in implementing the decision.

There are limitations to group decision making. It can be time-consuming; there may be a tendency to work toward compromise decisions; some people may dominate; some may shy from participating; and **group think** may develop. Group think exists in cohesive groups with high commitment and loyalty to the group; there is a reluctance to disagree and a feeling of invulnerability. The frequent result is a poor decision.

Group think All members of a group think the same way because of high commitment and loyalty to the group; there is a strong reluctance to disagree and a feeling of invulnerability. The usual result is poor decisions made by the group.

MANAGING MANAGEMENT GROUPS

In the material described so far about groups, you have been placed in the role of manager. We have suggested that information about formal and emergent groups helps make the management of groups easier; however, there are other instances when managers relate with groups in a totally different context. They relate without formal authority.

Managers, especially at the middle and higher levels of an organization, spend many hours and much effort as members of committees and project teams. There is not a great deal of empirical research on this topic—most of the insights on human groups come from research using hourly workers and operatives as the data base. However, there are some observations common to most managerial groups that provide a better understanding of the world managers face.

Observations

- Many groups are temporary in nature. Oriented to a specific task or project, these groups function until the task is completed, and then their life is terminated.
- Peers are the participants in such groups.
- The chairperson or leader of the committee or project team is usually appointed by some higher management level.
- There are few written rules for the behavior or roles of group members.
- Much of the behavior is of a political nature. You must be aware that your performance in these temporary groups may have an important impact on your career. Success at operating with no formal authority will open opportunities for you to move up the managerial ladder. It is therefore imperative that any discussion of managing include a discussion on the topic of power and politics, the title of our next chapter.

SUMMARY

This chapter has been full of ideas about individual behavior in groups. We have seen how individuals make up groups and how groups relate to individuals. In the beginning of the chapter, the concept of the group was described through the use of examples and a discussion of group functions. Then, several ways of systematically examining emergent- or informal-group behavior were explained. With this background in mind, you were asked to turn your attention to the practical alternatives for managerial action when relating to group behavioral problems. Leadership and the organizational structure were the primary sources of the manager's plan of action.

KEY TERMS

Group A unit of two or more people who work together to achieve a common purpose or goal.

Formal groups A group given structure, a mission, authority, and legitimacy by an organization.

Informal groups A work group that emerges from the formal group. It has no legitimacy, no authority, but has structure and mission; it fills the gap of the formal work.

Culture Those acquired and learned behaviors which have persisted in human groups through traditions.

Activity Something that a group or individual does.

Interaction Communication between people.

Sentiment An idea, a belief, or a feeling about something.

Informal leader A person in a group who is not officially appointed as leader yet assumes the leadership role to give the group direction and establish group norms.

Status symbol A visible sign of one's social position, e.g., the corner office or the Mercedes.

Group think All members of a group think the same way because of high commitment and loyalty to the group; there is a strong reluctance to disagree and a feeling of invulnerability. The usual result is poor decisions made by the group.

STUDY ASSIGNMENTS

1. At the Adam-Carey Company, how did group values and behavior affect the productivity of the organization?

2. What is the difference between a formal group and an informal group? Identify and describe a formal group that you are a part of, and then describe any informal groups that exist within the formal group.

3. What is meant by the statement that there is a dual character to work groups? Why is it important for a manager to understand this dual character of work groups?

4. What are some of the functions that groups fulfill for individuals? What are some of the different reasons that people join groups? Identify a group that you have joined and explain why you joined that group.

5. What role do norms play in defining the relationship between the group and its individual members?

6. Explain how a manager can use the Homans/Whyte A-I-S Method to gain an understanding of the nature and character of an informal group.

7. What is the relationship between the formal and informal leaders of any work group? What kinds of problems can occur in this relationship? What kinds of benefits can result from this relationship?

8. Why should managers accept the notion that informal groups are a valuable and critical feature of any work group?

9. How can managers use the leadership techniques discussed in earlier chapters to positively influence group behavior in the workplace?

10. Identify what you consider to be characteristics of a highly effective work group. Describe a work group that you consider to be a highly effective group.

11. How are group behavior and performance influenced by organizational factors such as structure, technology, authority, and status?

12. What are the pros and cons of an organization's creating special groups to resolve unique problems or complete specific tasks? (Consider special groups such as quality circle groups or project management groups.) How do these special kinds of groups differ from the existing formal and informal groups?

Case for Discussion

THE CARLSON PACKING COMPANY

It would be a meeting that most managers had expected for months. Brad Carlson, president of Carlson Packing, had hoped to avoid calling such a meeting. However, business was declining rapidly, and Carlson, along with most of his managers, believed that the company could not survive much longer without making some significant operational changes. So Carlson and his top managers were meeting to decide what actions they needed to take to keep the company from going out of business.

Carlson Packing had been a leading meat-processing company for about twenty years. During most of the twenty years, the company had been rather profitable and had expanded its Midwest operations rather cautiously. The relationship between Carlson's management and its unionized employees was usually confrontational and always strained. During the past two years, the recession and a number of dramatic changes in the meat-packing industry had made it increasingly difficult for Carlson Packing to remain profitable and competitive.

After calling the meeting to order, Brad Carlson reviewed the situation facing the company. He began by noting that sales were continuing their substantial decline and that the company was unsuccessful in renewing contracts with some of its major customers. In his review, he emphasized that the loss of sales had nothing to do with either the reputation of the company or the quality of its products, both of which were considered to be quite good. Rather, Brad stated that Carlson Packing had simply failed to be competitive in price. He commented that although the firm constantly endeavored to upgrade its equipment and processes, the cost savings gained from improved operating efficiency were not enough to allow the company to lower its prices to a competitive level.

Brad asked the group to comment on why Carlson Packing could not be competitive. Almost every manager said that the high labor costs of Carlson Packing were the problem. Someone noted that one of the most significant changes in the meat-packing industry in recent years was the reduction of labor costs. Labor costs were falling because packers either were forcing unions to make wage concessions or were going out of business. Everyone agreed that this trend began when one of the major meat packers successfully broke an expensive long-term union contract by filing for Chapter 11 (reorganization under the bankruptcy law). When the packer did this, it was able to cut its labor costs by about half. Another manager pointed out that the other trend in the industry was the rise of nonunion packers. Many of these nonunion packers were formerly unionized operations that chose to go out of business to start a new company that could operate with lower labor costs.

Brad interrupted to comment on the status of Carlson Packing's current union contract. He pointed out that the company was in the second year of a three-year contract and that the third year's contract called for a substantial increase in the hourly wage along with a cost-of-living adjustment. Everyone in the meeting agreed that if the company were to comply with the provisions of the third year of the union contract, the company would surely go out of business.

The discussion then turned toward considering alternative actions to reduce labor costs. A number of managers favored asking the union to make concessions, but others observed that such an alternative would not work because the national union was pressuring the local unions to stop making wage concessions. After a while, the discussion focused on the Chapter 11 option. When some of the managers realized that Brad favored the Chapter 11 option, they began to argue against it. These managers emphasized that such a move would certainly be met with union resistance and would cause considerable labor conflict for Carlson Packing. Brad cut their argument short by saying, "We can get anyone to cut meat for $6 an hour, so let them strike! I want us to file for Chapter 11 as soon as possible." With that statement, he closed the meeting.

Chapter 15

Power, Politics, and Tactics

Learning Objectives

1. **Distinguish** among the definitions of the terms authority, power, and influence.
2. **State** and **Describe** at least five sources of power.
3. **Differentiate** between the negative and positive faces of power.
4. **Identify** the relationship between power, influence, and dependence.
5. **List** five personal examples of negative power.

I WONDERED what had happened to Dan. He seemed to be walking on air. I hadn't seen him so excited since he had described in detail his catches of big fish. Finally, he came into my office, with a twinkle in his eye and a bounce to his step. "Okay, Dan," I said, "what is it?"

"Burke, I've got a tremendous offer for another job! It's the kind of thing I've always wanted. In fact, you'd probably like it, too. Why not come along with me?"

"Whoa! Before you get me to come along with you, why don't you start from the beginning and fill me in on all the details."

"Well, you know how we've always wanted to be in positions of power and influence so that our ideas about education could be put into effect? Well, this is our chance. I'll be able to see that all new courses developed in the program will have a behavioral orientation. You know how often both of us have said that teaching behavioral science courses by themselves doesn't give students any feel for the area—they don't know how to relate the ideas in the social psychology courses to the business world—and that what should be done is to have behavioral science concepts taught as part of the finance, marketing, management, and quantitative courses. Now's my chance to see that that happens."

I was still confused, but I could see that Dan was too excited to be organized, so I thought I'd better ask questions about the situation rather than try to get the story straight out.

"What kind of job is it? Where's the school? What's the teaching load? And how much money is involved? What's your title?"

"I'll be assistant to the president. It's a new university. In fact, the students won't start until a year after I arrive, so I'll have a year to develop curriculum

and hire faculty members. The president, a friend of mine, wants me to make the behavioral science inputs. The other deans and chairpersons are coming from first-class schools all over the states, and we should have a great university. I'll have to hire 50 people the first year, and then 25 each of the next two years until we get a faculty of 100. Just think of the opportunity to make a significant impact on business education!"

The phone rang, and my secretary reminded me that I was already late for an ad hoc university committee meeting on a faculty appeals case.

"Dan, I'd like to talk with you and Phyllis about the new job. I have more questions I want to ask. Why don't Marilyn and I run over to your house for coffee tomorrow night, and we can talk?"

I didn't listen very well to the vice president's introductory comments about the procedures for our appeals committee—my mind was recalling the events of the past five years. Dan had been hired from a West Coast school by the man who had preceded me as chairperson of the department. His first full year as a faculty member was my first full year as a department chairperson, so we grew and developed together. Dan quickly proved to be an invaluable faculty member. He was an excellent committee member, too, willing to put in the kind of time needed to get a project completed. In fact, it was Dan who helped me put together our new graduate program in business. Dan seemed to thrive on developing ideas, analyzing events of the past and putting them into the context of the present, anticipating problems of program implementation, and planning for the execution of the whole project. He was an excellent staff man.

But Dan was also outspoken, and in recent years he had provoked a number of faculty members and others in administrative positions. And because he was reluctant to publish just anything, he had not been productive enough in the eyes of the present administration. Consequently, his ideas were not given much support. It seemed to me, coming back after I had resigned as chairperson and taken a sabbatical leave, that Dan was being tolerated rather than encouraged and supported by faculty and administration. As an ex-administrator, I could see the situation from both sides and did not feel particularly hostile to the faculty or the administration. Dan was unable to function the way he wanted, and the environment had changed for him. In all honesty, I had to say that Dan was not receiving respect from either his superiors or his peers. In both groups, the absence of "professional productivity" set the stage for a holding operation. I could see that a move by Dan at this time could be beneficial to him and would be one way of resolving the conflict. But there was something he needed to know about becoming effective in organizations. Dan had to learn how to become political.

The next night, I tried to show Dan that he needed to develop many bases for power—he needed to get faculty as well as administrative support. He replied by saying that he would have all the power he needed. "My authority as assistant to the president will be enough." I wondered if indeed it would be enough. ■

For the full reality of the manager's world to be understood, another dimension of managerial activity must be explored. In earlier chapters, the attributes of the twenty-first-century executive were mentioned. Managers must perform as

- Global strategists
- Masters of technology
- Politicians par excellence
- Leaders/motivators

In Parts I–III you have viewed managers as leaders/motivators and masters of technology, and you have seen the global world of management. In this chapter, you will be introduced to another dimension of a manager's world—the world of power and politics.

It is no longer enough for people to demonstrate talent in one narrow area (technology, for example); they may find themselves ineffective because of their ignorance in other critical dimensions. One such area is power, politics, and tactics,[1] sometimes referred to as the invisible, unofficial aspect of managing.

Organizations worldwide are filled with case histories of intelligent, well-educated, trained individuals who lacked the "organizational smarts." These people were naive in thinking that the official organizational world was all that counted.[2] Even experienced political fighters are frequently surprised by the turn of events in organizational politics. Politics plays a very dominant role in the careers of people in the U.S. auto industry, but Detroit and many executives at Ford Motor Company were surprised when Lee Iacocca was fired by Ford after so many years of success.[3]

If you review the opening case, you will see how important the nontechnical area is to Dan. You can sense the different "readings" each man has of the reality of organizational life. Dan sees that life in very simplistic terms: "If I have authority, people will do as I say and I'll be successful as an administrator." Burke, on the other hand, displays an organizational wisdom honed from personal wars. He is trying to explain the other world of organizational life. This other world, the unofficial world, does not exist on charts or diagrams. In fact, to some people it is invisible. It's the world of power and politics. It's the world often labeled

- The real world
- The jungle
- The world of hard knocks
- Being in the trenches
- The world you don't learn about in school

Although there is no substitute for on-the-job experience, an understanding of this world will prove beneficial and may sensitize you to its existence.

Figure 15-1 provides a good start for understanding because it depicts three sectors of a manager's world. Sector 1 contains the information and skills applied to the nonbehavioral aspects of the organization. Most of the materials in Part II dealt with developing the nonbehavioral management skills in decision making, planning, organizing, and control. Sector 2 identifies the behavioral dimensions of leadership—the relations between the leader-manager and others (bosses, peers, subordinates, groups, and so on).

FIGURE 15-1 The Three Dimensions of a Manager's World

1. MANAGING

Planning
Organizing
Decision making
Controlling

Authority   2. LEADERSHIP

Consideration
Initiating structure

3. POWER AND POLITICS

Contingency approaches

Legitimate power

Whom you know

Influence

Bluffing

Sector 3 is the focus of the present chapter. As a leader-manager, your success may be limited if you don't see the factors of power, politics, and tactics operating in your organization. To survive organizational life, you need a level of sophistication in this subtle, unofficial, but critical world. To some, this picture will appear bleak and unattractive; to others, it will support perceptions they have had throughout earlier sections of this book; the whole truth was not being told. To both groups, we offer suggestions for coping successfully and effectively.

We begin our exploration of this new world by first presenting a brief description of its characteristics. We provide more insight by looking first at concepts in this political world (influence, authority, and power) and then at the ways of getting, keeping, and exercising power—the use of politics and tactics.

CHARACTERISTICS OF THE POLITICAL WORLD OF ORGANIZATION

The topics of power and politics have been absent from much of the history of management. The early writers and researchers treated the subjects as though they were a disease or a plague. Those proponents of the scientific school of management believed that power and politics were the by-products of poor management. If you had sufficient authority and executed the management functions correctly, there would be no need for power or politics. (In all fairness to the early writers, it must be remembered that they were writing primarily for the first levels of supervision in manufacturing plants where there was a surplus of labor.)

Interest in the field of managerial power and politics is slowly growing. Power and politics belonged to the political scientists who focused primarily upon the governmental use of these topics. In this introductory book, therefore, it is possible to provide you only a brief glimpse of the world of power and politics, and a few generalizations will get us started.

It exists in every firm.   Politics is unavoidable. Power exists in every group, organization, or business. In any group, even one consisting of only two people, there is power. In every firm, there's an "informal organization" with centers and networks of power that are very often different from the formal organization charts.

It's subjective.   The political world judges behavior by a different set of criteria. In a study of 3,000 U.S. businesspeople, Dale Tarnowleski, director of the American Management Association survey, reported that "52% of all respondents believe that advancement and promotion . . . are most often based on a largely subjective and arbitrary decision; . . . 88% say a dynamic personality and the ability to sell yourself and your ideas is more of an attribute to the manager on the move today than is a reputation for honesty or firm adherence to principles; 82% believe that pleasing the boss is the critical factor in determining promotability in today's organizational environment."

It's on the rise.   There are some who believe that power and politics become more noticeable, more necessary, during periods of uncertainty and stress. The last two decades have been periods of immense uncertainty and stress, particularly in corporate America. (See Table 15-1 Stresses and Strains.) When organizations are filled with uncertainty and stress, many traditional values are questioned, threatened, or lost. A manager's reaction to such culture change and value stress is to seek political solutions—solutions based upon expanding the unofficial basis of power.

Global Application

The Politics of Global Competition

At one time, all a business had to worry about was getting its products or services to its customers and meeting customer expectations. But nowadays, businesses are finding that to compete on a global basis, they must address issues that go beyond simply making and selling a product and that they must be able to understand the nature and dynamics of international politics.

American businesses have long been frustrated by the difficulties of entering the Japanese markets, and they are amazed at how easily the Japanese overcome the numerous political hurdles they face in operating in the United States. Japan-bashing is a politically popular and ongoing activity in Washington. Debates over "unfair trading practices" always surface around election time. Politicians can be counted on to make TV-worthy statements about the need to limit Japanese access to the U.S. markets and how to force American products on Japan.

Despite what would appear to be a very negative political climate for doing business, the Japanese firms continue to expand their presence in the American market. Part of the reason is that they have developed a clear understanding of what it takes to influence U.S. political forces. For instance, although the practice of corporate charity is almost unheard of in Japan, Japanese firms have become big contributors to American charities and highly visible sponsors of community events. The Japanese realized that this kind of giving yields considerable benefits and is essential in gaining political support. Five years ago, Japanese firms gave little more than $30 million to American charity organizations. Now, Japanese firms are giving more than $500 million annually. This giving is designed to improve the image of the Japanese and reduce political pressure.

On the other hand, American firms are still struggling to understand Japanese politics. It is confusing that every time a Japanese prime minister agrees to new trade concessions, no one in Japan seems to comply with the agreements. For instance, firms operating in the silicon-chip industry have experienced a steady erosion of their market position. They have been frustrated in their attempts to penetrate the Japanese market, and they keep losing domestic sales to imported Japanese chips. Although a number of trade agreements have been negotiated, the competitive situation of American chip manufacturers continues to deteriorate. Yet, the Japanese argue that they are complying with the agreements and suggest that it may be a matter of how various provisions of the agreement are interpreted. In competing on a global scale, it is important to understand the dynamics of international politics, because having the best product is no guarantee that a firm will have access to a particular foreign market. The way to play the global game is to adjust tactics to the competitor's rules and field.

References: Neil Gross, "Making Deals—Without Giving Away the Store," *Business Week,* June 17, 1991, p. 96; S. Alexander, "Japanese Firms Embark on a Program of Giving to American Charities," *Wall Street Journal,* May 23, 1991, p. B1.

TABLE 15-1 Stresses and Strains

CHANGES	RESULTS	VALUE LOST
Mergers and hostile takeovers	Reduction of work force, both blue and white collar	Certainty
		Job security
	Intrusion of new culture and values into old culture and values	
Downsizing of the labor force	Elimination of jobs	Trust
	Elimination of managerial jobs	Loyalty to the organization
	Reduction of nonunion labor force	
	Combining of jobs	
Foreign ownership of manufacturing plants in the U.S.	New culture	National identification
	Development of a we/they work force	
	Conflict of national interest issues	
Short product and technology life cycles	Pressure for rapid return on product-development investment	Pure research efforts
		Planning time for quality product
	Greater job specialization	Commitment to the whole process or product
		Pride in output

Organizational politics is important to aspiring and practicing managers. Whereas some people see office politics as an effective way of short-circuiting red tape and paperwork, and of promoting their favorite people and ideas, others see politics as a destructive force in business. According to the Research Institute of America, "Today, when business can least afford a dissipation of effort, office politics is on the rise within many companies. As a menace to individuals and organizations alike, it deserves more concentrated study than anyone has given it. The price of office politics is tremendous, both to management and the individual. . . . To ignore the existence of company politics, when others in an organization are dedicating much of their time to it, can be as impractical as assuming that the right-of-way is always an assurance of safety in traffic."

With this background, we are now ready to explore more fully the specific features of the political world—influence and power. Let us begin with the relationship between influence, power, and authority, terms often used interchangeably.

THE RELATIONSHIP AMONG INFLUENCE, POWER, AND AUTHORITY

Influence Any behavior by one person that produces an effect on the behavior of another person.

In one way of thinking, the objective of most interpersonal acts by managers is influence. Put simply, **influence** is any behavior by one person that produces an effect on the behavior of another person.[4] It is also a psychological force. As a manager, you might like your subordinates to produce more, to produce at an even rate, to reduce the number of processed defective parts, to accept a new person into their work group, or to become more cooperative. This attempt to influence behavior is not limited to subordinates, for you also want to affect the behavior of your boss, peers, staff, and customers. Thus, for our purposes, influence will be considered a very general term.

The relationship among influence, power, and authority appears in Table 15-2. In this table, you see that influence is the most general, inclusive term; that power is one way to get influence; and that **authority** is one way to get power. Recall that we made a distinction between authority that exists in the formal organizational position—authority that gives you the right to command—and effective authority based upon acceptance by others. In Chapters 2 and 9 specifically, we acknowledged Chester Barnard as being the proponent of the acceptance theory of authority. His contribution highlights the importance of perception and dependence.

To some traditionalists, subordinates are dependent upon you as a manager to give them commands, information, direction, and so on. You will be effective if you plan well, organize tightly, and use high levels of control over subordinates. Barnard believed that the manager is the one who is dependent upon subordinates for their acceptance of orders, directives, and information. If your subordinates do not believe that you have authority or do not perceive you to have authority, you will not be effective.

Managers need the formal designated authority that comes from a position and title (Manager of Sales for the Eastern Region, Head Nurse of Intensive Care, Maintenance Supervisor of the evening shift, Duty Officer, and the like). They also need to be aware that such designated position authority provides them only the potential to become effective. If managers act with the insights of a Chester Barnard, they will realize their potential. An understanding of this authority cycle (formal positional authority plus acceptance theory) is essential in today's world because so many managerial jobs are broadly defined and loosely configured. An illustration will demonstrate this point.

In Chapter 7, on organizing, we talked about the idea of authority. You read that when people join an organization, they are usually put into organizational positions or jobs with a list of duties and expectations. If you become a manager of a bowling center, the owner will neither tell you what to do nor hand you a sheet of paper that describes what it is you are to do. You may be expected to open the bowling center, to check the roster of people assigned for the day's work, and to see that they get started on their jobs. You may have a maintenance group cleaning the lanes, cleaning out the ashtrays, and picking

Authority   The right to decide or act.

What does authority mean to a manager of a bowling center?

TABLE 15-2	**Relationship Among Influence, Power, and Authority**
TERM	**FEATURE**
Influence	Broad . . . An objective of interpersonal relations. Something someone does. Active effort.
Power	Less broad . . . A means to achieve influence. Describes the capacity you have to influence. Deals with potential acts.
Authority	Most restricted term . . . A form of power. Power associated with a given organizational position. The right to command.

Formal authority is important in many positions, especially when decisions must be made and followed quickly. Emergency room situations frequently require the team to follow the commands of the person given the formal authority. Even in a simple training situation, formal authority can be useful in transmitting information to others.

up litter from the previous night; you may have people working in other areas—selling soft drinks and other refreshments, or bowling accessories.

There are many things that have to be done before the bowling center opens for business. You might have to make a physical count of cash and a physical check of inventory, and place some orders for materials that you anticipate needing in the future. The owner may expect you to hire part-time help, to see to it that ads are placed in the paper, and to make sure that innovations and special promotions are communicated to the public. There are numerous things that have to be done to run a bowling center, and you, as the manager, are probably the one responsible for getting everything done. We could go on with the various duties you would have, but perhaps the point becomes obvious—the complete description of the job might take more paper than this textbook.

It is likely that if a job description is written, the statements are very broad and lack detail. How a manager gets a job done is usually a matter of individual and personal discretion. What the owner will do, however, is identify for the manager the rights and authority that are part of the job. A manager will know how much money can be spent, who can and cannot be hired and fired, what disciplinary action can be taken, and what rewards may be passed out. The job has authority, which is the right to command action from others. Thus, authority is a source of power to influence behavior.

POWER

Why is one manager more effective and successful than another?

Suppose you are the owner of a number of car-wash operations in a city and have a local manager for each of them. As you look over the performance of these operations, you find that one is more successful than another. You might ask why, for all are located in a similar traffic pattern, and all the managers are approximately the same age, have approximately the same training, and supervise the same number of employees.

If you were to visit the car-wash operations and make yourself invisible, you might find that the difference among the managers could be best described by the power that each has. You might find that all the managers started with the same authority, yet one seems to be more successful in dealing with subordinates than another is. The power of one is greater than that of others. Why is that so? The answer may be found in an understanding of the nature and sources of power.

The Nature of Power   Korda

Power | The force that others perceive one to have that gives that one the capacity to influence them.

Power is a topic of relatively new interest in organizations. Swept under the carpet for years, the subject was the theme of a best-selling book by Michael Korda in the mid-1970s.[5] Korda viewed power as an instinct in men and women and said that the will to have power is an essential expression of our humanity. Korda also stated that although there are primarily four reasons for working—habit, pleasure, money, and power—it is primarily the desire for power that keeps most people working. He cautioned, however, that power must be your servant, not your master.

Robert N. McMurry, management consultant, spoke dramatically of this topic when he stated that "the most important and unyielding necessity of organizational life is not better communications, human relations or employee participation, but power."[6] To these two writers, power is natural and expected to exist among people in organizations. You have heard power called an instinct and a necessity. Conceptually, power has another meaning.

From reviewing Figure 15-2, you see that power can be defined as that force others perceive you to have that gives you the capacity to influence them.[7] Power refers to a potential set of acts, not a specific act occurring at the

FIGURE 15-2 What Power Is

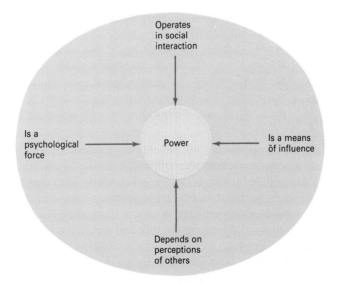

present time. As we mentioned earlier, the objective of power is influence over others.

When we talk of influence, we speak of it as a psychological force. For example, when one person wants something that another person has, he or she attempts to influence the second person to get it. The manager who wants subordinates to work harder attempts to influence them to do so. The secretary who wants to appear valuable to the boss will try to seem indispensable.

Power also operates in social interaction. A person marooned on an island has little power or influence if no others are on that island. Power and influence are forces that exist among people—that operate in social interaction.

The nature of power, then, becomes clearer to us. A person can be said to have power over others when those others believe that they should act the way that person wants them to act. Power, then, depends upon the perceptions that people have of one another and the situation that they are sharing. It is a psychological force and one that deals with the potential acts of others.

In a traditional sense, we know how a person gets authority—by being appointed into the hierarchy of the organization. When people become managers, they also become people with authority. But how do managers with authority establish their power? How do they develop this potential capacity to exert influence over others? We have seen in earlier sections of this book that when we talk about leadership, we talk about the leadership act, an act that may be exercised by people not in formal positions of authority. This same thinking applies to power. Power can be held by people who are not in the formal, official chain of command. Earlier reference to informal leaders and the power they have from their fellow workers suggests that a manager not aware of such power could possibly make grave errors in judgment. To avoid errors in judgment, you must realize that power may come from a number of sources.

Expert power enables an individual to receive the respect and response from others. In this picture the instructor has the attention of management trainees because of his knowledge and expertise.

Sources of Power

Power comes in many sizes and shapes. Power sources are also situational and change over time. For example:

- Amy has power as a police officer and gives you a ticket for speeding.
- Jose has power because he knows the best route to take to a ball game in Houston.
- Larry has power through his physical strength and street-fighting ability.
- Julie has power as a secretary to the most important manager in the division. She frequently tells us the unofficial news before it becomes official.
- Ed has power as a member of the internal auditing team coming to our plant for its biannual visit.

You can see the situational character of each example: Once we all know the best route to the ballpark, Jose's power is diminished; if we don't expect a street fight, Larry's power is not needed; no one pays any attention to Ed if he visits the plant when it's not time to be audited. Thus, power has many sources and is situational. These simple illustrations have theoretical roots and will be expanded upon; Figure 15-3 will serve as a base.

You may do what someone tells you to do because that person is your boss. Your boss has a position in the organization that carries the right (author-

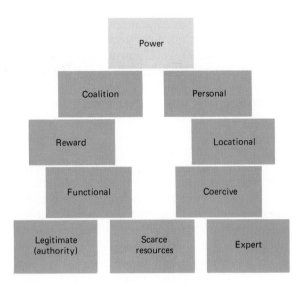

FIGURE 15-3 Sources of Power

Legitimate positional power Based on position in an organization.

Why do certain people emerge from a group as leaders?

Expert power Based on valued knowledge.

Functional power The power that rests with the people who usually perform certain functions.

ity) to do many things. That power is called **legitimate positional power,** and it comes primarily from the organization. You will have legitimate positional power when you become a member of the organization and when others in the organization expect you to have power and accept your possession of power. Authority, thus, is a source of legitimate power.[8]

Suppose a group is interested in playing volleyball and only one member is familiar with the rules. After a number of heated arguments between the two teams because of a lack of rules, one person may emerge from either side as an arbitrator of disputes and arguments. Members of the group allow their behavior to be influenced because they realize that knowledge of the game is important for playing it. All those on a team have decided that they would like to compete and even win, but they recognize that they are unable to win without someone to direct their efforts. When they sense the need for a leader with knowledge of the rules and strategy of the game, they give power to such a person and allow their behavior to be influenced. That person has **expert power.**

In the business world, expert power is frequently in the hands of engineers, accountants, financial and technical experts, or people who have been in the company for years and who know things that others do not know. Whatever the shape and form, what is true about expert power is that people sense the need for this knowledge and willingly yield to its influence. A perfect example of this point would be the increased value given to the director of industrial relations when a company and union are nearing a strike deadline. The director may be given the authority to call the president of the company any time of day or night. At this particular time, the director is a person with power.

Power frequently rests with those people who perform certain functions; this could be called **functional power.** For example, if an organization is very conscious of its spiraling costs, the members who keep records and report back to higher management about cost information undoubtedly have power. Often, older, experienced, "tough" managers will respond very meekly to the young clerk who is checking on cost information because they sense the power that the clerk has, owing to the function he or she performs. The founder of Ford Motor Company, Henry Ford, had no use for accountants or financial people. He admired people like himself: mechanics, workers who turned out a real product. Years later, Henry Ford II took over the company and discovered it was near bankruptcy. He brought in a group of nonautomotive "Whiz Kids" who knew how to use statistics, accounting, and finance. In a short time, the "power" group at Ford changed from the engineers to those who collected data and controlled costs.

Coercive power Based on fear.

Another kind of power is **coercive power.** This is power that is based on fear. The fear can take many forms, and the punishment that is potentially forthcoming from the person can also take many forms. You may have been a member of a group in which you were readily influenced by a more powerful person because if you did not do what you were told, you would get a sharp punch, which might be painful. Or if you want very much to be a member of a group, for example, and it is obvious who its leader is, you will allow yourself to be influenced by that leader so that you become a member of that group. Coercive power with physical punishment is not very common among managers of organizations, but the notion of coercive power and some of the nonphysical punishments is one that should not be overlooked or forgotten.

Reward power Based on desired results.

Reward power is very different from coercive power. In this case, you recognize that there is someone who gives the rewards, and you willingly allow that person to influence your behavior. You perform the desired behavior because you want the reward. In some instances, the reward may be monetary, and thus the person has two power sources (reward and legitimate) because he or she is probably your boss. In other cases, however, this person may have no formal authority yet reward you with a compliment or with a statement that gives you a feeling of being accepted. A group or an informal leader, for example, can be the source of reward power in organizations.

Your actual physical location or position in an office may give you power. For example, if you are located near the water cooler or the copy center and thus have opportunity for a great deal of contact, interaction, and communications with others, you undoubtedly have power. Another simple example of

Locational power Based on physical place in a work flow.

locational power is in a workplace where the work of one person is linked with the work of a second, then a third, and so on. If the first person does not perform correctly, the others are not able to continue with the task. Thus, the position in the flow of work gives rise to different positions of power and potential influence. Locational power exists in more subtle ways.[9]

Michael Korda devotes one chapter of his book to location power; he calls it the power spot. Offices are filled with power spots—corner offices, offices with a view, and offices with proximity to important people are more powerful locations. Corners are power spots at office parties but not necessarily at conference meetings. The power spot is at 12 on a clock face; the second most powerful person is usually at 1 o'clock and the least powerful at 11.[10]

Anyone with military experience should recognize the next source of

Coalition power Based on number of people presenting a united front.

power—**coalition power.** A high-ranking military officer desired some medical supplies for his wife but found the normal channels blocked. His drafted clerk assistant made a few phone calls to other drafted low-ranking personnel and produced the medical supplies. These people were part of an elaborate network, a coalition. In all large organizations, there is a powerful, unofficial, informal organization that is a coalition of people with some common bond.

Personal power Based on personality or physical attributes.

People may have power given to them because of their personalities or physical attributes. This **personal power** may be as simple a thing as physical attractiveness. Saul, in the Old Testament, was admired because he stood at least one head above his contemporaries. The Churchills and the Napoleons of the world may not have had the physical stature of a Saul, but they had other personality features that made others willingly yield influence to them.

A final source of power we will list here is called the **power of scarce resources** (this could be money, time, material, information, and so on).[11] Think how often people are given power when they have information that others want, and in some cases, that information may be on the grapevine. There is a simple lesson revealed from the section on grapevine politics: The grapevine contains information wanted by people—if you want power, know what's on that grapevine.

Power of scarce resources The power a person has when in control of scarce resources such as money and information.

The list of sources of power could continue for pages. Perhaps it is time to look at the topic from a different perspective. Table 15-3 is a table for managers, for it organizes the sources of power on the basis of the ability to be influenced or managed. As a manager, you can assign people to power spots. You can designate personnel with position descriptions and titles. You can give rewards to others. There is much you can do to gain power or distribute it throughout your unit.

Is dependency healthy?

At this point, you may be rather concerned about the frankness of our discussion of power. You may resent and feel uncomfortable with the statement

---

Management Application

Grapevine Politics

Susan RoAne provides counseling and training for business people, especially help on careers. She writes that grapevine politics can serve as an important career management tool. To aspiring and practicing managers, she addresses a series of questions to help improve their awareness. For example, do you

- Observe your colleagues, subordinates, and supervisors to see who eats with whom, works out together, commutes together?
- Read the company's annual reports, brochures, and newsletters so as to get an informational base?
- Listen to conversations in elevators, staff rooms, nearby restaurants, and even washrooms for birthdays, anniversaries, promotions, and so on, and then take action to recognize these events?

Many people feel uneasy with this short quiz. But Ms. RoAne tries to improve her client's savvy quotient; tries to have people see that, if used properly, "the grapevine can be a powerful resource and career aid." Her tips for cultivating your grapevine include the following:

- Determine who has access to relevant, powerful sources of information.
- Trade information when it is required.
- Buy lunch or dinner for people who are prime grapevine sources.
- Become aware.

Source: Susan RoAne, "Grapevine Politics: An Office Goldmine; a Career Management Tool," *the Woman CPA* (January 1986), pp. 32–33.

TABLE 15-3 Manager Influence over Power Sources	
AMOUNT OF MANAGER INFLUENCE	POWER SOURCE
Great deal	Legitimate power
	Functional power
	Coercive power
	Reward power
	Locational power
Some	Expert power
	Scarce resource power
Little or none	Coalition power
	Personal power

that others must be dependent on you,[12] with the subjects of how to become a powerful and influential manager and how to be successful through the manipulation of behavior. Many people are suspicious of power figures. This is particularly true in America, where people came to escape dictatorships and oppression. The American governmental structure (with its checks and balances) attempts to divide power sources and create a pluralistic type of society, where all voices are heard and a form of representative government protects minorities from majority manipulation.[13] It would therefore be natural for you to feel uneasy with some of the previous statements about power. Yet power, influence, and authority are factors of organizational life. They are terms used in objective descriptions of behavior and as such are neutral in feeling. Actually, power may be viewed as having both negative and positive features.

Negative and Positive Power

Negative power Domination over others.

What will positive power do?

Positive power Inspires others to work toward goals.

David C. McClelland believes that there are two faces of power,[14] a negative and a positive face, and that too many of us think of power only in the negative way. In the **negative** sense, **power** is domination over others, submission of one person to another, and the use of all necessary maneuverings to gain an end. Such power is antisocial and obviously destructive and dangerous to any organization.

The second face of power is more attuned to society. This is the type of power that you can develop and use. A person with this type of power motive does not make the other person feel drained of energy. Rather, the other person feels inspired, confident, willing, and interested in moving with the power figure; the power is shared. **Positive power** is based not on coercion but on identification with goals. In the illustration given earlier about volleyball, the emerging leader is not dominating the group; the group recognizes the necessity for the leadership and use of power and willingly submits to that type of influence. This more positive face of power is supported by the motivation concepts discussed earlier. It is a kind of management and leadership that may be difficult to achieve, may not be applicable in all situations and at all levels, but definitely is a worthy goal.

With this background on the topic of power, you are now ready to pursue the managerial questions about power: how to get it, keep it, and exercise it. These questions identify the areas of politics and tactics.

POLITICS AND TACTICS

Politics Those actions a person takes to get and keep power.

Tactics The way an individual uses power.

Managers want the answers to the following questions when dealing with power: (1) How do you get and keep power? In this chapter, we define **politics** as those things a person does to get and keep power. (2) Once you have power, how do you use it? Using the power you have is defined here as **tactics;** that is, the specific ways you exercise the power. (3) Finally, what can a manager do to increase or decrease the power of subordinates, peers, rivals, and bosses? Politics and tactics are both used in this area to achieve effective influence over others.[15]

In the next few pages, specific suggestions are offered that help answer all three questions.

The Scope of Politics and Tactics

Politics deals with the tactics that people use to get and activate their power potential. (See Figure 15-4.) Changing behavior through influence is still the objective, but now the manager wants to make use of the power for a constructive, positive end. Ironically, most people probably think of power as a top-down, dominating force; in the discussions in Chapter 9 on leadership, the true character of these concepts comes forth—the manager can only exercise power given by others.[16]

As is true in leadership and authority, the ultimate source of power is in the group; it is the group that decides how effective a manager will be. Thus, the real question that must be asked is: What is it that managers can do to influence the group, to have it give them power, to have the group accept the manager's leadership and authority, so that the goals of both the organization and its members are met?[17]

With the scope of politics and tactics in mind, we present two examples of politics and tactics: one dealing with interpersonal dimensions and one dealing with the tactics of organizational bluffing.

Some Tactics of Politics

In a penetrating and classic article in the *Harvard Business Review,* Norman Martin and John Howard Sims offered a number of tactics for the purpose of improving power.[18] To discover these tactics, they searched the biographies of

FIGURE 15-4 What Politics Is

leaders throughout history, explored the lives of successful industrialists, and interviewed a number of contemporary executives. The listing that follows corresponds very closely to their article, although the illustrations and examples differ. The question that these men asked themselves was this: What are the tactics that have proved successful for controlling and directing the actions of others?

Taking Counsel

What are some ways of being political?

An effective manager is very cautious in deciding when to seek advice. Able executives can get advice from others all too easily; they must take great care that in asking for advice, they do not show any weakness in themselves or their position.

Alliances

Many young people in organizations have quickly learned to form alliances with others above, at the same level, and below in the organization who seem to have those characteristics and abilities that the organization wants. These are the people who are most likely to be promoted in the organization and whom the manager has easy access to, communication with, and confidence in. These alliances also help the manager gain a degree of respectability from subordinates, for they know that their boss has access outside the specific work unit.

Maneuverability

The idea of maneuverability was developed early in the first chapter of this book when we suggested that you must be careful about staying too long on a sinking ship. This tactic suggests that you be aware of what the organization is looking for and try to grow with those needs. You should also maintain contacts outside the company or industry, thus developing a great deal of flexibility and maneuverability within the organization. The adage that "you are worth more to us if you are worth more to someone else" applies here.

Communication

The communication tactic would suggest that the manager is able to identify those people who have important, critical, and frequently confidential information. The insightful manager also wants to have information that other people need to become more powerful. This frequently means that you will seek out informal channels rather than holding rigidly to formal channels, which are often slow with important information. People in certain positions in an organization are good sources of communication. For example, security personnel will have information at certain times, as will mailroom personnel or others who happen to be crossing over routine and rigid lines of organizations. You must also know when to limit information.[19]

Compromising

This tactic will be obvious to those of you who already are masters of conflict resolution. You frequently see people who are able to win one battle but in the process create enemies and thus lose the war. There is definitely an art to compromising and giving up insignificant points while being willing to fight for those points that are critical and important. A successful manager, by being able to recognize the stakes that people have in various matters and the potential alienation and power they have, is sure to move with the flow that is important.

Negative Timing

Frequently, a lower-level manager cannot get into direct confrontation with a boss about certain projects. You will be able to sense when your boss wants no more discussion but action. It may be possible to delay the implementation of action by negative timing, a technique in which the manager starts the project in motion but calls for additional planning, additional studying, additional feedback; thus, the movement of the project is retarded. Obviously, the manager must be fully aware of the costs and consequences of taking such negative timing and be prepared to shift into a faster gear if the boss insists upon the project or if, in hindsight, the manager feels that the project is a legitimate one that should be expedited quickly.

Enthusiasm

This technique deals with nonverbal communication. People "read" both what you say and how you say it, and, therefore, the manager must be aware that both these aspects are important. A successful manager should have the skill (expert power) of selling products and conveying an excitement and a tone that commit others to projects.

Confidence

Confidence is a must for managers. Confidence is obviously something that others see in you; yet, there are techniques, skills, and tactics that you may develop that will improve the probability of others' viewing you as confident. Someone who is optimistic is usually viewed as confident, whereas someone who is always pessimistic may be viewed as having no confidence. A manager who reports to peers, bosses, and subordinates in optimistic tones may well exude an air of confidence that will enhance a power position. Frequently, managers must act as if they know what they are doing when, in fact, there may be some doubt and uncertainty. In some cases, they are able to share with subordinates their doubt and uncertainty, realizing that these people are mature enough to understand that no one in the situation has certainty. But in other instances, transmitting the feeling of uncertainty to a group that needs certainty would destroy the possibility of success. Thus, being confident is a delicate but invaluable power tactic.

Always Being the Boss

Subordinates do not want bosses to become subordinates. A boss cannot be a boss and a subordinate simultaneously. As long as organizations have hierarchy and positions of authority and responsibility, there will be bosses and there will be subordinates. This does not mean that the boss must be constantly isolated from subordinates. But it does mean that boss and subordinate have a mutual respect for the roles and psychological demands that are called for. The boss must stay away from some group meetings where workers will be critical. The criticism, the "getting it off the chest," may be very healthy for the group, and an outside presence would just destroy the solution. Subordinates also want you to show evidence of your status and power. Their own power is enhanced if they work for a powerful boss.

Managing Status Symbols

You can affect your own power and that of others by managing the symbols of power and status. Recall that author Michael Korda mentioned the existence of a power spot in an office. You might have the authority, for example, to move people into or out of the power spot, or to improve their status by giving them more "status-looking" desks. Gold-plated thermos jugs, personal computers, type of car, and number of telephones are also symbols subject to your management.

Managing the Sources of Power

In Table 15-3, we showed the amount of management control over sources of power. For example, as a manager, you have authority over legitimate, functional, locational, and reward power sources. Using this authority will enhance the possibility that others will perceive you as having power.

The Tactics of Bluffing

Why must you bluff?

The idea of organizational bluffing comes to us from an article by Albert Z. Carr in the *Harvard Business Review*[20] that generated a great deal of discussion and reaction because of its openness and frankness.

As we present some of Carr's ideas and positions, we would have you remember that the term *business* in this context could very easily be replaced by the term *organization*. We have said repeatedly that managers in the future will be managers of many different kinds of organizations and that the behavior found in the business organization is likely to be found in other types of organizations.

Carr believes that the ethics of a business are not necessarily those of society but are, rather, those of the poker game, and he uses the analogy of a poker game to illustrate his point. He says that in poker, as in business, the element of chance exists, yet the person who plays with skill is most likely to come out the winner in the long run. Now, what are the rules or elements in a poker game that might also relate to a business world? In both games, according to Carr, "the ultimate victory requires intimate knowledge of the rules, in-

---

Ethics Issue

Bluffing

In an article from the *Journal of Business Ethics,* author John Beach examines Carr's ideas on business bluffing. Beach looks at Carr's examples and questions whether bluffing should be used when the act may be legal yet deceptive. To Beach, the deception can be active (management or union people deliberately misstating data to create a certain impression) or passive (an individual omitting information relevant to an issue). He even adds a concept (puffing)—an expression of opinion not made as a representation of fact—and believes that "business bluffing is an act of puffing at best and misrepresentation or fraud at worst."

Source: John Beach, "Bluffing: Its Demise as a Subject unto Itself," *Journal of Business Ethics,* 4 (1985), 191–96.

sight into the psychology of the other player, a bold front, a considerable amount of self-discipline, and the ability to respond swiftly and effectively to opportunities provided by chance." Thus far, the rules sound very similar to some of the insights we have been identifying throughout the previous chapters.

Carr maintains that there is a certain code of ethics, a certain expectation, in a poker game that is different from the expectation of behavior in church. It is expected in a poker game that one player will try to bluff another even if that other player is a friend. Good poker players are able to keep a straight face and be careful about displaying communication signals. They do not want to give the other people in the game any knowledge of the cards they hold or the excitement they feel when dealt a winning hand. Certain poker players use a strategy of voluntarily losing early games to encourage opponents to stay in the game in anticipation of winning a big pot at the end of the evening. Carr identifies the special ethics in poker and says these ethics are not dishonest. A player who cheats at the game will receive punishment from the other players, and Carr is not suggesting that businesspeople become cheaters.

Carr gives more meaning to the brand of ethics used in poker: "The game calls for distrust of the other fellow. It ignores the claim of friendship. Cunning deception and concealment of one's strengths and intentions, not kindness and openheartedness, are vital to poker." If a special brand of ethics is applicable to the poker game, should not a special brand of ethics be applicable in certain business transactions?[21]

Ethics was discussed in Part I, but just think for a few moments of the many situations to which Carr's brand of ethics applies. Would you expect the first offer of a union official at a collective bargaining session to be the final offer? Is it not true that both the public and the parties involved in negotiation expect a bargaining relationship to exist? Do you expect the first figure quoted by a car salesperson to be the final offer, or one that can be negotiated? Do you make a monetary bid for a car that is the only bid, or do you anticipate a kind of "auction ethics" in which there will be negotiations and a great deal of give-and-take between buyer and seller?

There are some areas in the relationships among people that are not bargainable. We are not saying here that people expect negotiation and compromise in all areas. If you are given a ticket for speeding and must appear before a judge, it is unlikely that you and the judge will enter into negotiations concerning the amount of the fine. If you and your boss are having a performance appraisal, and your performance is measurable and the evidence is clear-cut, you probably do not enter a bluffing and bargaining contest with your boss. You may resort to other tactics—passing the buck or finding a scapegoat—but it is unlikely that you would bluff your boss in this kind of exchange.

A few statements concerning bluffing as an ethical consideration may summarize this discussion:

1. The strategy and tactics a manager uses must relate to the mores, culture, and standards of the organization.
2. Using ethics or standards that are foreign to the organization may result in a breakdown of relationships in the organization.
3. Conforming to the expectations of other people is not an unethical or illegal practice.
4. Business bluffing (or organizational bluffing) seems to be a natural feature of organizational life and probably applies in many instances.

SUMMARY

The preceding descriptions of power give us a glimpse into the manager's political world. We started by examining the nature of that world; then, we explained several types of power. As we have said before, the words *power* and *politics* are neutral. They become moral questions when the ends are selfish. Although the definition of "good" is always debatable, the power of managers is a fact of organizational life. Managers must be made aware of this power, its generation, its sources, and its political usefulness.

The section on managerial tactics outlined just a few of the ways that politics and tactics can be used for managing during the active implementation of strategy.

Note that the theme of modification of traditional approaches permeates the ideas in this chapter. Armed with these new views of strategy and tactics, you should now be a bit more aware of the subtle qualities required in the manager.

KEY TERMS

Influence Any behavior by one person that produces an effect on the behavior of another person.

Authority The right to decide or act.

Power The force that others perceive one to have that gives that one the capacity to influence them.

Legitimate positional power Based on position in an organization.

Expert power Based on valued knowledge.

Functional power The power that rests with the people who usually perform certain functions.

Coercive power Based on fear.

Reward power Based on desired results.

Locational power Based on physical place in a work flow.

Coalition power Based on number of people presenting a united front.

Personal power Based on personality or physical attributes.

Power of scarce resources The power a person has when in control of scarce resources such as money and information.

Negative power Domination over others.

Positive power Inspires others to work toward goals.

Politics Those actions a person takes to get and keep power.

Tactics The way an individual uses power.

STUDY ASSIGNMENTS

1. In the opening case, why does Burke feel that Dan's current problems are the result of Dan's failure to understand the role of power and politics in getting things done in an organization?

2. How does the power and politics dimension of the manager's world differ from the management dimension and the leadership dimension?

3. Why does appreciating and exercising power and politics influence a manager's ability to survive organizational life?

4. Why do some observers feel that the significance and impact of power and politics in organizations have been on the rise in recent years?

5. With respect to the managerial process, compare and contrast the terms *influence, power,* and *authority.*

6. Discuss the nature of power and its role in facilitating a manager's ability to get things done. What role does power play when a manager needs to get nonsubordinates to perform work and to get things done?

7. Compare and contrast the different types and sources of power.

8. What did McClelland mean when he said that there are two faces of power? Why should managers focus more on utilizing the positive face of power?

9. How does a manager use tactics to keep and exercise power? What are some examples of how managers use tactics to exercise power?

10. What are the ethical issues raised when managers use bluffing as a tactic in exercising power?

Case for Discussion

E. F. HUTTON

For years the advertisements announced that "when E. F. Hutton talks, people listen." But in December 1987, what people were listening to was the announcement that after eighty-three years of operation, E. F. Hutton would no longer exist. To avoid total collapse, E. F. Hutton's board of directors had accepted an acquisition offer from Shearson Lehman Brothers.

Many analysts attributed the demise of the once reputable and highly profitable brokerage house to a series of problems that began with Hutton's conviction for illegal check-floating activities in 1985 and ended with the stock market crash of October 1987. But other observers have suggested that it was internal politics and a power struggle between Hutton's top two managers, Robert Fomon and Robert Rittereiser, that ultimately brought about the firm's failure.

In June 1985, Hutton's chairman and CEO of fifteen years, Robert Fomon, recruited Robert Rittereiser from Merrill Lynch in an effort to restore the firm's reputation and to reorganize Hutton's operations in the wake of the check-floating catastrophe. What Rittereiser found on his arrival at Hutton was an organization that was managed without an authority structure, budgets, or controls.

The retail brokers who acted like free agents received unusually high commissions. In addition, Rittereiser discovered that most offices and divisions were operated like fiefdoms plagued with conflict, intrigue, mismanagement, and declining profits.

Rittereiser moved cautiously to revamp Hutton's operations. He soon realized, however, that his cost-reduction suggestions would be undermined because Fomon exempted his favorite subordinates and operations from any cuts. In addition, he recognized that the needed cuts in the brokers' commission rates would be difficult to implement; he needed their support for other planned changes. Rittereiser's difficulties were further compounded when his relationship with Fomon began to deteriorate. Suddenly, he found himself in a power struggle with Fomon.

In time, it became evident to some board members and top managers that Rittereiser was unable to create change with Fomon continuing as chairman and CEO. In November 1986, Hutton's board made Rittereiser CEO, hoping that the situation would improve. Instead, the conflict grew worse, and soon the board members and the managers began taking sides. Fomon continued to undermine Rittereiser's reform efforts and, on his own, began negotiating with other firms for their acquisition of Hutton. (Fomon would benefit financially from such acquisition.) When some of Hutton's top managers discovered what Fomon was doing, they feared for their jobs and threw their support behind Rittereiser. But Rittereiser remained indecisive and ineffective, unable to exploit any allegiances he had developed. By the spring of 1987, he had lost the confidence of most of the board members and of Hutton's managers.

In May 1987, Hutton's board removed Fomon from the chairmanship, noting that his presence was no longer in the best interest of the firm. Nevertheless, Fomon was still able to exercise influence until Hutton's end, partly because the board chose not to promote Rittereiser to chairman. Rittereiser was unable to control Fomon's influence or gain the necessary support to revive Hutton. In the aftermath of the October 1987 crash, which devastated Hutton financially, Rittereiser had no other option but to negotiate Hutton's acquisition by Shearson. In the battle for power between Fomon and Rittereiser, everyone lost.

Chapter 16

Change

Learning Objectives

1. **Identify** some of the changes in a manager's world.
2. **Discuss** opportunities and problems.
3. **Identify** environmental changes.
4. **Describe** planned change and resistance to change.
5. **Describe** approaches to managing change.

"I WONDER where I went wrong. Did I get bad advice, or didn't I implement the advice right? Should I call Professor Elsea again?"

Pam Baugher had many second thoughts about the organizational changes she had made. At first, when she had started to implement her plan, things seemed to go just the way the professor had predicted. Actually, the professor had answered Pam's questions with a series of other questions, as professors frequently do. At the business school, Dr. Elsea had suggested that those in positions of leadership in organizations use information and knowledge from the behavioral sciences. And that's exactly what Pam had tried to do. She decided to write the professor a letter, since getting things down on paper frequently helps clear up the problem. The letter read as follows:

Dear Professor Elsea:

I am faced with an organizational problem I would like to share with you. You may recall our phone conversation two years ago, dealing with the specific problem of reorganization in my department. I know you recall the problems the department had when our president-appointed task force uncovered many morale problems using the survey you conducted.

You may also remember that when I pressed you for solutions at the debriefing meeting, you replied that since I was the one who had to be part of the dynamic plan of action, I should be the one to develop the solution. At the time, frankly, I felt you had let me down. I guess I was hoping for some miraculous, university-endorsed solution. You turned out to be very prophetic.

You asked me to recall some of the information from your course, Analysis of Organizational Behavior, and use some of the tools and techniques of analysis as well as some theoretical models of organizational behavior. You agreed that Homan's A-I-S thoughts and Leavitt's Structure-Technology-People model might apply. Using those ideas, I developed a scheme that my boss approved.

I asked my secretary to draw up a blueprint of the physical location of all forty people in the department. Next, I had a management trainee in the company do a kind of work-flow analysis. After looking at both the reports and the diagrams, I decided to make structural changes in the physical locations of the people so that their behavior might be changed.

Based on my analysis of the type of work to be performed, I grouped together the names of all the workers engaged in a similar function. Next, I took a blueprint of the office space and diagramed where each of these functional groups should be located and had the Office Construction Department erect partitions in what was the large "bullpen" area. Now the large area was divided into five subareas. I also asked the construction people to make signs designating the functional title for each area. Knowing how people sometimes resist change, I informed all employees of the impending change, and on a holiday weekend, we paid double time to have the partitions put up.

Initially, there was a little static and resistance, but most of the people responded and adjusted quickly. Within six months, communication improved within each of the functional divisions, new cliques formed, workers identified with the goals and norms of the functional unit, and the process time for auditing functions in the whole department speeded up. With all this success, you probably wonder why I am writing you with a problem.

Coordination among the functional units is at an all-time low. Where I have been able to promote identification within the unit, I now find that there is almost no identification with or loyalty to the department I manage. While there seems to be good cooperation and communication within the units, there is almost no cooperation or communication on projects that take the efforts of more than one auditing unit. Whenever I have staff meetings with the highest-grade personnel from each of the units, there seems to be a great reluctance by any of the units to do anything for the sake of another unit. I can even sense that the units are becoming jealous of each other, and I have to be very careful with the verbal rewards I make.

I guess I had to give something up in order to gain the within-unit cohesiveness. Now, what I want to know from you is what to do about getting identification on group projects. Surely, if the behavioral science theory and research studies were able to contribute so much to my first success, they should be able to help me out with this new problem.

I look forward to your reply and also a possible visit from you. Is there an ethical question involved when I make use of the behavioral science data to change—or, as some say, "manipulate"—the environment or structure and thus have people do what I want them to do?

Sincerely,

Pam S. Baugher, Manager
Auditing Department
Smyth Industries, Inc.
Wadsworth, Ohio ■

Sometimes, it seems that managerial solutions take us from the frying pan into the fire. Certainly Pam, manager of the auditing department of Smyth Industries, Inc., thinks so. One of the harsher realities in business is that a vital, growing organization will constantly have problems because growth means change.

Change is one of the basic facts of organizational life. By definition, any living organism is constantly undergoing change. Managers are part of this changed environment in a number of ways: They are changing because of their own biological and sociological composition, their work world is constantly changing, and the people they work with are under constant conditions of change. (See Figure 16-1.)

Saying that change is natural and should be expected is not enough for managers preparing to tackle the organizational problems of the twenty-first century.[1] Because there is no way to get around or avoid change, we must deal

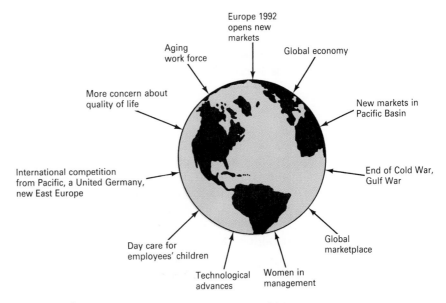

FIGURE 16-1 Some Changes in a Manager's World

with it directly. Thus, our approach is to examine more closely where the manager's world is changing and the elements of planned change. Then we address some approaches to managing change.

CHANGES IN A MANAGER'S WORLD

To be accurate, this section should be written in fading ink and on loose-leaf pages, for what are "truths" today may not be "truths" tomorrow. Many products you use daily may not exist in a few years, and much of your future living style is already on the drawing boards of firms throughout the world. What follows, therefore, are a few examples of change trends in areas that may have a direct effect on you personally.

Changing Opportunities and Problems

The changes presented are in the form of opportunities, challenges, and problems. In many instances, one situation may be an opportunity or a problem.

Service-Oriented Economy

What is a service-oriented economy?

In the 1970s, the United States moved into a service-oriented economy. More and more people found employment in

■ Education

■ Wholesale/retail trade

■ Hotel/motel business

- Airlines
- Health care organizations
- Banks and financial institutions
- Restaurant and fast-food services
- Medical and legal careers
- Leisure services

Most estimates are that the trends in the service area will grow both domestically and internationally. McDonald's, Kentucky Fried Chicken, and Wendy's, for example, have operations around the globe; Arthur Andersen has 450 offices in 82 countries to provide accounting, auditing, tax, and management consulting services; and most hotel developers have China as an area for expansion during the next decade. The merger mania, so dominant in the mid-to late 1980s, will be exported to other parts of the globe, thus providing more opportunities and changes for managers.

Public-Sector Challenges

New opportunities in federal, state, and local government, an employment area of approximately 20 million jobs, will offer you challenges full of uncertainty and excitement. Work in the public sector will become increasingly important as the government tackles such issues as drugs, environment (everything from oil spills off the coast of Alaska to dead oceans to the destroyed ozone layer), crime (Washington, D.C., is now more noted for being the murder capital of the world than for being the nation's capital), nuclear disarmament, illiteracy, technology, education, and poverty. All these complex and difficult problems demand new ideas and approaches and new partnerships between government and business.

Small-Business Opportunities

In recent years, most of the new jobs in the economy have been created by small businesses (firms with fewer than 100 employees). Opportunities in small business appear daily. Many enjoy the ownership, the freedom to work at their own pace, and the opportunity to control growth and expansion as it relates to a personal value system about the role of work in life.

Opportunities also abound for the nonowner managers of small businesses. For a person who wants variety of work, broad position descriptions, and involvement in many aspects of the total output of products or services, the small-business world may be the answer.

Entrepreneurship

The decline of the smokestack industries of the Midwest, the downsizing of staff by most major corporations throughout America, and the exporting of work to offshore countries worldwide have contributed to an awakening to opportunities for the entrepreneur.[2] Business schools in the United States are introducing or expanding their course offerings to people who want to start their own organizations, and there are good reasons to believe the trend will continue.

The entrepreneur can respond almost instantly to opportunities in his or her environment—an environment that is no longer limited to the state or geographic area of the company founder. International marketing channels have uncapped the potential markets for entrepreneurs.

Has America Run Out of Time?

In 1967, a Senate subcommittee heard testimony that by 1985, the average American would be working an average of twenty-two hours a week or only twenty-seven weeks each year at forty hours per week. The testimony also stated that people would be able to retire at age 38. A great concern at that time was what people would do with all the leisure time labor-saving technology was supposed to provide. Robots, computers, satellites, and other technological advancements were supposed to improve work efficiency, increase GNP, and reduce work hours.

Wrong.

In the early 1990s, people are working more hours, not fewer. According to a Harris survey, leisure time has decreased over 37 percent since 1973. Some professionals—accountants, doctors, lawyers, managers—work eighty hours a week or more. The average work week is nearly forty-seven hours. Vacations have become long weekends. Coordinating schedules in a family takes a home computer. Hallmark has developed cards for parents to send their young children: "Wish I were there to tuck you in." Service industries are booming as people pay others to wait in line, shop, walk the dog, and open the mail. Even with all the "modern conveniences"—microwave ovens, dishwashers, and portable telephones—people feel that there still are not enough hours in the day to get everything done. Some sociologists feel that the family is at its breaking point and on the verge of collapse.

How did we get into this situation?

Some feel that technology has quickened the heartbeat of America, with computers that have a response time of a trillionth of a second. People are continually inundated with information, with new facts. Even the worker on the factory floor must become familiar with computers, because computers operate and coordinate the machinery. The half-life of job skills is decreasing at faster and faster rates.

Technology is only partly responsible for the decrease in leisure time. Economics is another factor. The American dream—to own a home, to be at least middle-class—is still very much a part of American life. However, it now costs more than it did in 1967. Two incomes are needed for most families to maintain a middle-class status.

Self-worth is the third primary factor. Some people work long hours because they see success in a career as their measure of self-worth. If they are successful in their career, they think that they are also successful in life.

Many people are now exhausted. And sociologists and others are concerned with the long-term effects of such exhaustion. Physically, it could mean ulcers, strokes, heart disease, drug addiction, or hypertension. Emotionally and spiritually? There's no time left to reflect on the meaning of life, no time left to think, to be creative. And, with not enough time to sleep, there's not enough time to dream.

Source: Nancy Gibbs, "How America Has Run Out of Time," *Time,* April 24, 1989, pp. 58–67.

Work Is Changing

The concept of work and its contribution to the growth of the economy change constantly. Compare your own generation's ideas and experiences with those of your parents and your grandparents, and you will find radical change in such things as number of hours worked per week, paid vacations and holidays, retirement plans, and working conditions. Grandparents and great-grandparents may have worked long hours six or seven days a week under poor conditions for low pay. Parents may have lived and thrived during the post–World

407

War II prosperity into the 1970s, when labor-saving devices provided more leisure time. Inflation and severe recessions in the 1970s and 1980s had an impact on the work force. More women entered the labor market. Others took on second or third jobs. Today's workers are apparently caught up in a "rat race," with time itself being an extremely valuable commodity. What will happen next is impossible to predict.

Physical labor has increasingly been reduced by machines; work requires more knowledge and mental effort, resulting in greater challenges to unique human qualities. Education, information, and technology are very important in today's work world. Both managers and subordinates are very likely to have computers sitting on their desks at work. Many subordinates may not even be "at work," because it is becoming more popular and accepted for employees to work at home, sending their "output" to their employer by means of computer and telephone lines. Continuing education creates greater opportunities for promotion and also for changing careers. A person no longer needs to feel that "getting in a rut" is inevitable. Whereas the last generation may have held on to their jobs for thirty or forty years, this generation will change jobs and career fields numerous times during their years in the work force. There is no such thing as job security, anymore; even the concept of career security is shaky.

Is job security a thing of the past?

Education has also changed the way employees are treated in the work force. Since subordinates are now better educated, they are now more likely to want a voice in decision making. Opportunities are changing and new challenges are opening up daily.

Environmental Changes

What kind of manager is needed for all these changes?

Changes in the wider environment are so varied and pervasive that we shall list only a few of the principal ones.[3] Each of these will affect you and your managing processes significantly.

To most Americans, the changes in air travel have made the world smaller for them. To business, the changes in air express have solved many transportation problems. Few places in the world are more than one day away for an air express delivery like Federal Express.

Changing Population Patterns

Population will continue to grow, but at a decreasing rate. Family planning and changing life styles have affected the birthrate. The "traditional" family, with one spouse (normally the father) working and the other spouse staying home with the children, now represents only 4.6 percent of the population of the United States. If there are two parents in the family, both of them are usually employed. Single-parent families are common, as are stepfamilies. Many children have divorced parents, stepparents, and four sets of grandparents. Some families have no children at all. A popular term was coined for these families in the late 1980s—**DINKs** (Dual Income, No Kids). All these individuals bring different expectations, goals, and objectives to the workplace. This text has attempted to show you some of the struggles facing these people and their impact upon managers. Both subordinates and managers struggle daily with such things as career-versus-family decisions, lack of time, and day care. The problem of day care is not just for their children anymore, but also for their own elderly parents. As the population grows older, more and more people are faced with caring for their elderly parents. People are living longer; there are now many people in their 70s, 80s, and 90s. More and more are surpassing the 100-year-old mark. Although some remain healthy and independent, others need to be cared for on an almost constant basis.

DINKs Acronym for Dual Income/No Kids. Refers to couples where both have careers and no children, generally having more disposable income.

In addition, because the population is growing older, the work force is changing. Teenagers are in short supply, so many employers are relying on older (over 65) employees to fill in, particularly in entry-level jobs at McDonald's, Carl's Jr., and other organizations. It is not unusual for a manager to be much younger than the subordinates.

It's a possibility that the manager may not even speak the same language as the subordinates. Changing demographic patterns show a growing number of Hispanics and other ethnic groups in the United States. **Diversity** is the norm in the work force. In addition, business is now very much international. It would be very helpful if managers were bilingual so as to deal better with clients, customers, bosses and subordinates, suppliers, and government officials.

Diversity A term describing a work-force that contains people of different races and cultures.

Urbanization will continue. It is predicted that stretches of land 300 to 400 miles long will become belts of megalopolises, with one city merging into the next. An excellent example of this is the stretch of land from Los Angeles to San Diego; it is very nearly one city after another all the way down the coast. These megalopolises will require that managers concentrate on the interrelationships of a large number of people in groups and subgroups—central cities, suburbs, and community centers. The impact of this concentration of people will be evident in the need for improved planning, organization, and control of new clusters of people. The demand for managing skills will clearly be tremendous.

Technological Changes

How will new technology affect your life?

The rapidity of technological changes is evident to every person in modern society. Technological means for improving society have been discovered at a much faster rate than have the social means for accommodating them. Managers will continually be faced with having to adapt to rapid obsolescence of their present plants and equipment. Let us list some of the areas in which technological improvements will continue to add pressures on the manager's world:

1. New products have more impact upon the American scene than just creating new jobs. Since 1960, the products have also produced changes in life styles, aspirations, and expectations. New products and ideas have a way of creating new subcultures.

Consider how dependent we have become upon television, VCRs, copying processes, credit cards, computers, pocket calculators, transistors (and soon superconductors), electron microscopes, frozen foods, the microwave, the jet engine, and birth control procedures. There are hundreds of products in the development stage that will affect your life style in the next decade. It is the wise manager who is constantly aware that many present products and procedures will soon be replaced.

2. New transportation methods will result in even-greater speed of air, land, sea, and space vehicles and will contribute even more to bringing people closer together. On one hand, improved transportation will help the manager, but on the other hand, it will provide the manager with new challenges. The manager will need to give more attention to the need for planning unified networks of all transportation systems and will have to respond to claims of damages transportation systems may cause to the environment.

3. Communications already bring faraway plants and offices into instant contact, and new technology in this area will improve communications even more. Today, information is transmitted almost instantaneously through computer and telephone lines and through satellite systems. One office on the East Coast can receive from an office on the West Coast a picture of a person, or a report, in seconds with fax machines, which are becoming common in offices. Electronic mail is also becoming common in the workplace. Information can be sent anywhere in the world in seconds. This instant access to information creates both challenges and opportunities for the manager.

4. New sources of energy must provide answers to current worries about power shortages. Further study of the energy problem should result in new

Historians have theorized that the neolithic standing stone provided some sort of communication system for people in prehistoric England. Mounted next to the ancient is a modern communication system—the satellite receiving dish that is part of an instantaneous communication network that spans the globe. The satellite dish is part of British Telecom's international telecommunications network. Both the dish and the standing stone can be seen at Goonhillie Down, Cornwall, England.

technology for energy sources. Some sources explored so far include solar, wind, water, and nuclear power. Additional sources may develop through the exploration of space and through other scientific investigations. Both public and private managers will need to be concerned about energy. In addition, the need for changes in attitudes toward conservation of energy (and other expendable resources) will pervade all issues facing managers in the future.

5. Technological support for life processes will improve health and extend life. Control of disease in animals, plants, and humans; new foods and new packaging of foods; better fertilizers; new pharmaceuticals; and many other health aids will improve the quality of life. These improvements will offer new opportunities to perceptive managers. Environmental protection can be viewed not only as a problem for and a constraint on managers but also as an opportunity for managers who recognize change.

Global Interdependence

Because of improved transportation and communication, the entire globe has become closely interdependent. What happens 10,000 miles away can immediately become important to a nation or a local community.

International markets and sources of supply are available for even the small firm that in the past thought in terms of a radius of 100 miles. Effects of unstable international money markets, shipping strikes, changes in international transportation rates, and changes in the weather in some faraway place may now have an immediate effect on managing in the local plant or shopping center. Damages to planet earth from pollution of the oceans, oil spills in Alaska, and destruction of the ozone layer and the resultant greenhouse effect

Global Application

The Supereconomy of Europe

On December 31, 1992, the twelve nations of the European Economic Community remove their restrictions on trade, migration, and capital flow to form one vast trading market of 320 million people. The idea, drawing its first breath in 1967 when the Coal and Steel Community merged with the European Economic Community and the European Atomic Energy Community, seems appropriate to the 1990s and the twenty-first century.

Western Europe, once the economic and military power of the world, hopes to become preeminent again and reposition itself in a global marketplace. The USSR presents a huge question mark on the road to this objective. Mikhail Gorbachev's policies of glasnost and perestroika, conditioned by the desire for independence by some of the Soviet republics, are creating new uncertainties for Eastern Europe; the European Common Market is not sure how to take advantage of this situation.

The new economic power of the EC is expected to provide greater balance with the economic forces of the United States and Japan and to stimulate global competitiveness.

Sometimes the old saying, "The more things change, the more they stay the same" is true. McDonald's started as one small restaurant with golden arches in Texas and is now an international business, with restaurants all over the United States, Mexico, Canada, Europe, and the Soviet Union. The menus may vary just a little (in Germany, for example, the McDonald's has beer on the menu) but the employees are the same—bright, happy, caring with warm and personal service. These particular employees are in Moscow.

now have an impact on all residents of earth. Managers have both the challenge and the opportunity to reverse the damage and preserve the planet. In addition, managers will feel the impact of this global interdependence in the following areas:

1. Multinational firms have expanded in the manufacture of automobiles, electrical products, petroleum products, pharmaceuticals, information processing equipment, and many other products in daily use.[4] These firms have seen the economic advantages of viewing the entire world as a market and have expanded accordingly. Competition in an increasing number of industries is now international.

2. Intercultural exchanges of ideas, products, and customs have enriched the variety and diversity of formerly isolated, separate cultures. Modes of dress, philosophy and religion, language, methods of expression in music and the fine arts, and new ideas of social organization are rapidly influencing even the most provincial sectors of society. These changes at times cause disruptions in the old ways of living and force people to come to some accommodation with an increasingly diverse and pluralistic society, where differences must not only be tolerated but also be encouraged.

3. Businesspeople in small firms who were domestically oriented will find that tremendous opportunities await them if they tap the resources available in world markets. For example, a small retail store can specialize in exotic products from foreign countries, a lumber processor can import unique woods for furniture and houses, a local travel agent can promote charter flights to faraway places, a photography specialist can offer products made in four or five foreign countries. The horizon for new opportunities for managers in a variety of endeavors is unlimited if only the effects of global interdependence are recognized.[5]

MANAGERIAL PLANNED CHANGE

Can change be managed?

The preceding section on the changes in a manager's world represents one facet of change. Many of those changes are beyond the manager's control and influence; all you can do is to respond to or be affected by them. In Chapter 1, we said that the manager's job was one of action as well as response, and it is to the action phase of change that we now move. In this section, we look more carefully at the process of planning change, followed by some approaches to managing change.[6]

The Setting for Planned Change

Planned change Change that occurs as the result of a manager's determining what elements in a situation are unsatisfactory and cannot remain.

Planned and managed **change** is the preset method a manager uses to move a situation toward a specific, predetermined objective or goal.[7] Figure 16-2 pictures the scope of planned-change activities. At T_1 (Time 1), some situation develops that is not wanted: Production or sales drop, there is a possibility of a labor strike, personnel turnover is higher than anticipated, the government changes a regulation, a competitor comes on the market with a new product, or, as in the case of the European Economic Community, a staggering challenge and opportunity comes on the horizon. As the manager in charge, you would want to be in a more favorable situation at T_2, the future.

The following steps might be taken by a manager or a management team planning to manage change.

1. A situation evaluation takes place that results in dissatisfaction with the present condition, so that
2. A new objective or goal is set, and then
3. A plan is developed to reach the goal.
4. The manager implements the plan using the resources of the organization.

FIGURE 16-2 The Scope of Managerial Planned Change

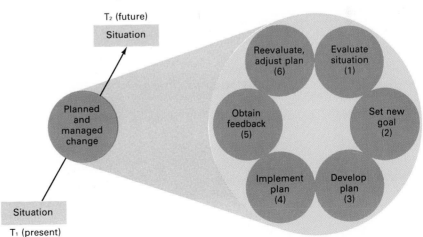

5. Next, the manager gets feedback on the results of the plan and

6. Reevaluates and adjusts the objectives or the plan itself.

The process is frequently repeated. Because the steps of this process may seem very logical to you, you may fail to find the potential problem areas in the change process. What's so difficult about moving from T1 to T2?

Human interpretation and individual differences present most of the challenges in planned and managed change. In every one of the steps in the foregoing change process, you might expect at least three different responses from all the people involved:

Acceptance and positive support. In this response, your people accept the change and strongly support it. They may help persuade others to accept the change, or they may innovate procedures or methods so that the change will be more effectively implemented. This response is the one you hope to receive in all situations.

Compliance and minimal support. Here, people will do only what is required. If the change requires innovation, workers may do only what they are told and no more. These people do not seem to have their hearts in the project and go through the motions to meet the minimum standards of performance. Although not as preferable as the first response, it is not as bad as the last response.

Resistance. This response has many options. The resistance may be open or hidden. An example of a hidden response is sabotage by the employee. If this response exists, you may be faced with more problems than if you had not implemented any change.

These three conditions can occur at any point in the change process. For example, not everyone may agree with your evaluation of the situation or with your objective, plan, or method of implementation. Frequently, your decision is based upon your personal interpretation, your values, and your priorities. Everyone around you—your boss, subordinates, and peers—may have opinions directly opposed to yours. The managerial challenge is to deal with all the problems created by planned change.[8]

Unfortunately, resistance of some kind is usually present when change is attempted. It seems appropriate, therefore, to present a few special insights on this topic before discussing approaches to managing change.

Resistance to Change

Why don't all people change?

At the base of all change is uncertainty. By definition, if something is to change, the state of the event in the future will be different from the state of the event in the present. It is not always possible to know in advance the exact state of the event in the future. Thus, you must deal with uncertainty.

We know from earlier chapters on human motivation and individual behavior that people come into an experience with different self-concepts, dominant needs, and perceptional frames of reference. This means that an event that is really a changing event may be perceived favorably by one person and unfavorably by another. You know of people who are eager to change, to get

Resistance to change
All those reasons why an individual wants to remain with the present condition.

themselves out of patterned, routine behavior. You also know people who prefer the status quo. Therefore, the spectrum of acceptance or **resistance to change** is broad. For what other reasons might people resist change and the uncertainty that follows?

■ The change may threaten someone's psychological safety.
■ The change may require a shakeup and revision of a person's psychological world.
■ The change may have an economic impact on one or more of the people involved.

To many people, change and uncertainty present the possibility of personal failure, and thus they have an emerging sense of fear. To the person who is not self-confident (has a weak self-concept), new and changing situations with a great deal of uncertainty will be perceived as threatening to psychological safety.[9]

Change also requires a revision in the behavioral processes of perception. New stimuli must be filtered and interpreted, and the changing motives of people will also come into the picture. Traditional defense mechanisms must now be revised. All psychological processes that perhaps placed a person at a point of psychological equilibrium will be affected because of the newness of the situation. Certainly, change will demand at least a reorganization of the behavioral processes.

Not all resistance is only psychological. There are changes in jobs or duties that will alter the worker's productive capacity and thus the opportunity for organizational rewards. One obvious reward is money, and if the change results in a change in the person's economic condition, there may be resistance to it. The psychological and social aspects of economic change, however, must not be overlooked. A simple illustration will demonstrate this point.

Assume there is a change in the nature of a job that results in a financial change, either a gain or a loss. A person may resist the change if some peers receive greater gains, or if the change brings about a difference in the rankings within the present work group. Figure 16-3 portrays this situation.

Note that all five workers ranked in Figure 16-3 could resist the changes in pay, Harry and Manny in particular. Even Tom may feel threatened if he feels that Kay and Georgette moved up in their rankings because of their sexual status rather than their performance. Different explanations are possible for all

FIGURE 16-3 The Social Consequences of Change

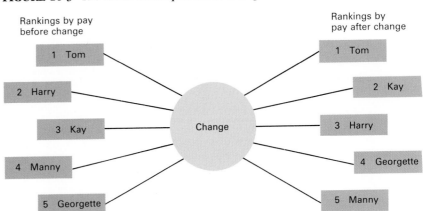

Rankings by pay before change

1 Tom
2 Harry
3 Kay
4 Manny
5 Georgette

Change

Rankings by pay after change

1 Tom
2 Kay
3 Harry
4 Georgette
5 Manny

Ethics Issue

Pregnancy in the Workplace

Sometimes, the need for managing change in the workplace arises as a result of social changes. When that occurs, managers often find themselves in difficult and compromising situations that may conflict with their own personal values and ethics. Such is the case with handling employee pregnancy in the 1990s.

Twenty years ago, when a working woman became pregnant, she was expected to quit on her own or be terminated. Only a handful of businesses provided the pregnant employee with maternity leave or any kind of option to return to work after the child's birth. But as more and more women entered the work force, social and political forces began pressuring businesses and managers to change their attitude toward and handling of pregnant employees. The Pregnancy Discrimination Act of 1978 made it illegal to fire, withdraw benefits from, or deny employment to a pregnant employee. Today, over 70 percent of the women who become pregnant do so while employed.

Recent studies have shown that little has really changed in the way firms handle their employees' pregnancies, and if anything, attitudes about pregnancy in the workplace have deteriorated. Although firms ensure that they comply with the legal requirements pertaining to pregnant employees, many pregnant employees find that there is considerable, albeit subtle, behavioral discrimination against them. It is not unusual for pregnant employees to be given less-important assignments and fewer responsibilities.

Pregnant employees experience a number of problems related to their pregnancy. One of the biggest ones is the change in attitude on the part of their colleagues, associates, and even customers. Studies found that co-workers are often resentful of the pregnant employee. Pregnant workers observed that colleagues became more patronizing toward them and usually, over time, began to question the pregnant employees' competency.

Some managers argue that pregnant employees must be treated differently, and that by doing so, firms are acting in a socially responsible manner. There was an important court case involving a manufacturer of car batteries who closed jobs to any woman employee who was or could become pregnant. The firm was concerned that it would be liable for any birth defects that might result from the employee's exposure to the lead materials used in making the batteries.

Businesses cannot afford to handle employee pregnancy as they have in the past because both the employees and the firms lose. A returning employee is a valuable asset and a known commodity. Studies found that over 70 percent of employees return from maternity leave within a year of their child's birth. Unfortunately, when they return, even if it is to their old job, they find that they have lost professional, promotional, and compensation opportunities.

References: Kathleen Hughes, "Pregnant Professionals Face Subtle Bias at Work," *Wall Street Journal,* February 6, 1991, p. B1; Kathleen Hughes, "Mothers-to-Be Sue, Charging Discrimination," *Wall Street Journal,* February 6, 1991, p. B1.

five people. If you recall our discussion of groups in Chapter 14, you will remember that not all may want to disturb the cohesiveness, norms, or status positions already established.

Usually, resistance is a warning signal to the manager, for nearly all change brings a change in the social patterns and individual behavior processes. Managers should expect resistance when change occurs and, to the extent possible, act to minimize the ensuing problems.

With a sense of the changes in a manager's world, the planned-change process, and resistance to change, we now turn to a few approaches managers can take when facing change.

APPROACHES TO MANAGING CHANGE

What are some approaches to managing change?

The approaches to change described in this section are based upon the assumption that a manager is interested in reducing any resistance harmful to the organization.[10] In one way of thinking, the approaches could be classified as those in which

- The structure is changed.
- The technology is changed.
- The decision-making techniques are changed.
- Organization development techniques are used.

In these general approaches, the objectives are still the same: to create the desired behavior. In some cases, the approach works more on attitudes than on behavior, but the ultimate objective is still the behavior change. (See Figure 16-4.)

Changing the Structure

This method of change is probably obvious to you from reading the previous chapters. In this approach, the manager who has direct authority and influence over the structure of the organization changes behavior by changing the structure.

Assume that you are a political appointee in the state office of personnel. When you come into your new job, you find that the people (managers and nonmanagers) are either political appointees or those who are in the positions

FIGURE 16-4 Managed Change

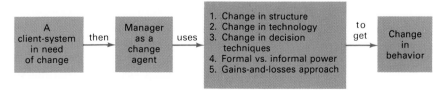

as professionals. Because part of the work force is federally controlled through civil service (employees cannot be fired arbitrarily after each election), you find yourself with a very mixed group. Some are politically independent, some are from a previous Democratic administration, and some are from the present Republican administration. One person in your office has an exceptional amount of power over the people in the political arena of the state capital, and she is fully aware of that power, as are the other members of the work force.

She is a problem employee. She is unproductive and a disruptive force among the rest of the work group. You seek counsel and are told that the situation must be accepted as a fact of political life and cannot be changed. You are at a loss to make any shift through firing and/or job rotation.

You ask a consultant to perform a work-flow analysis of the materials being processed in your unit. The consultant submits recommendations and you implement most of the suggestions. The results amaze you.

Under the previous situation, your problem employee was allowed to behave in a very annoying manner. Under the new situation, she is placed in a position along the flow of work that gives her something to do and makes her dependent on others in the office. It is not long before she finds the situation intolerable and resigns. You find later that she makes no political waves and that the department has been improved by her absence. The work study and subsequent redesign of the organizational structure proved effective.

Changing the Technology

Managing an organization's technology is another approach to changing attitudes and behavior. In the research studies of Leonard Sayles,[11] he identified four work groups of people who displayed similar behavior: apathetic, erratic, strategic, and conservative. He suggested that the behavior of each group was influenced by the type of job performed. The conservative group, for example, was the most skilled and the oldest workers; the strategic work group was younger and worked in the most important jobs in the plant. Any action they took directly affected the output of the organization.

It follows from the insights of that research study that a manager can influence the behavior of work groups through decisions about types of work to be done in the organization.

Another research study, done by William Foot Whyte[12] in the restaurant industry, reveals the impact that work flow (technology) has upon the behavior and satisfaction of work groups. Whyte found that there was a difference in the satisfaction and tension of waitresses, depending upon the work-flow demands on and the status of individuals. When the work flow demanded a person of lower status, in this case the waitresses, to start the interaction with someone with higher status, cooks, neither group felt satisfied and tension was obvious. The technology of the workplace was changed so that waitresses did not initiate the interaction with the cooks; satisfaction of both groups improved and tensions were reduced.

More illustrations are possible, but perhaps the point has already been made: the manager of an organization has available at least two approaches to influencing and changing behavior—affecting the structure or affecting the technology. The third approach to be discussed deals with the decision-making techniques of the manager.

Changing the Decision-Making Techniques

In most organizational decisions, the manager has at least three general options: to make decisions alone, to let subordinates make the decision, or to participate in a joint decision-making experience.

If you recall the steps in the planned-change process, you can see the possibility of the three decision-making options in the problems of evaluation, objective setting, plan development, and implementation. Is there a management decision-making approach or technique that will improve the success of planned change and the reduction of resistance to change? Setting objectives or goals is one area where we have some insight into knowing how to manage change and reduce resistance.

There is a growing body of research that suggests that goal setting is directly related to goal achievement; that is, the conscious setting of goals results in behavior that works toward that goal. Kolb and Boyatzis[13] identified characteristics of the goal-setting process and found that five factors were important for goal setting to result in goal achievement: awareness, expectation of success, psychological safety, measurability of the change goal, and self-controlled evaluation. To have successful participation in goal setting that will lead to the planned behavior change, you will want to be sure these characteristics exist.

If awareness exists, it means that the subordinate in an objective-setting session is able to focus clearly on the role required for the goal achievement. Such a person will be more aware of the forces that are related to the change goal and will be realistic rather than naive.

A person who expects to succeed will be confident that the goal is possible, feasible, and within reach. Thus, the expectation of success may help one to achieve and be successful.

With psychological safety, the person feels psychologically free and safe and is therefore open to realistic feedback and results. There is less likelihood of defense mechanisms to cover up weaknesses.

The measurability of the change goal is also a critical characteristic, for if a goal does not have the potential of being measured, feedback and progress toward that goal will be superficial and unreal. If people have identified a goal with a specific target date and specific methods of achieving it, they should be able to get feedback on progress and move more successfully toward that goal. It may even be necessary for them to make modifications in their productivity rate or in methods, or even in the goal itself, as feedback flows from their efforts.

The final characteristic is the self-controlled evaluation. The person will only be going through the motions if the goal that is set comes from the organization or the boss and progress is viewed as a requirement. If the person has some control over the process and the goal-setting method, the whole process will be improved.

Other Approaches to Managing Change

There are some other methods that may affect behavior and attitude simultaneously. The logic behind these methods is very simple. Rather than getting involved in debate over which comes first—attitude or behavior—the proponents of these methods are concerned with the immediate output of change more than whether intervening variables are changed before other variables. There are two approaches that we want to share with you: the formal-versus-informal power approach and the gains-and-losses approach.

Formal Versus Informal Power

This approach to attitude-behavior change can best be illustrated by a concrete example. A group of churches was sponsoring a people's organization in a predominantly black, low-income area. The neighborhood people wanted to plant gardens in their backyards and asked for assistance from the agricultural division of the local university and other groups in town. They received the seeds and planted them.

A drainage problem developed, however, during one of the first big rainstorms of the season. Directly across the street, the drainage pipes from tobacco warehouses were turned in the direction of the vegetable gardens. The water from the storm washed away most of the seed. The local people wanted to replant and sought help with the drainage problem.

The situation was brought to the church board of directors, and two approaches were suggested. One approach required using formal channels of communication and power, even to the point of a protest march on the homes of the warehouse owners. The other approach was to use more informal and subtle techniques. The owner of the warehouses was identified and found to be a member of one of the affiliated churches. A phone call was placed to the minister of his church, and the minister in turn relayed the request and problem to the manager of the warehouses. Soon the drainpipes were realigned so that the flooding stopped.

In this example, the informal, nondirect approach seemed preferable to the direct use of power through formal channels. In another situation, formal power might have been more effective. In our case, however, the parties were never given an opportunity to generate resistance to change. They were not put into embarrassing situations where they might lose face. The issue was fed through the informal channels, where the action was immediate and successful.

Gains-and-Losses Approach

In this approach, the manager performs a process of analysis before taking any action. He or she makes up a simple T-account-type form and asks one question: If the proposed change were to take place, what would be the gains and the losses to the people affected by the change? In Table 16-1, for example, the proposed change from assigning secretaries to a specific boss to assigning them to a group (that is, a secretarial pool) may have economic advantages but psychological disadvantages. In this case, the manager would list the gains and the losses from the viewpoint of the managers, the secretaries, and others. From the analysis come insights and areas of potential danger whenever the decision is made and the action implemented.

This approach takes into account some important features of change. Looking at change from the perspective of the people involved reminds us of the importance of individual processes, especially the process of individual perception.[14] The changes contemplated by any manager have a meaning above and beyond the meaning that the manager simply states. Much friction, frustration, confrontation, and organizational disarray can be prevented by the use of so simple a process as this behavioral analysis of change.

The managerial role in change has purposely been narrow. Dealing with

TABLE 16-1 The Gains-and-Losses Approach to Proposed Change of Secretaries from Personal to Pool Assignment	
Gains	Losses
To Secretaries	
More money	No sense of loyalty
Specialization of talent	Loss of pride and identity with
Greater socialization with other	specific job
secretaries	Boredom
	Less chance to broaden growth
	through varied experience
To Bosses	
Greater efficiency	Possible loss of power
Reduced manpower costs	Loss of status symbol
Impersonal—few personnel problems	Loss of personal services

change can be a very depressing and frustrating experience because so much of change is beyond our influence and authority. Few managers will influence the country's economic policies or reduce cutthroat competition in an industry. Few may be in a position to alter the prices of products or request more rigorous testing of new products. But there is a world that may respond to managerial influence—the immediate, interpersonal world.

As a manager, you may be able to change work procedures so that performance improves; you have the authority to rearrange the location of people in an office so that a project writer is freed from interruption and distracting noise; and you may be able to convince your boss that more of the staff should participate in decision making that involves them.

Much of the material presented so far is applicable and useful when you find yourself in these roles. But the topic of change, and especially organizational change, is much broader and more complex. What approaches are taken when the scope of the problem is broad and affects more than one or two people, one or two departments?

Using Organization Development Techniques

Organization development A comprehensive organization-wide approach to change; usually this approach requires strong top management commitment.

Organization development (OD) is "an effort (1) planned, (2) organization-wide, and (3) managed from the top, to (4) increase organization effectiveness and health through (5) planned interventions in the organization's 'processes,' using behavioral science knowledge." When this definition is compared with earlier ones in this chapter, you realize that items 2 and 3 are different. Planning for change so as to create effectiveness and health by managing approaches (or interventions) with the insights and experiences from the behavioral sciences is a description of the present chapter. The distinction occurs when we add the notion that the planning is to be organizationwide and should involve the participation and support of top management. Organization development requires the involvement of many personnel in a firm and should include many parts of the system. For example, change interventions would include the effect upon pay systems, promotion, career paths, shifts in personnel, interacting departments, and even the consequences in the marketplace to both consumers and competitors. OD is a larger, broader, more encompassing form of managing organizational change.

Although OD is process oriented, it is not value-free. Writers like McGregor, Sayles, Maslow, Likert, Blake and Moulton, Argyris, and others value the human resources of an organization and believe there is a preferred way of managing that brings out the best in people. The theories and practices are based upon a set of democratic, humanistic values. After an organization performs an assessment of its present state (using surveys, interviews, and other measures), there is an evaluation of the results, and then a determination of the preferred state. This assessment, evaluation, and determination, although supported by top management, is not performed exclusively by them. Many people contribute, so that the decision-making base is broadened and power is distributed throughout the organization. Developing strategies and action plans plus managing the transition period (the state between the present and the preferred) should be given top priority by all management. Piecemeal efforts create piecemeal results.

Many techniques described throughout this book become part of the OD technology. Some of these are job enrichment, MBO, job design, management training, team building, managerial grid, and career planning.

Since change is such a constant companion of organizations and managers, OD approaches recommend continuous monitoring and feedback to the participants of change. Managing change through individual or organizational means is so critical that all managers need to become familiar with and proficient in the concepts and the technology.[15]

SUMMARY

Among various approaches to the management of change, we found changing the structure, the technology, and the decision-making technique, and others. You will remember that we arrived at the discussion after first discerning the ways the manager's world changes and then analyzing the change process itself.

The manager of an organization will have to learn to live with change. Frequently, change is like the wind, in that it is neutral in its effect. There are times when the wind can be refreshing, and there are times when it can be destructive. We believe the ideas presented in this chapter give you a perspective on the topic of change that will allow you to approach the organizational world with confidence rather than fear.

KEY TERMS

DINKs Acronym for Dual Income/No Kids. Refers to couples where both have careers and no children, generally having more disposable income.

Diversity A term describing a workforce that contains people of different races and cultures.

Planned change Change that occurs as the result of a manager's determining what elements in a situation are unsatisfactory and cannot remain.

Resistance to change All those reasons why an individual wants to remain with the present condition.

Organization development A comprehensive organization-wide approach to change; usually this approach requires strong top management commitment.

STUDY ASSIGNMENTS

1. In the opening case, why did Pam Baugher achieve only limited success in her efforts to "manipulate" the workplace and alter the performance of her subordinates?

2. Identify some of the recent changes in the manager's world and explain how these changes affect the managerial process. How should managers prepare for future changes in their environment?

3. How has the typical individual work week changed since 1970? What are the implications of this kind of change for managers?

4. What are some of the significant changes in the population patterns, and how have those changes influenced employee behavior and work performance?

5. How have recent technological changes placed new pressures on today's managers?

6. Discuss some of the changes and adjustments managers must make to work and succeed in the increasingly global business environment.

7. What can today's managers do to facilitate change in their work and organizational environment? Can change really be managed?

8. What are some of the reasons that people resist change? Why do people resist change even when it is needed and when it is in their best interest to change?

9. Compare and contrast some of the different approaches to managing change that a manager can utilize to improve individual, group, and organizational performance.

10. How does implementing change that affects an individual or a small group differ from implementing broader and more complex organizational changes?

Case for Discussion

THE BRANCH BANK EXPANSION AT SECURITY NORTHERN BANK

When word came to the employees of the Craigmont branch of the New York Security Northern Bank that they would soon be moving to a new location, there seemed to be an immediate surge in morale. The growth in business had convinced the bank's top management that the Craigmont branch facilities were already inadequate. So, when the opportunity came to relocate the branch in a new and considerably larger building fifteen blocks away, top management decided to make the move.

On the last day of work at the old location, a few of the approximately one dozen employees of the branch expressed a slight note of sadness about having to leave the building they had grown to both love and hate over the many years. Even Jean O'Sullivan, the branch manager, said she would be sorry to say farewell to the four walls, the leaky roof, and the warped and well-worn hardwood floors that she and the other employees called their "work home." They forgot about the breakdowns in the air-conditioning system during the hottest week of the summer and the clanking steam pipes during the winter months. There was even a string of stories about a wild animal that lived under the building. Some employees claimed it was a woodchuck, others thought it was a badger, and one (unnamed) employee joked it was the state bank examiner.

At about the same time the move took place, Jean O' Sullivan received a major promotion. She was named vice president of personnel for the entire bank, reporting directly to the president. When the personnel V.P. position opened up, the management asked, "Whom do we have who really understands people and can manage a major area of activity that will increase in importance?" The answer was obvious. Jean's branch was well known for having the most friendly and efficient employees. Although Jean demanded first-rate performance from those who worked for her, she was also understanding and respectful of them. Her subordinates were sad but certainly not surprised by her advancement.

Audrey Cummings, who had been head teller at the bank's largest branch, in Evinrude, some thirty-two miles away, was selected to replace Jean as manager of the new Craigmont branch. Audrey was an "up and comer," sometimes referred to as a "fast track" employee. She was about twenty years younger than Jean and had earned a reputation for thoroughness and good judgment. Audrey was thirty-six years old and obviously very career oriented. She wanted to advance as far and as rapidly as possible. She considered it important for her subordinates to perform well so she could continue to move ahead in the bank. Thus, she watched everything that went on very closely to assure there were no slipups.

A short while after the move was made, eight employees were added to the branch to handle the already increased volume of work and in anticipation of the continued growth in the banking industry. With the increases in work load and staff, Audrey found it necessary to reorganize the branch and reassign the duties and the responsibilities of employees.

Under the new system of organization, each employee became accountable for a specific function. Some employees had more than one. Audrey believed that this would give each person a sense of responsibility and also make it easier for her to assess the work performed by each person. Under the old system, the division of work was less specified, but the greatly increased level of activity seemed to call for a change.

The new location was brighter, cleaner, and far more spacious than the old one. The carpeted floor made the new location much quieter, too. There was even a good parking lot for employees just behind the new location, as well as better places to go for lunch.

Eight months after the move, noticeable changes had taken place at the Craigmont branch. One change was that three of the long-time employees had quit to work at other banks in the area, and rumors floated about that several others had intentions of leaving, also. "It's all part of change," thought Audrey as she concentrated on making the branch perform efficiently. This was borne out in the third-quarter report showing record-setting growth in deposits, loans, and other services. Audrey worked hard to make the Craigmont branch a success. She usually came in one or two hours before the normal starting time and frequently worked late into the evenings and on Saturdays.

About a year after her promotion, Jean became concerned about the changes at the Craigmont branch. Turnover there persisted. Discipline problems, particularly with some of the younger employees, were brought to her attention. Jean wondered how she might be perceived by the bank's president and the executive vice president of banking operations if she approached them on the issue of the personnel problems and the soured attitudes she could see at her old branch, especially in view of the fact that the branch was operating at a higher level of business volume and growth than when she was there running things. Would it sound like "sour grapes"? "Perhaps," she thought, "it might be a good idea to talk directly to Audrey. But how?" There didn't seem to be an easy solution as to what to do or say.

Chapter 17

Managing Information

Learning Objectives

1. **Identify** the fundamental concepts of information systems.
2. **Distinguish** between data and information.
3. **Explain** how information systems provide support in implementing managerial functions.
4. **Discuss** the application of information systems in managerial problem solving and decision making.
5. **Identify** the principal issues in implementating and using information systems.

- The site: The Executive Conference Center on the outskirts of San Diego, California
- The participants: Twenty-five middle-level managers and administrators from diverse organizations—public and private, manufacturing and investment and marketing and banking, large and small, profit and nonprofit. Some are line managers, some are staff personnel.
- The topic: Developing Information Systems
- The scene: Opening session in the conference room

"Good morning. What a great day we have in sunny California for the first day of this three-day conference! My name is Larry Tarpey, and my associates and I will be with you during your stay here. Les Poff, that cheerful woman who registered you early this morning, tells me that this is a very diverse group. We have people here from many different organizations and from different functions within those organizations. That's good, because what we want to develop at this conference is a process and a way of thinking about data and information in any organization. Many training-consulting outfits will teach you specific techniques or methods of dealing with specific problems, and this approach works fine if you continue to face the same problems. We would rather have you understand why the problems exist, what objectives are to be achieved, what the capabilities are of all forms of information systems, and most importantly, what personnel must still do after the data are collected so that they can become useful managerial information—but I'm getting ahead of myself.

"To get us off on the right foot, I'd like each of you to identify for us one of the problems you're facing in your organization. Briefly describe the situation that seems to be crying for a managerial solution. Why don't we start with all of you outlining on the pads in front of you the basic elements, and then we'll have a few of you give us oral reports so that the whole group can sense the flavor of the problems."

(A few minutes pass.)

Larry: All right, I see that most of you have written something down, and I'm looking forward to these reports because I saw many smiles and chuckles while you were outlining your situations. Let's start with your examples. Give us your name, organization, and job function. In a short time, you'll know each other.

Wendy: I'm a personnel manager for a small machine tool manufacturer, which employs about 500 people. Because we have a number of federal contracts, we periodically have to complete and file EEO reports. This is a time-consuming exercise, particularly because we have not computerized any of our personnel operations. I would like to know if an information system would improve our operations and make it easier for us to comply with EEO reporting requirements.

Joe: We had a recent incident at our facility where an employee was denied a promotion based on material contained in her personnel file. She filed a grievance, and in the processing of the grievance, someone discovered that some data in her file had been inappropriately entered on her records. Actually, the data pertained to another employee. Needless to say, we were rather embarrassed by the incident. How can we prevent such an occurrence in the future?

Tori: Our firm has gone into office automation in a big way—not just the personnel department, but all administrative offices. Recently, some of my friends and fellow workers have expressed how much they dislike working in the place since the computers arrived. A couple believe that productivity has actually declined. I think the system is great, and I don't understand what their problems are with the system. I'm comfortable with the system.

Karen: I'm the staff supervisor for the data-processing department of the Detroit public schools in Michigan. In one of our school systems, they file student records by birth date, and it makes it impossible to locate a file unless you know when the student was born.

Larry: These are good examples and illustrations. While some of them may have seemed crazy to you, they are the very ones that can bring a sophisticated, expensive information system to its knees. If I can summarize these examples and problems, they might look like this:

- What data can you ask for?
- How can you get valid data?
- How can you keep data current?
- How do you maintain the integrity of your information system?

With these questions written on the board, Larry then spent the rest of the session presenting materials to answer these and other questions about effective information systems. ■

The experiences related to Larry by the seminar participants reflect the type of informational demands and problems facing today's managers. How effectively managers respond to these demands and problems depends largely on their willingness and ability to utilize information systems to solve problems, make decisions, and facilitate operations. In recent years, there has been an explosive growth in the demand for information and application of information systems. Managers now face the challenge of how to fully incorporate the principles and technologies of information systems into the managerial process.[1]

Why have an information system?

Because organizations are functioning in a highly competitive and rapidly changing environment, today's managers need to be able to quickly access and analyze critical data and information. Having these data and this information readily available is absolutely necessary if managers are to make sound and appropriate strategic and operational decisions. Incorporating the capabilities and output of information systems into the decision-making process is becoming essential to organizational survival.[2]

Despite the growing need for information systems and the support these systems can provide the managerial process, few organizations have been able to fully implement and successfully use information systems. In many organizations, managers are engaged in a constant struggle to manage information and to efficiently use information systems to enhance individual and organizational performance. Many managers and organizations have never had the opportunity to experience the benefits that information systems provide.[3]

Researchers have found that the degree of implementation and use of information systems is a function of managerial attitude. Some managers fear that information systems and the new computer technology associated with those systems will adversely affect the workplace and possibly undermine their own authority. This kind of managerial attitude is rather common and usually results in resistance to or grudging acceptance of information systems. In this case, managers typically choose not to use the system's new technology, or they use the system to perform only the simplest of tasks. The end result is underutilization of valuable resources and a decline in organizational performance.

Opinions about the purpose, merits, and performance of information systems vary greatly. Advocates of information systems argue that managers who are computer and systems illiterate will soon find themselves "organizationally dysfunctional" and unemployed. In contrast, other managers suggest that computer programs and information systems fail to satisfy their informational needs and fail to fulfill managerial expectation.

Today's managers must understand that analysis of data and access to information are essential for making strategic and operational decisions and for facilitating the organization's ability to respond to changing competitive and environmental conditions.[4] Information systems support problem solving and decision making, and thus facilitate the managerial process. For information systems to work and for managers to derive the full benefit from them, managers must understand (1) the concepts of information systems, (2) the rationale for implementing new systems technology and methods, (3) the human issues associated with information systems, and (4) the concerns and objectives that an organization has for making better decisions and having efficient resource management. This understanding will help managers balance the human concerns about information systems (concerns for job security, quality of work life, individual privacy rights) with the organization's needs for information to make decisions and manage operations.

In this chapter, we will focus on some of the concepts, practices, components, and uses of information systems. We will examine how information systems facilitate the managerial process, and we will close the chapter with a discussion of the emerging issues related to the use and implementation of information systems.

FUNDAMENTAL CONCEPTS AND FUNCTIONS OF INFORMATION SYSTEMS

MIS Management Information Systems. An integrated, structured complex of people, machines, and procedures for supplying relevant data, i.e., information from both external and internal sources to aid managers in performing their functions.

DSS Decision Support Systems. A process-oriented system focusing on how information systems are used to provide managers with the appropriate information to make intelligent decisions.

Before exploring how information systems are used in the managerial process, we need to examine some of the fundamental concepts of information systems. First of all, we should note that we are taking a broad-based orientation to defining information systems, focusing primarily on how information systems relate to the managerial process.

However, there are some other perspectives and variations on the nature and character of information systems. For instance, you will sometimes hear information systems being referred to as management information systems, or **MIS**. MIS is more technological, emphasizing computer applications in the processing and analysis of data and information. Another variation is Decision Support Systems, or **DSS**. DSS is process oriented, focusing on how information systems are used to provide managers with the appropriate information to

Information system
A planned procedure to develop accurate, timely, comprehensive, and appropriate information that will support managerial decision making.

make intelligent decisions. You will find that we integrate the concepts and principles of both MIS and DSS in our broad-based view of information systems, as it relates to the managerial process.

The primary purpose of an **information system** is to support managerial decision making with information that is accurate, timely, comprehensive, and appropriate.[5] Managers will be better equipped to make strategic decisions if they have information gathered from both internal and external sources. Managers need to be aware of and sensitive to both change and interdependence in the external and internal environments.

The conceptual model of an information system is depicted in Figure 17-1. This model demonstrates the flow and interrelations among various components and functions of an information system. For instance, information about market conditions can be used to determine a marketing strategy for an organization; employees' time cards become the input to the payroll department.

Operationally, an information system is a computer-based network that integrates into a single system the following functions:

■ Collecting, storing, and retrieving data
■ Processing, analyzing, and transforming data into information
■ Distributing data and information to appropriate individuals

These functions need some elaboration for your full understanding of concepts in information systems.[6]

Data Collection

Data collection A function that identifies data sources, obtains data from those sources, encodes those data, and then enters or loads the data into the data bank of the system.

As we noted earlier, data can be found in a variety of forms and places. The collection function identifies data sources, obtains data from those sources, encodes those data by translating all the various forms into electronically read symbols, and then enters or loads the data into the data bank of the system for storage.

The quality and strength of any information system depends on the comprehensiveness of the data contained in the data base of the system. A primary concern of the collection function is how easily available data can be converted into a form that can be stored and retrieved for analysis or other processing

FIGURE 17-1 Simplified Conceptual Information System Model

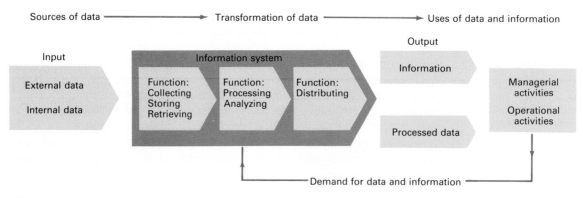

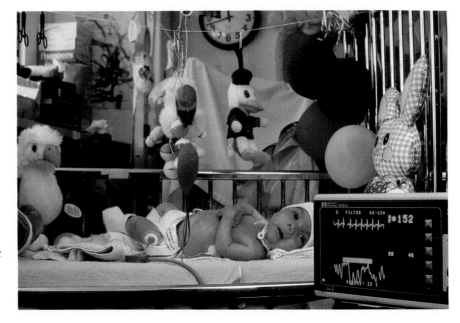

Countless people have benefitted from the innovations in information system technology. A critically ill child in Australia, for example, can receive the best diagnoses possible from specialists in Paris, London, or the Mayo Clinic in Minnesota through the transmission of data accumulated through a computer monitor.

Internal data Data obtained from sources within the organization such as annual reports, production and marketing forecasts.

External data Data obtained from sources outside the organization such as data from Standard and Poor's Industrial Surveys, census material, and reports from data collecting institutions.

purposes. Quantitative data sources—such as sales figures, time cards, production records, demographic material, and inventory levels—can be stored on magnetic tape or disks. However, data contained in subjective documents, such as performance appraisals, job descriptions, legal materials, grievance proceedings, and decision papers, are not easily converted to electronically read symbols. In this case, either the documents are microfilmed and given an electronically coded reference identifier, or the critical data are abstracted from the document in a standardized pattern.[7]

Another element of the collection function is the source of the data—that is, whether the data are internal or external. **Internal data** are obtained from sources within the organization, such as annual reports, production forecasts, personnel records, pay schedules, and marketing plans. **External data** are obtained from sources outside the organization, such as data from *Standard and Poor's Industrial Surveys,* census material, and reports from institutions that provide economic and political forecasts.

Data Processing and Analysis

Data processing and analysis A process that refines and transforms data into another form that can be used to support managerial activities; value is assigned to the data that enhances their interpretation and meaning.

The purpose of **data processing and analysis** is to refine data and transform them into a form that can be used to support managerial and organizational activities. In the collection and storage function, no value or context is applied to the data. But the data-processing and analysis function transforms the data by assigning some value to the data, interpreting the meaning of the data, and placing the data into some context. This could be anything from data that have been simply classified or categorized to information that is highly analytical in nature. The type of data and information produced by the data-processing and analysis function depends on the purpose for which the data and information are to be used, the technical capabilities of the equipment, and the programming of the system.

The Distributing Function

Distribution function
The function that transfers data and information from the system to various individuals and users in the organization.

The **distribution function** of an information system transfers data and information from the system to various individuals and users. The distribution function electronically transmits information from the information system to any terminal location in the organization. The function also can route information from one terminal to another, even if the other terminal is located across the country. Usually, the information is distributed to users in a given format and can be received by the users as a reproduced document, an image on a monitor, or a computer printout. The distribution function can also be designed to transmit information simultaneously to designated terminals and individuals. The only real barrier to distribution is the compatibility of different equipment. Because there are variations in how information is encoded, the equipment must be compatible if the information is to be transferred and distributed accurately. In the distribution function, the information is not altered in any way, but merely transferred from one point to another in the system or from the system to individual users.

THE DISTINCTION BETWEEN DATA AND INFORMATION

Are data and information the same?

In the past few pages, you may have assumed that data and information are the same. Such is not the case, as the discussion in this section reveals.

Data

The basic units of any information system are the raw data. The quality, applicability, comprehensiveness, and integrity of the data will determine how beneficial an information system is. But what are data, what are the sources of data, and in what forms do data exist?

Data Facts, statistics, opinions, or predictions. Can be classified on some basis for storage, processing, and retrieval in computer systems.

Data can be characterized as reliable and verifiable records or measurements of an event or a condition. In a sense, data are knowledge; but they are knowledge that exists without meaning, context, or value. Data can be as simple as an employee's birth date or as complex and detailed as the 1990 census. The source of the data may be internal, such as monthly sales reports or production schedules, or it may be external, such as the index of leading economic indicators or an economic forecast from the Rand Corporation. Data can be in the form of a document, an instrument reading, a statistic, or a graphic representation. Data can exist in every imaginable form. An example of this diversity can be seen in the extensive listing and categorization of human resource management data by the American Society for Personnel Administration (ASPA) in their *Handbook of Personnel and Industrial Relations*. (See Table 17-1.)

Information

Information Data that are relevant to the performance of the manager's functions.

Information consists of facts that have been analyzed and interpreted in the context of human or business objectives. It describes the relation between a

Table 17-1   Examples of a Human Resource Data Base

Personal data
Name
Pay number or social security number
Sex
Date of birth
Physical description of employee
  (height, weight, color of eyes, etc.)
Names, sex and birth dates of
  dependents
Marital status
Employee association participation
United Fund/Community Chest
  participation
Minority group classification

Work experience data
Names and locations of previous
  employers
Prior employment chronology
Military service
Job skills possessed
Product line experience
Managerial or supervisory experience
Foreign languages spoken, written,
  read
Publications authored
Special skills or hobbies of potential
  value to the business
Patents held
Elective governmental positions
Security clearances held

Educational data
College degree, high school diploma,
  level of educational attainment
Field of degree
Date of degree
School attended
Special employer-sponsored courses
  completed
Professional licenses held

Benefit plan data
Medical and/or life insurance plan
  participation
Pension plan participation
Savings plan participation (U.S. bonds,
  etc.)
Pay for time not worked (vacation,
  illness, lost-time accidents, personal
  time off, death in family, jury duty,
  military reserve duty, etc.)
Tuition refund plan participation
Etc.

**Performance evaluation/
  promotability data**
Personal interests
Work preferences
Geographical preferences (for
  multiplant operations)
Level of aspiration
Rank value of contribution in current
  work group
Special nominations and awards
Appraisal reports
Date of last appraisal
Growth potential as rated by manager
Previous promotions considered for,
  and dates of consideration
Dates of demotion
Reason for demotion
Date of last internal transfer
Dates considered for apprenticeship
  or other special training
Reasons for elimination from
  consideration for apprenticeship or
  other special training
Dates of, type, and reason for
  disciplinary action

Employee attitude morale data
Productivity quality measures
Absenteeism record
Tardiness record
Suggestions submitted (usually to a
  formal suggestion plan)
Grievances
Anonymous inquiries/complaints
Perceived fairness of management
  practices regarding employees
Perceived fairness and soundness of
  management philosophy
Attitudes about credibility/honesty of
  management
Attitudes toward work, pay,
  supervisor, etc.

Labor market data
Analysis of local staffing availability
Unemployment levels by skill,
  occupation, age, sex, etc.
Predicted future staffing needs
Identification of scarce and surplus
  staffing pools
Wage and salary, shift differentials,
  etc.

Source: Adapted from Glenn A. Bassett, "PAIR Records and Information Systems," in D. Yoder and H. G. Heneman, eds. *ASPA Handbook of Personnel and Industrial Relations* (Washington, D.C.: Bureau of National Affairs, Inc., 1979), pp. 66–68.

Management Application

Information Power

Companies around the world are using information power to create new markets, attract new customers, provide quality service, and edge out competitors. Here are some examples.

- The Red Lion Inn chain of over fifty-two hotels uses a minicomputer at its Vancouver, Washington, headquarters as a kind of inventory-control system to make sure its 11,000 rooms in eight western states are filled.

- AT&T uses its information system to find the most efficient and effective routes for customers' long distance calls in an effort to avoid the recording "all circuits are busy" and thus improve customer service.

- The Tragessor Ford dealership has a direct link to the Ford manufacturing plants in Detroit. Customers' new-car orders are entered electronically. Salespeople can check on manufacturing dates, available options, and updates and receive an almost instant response from the factory.

- Allstate representatives carry a laptop computer with them to demonstrate to the at-home customer the advantages of the universal life policy. The computer also lets them figure premium rates for any person, any age, any time.

- American Airlines provides its Sabre reservation system to travel agents. This system lists the flight schedules of every major airline in the world.

- Akzo Coatings sets up an information system for its automobile body repair shops throughout the world. This gives repair shops instant access to spare-parts lists, new repair procedures, and labor-hour guides for some 2,000 car models. Shop personnel access all this information through PCs and can give customers nearly instant estimates for repair work.

- The power of information has also been noticed by the government, notably the IRS. Delinquent taxpayers receive three computer-generated dunning letters before receiving a computer-generated telephone call from ACS—the Automated Collection System. The computer dials the telephone number. If the line is busy, or if no one answers, the computer automatically redials in two hours. If someone answers, the computer tells an IRS employee to come on the line to talk to the delinquent taxpayer.

characteristic or an event and the goals and purpose of an organization's actions. Like data, it is knowledge. Unlike data, however, it is knowledge that provides insight into and sheds light on the unknown. For example, an employee's birth date is a piece of data, but when it is used in determining adjustments to pension funding or deciding on recruitment strategies to replace personnel, it becomes information. Information is a powerful tool in business and other organizations; it has been said that information is power.

There are other factors to consider. First, information is always relative. A particular bit of information may be a valuable resource for one manager, whereas another manager may view the same bit of information as totally irrelevant. Also, because information is contextual (that is, how you view information depends on your perspective) and subject to considerable interpretation, managers must be sensitive about the quality, timeliness, accuracy, and appropriateness of information provided to them. Quite simply, information derived from information systems is highly subjective, and that subjectivity must be considered before making decisions.

With respect to the managerial process, information can be categorized into three general areas: (1) strategic planning information, (2) management control information, and (3) operational information.

Strategic planning information relates to the task of top management to decide upon the objectives of the organization, the levels and kinds of resources for attaining the objectives, and the policies that govern the acquisition, use, and disposition of the resources.[8] Strategic planning depends heavily upon information external to the specific organization. When the external data are combined with internal data, management can make estimates of expected results. The specifics of this information are often unique and tailor-made to particular strategic problems.

Management control information Information that helps managers take the actions that are in the best interest of the company; managers are also able to see that resources are being efficiently and effectively used.

Management control information sheds light on goal congruence; it helps managers take the actions that are in the best interest of the organization and enables them to see that resources are being efficiently and effectively used in meeting the organizational goals. Robert Anthony has pinpointed three types of information needed for management control: (1) costs by responsibility centers, (2) direct program costs, and (3) full program costs (including allocation of indirect costs). Management control information ties together various subactivities in a coherent way so that managers can gauge resource utilization and compare expected results with actual results. Management control information is often interdepartmental, in that the inputs come from various organizational groups, cutting across established functional boundaries.

Operational information pertains to the day-to-day activities of the organization and helps ensure that specific tasks are performed effectively and efficiently. It also includes routine and necessary information, such as financial accounting, payrolls, personnel rosters, equipment inventories, and logistics. Because this information relates to specific tasks, all inputs generally come from one established department.

These three categories, illustrated in Figure 17-2, are useful when developing management information systems, because they identify the different types of needs managers have and because they point out a continuum, from the typically well defined operational information to the other extreme of the characteristically ill defined strategic planning information.[9]

FIGURE 17-2 Management Information Categories

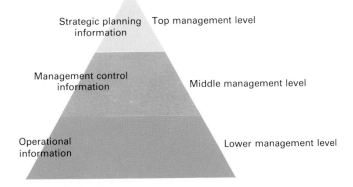

Strategic planning became a household word during the Gulf War of 1990–1991. Allied forces used sophisticated devices to collect data for analysis and subsequent military planning and action. Generals Norm Schwarzkopf and Colin Powell (seen briefing the press) also used information to keep Americans informed and committed to the Allied cause.

APPLICATIONS OF INFORMATION SYSTEMS

What are some applications of information systems?

Primarily, there are four areas where information systems can be used to support managerial and operational activities: (1) transaction processing, (2) reporting, (3) query and retrieval, and (4) decision support. We will examine how the functions of information systems are generally applied in each of these areas, then look at how they can be specifically applied in the area of human resource management, and finally consider the emergence of an integrated information industry.

General Applications

Transaction Processing

Transaction processing One of the simplest uses of an information system. This process takes data and uses them to perform an operation or administrative task.

Providing data for **transaction processing** is the simplest use of an information system. Data are collected, processed, and then used to complete some operation or administrative task. An example of transaction processing is automatic payroll preparation. The employees' time cards record each employee's work periods, so that when all the cards are collected, they can be easily entered into the information system for processing. Data from the time cards are integrated with other employee data, such as pay scales, deductions, and tax rates, enabling the accounting department to process and compute the payroll and employees' paychecks.

Reporting

Reporting The reporting function may require complex operations. Data are collected from selected sources and then processed by sorting, classification, and other procedures.

When used for **reporting** purposes, the operations and activities of information systems are far more complex. There are substantially more interactions among the various functions of the entire information system. Typically, data are collected from selected sources and then processed by sorting, classification, and other procedures.[10] Some of the processed data undergo simple analysis, such as examination for comparison purposes. The final processing procedures consist of arranging the data in a given report format, which can be either retained in the data bank for future reference or converted into a physical document. The finished report can then be distributed to the appropriate areas.

Query and Retrieval

Query and retrieval
A process where users will ask the system to search for, identify, and retrieve information from the data bank.

A common demand placed by users on information systems is to search for, identify, and retrieve data and information contained in the data bank of the system. This use of an information system is referred to as **query and retrieval**. Essentially, the query-and-retrieval procedure operates in the following manner. In response to a user's request,[11] the system conducts a search of the data bank for references to sources of the requested data and information. If the specific data and information cannot be identified, the system then searches for variations or alternative sources. The user is instructed by the system about the nature and availability of the requested data and information. If the identified material meets the user's needs, the system, upon the direction of the user, retrieves the data and information in completed form from the data bank. This procedure is still technically simple and requires the system to perform only elementary analytical operations. However, it is more complex than both the transaction processing and the reporting applications of information systems.

Support of Decision-Making Activities

The most effective application of an information system is the generating and providing of information in support of decision-making activities.[12] To accomplish this, an information system requires technical sophistication and complexity in both the hardware and the software of the system. When supporting

The laptop personal computer is portable and thus allows managers, engineers, and salespeople total freedom to travel to a client, project, or trouble area and have access to data banks at the home office. Query and retrieval capability allows for immediate and improved decision making.

decision-making activities, the focus of the operation is on analysis of data and the transformation of the data into information. The system provides a user with information that has been interpreted, has been given meaning, and has been placed into a context that demonstrates its significance. In addition, when systems are being used to support decision making, they can be used in problem-solving situations and for assessing the impact of alternative courses of action. As noted earlier, using information systems in the decision-making context is the primary reason for an organization to design and implement an information system.

Summary Statement on General Applications

How extensively and effectively any information system is integrated into the operations of an organization depends in large part on how well managers understand the workings and benefits of information systems. We have just considered some of the concepts, components, and uses of information systems in the most introductory of terms. Much of what we have focused on is illustrated in the enhanced model of an information system shown in Figure 17-3. Neither

FIGURE 17-3 Enhanced Conceptual Information System Model

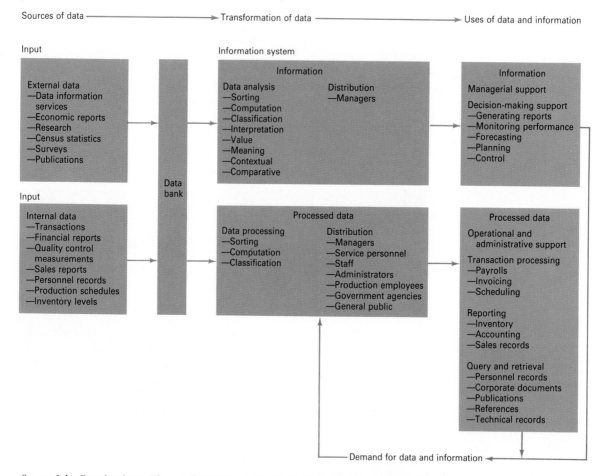

Source: John Douglas, Stuart Klein, and David Hunt, *The Strategic Managing of Human Resources,* New York: John Wiley and Sons, 1985, p. 149.

our discussion nor this graphic model adequately reflects the complexities and details involved in operating an information system. We believe that the critical concern for managers should be the effective use of information systems in the operational and managerial activities, and not the technical workings of the system. One does not have to be an automotive engineer to know how to drive a car, just as one does not have to be a computer or systems specialist to know how to use and integrate an information system into the work context.

Illustrations of Specific Applications

How does an information system work?

To gain an appreciation of how information systems can support managerial decision making and operational activities, we need to develop an understanding of how information systems operate. In addition, our examination of two applications of information systems will provide some insights into the problems associated with implementing and using information systems.[13] The first example illustrates how a national department-store chain developed and implemented an information system, and the second example illustrates how a New York City hospital used its information system to help solve morale problems.

How an Information System Supports a Department Store's Operations

Recently, a national department-store chain developed and implemented a comprehensive information system to enhance organizational performance. The firm created a nationwide network of data-processing and information systems. Although the system operates on essentially three levels (corporate, regional, and individual store), the system is fully integrated and capable of providing managers and other users with a wide range of information and administrative support.

The best way to demonstrate the system's integration and utilization is to examine a few of its key components. Perhaps the most critical component of the system is the in-store terminal, more commonly known as the cash register. The registers operate on-line, so that every time a customer makes a purchase, the transaction is recorded on the register tape and is also transmitted to a regional data-processing center. Each time there is a customer purchase, the salesperson enters more data than just the price of the item. The data entered into the register include the store code, the employee's identification number, the date, the department code, the merchandise stock number, the price of the item, and the amount of tax on the sale.

In some cases, a scanner system may be used, in which a magnetic or graphic code on the merchandise automatically registers the appropriate data about the merchandise. With the scanner operation, the data recorded do not come from the register; rather, the code is transmitted to the regional center, where it is interpreted. The regional center then transmits the data back to the register to complete the transaction. A credit purchase follows a similar procedure. The employee enters the customer's credit card number into the register, which then transmits the number to the regional center for verification. If the credit account is in order, the center signals the register to complete the transaction. However, if the account is not in order or if the card is a stolen one, the center signals the register to stop the transaction.

Although the recording, transmission, processing, and verification of this entire transaction takes only a matter of seconds to complete, the data collected during this transaction will become a permanent part of the system data base. The data base forms an inventory and a variety of information that will support managerial decision making and operational activities. A few examples illustrate this point.

In the store, the transaction data provide information for accounting purposes, such as cash receipts verification. It provides department supervisors with a breakdown of their salespeople's performance, to include sales volume, number of sales, and the types of merchandise sold. Promotional programs can be closely monitored. Because the information is generated daily, managers can make immediate adjustments to ensure successful promotions.

Another way to picture the operation of the system is to monitor the use of a particular piece of data. For instance, the merchandise stock number data are retrieved and used by a variety of individuals. When the warehouse operations manager in Dallas retrieves these data, he or she uses them to identify restocking requirements for each store. The advertising operations manager in New York City uses the data to provide information about the success of promotional programs on a comparative basis for different segments of the country. And buyers in Seattle can use the data to indicate how well a product is selling and if additional purchases are required.

Top management uses transaction data to generate strategic information. From top management, for example, comes information about trends, performance of the various segments of the firm's operations, and changes in the firm's financial position. The data are integrated with historical and external environment data, thus providing critical information for strategic decision making.

For the firm in our illustration, the information generated in the 1980s showed that performance was declining. Although some of the information revealed that the decline was a factor of the economy, other information suggested that the firm had reached its growth limits. In addition, the information indicated that the competition, with a different marketing strategy, was successfully taking away the firm's business. Without the information system's capability to routinely collect transaction data and then to transform those data into relevant information, the firm's top management would not have been able to identify the nature of the problems causing the firm's decline. Because of its information system, the firm was able to develop a successful strategy of diversification, which enabled it to be more responsive to the changing conditions in the environment. This strategy returned the firm to a condition of growth and profitability.

A New York City Hospital

How could low morale be related to information systems?

An administrator of nursing services in a major New York City hospital faced a problem of low morale and a high turnover rate among her nursing staff. The hospital had been expanding both its services and its staff in recent years. A clue to the problem came from the complaints of the nurses that the opportunities for promotions and pay raises were limited. She believed that this might be the reason for the poor morale and high turnover rate.

The hospital had computerized much of its administrative operations during its recent expansion, and the personnel department had developed and implemented a human resource information system, linked to the hospital's data-processing center. Thus, when the nursing administrator approached the head of personnel with her problems, the personnel manager suggested that the two of them meet with the hospital's systems analyst.

Selected data were retrieved from the personnel records of all nurses who had resigned within the past five years. This information showed that most of the nurses had worked from five to ten years; yet, only a few had been assigned to duty in the new specialized care units. Thus, the promotion rates for these nurses had been slow or nonexistent. In addition, most of the nurses had requested that references about their employment history be forwarded to other area hospitals.

Next, the hiring and promotion activity for the nursing staff during the past five years was examined. It was apparent that the opportunities for promotions had been limited because the positions required specialized training and certification. The new positions were typically filled by recent graduate nurses with limited experience but with advanced degrees that enabled them to obtain the necessary job certification. Information about recruiting of nurses in the New York City area revealed a critical shortage of certified nurses to work in the new specialized services. Because of the shortage, hospitals were required to offer premium salaries to certified nurses. Only a few of the nurses who had been at the hospital more than five years had received the necessary training or education to qualify them to work in any of the new specialized care units.

Supplementary data were collected from external sources concerning trends in the medical field, demographic changes, and hospital operations in the New York area. The information suggested that there would be continued demand for specialized treatment services and that the shortage of qualified nurses to provide those services would remain for some time.

The nursing services administrator determined the certification requirements for each nursing specialty required by the hospital. She discovered that certification could be achieved either through educational qualifications or through a combination of experience and supplementary training. When results were integrated with the personnel data of all currently employed nurses, the conclusion was that many of the nurses with five or more years employment would qualify for certification with some additional training.

After reviewing all the information generated by both the human resource information system and the hospital data-processing system, both the nursing administrator and the personnel manager realized that a professional-development program for the hospital nurses was needed. In addition, they believed that by coordinating the development program with long-run expansion plans, the hospital could reduce nursing personnel costs and improve the morale. Newly created positions could be filled by current employees, and any outside hiring could be limited to entry-level nursing positions. The costs of training nurses for certification would be more than offset by reduced recruitment expenses, because there was a bigger pool of nurses available for entry-level positions. Additionally, the increased opportunity for promotions would reduce the turnover rates in the nursing staff.

The nursing staff administrator and the personnel manager developed a final proposal for a nurses' professional-development program and presented the proposal to the hospital's administrative board for approval. The board approved, and in time the hospital experienced a reduction in the turnover rate of the nursing staff. In addition, the hospital was able to reduce annual expenditures for nurses' salaries, as well as reducing the costs of recruitment and hiring. As predicted, the morale of the nursing staff improved as the opportunities increased for promotion and training in new skill areas.

Emergence of an Integrated Information Industry

What opportunities does this field have?

The two examples just presented illustrate the growing need for information to facilitate problem solving and managerial decision making. This growing need has in turn created new opportunities for firms interested in providing information-based services. You find small and large firms not only supplying the equipment and programs needed for information systems, the hardware and the software, but also providing access to data bases and information banks. TRW maintains credit records on the majority of credit users in the United States. Mead Corporation's LEXIS system makes it possible for law firms to conduct legal research in a fraction of the time that it once took to review law books. Anyone with a personal computer can purchase access time from firms like Prodigy and CompuServe to retrieve data and information from a wide range of the data bases and information systems.

Xerox and other duplicating specialists are looking to become more involved in the emerging information industry. Book and magazine publishers have visualized that their industry will move toward information retrieval using means outside of printing. Libraries have moved toward information retrieval outside the mere storing and distribution of books and periodicals. Exxon and leaders in other industries have developed strategies to take advantage of the emergence of the new information industry.

Even the smallest companies can afford modern information systems without a large investment in hardware. Four alternatives are available, each with its pros and cons:

> *Service bureau:* Data-processing work and information flow can be contracted out to a specialized company that handles information needs. This alternative is often preferred at the early stages of developing a system, because it does not lock the company into a fixed type of technology and the capital investment can be kept low.
>
> *Time sharing:* Contracting for time sharing on an outside mainframe is similar to using a service bureau except that a terminal is installed in the user's location and connected by telephone lines with the service bureau's computer.
>
> *Commercial software packages:* The using company can purchase a complete system from a vendor from among the vendor's standardized types of systems. Many information problems and needs are similar to those of other companies; thus, this alternative is viable as long as the user can fit its needs to the available standard systems.
>
> *Custom system:* Our earlier discussion in this chapter described how managers should identify their needs first and then obtain the hardware and software that best fits those needs. The custom system is one that is tailored to the unique needs of the user company.

In this section of the chapter, we see that the industrial structure offers external economies to company managers in designing information systems. They also offer advantages for improvements, but they raise issues and problems to which we now turn.

Global Application

Don't Leave Home without a Laptop and a Fax

As more and more businesses globalize their operations, the information systems that support these businesses and the decision making of their managers have had to acquire global characteristics. Fortunately, the technology of communication and information systems has advanced to the point where support of global business operations is not very difficult.

Innovations in laptop computers, faxes, accessible data bases, and cellular phones have made it possible for firms and managers to operate throughout the world at any time of the day. For instance, the Motorola Corporation, a leader in cellular-phone technology, is planning to develop a cellular satellite system that enables people to take their phone and phone number wherever they travel, making it possible for just about anyone to reach them anywhere in the world. This is almost like a global call-forwarding system.

The accessibility that the new communications technology creates also has forced global managers to significantly adapt their work schedules and life styles. Global managers are finding that the new information technology means that they must live and work on a 24-hour schedule. The notion of flex-time is now being applied to both life and work. One manager found that because most of his business dealings were performed early in the morning (London) or late in the day (Tokyo), he could work at home and have more contact with his children. He also discovered that he didn't need to take vacation time to be able to take his children to a wide variety of summertime activities.

But sometimes, the new communication and information technology has a downside. There is a popular story about a manager who went to Luxembourg for his honeymoon. Unfortunately for his new wife, he took his laptop and a fax along. He ended up spending most of his time in his hotel room corresponding by fax and electronic mail with his home office and his clients.

Although some of the new communication and information technology intrudes on a manager's private life, it can also facilitate business activity in a way that gives managers more latitude and diversity in their personal and family life. An international consultant found that information technology enhanced her global travel and business dealings. Administrative, logistic, and decision-making support from the home office was only a phone call away, regardless of location. As a result, she was able to complete her business dealings in a shorter time, thereby gaining more time for personal travel and having to spend less time on the road. The globalization of business and the evolution of information systems that are capable of supporting global activities have not only altered the working and life-style patterns of people but also presented new opportunities for working men and women and their families.

References: Lourdes Valeriano, "Executives Find They're Always on Call," *Wall Street Journal,* August 6, 1991, p. B1; L. A. Winokur, "Vacations Are Becoming Part of the Job," *Wall Street Journal,* July 9, 1991, p. B1.

As you can see, the availability of information and opportunities to access and use it are widespread. In many ways, data and information are becoming more of a commodity, something that is easily moved, transferred, bought and sold. But achieving this level of accessibility and use has raised a number of complex issues concerning how information systems operate. In the last segment of this chapter, we are going to review a number of these issues and consider their managerial implications.

ISSUES

What are some critical issues in MIS?

In recent years, the innovations in computer technology and applications have resulted in an information revolution. However, despite the many benefits of data-processing and information systems, the rapid and uncontrolled growth of these systems has created numerous problems and raised questions about the need to establish guidelines for their use. Even early developers of the computer, such as Norbert Wiener, expressed concern about the disruptive potential of computers. Wiener stated that "machines can and do transcend some of the limitations of their designers, and that in doing so, they may be both effective and dangerous."[14] Because of the dramatic impact on individuals and the work environment, we will now examine some of the principal issues of the information revolution. (See Figure 17-4.)

Many of the issues related to the expanded use of data-processing and information systems center on the creation, storage, and exchange of the voluminous number of records people create about themselves. There are credit records, tax records, academic records, financial records, medical records, criminal records, and on and on. But one of the most significant and comprehensive records is the individual's record of employment, the personnel file.

FIGURE 17-4 Information System Issues

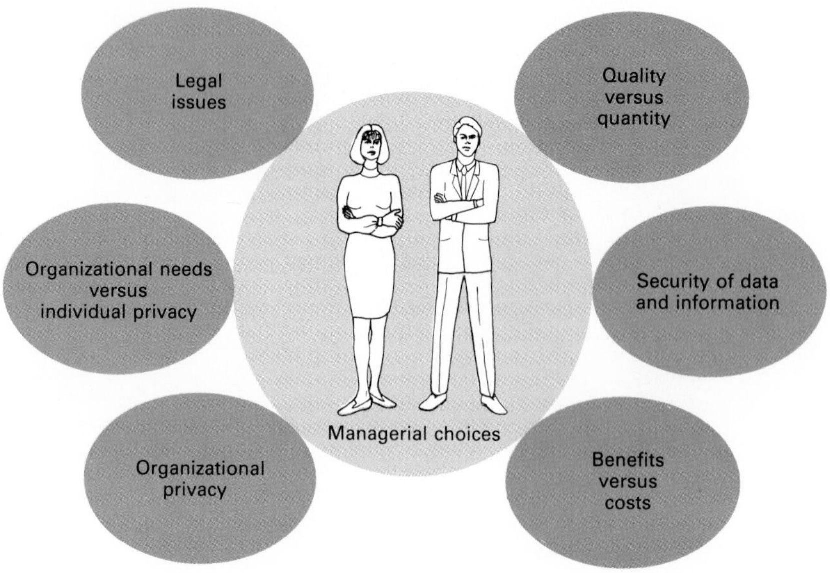

Just consider the potential data contained in the documents typically found in a personnel file. There is the individual's employment application, which usually details the individual's vital statistics, prior employment history, academic background, and technical qualifications. Also, there are medical records, insurance papers, performance appraisals, pay and compensation records, credit checks, results from psychological testing, security investigations, and more. As we noted earlier in the chapter, the technical sophistication of information systems makes it easy to store, retrieve, and collect data from these documents. Data from the personnel file, entered into the system's data bank, can easily be used to provide a variety of information about an individual to any person who has access to the information system. Needless to say, many people and organizations have become very sensitive about the maintenance, accuracy, and accessibility of data and information. These concerns are viewed as the most significant issues associated with the use and application of information systems.

Human Resistance to Electronic Rationality

The introduction of computer-based information systems into any organization naturally results in changes, and as you recall, the typical human reaction to change is resistance.[15] At the clerical and worker level, the fear of being displaced by machine is based on both real and imaginary grounds. The routinized and boring jobs may be eliminated by computers, but history shows that new and challenging types of jobs emerge.

At the managerial level, Chris Argyris[16] has warned that there is a potential loss of status and influence by the manager when information can be obtained from the computer by the lowest-level worker. The loss of power to regulate the flow of information by managers may be a threat to their status. Computers, thus, can trigger emotional problems and stress, not only for the lowest-level worker in the organization, but also for top management.[17]

Legal Issues

In general, laws and regulations governing the use of and access to all forms of personal data and records are extremely inconsistent. Laws allowing individuals to exercise the right to review the data and documents contained in their personnel files vary from state to state. Furthermore, compliance with federal laws and regulations such as the Privacy Act depends on the size of an organization and whether or not it has a federal contract. As a result, there are situations where employees cannot restrict access to or even review the contents of their own personnel files, while at the same time, other members of the organization may have unrestricted access to those data. When this situation exists, the individual has no way of verifying either document or data accuracy or completeness and appropriateness of the records. Because there is always a possibility of computer error or inaccurate employee records, how can managers be certain that the information they are using was derived from accurate and relevant data? The consequence of not providing employees an opportunity to review and correct their records is that managers run the risk of making decisions and taking personnel actions based on incorrect or inappropriate information.

Organizational Needs versus Individual Privacy

The issue of whether an employee has the right to restrict access to his or her records, or to determine how the data may be used, is not easily resolved. If employees could control their records, human resource managers would find themselves faced with an administrative nightmare accommodating the preferences of each employee. Such control would also seriously hamper the development of information essential to managerial problem-solving and decision-making activities. Reconsider the human resource problems faced by the nursing administrator and the government agency head discussed earlier. Without unrestricted access to the data contained in their employees' personnel records, neither manager would have been able to obtain the critical information needed to identify the nature of the problem and to select a course of action. The issue of control and use of data raises the question of how the human resource manager can balance the informational "need to know" of the organization against the employee's right to privacy. Unfortunately, there is no easy answer.

Organizational Privacy

The issues raised about the impact information systems have on individual privacy extend to the organization as well. An organization's data base contains a substantial amount of proprietary information about production, financial, and sales performance, as well as detailed product research and development information. Organizations would prefer to limit access to such information, but in the normal course of doing business, employees, customers, suppliers, and outsiders can casually or intentionally access information that may not fall into the realm of their "need to know."

Managers must consider how the information system's vast array of organizational information can be used against itself. For instance, the justice system has taken greater interest in the issues of employee rights to review their personnel records and the proper use of those records. In discrimination suits, the courts have generally ruled that an organization must provide the plaintiff employee all relevant data and information to support the case, even if the request goes beyond the individual's own personnel record. What this means for the organization is that managers may have to provide data and information that, when introduced as evidence, will reveal to the public the employment practices of the organization. Such evidence may prove to be embarrassing if the organization has questionable hiring practices or has not treated employees fairly.

Then there are the information services that specialize in collecting and processing large amounts of information about organizations, and make that information easily available to competitors, investors, creditors, and the general public. Some of the major information services specializing in collecting information on businesses include McGraw-Hill, Dun and Bradstreet, Value-Line, Standard and Poor, and the Harris Corporation. Managers need to recognize that information in the wrong hands can seriously undermine the organization's competitiveness or result in serious internal conflict.

Ethics Issue

Computer Hacking: For Fun or Profit?

Personal computers and modems have made working at home or away from the office much easier, and they have simplified access to a vast array of computer-based networks and systems. While this development has provided businesses with a new degree of operational flexibility, it has also provided pranksters and criminals with the opportunity to exploit or vandalize valuable computer and information systems.

The computer revolution of the 1980s created a whole generation of computer hackers who became wrapped up in the game of electronically breaking into secured computer and information systems. Once in the systems, they stole data, disrupted the network, and freely used the services provided by the system. For instance, "phone phreaking" hackers would breach the security system of AT&T's long-distance operation and then manipulate the system to make free long-distance calls. What made matters worse for AT&T and other victims of these practices was that hackers typically collaborated with one another, sharing techniques and exchanging deciphered access codes.

As AT&T and other long-distance carriers learned to control the problem of hackers, the hackers began preying on other systems. For the hackers, there was always a new challenge to overcome, a new way to beat or to disrupt a system. Hackers easily discovered ways to penetrate sensitive governmental, military, research, and business information systems.

Efforts to thwart hackers' access sometimes had disastrous results. In one instance, system managers at Stanford University detected the presence of a hacker in their system. When they ordered him off their system, he initiated a computer virus program that brought Stanford's system to a halt within minutes.

Corporate voice-mail systems have become targets for today's hackers. These systems do not have the extensive security precautions that have been introduced at AT&T and at various government agencies and military installations. Once into a voice-mail system, for example, the hackers gain access to and use a business's long-distance lines. The business is then stuck with the cost of the hackers' phone calls. Hackers have also had "great fun" making the voice-mail system inaccessible to the system's legitimate users, erasing transactions between the business and its customers and suppliers, and placing obscene greetings in the system.

When caught, hackers seldom show any remorse for their activities. They argue that they were just having fun and meant no harm. But the hackers' activities have cost U.S. businesses millions of dollars in additional phone costs, lost sales, added security measures, and system downtime. While businesses face the question of whether or not to prosecute hackers as criminals, American society faces the bigger challenge of recognizing that hacking is more than just mischief; rather, it is a breach of social standards and values.

References: Katie Hafner and John Markoff, *Cyberpunk: Outlaws and Hackers on the Computer Frontier* (New York: Simon & Schuster, 1991); John Keller, "Hackers Open Voice-Mail Door to Others' Phone Lines." *Wall Street Journal,* March 15, 1991, p. B1.

Security of Data and Information

Another issue, somewhat related to the question of access, is that of system security. Technological innovations have made it easier to establish connections between various systems and distant terminals; for instance, managers now have the ability to link their home computers and their office information systems by telephone. In addition, the information derived from the exchange of data between systems can be very beneficial in enhancing managerial decision making. The technological innovations have also made it easy to duplicate the software of a system and to make backup copies that can be stored at other locations.

The ease of access and data transfer has likewise made it possible for unauthorized individuals and organizations to gain entry into systems. There have been numerous newspaper accounts of amateur teenage computer operators who managed to gain access to everything from a government information system containing highly sensitive military information to AT&T for free long-distance calls. Braniff Airlines claimed that one of the principal reasons for the collapse of its operations was that American Airlines had gained access to their computer reservation system and altered the reservation dates.

Some system managers try to restrict access by using passwords and authentication codes. However, these minimal security measures have been easily surmounted by resourceful individuals, enabling the stealing of data without the need for physical removal of tapes or disks containing the data. Thus, the problem facing managers and systems analysts is how to ensure the security of the information system and its data resources without reducing the potential benefits derived from enhanced accessibility and the ease of data transfer between systems. The answer depends on managerial preferences and priorities.

Quality versus Quantity

An issue of a different nature is that of how much data and information is enough. Early proponents of data-processing and information systems argued that more data and more information would mean better decisions. That attitude, together with technological changes that substantially increased the storage capacity of systems, encouraged managers and systems analysts to collect data and retain information "just in case." The problem with that approach was that managers became overloaded with data. They did not have the time to sort through vast quantities of information to find out what was relevant and what was not. Managers were receiving quantity, not quality. In the end, much of the data and information provided on the printouts were never used.

Balancing the Benefits

Managers are recognizing that their organizations are operating in an environment that is increasingly complex and competitive. They realize that the survival and viability of the organization depend on its ability to respond to changing conditions. Therefore, managers have turned to the use of data-processing and information systems as a means to make the operations of the organization more effective and efficient. In initiating these systems, however, many managers fail to consider the human dimension involved in their design of the system. Few understand that a balance must be achieved between the needs of the organization and the needs of the individual if information systems are to operate effectively and without conflict. Given the impact that information systems have on the employees and the work environment of an organization, human resource managers must develop an understanding of the issue involved and must assume the responsibility for determining a proper balance.

SUMMARY

By now, you should have a good understanding of the importance of managing information and of the role information systems can play in facilitating the managerial process. In today's economic and social environment, information systems are playing a critical role in strategic and operational decision making and are becoming a principal factor influencing the competitiveness of any organization.

You should also have appreciation for the distinction between data and information, and how information systems work in both general and specific applications. But most important, you should have some insights into the issues that surround the implementation and use of information systems. The effectiveness of any organization's information system depends on how well managers address the issues of resistance, individual privacy, legal implications, and the quality of information. Unfortunately, many organizations have spent considerable time and resources on information systems, only to see the systems fail because managers did not resolve these critical issues. Managers need to recognize that information systems are valuable resources that support and enhance organizational performance.

KEY TERMS

MIS Management Information Systems. An integrated, structured complex of people, machines, and procedures for supplying relevant data, i.e., information from both external and internal sources to aid managers in performing their functions.

DSS Decision Support Systems. A process-oriented system focusing on how information systems are used to provide managers with the appropriate information to make intelligent decisions.

Information system A planned procedure to develop accurate, timely, comprehensive, and appropriate information that will support managerial decision making.

Data processing and analysis A process that refines and transforms data into another form that can be used to support managerial activities; value is assigned to the data that enhances their interpretation and meaning.

CHAPTER 17 MANAGING INFORMATION

Data Facts, statistics, opinions, or predictions. Can be classified on some basis for storage, processing, and retrieval in computer systems.

Data collection A function that identifies data sources, obtains data from those sources, encodes those data, and then enters or loads the data into the data bank of the system.

Internal data Data obtained from sources within the organization such as annual reports, production and marketing forecasts.

External data Data obtained from sources outside the organization such as data from Standard and Poor's Industrial Surveys, census material, and reports from data collecting institutions.

Distribution function The function that transfers data and information from the system to various individuals and users in the organization.

Management control information Information that helps managers take the actions that are in the best interest of the company; managers are also able to see that resources are being efficiently and effectively used.

Information Data that are relevant to the performance of the manager's functions.

Transaction processing One of the simplest uses of an information system. This process takes data and uses them to perform an operation or administrative task.

Reporting The reporting function may require complex operations. Data are collected from selected sources and then processed by sorting, classification, and other procedures.

Query and retrieval A process where users will ask the system to search for, identify, and retrieve information from the data bank.

<table>
<tr><td rowspan="10" valign="top">

STUDY ASSIGNMENTS
</td><td>

1. What advice would you give the managers attending the executive conference on how to use information systems to help solve their managerial problems?
</td></tr>
<tr><td>2. What are some of the reasons why managers need to know how to use information systems in making decisions and managing operations?</td></tr>
<tr><td>3. Based on the information system model, develop an example of how a manager can use an information system in managerial problem solving.</td></tr>
<tr><td>4. Compare and contrast data and information. Identify some examples of data and illustrate how those data can become information.</td></tr>
<tr><td>5. What are some of the problems associated with generating, analyzing, and interpreting information?</td></tr>
<tr><td>6. How can various general applications of information systems be used to support the managerial functions discussed in Chapters 5 through 11?</td></tr>
<tr><td>7. What role can integrated information services play in supporting managerial decision making?</td></tr>
<tr><td>8. What do you consider to be the primary issue facing managers in their implementation and use of information systems?</td></tr>
<tr><td>9. Why would there be so much managerial and nonmanagerial resistance to the use of information systems? How can managers work to reduce resistance to information systems?</td></tr>
<tr><td>10. How can managers use information systems to enhance the effectiveness, efficiency, and competitiveness of the organization?</td></tr>
</table>

Cases for Discussion

I. STANDARD ELECTRONICS

Standard Electronics has prospered in the area of high technology. In the last ten years, it has substantially increased its sales, the size of its production facilities, and the number of personnel. Standard has built a strong reputation based on innovation and quality—essential elements for achieving success in the highly competitive high-tech industry. It has also acquired a reputation for hiring very qualified and intelligent individuals who are paid top wages and salaries.

Demand for Standard's products currently exceeds its production capabilities. All the facilities are located in the Silicon Valley in California, which has one of the highest concentrations of high-tech firms in the country. Top management of Standard must decide whether to expand their present facilities one more time or to relocate the entire operation to another area of the country. Although its present location has contributed greatly to the success of the firm, operating in the valley has become extremely expensive.

The valley area has a large number of academic and technical institutions, which have provided the high-tech businesses operating there with a pool of highly trained and qualified individuals. The institutions have established a good working relationship with the high-tech firms and have adjusted their programs to meet the specific needs of these firms. The continuing expansion of the high-tech industry in the valley, however, has created demands for trained personnel that exceed the training capabilities of the local institutions. As a result, there has been a critical shortage of qualified high-tech personnel in the valley area.

The shortage has forced firms to offer premium wages and salaries to attract and retain qualified individuals. The shortage has also caused firms to have higher personnel turnover rates. Firms operating in the valley typically try to lure high-tech personnel from competition firms by offering lucrative compensation and benefit packages. For Standard, this turnover problem means that the cost of recruiting, employee morale, product development, and organizational stability is extremely high.

The prosperity of the high-tech firms has had a significant impact on the valley's economy and quality of life. The region has been growing in the same manner as the high-tech industry. Such economic growth in the valley has caused the area's cost of living to rise, making the valley one of the most expensive places to live in the entire country. The high cost of living has driven up wage and salary scales, which in turn have driven up operating and overhead costs. In some instances, the high cost of living has also contributed to the turnover problem. Many high-tech employees, including some of Standard's former employees, have quit to relocate to other areas of the country.

A number of Standard's competitors either have already moved or have been considering relocating or expanding operations in other parts of the country. Likewise, Standard's top management recognizes that to remain competitive, it must expand its production capacity. At the same time, management also understands that further expansion in the valley area could adversely affect the firm's profitability and that personnel costs would continue to escalate. For those reasons, the top management of Standard must seriously consider the relocation alternative.

II. CLAYTON-McGREGOR PAPER COMPANY

The Clayton-McGregor Paper Company is a distributor of paper and industrial supplies. It buys products from manufacturers and then inventories, sells, and distributes that merchandise to customers. Headquartered in Chicago, Clayton-McGregor operates five distribution centers, which serve the states of Illinois, Indiana, Wisconsin, Michigan, and Iowa. Each center supplies customers with four lines: (1) packaging and shipping room supples, which include lines of protective packaging, bags, closure products, tags, envelopes, and special-purpose tapes; (2) janitorial and maintenance products, which include floor-cleaning chemicals, floor-care equipment and supplies, washroom products, and general housekeeping supplies; (3) printing/office paper and supplies, which include lines of printing paper, envelopes, supplies, and office products; and (4) food-service products, which include tabletop disposables and supplies.

C-MP Company purchases its products from more than seventy-five well-known manufacturers, such as 3M, American Can, Union Camp Corporation, Scott Paper Company, Mobile Chemical, and Fort Howard Paper Company. The products are kept in inventory in the five distribution centers. Upon receiving orders, the centers assemble the products and ship them to customers in C-MP's fleet of trucks.

The company's customers are virtually any business organization that uses paper, cleaning supplies, packaging materials, or food-service products. They may be schools, churches, libraries, museums, governments, restaurants, printers, advertising firms, newspapers, manufacturing firms, and so on.

Each distribution center employs between eight and twelve sales representatives who call on customers in their respective territories. Orders are then sent to the distribution centers the salesperson represents. An office staff at each center prepares its own bills and collects from customers.

In total, C-MP handles nearly 4,000 products and sells to roughly 30,000 accounts. Sales personnel are evaluated and rewarded on the basis of their sales dollars generated, which are collected within sixty days of billing. Some customers purchase enormous amounts from C-MP, and others purchase less than $30.00 annually.

To be successful (profitable), it is important that C-MP Company be very efficient and reliable and that it control its costs of selling, taking inventory, billing, and collecting on a timely basis.

The president of C-MP has become concerned about his firm's ability to compete in a business that has small profit margins and escalating costs. He is also concerned that the board of directors has not yet approved the purchase of computers and an integrated information system for the company. He feels that it is hopeless to try to compete any longer without one.

Chapter 18

Managing Operations

Learning Objectives

1. **Define** operations management and the scope of its impact.
2. **Diagram** the production process.
3. **Cite** examples of the structural process designs.
4. **Compare** the operations management functions with other managerial functions from Part II.
5. **Explain** the objectives of scheduling techniques.
6. **Describe** the Japanese approaches to production and total quality control.

The Plant Manager

"Chuck, I need to see you sometime today. Sales tells me that we have been letting them down by not being able to fill orders. What's the story?"

"Sure, Paul. I just noticed on my shipping report that we had a problem yesterday with the strawberry jam. I'll look into it and get back to you soon."

"Thanks, Chuck. I'll see you later."

Chuck thought about the problem that Paul had brought up. It was not totally unexpected. Two days ago, the scheduler had told Chuck that the inventory of strawberry jam would not cover the orders received so far this week and that there was too much orange marmalade on hand. Given the fact that strawberry jam was featured this month with special advertising and a discount price, the shortage would only get worse. Also, the next open time on the production schedule was four days away.

Chuck knew that Paul would be sympathetic to his situation; after all, Paul had been the plant manager and understood the challenges of the job—the significant errors in sales forecasts, the inaccuracies in inventory reports, the limited space in the warehouse, and the difficulty in scheduling the correct items to manage the best use of plant capacity. Yet, Chuck knew that because of his experience as plant manager, Paul would expect him to have a carefully developed plan to deal with the problem.

If a solution to the problem existed, the combined wisdom of the plant superintendent, the production scheduler, and the shipping department manager would be needed to get ready for the meeting with Paul. If they had had more accurate information, the plant could have had enough stock of all the finished goods.

I wonder if the fact that the sales of strawberry jam are higher than expected is making the salespeople a little nervous. They may be trying to shift the blame to manufacturing. I wonder if we have enough frozen strawberries to produce the jam even if we expedite production. I wonder if our Memphis plant has any in stock that we can use. With these thoughts in his mind, Chuck knew he had to get started finding a creative way to manage this situation.

"Sally, call Bob, Vern, and Doug and set up a meeting in thirty minutes in the conference room. Tell them to bring their reports of orders received and stock status. Thanks."

The Outstanding Worker

Sandi had been a real surprise to Gene. She had joined his work team two months ago and was now the outstanding producer. There were six workers in a team, each assigned to one station. The worker at station 1 would perform a set of operations, and the product would move on a gravity belt to station 2, where a second operator would perform different tasks. After station 6, the products would go to the paint department.

Sandi worked at station 3 and was really fast. Gene had observed that the worker at station 4 had a backlog of parts to be worked on, and Sandi usually stood waiting for the work from station 2.

Gene thought the competition this new woman brought to the group was healthy. In fact, last week he had authorized a wage increase (legal under the contract but rarely done in practice) for Sandi. Recently, he had noticed an increase in the number of rejected units from this team and a lowering of worker morale.

The Long-Term Care Administrator

Jess had never faced a problem as thorny as the one she now faced. She had jumped at the opportunity to move from the directorship of hospital support personnel at Good Samaritan to director and chief administrator of the Maple Crest Long-Term Care Retirement Center. This center was an eighty-two-bed, not-for-profit unit with an established reputation for providing excellent retirement and nursing services.

The former director, Al Harbit, had been a member of the old school of Long-Term Care Retirement Center administrators. He kept few records, made many arrangements with residents by oral contracts, and wanted to run a happy operation. He would not tolerate criticism from any of his staff.

Some of the residents were under life-term contracts—they were paying a fixed entry fee and were guaranteed care until death. A few had come into Maple Crest in the 1960s and were now in their nineties. Health care costs had zoomed as their health care needs increased, and the revenue base of the entry fee no longer covered the costs. Luck had been with the institution; for most of those twenty-five years, some of the residents had willed money from their estates to Maple Crest, and deaths had meant new operating funds. Al really seemed relieved to retire and turn the operation over to Jess.

Jess looked at the list in front of her. It was a mixture of problems, causes, solutions, and frustrations.

1. Is there any way to "rewrite" the oral contracts of residents to cover their costs more realistically?
2. The number of wealthy residents seems on the decline.
3. Inflation demands are forcing labor costs up. There are sixty-two members, ranging from the director of nursing to nursing aides, the maintenance chief, the head dietician, and the physical therapist.
4. Many members of the board of trustees, the governing group, are the adult children of elderly residents.
5. A recent report from a graduate student in gerontology (on an internship at Maple Crest) shows a wide variety of mental and physical capabilities among the residents. Some need much assistance, whereas others are accustomed to four or five meals per day and wander in and out of the kitchen looking for snacks.
6. A recent report from an accounting firm shows a $10,000 per month negative cash flow.

Jess had just returned from a workshop held by the local chapter of the American Production and Inventory Control Society (APICS). The topic had intrigued her: The Application of Operations Management in Not-for-Profit Service Organizations. She wondered if any of their concepts or techniques applied in her organization. ■

Chuck, Gene, and Jess are all involved in the same process—managing operations. To each, this process becomes increasingly complex and challenging. Chuck hopes his efforts will satisfy his boss and salespeople. Gene was probably overjoyed to find an outstanding worker but now worries about worker peer resistance to his decisions. Jess knows that resolving the resident-contract issue does not solve all her problems. Each of these individuals possesses an expertise that has brought him or her to his or her current position; yet, all of them find that their previous experiences and training don't seem to have prepared them for the problems they are currently facing.

Ethics Issue

Outsourcing both Jobs and Ethics

In the early 1980s, many American firms shut down their domestic manufacturing operations and moved production activities south of the border or to countries located on the far eastern part of the Pacific Rim. At the time, there was considerable public and political outcry against these plant closures, and many suggested that the firms were reneging on the moral obligations they had to their employees and communities.

The firms argued that because of competitive pressures, they had no choice but to go ahead with the closures. They maintained that lower labor costs and a more favorable business climate made manufacturing in developing countries an appealing opportunity. Political and ethical concerns about plant closings and the practice of outsourcing manufacturing operations to foreign countries faded with the economic recovery and expansion of the mid-1980s.

In the 1990s, businesses started relocating their overseas manufacturing operations. They shut down production facilities in southeast Asia and China and established new operations in Mexico. Ironically, the same need-to-remain-competitive argument used to justify plant relocation in the 1980s was again being used to justify moving manufacturing operations back to the North American continent.

Mexico had become a more desirable manufacturing location than China and most Southeast Asian countries because of its proximity to the U.S. market (reducing transportation costs and time), ease of control (U.S. managers could easily travel to their Mexican facilities), and the expectation that a North American free-trade zone would soon be a reality. Although labor costs in Mexico were typically higher than at the Asian locations, this was not a problem, because Mexico's business environment had little regulation and the new locations improved the firms' ability to be more responsive to changing market conditions.

Few individuals or groups questioned the ethics of this new wave of plant shutdowns and relocations or its impact on the people, communities, and countries losing the plants. Although some firms felt that the political uncertainty of operating in China necessitated shifting operations from China to Mexico, most firms simply based their relocation decision on fundamental economic factors. Likewise, no one expressed any concern that there was a lack of labor laws in Mexico and that a bulk of Mexico's labor force comprised underage workers.

The manner in which global businesses shift manufacturing operations raises some serious questions about whether firms are acting or should be acting in a socially responsible manner. For the moment, it appears that plant closings and relocation decisions continue to be made simply in the name of cost and competition.

References: Stephen Baker, "Assembly Lines Start Migrating from Asia to Mexico, " *Business Week*, July 1, 1991, p. 43; Matt Moffett, "Working Children—Underage Laborers Fill Mexican Factories," *Wall Street Journal*, April 8, 1991. p. A1.

How important is the
operations manager?

Just a few years ago, the average person knew very little about the production of goods and services. Now, topics like quality, productivity, just-in-time manufacturing, and robots are often in the news.[1] These topics are part of operations management. Operations is a field within business, as are marketing and finance, operations being the processes by which a firm produces its products or services. Many American firms realize that they have been producing their product or service all wrong. The success that Japanese firms have had in capturing the America consumer has helped American firms come to this realization. Now, operations managers everywhere are analyzing their operations and finding that it is no longer good enough to "just do it." Instead, they seek ways to "do it better."

CHALLENGES FOR THE OPERATIONS MANAGER

The job of an operations manager is a challenging one. The operations manager coordinates the efforts and activities of people who perform a wide variety of functions. There may be a mix of education and training that creates opportunities, challenges, or problems, depending upon the managerial skills of the operations manager.

Three additional factors create further challenges. One of these is the *time available* for decision making. The decision time frame can be very short. Think, for a moment, of the different settings of a trauma center and a doctor's office. In one, emergencies are routine and decisions must be made quickly; in the other, emergencies and quick decision making are the exceptions.

Another factor is that *managerial authority is more often questioned* in operations than in many other functional areas of the organization. For example, if a company is unionized, it will be in the operations area. (Union leaders realize that their power is increased when production workers are part of the collective bargaining unit; management obviously responds to a potential strike threat in the production area more quickly than they would to a strike threat in the records department.)

The final element that presents challenges for operation personnel is the *rate of innovation.* To remain competitive, firms are continually looking for newer and better ways to produce their products and services. The development of technology and techniques like computers, robots, CAD/CAM (computer-aided design, computer-aided manufacturing), flexible manufacturing systems, and just-in-time manufacturing has created both opportunities and problems. The operations field is a dynamic one, and if a company or a manager falls behind in the implementation of new production techniques or processes, the company's future is in jeopardy.

This chapter describes the management and control of operations. The first part of the chapter addresses broad questions like: What is operations management? Why is it important? The second portion of the chapter becomes more specific and presents various operations issues. In presenting this material, we intend to make you aware of some of the managerial aspects of the operations function. Further reading or on-the-job training will be needed if you wish to specialize in operations management.

MANUFACTURING AND SERVICE OPERATIONS

The basic purpose of any organization is the production of goods or services for consumption in the marketplace. For example, a restaurant produces food and also perhaps a particular atmosphere; an automobile company produces cars; a university provides education. In essence, every organization exists to transform inputs into outputs. The process of converting those inputs into outputs is called the **production function.** Figure 18-1 is a simplified view of the production function.

Production function
The process of converting or transforming various inputs into a distinguishable output.

The Production Function

All organizations use inputs to create their outputs. From Figure 18-1, we see that the inputs may include workers, managers, staff, materials (that is, steel, rubber, purchased parts, services, and so forth), energy, and money. Without managerial direction or planning, these inputs have limited organizational utility. They become converted or transformed when managers use facilities, machines, and processes to produce an output of goods and services. For example, managers hire and train young men and women to use the machines and work procedures to cook chicken or make hamburgers that will make a tasty lunch or dinner for a customer; a skilled team of renal intensive care nurses and doctors use a dialysis machine to correct a kidney malfunction in a severely burned patient; and managers of athletic sports teams use game plans, scouting reports, and motivational schemes to mold a collection of individuals into a functioning and productive unit.

The transformation process takes many forms. It may be physical (for example, the cutting, painting, and assembly of a car); it may be physiological, as in health care; it may occur through storage (for example, the cellaring of wine); or it may occur in transportation (for example, airlines or garbage removal). Through whatever form, the transformation process increases the value of the inputs so that they may be sold as an output for a profit. Hence, the transformation process is also often called the *value-added process.*

To monitor and control the efficiency and effectiveness of the transformation process, several feedback mechanisms are needed. This feedback may provide information on customer satisfaction with the product or the service,

FIGURE 18-1 The Production Function

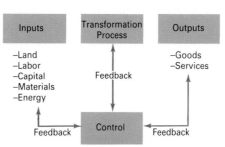

the quality of the product or the service, the amount of material being used to produce the product or the service, or perhaps the availability of necessary materials or labor.

Operations management
The process of managing all the activities required to produce a good or service.

Operations management is the process of managing all those activities that are required to produce a good or provide a service. In broad terms, operations management is responsible for determining and acquiring the appropriate inputs, processing those inputs, and controlling the performance of the process. To meet these responsibilities, an organization must perform a wide variety of activities.[2]

The terms *production* and *operations* are often associated with manufacturing firms, but they apply equally well to service organizations. For example, operations techniques are being used in many health care, educational, financial, and government organizations to help control escalating costs.

Both manufacturing and service organizations produce an output from various inputs, and they have similar concerns about operations. Each organization needs to acquire a constant supply of materials, labor, and other inputs and is concerned with scheduling its people and equipment.

- A hospital needs medical equipment, skilled doctors, pharmaceuticals, and so on, to produce its medical services, and a clothing manufacturer needs inputs of cloth, sewing machines, sewers, and maintenance people to produce its products.
- A doctor's office schedules doctors and examination rooms for patients, and an auto manufacturer schedules people and equipment to process a product through the cutting, painting, and assembly process.

Further, each organization is concerned with producing a quality output at a competitive cost.[3] The output of neither a service nor a manufacturing organization will be demanded by customers if it doesn't meet their quality requirements at a price they're willing to pay.

The Impact of Operations Management

The effectiveness with which a hair salon, a restaurant, a university, an airline, or an auto manufacturer operates depends upon how well the operations functions are managed and controlled. You have experienced poorly run operations: long lines at checkout counters; textbooks that are unavailable at the bookstore; a mechanic who promises your car by noon but doesn't have it ready until 2:00 P.M.; or a pair of athletic shoes that fall apart after two wearings. If poorly performed, operations functions can certainly create problems: frustration for the customer; reduced sales, market share, and profit for the company; and, if widespread, reduced competitiveness for the United States. On the other hand, well-managed operations functions are a joy for the customer: an auto that rarely breaks down and needs only basic maintenance; a supermarket that opens another checkout counter when there are three or more people in line; an auto-repair shop that picks up and delivers your car; a restaurant that serves quality food in a quality atmosphere; clothing that lasts for years; and an airline that provides quality food and service at a reasonable price.

The operations function can focus on a number of areas. These areas typically include low product cost (price-competitive), high quality (better overall workmanship), superior reliability (consistent performance), flexibility (ability to easily produce a variety of outputs or quantities), and availability (fast provision of the product or the service). Many Japanese firms have become quite successful following a strategy of low product cost, with quality being a key element in their strategy. Today, the issue of time is also becoming a popular competitive element—having a variety of products available in a short period of time (represented by product or service flexibility and availability).

Managing the Operations Area

What does the operations manager do?

The primary responsibilities of the operations manager are depicted in Figure 18-2. In the areas discussed in this chapter, the operations manager performs all those managing functions mentioned in Chapters 5–11. Our approach will be to study the various operations areas and address manager functions, issues, problems, and challenges as we go.

The operations manager does a great deal of planning. In developing these plans, the operations manager makes decisions that require substantial investment by the organization and will typically have a long-term impact on the performance of the firm because the decision is not easily reversed (decisions in the areas of product and process design, selection of capital equipment, capacity planning, location and layout of facilities, and work design).

Product Design

Once the need for the firm's products or services is determined, the firm must completely design those products or services. One recent approach to product design that is receiving considerable attention is that of "design for producibil-

FIGURE 18-2 **Responsibilities of the Operations Manager**

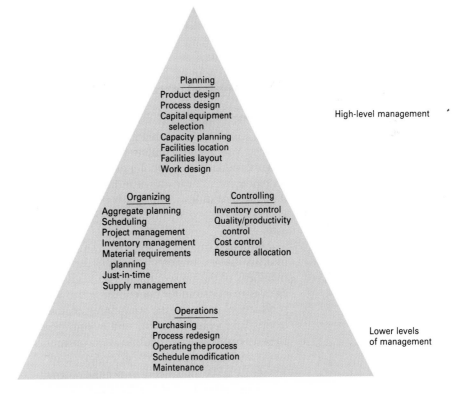

ity." Often used by the military in the design or purchase of new systems (and quickly being adopted by commercial firms), the approach considers elements of producibility, cost, consistent quality, and reliability in the design of the product.

Producibility considers the extent to which the firm's people, equipment, and technology can produce the product within its current production system. *Cost* refers to the total cost of producing the product, including the costs of materials, labor, energy, equipment, and transportation. *Quality* refers to the excellence or superiority of the product. In design for producibility, the ability to consistently produce a quality product is emphasized. *Reliability* is the extent to which the consumer can depend upon the product to perform its intended function. If an automobile performs its intended function of providing transportation without breaking down, the product is said to be reliable.

Successfully using the concept of designing for producibility requires the coordination of many functions. Marketing, operations, finance, accounting, and engineering must all work together to design a product that meets all the requirements of producibility.

The design of services also uses the concepts of designing for producibility, but there are some differences. First, a service is often sold as a "package,"—that is, a product, a service, atmosphere, and response time might all be considered—whereas a manufactured good is generally considered by itself. Further, in services, the method of producing the service is developed with the service itself, whereas in manufacturing, process design (the method of producing the product) generally follows the design of the product.

Process design
Determining the production system to use in manufacturing the product.

Once the product or the service has been designed, the next step is to determine the production system by which the product or the service is to be produced. This activity is known as **process design.**

Process Design

Process design decisions are basic to the efficient and effective operations of any firm. The nature of the product or the service and the volume to be produced determine the way the product is made—that is, using project, job or intermittent, repetitive, or continuous production.

Project production
A system with limited life and budget designed to bring a particular project to completion; example would be a launch of the space shuttle.

If the product or the service is a complex, large-scale, special-purpose job requiring a unique set of activities, **project production** is usually used. Because this production system has a limited life (production ends when the project is completed), a budget and a time constraint are usually assigned to the project. You are all familiar with the concept of project production in which you and other members of a group must develop a term paper or an oral presentation by a particular deadline. In performing the project, you may divide the responsibilities so that each of you becomes an expert in a particular area of the topic. Additionally, one of you will tend to coordinate the group's efforts.

Although smaller in scope than most projects, this process is similar to the industry use of projects in which experts from various functional areas are members of the project team. The leader of the team, called the project manager, is responsible for coordinating the activities of all team members. Project production includes the launching of the space shuttle; the movement of troops and equipment to, and within, the Persian Gulf during Operation Desert Storm; and the planning and promotion of a new product line.

If a variety of products or services is to be produced and each product or service is to be produced in relatively small quantities, **job** or **intermittent**

Job (intermittent) production Production work is unique for each "job." Job may include custom home; television repair; restaurant meal.

production is generally used. In a job shop (a commercial printer, tailors, or restaurants), work is unique and done in small quantities. Many different jobs go on at any one time and require different tasks. Thus, the work flows through the organization in various directions. In this system, workers have a wide range of production skills, and the production equipment and materials tend to be general rather than specialized.

If, on the other hand, a rather standardized product is to be produced in large quantities, neither project nor job production is the most economical design. Rather, **repetitive production** is used. This system is what you would recognize as the assembly or production line. With a production line, the manufacturing tasks are repetitive and the workers and the equipment perform specialized tasks in a prescribed sequence of production steps. This assembly or production line can be either machine-paced, in which the product automatically moves from station to station, or worker-paced, in which the product flow is controlled by the worker. On a worker-paced line, the job contents and the production pace vary throughout the worker's shift, whereas the machine-paced line will operate at a constant pace. Automobiles, pencils, and bicycles are good examples of products using a machine-based line, whereas the fast-food industry uses a worker-paced line. A worker-paced line will generally be used when greater flexibility is needed in the process.

Repetitive production Traditional assembly line where workers do same tasks over and over again.

The production of a product using a machine-paced repetitive process requires tremendous initial analysis because once this production process is established, it is very difficult and expensive to change. Consider the effort that would be involved in changing an automobile assembly line.

Figure 18-3 shows a diagram of this concept of operations management applied to the production of hamburgers. It shows the process flow for a Burger King Restaurant in Noblesville, Indiana.

Continuous production Manufacturing system used to produce highly homogenous and standardized products (i.e., oil, dog food); highly automated and capable of running 24 hours per day.

If the product to be produced is extremely standardized and is not measurable by discrete units, **continuous production** is used. These products

FIGURE 18-3 Production System for Hamburgers

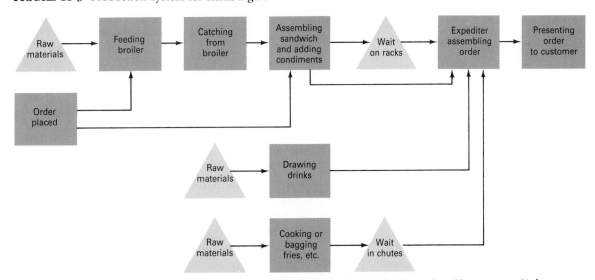

Source: Reprinted by permission of MacMillan Publishing Company from *Production/Operations Management,* 4/e by Roger W. Schmenner. Copyright © 1990 by MacMillian Publishing Company, New York, p. 164.

Design and engineering improvements in machinery have given workers many advantages. The new machines are usually safer, require less physical energy to operate, and allow the operator to achieve higher productivity. Some machines perform basic operations for different jobs and are called **general purpose**. Others, like this one shown in an aircraft parts assembly operation in California, are designed for a specific purpose and are thus called **special-purpose machines**.

are often in the process industries and include items like steel, petroleum, beer, and many foods. In continuous flow, individual operations do not exist. The inputs (crude oil, for example) are gradually converted to outputs through a continuous-flow process. From barrels of crude oil, a refinery produces gasoline, jet fuel, kerosene, lubricants, and other by-products. Because a continuous production system tends to be capital-intensive, highly automated, and computerized, the primary emphasis is placed on the initial design and planning aspects of the total process. Additionally, it is generally desirable to run the operation twenty-four hours a day to avoid expensive shutdowns and start-ups.

Once the design of both the product and the process is complete, operations managers turn their attention to the problem of determining the type of capital equipment or the level of technology to use in the production of the product or the service.

Selection of Capital Equipment or Technology

The rate of technological development makes the decision about capital equipment a very complex one.

One distinction in equipment is between **general-purpose** and **special-purpose** machines. General-purpose machines perform many operations or perform operations useful to many products. Sanding, cutting, and polishing machines are illustrations of general-purpose machines. Equipment in oil refineries, ore-extraction industries, and brewing firms illustrates special-purpose machines. The skill required on a special-purpose machine is less than on a general-purpose machine, because the skill is built into the special-purpose machine.

At one time, the only choice to be made in the selection of equipment was the one just described. With the advent of mechanization and automation, however, the selection of capital equipment has become much more difficult for operations managers. Great advances have been made in automation, including the development of machining centers, numerically controlled machines, industrial robots, computer-aided design and manufacturing (CAD/CAM), flexible manufacturing systems, and computer-integrated manufacturing.

Machining centers can automatically control a machine and also change the tooling on the machine. The operations of numerically controlled machines (NC machines) are totally controlled by a computer program. The computer will position the machine and make any needed corrections. An NC machine is used in many fabrication shops to position sheets of steel and drill holes where needed. A **robot** is a mechanical device that can be trained to do its job through the use of a teaching box. The movements of a robot's arm are stored in a computer program, and the robot then does exactly as the program demands. Robots generally do the boring welding, spray painting, loading, and unloading as well as more difficult and dangerous tasks in the firm.

"Second-generation" robots exist and are becoming more common in traditional white-collar work. These robots are able to design products and even schedule factory work. The term *generation* in this field defines a very short time frame, for the "third- and fourth-generation" robots are already among us. These are the robots with artificial intelligence. Aided by sophisticated sensors and computer software, these "smart machines" are being developed to learn—that is, to respond to outside changes, make judgments, communicate

Robot A reprogrammable multifunctional manipulator designed to move material, parts, tools, or specialized devices through variable programmed motions to accomplish a variety of tasks.

What are some applications of robot technology?

with human operators, and process information. These robots clean up nuclear plants, participate in the rescue of disaster victims, and work in deep underwater projects. The number of applications for these robots is increasing every day, and new uses seem more fantastic than the previous ones. Because Japan has more than 60 percent of the world's robots (compared with less than 20 percent in the United States, although it is growing rapidly now), the illustrations that follow come from Japanese companies. These applications make use of the field of robotics and integrated technology involving mechanical engineering, computer software, and electronics.[4]

■ Kaiho-Jitsugyo produces a lumberjack robot. It climbs up a tree spirally with a set of wheels and with a chain saw lops off branches as it goes.

■ Suzujo Machinery Works began selling a sushi robot in 1982 with a robotic arm and claws that make rice patties. It produces three times more than an experienced sushi chef.

■ Hitachi has a sixty-four-pound, highly portable robot. It can go where the work is rather than having the work brought to the machine. It moves along the giant steel structures that make up the skeleton of big ships and does welding.

■ Toshiba's robot (the "elephant's nose") has one seven-foot-five-inch arm with eight joints, touch sensors, and a tiny television camera. It does inspection in dangerous places.

■ Nachi-Fujikoshi makes an electrically driven spot-welding robot to supplant the larger, less energy-efficient hydraulic-powered machines used in the past.

There is little doubt about the future development and use of robots.[5] They are part of the new information technology revolution spreading to all parts of the world. Their use is not in question; their impact is what concerns many people. Robots are replacing workers in various tasks, but where possible, these workers are retrained for other, safer, more satisfying tasks. However, as robots continue to perform a wider variety of tasks, concern about worker displacement grows.

Unions have embraced the introduction of robots to do dirty and hazardous work. Will they be so charitable when robots begin replacing more blue- and white-collar workers? There could be social unrest and even violence if the robot revolution bumps thousands of workers out of their jobs. In 1990, over 200,000 robots were in place in U.S. factories. By 2025, robots could replace humans in almost all manufacturing jobs. There are activities that robots will never be able to do. Table 18-1 depicts the potential uses and "nonuses" for a robot. The basic question, however, is whether America can afford *not* to make full use of the capabilities of robots. The Japanese are already ahead of us in using robots to cut costs and improve quality in operations.

Computer-aided design (CAD) The design of products, processes, or systems with the help of a computer.

Computer-aided manufacturing (CAM) Use of a computer to design and control the manufacturing process.

Flexible Manufacturing System System combining automated equipment, computer control, and automated material handling to create flexibility in production.

Technologies

Computer-aided design and **computer-aided manufacturing (CAD/CAM)** uses a computer to link the design of the product and the production process. With a CAD/CAM system, you are able not only to view the product from different angles but also to evaluate various product or process changes. Such a system (currently expensive) allows the design process to occur much faster and with higher quality levels.

A **flexible manufacturing system (FMS)** combines automated equipment, computer control, and automated materials handling to create an automated manufacturing "cell." These systems are able to produce a number of

TABLE 18-1   Current and Future Computer Uses

THINGS PRESENT (OR PAST) ROBOTS CAN DO	THINGS NEXT GENER-ATION ROBOTS WILL BE ABLE TO DO	THINGS A VERY SOPHISTICATED FUTURE ROBOT MAY BE ABLE TO DO	THINGS NO ROBOT WILL EVER BE ABLE TO DO (PROBABLY)
Play the piano	Vacuum a rug (avoiding obstructions)	Set a table	Cut a diamond
Load/unload CNC machine tools	Load/unload a glass blowing or cutting machine	Clear a table	Polish an opal
Load/unload die casting machines, hammer forging machines, molding machines, etc.	Assemble large and/or complex parts, TVs, refrigerators, air conditioners, microwave ovens, toasters, automobiles	Juggle balls	Peel a grape
Spray paint on an assembly line	Operate woodworking machines	Load a dishwasher	Repair a broken chair or dish
Cut cloth with a laser	Walk on two legs	Unload a dishwasher	Darn a hole in a sock/sweater
Make molds	Shear sheep	Weld a cracked casting/forging	Play tennis or Ping Pong at championship level
Deburr sand castings	Wash windows	Make a bed	Catch a football or a Frisbee at championship level
Manipulate tools such as welding guns, drills, etc.	Scrape barnacles from a ship's hull	Locate and repair leaks inside a tank or pipe	Pole vault
Assemble simple mechanical and electrical parts: small electric motors, pumps, transformers, radios, tape recorders	Sandblast a wall	Pick a lock	Dance a ballet
		Knit a sweater	Ride a bicycle in traffic*
		Make needlepoint design	Drive a car in traffic*
		Make lace	Tree surgery
		Grease a continuous mining machine or similar piece of equipment	Repair a damaged picture
		Tune up a car	Assemble the skeleton of a dinosaur†
		Make a forging die from metal powder	Cut hair stylishly
		Load, operate, and unload a sewing machine	Apply makeup artistically
		Lay bricks in a straight line	Set a multiple fracture
		Change a tire	Remove an appendix
		Operate a tractor, plow, or harvester over a flat field	Play the violin‡
		Pump gasoline	Carve wood or marble
		Repair a simple puncture	Build a stone wall
		Pick fruit	Paint a picture with a brush
		Do somersaults	Sandblast a cathedral
		Walk a tightrope	Make/repair leaded glass windows
		Dance in a chorus line	Deliver a baby
		Cook hamburgers in a fast-food restaurant	Cut and trim meat
			Kiss sensuously

* Assuming the other vehicles are not robot controlled.
† Admittedly a computer could provide very valuable assistance.
‡ But it could "synthesize" violin music.
Source: Robert U. Ayres and Steven M. Miller, *Robotics: Applications and Social Implications* (Cambridge, Mass.: Ballinger Publishing, 1983), p. 25.

similar products, providing a flexibility that is needed to provide products faster at a low cost. Compared with traditional manufacturing methods, a FMS is able to provide lower labor costs and higher quality while offering more flexibility and less capital investment than traditional forms of automation.

Computer-integrated manufacturing A computer system that links together engineering design and test, production, inspection, inventory control, etc.; eliminates paperwork, reduces errors, creates flexibility.

Computer-integrated manufacturing (CIM) links all or selected production functions—for example, the functions of design, test, manufacture, inspection, purchasing, inventory control, scheduling, and materials handling—through an integrated computer system. Such an integration of functions eliminates paperwork and errors while creating a faster, more responsive system.

Technology improvement promises great economic gains, but it can also create social and psychological costs for workers. Our society in general, and American management in particular, must prepare its citizens for the coming of the high-technology age. Education and training of the workers are necessary elements if technology is to be used to its fullest potential.

Corporate managers must also learn from the experiences of the past as well as the experiences of other industrial societies. Norwegian strategy uses union–management committees to devise new technology agreements, and the Germans and the Japanese also involve their work forces in the decision-making process. The consequences of the rapidly changing technology and its impact on the quality of work life cannot be left to chance.

Many technological changes are anticipated and have already begun in response to world-class competition. Although productivity in the United States is still quite high, it has been virtually equaled in recent years by Japan, France, and the former West Germany. Additionally, unit labor costs in the United States have been higher than those in its principal competitors. To become more competitive in the future, advanced technologies, including the use of the computer, will play a greater role. The use of computer-aided design (CAD) and computer-aided manufacturing (CAM) is increasing. Computer-integrated manufacturing (CIM) is also getting much attention and is being rapidly developed within organizations. It is intriguing to think about what the factory of the future will really look like. Will our products actually be produced without the touch of a human hand? Will we develop a robot society? How much technological advancement can we as a society accept? These questions and more will have to be answered soon.

Facilities Layout

Facilities layout deals with the placement of departments and equipment, the purpose being to minimize the cost of moving materials or customers through the facility. Layout decisions, like location decisions, are expensive; they're a long-term commitment, and they will have a substantial impact on the efficiency of the firm's operations.

Once the production system has been decided upon, a big step has been taken in determining the appropriate layout, because the type of layout roughly corresponds to the production system. Each layout has its own set of advantages and disadvantages. The traditional layouts are these:

- *Product:* Usually associated with repetitive production. Equipment is arranged in the order in which the product is produced or assembled, with the resulting arrangement being an assembly or a production line.
- *Process:* Usually associated with job production. In this layout, similar functions are grouped together—for example, X-ray, maternity, and surgery departments in a hospital.
- *Fixed-position:* Often associated with project production. In this layout, the product or the service remains stationary and the workers, equipment, and materials revolve around it. For example, the building of a bridge occurs at the location of the bridge, and all the workers, bulldozers, cement, steel, and the like, are brought to the bridge site.

Global Application

Operating Global Partnerships

One of the ways that U.S. firms have enhanced their ability to compete on a global basis is through the formation of joint ventures with their suppliers, customers, and even competitors. Firms engage in international joint ventures to facilitate implementation of their global strategies.

Global joint ventures are typically complex arrangements, with the participating firms pooling financial resources and establishing joint operations. One of the most successful examples of global joint ventures is the fifty-fifty partnership between General Electric and its French counterpart, Snecma. The two have been partners in CFM International for over eighteen years, and they have taken orders to make over 10,000 jet engines valued in excess of $38 billion. Noting the success of CFM, Boeing is now developing a joint venture with the Japanese firms Kawasaki, Fuji, and Mitsubishi to produce the new 777 commercial jet.

The use of global joint ventures as comparatively inexpensive means to quickly enter global markets continues to grow in appeal. Even typically "go it alone" firms like IBM and AT&T are participating in such arrangements. However, forming a joint venture remains a highly volatile and risky endeavor. Because global joint ventures require a great deal of give and take between the venture's participants to make it work, they have a rather high failure rate. Quite often, there is considerable conflict between the participants' corporate cultures and the egos and personalities of the ventures' executives. One study of executives working for

global ventures discovered that more than 60 percent were dissatisfied with the way the ventures were working.

Even in ventures based on fifty-fifty arrangement, usually one side begins to feel threatened by the relationship. There is the fear that the other partner in the venture is using the venture to steal the technology and trade secrets from its partner and, even worse, that one partner or the other is in the venture to acquire its partner's assets and operations.

What partners get out of their ventures varies quite a bit. The GM–Toyota joint venture with the Nummi production operation in Fremont, California, gave Toyota a unique opportunity to learn about manufacturing in the United States before making the commitment to establish its own plant in Georgetown, Kentucky. For GM, it was an opportunity to learn about Japanese management techniques as they could be applied in an American setting, but unfortunately for GM, little effort was made to apply the lessons it learned at Nummi elsewhere in the organization.

For most American firms, global joint ventures represent both an opportunity and a threat, and they recognize that participation in this kind of venture is absolutely essential if they are going to be competitive on a global basis.

References: J. Main, "Making Global Alliances Work," *Fortune,* December 17, 1990, p. 121; Michael Schroeder, "Inland Rolls Out a Sheet of Disappointment—Nippon Steel Joint Venture," *Business Week,* May 20, 1991, p. 114.

Cellular layout
Manufacturing floor layout that groups machines together into "cells" that function as mini production lines; allows for flexibility in production.

A more recent layout is a **cellular layout,** in which machines are grouped together into what is known as a cell. This group of machines essentially becomes a mini–product layout in which all parts entering the cell flow through the machines in the same order and then leave the cell to go elsewhere in the plant. The layout is based upon the ability to group parts into families (a situation in which a number of parts go through a set of machines in the same order). Where possible, the cellular layout is replacing process layouts because the use of cells allows the product to move more efficiently through the processes.

Scheduling

Scheduling The process of assigning a time dimension to the resources of an organization to transform objectives and plans into goods and services.

Scheduling involves the timing of operations. A manufacturing plant must schedule workers, machines, and materials; a university schedules classrooms, instructors, and students.

Scheduling is the process of putting a time dimension to the resources of the organization to transform the objective and plans into goods and services. A schedule is a blueprint, a guide, a tool, and an aid. Scheduling integrates your objectives with your organizational resources. You may know where you want to be or what you want to achieve three weeks from today. You may even have all the necessary equipment, materials, and people. Unless these resources are scheduled (put into a time framework), success may be only a dream.

The nature of the scheduling activities depends upon the volume of output and the type of production process. The type we have selected to illustrate is the most-used one, a low-volume system (job production).

In job production, products or services are produced for a particular customer, and each order tends to require different materials, processes, and time. This feature creates a difficult scheduling task, because customers may cancel or change their orders, creating more complexity in the scheduling task.

What is a Gantt chart?

Gantt chart A bar chart with time on the horizontal axis and a factor (job) to be scheduled on the vertical axis.

One scheduling tool is the **Gantt chart.** The Gantt chart, developed by Henry L. Gantt, is a general-purpose tool for scheduling. Its purpose is to visually show the use of resources during a period of time. In most cases, it is in the form of a bar chart, with time on the horizontal axis, the factor to be scheduled on the vertical axis, and the use of resources in the body of the chart. Gantt charts can be used as charts of the various products or services to be produced, charts of the times at which different jobs are planned, and order charts, to indicate the time to start different orders and the time of completion. These charts are an extremely valuable planning and scheduling tool for the operations manager. A few illustrations appear in Figure 18-4.

The insights provided by these charts help the operations manager manage resources. One look at the Gantt charts tells a manager what jobs are finished, what jobs to start, what machines and workers need to be ready for assignment, where coordination is required, and so forth. In the second example, in the scheduling of a complicated table order, machine B must be scheduled in department 1 if the order is to be processed by the due date in eight weeks. Department 3 can plan to overlap the assembly and painting operations even though assembly requires double the time. All tables assembled in the sixth and seventh weeks can be painted during the seventh week.

The Gantt chart approach to planning and scheduling is very appropriate to small operations or small firms. You can even schedule your own study time during a week, month, or term. Automobile service department managers can schedule workers or jobs using Gantt charts and determine when changes or corrective actions are needed. Use of the charts for classroom scheduling would promote efficient use of classrooms and prevent the scheduling of two classes in the same room. The simplicity of the Gantt chart makes it a useful and widely used technique.

A new method of managing the production system in such an environment

(a) Work Orders

Job order

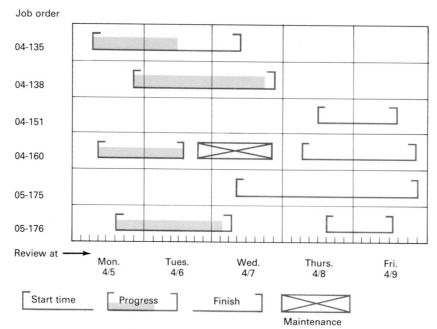

Review at ⟶ Mon. 4/5   Tues. 4/6   Wed. 4/7   Thurs. 4/8   Fri. 4/9

| Start time | Progress | Finish | Maintenance |

Source: Reprinted by permission from *Fundamentals of Production/Operations Management,* 4/e by Harold E. Fearon, et al. Copyright © 1989 by West Publishing Company. All rights reserved. Figure p. 103.

(b) Schedule of Table Order

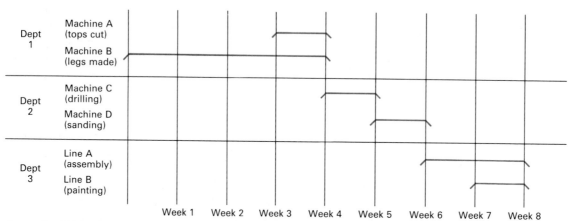

Dept 1 — Machine A (tops cut), Machine B (legs made)
Dept 2 — Machine C (drilling), Machine D (sanding)
Dept 3 — Line A (assembly), Line B (painting)

Week 1   Week 2   Week 3   Week 4   Week 5   Week 6   Week 7   Week 8

Source: David J. Rachman and Michael H. Mescon, *Business Today,* 4/e (1991), McGraw-Hill. Reproduced with permission of McGraw-Hill, Inc.

FIGURE 18-4 Gantt Chart Illustrations

Synchronous production System that requires all phases of the production to work together to achieve firm's goal of making money; no department can excel at the expense of the firm overall.

is to focus on scheduling the bottlenecks—those operations that have the least capacity, or are able to produce the fewest units. This method, known as **synchronous production,** is based on the assumption that bottleneck operations affect the entire plant; therefore, the best way to schedule the plant is to schedule the bottlenecks and maximize their output. The nonbottleneck operations are not critical and can be treated differently.

Traditionally, manufacturing firms have tried to *balance* capacity; that is, each machine or work center is designed to produce the same rate of output. Synchronous production, on the other hand, uses a system of *unbalanced* capacity, in which effort is made to smooth the flow of product through the system rather than balancing the output of each work center. Each production process tends to have normal variation in production time. For example, the time needed to fry a hamburger varies with the heat of the grill and the size and thickness of the patty, but even with burgers of the same size and thickness, variation in cooking time will occur if a number of patties are fried. Given this normal variation, if all processes are producing at the same rate, the variation tends to create a backup or idle time in the system. Balancing the flow of product through the entire system creates a more stable system.

Synchronous production requires that all phases of the production system work together toward the achievement of the firm's goal of making money. This integration of activities reduces the possibility of any functional area performing well at the expense of the firm. Emphasis is placed on total system performance.

The concept of synchronous production has gained a number of "followers," but because it is relatively new, firms have only recently begun to use the system. Therefore, documented benefits from this type of scheduling system are not yet available.

Project Management

The management and scheduling of projects is very different from the other forms of production. You'll recall that a project is a unique, large-scale production in which a set of activities must be completed within a particular time frame. Most projects have a large number of activities that must be planned and coordinated if the project is to be completed on time without excess costs. In managing a project, the manager must set goals and priorities, identify required tasks and the time to perform those tasks, and monitor project progress. Very simple projects can often be managed with the Gantt charts just discussed, but this technique is inadequate for larger projects. Instead, two techniques, **PERT** (program evaluation and review technique) and **CPM** (critical path method), are most widely used to schedule and control projects.

PERT and CPM were independently developed during the 1950s. PERT was developed by Lockheed Aircraft, the U.S. Navy, and the firm of Booz, Allen, and Hamilton to speed the development of the Polaris missile. CPM was developed by E. I. Du Pont de Nemours & Company in conjunction with the Remington Rand Corporation to improve the scheduling of large maintenance projects. Although these two techniques were developed separately, they have many features in common, and the initial differences have practically disappeared. For all practical purposes, the techniques are the same; therefore, the following discussion will apply to the use of both CPM and PERT in managing a project.

One of the main features of PERT and CPM is the use of a network or precedence diagram. This diagram provides you with a visual display of all the principal activities (tasks) of a project. The diagram shows the interrelationships of the activities as well as when the start of one activity depends upon the completion of another.

To produce a project network, you must first divide your project into manageable, identifiable tasks or activities. Then, determine the sequence of your activities. For each of the activities, you must develop an estimate of time. How long do you estimate it might take to paint a house, type a term paper, sew on buttons, weld, sand, and so forth? Your estimate may come from your own production records (experience) or from an industry standard for performing such a task. You may even want to estimate the most optimistic, the most likely, and the most pessimistic time to arrive at an expected time.

How do PERT and CPM work?

Program Evaluation and Review Technique (PERT) Technique used to schedule and control projects; uses a diagram as a visual display of all the major activities of a project.

Critical Path Method (CPM) The path that must be managed most closely in a PERT diagram project.

TABLE 18-2   Plant Construction Activities

ACTIVITY	TIME(MONTHS)	ACTIVITY DESCRIPTION
A	2	Determine site location
B	2	Formulate final building plans
C	10	Construct facility
D	3	Select and purchase equipment
E	4	Determine plant layout
F	9	Equipment delivery time
G	2	Install equipment
H	1	Open plant

With these data, you then develop the network diagram. In Table 18-2, we have the activities for a plant opening, and in Figure 18-5, the precedence network. This simple diagram does a number of things for an operations manager. First, it provides a visual display of the activities and their interrelationships, so that it is easy to see the order in which activities must be performed. For example, installing the equipment (Activity G) cannot be done until the facility has been built, the layout has been determined, and the equipment has been ordered and delivered. Second, it is now possible to create new diagrams for each of these activities to further define and clarify each task. Third, the actual on-time completion of this project carries with it a reward; there is more likely a penalty if it is not done on time. As you look at Figure 18-5, there is a way to determine the time it will take to complete this project. Add up the time required to complete each task as you proceed from left to right. For example, taking the path A–B–D–F–G–H requires a total of nineteen months. The path A–B–D–E–G–H requires fourteen months. The longest path possible for a diagram is called the critical path. The critical path identifies how long the project may take and also which activities are critical to the on-time completion of the project.

If the activities on the critical path are not done in the time allowed, the duration of the project will be extended. In this example, the critical path involves activities A–B–D–F–G–H. Special attention must be given to these activities to keep the project on time. The activities not on the critical path may be

FIGURE 18-5 CPM Diagram for Plant Construction

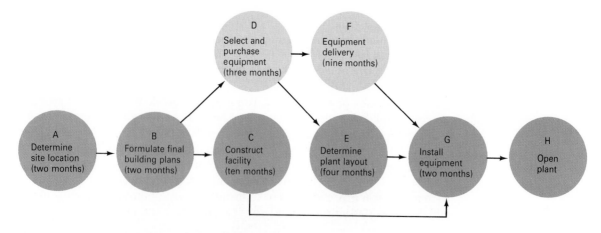

delayed somewhat and still keep the project on schedule. For example, activity E may take as long as nine months without changing the completion date of the project.

The nature of the scheduling activities may vary depending upon the type of production environment, but the purpose of scheduling is still to determine the *timing* and *sequencing* of resources to perform the tasks and operations for the desired product or service. In manufacturing, if too many products are scheduled or the wrong products are scheduled, the firm will create excess product. This extra product is called inventory.

Similarly, the scheduling of too few products can produce stockouts for the firm. Obviously, a firm doesn't want to have too much inventory because it's expensive, but it also doesn't want to have many stockouts because it may lose customers. Determining the specific items to produce, in what quantities, and when they should be ready for use is addressed in the operations activity of inventory management.

Inventory Management

Effective management of inventory is critical to an organization because of the cost that it represents as well as its impact on operations. A firm needs an inventory to use in the production or sale of its product or service. A firm generally has four types of inventory:

- *Raw materials and component* parts are the basic inputs to an organization's production process. These include steel, transistors, plastic, and paint for a computer manufacturer and meat, buns, relish, and potatoes for a fast-food restaurant.

- **Work-in-process (WIP)** inventory is the materials that are moving through the production process but have not yet become a finished product. Partially completed computers are WIP for the computer manufacturer, and french fries in the fryer or hamburgers on the grill are work-in-process inventory for the fast-food restaurant.

- *Finished goods* are the final output of the firm. French fries, hamburgers, and computers are finished-goods inventory.

- **Maintenance, repair, and operating supplies (MRO)** are those items that are needed to produce the firm's product or service but do not go into the product itself. Oil for the fryer and towels are MRO for the fast-food restaurant.

Effectively managing inventory generally addresses two questions: *When* should an item be ordered or produced? *How many* units should be ordered or produced? The method of answering these questions depends upon the particular item and whether the demand for the item is *independent* or *dependent*.

The method of managing finished goods and MRO inventory is somewhat different from that for raw materials, components, or subassemblies. The demand for finished goods or MRO is viewed as "independent," whereas the demand for raw materials and work in process is "dependent" upon the item being made. For independent items, demand is usually linked to past or historical demand.

Demand for dependent items is generally regarded as "lumpy" because production is normally done in lots. When a lot is planned for production, all the raw materials and subassemblies are ordered in preparation for the production run; hence, there is a "lump" in demand. Because it can be determined when the production run will occur, it is possible to order these dependent-demand materials so that they arrive when they are needed.

Work in process (WIP) Units of product partially completed. One of three inventories (finished goods, raw materials are the other two) held by a manufacturing company.

Maintenance, repair, and operating supplies (MRO) Indirect materials used in the production of the product but not in the product itself. Example: oil used to produce french fries.

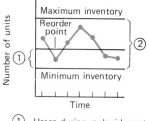

① Usage during replenishment cycle

② Economic order quantity

FIGURE 18-6 EOQ/ROP Inventory System

Material requirements planning (MRP) A manufacturing planning and control technique that works backward from planned-quantities and completion dates for end items on a master production schedule to determine what and when individual parts should be ordered.

Items that have independent demand are normally managed and controlled through systems that determine economic order quantities (EOQs) and reorder points (ROPs), whereas items with dependent demand are generally managed through a system called **material requirements planning (MRP).** Managing independent demand will be briefly discussed first, and then the more recent technique of MRP will be described.

EOQ/ROP Inventory Systems

In managing independent-demand items, targets must be set for four elements of inventory: maximum inventory, minimum inventory, the reorder point, and the economic order quantity (EOQ). Figure 18-6 illustrates how these four targets relate to one another. When such a chart is used for control, actual performance is plotted on the same sheet so that comparisons can easily be made. For example, use of the product causes the quantity on hand to decline. Before the minimum inventory is reached, at the reorder point, an order must be issued for the amount of the economic order quantity. When it arrives, the quantity on hand reaches the maximum level. If the replenishment process is dependable, the minimum inventory can be set very low, because the chief reason for having minimum inventory above zero is to serve as insurance against delays and to reduce the chances of needing continual corrective action.

Various versions of the EOQ/ROP model are available for different situations. For example, unique models are available for situations in which quantity discounts are used, the product is produced rather than purchased, or uncertainty exists in the demand or delivery time.

In managing dependent demand, material requirements planning (MRP) is used. As indicated in Table 18-3, the components of MRP allow an operations manager to address the necessary issues of managing inventory.

TABLE 18-3 Purposes of MRP Components

INVENTORY ISSUE	MRP COMPONENT
1. What products do we make and when?	Master production schedule (MPS)
2. What components go into them?	Bill of materials (BOM)
3. What is available now?	Inventory data
4. What do we need to buy or manufacture and when?	Materials requirement planning (MRP)

	Week							
	1	2	3	4	5	6	7	Quantity needed
3-pac razor	6	12	8	5	24	13	7	

FIGURE 18-7 A Master Production Schedule

Material Requirements Planning

MRP is a computer-based information system driven by the master production schedule, which determines *what* is needed, *when* it is needed, and *how much* is needed. With MRP, operations people can see in advance if they have the correct numbers and types of machines, materials, and people to meet expected demand. It may be that they cannot meet customer orders under the present conditions; they may have to request subcontracting to other firms, prepare the personnel department to hire additional people, or inform supervisors to put workers on overtime. They may not have enough materials in stock or on order, and plans must be made to purchase the needed parts. Additionally, the operations people can use MRP to generate different "what if" scenarios—for example, "what if" materials don't show up on time? One simple illustration of the MRP system follows.

Assume you manufacture a three-pack disposable razor. You would first develop a **master production schedule (MPS),** and it might contain the data as shown in Figure 18-7. This schedule shows both the quantity of razors that must be produced and when they are due for this seven-week period. The quantities in the MPS may represent both firm customer orders or forecasted demand.

The next step is to develop a statement of the components required for the final product, known as a **bill of materials (BOM).** The bill of materials for the razor is shown in Figure 18-8. To produce one three-pack disposable razor, three of the razor assemblies are needed. Each of these assemblies requires a handle, blade, retainer, and guard.

An inventory check is made to find the on-hand status of handles, blades, retainers, and guards. The MRP process then takes the end-item production quantities from the MPS and uses the BOM file as well as inventory status data to determine component material needs and their planned order releases. This explosion process is logically simple but can involve hundreds or thousands of calculations for complex products.

Master production schedule (MPS)   Tells quantity of and time each item is wanted; it is developed from the end-item forecasts and customer orders.

Bill of materials (BOM) A list of the components required for producing the final product.

FIGURE 18-8 A Sample Bill of Materials

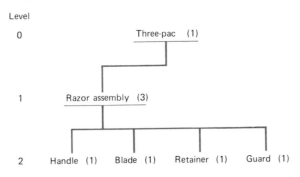

Level	
0	Three-pac (1)
1	Razor assembly (3)
2	Handle (1) Blade (1) Retainer (1) Guard (1)

The development of MRP demonstrates the gains from both the computer and the information revolutions. Computers allow operations managers to simulate future options and thus generate flexibility in production decisions. MRP essentially allows vision into the future, enhancing the ability of the production function to perform and to respond to changes. Firms that have implemented MRP have realized many benefits, such as reduced inventory, better customer service, better response to market demands, increased sales, reduced sales price, and reduced idle time.

Currently, applications of MRP in services are rare because the logic of MRP programs has been based upon the control of inventoriable items. As MRP systems continue to develop, they will be able to control all resources, including materials, facilities, equipment, and labor.

In the foregoing discussion of MRP, MRP included only the production and inventory functions; however, as the abilities of computers have increased, more functional areas have been integrated into MRP systems. With the inclusion of more functions, the name of the system has been changed to manufacturing resources planning, or MRP II.[6]

Manufacturing resources planning (MRP II)
Applies the scheduling concepts to all segments of the organization, not just manufacturing; includes finance and marketing.

Manufacturing resources planning (MRP II) adds new dimensions to material requirements planning (MRP). MRP II plans and monitors all the resources of a manufacturing firm, bringing all segments of the organization together. Like synchronous production, MRP II is a company game plan. It requires participation from all members of the corporate team. There must be a common language, which is the one data base. In one way, it is a new philosophy of management.

MRP is known as a *push* production system because it schedules each operation in the production process, forcing the product through the system. MRP also uses what would be called backward scheduling, in which production is scheduled at operations working backward from the desired completion date. On the other hand, synchronous production is becoming known as a *squeeze* system, because it focuses on squeezing material through the bottlenecks. This system uses forward scheduling, in which the critical (bottleneck) operations are scheduled into the future with work to ensure that they are always busy.

Just-in-Time Production

How does JIT work?

Within the last decade, another approach to managing production and inventory has been developed. This system, called **just-in-time (JIT),** was developed by Mr. Taiichi Ohno at the Toyota Motor Company of Japan. Currently, it is being introduced into manufacturing firms throughout the United States. JIT can offer tremendous benefits if used correctly within an organization.

Just-in-time (JIT)
Production and delivery of finished goods just in time to be sold, of sub-assemblies just in time to be assembled into finished goods, of fabricated parts just in time to be used, and so on.

The Japanese have made great inroads into the manufacturing superiority of America by employing this concept. The ideal in a Japanese factory is zero inventory and unit production.

Just-in-time is built upon two primary principles: the elimination of waste and respect for people. The first principle may have developed because Japan is a nation with few natural resources, and as such, they have become quite aware of waste and inefficiency. In addition to just-in-time production to eliminate waste, the Japanese employ several other concepts. First, their plants are small and specialized. The Japanese also use a layout based upon manufacturing cells in which the processes are grouped so that the parts do not have to be moved between departments for processing. Another concept to eliminate waste is the use of a kanban production control system. The **kanban tech-**

Kanban Techniques
A manufacturing control system using simple manual cards to indicate when to deliver or produce more units; a pull system since only the final output is scheduled.

nique is a simple manual card system that controls the manufacture of units.[7] The card, attached to a container, signals the need to deliver or to produce more parts. This system is often referred to as a *pull* system because only the final output is scheduled and each user must draw materials from the preceding stages when needed. Minimizing setup and order costs is also a waste-reduction component of JIT. If small quantities are to be produced frequently, the cost to place the order or prepare the machines to produce the order must be reduced. Another way to reduce waste is to improve quality. In JIT, every worker is responsible for controlling the quality of his or her process.

The Japanese, realizing that people are an important element in the system, have great respect for the people who work in their firms. To show this respect, lifetime employment is granted to critical individuals; machines, rather than people, perform any degrading tasks; and the employees are given the opportunity to use their potential. Additionally, company unions include employees and management as members. This enhances cooperation among workers and helps focus all employees' efforts on the goals of the company.

Another way to show respect for people is to allow them to make decisions. An important element of JIT is a management approach in which decision making is pushed to the lowest level possible within the organization. With this approach, individuals on the shop floor are responsible not only for the quality of their product but also for deciding when to maintain equipment and when to order more materials. Often, these decisions will be made through a *quality circle*—a group of volunteers who meet regularly to discuss their function, the problems they are encountering, and possible solutions. Allowing the workers to make the decisions related to their jobs not only gets them more involved in the production process but also allows management more time to perform the planning activities.

Inventory management under the JIT philosophy and practice means that production is in small batches, inventories are in small lots, and deliveries are made frequently by suppliers. Suppliers in Japan are partners in achieving the total corporate goal of a quality good at a competitive price. Suppliers frequently build factories or warehouses close to the production plants so that delivery times can be minimized, and suppliers are often consulted if production problems arise in the main plant. Everyone works for the same objective.

JIT practices also encourage simple means to solve problems.[8] The use of computer techniques is not a requirement for JIT; rather, manual techniques like kanban are often used. The Japanese have found that simple techniques reduce waste and confusion because the workers can understand the techniques. The Japanese method of managing production is based upon just-in-time production. It requires the production of precisely the needed quantity of items at precisely the right time. Because only the needed quantity is ordered from suppliers or produced in-house, there is no slack and each unit must be a quality product. Also, because materials arrive "just-in-time" for production, changes in the master schedule would ruin the timing of the incoming material and are not allowed. You know that it would be difficult to complete a term paper "just-in-time" if the due date and requirements kept changing.

Although JIT has a wide range of applications in both manufacturing and service firms, it is designed primarily for a repetitive manufacturing process. A large volume of a particular finished product does not necessarily have to be produced (although it is helpful), but it is essential that the parts for which JIT is to be used be produced over and over again.

Many U.S. and European firms have implemented the JIT approach to managing production and report benefits in reduced inventory, throughput and setup times, and increased productivity. There is no doubt that we will see increasing use of JIT in both service and manufacturing firms.

So far, we have focused primarily on the management of the product *within* the firm, but what about all the materials, components, and subassemblies that are purchased from other companies?

Supply Management

Supply management
A field management specializing in maintaining a consistent flow of quality materials and services needed to produce products at the lowest total cost to the firm.

Managing and controlling the process of acquiring inputs from outside suppliers is called supply or procurement management. A few years ago, **supply management** was seen more as the simple task of placing orders, but that view has changed. Supply management is a field of its own, with managers performing planning, organizing, and control activities as well as the other managerial functions.[9]

To operate efficiently and effectively, a firm needs to have a consistent flow of quality materials and services. Because these materials contribute to the cost of the finished product, they must be procured at a competitive marketplace cost. This doesn't mean that the lowest-priced materials are purchased; rather, materials are purchased that provide the lowest total cost, where total cost includes things like price, quality, service, delivery time, and delivery reliability.

Supply management is becoming more important for a number of reasons. First, the average manufacturing firm spends about sixty cents of every dollar received in sales on outside purchases, and that number is growing as firms continue to buy more and make less. Second, as the marketplace becomes more competitive, procurement spending is a logical area in which to try to reduce costs. Third, products, processes, and techniques (like JIT) are placing new demands on the suppliers, and procurement personnel must help suppliers meet these demands.[10] Procurement personnel must work more closely with suppliers on issues of total quality control and improvement; in many cases, a partnership relationship is being formed to achieve these goals.

Briefly, the role of the supply manager is to develop and maintain a continuous flow of required materials and services while achieving the best combination of price, quality, and service; determine which firms to buy from and develop close relations with those suppliers; calculate how much to buy so that extra material isn't purchased; analyze the market trends to determine when to buy; remain current with technological developments to improve the firm's productivity whenever possible; perform other managerial activities of training and motivating personnel; controlling individual and function performance; and planning future supply requirements.

As organizations try to become more competitive, a number of changes are occurring in supply management. Firms are now buying from fewer suppliers so that procurement people may spend more time with selected suppliers, communication costs are reduced, and quality levels are improved.

Countertrade A situation where a firm is required to buy materials, components, or labor from a country in exchange for selling its products in that country.

Another change is that procurement is "going international." Again, to reduce costs and improve quality, procurement is doing business with more and more overseas firms. These firms may be supplying a plant located overseas or one located in the United States. Procurement is also being asked to handle the issue of **countertrade**, in which a firm is often required to buy materials, components, or something else from a country in exchange for selling its products to that country. This can often be a big problem because the country is often underdeveloped and cannot easily provide items the firm can use in its production process. In that case, the firm may buy a commodity and sell it to another organization.

Quality and Productivity Control

Within the past decade, the issue of quality has become extremely important as Japanese manufacturers have been able to successfully produce goods of higher quality than U.S. manufacturers do.[11] The quality issue continues to be important because the production of quality products and services greatly affects a nation's ability to compete in the world marketplace.

A primary concern in controlling quality is learning to remove the causes of variation in the manufacturing process. The technique used to accomplish this is called **statistical process control** (SPC). Essentially, SPC gauges the performance of the manufacturing process by carefully monitoring changes in whatever is being produced. The objective is to determine potential problems before poor-quality products are produced and to then identify the reasons for the deviation and adjust the process to make it more stable.

The quality targets are set by engineers. Samples of products in production are tested at intervals to provide data on the current quality. These samples yield data that may vary from standard for two reasons: (1) the chance selection of the items in the sample and (2) the "real" cause of poor quality, such as the wearing of a cutting tool. The problem of using samples to control quality is in differentiating between these two factors so that corrective action is taken only when it is needed.

Statisticians have provided tables for determining the size of samples and the degrees of risk for inference from samples and other data, using probability reasoning. The important skills needed by the nonstatistics-oriented manager are (1) a familiarity with the powerful tools provided by statisticians and (2) an ability to interpret the output of their work. Quality-control charts offer a graphical means by which the manager can interpret the information supplied by the statisticians.

Statistical process control A method used to monitor and adjust production to prevent variations in the manufacturing process; the goal is to maintain high quality, the control function.

More American firms are committing themselves to the philosophy and practice of quality thoughout their operations. In many instances it may take more than 10 years of training before a quality perspective exists among workers, managers, and staff. Ford Motor Company believes that a quality focus will sell more cars as they tell their readers that "Quality is Job 1."

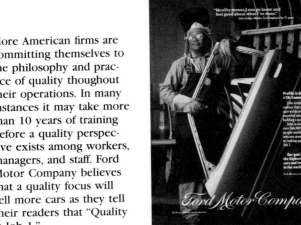

The section on inventory management and JIT suggested the interrelationship between productivity and product quality. Too often, these terms have been viewed as distinct from each other. Traditionally, quality has meant prestigious, special, and expensive. You expect quality from a Rolls Royce, a Mercedes Benz, or a Cadillac, and you pay for it. Americans have felt that mass-produced products could not stand up to the test of quality. The success of other countries, especially Japan, in producing quality and competitively priced automobiles has done much to change the customer's expectation of quality.

Japan's success has also begun to change the concept of managing quality in the United States. The change will not come easily or without cost because some basic elements are involved. The following quote is from a Special Report on Quality in *Business Week.* "Managing for quality means nothing less than a sweeping overhaul and a permanent commitment to seek continuous improvements."[12] Such a change will bring American industry in line with other global competitors; in fact, the new position will most likely contain many features of the Japanese total quality-control concepts that follow:

- A goal of continual quality improvement, project after project (rejection of the Western notion of an "acceptable quality level")
- Worker responsibility (not quality-control department responsibility)
- Quality control of every process, not reliance upon inspection of lots for only selected processes (defect prevention, not random detection)
- Measures of quality that are visible, visual, simple, and understandable, even to the casual observer
- Automatic quality-measurement devices (self-developed)

Ironically, the concepts of total quality control stem primarily from the contributions of three Americans: Joseph M. Juran, W. Edwards Deming, and A. V. Feigenbaum. The Japanese, however, are the ones who have been able to successfully apply the concepts to their manufacturing processes. The worker quality circle is also a technique borrowed from American quality-control experts. Developed in Japan, it is now returning to U.S. manufacturing firms (recall, however, the reservations on quality circles mentioned in Chapter 14).

Quality Circles (QCs) is a Japanese technique receiving attention and credit for worker productivity and quality gains during the past ten years. Membership in these groups is voluntary, although the climate in the workplace shows strong management support for such voluntary involvement. The QC members come from the same shop or work area, and the supervisor is usually, but not always, the leader of the circle.

Within the circle, however, the supervisor does not issue orders or make decisions. Circle members choose the problems and projects to work on, gather all the information, analyze it, and make decisions. Some management authorities state that the secret of Japanese success with QCs is the emphasis on worker participation in the process of improving the quality of the firm rather than an emphasis on the control of quality. QCs allow a revision in the authority system and tap the knowledge and experience of workers, those persons who in the last analysis actually determine product and service quality.

A quote from the *Canadian Business Review* perhaps best highlights the importance of total quality control in firms: "To achieve competitiveness, total quality must permeate the organization. Those who adopt and adapt, prosper. Those who do not, disappear."[13] As you might guess, operations managers are working exceptionally hard to consistently produce a quality product or service.

Quality also affects the productivity of a firm or a country. Productivity is often associated with competitiveness because it is a principal element of competitiveness. In its broadest form, productivity is found by this measure:

$$\text{Productivity} = \frac{\text{Inputs}}{\text{Outputs}}$$

An organization wants the ratio to be as large as possible because that means that fewer inputs are being used to produce the outputs, also meaning that the products or the services are being produced at a lower total cost. If a product or a service is produced at a lower cost, then it can also be economically sold at a lower price in the marketplace.

The foregoing productivity measure is a total measure in which all inputs (labor, materials, capital, and energy) are included. If a firm wished to see what was happening to the productivity of an individual input—for example, how effectively and efficiently labor was performing—a partial productivity index would be calculated. Productivity measures are generally stated in units to avoid the fluctuations in currency. These measures also capture the impact of poor quality because products that need rework, or scrap that is produced, will increase the inputs used but not the outputs, thereby reducing the productivity levels.

The United States still has one of the highest absolute levels of productivity,[14] but there is concern because U.S. productivity growth is very small, whereas the productivity of other countries continues to increase substantially. By the year 2000, several countries could potentially surpass U.S. productivity levels, making it very difficult for the United States to compete in products and services. In some instances, however, the United States is still competitive.[15]

According to a recent survey by the MIT Commission on Industrial Productivity, to turn U.S. productivity around, business must make the following changes.[16]

1. Place less importance on short-term financial results and invest more in research and development.
2. Revise corporate strategies to respond to foreign competition. This includes greater investment in people and equipment to improve manufacturing capability.
3. Eliminate communication barriers within the organization and between the organization and its suppliers.
4. Recognize the importance of the work force and nurture it.
5. Get back to basics in managing production operations. Build in quality at the beginning, and focus on process improvement as well as product improvement.

As you can see, many of these elements deal with the operations manager and the production function. Operations managers will indeed have a challenging decade ahead of them.[17]

America is faced with many threats and challenges. Military threats seem to be a constant companion, but we have experienced those threats before. Economic threats are new to us. The oil crisis, the recession, staggering unemployment, environmental concerns, and the gloomy prediction about the future of our basic industries are all unfamiliar territory for Americans. The Japanese

In spite of the negative press that some U.S. firms receive, Americans do make good products. From a list of 100 good American products, you can see three of Apple Computer's line: the MacClassic, IIsi, and LC. Apple has achieved success by designing its products to be very "user" friendly.

Management Application

Good American Products

- All-electric plastics injection-molding machines: Cincinnati Milacron
- Aluminum foil: Reynolds Wrap
- Ballpoint pens: A. T. Cross
- Balloon and laser angioplasty catheters: C. R. Bard, Eli LIlly, Trimedyne
- Bed sheets and towels: Burlington Industries, Dan River, Dundee Mills, Fieldcrest Cannon, J. P. Stevens
- Biotech drugs: Genentech
- Boots and hunting shoes: Timberland, L. L. Bean
- Camera film (color): Eastman Kodak
- Central office switching equipment: AT&T
- Charcoal briquettes: Kingsford
- Clothes dryers: Whirlpool
- Combines: Case IH, John Deere
- Copiers: Eastman Kodak, Xerox
- Digital plotters: Hewlett-Packard
- Dishwashers: General Electric
- Electrodeposition primers: PPG Industries
- F-16 jet fighters: General Dynamics
- Fast foods: McDonald's

- 501 jeans: Levi Strauss
- Flutes: Wm. S. Haynes
- Heating controls: Honeywell
- Heavy earthmoving equipment: Caterpillar
- Instant camera films: Polaroid
- Jet engines: General Electric
- Lycra spandex fiber: Du Pont
- Microwavable food: General Foods
- Microwave ovens: Litton Industries
- Minicomputers: Digital Equipment, Hewlett-Packard, IBM
- Pacemakers: Medtronic
- Paper towels: Procter & Gamble
- Personal computers: Apple Computer
- Pianos: Steinway & Sons
- Soft drinks: Coca-Cola
- Teflon: Du Pont
- Tillage equipment: Krause Plow
- Tractors: John Deere
- Washing machines: Maytag, Whirlpool

Source: "100 Products That America Makes Best," *Fortune,* March 28, 1988, p. 54.

have leaped forward in productivity and quality, and the Third World countries are becoming the suppliers of low-cost labor.

If solutions are to be found for the turnaround, they will only be as effective as the foreman and the supervisor on the plant floor. Will these first-level managers be able to cope with the awesome task of creating a work force that is flexible, productive, and concerned about the quality of the goods and services produced? Managers need every bit of help they can get to face the many challenges in today's competitive environment.

SUMMARY

Operations management is an exciting, challenging managerial area of the 1990s. In this chapter, you read about the nature of this area and of some of the developing techniques. The management functions (especially planning, organizing, and control) were woven throughout the operations area.

Changes and challenges in the field of operations management were also very much a part of this chapter—from fourth-generation robots to Japanese inventory techniques. Techniques alone, however, will not answer the challenges for quality and improved productivity—the human factor remains as one of the most critical in the whole process.

KEY TERMS

Production function The process of converting or transforming various inputs into a distinguishable output.

Operations management The process of managing all the activities required to produce a good or service.

Process design Determining the production system to use in manufacturing the product.

Project production A system with limited life and budget designed to bring a particular project to completion; example would be a launch of the space shuttle.

Job (intermittent) production Production work is unique for each "job." Job may include custom home; television repair; restaurant meal.

Repetitive production Traditional assembly line where workers do same tasks over and over again.

Continuous production Manufacturing system used to produce highly homogeneous and standardized products (i.e., oil, dog food); highly automated and capable of running 24 hours per day.

General purpose machines Equipment that can be programmed to manufacture different products with only minor modifications to the equipment; useful in many areas of production.

Special purpose machines Equipment designed to manufacture just one product or to do one specialized part of the manufacturing sequence.

Robot A reprogrammable multifunctional manipulator designed to move material, parts, tools, or specialized devices through variable programmed motions to accomplish a variety of tasks.

Computer-aided design (CAD) The design of products, processes, or systems with the help of a computer.

Computer-aided manufacturing (CAM) Use of a computer to design and control the manufacturing process.

Flexible Manufacturing System System combining automated equipment, computer control, and automated material handling to create flexibility in production.

Computer-integrated manufacturing A computer system that links together engineering design and test, production, inspection, inventory control, etc.; eliminates paperwork, reduces errors, creates flexibility.

Cellular layout Manufacturing floor layout that groups machines together into "cells" that function as mini production lines; allows for flexibility in production.

Scheduling The process of assigning a time dimension to the resources of an organization to transform objectives and plans into goods and services.

Gantt chart A bar chart with time on the horizontal axis and a factor (job) to be scheduled on the vertical axis.

Synchronous production System that requires all phases of the production to work together to achieve firm's goal of making money; no department can excel at the expense of the firm overall.

Program Evaluation and Review Technique (PERT) Technique used to schedule and control projects; uses a diagram as a visual display of all the major activities of a project.

Critical path method (CPM) The path that must be managed most closely in a PERT diagram project.

Work in process (WIP) Units of product partially completed. One of three inventories (finished goods, raw materials are the other two) held by a manufacturing company.

Maintenance, repair, and operating supplies (MRO) Indirect materials used in the production of the product but not in the product itself. Example: oil used to produce french fries.

Material requirements planning (MRP) A manufacturing planning and control technique that works backward from planned-quantities and completion dates for end items on a master production schedule to determine what and when individual parts should be ordered.

Master production schedule (MPS) Tells quantity of and time each item is wanted; it is developed from the end-item forecasts and customer orders.

Bill of materials (BOM) A list of the components required for producing the final product.

Manufacturing resources planning (MRP II) Applies the scheduling concepts to all segments of the organization, not just manufacturing; includes finance and marketing.

Just-in-time (JIT) Production and delivery of finished goods just in time to be sold, of subassemblies just in time to be assembled into finished goods, of fabricated parts just in time to be used, and so on.

Kanban Techniques A manufacturing control system using simple manual cards to indicate when to deliver or produce more units; a pull system since only the final output is scheduled.

Supply management A field management specializing in maintaining a consistent flow of quality materials and services needed to produce products at the lowest total cost to the firm.

Countertrade A situation where a firm is required to buy materials, components, or labor from a country in exchange for selling its products in that country.

Statistical process control A method used to monitor and adjust production to prevent variations in the manufacturing process; the goal is to maintain high quality, the control function.

STUDY ASSIGNMENTS

1. Using the three situational cases at the beginning of the chapter as examples, answer this question: What lessons can managers learn by observing the production and operational practices of others?

2. Why would managerial authority be questioned more in the operations and production area of an organization than it would be in any other functional area of the organization?

3. Compare and contrast the operations of manufacturing firms and the operations of service firms.

4. What impact can or does operations management have on the performance and competitiveness of an organization? How has the role of operations management changed in recent years?

5. Compare and contrast the product design function of operations management and the process design function of operations management.

6. What are the principal forms of production? What determines which production form an organization uses to manufacture its products?

7. What are some of the new manufacturing technologies being used by businesses? How is the new technology changing the way work is done?

8. What are some of the recent changes in inventory management, and what are the strategic and operational implications of those changes?

9. Compare and contrast the use of just-in-time and the use of more traditional inventory management approaches, such as EOQ, MRP, and MRP II. Why have more and more manufacturing firms been adopting a just-in-time approach for their operations?

10. What is the role of quality control in the area of operations management? Why has the issue of quality become so important for U.S. businesses in recent years?

Cases for Discussion

I. ZENITH BUSINESS FORMS, INC.

Joe, Charlie, Mike, and Kathy, officers and managers of a small printing company, must decide how to reduce the production capacity of one of their production facilities. The situation has significant implications for the firm's financial situation as well as the future positioning of the firm in the marketplace.

Zenith Business Forms, Inc., is a produce-to-order printing company serving three distinct markets. Two years ago, the company was purchased from a *Fortune 500* firm as a "levered buyout"; therefore, Zenith's assets are financed almost entirely with borrowed capital. The markets that Zenith serves are (1) single or "snap-apart" business forms (purchase orders and the like), (2) computer or "continuous" business forms (payroll checks and the like), and (3) mailers (grade reports sent out at the end of the term, W-2s sent out by employers, and so on). Over the last few years, the market for the snap-apart products has rapidly diminished while during the same period, more and more producers of the product have entered the market. As a result, the capacity of the industry to produce the product far exceeds the market demand for the product. During the same period, the market demand for the continuous products has been growing at a modest rate; however, the industry's capacity to produce these products has grown rapidly. Most experts expect that the natural economic interactions of supply and demand will eventually create unfavorable pricing pressures on producers in both the snap-apart and the continuous product lines. The mailer product, however, is in its infancy. The demand in the marketplace for these products is growing rapidly while the capital requirements and production technology requirements have limited the number of new producers who can effectively produce this product line.

Zenith Business Forms began as a producer of snap-apart forms and gradually expanded into the production of continuous business forms. At the present time, the management of the company knows that they must reposition the firm's production capacity; the more complex issue involves addressing the timing of this repositioning. Some of the specific issues that Joe, Charlie, Mike, and Kathy are considering have been framed by the following questions:

1. Given the highly leveraged nature of the company, should the firm gradually reposition its production capacity, or should it set a definite date and stop all production of its troubled product lines?

2. Should the firm expand production capacity to produce a product line that "everyone in the industry" recognizes as having a favorable imbalance of supply and demand, or should the company seek to expand production capacity on the "next generation" products that may be demanded in the marketplace?

3. What are the financial, marketing, and personnel issues that need to be considered as the managers make their decision about the repositioning of the production capacity of the firm?

II. THE JELLY FACTORY

Imagine that you manage a jelly factory. Each week, the master production schedule identifies which products (flavors, size of containers, types, and so on) you will make, based upon customer orders and your forecasts. The bill of materials identifies the components that go into each product. The inventory status for each item is checked to determine what components are on hand and which components will need to be ordered. The material requirements planning (MRP) system identifies the materials needed to make the jelly and the glass containers required to store the jelly, based upon what is on hand and the number you plan to make. The MRP process does this through the computer and extends the material requirements many weeks into the future. In this way, materials that require a longer lead will be ordered when appropriate so they arrive when they are needed.

All these materials, including the glass containers, are taken from inventory and brought to the assembly line so that the day's production can begin. The glass containers must be carefully washed and sterilized before use. Currently, once the jelly is made, it is placed in the glass containers, packaged, and then shipped.

The glass containers are delivered to the factory by truck. Deliveries are made several times each day from plants approximately an eight-hour drive away. Once the glass has arrived, it is unloaded, inspected, and placed into storage until the containers are needed.

As you examine the procedure used for the glass containers, it becomes clear that placing the glass containers in storage is an extra process that requires at least three additional processes at the time the containers are used: (1) locating the specific containers in storage, (2) preparing them for use, and (3) moving them to where they will be needed in the manufacturing process.

The present operation does not use the just-in-time (JIT) system. The JIT concept is to have materials arrive just in time to be used in the next step or phase of the manufacturing process. Is it possible to apply the JIT approach only to the glass containers? If it is, how would this be done? What specific savings (processes, space, and so on) would result from the JIT approach applied only to the glass containers? What safeguards, if any, would you want to put in place to ensure a continuous operation?

Chapter 19

Lessons
from Managerial
and Organizational
Performance

Learning Objectives

1. **Explain** why studying the performance of other organizations can be beneficial to a manager's own performance.
2. **Identify** some of the criteria used in appraising managerial performance.
3. **Discuss** the applicability of Sloan's, Watson's, and Wood's managerial and organizational concepts in today's business environment.
4. **Discuss** the importance of growth for a manager and for an organization.
5. **Explain** the concept of flexibility with respect to an organization's ability to survive and maintain growth.
6. **Compare** the effectiveness of managerial performance in Apple, McDonald's, and Caterpillar.
7. **Explain** the significance of the renewal concept with respect to established enterprises.

THE history of the American automobile industry is punctuated by success, failure, innovations, turnarounds, and personalities. It also provides countless examples of how organizations and managers adapt and survive in a dynamic and hostile environment. The Chrysler and American Motors corporations (AMC) exemplify the ever-changing fortunes and misfortunes of firms operating in the automobile industry. Throughout their history, both firms have characteristically done the right thing at the wrong time, and in the end, only one of them succeeded in overcoming the consequences of bad timing and inappropriate decisions. The history of each provides colorful reading as well as valuable lessons that other managers can apply in their own managerial practice.

Chrysler's history began in 1921, when Walter P. Chrysler founded the company. At the time, he felt that for the company to succeed, it would have to offer a full range of cars, just like GM. The strategy worked, and by 1936, Chrysler was the number two auto producer. Unfortunately, at the moment that Chrysler achieved its greatest success, its management made a decision that would contribute to the eventual decline and near bankruptcy of the firm.

In 1934, Chrysler introduced a radical change in the design of its automobile. The Chrysler Airflow design emphasized aerodynamics and unibody construction. The design was a commercial failure, and Chrysler lost both sales and market share. (Ironically, fifty years later when Ford made the same radical design change, it proved to be a huge success, and according to many observers, the design change saved Ford.) In response to this setback, Chrysler's management decided to avoid ever again making innovative and radical design changes. They chose to focus on engineering and on following industry trends.

In the 1950s, Chrysler's conservative strategy began to adversely affect the company. It was unable to respond to the reemergence of Ford as the number two auto producer. Chrysler remained committed to the production of large cars, even into the 1970s, when both GM and Ford developed compact cars in response to market demands, foreign competition, and the oil crisis. To complicate the situation, Chrysler's top management was made up primarily of accountants who had no interest in or flare for marketing. By 1979, the company was rapidly losing market share and was on the verge of bankruptcy. In an effort to turn things around, Chrysler's board hired Lee Iacocca. Iacocca's turnaround of Chrysler has become a legend. He redefined Chrysler's strategies, took enormous risks, focused on marketing and production of a quality product, and, most of all, provided Chrysler's management with leadership. He challenged them to be the best.

AMC's story is somewhat different. Although its origins can be traced back to 1902 (the one-cylinder Rambler), the company was created in 1954 through a merger of the small independent auto manufacturers Nash-Kelvinator and Hudson Motors. AMC's management, headed by George Romney, determined that AMC would be an innovator and would not follow the "Big Three." Romney championed the small-car strategy, creating a new niche in the market for low-cost and fuel-efficient cars. AMC performed well in that market until Romney departed for a political career in 1958 and foreign automobile producers began competing for the small-car market. Soon, AMC abandoned the small-car market and began producing larger cars that were characterized as boring cars made for equally boring people. The only bright spot for AMC in the 1970s was its purchase of the Kaiser Jeep Corporation, which proved to be the only real moneymaker for the firm. AMC continued to flounder, even after France's Renault Corporation acquired an equity interest in the firm in 1980. In the 1980s, poor vehicle designs, quality problems, lack of direction and leadership, labor strife, and high production costs continued to plague AMC's management. The firm proved to be a financial drain for an embattled Renault (Renault was having a difficult time preserving its position in the European market). Renault sold its interest in and control of AMC to Chrysler in March 1987. With that transaction, AMC's twenty-three-year struggle to become a viable enterprise ended.

Chrysler's newfound success is continuing into the 1990s because Chrysler's management, led by Lee Iacocca, vigorously adapted to a changed environment. Chrysler's management adjusted strategies and managerial practices by understanding its own history and learning from the experience of other enterprises. Unlike AMC, Chrysler was able to emerge from its own past and move into the future. ■

This last chapter tells what every reader wants to know: how to be effective, both from a managerial and from an organizational perspective. You will learn that there is no magic formula. Instead, you will have to discover, identify, and

American Motors offers an excellent history lesson in management. In spite of numerous attempts, and various strategies, American Motors was never quite successful in achieving its goal of being a major force in the automotive industry.

adopt the managerial approach that is best suited to you and to the organization. To this point, this book has exposed you to a wide range of managerial techniques. Now, it is time to stand back, to observe, to evaluate, and to decide which approach really contributes to organizational effectiveness.[1]

Managerial skills are acquired, developed, and influenced through a mixture of education, observation, and personal experience. Through education, a manager learns the concepts and principles of management. By observing how other managers and organizations work, a manager can gain insights into how successful or unsuccessful application of those concepts and principles influences performance. And by the trial and error of personal experience, a manager can discover how to use the skills and insights that he or she has acquired through education and observation.[2]

In previous chapters, the emphasis was on introducing you to the fundamental concepts and principles of management. In other words, the focus was on the educational dimension.

In this chapter, however, the focus shifts. We are now going to examine how managers can acquire, develop, modify, and even broaden their managerial skills by observing and analyzing the performance of other managers and organizations. We will begin by considering how the performance of a manager or an organization is evaluated and judged.

Can you learn from failure?

Managers can learn valuable lessons not only by studying successful managers and organizations but also by examining managerial and organizational failures. From our opening case, we can see that Chrysler, under Lee Iacocca, has come a long way. The Chrysler story is now viewed as a model of sound managerial and organizational performance. As a result, countless managers, journalists, researchers, and students have written about this unique success story. The turnaround at Chrysler has become a model that many managers use in formulating and executing their own decisions.

Likewise, managerial errors and organizational failures, such as those at American Motors Corporation, merit investigation and comment. Often, we learn more from managerial and organizational failures than from successes. AMC's failure provides us with a unique opportunity to closely examine what circumstances and actions contributed to the decline of an organization. Through such an examination, managers can gain insights into the consequences of poor decisions, and they can learn how to avoid making similar managerial and organizational errors.[3]

One final note before proceeding. Quite often, managers and organizations fail to recognize that yesterday's, or even today's, success does not guarantee success in the future. There are countless examples of corporations that were industry leaders one day and out of business the next. For instance, many of the successful conglomerates of the 1970s, such as ITT, LTV, Litton, and American Standard, have had to undergo painful restructuring, downsizing, and even bankruptcy proceedings in the 1980s. Recall that Donald Burr's highly praised employee-oriented managerial practices and the incredible success of People Express in taking advantage of the airline industry's deregulation proved to be of little significance when Burr and his airline were unable to adapt to changing conditions. Despite his early success, Burr, in the end, was forced to sell People Express to the Texas Air Corporation.

This is not to suggest that managers and organizations can never make mistakes if they are to be successful or considered the best. IBM, McDonald's, AT&T, Sears, and Hewlett-Packard have all made serious errors. Ford has undergone a number of up-and-down periods since its founding. Ironically, in the early 1980s, a number of analysts and observers predicted that it was only a matter of time before Ford would go out of business. By the end of the 1980s, however, Ford was successfully challenging GM for the leadership position of the automobile industry.

It is important to remember that the environment in which managers and organizations work and operate is dynamic and hostile. Organizations need to be responsive and flexible in their managerial practices and organizational actions if they are to succeed over the long run. It is this ability to adapt to changing conditions over time that should be the basis for evaluating the effectiveness of managerial and organizational performance. With that in mind, we will now consider some notable examples of managerial and organizational performance.

This chapter is devoted to viewing management in practice and focuses on lessons learned by managers working in the business world. As you study these examples, you should ask yourself what valuable lessons can be learned by observing and evaluating these and other examples of managerial and organizational performance.

APPRAISING MANAGERIAL PERFORMANCE

How do we determine whether a manager or an organization is successful? What criteria does one use to make such a judgment? Are all measures of performance the same, and are they applicable in all situations? Unfortunately, there are no clear-cut answers to these questions. For the most part, the way one evaluates managerial and organizational performance is a matter of perspective. How employees judge their managers and organization can be substantially different from how shareholders judge the organization and its managers. Likewise, a community's view of an organization can be substantially different from the assessment made by financial analysts. To enhance your appreciation of the diverse criteria and methods that can be used in judging managerial and organizational performance, let us first consider some of the most recognized approaches.

Stock Performance

One of the simplest measures of managerial and organizational performance is the movement of the firm's stock price. This pragmatic method has been used for years by securities analysts, investors, and market observers. It is assumed that the stock price and the market value of the firm provide a means to measure the quality of the managerial performance as well as organizational performance. For many, the expectations of long-term growth and increased earnings serve as an objective indication of the managerial performance. One such example of this approach is *Business Week's* annual survey of executive pay. In Table 19-1, *Business Week* compares executive compensation with shareholder return as a means of measuring managerial performance.

TABLE 19-1   Pay for Performance—The 20 Highest-Paid Chief Executives . . .

	COMPANY	1990 SALARY AND BONUS	LONG-TERM COMPENSATION	TOTAL PAY
		THOUSANDS OF DOLLARS		
1. STEPHEN M. WOLF	UAL	$1,150	$17,151	$18,301
2. JOHN SCULLEY	Apple	2,199	14,531	16,730
3. PAUL B. FIREMAN	Reebok	14,822	—	14,822
4. DEAN L. BUNTROCK	Waste Management	1,582	10,708	12,290
5. LEON C. HIRSCH	U. S. Surgical	1,128	10,548	11,676
6. MICHAEL D. EISNER	Walt Disney	11,233	—	11,233
7. JOSEPH D. WILLIAMS	Warner-Lambert	1,585	6,898	8,483
8. DAVID O. MAXWELL	Federal National Mortgage	1,039	6,529	7,568
9. GEORGE V. GRUNE	Reader's Digest	1,192	6,271	7,463
10. P. ROY VAGELOS	Merck	2,092	5,050	7,142
11. RAND V. ARASKOG	ITT	3,844	3,179	7,023
12. RICHARD D. WOOD	Eli Lilly	1,781	5,104	6,885
13. DANIEL B. BURKE	Capital Cities/ABC	1,033	5,584	6,617
14. WILLIAM S. EDGERLY	State Street Boston	953	5,561	6,514
15. ROBERT P. LUCIANO	Schering-Plough	1,695	4,691	6,386
16. MARTIN S. DAVIS	Paramount Communications	3,646	2,614	6,260
17. JAMES E. PRESTON	Avon Products	1,188	5,061	6,249
18. ROBERTO C. GOIZUETA	Coca-Cola	3,142	3,100	6,242
19. H. WILLIAM LURTON	Jostens	880	5,099	5,979
20. ROBERT E. CAWTHORN	Rhone-Poulenc Rorer	1,054	4,835	5,889

. . . And 10 Who Aren't CEOs

	COMPANY	1990 SALARY AND BONUS	LONG-TERM COMPENSATION	TOTAL PAY
1. JOHN A. SHIRLEY Pres.*	Microsoft	$ 414	$25,594	$26,008
2. FRED W. LYONS JR. Pres.	Marion Merrell Dow	1,178	9,091	10,269
3. ERNST WEIL Exec. V-P	Salomon	6,640	800	7,440
4. THOMAS S. MURPHY Chmn.	Capital Cities/ABC	1,012	5,605	6,617
5. DONALD R. KEOUGH Pres.	Coca-Cola	2,103	4,299	6,402
6. FRANK G. WELLS Pres.	Walt Disney	5,642	—	5,642
7. JOHN C. POPE Vice-Chmn.	UAL	655	4,720	5,375
8. LEONARD COHEN Pres.	National Medical Enterprises	1,408	3,751	5,159
9. EUGENE L. STEP Exec. V-P	Eli Lilly	914	4,193	5,107
10. JOHN E. LYONS Vice-Chmn.*	Merck	1,133	3,955	5,088

*Resigned or retired
Data: Standard & Poor's Compustat Services Inc.
Source: Reprinted from May 6, 1991 issue of *Business Week* by special permission, © 1991 by McGraw-Hill, Inc.

Management Audits

One of the earliest efforts to systematically evaluate management performance was developed by the American Institute of Management. Its "management audits" rated many operating companies on a point system using ten categories, which were weighted subjectively as to their relative importance. The ten categories were

1. Economic function
2. Corporate structure
3. Health of earnings
4. Service to stockholders
5. Research and development
6. Directorate analysis
7. Fiscal policies
8. Production efficiency
9. Sales vigor
10. Executive evaluation

This early attempt to systematically publish management audits had limited success because the appearance of measurability through the quantitative point system masked the subjective weighting and assignment of points to the ten categories.

Fortune's **Annual Survey of the Most-Admired Firms**

Who's the Best?

Another method of assessing managerial and organizational performance has been used by *Fortune* magazine. To determine which are the most-admired firms, the editors of *Fortune* annually survey executives from their *Fortune 500* list. The survey's participants use the following eight attributes in assessing managerial and organizational performance.

1. Ability to attract, develop, and keep talented people
2. Value as a long-term investment
3. Community and environmental responsibility
4. Innovativeness
5. Financial soundness
6. Quality of management
7. Quality of products or service
8. Use of corporate assets

The strength of this survey method is that the appraisal is made by individuals who are actively involved in managing major American corporations. The weakness of this method is that the appraisal does not use the type of objective measures that would normally be employed by observers from outside the business community. However, the wide publication of the results provides interesting insights into how managers view the managerial and organizational performance of their peers. Table 19-2 summarizes the survey results for 1989 and 1990.

In Search of Excellence Criteria

Popular interest in evaluating managerial and organizational performance increased during the 1980s, and it is expected to continue throughout the 1990s.

TABLE 19-2 *Fortune's* Survey of Most-Admired Companies: At the Top and Bottom of 306 Companies

THE MOST ADMIRED

Three drug companies rank in the top ten. By now Merck has squatter's rights on first place; Johnson & Johnson returns after four years; and Eli Lilly makes its debut.

RANK	LAST YEAR	COMPANY	SCORE
1	01	**Merck** Pharmaceuticals	8.86
2	3	**Rubbermaid** Rubber and plastics products	8.58
3	4	**Procter & Gamble** Soaps, cosmetics	8.42
4	6*	**Wal-Mart Stores** Retailing	8.35
5	6*	**PepsiCo** Beverages	8.19
6	8	**Coca-Cola** Beverages	8.12
6	5	**3M** Scientific and photo equip.	8.12
8	12	**Johnson & Johnson** Pharmaceuticals	8.01
9	11	**Boeing** Aerospace	7.92
10	29	**Eli Lilly** Pharmaceuticals	7.90
10	13	**Liz Claiborne** Apparel	7.90

*Wal-Mart Stores and PepsiCo were tied in score last year.

THE LEAST ADMIRED

These days you would expect four of the bottom ten to be thrifts, but back again by popular demand are Wang, Continental Airlines, Unisys, LTV, and Control Data.

RANK	LAST YEAR	COMPANY	SCORE
306	—	**Goldome** Savings institutions	2.83
305	270	**Great American Bank** Savings institutions	2.98
304	288	**CrossLand Savings** Savings institutions	3.06
303	304	**Wang Laboratories** Computers and office equip.	3.10
302	302	**Meritor Savings Bank**[1] Savings institutions	3.16
301	301	**Continental Airlines Hold.**[2] Transportation	3.33
300	295	**Mack Trucks**[3] Motor vehicles and parts	3.40
299	296	**Unisys** Computers and office equip.	3.57
298	300	**LTV** Metals	3.81
297	303	**Control Data** Computers and office equip.	4.00

[1] Name changed from Meritor Financial Group.
[2] Name changed from Texas Air.
[3] Acquired by Renault Véhicules Industriels SA, 10/4/90.

Source: Alison Sprout, "Corporate Reputations: America's Most-Admired Corporations," *Fortune,* February 11, 1991, pp. 52–58. Reprinted with permission from *Fortune,* the Time Inc. Magazine Company. All rights reserved. The survey includes 306 companies in 32 industries of the 1990 Fortune 500 and Fortune 500 service 500 directories. More than 8,000 senior executives, outside directors and financial analysts rate the largest companies on the attributes of quality of management; quality of products and services; innovativeness; long-term investment value; financial soundness; ability to attract, develop, and keep talented people; community and environmental responsibility; and wise use of corporate assets.

Procter & Gamble was recognized by Peters and Waterman in their book *In Search of Excellence* as one of the best-managed corporations in the United States. There is a great deal to be managed at Procter & Gamble. Consumer brands include Pampers, Charmin, Tide, Cheer, Joy, Ivory, Sure, Pepto-Bismol, Crisco, and Noxzema.

Procter & Gamble Consumer Brands

This interest is a result of the threat that foreign competition poses to American businesses. This threat has resulted in a reexamination of American managerial practices and in a national effort to revitalize and restructure American industry.

This popular interest in appraisal of management performance is evidenced by the fact that several books on the subject have become best sellers. One such best seller is *In Search of Excellence* by Thomas J. Peters and R. H. Waterman, Jr.[4] The authors of this book, using their experience as management consultants, describe the basic characteristics of the best-managed companies. They found that excellent managers have the following eight important attributes:

1. They are action oriented.
2. They are close to their customers.
3. They seek autonomy and emphasize entrepreneurship.
4. Their focus is on production through people.
5. They emphasize underlying values and try to use values in practice.
6. They "stick to their knitting" and do not attempt to perform in areas outside their expertise.
7. They seek a simple form of organization and keep their staffs lean.
8. They keep tight controls, yet they allow loose means of maintaining controls.

Peters and Waterman based their conclusions on structured interviews and reviews of literature over a twenty-five-year period in forty-three companies. Among those studied in greatest detail and receiving the highest ratings are

- High technology: Amdahl, Digital Equipment, Emerson Electric, Hewlett-Packard, IBM, Schlumberger, and Texas Instruments
- Consumer goods: Eastman Kodak, Johnson & Johnson, and Procter & Gamble
- General industrial: Caterpillar Tractor, Dana, and Minnesota Mining & Manufacturing
- Service: Delta Air Lines, Marriott, and McDonald's
- Project management: Bechtel, Boeing, and Fluor
- Resource-based: Exxon

Evaluation by Observation

Practitioners, academicians, analysts, and consultants devote a considerable amount of their time to appraising and rating managerial and organizational performance. Most of this effort focuses on those firms and managers who are recognized for their excellent performance and effective managerial practices. You should realize, however, that valuable insights into strategies, operations, and managerial techniques can also be gained by analyzing failures and learning from the mistakes of others. So as you continue reading in this chapter, do not only consider what the firms and managers did right, but also pay attention to the errors they made and note how they responded to and learned from those mistakes.

LESSONS FROM BUSINESS LEADERS OF THE PAST

In the development of American business and managerial practices, there have been a number of unique individuals whose skills and personalities shaped and determined not only the direction of their own organizations but the American economy as a whole. The concepts and principles that they developed and applied continue to influence the performance of today's managers. Essentially, these individuals could be characterized as either initiators or organizers.

Initiator An entrepreneur, a promoter, an inventive person.

Organizer A manager who builds the structure and lays the foundation for the permanent life of a corporation.

1. The **initiator**—an entrepreneur, a promoter, and an inventive person.
2. The **organizer**—a manager who builds the structure and lays the foundation for the permanent life of a corporation (not dependent on the life of any single individual). This person utilizes managerial specialists and staffs the company with professional managers.

We shall see that the primary source of new basic managerial concepts is the person who has served in the second role, that of the organizer. The role of the initiator is dependent on personality traits, such as charm, imagination, brilliant flashes of insight, intuition, hunches, venturesomeness, which are not learned easily through intellectual endeavor and thus are less transferable to others through study. Therefore, let us look at some of the basic organizing ideas and identify the great organizers who have contributed them.

We have chosen three very large and well known companies to represent the strategic sector of the American economy: General Motors Corporation, the world's largest manufacturing firm; IBM Corporation, the leader in the computer industry; and Sears, Roebuck & Company, a leader in mail-order and retail sales. Each of these firms has become so large that it may give an initial appearance of an impersonal entity; however, each is a product of one or two great organizers. Although the histories of these corporations and the biographies of their organizers are interesting, we are interested primarily in the ideas that have contributed to the successes of these firms.

General Motors Corporation developed through the two stages of leadership just discussed. William C. Durant created General Motors in 1908, using the Buick Motor Company as his base. With great vision and energy, he included Oldsmobile, Oakland, and Cadillac in early consolidations. Durant's financial skill and sales-promotion ability were essential elements in the rapid growth of the company.

Durant was prone to keep information in his head, to take risks without analyzing detailed facts, and to run the company as a one-man operation. In the early days of the company, this approach fostered growth through flexibility and informality. However, during World War I and immediately thereafter, Durant, failing to use accounting information and inventory control, ignored advice from his experts and faced a business-cycle crisis with few resources to combat the problems. The result was that in 1920, General Motors faced collapse, which was averted only by the prompt action of key stockholders.

Alfred P. Sloan, who was already a part of GM, presented a comprehensive organization plan to the board of directors in 1920 and, in 1923, was made president of the corporation.[5] (He remained president until 1937, after which he served as chairman of the board until 1956.) Sloan's twenty-eight-page program for GM, prepared in 1920, provided new administrative ideas that have served as guidelines for GM management to the present day. Sloan's program was based on two concepts:

1. The responsibility attached to the chief executive of each operation shall in no way be limited. **(Decentralization of Operations)**
2. Certain central organization functions are absolutely essential to the logical development and proper coordination of the corporation's activities. **(Centralized Staff Services)**

Decentralization of Operations The responsibility of chief executive of each operation shall in no way be limited.

Centralized Staff Services Certain central organization functions are absolutely essential to the logical development and proper coordination of the corporation's activities.

Sloan early saw the necessity for group management in a large organization and the advantages of giving full authority to operating-division managers, who could make decisions coordinated by the general policies set by the central office. An elaborate control system was defined so that the central office would have detailed information about the activities of the divisions and their profitability.

Over the years, the basic ideas instituted by Sloan at General Motors were adapted by many other organizations, and those ideas continued to serve as the foundation of GM's managerial practices through the 1980s. However, GM and many other organizations found it difficult to adhere to Sloan's concept of decentralization. As these organizations became larger, there was a tendency to create vast administrative and bureaucratic structures, which all but eliminated the benefits gained through decentralization. This condition was particularly evident at GM. Many auto industry analysts attributed the decline of GM during the 1980s to the failure of GM's management to adhere to Sloan's concepts. Declining sales, market share, and profitability finally forced GM to initiate a large-scale restructuring program during the late 1980s in an effort to regain its competitive position.[6]

The spectacular growth of IBM can be explained by a number of factors, such as the rapid growth of the new computer industry and fortunate events outside the company's control, but we are most interested in learning the management ideas and beliefs that have made it possible. Again, the original concept of the firm was developed by one man, Thomas J. Watson, Sr., who came to the corporation in 1914 and was active in management until his death in 1956.[7] His son, Thomas J. Watson, Jr., continued to emphasize certain tenets of management established early in the history of the company. He summarized those tenets in a series of lectures in 1962, as follows:

1. Respect for the individual and development of the human resource
2. Emphasis on service to customers by helping them solve their problems
3. Superior effort as a way of life

Using these three tenets, Watson outlined some of the lessons that the company learned from its experiences. Since these lessons have wide applicability, we quote them here:

1. There is simply no substitute for good human relations and for the high morale they bring. It takes good people to do the jobs necessary to reach your profit goals. But good people alone are not enough. No matter how good your people may be, if they don't really like the business, if they don't feel totally involved in it, or if they don't think they're being treated fairly—it's awfully hard to get a business off the ground. . . .
2. There are two things an organization must increase far out of proportion to its growth rate if that organization is to overcome the problems of change. The first of these is communication, upward and downward. The second is education and re-training.
3. Complacency is the most natural and insidious disease of large corporations. It can be overcome if management will set the right tone and pace and if its lines of communication are in working order.
4. Everyone—particularly a company such as IBM—must place company interest above that of a division or department.
5. Beliefs must always come before policies, practices, and goals. The latter must always be altered if they are seen to violate fundamental beliefs.[8]

IBM has become well known throughout the world not only as a rapidly growing, profitable business organization but also as an innovator of managerial practices based on the foregoing beliefs. IBM has expanded its internal educational activities through company schools for employees, customers, and other educators, and it has sent many of its managers to executive-development programs sponsored by universities. And it has continued to lead its industry in making its sales organization service oriented.[9]

IBM not only has succeeded in attaining large size, maintaining rapid growth, and sustaining high profitability, but also has participated with educational and government institutions in the development of management thought. The company pays special attention to research and spends a great deal of money on it. As a result, IBM's practice of management has been in close contact with the development of management theory as discussed in this book.

Sam Walton is the CEO of one of the most admired and most profitable corporations in the world—WalMart. Walton is shown in this picture at the opening of yet another new WalMart store in Conway, Arkansas. WalMart includes Sam's Wholesale Club and Sam's Club stores throughout the United States. Walton's emphasis on quality, service, and reasonable prices has made WalMart a leader in the retail and wholesale industries.

Sears, Roebuck & Company also illustrates the different effects that an initiator and an organizer can have on organizational performance.[10] It was created before the turn of the century by one man, Richard Sears, who was an expert promoter and salesman and a spectacular advertiser. Sears responded to the needs of the isolated farmers of the late nineteenth century through the innovation of direct-mail advertising and direct mailing of products. Under Sears, the company's operations were more a series of astute purchasing deals and mass distributions than a coordinated, long-term business venture.

Managing the large number of transactions began to create serious problems, and again an organizer appeared who could build a firm foundation for the large organization. Between 1895 and 1905, Julius Rosenwald originated several basic ideas that have continued to serve the company through the years: (1) systematic development of low-cost merchandising sources, (2) a factual, comprehensive mail-order catalog, (3) implementation of the policy of "satisfaction guaranteed or your money back," (4) scheduling and routing of the large, central mail-order plant, and (5) recruitment of professional managers. Supporting the fifth idea was Rosenwald's recruitment and backing of another innovator, Otto Doering, who supervised the building of the first large mail-order plant in Chicago in 1905. Doering concentrated on operating efficiencies by breaking down work into simple, repetitive operations at the time that Frederick W. Taylor was becoming known as a scientific manager in manufacturing firms. Doering used the mass-production techniques of the conveyorized assembly line, standardized and interchangeable parts, and detailed planning and control in the Chicago plant almost a decade before Henry Ford became known as a mass producer in the automobile industry.

Julius Rosenwald was the leading organizer of Sears during the peak centralized mail-order phase of distribution; however, Sears's continued success in the marketing field was fostered by a second principal organizer, General Robert E. Wood, who appeared when marketing channels changed as a result of widespread use of the automobile. Wood contributed new ideas to meet the different situation that developed in the 1920s—the growth of chains of retail outlets. Management concepts thus were adapted to the changing situation by providing the following:

1. A strong, decentralized organization, with managers who could make most decisions at the store level
2. An incentive system through profit sharing and stock ownership
3. Strong emphasis on the human element

Sears continually faced changing social and economic conditions. Yet in the 1970s, after leading in the move to suburban shopping centers, Sears was slow to adjust to increasing competition from discount chains. Shifting its strategy to higher-priced items, it lost part of its traditional market to others. In the last decade, the Sears management has expanded into insurance, investment brokerage, and banking in an effort to capitalize on its resources outside its traditional retailing field. Even successful managements must continually be alert to environmental changes and adjust strategies to meet new situations.[11]

Many other interesting historical and contemporary examples of successful management of large firms could be studied in detail, and you will want to continually search for those ideas that have proved useful in practice. These three companies are especially important, for all three found answers to the demanding problems of directing and controlling large, complex organizations. All three have also led their industries in research and innovation. All three have achieved a dominant position in the American economy.

LESSONS FROM GROWTH COMPANIES

Little more than a decade ago, some of today's premier companies either were nonexistent or were struggling to survive. Names like Apple, Nike, Liz Claiborne, Lotus, Federal Express, Genentech, KinderCare, Toys 'R' Us, and Compaq were hardly household words. But over the past ten years, these firms have achieved phenomenal success, and as a result, they are considered model "growth" companies.

The growth these firms experienced was not only in revenues, profits, and assets but also in market share, reputation, and the nature and scope of their businesses. Based on their record, many observers concluded that these organizations reflected the best in managerial and organizational performance. Part of the reason that they were so successful was that they typically adopted managerial practices that enabled them to be responsive to changing environmental conditions. Furthermore, they exploited demographic trends, stressed innovation, introduced unique approaches to human resource management, and applied advanced technologies to improve productivity. But most of all, they took risks.

Flexibility Adaptability to external changes, resiliency of policies, and responsiveness of the entire organization to meet new problems.

There are other factors that influence a firm's ability to sustain growth. The most notable factor is "flexibility." **Flexibility** refers to the adaptability of the firm, the resiliency of its policies, and the ability of the entire organization to identify and solve emerging problems. An organization can also sustain growth by

1. Introducing innovative product and service designs
2. Continual innovation of the operations process
3. Being responsive to competitive challenges
4. Being able to redefine markets
5. Constantly identifying and creating new niches
6. Maintaining an informal organizational structure
7. Having the ongoing desire to seek and exploit emerging opportunities

Is there a lesson from growth companies?

In this context, it is critical that you understand how important it is for managers to observe and analyze growth organizations. There are many valuable lessons that can be learned by observing how growth organizations use these factors and how they apply the concept of flexibility. Some firms, as we have noted, do this quite well, whereas others repeatedly fail in their attempts to maintain organization momentum and growth.

There are numerous examples of the importance of observing growth organizations in action. For instance, when the airline industry was deregulated in the early 1980s, many of the well-established domestic airlines struggled, and in some cases failed, as a result of this significant change in the competitive environment. At the same time, countless small commuter airlines were started or expanded. They experienced substantial growth simply by redefining the market and by recognizing that the major air carriers needed "feeder lines" to adequately serve their customers.

Another example of the potential responsiveness of some of these growth companies is provided by a company known as Nucor. While the basic steel industry was in decline as a result of foreign competition, the recession of the early 1980s, and a considerable amount of self-inflicted injury, Nucor discovered that it could successfully operate in the steel industry by using innovative production technologies (a process known as continuous-casting minimills), identifying and targeting unique market niches, and implementing creative human resource management techniques. In that way, Nucor was able to produce 700 tons of steel per employee, as opposed to an industry average of 350 tons per employee. Thus, in the midst of the decline of the American steel industry, Nucor demonstrated that a steel company can compete against foreign producers without protective trade legislation.

This concept of growth is not peculiar to young, entrepreneurial types of companies. Growth is a critical factor in sustaining performance and successful operations in older and more-established organizations as well. Growth creates a dynamic tension in organizations. It creates an environment that both stimulates and challenges employees to achieve higher levels of performance. But growth also can be highly destructive, because by its very nature, it is a catalyst for change. Ironically, many enterprises that experience extreme growth in business volume and activity suddenly discover that they are out of business because they were unable to handle or sustain that level of growth. People Express, discussed earlier in the book, is an excellent example of a firm whose success eventually contributed to its demise. Likewise, many established firms found that they could achieve substantial growth in the 1970s by becoming conglomerates. However, in the 1980s, conglomerates such as Gulf & Western, Beatrice, LTV, Litton, ITT, Wickes, and RCA discovered that their growth strategy of rapid acquisition of hundreds of unrelated businesses would not work in the long run. Eventually, those firms experienced substantial restructuring, downsizing, mergers, and, in some cases, bankruptcy.

Given all of that, the question becomes, What lessons can we learn by examining the performance of growing firms? One lesson we will learn is that growth is an essential element for *maintaining vitality and momentum* in organizations. To understand this point better, we will examine how growth influences managerial practices and how it sustains organizational vitality and momentum. We will begin by looking at how Apple has been able to achieve substantial growth, and we will demonstrate how the effective management of growth can serve as a critical indicator of both managerial and organizational performance. Following that, we will examine, through a discussion of Honda, how many of these same growth issues are important in maintaining the vitality of well-established businesses.

Apple Computer, Inc.

Apple Computer, Inc., was incorporated in March 1977 by Steven Jobs and Steven Wozniak, and by 1982, it had made the *Fortune 500* list, with over $1.7 billion dollars in sales. The rapid rise of Apple amazed the media, investors, and analysts alike. Many credited Apple with single-handedly creating the personal computer (PC) market. From its beginning, it was clearly the industry leader, holding a 26 percent market share at the time it first appeared on the *Fortune 500* list. It had a reputation for innovativeness, aggressiveness, sound human resource management, and corporate culture that was noted for its casualness—managers typically wore jeans in the office, and the company paid for regular Friday afternoon beer blasts.

By 1980, not only was Apple's success getting attention from the media, investors, and analysts, but also its performance was being closely monitored by IBM. In 1980, IBM's market share in the PC industry was 0 percent. In fact, IBM did not enter the PC market until August of 1981. However, it took only thirteen months for IBM to overtake Apple as the industry leader. By 1983, there was concern that Apple's phenomenal growth was about to end. Some observers were predicting that Apple would soon fail, as had so many of the early PC manufacturers, such as Osborne, Eagle, and Sinclair, in the wake of IBM's entry into the PC market. For Apple's management, the problem was not just a matter of sustaining growth; the problem was also how to survive.

What problems did Apple face in the 1980s?

Apple faced one of the typical problems experienced by young companies introducing new products or services into the marketplace. To satisfy rapidly growing demand, these firms often had to undergo the very expensive process of quickly expanding their limited capacity. Then, as was so often the case, demand fell. What happened to them was that their product or service turned out to be a fad, or new competition entered the field, or someone developed a better variation of the product or the service. The firm was then stuck with excess capacity, declining revenues, and a huge debt load.

For Apple, it was not so much that demand fell as it was that the nature of the market shifted from domination by computer "hackers" and educational users to domination by professionals and business users. This new consumer group typically had an established relationship with IBM or recognized IBM's long-standing reputation for reliability and service. This group, therefore, greeted IBM's entry into the PC market with purchases and a demand that exceeded even IBM's expectation. Thus, the problem facing Apple's management was whether it could continue to effectively manage its growth by adapting to a new market and new competition.

Fortunately, Apple's management recognized the problem and directed Apple's resources toward the development of microcomputers designed specifically for professional and business users. Unfortunately, Apple's management did not understand the nature and character of their new market. The introduction of the Apple III business computer was a disaster. The computer was plagued by technical and mechanical problems, and Apple's service performance, in comparison with IBM's, was a joke. As the mistakes were compounded, IBM took more and more of the potential market away from Apple.

Despite the setbacks, Apple's management remained flexible. Like most analysts, they recognized that the IBM product line was not exceptionally good. What people were getting in an IBM was an average computer that had an endless variety of software options, and, most important for businesspeople, it came with an exceptional service network. So Apple's management moved to develop an innovative computer product, one that would be distinct from an IBM because of its user friendliness. This new computer was known as the Lisa.

But internal conflict, personalities, and lack of clear strategic direction were creating additional problems for Apple. Jobs had been excluded from the development of the Lisa, and in response, he created his own team to independently develop a similar computer that he felt could be more successful. His effort resulted in the Macintosh, which not only had greater capabilities than the Lisa but also was priced substantially lower. The introduction of the Macintosh killed the Lisa, created considerable internal strife, and did nothing to thwart IBM's growing dominance of the PC industry.

To Jobs's credit, he recognized, at the beginning of 1983, that if Apple was to survive, it had to be competitive in the professional and business sector of the PC industry. Even though Apple was continuing to grow in revenue, Jobs realized that Apple needed a thorough overhaul of its operations and culture to sustain growth in profitability and to expand the nature and scope of the business. Apple needed to grow up. In May 1983, Jobs hired John Sculley, the former president of PepsiCo, to become Apple's president.[12]

John Sculley came from a mature but growth-oriented firm. He had considerable experience in competing against other mature and highly competitive businesses. Although Apple's board and outside observers welcomed the fact that Sculley was joining the company, many employees at Apple were concerned that Sculley would reshape the character and direction of Apple. They were correct. By 1985, Sculley had substantially restructured Apple. He did away with Apple's "laid-back" management style and instituted rules and reporting procedures designed to eliminate internal conflict and to provide clarity, direction, and effective utilization of resources. In time, the culture of Apple was so changed that even Steven Jobs no longer felt comfortable working there.[13]

When Jobs left Apple in 1985, he left a company that had changed radically from the freewheeling and entrepreneurial culture he had created. Under Sculley's leadership, the firm had transformed itself into a mature venture, and it reestablished itself as an innovative, growth-oriented firm. Today, Apple continues as a leading force in the PC industry, particularly in the area of desktop publishing. Sculley has developed the Macintosh into an alternative for businesses considering IBM PCs or IBM PC clones. As the firm moves into the 1990s, it is well positioned to give IBM a competitive headache.

What happened at Apple demonstrates some of the problems of growth. But in this case, the growth we are talking about is not simply one of revenues or profits or market share; it is a maturing process for the organization, its employees, and, most of all, its managers. Today, Apple is a viable enterprise with a strong future because its management had the ability to recognize and respond to the need for change, even at the cost of their own styles, practices, and positions. Under Sculley's leadership, Apple is now managing growth. How well Apple manages its growth is demonstrated by its ability to realize greater profits, to achieve competitive advantages, and to successfully challenge IBM for business customers.

Honda

What is the lesson at Honda?

Honda's situation is rather different from Apple's.[14] Unlike Apple, Honda is an old, established business, which has been for years the unquestioned leader of the motorcycle industry. Honda took control of the domestic Japanese motorcycle industry in the 1950s and proceeded to take the worldwide leadership position in the 1960s. It achieved all of that through aggressive marketing, continuous product innovation, and establishing quality standards that are second to none. Challengers to Honda's position have been easily crushed, both at home and abroad. Despite its success, however, Honda faced a serious dilemma in the 1970s. The motorcycle market had matured and was saturated. There was little growth possible, except the rather costly and at some point unproductive approach of trying to take market share away from the competition. Honda's management faced the problem of maintaining the organization's vitality while providing its management with the type of challenge that would keep the organization competitive and growing.

Unlike many American and Japanese firms in the 1960s and 1970s who chose to achieve growth by diversification, Honda decided to seek new opportunities for growth by expanding within its area of expertise, motors and motor vehicles. After assessing the environment, the markets, and their own capabilities, Honda's management felt that the most natural extension of their business would be the production of automobiles. With the decision made, Honda, under the leadership of its founder, Soichiro Honda, began expanding into automobile manufacturing in the early 1960s.

The news that Honda would move into the automobile industry was not well received by Japan's influential Ministry of International Trade & Industry (MITI). Bureaucrats in MITI worked to discourage Honda from expanding beyond its motorcycle business, and they provided little support in Honda's effort to establish automobile export operations. But Soichiro Honda was not to be stopped. He recognized that Honda had little chance of making any inroads into a domestic market dominated by Toyota and Nissan, particularly when Honda lacked MITI's approval. In light of that situation, he and his management team concluded that Honda's best opportunity for growth would be in foreign markets, most notably the United States.

Honda's management realized that the firm could not achieve the type of growth it wanted by merely selling its automobiles in the United States. They recognized the need to make a bold move that would give Honda a competitive edge over its Japanese counterparts in the U.S. market. The bold move came in the form of a decision to establish manufacturing operations in the United States. At the time, the late 1970s, this action was considered risky and highly unusual for a Japanese firm. Nevertheless, Honda's management pressed ahead.

Honda began its U.S. strategy by first building a motorcycle assembly plant in Marysville, Ohio. Honda's management recognized that they needed some time to learn about manufacturing in the United States, and it was easier to start with assembling motorcycles, which had a well-established reputation in the U.S. market. This approach proved to be quite successful. Honda discovered that it could introduce a wide range of Japanese managerial techniques to its American work force and that American workers could achieve the same quality levels as their Japanese counterparts.

While it was gaining expertise on how to manufacture in the United States, Honda was redesigning its cars (upgrading them from the low-cost end of the market) and establishing a reputation for producing quality automobiles. In 1980, Honda began construction of a Honda Accord assembly plant in Marysville, Ohio. At the time, Honda was behind Toyota and Nissan, holding 4.2 percent of the market.

By 1987, Honda had become the number one foreign automobile company in the United States, ahead of both Toyota and Nissan. A year later, Honda began exporting Accords made in the United States back to Japan (Honda plans to annually export 50,000 U.S.–made cars to Japan by 1991.). Not satisfied with this success, Honda's management established a new goal for the 1990s: to overtake Chrysler's position in the U.S. market. To accomplish this, Honda began construction on both a new U.S. assembly plant and a U.S. engine-manufacturing plant in 1988. What is remarkable about the successful U.S. expansion of Honda's automobile business is that Honda accomplished it without being unionized and it achieved this growth during a time when GM, Ford, and Chrysler were reducing their U.S. production capacity.

Honda's ability to sustain growth and achieve exceptional organizational performance demonstrates the importance of being flexible and responsive to changing environmental conditions. Honda could have chosen a more conservative route, one oriented to preserving its leadership position in the motorcycle industry. But like its motorcycles and later its automobiles, Honda has developed a reputation for high performance. That level of performance is stimulated and driven by a growth strategy that emphasizes innovation, gaining competitive advantage, vision, and managerial leadership. Honda's story is one of overcoming the odds, of discovering a way to succeed, and it is in observing this effort and performance that managers can gain valuable insight into what constitutes effective managerial and organizational procedures.

LESSONS FROM MATURE ORGANIZATIONS

Do mature firms just fade away?

The vast majority of American enterprises are considered mature organizations operating in mature industries. There is little growth in the demand for the products or the services that these firms provide, and in some instances, the demand is actually declining. For many of these firms, the sole function of management is to maintain and preserve market position and profitability.

More often than not, the managerial and organizational performance of many of these firms has been lackluster at best. For a long time, this less-than-dynamic performance was not critical to a firm's survival. Then came the 1980s. During that period, many marginal firms found themselves at risk. First, there was the recession; then, foreign competition moved into their markets, followed by aggressive "lean and mean" domestic firms; and, last, there were the raiders. As a result, many older, well-established, dead-in-the-water firms were sold off, acquired, broken up, placed into bankruptcy, or simply driven out of business by competition. The list of marginal firms that failed to adapt and respond to changing conditions includes such notable firms as Gulf Oil, Federated Department Stores, Pillsbury, Republic Steel, Braniff Airlines, Firestone, RCA, Howard Johnson's, and BankAmerica.

But not all mature firms are boring, passive, and marginally productive endeavors. Many are very dynamic and viable enterprises. They operate with a certain intensity that is reflected in the quality of their products and services and in the energy, enthusiasm, and commitment of their employees. They possess what Robert Waterman suggested in his book, *The Renewal Factor: How the Best Get and Keep the Competitive Edge,* [15] are certain renewal factors that help sustain organizational competitiveness and vitality. (See Table 19-3.)

Highly Adaptive Organizations

Firms like IBM, Johnson & Johnson, UPS, United Airlines, and Sears are highly adaptive operations. Like their growth-oriented counterparts Apple, Genentech, Federal Express, Texas Air, and The Limited, they are flexible and respon-

---

Table 19-3   Lessons in Corporate Renewal

WHAT ARE THE MOST IMPORTANT ATTRIBUTES OF RENEWING COMPANIES? EIGHT MAJOR THEMES EMERGE IN ROBERT H. WATERMAN'S *THE RENEWAL FACTOR.*

INFORMED OPPORTUNISM

Information is their main strategic advantage, and flexibility is their main strategic weapon. They assume opportunity will keep knocking, but it will knock softly and in unpredictable ways.

DIRECTION AND EMPOWERMENT

Managers at renewing companies define the boundaries, and their subordinates figure out the best way to do the job within them. Managers give up some control to gain results.

FRIENDLY FACTS, CONGENIAL CONTROLS

Renewing companies have information that provides context and removes decision-making from the realm of mere opinions. Their people regard financial controls as the benign checks and balances that allow them to be creative and free.

A DIFFERENT MIRROR

Leaders are open and inquisitive. They get ideas from almost anyone in and out of the hierarchy—customers, competitors, even next-door neighbors.

TEAMWORK, TRUST, POLITICS, AND POWER

Renewers stress the value of teamwork and trust their employees to do the job. While relentless at fighting office politics, they acknowledge politics are inevitable in the workplace.

STABILITY IN MOTION

Renewing companies undergo constant change against a base of underlying stability. They understand the need for consistency and norms. But they also realize that the only way to respond to change is to deliberately break the rules.

ATTITUDES AND ATTENTION

Visible management attention, rather than exhortation, gets things done. Action may start with the words, but it has to be backed by symbolic behavior that makes those words come alive.

CAUSES AND COMMITMENT

Commitment results from management's ability to turn grand causes into small actions so that everyone can contribute to the central purpose.

---

sive to the changing environment. But unlike their younger competition, they have to constantly overcome organizational inertia. Size and prior success work against them, and sometimes they are a little slow in responding (like IBM to Apple's PC, like UPS to Federal Express's overnight delivery), but they do respond, and when they respond, they commit the full force of their resources to achieving their goals. And unlike many of their mature counterparts, they are willing to take risks and to learn from their mistakes (like Johnson & Johnson's unsuccessful entry into the disposable diaper market, like Sears' unsuccessful expansion in the area of financial services).

As with growth organizations, there are many valuable lessons that managers can learn by studying how mature firms operate and how they remain visible and responsive enterprises. In many ways, managers in mature organizations face far greater performance challenges than their peers who work in growth organizations. For managers in mature organizations, the ultimate challenge is to avoid falling into a "preserve the status quo" mentality. The ultimate risk in not continually pursuing change and making renewal an ongoing process is failure of the enterprise.

Caterpillar

One organization that faced just such a situation is Caterpillar. Before 1980, Caterpillar was the unquestioned leader in the heavy-equipment industry. It had experienced more than fifty years of uninterrupted profitability and successful performance. Peters and Waterman cite Caterpillar as a model of corporate excellence in their book *In Search of Excellence.*[16] Given this record, it should not be a surprise that at the time, Caterpillar's management was seen as smug, aloof, and inflexible. Why change a winning formula?

But in the 1980s, Caterpillar's operating environment changed dramatically. The recession in the construction industry caused a collapse in their market. The era of mega–construction projects (such as the interstate highway system) had come to an end, and the oil industry went into decline. And to make matters worse, suddenly there was new competition from a Japanese company, Komatsu, who aggressively went after Caterpillar's remaining market, undercutting Caterpillar's prices by as much as 40 percent.

At the time, Caterpillar, unlike most mature, old-line American manufacturers (who refused to adapt to the changes in the environment and instead chose to blame everything and everybody for their declining fortunes), recognized and accepted the need to initiate a radical transformation of the firm. After examining the performance of their competitors, Caterpillar's management understood that the overhaul of the corporation's strategies, managerial practices, and manufacturing processes was essential to the firm's survival. They realized that their past was not relevant to their future. With that change in managerial attitude, Caterpillar began the long and hard struggle to regain its competitiveness.

What did Caterpillar do?   One of the earliest decisions Caterpillar's management made in their renewal effort was that the firm would make every effort to defend its position in the market. Management began by cutting Caterpillar's equipment prices to match those of Komatsu, choosing to lose money rather than lose market share. At the same time, they began an intensive effort to drive down Caterpillar's production costs. This effort entailed not only a restructuring of the organization but also a substantial investment in new equipment, production methods, and facility rehabilitation. Finally, top management developed a new vision to fulfill Caterpillar's potential. In time, Caterpillar's employees became committed to a concept known as PWAF. As a team, they were to create "plants with a future."

In addition to implementing employee participation programs, reducing inventory levels, cutting assembly time, and improving quality, Caterpillar redesigned, innovated, and downsized many of its products. Caterpillar took a great risk in developing these new products, because with the change in product line, Caterpillar found itself operating in unfamiliar markets. There was well-established competition, like John Deere and Case, in these new markets. The customers were different as well. In the new market, the customers were smaller, owner–operator businesses, whose concerns and needs were significantly different from those of Caterpillar's traditional customers (the purchase of a $500,000 piece of equipment was routine for firms like Bechtel, Kaiser, or Turner). In this new market, Caterpillar had to find a niche, and it had to develop a new way of doing business.

Leadership was the final component of Caterpillar's renewal effort. When he was promoted to Caterpillar's CEO in 1985, George Schaefer did not have

Caterpillar is classified as a mature organization and at one point in time was the leader in the heavy-equipment industry. When challenged by the Japanese firm Komatsu, Caterpillar responded aggressively. It cut prices, reduced production costs, restructured the organization, invested in new equipment, production methods, and facilities. To survive, it showed all the signs of growth organizations.

the image of a high-profile leader. He was an accountant by discipline, and he had worked his way up through the organization in the traditional manner. When he took the CEO's position, he understood that he had to assume more of a leadership role than his predecessors had, to ensure that Caterpillar successfully accomplished its transformation. He focused on improving communications and employee involvement, and he challenged Caterpillar's employees to restore the firm's reputation for outstanding performance. To accomplish all of that, Schaefer willingly accepted the risk of sacrificing short-run profitability for long-term gains.

As Caterpillar moved into the 1990s, its transformation was succeeding. Caterpillar had reestablished itself as the unquestioned leader in the heavy-equipment industry. Komatsu was in retreat, and profitability was returning. Revenues, productivity, and quality were up; production costs were down. In addition, Caterpillar was successfully making inroads into new markets. Over a period of ten years, the firm had changed its nature, culture, and managerial practices and, in doing so, had renewed its competitiveness.

Caterpillar's story provides managers with many valuable lessons. One of the most important is that to survive, mature firms need the same type of vitality and effective managerial performance that is so essential to growth organizations. Many of the actions that Caterpillar initiated in its turnaround effort are quite similar to those actions routinely taken by growth-oriented enterprises. Caterpillar innovated in product design and production processes, it redefined markets, and it sought new opportunities. Its top management assumed leadership in creating for Caterpillar's employees a vision and a challenge that motivated individual performance. Caterpillar's success in restoring its competitiveness equals any of the successes achieved by the best of the growth companies. Caterpillar demonstrates the need of an organization to be flexible and responsive. And much of Caterpillar's success can be attributed to a willingness on the part of its managers to learn from the successes and failures of other organizations.

CONCLUDING THOUGHT

In Chapter 1, you were introduced to the manager's world. You read of the complexity in this world brought about by the expansion of business into international markets containing both new customers and new competitors. In the other chapters in Part I, the complexity described included problems of ethics and corporate social responsibility. After all, if people in organizations are not concerned about the ethical and social issues of this world, who will be?

Parts II and III presented you with information on the management functions and the behavioral and political contexts within which managers must act and exist. In Part IV, we turned to three issues that seem to be of critical importance to managers in these last years of the twentieth century.

Change is a part of the contemporary environment, and managers have no choice but to address the issue head on. Part of the problem of and the solution to the dynamic changes in the contemporary environment is the information explosion. At times, managers will feel they are drowning in a vast sea, but once again, the successful survival of our economic system requires that we use the new technology to "manage information."

Perhaps no other message has been more clear in the past twenty-five years than that customers place great importance on the quality of the products and the services they buy. Rather than running from the quality questions, American managers must understand that customers' quality expectations are legitimate and cannot be ignored. Don't we all expect improvement?

Many critics of American management believe we have lost the will to compete. They cite the increasing crime rate and the increasing use of drugs in our cities, problems in providing educational opportunities for all, and the difficulty that both the executive and the legislative branches of our government have in setting priorities and direction for the next century.

There are many Americans who see the challenges that all nations have in an increasingly complex world. These Americans believe the challenges will be addressed, for they sense the spirit of entrepreneurship, determination, and courage that made the United States what it is.[17]

To succeed in this pursuit, more voices must participate in the critical decisions. American men and women of every race and religion are the true power that needs to be unleashed. Managers must play a leading role in creating an environment that encourages experimentation, open criticism, trust, and a desire to direct personal productivity into quality products and services. The opportunities are endless.

SUMMARY

As we have seen in other parts of the book, management practices and organizational performance can be improved through empirical research and conceptual model building. But management practices and performance can also be enhanced through the study and analysis of the histories and experiences of successful and unsuccessful managers and businesses. In this chapter, we have learned valuable lessons by reviewing the experiences of General Motors, IBM,

Sears, Apple, Honda, and Caterpillar. Our chief purpose in this chapter has been to focus on the ideas and managerial approaches of practicing managers.

We have tried to find those ideas and situations that are transferable to you so that you can be successful in your own managerial performance. Therefore, we shall summarize some of these ideas.

1. One of the keys to improving individual managerial performance is to learn lessons by observing and studying the performance of other managers.
2. Managers and organizations need to understand that yesterday's success does not guarantee future success. Therefore, managers and organizations should endeavor to be flexible in their practices and responsive in their strategies for environmental change.
3. It is important for both growth and mature organizations that top management create a vision and maintain a certain amount of "dynamic tension" as a means to preserve the organizational vitality so essential for employee motivation and the survival of the venture.
4. Because of their flexibility and informality, smaller, growth-oriented firms have significant advantages in their ability to respond to new opportunities.
   a. By identifying niches for operations and understanding clearly the guiding concepts of the firm, growth-oriented businesses may find tremendous opportunities that are ignored by their larger competitors, who must overcome inertia.
   b. As a firm grows, there is an increased need to pay attention to explicit organizational problems.
5. Rapid expansion or organizational transformation requires more than ambitious targets. Success requires leadership, commitment, close attention to building a management team, responsiveness to environmental changes, and a willingness to take risks, by accepting and learning from failure.

KEY TERMS

Initiator An entrepreneur, a promoter, an inventive person.
Organizer A manager who builds the structure and lays the foundation for the permanent life of a corporation.
Decentralization of Operations The responsibility of chief executive of each operation shall in no way be limited.

Centralized Staff Services Certain central organization functions are absolutely essential to the logical development and proper coordination of the corporation's activities.
Flexibility Adaptability to external changes, resiliency of policies, and responsiveness of the entire organization to meet new problems.

STUDY ASSIGNMENTS

1. Explain how each of the methods we considered for developing management skills can contribute to your own personal development.
2. Compare and contrast *Fortune*'s eight attributes and the eight attributes used by Peters and Waterman as measures of effective managerial and organizational performance.
3. Describe the characteristics of the initiator and the organizer, and show how they are different.
4. Explain how Sloan's basic concepts supplement the discussion of organization structure in Chapter 7.
5. How do T. J. Watson's tenets for IBM relate to McGregor's theory?

6. How do the stories of Sears and Caterpillar illustrate the need for an organization to be adaptive to change?

7. Why was it necessary for Apple to change its top management, from Jobs to Sculley, to ensure survival and continued growth?

8. Why do growth firms experience such tremendous difficulties in expanding the scope of their business, even when there is increasing demand for the firm's products or services?

9. With respect to influencing organizational and managerial effectiveness, compare and contrast the growth factors we noted and the renewal factors Waterman identified.

10. How does Honda's approach to sustaining growth differ from Caterpillar's effort to maintain a leadership position in the heavy-equipment industry?

Case for Discussion

CORPORATE PRACTICES TODAY

A look at the American business scene today reveals many interesting yet not widely known management policies and practices. Robert Levering, Milton Moskowitz, and Michael Katz have uncovered many of these and report on them in their book, *The 100 Best Companies to Work for in America.*[18]

1. Dana Corporation

Dana makes axles, transmissions, clutches, and universal joints for cars and trucks, as well as a variety of valves, pumps, and motors for industrial equipment.

Organization charts, policy manuals, a large corporate staff, written reports, and memos have fallen by the wayside at Dana. The company president, Ren McPherson, is said to have plunked a foot-high stack of policy manuals on the boardroom table and asked which ones were really important. When he didn't get a satisfactory answer, he tossed all the manuals into a wastebasket and said he would put everything essential from the manuals onto one piece of paper. Dana today has no policy manuals.

2. Donnelly Mirrors, Inc.

Donnelly Mirrors makes nearly all the rearview mirrors found in U.S. automobiles. Donnelly operates on the notion that people can be responsible human beings, even in the workplace. They don't have to be told what to do; they can decide for themselves.

At Donnelly Mirrors, time clocks have been removed and everyone is salaried. A Donnelly employee works in a team of ten people. You are trusted to keep your own records, but you are responsible to other members of the team. If you're late because of an illness in the family, for example, your work will be covered by another team member. If you are constantly absent or not performing well during working hours, you have to answer not to the company but to the other members of your team.

3. H. B. Fuller Company

Fuller is one of the world's largest makers of glues, adhesives, and sealants.

Once a year, Tony Anderson, president of H. B. Fuller Co., makes himself available to everyone in the company through "The President's Hot-Line." Employees can call him on that day on a special toll-free number to complain about their supervisor or to make suggestions for improving their products or to talk about anything else on their minds.

4. W. L. Gore and Associates, Inc.

Gore makes synthetic fiber called Gore-tex, used in camping equipment, among dozens of other products.

Bill Gore uses a system he calls the "lattice organization," in contrast to the pyramid organization typical of most companies. Instead of people relating to others within a hierarchy, each person in a lattice can interact directly with every other person. A lattice has several attributes, including these:

- No fixed or assigned authority
- Sponsors, not bosses
- Natural leadership defined by followership
- Person-to-person communication
- Objectives set by those who must "make them happen"
- Tasks and functions organized through commitment

5. Intel Corporation

Intel is one of the leading developers and makers of the microelectronic products that are the heart of the computer revolution: the microprocessor, memory chips, and computer systems.

Intel is an intense place, with few trappings of big business. There are no dress codes. The president of the company walks around with an open shirt showing a gold chain around his neck. You won't find any mahogany-lined offices. There is no executive dining room; everyone eats in the cafeteria. And there are no reserved parking spaces for top executives; you won't find "flex-time" or job sharing at Intel. You are expected to clock in at 8:00 A.M. The company wants you there, not for the bureaucratic reason of enforcing mindless discipline, but because it's anxious to have all the brains present to interact with each other.

6. The Maytag Company

Maytag makes washing machines, dryers, dishwashers, and other major appliances.

Harvey Jackson works in the machine shop at Maytag's plant in Newton, Iowa. Several years ago, while taking a vacation in the Bahamas, he went into a local boutique to buy a gift for his wife. As he was talking with the salesperson, he discovered she had a new Maytag washer that didn't work. Concerned about his company's reputation, Jackson reported the problem machine to people in Newton. Within a matter of days, Maytag had sent a replacement machine to the hotel. The defective machine was returned to Iowa and put in the "boneyard" where quality-control experts examined it carefully to find out what had gone wrong.

7. McCormick and Company, Inc.

McCormick is the largest spice maker in the United States.

Charles McCormick's legacy continues in the form of "Multiple Management" boards that operate throughout the spice and seasonings company founded by his uncle. Each of the thirteen boards functions like a junior board of directors for the company's major operating divisions. They parallel the divisional boards composed of the key functional executives within each part of the company. While the divisional boards concentrate on basic administrative questions, the Multiple Management boards analyze and offer solutions to a wide variety of nuts-and-bolts problems. New ideas are hashed over and worked out.

8. Merle Norman Cosmetics

Merle Norman makes its own brand of cosmetics in Los Angeles and sells them through 25,000 privately owned Merle Norman studios in the United States and Canada.

The perks and family feeling at Merle Norman have resulted in a company with negligible turnover. Statistics on perfect attendance are impressive. To recognize those who achieve perfect attendance, the company offers gifts:

- One year: A gold engraved watch
- Two years: Either an Atari video game, a Farberware cookware set, or Oneida stainless flatware
- Three years: Either a Toshiba personal stereo or a Panasonic portable TV
- Four years: Either a Sunbeam or a Cuisinart food processor
- Five years: A Nikon 35 mm camera
- Six years: A Panasonic AM/FM stero cassette player with two-way speakers
- Seven years: An RCA 19-inch color TV
- Eight years: A Panasonic microwave oven
- Nine years: A specially designed ring
- Ten years: A two-week, all-expense-paid trip to Hawaii for two (in 1983, three employees and their spouses took the trip)
- Fifteen years: A two-week, all-expense-paid trip to anywhere in the world for employee plus spouse, relative, or friend

9. The Morgan Bank

The Morgan Bank is the fifth largest U.S. bank in terms of deposits and assets.

Morgan employees don't expect such patrician generosity, but they do get a free lunch. Every day, Morgan serves a free lunch to nearly 10,000 employees. The fare ranges from a top-rate corporate cafeteria for most of the employees, to an excellent buffet-style spread for the junior executives, to a four-star multicourse repast for top executives and their guests. The bank spends $6 million a year on the noontime perk.

10. The Tandy Corporation

Tandy is America's largest retailer of consumer electronics.

The open door is Tandy doctrine. The employee handbook puts it explicitly: "Any employee is welcome to walk through the door of any member of management to discuss business-related problems. There are no closed doors in our corporation." The policy even extends to the architecture of the Tandy Center in Fort Worth. Top executives work in offices with glass walls and doors, accentuating everyone's accessibility.

Endnotes

Chapter 1

1. Malcolm McConnell, *Challenger: A Major Malfunction: A True Story of Politics, Greed, and the Wrong Stuff* (New York: Doubleday, 1987).
2. Myron Magnet, "Putting Magic Back in the Magic Kingdom," *Fortune,* 115, no. 1 (January 5, 1987), 65.
3. "Profiting from the Nonprofits," *Business Week,* March 26, 1990, pp. 66–74.
4. Sally Helgesen, *The Female Advantage* (New York: Doubleday, 1990).
5. "Profiting from the Nonprofits," pp. 66–74.
6. Kenneth Labich, "Can Your Career Hurt Your Kids?" *Fortune,* May 20, 1991, pp. 38–60.
7. Fern Schumer Chapman, Looking Ahead/Cover Story. "Executive Guilt: Who's Taking Care of the Children?" *Fortune,* February 16, 1987, pp. 30–37. ©1987 Time Inc. all rights reserved.
8. Thomas A. Steward, "Do You Push Your People Too Hard?" *Fortune,* October 22, 1990, pp. 121–32.
9. Thomas J. Peters, *Thriving on Chaos: Handbook for Management Revolution* (New York: Knopf, 1987).
10. Susan B. Garland, Laura Zinn, Christopher Power, Mario Shao and Julia Flynn Siler, "Those Aging Boomers," *Business Week,* May 20, 1991, pp. 106–12.
11. John Naisbitt, *Megatrends: Ten New Directions Transforming Our Lives* (New York: Warner Books, 1984).
12. John Naisbitt and Patricia Aburdene, *Ten New Directions for the 1990s: Megatrends 2000* (New York: Morrow, 1990).
13. Alecia Swasy, "Changing Times," a special report on marketing in the 1990s, in the *Wall Street Journal,* March 22, 1991, p. B6.
14. "The 21st Century Executive," *U.S. News and World Report,* March 7, 1988, pp. 48–51.
15. Alan M. Webber, "Corporate Egotists Gone with the Wind," *Wall Street Journal,* April 15, 1991, p. A14.

Chapter 2

1. Daniel Wren, *The Evolution of Management Theory,* 3rd ed. (New York: John Wiley, 1987).
2. Charles Babbage, *On the Economy of Machinery and Manufactures* (New York: Charles Knight, 1832. Reprint. New York: Augustus M. Kelley, 1963).
3. Frederick W. Taylor, *Shop Management* (New York: Harper & Row, 1903).
4. Frederick W. Taylor, *Principles of Scientific Management* (New York: Harper & Row, 1911).
5. Edwin A. Locke, "The Ideas of Frederick W. Taylor: An Evaluation," *Academy of Management Review,* 7, no. 1 (January 1982), 14–24.
6. H. C. Metcalf and L. Urwick, eds., *Dynamic Administration: The Collected Papers of Mary Parker Follett* (London: Pitman, 1941).
7. Elton Mayo, *The Human Problems of an Industrial Civilization* (Boston: Harvard Business School, 1945).
8. Chester I. Barnard, *The Functions of the Executive* (Cambridge, Mass.: Harvard University Press, 1938).
9. Herbert A. Simon, *Administrative Behavior* (New York: Macmillan, 1947); *Administrative Behavior,* 3rd ed. (New York: Free Press, 1976).
10. James G. March and Herbert A. Simon, *Organizations* (New York: John Wiley, 1958).
11. Douglas McGregor, *The Human Side of Enterprise* (New York: McGraw-Hill, 1960).
12. Henry Mintzberg, *The Nature of Managerial Work* (New York: Harper & Row, 1973); *The Nature of Managerial Work* (New Jersey: Prentice Hall, 1980).
13. William G. Ouchi, *Theory Z: How American Business Can Meet the Japanese Challenge* (Reading, Mass.: Addison-Wesley, 1981).

Chapter 3

1. *Europe 1992: The Single Market,* produced and distributed by Ernst & Whinney, 1988.
2. Karen Elliott House, "Europtimism Dies; Two Suspects Held Responsible," *Wall Street Journal,* May 9, 1991, p. A9.
3. Matt Moffett, "Salinas Goes on Tour to Push Free Trade," *Wall Street Journal,* April 15, 1991, p. A10.
4. Rudiger Dornbusch, "If Mexico Prospers, So Will We," *Wall Street Journal,* April 11, 1991, p. A8.

5. Michael A. Hitt, Robert E. Hoskisson, and Jeffrey S. Harrison, "Strategic Competitiveness in the 1990s: Challenges and Opportunities for U.S. Executives," *The Executive,* May 1991, pp. 7–22.
6. "Reshaping Europe: 1992 and Beyond," *Business Week,* December 12, 1988, pp. 48–51.
7. Richard M. Steers and Edwin L. Miller, "Management in the 1990s: The International Challenge," *The Academy of Management Executive,* February 1988, pp. 21–22.
8. "U.S. Exporters That Aren't American," *Business Week,* February 29, 1988, pp. 70–71.
9. Walter B. Wriston, "The State of American Management," *Harvard Business Review,* January-February 1990, pp. 78–83.
10. John D. Daniels and Lee H. Radebaugh, *International Business,* 5th ed. (Reading, Mass.: Addison-Wesley, 1989).
11. Michael E. Porter, "Competitive Advantage of Nations," *Harvard Business Review,* March-April 1990, pp. 73–93.
12. Udayan Gupta, "Small Service Companies Find High Profits Overseas," *Wall Street Journal,* March 29, 1991, p. B2.
13. "U.S. Exporters That Aren't American," pp. 70–71.
14. Philip M. Rosenzweig and Jitendra V. Singh, "Organizational Environments and the Multinational Enterprise," *Academy of Management Review,* April 1991, pp. 340–61.
15. "G.E. in Hungary: Let There Be Light," *Fortune,* October 22, 1990, pp. 137–42.
16. Raj Aggarwal, "The Strategic Challenge of the Evolving Global Economy," *Business Horizons,* July-August 1987, pp. 38–44.
17. Howard V. Perlmutter, "Social Architectural Problems of the Multinational Firm," *Quarterly Journal of AIESEC International,* 3, no. 3 (August 1967).
18. Joseph L. Massie and Jan Luytjes, *Management in an International Context* (New York: Harper & Row, Pub., 1972).

Chapter 4
1. "Is Ethics Good Business," *Personnel Administrator,* February 1987, pp. 67–74.
2. John D. Hatfield, "An Empirical Examination of the Relationship between Corporate Social Responsibility and Profitability," *Academy of Management Journal,* June 1985, pp. 446–63.
3. Kenneth R. Andrews and Donald K. David, *Ethics in Practice: Managing the Moral Corporation* (Boston, Mass.: Harvard Business School Press, 1989).
4. Thomas Donaldson, *The Ethics of International Business* (New York: Oxford University Press, 1989).
5. David Stipp, "Throwing Good Money at Bad Water Yields Scant Improvement," *Wall Street Journal,* May 15, 1991, pp. A1, A4.
6. Gordon F. Shea, *Practical Ethics* (New York: AMA Membership Publications Division, American Management Association, 1988).
7. Frank Edward Allen, "McDonald's Launches Plan to Cut Waste," *Wall Street Journal,* April 17, 1991, p. B2.
8. David Kirkpatrick, "Environmentalism: The New Crusade," *Fortune,* February 12, 1990, pp. 44–50.
9. "What Led Beech-Nut Down the Road to Disgrace," *Business Week,* February 22, 1988, pp. 124–28.
10. "What Led Beech-Nut Down the Road to Disgrace," pp. 124–28.
11. Frank Rose, "A New Age for Business," *Fortune,* October 8, 1990, pp. 156–60.
12. Michael Hoffman, Robert Frederick, and Edward S. Petry, *The Corporation, Ethics, and the Environment* (New York: Quorum Books, 1990).
13. Janet P. Near and Marcia P. Miceli, "Retailiation Against Whistle-Blowers: Predictors and Effects," *Journal of Applied Psychology,* February 1986, pp. 137–45.
14. Amanda Bennett, "Unethical Behavior, Stress Appear Linked," *The Wall Street Journal,* April 11, 1991, p. A4.
15. Rose, "A New Age for Business, pp. 156–60.

Chapter 5
1. G. P. Huber, *Managerial Decision Making* (Glenview, Ill.: Scott, Foresman, 1980).
2. E. Frank Harrison, *The Managerial Decision Making Process,* 3rd ed. (Boston: Houghton Mifflin, 1987).
3. Huber, *Managerial Decision Making.*
4. A. Elbing, *Behavioral Decisions in Organizations,* 2d ed. (Glenview, Ill.: Scott, Foresman, 1978).
5. Orlando Behling and Norman L. Eckel, "Making Sense out of Intuition," *The Executive,* February 1991, pp. 46–54.
6. Charles E. Lindblom, "The Science of Muddling Through," *American Society for Public Administration,* 19, no. 2 (Spring 1959); and *The Policy Making Process* (Englewood Cliffs, N.J.: Prentice Hall, 1968).
7. Thomas M. Jones, "Ethical Decision Making by Individuals in Organizations: An Issue-Contingent Model," *The Academy of Management Review,* April 1991, pp. 366–95.

8. Philip Revzin, "East European Market Beckons, Then Proves Daunting to U.S. Firm," *Wall Street Journal,* May 13, 1991, pp. A1, A10.
9. Herbert A. Simon, *Administrative Behavior* (New York: Macmillan, 1947).
10. Robert L. Rose, "How 3M, by Tiptoeing into Foreign Markets, Became a Big Exporter," *Wall Street Journal,* March 29, 1991, pp. A1, A10.
11. Bruce F. Baird, *Managerial Decisions under Uncertainty: An Introduction to the Analysis of Decision Making* (New York: John Wiley, 1989).
12. Ray H. Garrison, *Managerial Accounting,* 6th ed. (Plano, Tex.: Business Publications, Inc., 1991).

Chapter 6
1. Thomas Peters and Robert Waterman, Jr., *In Search of Excellence,* (New York: Harper & Row 1982).
2. Michael E. Porter, *Competitive Advantage: Creating and Sustaining Superior Performance* (New York: Collier Macmillan, 1985).
3. Michael E. Porter, *Competitive Strategy: Techniques for Analyzing Industries and Competitors* (New York: Free Press, 1980).
4. James Bryan Quinn et al., Strategy: Cases, Concepts, and Contexts (Englewood Cliffs, N.J.: Prentice Hall, 1991).
5. Spyros Makridakis, *Forecasting, Planning, and Strategy for the 21st Century* (New York: Free Press, 1990).
6. Thomas E. Milne, *Business Forecasting: A Managerial Approach* (New York: Longman, 1975).
7. Bill Richardson, *Business Planning: An Approach to Strategic Management* (London: Pitman, 1989).
8. Craig Rice, *Strategic Planning for the Small Business: Situations, Weapons, Objectives, and Tactics* (Holbrook, Mass.: Bob Adams, 1990).
9. "The Rage for Faster Forecasts," *Business Week,* October 1983, pp. 135–36.
10. Derek F. Abell, *Defining the Business: The Starting Point of Strategic Planning* (Englewood Cliffs, N.J.: Prentice Hall, 1980.
11. Arthur Thompson, Jr., and A. J. Strickland III, *Strategic Management Concepts and Cases,* 3rd ed. (Plano, Tex.: Business Publications, Inc., 1984).
12. R. Edward Freeman, *Strategic Management: A Stakeholder Approach* (Boston: Pitman, 1984).
13. R. Edward Freeman, *Corporate Strategy and the Search for Ethics* (Englewood Cliffs, N.J.: Prentice Hall, 1988).
14. Henry Mintzberg, "Strategy-making in Three Modes," *California Management Review,* 16, no. 2 (Winter 1973), 45–53.
15. William H. Newman, "Shaping the Master Strategy of Your Firm," *California Management Review,* 9, no. 3, 77–88.
16. David Halberstam, *The Reckoning* (New York: Morrow, 1986).

Chapter 7
1. Henry Mintzberg, *Structuring of Organizations* (Englewood Cliffs, N.J.: Prentice Hall, 1979).
2. Elliott Jaques, "In Praise of Hierarchy," *Harvard Business Review* (January-February 1990), pp. 127–33.
3. Clay Chandler and Paul Ingrassia, "Just as U.S. Firms Try Japanese Management, Honda Is Centralizing," *Wall Street Journal,* April 11, 1991, pp. A1, A10.
4. Max Weber, *The Theory of Social and Economic Organization* (New York: Oxford University Press, 1947).
5. Rensis Likert, *The Human Organization* (New York: McGraw-Hill, 1967).
6. Ibid.
7. T. Burns and G. M. Stalker, *The Management of Innovation* (London: Tavistock, 1961).
8. M. Crozier, *The Bureaucratic Phenomenon* (Chicago: University of Chicago Press, 1964).
9. John Milliman, Mary Ann Von Glinow, and Maria Nathan, "Organizational Life Cycles and Strategic International Human Resource Management in Multinational Companies: Implications for Congruence Theory," *The Academy of Management Review* (April 1991), pp. 318–39.
10. Joan Woodward, *Industrial Organization: Theory and Practice* (London: Oxford University Press, 1965).
11. Ibid.
12. Paul R. Lawrence and Jay W. Lorsch, *Organization and Environment* (Homewood, Ill.: Richard D. Irwin, 1969).
13. Mintzberg, *Structuring of Organizations.*
14. K. R. Thompson and A. C. Meadors, "Reconfiguring an Industry to Meet Changing Demands in the Environment: A Case Study," *Conference Proceedings,* ed. Thomas C. Head and H. Randolph Bobbitt, Jr. (Midwest Division, Academy of Management 34th Annual Meeting, Cincinnati, Ohio, April 10–14, 1991), pp. 43–48.
15. Erik W. Larson and David H. Gobeli, "Matrix Management: Contradictions and Insights," *California Management Review* (Summer 1987), pp. 126–38.

16. Gareth Morgan, *Images of Organizations* (New York: Sage Publications, Inc., 1986).
17. Gareth Morgan, *Creative Organizational Theory* (New York: Sage Publications, Inc., 1989).

Chapter 8

1. John Douglas, Stuart M. Klein, and David Hunt, *The Strategic Managing of Human Resources* (New York: John Wiley, 1985).
2. Lin Grensing, *A Small Business Guide to Employee Selection: Finding, Interviewing and Hiring the Right People* (Vancouver, B.C.: International Self-Counsel Press, 1986).
3. Joseph Boyett, *Workplace 2000: The Revolution Reshaping American Business* (New York: Dutton, 1991).
4. Mike Smith and Ivan Robertson, eds., *Advances in Selection and Assessment* (New York: John Wiley, 1989).
5. Richard D. Avery, *Fairness in Selecting Employees* (Reading, Mass.: Addison-Wesley, 1979).
6. Walter Galenson, *New Trends in Employment Practices: An International Survey* (New York: Greenwood, 1991).
7. Robert D. Gatewood, *Human Resource Selection* (Chicago: Dryden Press, 1990).
8. *ASPA Handbook of Personnel and Industrial Relations: Official Handbook of the American Society for Personnel Administration* (Washington, D.C.: Bureau of National Affairs, 1989).
9. Clark Kerr, ed., *Industrial Relations in a New Age* (San Francisco: Jossey-Bass, 1986).
10. Performance Appraisal Form as currently used by Amy Milholland, CPA, Inc., Oxford, Ohio.
11. Joann S. Lublin, "The American Advantage: It Often Doesn't Pay to Work for a Foreign Company's U.S. Unit," *Wall Street Journal*, April 17, 1991, p. R4.
12. John Douglas, *The Strategic Managing of Human Resources* (New York: John Wiley, 1985).
13. John Fossum, ed., *Employee and Labor Relations* (Washington, D.C.: Bureau of National Affairs, 1990).
14. Douglas, *The Strategic Managing of Human Resources*, pp. 586–93.
15. Karen Elliott House,, "Europtimism Dies; Two Suspects Held Responsible," *Wall Street Journal*, May 9, 1991, p. A3.
16. Tom Juravich, *CHAOS on the Shop Floor* (Philadelphia: Temple University Press, 1985).

Chapter 9

1. Daniel Katz and Robert L. Kahn, *The Social Psychology of Organizations,* 2nd ed. (New York: John Wiley, 1978).
2. A. Paul Hare, *Handbook of Small Group Research* (New York: Free Press, 1962).
3. William E. Henry, "The Business Executive: The Psychodynamics of a Social Role," *American Journal of Sociology,* 54 (1949).
4. Edwin E. Ghiselli, *Explorations in Managerial Talent* (Pacific Palisades, Calif.: Goodyear, 1971).
5. Ralph M. Stogdill and A. E. Coons, eds., *Leader Behavior: Its Description and Measurement* (Columbus, Ohio: Ohio State University, Bureau of Business Research, Research Monograph 88, 1957).
6. Alan C. Filley, *The Compleat Manager* (Champaign, Ill.: Research Press Company, 1978).
7. Rensis Likert, *New Patterns of Management* (New York: McGraw-Hill, 1967).
8. Saul Gellerman, *The Management of Human Relations* (New York: Holt, Rinehart & Winston, 1966).
9. Fred E. Fiedler, *A Theory of Leadership Effectiveness* (New York: McGraw-Hill, 1967).
10. S. Kerr and J. Jermier, "Substitute for Leadership: Their Meaning and Effectiveness," *Organizational Behavior and Human Performance* (December 1978), pp. 375–403.
11. P. Hersey and K. Blanchard, *Management of Organizational Behavior: Utilizing Human Resources,* 4th ed. (Englewood Cliffs, N.J.: Prentice Hall, 1982).
12. Ibid.
13. Victor H. Vroom, *Work and Motivation* (New York: John Wiley, 1964).
14. Kerr and Jermier "Substitutes for Leadership," pp. 375–403.
15. Victor H. Vroom and Philip W. Yetton, *Leadership and Decision Making* (Pittsburgh: University of Pittsburgh Press, 1973).
16. Judy B. Rosener, "Ways Women Lead," *Harvard Business Review* (November-December 1990), pp. 119–25.
17. Charles L. Hulin and M. R. Blood, "Job Enlargement, Individual Differences and Worker Responses," *Psychological Bulletin,* no. 1, 1968.
18. W. Bennis, "The 4 Competencies of Leadership," *Training and Development Journal* (August 1984), pp. 15–19.
19. R. J. House, "A Path-Goal Theory of Leadership Effectiveness," *Administrative Science Quarterly,* 16 (1971), 321–38.
20. Leonard R. Sayles, *Leadership: What Effective Managers Really Do . . . and How They Do It* (New York: McGraw-Hill, 1979).
21. Kerr and Jermier "Substitutes for Leadership," pp. 375–403.

Chapter 10

1. Joseph Allen and Bennett P. Lientz, *Effective Business Communication* (Santa Monica, Calif.: Goodyear, 1979).
2. Henry Mintzberg, *The Nature of Managerial Work* (New York: Harper & Row, 1973).
3. S. King, "The Nature of Communication," in *Small Group Communication: A Reader,* 5th ed., ed. R. Cathcart and L. Samovar (Dubuque, Iowa: Wm. C. Brown, 1988).
4. Ibid.
5. Ibid.
6. D. Berlo, *The Process of Communication* (New York: Holt, Rinehart & Winston, 1960).
7. D. Barnlund, "Toward a Meaning-Centered Philosophy of Communication," *Journal of Communication,* 2 (1962), 197–211.
8. Otis W. Baskin and Craig E. Aronoff, *Interpersonal Communication in Organizations* (Glenview, Ill.: Scott, Foresman, 1980).
9. Charles Fombrun and Mark Shanley, "What's in a Name? Reputation Building and Corporate Strategy," *Academy of Management Journal* (June 1990), pp. 233–58.
10. William V. Haney, *Communication and Interpersonal Relations,* 4th ed. (Homewood, Ill.: Richard D. Irwin, 1979), pp. 126–40.
11. J. Powell, *Why Am I Afraid to Tell You Who I Am?* (Niles, Ill.: Argus Communications, 1969), p. 194.
12. David C. McClelland, *The Achieving Society* (New York: Van Nostrand Reinhold, 1961).
13. Baskin and Aronoff, *Interpersonal Communication.*
14. Ken G. Smith, Curtis M. Grimm, Martin J. Gannon, and Ming-Jer Chen, "Organizational Information Processing, Competitive Responses, and Performance in the U.S. Domestic Airline Industry," *Academy of Management Journal* (March 1991), pp. 60–85.
15. Jaclyn Fierman, "Do Women Manage Differently," *Fortune,* December 17, 1990, pp. 115–18.
16. Keith Davis and J. W. Newstrom, *Human Behavior at Work: Organizational Behavior,* 8th ed. (New York: McGraw-Hill, 1989).
17. J. Stewart, *Bridges, Not Walls: A Book about Interpersonal Communication* (New York: McGraw-Hill, 1990). See particularly Chapters 1 and 2.
18. J. Stewart and G. D'Angelo, *Together: Communicating Interpersonally* (New York: Random House, 1988). See particularly Chapter 2.

Chapter 11

1. Thomas E. Vollman, *Manufacturing Planning and Control Systems* (Homewood, Ill.: Dow-Jones-Irwin, 1988).
2. Jeffrey A. Alexander, "Adaptive Change in Corporate Control Practices," *Academy of Management Journal* (March 1991), pp. 162–93.
3. Robert Newton Anthony, *The Management Control Function* (Boston: Harvard Business School Press, 1988).
4. Jack N. Kondrasuk, "Studies in MBO Effectiveness," *Academy of Management Review* (July 1981), pp. 419–30.
5. Robert Newton Anthony, J. Dearden, and N. M. Bedford, *Management Control Systems,* 6th ed. (Homewood, Ill.: Richard D. Irwin, 1989).
6. R. K. Mautz, *Criteria for Management Control Systems: A Research Study,* prepared by the Financial Executives Research Foundation by R. K. Mautz and James Winjum (New York: The Foundation, 1981).
7. John W. B. Gibbs, *Practical Approach to Financial Management* (Englewood Cliffs, N.J.: Prentice Hall, 1980).
8. Robert Waterman, Jr., *The Renewal Factor: How the Best Get and Keep the Competitive Edge* (New York: Bantam Books, 1987).
9. Anthony, *The Management Control Function.*
10. Peter Lorange, Michael S. Scott, and Sumantra Ghoshal, *Strategic Control Systems* (St. Paul: West Publishing Co., 1986).
11. Ibid.
12. A. V. Feigenbaum, *Total Quality Control* (New York: McGraw-Hill, 1983).
13. W. Edwards Deming, *Quality, Productivity, and Competitive Position* (Cambridge, Mass.: Massachusetts Institute of Technology, 1982).
14. George Schreyogg and Horst Steinmann, "Strategic Control: A New Perspective," *Academy of Management Review* (January 1987), pp. 91–103.
15. Jeremy Main, "How to Win the Baldridge Award," *Fortune,* April 23, 1990, pp. 101–16.

Chapter 12

1. Frances J. Milliken, "Perceiving and Interpreting Environmental Change: An Examination of College Administrator's Interpretation of Changing Demographics," *Academy of Management Journal* (March 1990), pp. 42–63.

2. John Douglas, George Field, and Lawrence X. Tarpey, *Human Behavior in Marketing* (Columbus, Ohio: Chas. E. Merrill, 1969).
3. John William Atkinson, *Personality, Motivation, and Action: Selected Papers* (New York: Praeger, 1983).
4. Robert R. Carkhuff, *Human Processing and Human Productivity* (Amherst, Mass.: Human Resource Development Press, 1986).
5. Jon L. Pierce, Donald G. Gardner, Larry L. Cummings, Randall B. Dunham, "Organization-Based Self-Esteem and Managerial Behaviors," *Conference Proceedings* (Midwest Division of the Academy of Management Cincinnati, Ohio, April 1991), pp. 109–14.
6. A potential important role conflict may be coming if the ideas of Alan Webber become widespread. He foresees a reduction in the importance of the CEO as a dominant figure in American businesses. See Alan M. Webber, "Corporate Egotists Gone with the Wind," *Wall Street Journal,* April 15, 1991, p. A8.
7. A new culture change may be on the way because the "Baby Boomers" are now into their forties and coming into positions of influence. See the Cover Story, "Those Aging Boomers" and subsequent articles: "Not Exactly the 'Me' Generation"; "How to Fall Off the Corporate Ladder—and Thrive"; "This Is Not Your Father's CEO"; *Business Week,* May 20, 1991, pp. 106–12.
8. M. Roheach, *The Nature of Human Values* (New York: Free Press, 1973).
9. M. Roheach, *Beliefs, Attitudes, and Values: A Theory of Organization and Change* (San Francisco: Jossey-Bass, 1968).
10. See the article "Those Aging Boomers" in *Business Week,* May 20, 1991, pp. 106–12, for insights into possible new attitudes, beliefs, and norms.
11. C. Argyris, *Integrating the Individual and the Organization* (New York: John Wiley, 1964).
12. L. Festinger, *A Theory of Cognitive Dissonance* (Evanston: Ill.: Row, Peterson & Company, 1957).
13. J. Stacy Adams, "Towards an Understanding of Inequity," *Journal of Abnormal and Social Psychology* (November 1963), pp. 422–36.
14. W. R. Johnson and G. J. Johnson, "The Effect of Equity Perceptions on Union and Company Commitment," *Conference Proceedings* (Midwest Division of the Academy of Management, Cincinnati, Ohio, April 1991), pp. 215–20.
15. J. S. Adams, "Inequity in Social Exchange," in *Advances in Experimental Social Psychology,* vol. 2, ed. L. Berkowitz (New York: Academic Press, 1965).
16. Allen R. Russon, *Personality Development for Work* (Cincinnati, Ohio: South-Western Publishing Company, 1981).

Chapter 13

1. Richard Steers and Lyman W. Porter, *Motivation and Work Behavior,* 4th ed. (New York: McGraw-Hill, 1987).
2. The framework for this section is similar to that developed in John Douglas, George A. Field, and Lawrence X. Tarpey, *Human Behavior in Marketing* (Columbus, Ohio: Chas. E. Merrill, 1967), pp. 55–58.
3. Abraham Maslow, *Motivation and Personality* (New York: Harper & Row, 1954).
4. David C. McClelland, *The Achieving Society* (New York: Van Nostrand Reinhold, 1961); and John Atkinson, *Motivation and Achievement* (Washington, D.C.: Winston, 1974).
5. Victor Frankl, *Man's Search for Meaning* (New York: Washington Square Press, 1963). One can read more about the ideas of Victor Frankl in one of the best-selling books of the 1980s: Thomas J. Peters and Robert H. Waterman, Jr., *In Search of Excellence: Lessons from America's Best-Run Companies* (New York: Harper & Row, 1982). In Chapter 3, "Man Waiting for Motivation," they write, "The dominating need of human beings is to find meaning" (p. 76), "to control one's destiny" (p. 80) and for creative leadership—one who is able to institutionalize values. The institutional leader is "primarily an expert in the promotion and protection of values" (p. 85).
6. John Kelly, *Scientific Management, Job Redesign, and Work Performance* (New York: Academic Press, 1982).
7. Frederick Herzberg, Bernard Mausner, and Barbara Bloch Synderman, *The Motivation to Work* (New York: John Wiley, 1959).
8. B. F. Skinner, *Beyond Freedom and Dignity* (New York: Knopf, 1979).
9. Michael LeBoeuf, "The Greatest Management Principle in the World," *Working Woman* (January 1988), p. 70 ff.
10. Victor H. Vroom, *Work and Motivation* (New York: John Wiley, 1964).
11. Lyman W. Porter and Edward E. Lawler III, *Managerial Attitudes and Performance* (Homewood, Ill.: Dorsey Press, 1968).
12. Robert J. Greene, "Effective Compensation: The How and Why," *Personnel Administrator* (February 1987), pp. 112–16.
13. Sally Helgesen, *The Female Advantage: Women's Ways of Leadership* (New York: Doubleday, 1990).
14. Kenneth Labich, "Can Your Career Hurt Your Kids?" *Fortune,* May 20, 1991, pp. 38–60.

Chapter 14

1. Peter F. Drucker, "Don't Change Corporate Culture—Use It!" *Wall Street Journal,* March 28, 1991.
2. Marvin E. Shaw, *Group Dynamics—The Psychology of Small Group Behavior,* 4th ed. (New York: McGraw-Hill, 1985).
3. Gregory Moorehead and Ricky W. Griffin, *Organizational Behavior,* 2nd ed. (Boston: Houghton Mifflin, 1989).
4. Ibid.
5. John Douglas, Stuart Klein, and David Hunt, *The Strategic Management of Human Resources* (New York: John Wiley, 1985), p. 479.
6. Gareth Morgan, *Images of Organizations* (Newbury Park, Calif.: Sage Publications, 1986).
7. G. J. DeSouza, "Social Influences on Group Member Goal Commitment," *Conference Proceedings,* Midwest Division, Academy of Management, 34th Annual Meeting (Cincinnati, Ohio, April 10–14, 1991).
8. Linda N. Jewell, *Group Effectiveness in Organizations* (Glenview, Ill.: Scott, Foresman, 1981).
9. George G. Gordon, "Industry Determinants of Organizational Culture," *The Academy of Management Review,* 16, no. 2 (April 1991), 396–415.
10. George C. Homans, *The Human Group* (New York: Harcourt Brace Jovanovich, 1950).
11. William F. Whyte, *Men at Work* (Homewood, Ill.: Richard D. Irwin, 1961).
12. George C. Homans, *Social Behavior: Its Elementary Forms* (New York: Harcourt Brace Jovanovich, 1961).
13. Moorehead and Griffin, *Organizational Behavior.*
14. Rensis Likert, *New Patterns of Management* (New York: McGraw-Hill, 1961).
15. Leonard R. Sayles, *The Behavior of Industrial Work* (New York: John Wiley, 1958).
16. Richard Dunford and Peter McGraw, "Abandoning Simple Recipes and Benefiting from Quality Circles: An Austrailian Study," *Work and People,* 12, no. 2 (1986), 22–25.

Chapter 15

1. Douglas Yates, *The Politics of Management: Exploring the Inner Workings of Public and Private Organizations* (San Francisco: Jossey-Bass, 1985).
2. Samuel B. Bacharach, *Power and Politics in Organizations* (San Francisco: Jossey-Bass, 1980).
3. David Halberstam, *The Reckoning* (New York: Morrow, 1986).
4. Daniel Katz and Robert L. Kahn, *The Social Psychology of Organizations* (New York: John Wiley, 1966).
5. Michael Korda, *Power! How to Get It, How to Use It* (New York, Random House, 1975).
6. Robert N. McMurry, "Power and the Ambitious Executive," in *Management in the World Today: A Book of Readings,* ed. Don Hellreigel and John Slocum, Jr. (Reading, Mass.: Addison-Wesley, 1975).
7. Leonard Sayles, *Leadership: What Effective Managers Really Do . . . and How They Do It* (New York: McGraw-Hill, 1979). See particularly Chapter 6, "Gaining Power in Any Organization.".
8. Max Weber, *The Theory of Social and Economic Organization* (New York: Free Press, 1947).
9. Pamela Cuming, *Turf and Other Corporate Power Plays* (Englewood Cliffs, N.J.: Prentice Hall, 1985).
10. Michael Korda, *Power! How To Get It, How to Use It.*
11. T. O. Jacobs, *Leadership and Exchange in Formal Organizations* (Alexandria, Va.: Human Resources Research Organization, 1971).
12. Jeffrey Pfeffer, *Power in Organizations* (Marshfield, Mass.: Pitman, 1981).
13. Paul G. Swingle, *The Management of Power* (Hillsdale, N.J.: Lawrence Erlbaum Associates Publishers, 1976).
14. David C. McClelland, "The Two Faces of Power," in *Organizational Psychology, A Book of Readings* eds. David A. Kolb, Irwin M. Rubin, and James M. McIntyre, (Englewood Cliffs, N.J.: Prentice Hall, 1979), pp. 73–86.
15. Laton McCartney, *Friends in High Places: The Bechtel Story* (New York: Simon & Schuster, 1988).
16. Andrew J. DuBrin, *Winning Office Politics: DuBrin's Guide for the 90's* (Englewood Cliffs, N.J.: Prentice Hall, 1990).
17. Walter Kiechel, *Office Hours: A Guide to the Managerial Life* (Boston: Little, Brown, 1988).
18. Norman H. Martin and John Howard Sims, "Power Tactics," *Harvard Business Review* (November-December 1956), pp. 25–29.
19. Dennis K. Mumby, *Communication and Power in Organizations: Discourse, Ideology, and Domination* (Norwood, N.J.: Ablex Pub. Corp., 1988)
20. Albert Z. Carr, "Is Business Bluffing Ethical?" *Harvard Business Review,* 46, no. 1 (January-February 1968), 143–53.
21. Michael Lewis, *Liar's Poker: Rising through the Wreckage on Wall Street* (New York: W. W. Norton & Co., Inc., 1989).

Chapter 16

1. Joseph H. Boyett and Henry P. Conn, *Workplace 2000: The Revolution Reshaping American Business* (New York: E. P. Dutton, 1991).
2. Jeremy Main, "A Golden Age for Entrepreneurs," *Fortune,* February 12, 1990, pp. 120–25.
3. Frank Rose, "A New Age for Business," *Fortune,* October 8, 1990, pp. 156–66.
4. Heinz Weihrich, "Europe 1992 and a Unified Germany: Opportunities and Threats for United States Firms, *The Executive,* (February 1991), pp. 93–97.
5. Gareth Morgan, *Riding the Waves of Change: Developing Managerial Competencies for a Turbulent World* (San Francisco: Jossey-Bass, 1988).
6. Patrick E. Connor, *Managing Organizational Change* (New York: Praeger, 1988).
7. The change process of unfreezing, moving, and refreezing form the base for the interpretation of forty managers. Their interpretation stages used the words *anticipation, confirmation, culmination,* and *aftermath.* See Lynn A. Isabella, "Evolving Interpretations as a Change Unfolds: How Managers Construe Key Organizational Events," *Academy of Management Journal* (March 1990), pp. 7–41.
8. Michael Beer, Russell A. Eisenstat, and Bert Spector, "Why Change Programs Don't Produce Change," *Harvard Business Review* (November-December 1990), pp. 158–66.
9. Michael B. McCaskey, *The Executive Challenge: Managing Change and Ambiguity* (Boston: Pitman, 1982).
10. Douglas B. Gutknecht, *Strategic Revitalization: Managing the Challenges of Change* (Lanham, Md.: University Press of America, 1988).
11. Leonard R. Sayles, *The Behavior of Industrial Work* (New York: John Wiley, 1958).
12. William F. Whyte, *Men at Work* (Homewood, Ill.: Richard D. Irwin, 1961).
13. David A. Kolb and Richard E. Boyatzis, "Goal Setting and Self-Directed Behavior Changes," in *Organizational Psychology,* ed. D. Kolb et al. (Englewood Cliffs, N.J.: Prentice Hall, 1971), p. 333.
14. Isabella, "Evolving Interpretations as a Change Unfolds, pp. 7–41.
15. Craig R. Hickman, *Creating Excellence: Managing Corporate Culture, Strategy, and Change in the New Age* (New York: New American Library, 1984).

Chapter 17

1. The impact of new technology and product development will be significant. AT&T, for example, closed offices in ten states in 1991 by giving salespeople notebook PCs, modems, and printers. See Larry Armstrong, "Who Needs a Desk When You've Got A Lap?" *Business Week,* March 18, 1991, p. 124.
2. Gary W. Dickson, *The Management of Information Systems* (New York: McGraw-Hill, 1985).
3. Kenneth W. Clowes, *The Impact of Computers on Managers* (Ann Arbor, Mich.: UMI Research Press, 1982).
4. James B. Thomas and Reuben R. McDaniel, Jr., "Interpreting Strategic Issues: Effects of Strategy and the Information-Processing Structure of Top Management Teams," *Academy .of Management Journal* (June 1990), pp. 286–306.
5. Michael W. Davis, *Applied Decision Support* (Englewood Cliffs, N.J.: Prentice Hall, 1988).
6. *Information Systems Management* (Atlanta: Business Publication Division, College of Business Administration, Georgia State University, 1988).
7. John Douglas, Stuart Klein, and David Hunt, *The Strategic Management of Human Resources* (New York: John Wiley, 1985).
8. Thomas and McDaniel, "Interpreting Strategic Issues," pp. 286–306.
9. James Martin, *Strategic Information Planning Methodologies* (Englewood Cliffs, N.J.: Prentice Hall, 1989).
10. There will be an explosion in reporting data when the laptop boom gets into full swing. See Deidre A. Depke, Neil Gross, Barbara Buell, and Gary McWilliams, "Laptops Take Off," *Business Week,* March 18, 1991, pp. 118–24.
11. The growth of laptops for organizational personnel will expand the demand for query-and-retrieval information systems. See Depke et al., "Laptops Take Off," pp. 118–24.
12. Michael W. Davis, *Applied Decision Support* (Englewood Cliffs, N.J.: Prentice Hall, 1988).
13. Douglas et al., *The Strategic Managing of Human Resources.*
14. Norbert Wiener, *Science,* May 6, 1960.
15. Jane Carey, ed., *Human Factors in Management Information Systems* (Norwood, N.J.: Ablex Publishing Corporation, 1988).
16. Chris Argyris, "Management Information Systems, The Challenge to Rationality and Emotionality," *Management Science* (February 1971).
17. See two references to the developments in information technology and the impact upon organizational personnel: Tim R. V. Davis, "Information Technology and White-Collar Productivity," *The Executive* (February 1991), pp. 55–67; and Andrew Erdman, "CEOs Don't Share White-Collar Blues," *Fortune,* February 25, 1991, pp. 87–91.

Chapter 18

1. John F. Gilks, "Total Quality: Wave of the Future," *Canadian Business Review* (Spring 1990), p. 17.
2. Nicholas J. Aquilano and Richard B. Chase, *Fundamentals of Operations Management* (Homewood, Ill.: Richard D. Irwin, 1991).
3. "The Push for Quality," *Business Week,* June 8, 1987, pp. 131–32.
4. Steve Lohr, "What's New in Japanese Robotics," *New York Times,* July 3, 1983.
5. Customers can now select unique products. They can choose their personal-style bicycle from 11, 231,862 variations. See Susan Moffat, "Japan's New Personalized Production," *Fortune,* October 22, 1990, pp. 132–37.
6. Oliver Wight, *The Executive's Guide to Successful MRP II* (Englewood Cliffs, N.J.: Prentice Hall, 1982).
7. "Kanban: The Just-in-Time Japanese Inventory System," *Small Business Reports* (February 1984).
8. R. J. Schonberger, *Japanese Manufacturing Techniques: Nine Hidden Lessons in Simplicity* (New York: Free Press, 1982).
9. Keki R. Bhote, *Strategic Supply Management: A Blueprint for Revitalizing the Manufacturer-Supplier Partnership* (New York: AMACOM, 1989).
10. Richard J. Schonberger and James P. Gilbert, "Just-in-Time Purchasing: A Challenge for U.S. Industry," *California Management Review,* 26 (Fall 1983), 54–68.
11. Carla Rapoport, "The Big Split," *Fortune,* May 6, 1991, pp. 38–48.
12. "Spending Billions to Reinvent the Factory," *Business Week,* June 16, 1986, p. 102.
13. John F. Gilks, "Total Quality," p. 17.
14. Michael L. Dertouzoa et al., *Made in America: Regaining the Productive Edge* (Cambridge: MIT Press, 1989).
15. "100 Products That America Makes Best," *Fortune,* March 28, 1988, p. 54.
16. W. Edwards Deming, *Out of the Crisis* (Cambridge: MIT Press, 1986).
17. Brinton R. Schlender, "Chipper Days for U.S. Chipmakers," *Fortune,* May 6, 1991, pp. 90–94.

Chapter 19

1. Walter B. Wriston, "The State of American Management," *Harvard Business Review* (January-February 1990), pp. 78–83.
2. Susan J. Harrington, "What Corporate America Is Teaching about Ethics," *The Executive,* 5, no. 1 (February 1991), 21–30.
3. Richard A. Cosier and Charles R. Schwenk, "Agreement and Thinking Alike: Ingredients for Poor Decisions," *The Executive,* 4, no. 1 (February 1990), 69–74.
4. Thomas J. Peters and Robert H. Waterman, Jr., *In Search of Excellence: Lessons from America's Best-Run Companies* (New York: Harper & Row, 1982).
5. Alfred P. Sloan, Jr., *My Years with General Motors* (New York: Doubleday, 1964.)
6. John Z. De Lorean, *On a Clear Day You Can See General Motors: John Z. de Lorean's Look Inside the Automotive Giant* (Grosse Pointe, Mich.: Wright Enterprises, 1979).
7. Thomas J. Watson, *A Business and Its Beliefs: The Ideas That Helped Build IBM* (New York: McGraw-Hill, 1963).
8. Ibid, pp. 71–73.
9. F. G. Rodgers, *The IBM Way: Insights into the World's Most Successful Marketing Organization* (New York: Harper & Row, 1986).
10. Boris Emmet and John E. Jeuck, *Catalogues and Counters: A History of Sears, Roebuck & Company* (Chicago: University of Chicago Press, 1950).
11. Donald Katz, *The Big Store: Crisis and Revolution at Sears* (New York: Viking, 1987).
12. Lee Butcher, *Accidental Millionaire: The Rise and Fall of Steve Jobs at Apple Computer* (New York: Paragon House, 1988).
13. Frank Rose, *West of Eden: Apple Computer and the End of Entrepreneurship* (New York: Viking, 1989).
14. Robert L. Shook, *Honda: An American Success Story* (New York: Prentice Hall, 1988).
15. Peter H. Waterman, *The Renewal Factor: How the Best Get and Keep the Competitive Edge* (Toronto and New York: Bantam, 1987).
16. Peters and Waterman, *In Search of Excellence.*
17. Thomas J. Peters, *Thriving on Chaos: Handbook for a Management Revolution* (New York: Knopf, 1987).
18. Robert Levering, Milton Moskowitz and Michal Katz, *The 100 Best Companies to Work for in America,* (New York: New American Library, 1985).

Glossary/Index

Management by Objectives (MBO) *287. Management approach involving planning, motivating, and controlling consisting of joint planning sessions by superior and subordinate to establish attainable goals for the subordinate and joint evaluations after performance to check attainment of objectives.*

Management contracts, *59. A contract that usually describes providing specific services for a firm or party in another country; they usually do not require any capital investment.*

Management control information, *435. Information that helps managers take the actions that are in the best interest of the company; managers are also able to see that resources are being efficiently and effectively used.*

Management information systems (MIS), *429. An integrated, structured complex of people, machines, and procedures for supplying relevant data, i.e., information from both external and internal sources to aid managers in performing their functions.*

Managers, *10. The people in an organization who are primarily responsible for seeing that work gets done through the efforts of others.*

Manufacturing resources planning (MRP), *476*

Manufacturing resources planning II (MRP II), *476. Applies the scheduling concepts to all segments of the organization, not just manufacturing; includes finance and marketing.*

Maslow, Abraham H., *339*

Master of destiny concept, *69*

Master production schedule (MPS), *475. Tells quantity of and time each item is wanted; it is developed from the end-item forecasts and customer orders.*

Material requirements planning (MRP), *474. A manufacturing planning and control technique that works backward from planned-quantities and completion dates for end items on a master production schedule to determine what and when individual parts should be ordered.*

Matrix design (organizational structure), *181–83. The integration of both a product and functional structure for identifiable projects.*

Maximax, *117. Selecting a strategy for the possibility of receiving the greatest return.*

Maximin, *117. A strategy to maximize the least favorable result.*

Mayo, Elton, *80*

MBO. *See* Management by objectives

McClelland, David C., *341–42*

McGregor, Douglas, *36*

Theory X & Y, *172*

Mead, Margaret, *68*

Mechanistic model, *170. A model that suggests that the best way to organize a company is by planning rationally, objectively, and in advance; subjective and interpersonal adjustments are to be minimized.*

Mental set, *315. The tendency to act or react in a certain way to a given stimulus; one tends to "see" what one expects to see.*

Message competition, *277. Messages compete for attention and processing; some messages are processed more quickly than others depending upon communicator's perception of what is important.*

Message conflict, *277. Two messages contain contradictory directives, claims, or positions.*

Message distortion, *276. Changes to the message as a result of additions, deletions, or differences in the perception.*

Middle managers, *5. Managers at the mid-level of the organization who supervise first-level managers; judged on managerial skills, they are usually working toward being in top management.*

Milkin, Michael, *76*

Mintzberg, Henry, *38, 244, 256*

MIS. *See* Management information systems

Mission, *137–40*

MNC. *See* Multinational company

MNE. *See* Multinational enterprise

Model

causal, *134*

expectancy, *348–49*

mechanistic, *170*

OPA, *105*

organic, *171–72*

Morality, *78. Conceptual codes concerning how behavior conforms to established, socially accepted norms; addresses cultural notions of right and wrong.*

Moskowitz, Milton, *512*

Organization Index

PHOTO CREDITS